# DESIRE AND BELIEF

## Introduction to
## Some Recent Philosophical Debates

### Arthur E. Falk

## Hamilton Books

an imprint of
University Press of America,® Inc.
Dallas · Lanham · Boulder · New York · Oxford

**Hamilton Books**
4501 Forbes Boulevard
Suite 200
Lanham, Maryland 20706
UPA Acquisitions Department (301) 459-3366

PO Box 317
Oxford
OX2 9RU, UK

Library of Congress Control Number: 2003114210
ISBN 0-7618-2715-3 (paperback : alk. ppr.)

In memory of my father and my brother
Arthur Eugene Falk, Sr., 1913-2001
Richard Allan Falk, 1939-2001

# Contents

# List of Tables, Figures, and Video Clips

## VIDEO CLIPS

Philosophy International and Western Michigan University make available to you on video CD over an hour of W.V. Quine, and ten minutes of Noam Chomsky, discussing with other philosophers some of the issues raised in these notes. The video excerpts are formatted for Apple's Quicktime displayer, which can be downloaded free.

| | |
|---|---|
| Section B | D-B01 (4 minutes) on a controversy over the scientific respectability of the propositional attitudes. |
| Section C | D-B02 (5 minutes) on a controversy over regimentation. |
| Section D | D-B03 (5 minutes) on how Alfred Tarski exploited the concept of adicity to define truth. |
| Section E | D-B04 (5 minutes) on how to think of causes in a way that preserves substitutivity. |
| | D-B05 (2 minutes) on why philosophers must save propositional attitudes from logical disgrace, while letting modality die of embarrassment. |
| Section F | D-B06 (5 minutes) on the problems with interpreting modal logic as elucidating the concept of necessity. |
| | D-B07 (5 minutes) on explaining the intuition of necessity without appeal to anything objective. |
| Section G | D-B08 (2 minutes) on the identity conditions of propositions. |
| | D-B09 (5 minutes) on why accept vague particular entities but not accept attributes. |
| Section O | D-B10 (3 minutes) on the one and only meaning of existence. |
| Section T | D-B11 (6 minutes) on indeterminacy in ontology. |
| | D-B12 (5 minutes) on cosmic complements as one's proxy function. |
| | D-B13 (3.5 minutes) on whether one's own personal ontology is fully determinate. |
| | D-B14 (2 minutes) on whether the ontology of abstract objects is fully determinate. |
| Section U | D-B15 (5.5 minutes) on a problem with deriving observation reports from empathy. |
| | D-B16 (2.5 minutes) on whether empathy and objectivity are reconcilable. |
| Section Y | D-B17 (10 minutes, black and white) on there being no history of selection for the human mind's more spectacular traits. |

To purchase the CD, follow the instructions posted on the W.M.U. Philosophy Department's website: www.wmich.edu/philosophy/video

# Acknowledgments

My thanks to my students at Western Michigan University: Stephanie Fisher in 1993 and Kristin DeKam, Joseph Uhl, and Rachael Cabasaan in 1997, and Marshall Willman in 1998, for reading earlier drafts of various sections and patiently teaching me the art of writing clearly. In 2000 I discerned the salutary effect of the participants in my course on desire and belief: Craig Carley, Max Goss, Brian Mandock, Brian Spires, and Ming (Michael) Yang; also Professors Amita Chatterjee and David Newman. Professor Pranab Kumar Sen influenced my account of substitution in section E and forced me to see the need for section Z to defend a conception of philosophical method that emerges, starting in section H and continuing in parts III and IV. In 2001 Max Goss continued to provoke me to think about how to respond to his deep criticisms. In 2002 colleagues Marc Alspector-Kelly, John Dilworth, and Insoo Hyun helped me, as did my students in my course on desire and belief, especially Timothy Sherman.

Some paragraphs in sections M, N, O, P, T, U, Y, and Z appear in a publication of lectures I gave in India in 2001, *Darwinism and Philosophical Analysis: Utkal Studies in Philosophy*, vol 9, (New Delhi: Decent Books, 2003) ISBN 81-86921-24-9. They are reprinted with permission of the copyright holder, the Department of Special Assistance in Philosophy, Utkal University. Some paragraphs in section O also appear in *Philo* 5 (2002). Part of section Q is based on an essay that appeared in *Russell: the Journal of the Bertrand Russell Archives* 17 (1998); another part of Q is based on my article in *Realism: Responses and Reactions*. Section R is based on an essay that appeared in *Behavior and Philosophy*, 23/24 (1995/6). Material in section Y appeared in *Philosophy of Science*, 48 (1981) and *History and Philosophy of the Life Sciences* 17 (1995). Material in section Z appeared in *Russell* 18 (1999). My thanks to all the editors and copyright holders for permission to reuse the material.

# Introduction

These notes take you from A to Z on the structure of desires and beliefs, and not only because the sections are lettered from A to Z. The phrase "from A to Z" tells you to expect full coverage of a subject. I do intend to review the prerequisites for understanding the subject at hand: what it is to be a mind able to make choices. Beliefs and desires are the motors, so to speak, of deliberating and choosing.

### §1. How I propose to achieve both unity and comprehensiveness.

Alas, the words "from A to Z" may also suggest disconnection, as if these notes meet their encyclopedic goal by a mere list of information in alphabetic order. Instead of attempting comprehensive coverage that way, I zero in on what it is to have desires and beliefs, without which there could be no deliberation or choice. What one says of belief usually carries over to desire, so I emphasize belief, often leaving implicit the generalization to desire (and hope, anger, love, etc.). To study the many aspects of belief, I focus on an issue that enables me to encompass all the aspects, from A to Z, as I explore the issue. The issue is whether there are **relational beliefs** and, if so, what is it about them (and relational desires) that makes them relational. For the sake of unity, I stalk one issue through all its permutations, arguing for one side of the issue, defending it from the criticisms of the other sides and criticizing them.

    The phenomenon (possibly a chimaeric phenomenon) that we'll examine is close at hand: It seems sometimes a believer *comes into a distinctive relation to things*, and that relation, whatever it may be, results in her believing something about them; it seems to underlie and strengthen the belief and enable her to believe more about them. Thus the name, "relational beliefs." Here's a putative example of a relational belief—I say "putative" because, if the phenomenon is chimaeric, no examples are real—but here it is: You see this page, and your belief about it, that it's white, is a relational belief. Perception is one of the distinctive types of relation supposed to underlie relational beliefs, in this case your belief about the thing you perceive. On the other hand, your belief that dinosaurs are extinct is not relational. Whatever relation you may have to the extinct dinosaurs is a consequence of your believing it rather than a precondition for believing. We'll call that kind of belief notional.

The concept of relational belief could shed light on many areas of interest, for the range of relational beliefs, if there are any, might include much more besides those expressive of perceptions. For example, it might include even what occurs to someone who's experiencing religious conversion. Conversion can occur to someone who does not experience a change of mind about anything, just a change in *the way* some things are believed. Thus Job in the Bible tells God that, whereas formerly he had believed God's word without much effect, "now my eye seeth thee. Therefore I reprehend myself, and do penance in dust and ashes" (*Job* 42:5-6). Did Job's beliefs about God change only from being notional to being relational, and is that why they became more motivating? I raise the question here only to suggest the potential breadth of our topic.

Assuming for the moment that relational belief is a real phenomenon, what might the "distinctive relation" be, that's at the heart of the difference between relational and notional belief? Would you believe it is the essence of *Dasein*? You wouldn't? Oh . . . Well then, you'll have to plow through fifteen sections before the dust settles and an answer of sorts emerges, in section O.

## §2. Is the idea of relational belief a scientific idea?

These notes, besides describing the data, also address the question, is a rigorous science possible of such mentalistic phenomena as relational belief? The answer partly depends on whether we can analyze knowledge and belief rigorously. What we claim about them must be definite and internally coherent before the matter of the claim's truth even arises. Another way of putting our question is, can we make **folk psychology** self-coherent and rigorous so that the issue of its truth becomes worth considering? (Folk psychology[1] is our everyday way of thinking about one another's actions and states of mind. We think about actions in terms of the purposes or intentions they're supposed to fulfill, and we think about states of mind as composed of beliefs and desires. There's more on this topic in section H.) A scientific, experimental psychology, in contrast to folk psychology, may reject these terms, but should it? I think we can make folk psychology rigorous and self-coherent. In particular, the relational beliefs, which folk psychology posits, are not only real; they're suitable for science to theorize about.

Willard V. Quine, the key philosopher on this topic, came to deny that thesis, as have many other philosophers. So it can no longer be asserted without defense. These notes defend it, but only after they introduce Quine's classic presentation of the philosophical data. An introduction of technical terms goes along with the presentation; indeed it already began with the bold faced words. They're defined and indexed. The phenomenon we'll examine suggests that minds differ in a fundamental way from everything else we know about. Folk psychology attributes to minds the ability to picture to themselves their world; more generally, minds make models or representations of aspects of the world that are important for guiding their purposeful activities. Minds don't think about the models; they think about the things modeled. It's such a yawn-provoker to say just that, however, that we gussy up the claim by saying minds enter into the relation of *being about* something. Still a bland thing to say, despite being less intelligible. So we give it a contentious ring by saying that, even if a thing is absent from a mind's vicinity, even if it never exists at all, the mind can enter into the relation of being about it—*it*, not the idea or image of it, but *it*. You should now feel somewhat puzzled by the fact that, for example, I dream about my dog Smokey, dead now these fifty years, looking at me and panting so that, if he were here, I'd give him some water. How can absent things be present to mind, (aboutness and presence often being converse^ relations)? Another example to puzzle over: I and other readers of Dashiell Hammett's fiction are amazed how Sam Spade, private detective, tells he's being lied to. How can one and the same nonexistent thing, Sam Spade, be as present to others as it is to me? To clinch the puzzlement, the thesis that mental states are about things, all kinds of things, is given a fancy name, the **intentionality** of the mind.[2] (There's point in our using the fancy term instead of the more intuitive word "aboutness," since I'll later commandeer the word "about" to indicate a particular manifestation of intentionality and the term "directed toward" to indicate another manifestation of intentionality. The term "intentional" will then serve to cover them both generically.)

Many philosophers, taking the contrast between mind and nonmind at face value, say that the mind and the things that depend on mind, like the sentences we utter, are *about* things and states of affairs, and nothing else has this characteristic of being *about* something. I'm skeptical of this stark dichotomy; I think some things in nature are signs of ("of" = "about") other things independently of any minds, and even the simplest of organisms, an amoeba for instance, exploits some of them. Suppose, for example, a substance immersed in water sheds a chemical. The gradient of the dissolved chemical around the substance signifies its proximity and direction, whether or not it is so interpreted. When it is interpreted, no mind is needed for the interpreting: Unicellular organisms in the water sense the presence of either a nutritious or noxious substance by means of the type of chemical, and pursue or flee it, guided by the gradient. In view of the ubiquity of the phenomenon, a more cautious and more obviously true contrast to note is that

- only minds are about such a wide array of things, including falsities and nonexistent things.
- Only minds are about them so multiply, believing many things while desiring many other things, and
- so flexibly, at one moment about these, the next moment about those.

This more modest way of making the contrast is still consistent with folk psychology.

Belief is a mental state which would be pointless to have, were it not for its representing something. Since it's a prime instance of this aboutness, to focus on belief is to study the distinctiveness of the mind. Many philosophers think that this aboutness is the chief problem for philosophy today. So, however esoteric the discussion becomes as you read on, please recall that we're bringing into focus the core difference between minds and everything else, namely, their spectacular intentionality. As the pain grows, envision the gain.

## §3. Are these notes for you?

"Pain"? My candor forces the question whether you should read this book. I address the professional research scholar in the next paragraphs, and the intermediate or advanced student in this one. Let's review the situation of the students among you. If you studied elementary logic and contemporary philosophy of mind conscientiously, you've come quite a way in your understanding of philosophical problems concerning the mind. You studied debates about the reduction of beliefs to brain states and behavioral dispositions. Yet you may still be mystified by some of the more advanced discussions, which concern how exactly the mind's intentionality differs from everything else we know of. These discussions mystify because of all their technical jargon and arcane appeals to people's ways of reporting each other's beliefs. You may have an inkling that there's some ongoing debate about how to think of beliefs even apart from questions of reductionism, but despair of ever finding an intelligible introduction to it. You're already beyond introductions like those in textbooks and popularizations. Your teachers assume more than you know, however, when they discuss the debate, so much more that you fear it would take a special tutorial to get yourself up to speed. Yet you'd like very much to acquire on your own the further background that would enable you to understand the original articles and more recent ones published in philosophy journals. Perhaps you might add your critical and creative insights to the debate. If that describes you, these notes are for you.[3]

The hitch is that I do push my own views. Some prospective readers are professional philosophers specializing in this field, and now I address those of you who are experts. Since you've traveled from A to Z and back on these matters, are these notes for you? You may wish to know what position these notes take on the issues. Very well: The notes defend the view that there are relational desires and beliefs. They're distinct from notional ones, and they're objective and worthy candidates for scientific study. Contrary to what many philosophers assert, they're not attitudes toward singular propositions. Analogies to a similar distinction in modal logic are unrewarding in studying the anomalies that afflict them. The solution of the anomalies hints of ellipsis in the reporting of beliefs. The ellipsis is filled by a theory of the believer. Although I review much for the student with special attention to the most recent decade of publications (more than a quarter of the three hundred forty cited), I do propose some novelties. Perhaps one of the more original sections is section N, where I propose a theory of the believer that explains the interface between the intentional and the physical aspects of the believer. Also somewhat original are sections Q to U, where I propose that only names, no predicates, are symbols in the mind, and even they are distributed representations. Through linguistic analysis a picture unfolds of vestiges of the evolution of mentality. Indeed, a picture unfolds, explicitly in section Z, of a new kind of linguistic analysis, which reveals evolution. The most novel aspect of this view is that there's a dimension of philosophical analysis which is at once Wittgensteinian and evolutionary.

Otherwise I am syncretist^ about the contents of beliefs, finding some truth in sententialism and also connectionism, some truth in various versions of representationalism and nonrepresentationalism, some truth in semantic internalism and also externalism. Concerning the project of naturalizing the mind, my position emerges slowly, as motivation for it mounts, that evolution is the key to fruitful naturalization. I apologize for the sudden cold splash of "-isms"; each one is defined in the text. See also the glossary for an explanation of words followed by a superscript caret,^.

In a nutshell, I've tried to combine the virtues of a textbook and a research monograph in the same book. "But what about the pain?" Oh, forget the pain; there's fun to be had along the way to achievement. Let's have fun. I joke and tease to pique your curiosity. I catch you up in a debate with a cliffhanger ending.

## §4. "But where's the philosophy?"

Young philosophers are eager to prescribe to us what we ought to believe; they have no patience for merely describing what we do believe. The course I follow in these notes is contrary to their impulses, because first we do the work of describing and only afterward the work of prescribing. Shouldn't we be thoroughly familiar with that which we propose to revise? It turns out to be tricky business acquiring that thorough familiarity.

Our study is part of what we may call a *descriptive* metaphysics of the mind. For we may think of folk psychology as a metaphysics^ or a science. (Of course, this is controverted, as is just about everything in philosophy. We'll begin Part II by considering the controversy over whether folk psychology is a theory of mental states.) I acknowledge that there's also a revisionary or *prescriptive* metaphysics of the mind, which corrects or adds to folk psychology. We'll examine one such, the naturalization of the mind, briefly at the end in Part IV. The **naturalization project** embraces a variety of metaphysical positions, but they all make contemporary science the gold-standard of knowledge at least, if not the whole of knowledge. The project concerns folk psychology's coherence with science, whether it could be part of a scientific worldview and, if it could not as it stands, how much revision would make it so. All naturalizers agree that none of the mind's operations are exceptions to physical and chemical laws, however distinctive and unique the laws of those mental operations may be. The project of naturalizing the mind is part of a broader naturalism, which accepts only the ontology^ posited by the formal and empirical sciences' ideal comprehensive theory, and treats contemporary science as a reasonable guide to that. Using the words of its most famous critic (Kant), naturalism "asserts nature to be sufficient for itself."[4] An alternative project for philosophy, namely, the Kantian project of investigating, without assuming any science, the conditions for the possibility of science, puts philosophy before science, whereas the naturalization project puts philosophy with science and after it. The two projects, like two suitors for the hand of Lady Philosophy, are rivals in contemporary philosophy. Not that Kantianism considers naturalism a worthy rival; its archrival is skepticism, and the two of them think they alone exhaust the Lady's prospects, deeming naturalism to be a loser from the start. How wrong they are. I'll say virtually nothing about the Kantian and skeptical projects.

Disagreement arises even among the naturalizers over what it would take to show that folk psychology can hold its own within the scientific worldview. Some of them are more revisionary than others. Some would even abandon intentionality. They explain amoebic activities without imputing intentionality to the amoeba; they accept the challenge to explain human activities without imputing it to human beings. Well, good luck to them! I'm one of the less revisionary; I favor a naturalization that keeps the mind that folk psychology describes.

Here's a preview of the less revisionary kind of naturalization I'll defend in Part IV. One aspect of it is synchronic^ and ahistorical; the other is historical and evolutionary. My thesis will be that folk psychology is consistent when judged according to both the historic and the ahistoric aspects of the naturalization of folk psychology, but it cries out for expansion and completion in these dimensions. Folk psychology makes sense, but it makes more sense with these two naturalizing dimensions added to it.

First the ahistorical aspect: Although I accept the view that folk psychology was developed by our cavemen ancestors, and it's now embedded in the forms of thought we inherited from them, I reject the inference that it's through and through a superstition. I don't commit myself to the opposite extreme view either, that folk psychology uncovers primary qualities of mind just as physics and chemistry uncover those of matter. There's a middle ground between these views, between the view that folk psychology reveals things as they are really and the view that it succumbs to total illusion. Consider the analogy to sensory perception: The secondary qualities,^ which our sensory systems give rise to, do contain scientific information about their stimuli, although they're not simulacra. There is a science of secondary qualities, namely that branch of physiological psychology called psychophysics. The science of intentionality would be a part of that science, if it's legitimate to generalize in the following way: As our eye and the light impinging on it interact to construct in consciousness the visual secondary qualities, e.g., the color brown, and as our ear and the compression waves in the air interact to construct in consciousness the auditory secondary qualities, e.g., timbre, so our brain and the organisms it perceives interact to construct in our consciousness the perceived organisms' secondary quality of possessing intentionality. If we thus generalize the idea of a secondary quality to cover imputed intentionality, then the intentionality of organisms would be rather like the brownness of some surfaces and the timbre of musical instruments. Representations that impute intentionality to an organism contain scientific information just as these secondary qualities do, information about the organisms and their environments. Also just as it would be hopeless and pointless to try to see in a way that avoided having to see brown, or to hear in a way that avoided having to hear timbre, so it's hopeless and pointless to try to think of organisms in a way that avoids having to attribute intentionality to them. We might as well come to understand it better, secondary though it be.

The synchronic side of the naturalization project exploits the informational value of secondary qualities, but the theory of evolution helps us to achieve a more radical naturalization than the one the ahistoric or synchronic approach to naturalization would yield. For the synchronic approach has been schematic to the point of mere hand-waving. In contrast, relational beliefs and desires about oneself at the present moment will be revealed in these notes to be the primitive intentional states and a fundamental stratum of our own states. They'll be pivotal in their role at the frontier between the intentional and the physical. When Descartes pointed to the pineal body in the brain as the place where these two aspects of human beings interconnected, he did little to explain what was supposed to be going on there. I think our reflections on relational belief will put us in a position to say something insightful at long last about the interconnection. We'll then go further: The original contents of beliefs and desires were not linguistic; they were picture-like. After these primordial intentional elements were in place in organisms, mental names evolved, and only after all that's in place could public languages evolve. We'll reach these conclusions by a disciplined form of linguistic analysis which reveals traces of evolution and vestiges of the oldest forms of intentionality. Indeed by the end of these notes, not only will an evolutionary story of mentality have unfolded, but also a new evolutionary conception of analytic method for the advancement of the philosophy of mind.

Everything about folk psychology's portrayal of the mind betrays the fact that the mind is a product of evolution. The historical aspect of the naturalization of folk psychology exploits this insight. Folk psychology, in contrast, is not explicitly evolutionary; it presents the data in an ahistorical way, the human mind being at the apex of a scale of more or less mentality observed in other animals. The human mind's strata of capacities recapitulate some of that scale. When folk psychology is naturalized by taking evolution into account, it not only notes these layers of mentality; it explains the layering. It rejects any significant dichotomizing between mind and pre-mind, as an inappropriate ideal of precision for the kind of science it is, just as paleontology rejects as misconceived any search for Adam and Eve. Who's afraid of the sorites,^ the ever-popular offensive tactic of the dichotomizers? We're not.

Moreover the thesis that the human mind has evolved from more primitive forms of mentality not only affects the substance of folk psychology. It also affects the methods the philosophical analyst uses. Just as the Grand Canyon's strata reveal some of the previous two billion years of history, so the philosophical analyst will look for fissures in the mind that reveal earlier strata. (I reflect on this sort of analysis in section Z.) So my thesis about the naturalization project in both its ahistorical and historical aspects will be that folk psychology not only lends itself to naturalization, but it's rendered more coherent, more satisfyingly explanatory, and more scientific by being naturalized. And so is philosophical method. Patience, though; first comes the descriptive metaphysics.

### §5. The limits of our inquiry.

The data are what we start from in our analyses. We don't just assert, defend, and criticize in philosophy, as if we were lawyers; we also look to phenomena, as scientists do, especially to puzzling or paradoxical phenomena to discover what more needs explaining. Some phenomena look indeterminate to us, and we must decide whether we're lacking acuity, or whether the indeterminacy is objective. Sometimes we have to decide whether there is a phenomenon or just a chimaera. Let's look and see what's there to be analyzed. Sections A to G do that; section H starts the theorizing.

How we look at the data affects how we theorize about them. While our theorizing should be constrained by our data, it should not be constricted by a tunnel-vision view of them. So we'll vary our perspective on the data, seeing them now according to one conceptualization of them and now according to another. This shifting of standpoints increases our logical space for theorizing, because it raises new questions and issues. We then can ask, which of the ways of taking the data leads to the most illuminating theory of them?

Our theorizing will disappoint you if you want a science of mental statics and dynamics, which would tell you how our mental states are in equilibrium or change, and what things would cause those changes. Sorry, but we'll be stuck with the preliminaries to such a science. We'll only deal with the structure of its elements. We do anatomy merely, the anatomy of belief and desire. "We murder to dissect." So, yes, unfortunately our analyses wreak of formaldehyde. That's to say, we're describing the ontology^ of folk psychology merely: What's the nature of these characteristic items, the beliefs and desires which folk psychology is about, and is their nature such that one can theorize about them with scientific rigor?

To avoid the sense of being lost as you proceed, keep in mind the overall structure of these notes, which comes from four dichotomies. The distinction between descriptive and prescriptive theories we mentioned already. The contrast between theory and data should be familiar. The other two will be explained in later sections after some preparatory work:

- The data we theorize about — *Part I*
- The theories about the data.
    - Theories that are descriptive of folk psychology.
        - Theories of the nature of belief's aboutness — *Part II*
        - Theories of the nature of belief's directed-towardness — *Part III*
            - Representationalist theories of directed-towardness.
            - Nonrepresentationalist theories of directed-towardness.
    - Theories that are prescriptive and revise folk psychology — *Part IV*

## §6.  In defense of two stylistic choices.

First, if you failed to notice my frequent use of contractions, good. If you did notice, you'll soon get used to it. I use contractions because auxiliary verbs slow down thought; they're annoying except when the emphasis falls on them. Everyone uses contractions in speech; only starched collar stuffiness prohibits their use in scholarly writing.

Second, I put the notes at the end of sections to discourage you from reading them at the point they annotate. If I'd wanted you to read them there, I'd've incorporated them into the text there. The notes are for further study only.

# Notes

1.  In the early 1900s Wilhelm Wundt used the term *Völkerpsychologie* to refer to what we today call cultural anthropology and social psychology. Today, however, philosophers apply the term "folk psychology" to the mentalistic way of describing individuals. Daniel Dennett introduced this sense of the term "folk psychology" in 1975 in his "Three Kinds of Intentional Psychology" in Richard Healey, ed., *Reduction, Time and Reality*, 37-60; it has since become common usage even among those (like me) who reject the pejorative contrast between "folk" and "scientific." Dennett's essay is reprinted in David Rosenthal, ed., *The Nature of Mind* (1991).

2.  Roderick Chisholm's Introduction to his *Realism and the Background of Phenomenology* (1960) attributes the currency of the term to Franz Brentano, who

said in 1874 he was reviving a medieval concept. I suspect that Chisholm himself had much to do with its currency, however. The term "intentionality" was used to refer to this concept in 1924 by Oskar Kraus, the editor of the second edition of Brentano's *Psychology from an Empirical Standpoint.* See page 395 of the English translation. Although intentions in the narrow sense of purposes are intentional in Brentano's broader sense of representing states of affairs, just about all mental states are intentional in that broader sense. See Victor Caston, "Connecting Traditions: Augustine and the Greeks on Intentionality" in Dominik Perler, ed., *Ancient and Medieval Theories of Intentionality* (2001), 23-48, for a history of the concept and the term.

3.  Two other books that might serve your purpose are I. E. Mackenzie, *Introduction to Linguistic Philosophy* (1997) and S. Guttenplan, ed., *A Companion to the Philosophy of Mind* (1994).

4.  Immanuel Kant, *Prolegomena to Any Future Metaphysics* (1783), §60 (363). Kant defines a metaphysical^ naturalism, but some contemporary naturalists acquiesce in Kant's insistence on putting methodological matters before substantive ones. Contrary to Kant, however, their methodological naturalism asserts that all attempts to justify the scientific method by an antecedently justified method, including Kant's, have been embarrassingly fallacious. But there are the self-correcting procedures built into the scientific method to justify for the time being our continuing to trust in it. Quite perversely from Kant's point of view, these naturalists then default to a metaphysical naturalism. By "default to" I mean they throw the burden of proof on those who assert there's more to ontology than science's. As a consequence of applying the scientific method, substantive naturalism seems to them true; all human experience has been confirming it. If you know otherwise, you're requested to enlighten them, but expect to be held to the highest standards of rigor. And don't think that they assume that, if science determines the extent of ontology, science also exhausts all knowledge. That's a *non sequitur,* if there's extrascientific knowledge that has no extra ontological import. And there is—see sections M and N. The various naturalization projects are concerned with current science; they attempt to substantiate the boast of a ground for the metaphysics in what science already knows, and that's when the sparks fly.

# Part I: The Data, from A to G

The first part of these notes, consisting of seven sections, looks at the data for building and testing a theory of belief, desire, and other attitudes. We divide the phenomena of attitudes into notional and relational varieties, and distinguish these phenomena from the linguistic phenomena of reporting them. We "prepare" the data for theorizing about, by regimenting the formats of reports. Sections E, F, and G then examine the main problems that a theory of attitudes must account for.

Mindful of the needs of those new to this subject, I introduce in the course of the seven sections around ninety technical concepts (boldfaced), which are the barest minimum I need to present the material competently. If you memorize their definitions and use them in stating the various theses I'll be defending or criticizing, it will make the remaining parts more intelligible. I define the terms in the text as I use them. A million other technical concepts that are peripheral to our subject, coming from the sciences, logic, and other areas of philosophy, are marked in the text with a superscript caret, ^, and defined in a glossary.

Do I have your informed consent to lead you into this jungle of technicalities? In the interest of full disclosure, I must tell you that many astute minds, including the poet Wordsworth, warn against this sort of activity. Have you considered carefully his advice?

> Up! up! my Friend, and clear your looks;
> Why all this toil and trouble?
> Up! up! my Friend, and quit your books;
> Or surely you'll grow double:
>
> Books! 'tis a dull and endless strife
> Come, hear the woodland linnet
> How sweet his music! on my life
> There's more of wisdom in it.
>
> One impulse from a vernal wood
> May teach you more of man,

Of moral evil and of good,
Than all the sages can.

Sweet is the lore which Nature brings;
Our meddling intellect
Mis-shapes the beauteous forms of things:—
We murder to dissect.

(various stanzas from "The Tables Turned")

What's this? You're going to reject the poet's advice and turn to the next page? You think he's flirting with a false dichotomy? Very well, come along.

# A. The Two Varieties of Phenomena.

This section is a condensed introduction to the portions of the philosophy of language that are relevant to understanding the difference between relational and notional belief. It will turn out that, not only are there these two varieties of phenomena, there are two ways of understanding their difference that turn on concepts in the philosophy of language. I introduce both ways of understanding their difference, but favor the second way.

### §1. One of the ways of distinguishing relational and notional belief.

We approach belief by way of knowledge, since we should cadge what we can from the history of philosophy and philosophers have written more explicitly about knowledge than they have about belief. Consider our knowledge of individuals. There seem to be two ways of knowing a thing: The knower is remote from the thing in one of the ways, and her knowledge is reported by using **definite descriptions** of the thing known. Descriptions contain general terms that have to be combined to create an expression that would mean just the one thing. For example, by combining three general terms ("mother," "father," and "belonging to me") we get the definite description, "the father of the mother belonging to me" or more succinctly

"my mother's father."

Descriptions of a thing divide into definite and indefinite descriptions, depending on whether the description purports to be true uniquely of the thing it describes. For example, I may describe the north pole of the axis of the earth's rotation either as "a pole" or "the north pole." The latter is a definite description.

The article "the" preceding a description that isn't plural cues us to the description's purport of uniqueness, for the description that follows the definite article is supposed to be true of just one thing among all the things that we might be talking about. In contrast, a phrase consisting of an indefinite article "a" and the description following it, even when the description happens to be uniquely true of the thing described, does not *purport* to pick it out uniquely; that's not the job of the indefinite article.

(I'll use the word "description" in these notes to mean a definite description.)

This descriptive way is the way we know our great great grandparents. Even though we can know them by way of definite descriptions of each one, it is only pseudo-relational knowledge, because we're not put into any real relation with them simply by using some name like "my mother's mother's mother's father." I can refer to "the tallest of my ancestors," but who was that? In contrast, the knower is close up to the thing in the other way of knowing, and her knowledge is reported by using tag-names of the thing or demonstrative expressions pointing to it, which don't let general terms get in the way of knowing it directly. In contrast to definite descriptions, nondescriptive names that merely label nonfictional entities (**logically proper names**)[1] require that some relation brings the entities into our ken, and the relation suffices to establish that certain words are our names for them. This is the way we know our friends and refer to them. The adverb "logically" in "logically proper name" tips you off that we're stipulating here: Such proper names are defined to have no descriptive content. Consequently, the whole meaning of a logically proper name is the thing it names; its meaning is identical to the thing meant, pure and simple:

> Concerning the meaning of logically proper names,
> the meaning = the meant.

It seems to follow that only existing things can have logically proper names, for if, despite having no descriptive content, a mark is a name, then it names something existent; otherwise it names nothing and so is not a name.

You ask, "How close up to the thing known is this close-up knowledge?" Well, you're close enough to point to it. "But, but," you sputter in frustration at the spatial metaphor. You're quite right to demand more, but since I'll say more in later sections, let's leave it lamely metaphorical for now what this relation to an existent thing is, that puts a namer of the thing so close up to it, that she can tag or mark it without having to make her mark mean anything descriptive of it. A sufficient^ condition of sufficient closeness, though not a necessary one, is direct perceptual acquaintance.

The difference between the two ways of knowing seems to be one of kind, not degree. For we seem able to have either independently of the other: When you first glimpsed the person who would become your best friend, you had no descriptive knowledge of this person, but at the moment of the glimpse you acquired the second kind of knowledge, the directly relational kind. But the mere glimpse might give you no descriptive knowledge. On the other hand no increase in your descriptive knowledge of your ancestors will suffice to give you this second kind of knowledge of them. At least this difference in kind seems to hold for our knowledge of the things we can perceive, such as people; let's skip over our knowledge of things we cannot perceive, such as the natural numbers.[2]

Something like this distinction of ways of knowing was made by Aristotle and other European and Asian ancient and medieval philosophers.[3] Knowledge in the close-up way was to them twofold: first, our simple apprehension of the things we name, an apprehension they thought was a precondition for our complex knowledge of the truths about those things; secondly, our access *a posteriori*^ to the contingent truths about these things. The more remote kind of knowledge, which they did not dignify with the name "knowledge," calling it "opinion" instead, was not based on an apprehension of things, but required the knower's understanding of words.

In recent times, William James called attention to the distinction and noted that other languages have distinctive words to express the difference, in Latin *scire* and *noscere*, *wissen* and *kennen* in German, *savoir* and *connaître* in French. Bertrand Russell called the first way our **knowledge by description**, the second our **knowledge by acquaintance**.[4] He supposed us acquainted with universals and with particulars, the simplest particulars first and then the complexes in which they occur, these complexes being the contingent facts we are acquainted with. Russell analyzed the distinction and sharpened it in two successive theories of knowledge, the first theorizing that knowledge is a dual relation, which he held around 1905, and the second that knowledge is a multiple relation, which he held from 1910 to about 1917.[5] (Section D will explain dual and multiple relations.)

Consider some question about these kinds of knowledge, for instance, which of them is the more suited to be the object of scientific study? Part of the answer would have to concern belief. For the distinction between two kinds of knowledge depends on there being two kinds of belief. All knowledge is[6] a belief-content that's (i) believed, (ii) with justification, and (iii) is true. Since item (iii) won't distinguish the two types of knowledge, and item (ii)'s doing the job seems unpromising, the item that distinguishes the relational knowledge from the notional must be the belief. The belief in relational knowledge happens to be relational, as distinct from notional belief, which is part of knowledge by description. So whoever wishes to understand the ontology^ of the two types of knowledge must study the two types of belief. The stuff knowledge is made of is belief. Often belief is contrasted with knowledge, but belief in that contrastive sense is "mere" belief, that is, a belief occurs although the justification is missing for believing it. Not all belief is mere belief. So the question, which of the two sorts of knowledge is more suited to be the object of scientific study, is about the two kinds of belief. It's the question Quine asked, and we'll study his answer in section J.

You need to know alternative pairs of definitions of relational and **notional belief**, because philosophers argue about which one is correct. The first pair of definitions follows naturally from our discussion of knowledge, since it equates the relations underlying proper names with the relations underlying relational beliefs, and it's the one I'll argue against:

> ### THE CONTRAST I WILL ARGUE AGAINST
> A relational belief is one whose content is expressed by using proper names; a notional belief is one whose content does not require expression with proper names, but uses definite descriptions or quantifiers.^

Many philosophers accept this definition, but I don't—it assumes that the kinds of relation that underlie the use of logically proper names are all and only the kinds of relations that underlie relational belief. That may be true, but surely we may not assume it, for proper names are for communication by people who have language, and beliefs are mental states which even cats have despite their lack of language. We should be open to divergence of thought from language, not foreclosing its possibility through definition. So I'll soon give you an alternative way of making the distinction between the two. The argument between the two ways of defining the distinction will permeate our future discussions.

Although we eventually conclude in section U that the two kinds of belief overlap, some beliefs being instances of both, and we consider whether one of these kinds is a special case of the other, we'll start by assuming that relational and notional are dichotomous categories, that is, mutually exclusive and exhaustive of all the possible kinds of belief, just as it seems to be in the case of the two kinds of knowledge.

In 1956, Quine captured the Russellian intuitions of 1910-1917 concerning our judgments about the objects we know by acquaintance in his own theory of relational and notional beliefs. Quine sometimes referred to relational belief by these terms: transparent, attributary, triadic or polyadic, multigrade, and *de re* (Latin, pronounced "day ray"); he sometimes referred to notional belief by these terms: opaque, propositional, dyadic, *de dicto*.[7] In all this proliferation of terminology, there's just one contrast.

Note that Quine called notional belief "dyadic," since a notional belief relates (1) a believer to (2) a believed content (notion). For example, if Arthur believes that the dinosaurs are extinct, the relation of belief is relating Arthur to the notion that the dinosaurs are extinct. So notional beliefs are in that sense relational. But they are not relational beliefs in the sense we intend. Relational beliefs relate a believer to things as well as to the contents believed about those things. Thus Quine referred to the relational beliefs as being relations among more than two entities (so triadic, polyadic, or multigrade). Let's follow his example and use "relational belief" to exclude the merely dyadic notional belief.

I mentioned in the Introduction that Quine gave up his theory of relational belief. He gave it up, because around 1977 he ceased to believe there was a phenomenon about belief itself to be analyzed (as distinct from a phenomenon about the reporting of beliefs).[8] In the last decades of his life he thought relational belief, if not chimaeric, then amorphous to an extreme. Section J is devoted to this view. Now here's an irony: The two phenomena I refer to in this section's title are just the relational and the notional, and the philosopher who most effectively called our attention to these two phenomena came to doubt we should bother with the difference.

Whether relational or acquaintance-based beliefs should be equated with singular beliefs is a matter in contention. So we must not simply assume it, at least not at the outset and not without expressed reasons. A **singular belief** is a belief about one or more definite individuals. What makes a belief singular is not its being about just a single thing—it can be about more—but the fact that at least some of the things it's about are referred to in a way that singles them out. In other words, in a report of the singular belief there occur singular terms referring to the individuals. A **singular term** is a definite description or a logically proper name; we pretend[9] the latter kind of term includes ordinary proper names as well as demonstrative phrases and pronouns. (When I use the word "name" without appending qualifiers like "proper," it's a synonym for "singular term.") Here are singular terms: "the tallest person," "Napoleon Bonaparte," "this" (said while pointing to something), and "me" and "now." Singular terms, when they occur in sentences, refer to things so that the rest of the sentence, the predicates in it, can comment on them.

Beliefs that are not singular are **general**. (I give a positive account of generality in section E.) Singularizing and generalizing elements often occur together in a proposition, so this dichotomizing is artificial, though useful. As I define "singular belief," my believing that somebody loves me is singular, because it refers to me, and despite the fact that the word "somebody" expresses an element of generality. If I were distinguishing singular and general propositions within logic, rather than singular and general beliefs within the philosophy of mind, I'd define "general proposition" as any proposition containing a generalizing expression, such as a quantifier,^ and let singular propositions be all those that are not general. By that definition "somebody loves me" would be a general proposition, despite the occurrence of "me." So propositions that contain a mix of singular terms and generalizing expressions can be classified either way, if a purpose is served by doing it one way rather than the other. How one draws these lines depends on what the lines are good for. In these notes I call a belief "singular" to call attention to any singular terms in the belief's content, whether or not generalizing elements also occur there.

The classification of beliefs as singular and general is complicated by controversies over singular terms. Russell in 1905 discovered a way of analyzing definite descriptions so that they were not real singular terms. He analyzed them in context, that is, by analyzing whole sentences in which they occurred. For example, the sentence,

(i) The king of X is bald,

he analyzed into a sentence with three clauses:

(ii) Someone's a king of X, no one else is a king of X too, and he's bald.[10]

This paraphrase of (i) eliminates the definite article "the" which introduced a singular term in (i); the indefinite article "a" is in its place, and the phrase "king of X" has shifted into predicate position. The paraphrase eliminates the definite description and makes the whole sentence general. The general sentence contains a conjunction of three conjuncts. The first one makes a claim of existence of the subject, the second a claim of the uniqueness of the subject, and the third makes the predication of the subject. Yet, despite the reconstructive surgery, if either the original sentence or its analysis is true, the other must be true too. Since they are true together or false together, the main condition is met for saying that one is an analysis of the other.

What reasons did Russell have for claiming that the sentence (i) is not singular but general? In "On Denoting," published in 1905 when France was a republic and had no king, Russell gave one reason for being suspicious of the sentence's look of singularity:

... either 'A is B' or 'A is not B' must be true. Hence either 'the present King of France is bald' or 'the present King of France is not bald' must be true. Yet if we enumerated the things that are bald, and then the things that are not bald, we should not find the present King of France in either list. Hegelians, who love a synthesis, will probably conclude that he wears a wig.

In other words, to treat sentences like this one as singular when their subject terms might name nothing at all is to create a difficulty accounting for their falsity; they seem rather neither true nor false in that case, which violates logic. Russell's analysis solves this problem, because the general sentence it is analyzed into is clearly false since its first conjunct is false. Other virtues of his analysis will emerge in section B §1, particularly note 6, and section F §2.

Every philosopher must master Russell's technique of sentence paraphrase. But one must be circumspect about its philosophical implications. The paraphrase technique is only appropriate for one use of definite descriptions. Let's call this use of a definite description its **attributive use**[11]; when it's used attributively, for it to succeed in implementing the speaker's intentions it must be true of the thing it's supposed to refer to. A description's attributive use is in contrast to its **referential use**. The referential use of a definite description makes the description do in effect what a proper name would do, namely, simply refer, since the failure of the description to be true of the speaker's intended referent does not cause the reference itself to fail. (For example, at a party a lady tells someone, *"The person with the water glass* was rude." If her conversation partner tells her it's a glass full of gin, she knows her reference to the person succeeded. Her definite description did its job despite its false information, which was unimportant to her purpose anyway.) When a description is used referentially, does the false information in it make the speaker's whole sentence false? Philosophers of language disagree about that. If it does not, the referentially used description is functioning like a proper name in the sentence, and the speaker's sentence can be true despite the false description. But if it does make her sentence false, nevertheless what mattered was the truth of the sentence's predicate of the intended referent, for that's what she was thinking to say and her mind was directed toward the incomplete proposition expressed by the predicate. Two natural languages have distinct articles to differentiate attributive and referential uses of definite descriptions. They're Malagasy and Fering. The former's spoken on Madagascar, and the latter is a North Frisian dialect of Foehr and Amrun, islands in the North Sea.[12] It would be interesting to have the intuitions of speakers of these languages about how the falsity of referentially used descriptions affects the truth value^ of the sentences containing them.

Whether or not the descriptive content of a referentially used description counts in determining the truth value of a sentence, it seems misleading at best to apply Russell's technique to descriptions used referentially, since there's no convention of referential use of the sentences that result from Russell's technique. The truths conveyed would be displaced by the literal falsehoods expressed by the clauses of the analysis. But since indefinite descriptions are used attributively and normally definite ones are also, Russell's technique is generally applicable, since the sentences containing definite descriptions are analyzed into sentences using only indefinite descriptions.

Russell's technique is legitimated by supposing that a proposition's real logical structure may be different from its apparent logical structure. In that case, definite descriptions are singular terms only in a proposition's apparent logical structure, but don't exist as terms at all in the proposition's real logical structure. Russell's technique would then be a consequence of his discovery that real logical structure may be concealed by apparent logical structure. Let's continue to dally conservatively at the level of appearance where definite descriptions do occur in our propositions and occur as singular terms, until there's overwhelming reason not to. (We evaluate more reasons in sections B and F for supposing they don't really occur.) If they do occur, they are singular terms. On that supposition, my beliefs about, as I might say, the tallest man would be singular beliefs, *pace* Russell. But they are not relational beliefs.

## §2. A better way to distinguish relational and notional beliefs.

I want now to raise a doubt about the line of thought we've been following: Which is more fundamental to relational belief about things? Is it the use of a logically proper name to name that thing, or is it the relation established between the believer and the thing? Perhaps the latter, if the kind of singular term the believer uses is only a symptom of the kind of belief, and not always a reliable one. If so, we should shift our focus on to the essential aspect of the belief, its being relational. A strategic reason for shifting the focus is to reduce the dependence of philosophy of mind (of which folk psychology is a part) on the philosophy of language, from which we get such concepts as logically proper names, singular propositions, and definite descriptions used attributively. By the end of this section we'll see that the issues concerning proper names and singular propositions are fraught with paradox. If we tie the two fields of mind and language together too tightly and the philosophy of language falls down, won't the philosophy of mind come tumbling after?

Let's therefore be open to the possibility that general and singular beliefs can be either relational or notional beliefs. Perhaps we can have general relational beliefs, only because we have singular relational beliefs that imply them. We'll examine both singular and general kinds of relational beliefs. Also we can have singular notional beliefs; these beliefs would occur in knowledge by description. Here's a picture of the situation; instances fit all four boxes at least at first blush:

|                                | **singular beliefs**   | **general beliefs**   |
| ------------------------------ | ---------------------- | --------------------- |
| **relational beliefs** *(de re)*   | singular & relational  | general & relational  |
| **notional beliefs** *(de dicto)*  | singular & notional    | general & notional    |

Table A-1. A cross-classification of two dichotomies, implying their independence. We later cast suspicion on some instances in the upper right quarter (sections I and L) and the lower left quarter (sections T and U).

Some philosophers quarrel with our allowing the possibility of each of the four quadrants of the table being nonempty, saying a belief is relational or notional, depending on whether it's directed toward a complete singular or complete general proposition.[13] This seemingly economical way of proceeding follows from the considerations at the beginning of subsection §1. But singular propositions would be expressed by using logically proper names, and so this thesis is entangled in a problem with singular beliefs that I'll describe in subsection §4. We don't want to prejudge how that problem will be resolved. Moreover there are other questions begged. See the discussion of the validity of exportation in section E. So I prefer not to classify beliefs by the singularity or generality of the propositions they're directed toward.

The original way of stating the contrast between relational and notional beliefs, due to Russell and Quine, was this:

THE CONTRAST I WILL ARGUE FOR

If a belief is directed toward an *incomplete* proposition, whether singular or general, the belief is a **relational belief. Notional beliefs** are directed toward *complete* propositions, whether singular or general.

The terminology of complete and incomplete propositions is not Russell's or Quine's. I favor classifying beliefs as relational or notional by expanding the range of entities our attitudes may be directed toward, to include an entity analogous to a proposition. I try to draw your mind initially to that analogy by alluding to the completeness of the propositions they're directed toward, suggesting there are more, namely, the incomplete ones. Here's the proposal roughly: *That such and such be so* is the general form of a complete proposition. An **incomplete proposition** is like a complete proposition in this respect: A sentence expresses a complete proposition, a predicate expresses an incomplete proposition, and a predicate is like a sentence in every respect except that, where a singular term would be in a sentence, it has a ". . ." instead. Let me allude again to the underlying analogy by calling a predicate an incomplete sentence. "Incomplete sentence" is a natural name for something that expresses an incomplete proposition. My practice is to indicate an incomplete proposition by putting in place of the ". . ." a pronoun whose referent is not identified, for example, "he is a spy" instead of ". . . is a spy," because such phrases are used to report what an attitude is directed toward. The sentence with the pronoun is not incomplete grammatically, so I won't call it an incomplete sentence, but its interpretation is incomplete, because any complete proposition, in order to be expressed by it, waits upon something outside the sentence to specify the reference of the pronoun. Thus what the sentence expresses, the *such and such*, is still incomplete, in the sense that it's too incompletely specified to be the case or not the case. We may identify the incomplete proposition expressed by "he is a spy" with just that which is common to all the complete propositions which may be expressed by that sentence, using all the ways to make the pronoun's reference determinate. (I need a charitable and patient reader here. In return I promise to blow away some of the fog I just wrapped one of my central concepts in, but it will take the next six sections to do it. In section C I introduce pronominal anaphora, and in sections D and G I identify complete and incomplete propositions with abstract entities, of the kind called "attributes." The contrast of complete and incomplete will be recast in terms of the adicity of the attributes.)

In section H we'll note one reason to reject the idea that any belief in a singular proposition is *ipso facto* a relational belief. Later sections will try to refute more guarded claims that relational belief is belief in a certain kind of singular proposition that preserves the relationality of the belief.

## §3. Distinguishing reports of beliefs from the beliefs themselves.

Quine got at belief indirectly, through an analysis of reports of beliefs, of which he isolated two kinds, relational and notional reports. **Relational reports** report a person's relational beliefs, and I bet you guessed what **notional reports** report. Here's an example of a relational report:

> "About some guy (maybe this guy over there), Arthur believes that he is a spy."

The relation is between Arthur and this guy. Thus it is Arthur's belief *de re*, "about the thing"; the *res* or thing is this guy. We use "*de re*" as a synonym for relational. Note also the incomplete proposition expressed by "he is a spy." I'll assume the second way of making the contrast between relational and notional beliefs when I discuss reports. Here's an example of a notional report:

> "Arthur believes that some guy is a spy."

The notion is what's expressed by the clause, "some guy is a spy." Thus it's Arthur's belief *de dicto*, "about what is said"; the clause expresses what is said, the *dictum* which Arthur believes. We use "*de dicto*" as a synonym for notional. The idiom for reporting notional belief is like indirect discourse, that is, like our way of reporting what another says without committing ourselves to giving the other's exact words. I'll use the Latin terms for the two kinds of belief and report, and interchangeably with the terms relational and notional.

The way we talk about phenomena is also a phenomenon. The procedure of studying the talk about something (in our case, the reporting of relational and notional beliefs), in order to learn about the phenomenon talked about, Quine calls "**semantic ascent**."[14] Quine and Carnap think it's clarifying to talk about language use—about the contexts in which sentences are spoken and about the logical relations between sentences—when we're concerned with questions about what categories of things exist. For the basic categories reflect the language's structure. Also, where the alternative is to analyze states of mind hidden except to introspection, language is at least public.[15] Mysterious entities, like ego and subjectivity, look less mysterious when observed through their linguistic manifestations, like the pronoun "I" and the verb "seems." Concerning folk psychology in particular, we already noticed how the philosophy of language, especially the theory of meaning, has implications about what things are believed. Semantic ascent facilitates sorting out the interconnections of philosophy of mind and philosophy of language.

But it's not necessary to suppose that the philosopher is primarily concerned with linguistic idioms. Semantic ascent is simply a tool for studying the phenomena of the world, in this case, how the believer relates to the world. When semantic ascent becomes detached from scientific motivation and is pursued for its own sake, it's in danger, in Russell's words, of degenerating into the study of the different ways silly people can say silly things.[16]

Note that a report takes us into two minds simultaneously, the believer's and the mind of the person who reports the believer's belief. Quine gives us little help in disentangling the two people, to get a theory of belief as distinct from a theory of belief-reporting. One might even suspect (incorrectly) that the whole difference in the two ways of reporting beliefs lies in *the reporter's* mind or in the context of the reporting. For the relational mode of reporting another's belief looks like it avoids commitment to any account of the intrinsic properties of the belief, such as that a belief's a condition of the mind that represents a complete state of affairs, as if the condition were a mental sentence with mental names in it. The relational mode avoids full commitment to that, whereas the notional mode of reporting seems to commit to something representational being in the believer's mind, and the representation names things. At least in the case of notional belief the believed *dictum* is expressed by a representation that's true or false, depending on whether it represents a fact or not. These two approaches to a belief's nature, representational and nonrepresentational, i.e., the believed content naming things or not, do express the reporter's alternative commitments, however, in his adopting one of the alternative ways of reporting another's beliefs. I disentangle the belief's nature from the report's nature in Parts II and III.

As practice in using semantic ascent, let's look at the reports' structures to learn something about the structures of the beliefs reported on. Clearly the *de re* and *de dicto* are different beliefs, and concerning Arthur's beliefs about spies in the example above the FBI would only be interested in Arthur's first kind of belief. Both beliefs are directed toward propositions, the *de dicto* one toward the complete proposition, "some guy is a spy," and the *de re* one toward the incomplete proposition, "he is a spy." Although in this respect both kinds of belief are about (*de*) something, it will help to avoid confusion to use the phrase "**directed toward**" for the believer's relation to the propositional content of the belief. Let's now require that usage. I use the word "about" only in the *de re* report. The word "about" introduces the things the believer is related to, which complete the meaning of the incomplete proposition her belief is directed toward. The two reports about spies, which I gave at the beginning of this discussion of reports (§3), illustrate this structure.

It's appropriate to mark the two relations making up beliefs with the different words, "toward" propositions and "about" things, since the relations are opposites. Why "opposites"? As we'll see in section H, the "about" relations are based on a prior connection between the believer and the things believed about, typically a causal connection, but the "toward" relation must exist first between the believer and the proposition, before any causal power can be attributed to whatever the concrete thing is in the believer that expresses the proposition. For example, according to our folk psychology, if you see me approaching a water faucet with a cup, you explain my action by attributing a cluster of psychological states to me, including

>an intention *to fill a cup with water* because of
>my desire *to drink a cup of water* and
>my beliefs that *this* (in my hand) *is a cup* and
>that (over there) *is a faucet* and
>*by approaching a faucet with a cup, one is positioned to get a cup of water.*

Such singular and general propositions are factors in explanations only by psychological states being directed toward them and connecting them so that they constitute reasons for the action and causes of it.

The objects of the "directed toward" relation are propositions, but what are propositions? I already said that sentences express them, singular sentences expressing singular propositions, general sentences general propositions. So **propositions** are the meanings of sentences, or, if you prefer, they are the things meant by sentences. Different sentences express the same proposition, if they're synonymous. And I said that they have causal power on a believer's actions by way of something concrete that expresses them for the believer; that indirectness is because they are abstract entities. Abstract entities are inert causally. To copy a line from the good book, "the word became flesh," that is, meanings must be incarnated in something physical before they can do anything. We have more to say about propositions, but it's spread out: In section D we'll say propositions are an extreme form of attribute. In section G we'll give modal identity conditions for propositions. Part III is all about the objects of the directed-toward relation. Section V elaborates on their being public entities, not dependent for their existence on anyone thinking them. Section W argues that singular propositions don't exist!

## §4. What is the entity that a belief is directed toward?

It's controversial whether meanings are in fact the objects of the "directed-toward" relation. Perhaps the sentences themselves are the objects;
perhaps no abstract things are the objects, but rather those concrete things
that are the actual terms in causal relations are the objects. I already
introduced one idea that bears greatly on the issue, namely, logically
proper names, which occur in singular sentences. To set up the problem
of what sort of thing a belief is directed toward, we take note of this fact:
Anything that gets a label, that is, gets a logically proper name, might get
two labels. For example, I am Uncle Sonny to my nephews on my side of
the family and Uncle Arthur to my nephews through my wife's side. The
logically proper names "Arthur" and "Sonny" are mere labels, conveying
no descriptive content. There is only one meaning here, despite the two
names, and that's me. (Recall the equation, "Concerning the meaning of
logically proper names, the meaning = the meant.") Consequently two
sentences differing only in that one of them has "Sonny" where the other
has "Arthur" *must* express the same singular proposition, as Russell
noted.[17] By contrast, if descriptions had been used to refer to me, the
sentences would express different propositions, general ones if Russell is
right about definite descriptions, but at least two different ones. The
problem of determining the object of the directed-toward relation requires
the contrast of two sentences but only one proposition, so we'll stick with
proper names.

Someone new to my family might learn the name "Arthur" by listening
to one set of my nephews and the name "Sonny" by listening to the other
set, and never realize that they are names of the same person. Suppose she
has not yet had any direct perceptual acquaintance with me. She could
have proper names for me without being perceptually acquainted with me.
Given this section's introducing the subject of proper names by connecting
them to acquaintance, you may have been misled into thinking that *only*
those with direct acquaintance with things can use logically proper names
of them. But there is transmission of logically proper names from those
with direct acquaintance to those who lack it, as I'll suggest in section I,
for otherwise what use would they be in communication? So she acquires
the use of my two names from listening to my nephews. Or, we can keep
the connection to direct acquaintance by saying that each time she talks to
my nephews, they point me out to her as I dash nimbly in and out among
the trees, doing my Druid, Dionysiac, and Mithraic dances in various
costumes or conditions of undress. They yell, "And there he goes!" I am

the fleeting contorted apparition each time.

Has she in fact learned proper names of me, or is the name "Arthur" just a cover for the description, "an uncle of these boys," and the name "Sonny" for the description, "an uncle of those other boys"? We'll come down on the side of her having learned proper names, but we'll make a place for the descriptions. She has learned proper names, and the two descriptions are not part of their meanings, as though each name were synonymous with a definite description. For I would still be Arthur and Sonny even if I lacked nephews. (We'll return to this argument for distinguishing proper names from descriptions in section F.) But the descriptions are convenient **reference fixing** descriptions,[18] that is, they partly determine for her in a contingent way the references of the names. The contingency is not merely the contingency just noted, that I might not've had nephews, but also the contingency that she might not've associated my names with my having nephews. But, things having turned out as they have, among all the things she believes about Arthur, this one, that he's an uncle of these boys, currently has a privileged status, in that it would be the one she'd state if asked who Arthur is. As long as these descriptions have this privileged status for her, her statements, such as "Arthur is an uncle of these boys," would express truths in an *a priori* way for her. When a name is used by several people, the descriptions they use to fix its reference may vary, and the descriptions used even by a single person may vary from time to time. There's the limiting case where we all happen to agree on the description that fixes the referent, e.g., "Jack the Ripper," the serial murderer who stalked the streets of London in the 1890s, but the general case for reference fixing descriptions is one of idiosyncrasy and transience.

(Despite the similarity in nomenclature, reference fixing descriptions are not the same as referential uses of definite descriptions. Descriptions that fix the reference of names are usually attributive uses of the descriptions, since the most context-independent way to pick a thing out is descriptively, and descriptions so used, in contrast to referential uses, must be true of the thing to be named, and they may be indefinite, i.e., true of more than one thing, as is the case here since both sets of boys have other uncles. Since referential uses of descriptions may be false of the object the speaker intends to refer to, they are themselves in need of reference fixing, in their case by something about the context of their use, perhaps the knowing glance of the speaker toward the referent. We'll say more about reference fixing in sections F and L.)

Applying this conceptual tool to our example, the reference fixing description helps fix for my new relative the referent of a proper name, yet it's not the name's meaning for her. For it's not an analytic^ truth that Arthur is an uncle of these boys. If the description had been the name's meaning, then this would've been an analytic truth. (We return to this distinction between a meaning and a reference fixer in section F.) So, the proper names, when used in the course of expressing propositions, don't import into those propositions any descriptive content, not even the content of the descriptions that fix their referents.

End of digression on proper names; we return to the problem of determining the object of the directed-toward relation. My new relative is heard to mutter sentences of the form, "Sonny is a real so and so, but thank goodness Arthur isn't." We look to such remarks for guidance concerning what any belief of hers is directed toward. Since logically proper names differ from descriptions in the way pairs of them with the same referent, when interchanged in a sentence, affect the sentence's expression of a proposition, the account we gave of the meaning of logically proper names and of singular propositions (part of the philosophy of language) makes a prediction concerning the "directed-toward" relation (in folk psychology):

If

some new member of the family, after listening to all my nephews and unaware that I have two proper names, believes *de dicto* something complimentary about me, expressing it with the name "Arthur,"

then,

if

(i) propositions are the objects of the "directed-toward" relation, not the sentences which express them, and

(ii) logically proper names are merely labels conveying no description, not even a reference fixing description, into the propositions they're used to express, and

(iii) it's unreasonable in this instance to attribute to her any self-contradiction, which would be her both believing and disbelieving the same proposition, and

(iv) she does believe what she tells us she believes, and disbelieves what she tells us she disbelieves, and

(v) [here go all the other premises I'm not aware of having assumed],

then

she believes *de dicto* that same complimentary proposition about me, even if it's expressed with the name "Sonny."

Let's test the prediction. We ask her to assent to the same compliment with the name Sonny replacing the name Arthur. What? She denies it! By premises (iii) and (iv) her denial is evidence that the prediction fails. While I go find out what my nephews on my side have been saying about me, you reflect on which of the four known premises of our prediction to jettison, or uncover a hidden premise to jettison. One option is that propositions are not the objects of the "directed-toward" relation after all; the sentences themselves are, or they both are conjointly. That would be to deny premise (i). Might one hidden premise (v) be that there is a directed-toward relation? We might deny that. Then there'd be no problem of determining its objects. But there are many ways to distance ourselves from the embarrassing prediction our philosophy of language has foisted on us.

It's tempting to reach for the compromise solution: "She believes complimentary things of Sonny, but she doesn't realize it." We might just as well have said she believes uncomplimentary things of Arthur, but she doesn't realize it. In effect, the attempted compromise transmutes the problem into one of *de re* belief, my new relative believing of me that I'm both a so-and-so and not a so-and-so, only she doesn't realize it. We'll develop that problem for *de re* belief in section K. It's no concern of ours now, because the solution won't turn on the nature of the object of the directed-toward relation. But let's suppose we're now only testing predictions about the objects that *de dicto* beliefs are directed toward. Are they complete sentences or complete propositions? The attempted compromise is that my relative believes a complete proposition to the effect that something complimentary applies to Sonny, only she doesn't realize it.

Doesn't that solution replace one mystery with another, namely, *de dicto* belief without the believer realizing what her belief is directed toward? The situation is not one of subliminal belief nor Freudian repression. Nor is it that she's committed to believing something complimentary of Sonny without being aware of it, in the sense that the great Frege was committed by his theory of sets to believing there's a set which is both a member of itself and not a member of itself. Frege was not aware of his commitment to its existence until Russell informed him of the result. But my relative's situation is not Frege's. His commitment followed from things he believed. Her's follows only with the help of something she does not believe, namely, that Sonny is the same person as Arthur. So she's not committed by her believing complimentary things of Arthur to believing the same complimentary things of Sonny. I submit that the attempted compromise solution, namely, that she believes something *de dicto* without realizing it, is just words that tumble easily from the lips but don't express a coherent thought. Your reflections need not settle right now which of the premises leading to the false prediction is itself false. The exercise is just to sensitize you to the fact that certain theories of the meaning of proper names are on a collision course with the theory of belief over the issue of the object of the "directed-toward" relation. The crash will come in Part III. But we'll assume for the time being that belief is directed toward propositions. The word "proposition" functions in these early sections as a placeholder for the terminus of the "directed-toward" relation, whatever it turns out to be.

# Notes

1. This term was coined by the logician, L. Susan Stebbing, *A Modern Introduction to Logic* (1930), ch. 3, to convey the idea of a proper name that Bertrand Russell had expressed a decade earlier. The qualifier, "logically," is there to warn the reader that perhaps ordinary proper names do have descriptive content, although earlier proponents of this theory, for example, John Stuart Mill, thought them nondescriptive marks. See Mill's *A System of Logic*, ch. 2, §5. Mill thought this theory of proper names went back to the middle ages.

2. Not to be too mysterious, I'm alluding to the speculation that perhaps enough knowledge, of a clear and distinct sort, lifts the veil off unperceivable objects, disclosing the objects themselves to us despite their imperceptibility. In other words, enough of the first kind of knowledge of unperceivable objects just is the second kind of knowledge of them. I think this is the hope of rationalists like Anselm and Descartes. I suspect that much of the controversy about certitude is misdirected and really is about relational knowledge. For there's an infallibility about that which a relational belief is about, namely, that it exists. Could it be that enough clear and distinct predication ensures the existence of that of which it's predicated?

3. Aristotle, *Metaphysics*, VII.15: 1039b30ff; IX.10: 1051b24; *De Anima*, III.6. In India philosophers distinguished *savikalpaka* perception, comparable to perception yielding knowledge by description, from *nirvikalpaka* perception, comparable to perception yielding knowledge by acquaintance. See ch. 9 of Satischandra Chatterjee, *The Nyaya Theory of Knowledge*, 2nd ed. (1950). The function of *nirvikalpaka* perception in establishing reference is stated on p. 199.

4. William James, *The Principles of Psychology* (1890), ch. VIII, and Russell, "On Denoting," *Mind* (1905). I insist on the difference in kind between the two ways of knowing, whereas James did not, thinking that acquaintance always brought with it some descriptive knowledge. That's true, but not a good reason to make the distinction one of degree. James called knowledge by description

"knowledge about," which conflicts with my reserving the preposition "about" for reporting knowledge by acquaintance.

I also dissociate my use of "acquaintance" from three doctrines that Russell built into his notion, and which most readers of Russell today ignore and rightly so: (1) When we seem to be acquainted with external objects, really we are only "immediately" acquainted with sense data. Russell himself often downplayed this feature of his account of acquaintance. (2) The self contains no semantically relevant complexity; it is a logically simple subject of the relation of acquaintance, and (3) the acquaintance relation is the irreducibly primordial intentional (i.e., aboutness) relation; the aboutness relation is not constituted contextually. Russell himself discarded both the latter notions when he developed his theory of noticing in 1940 (*An Inquiry into Meaning and Truth*, chs. 3 and 24). I tell the story in my "The Judger in Russell's Theories of Judgment," *Russell: the Journal of the Bertrand Russell Archives*, new series 17.2, (Winter 1997-98) 116f. Russell tells the story in his *My Philosophical Development*, ch. XII.

5. Russell, *The Problems of Philosophy* (1912), ch. 12.

6. Not "is defined as," because of the problem that one's evidence may only justify the truth that one believes by way of a falsehood. That sort of justification for a true belief is inconsistent with the belief being knowledge. This is the so-called Gettier problem for the definition of knowledge. Since we're doing ontology,ˆ not epistemology, we need only avoid the problem, not solve it. For a review of the first attempts to solve the problem, see Robert K. Shope, *The Analysis of Knowing* (1983).

7. "Quantifiers and Propositional Attitudes," *Journal of Philosophy* 53 (1956), and reprinted in his *The Ways of Paradox* (1966), uses relational versus notional beliefs. In his *Word and Object* (1960), §31 (also §35 and §44) he uses transparent versus opaque beliefs. In "Speaking of Objects" (1965) *Ontological Relativity and Other Essays*, 21f, he uses attributary versus propositional beliefs. In his reply to Kaplan in Davidson and Hintikka, eds., *Words and Objections: Essays on the Work of W. V. Quine*, 341, he uses triadic versus dyadic beliefs; on p. 344 he expands triadic to polyadic, and he cites Chisholm's use of *de re* and *de dicto*. In "Intensions Revisited" in French, Uehling, and Wettstein, eds., *Contemporary Perspectives in the Philosophy of Language* (1979), he adopts these terms and adds multigrade for *de re* beliefs.

8. "Intensions Revisited" in French, Uehling, and Wettstein, eds., *Contemporary Perspectives in the Philosophy of Language* (1979), reprinted in Quine, *Theories and Things*, ch. 13. See also his "Reactions," section VI, in P. Leonardi and M. Santambrogio, eds, *On Quine* (1995).

9. Ordinary proper names fail to be unique labels; I've known three other Arthur Falks. Social security numbers are better in this respect, but are partly descriptive, for instance, those that begin with a 900 number are resident noncitizens.

10. The paraphrase I give is equivalent to the one Russell actually offered in his "On Denoting."

11. Keith Donnellan, "Reference and Definite Descriptions," *Philosophical*

*Review* 75 (1966). Philosophers know the distinction from Donnellan's article. He framed the idea, contrasted it against another idea as a foil, and provided contrastive names, thus forcing the issue, but the idea itself can be found earlier, even in Russell's elder contemporary and coauthor with him of the *Principia Mathematica*, Alfred North Whitehead. See pp. 7-8 of the University of Michigan reprint of his *The Concept of Nature* (1920). For further reflections on the complexity of questions of priority in the field of conceptual innovation, see the last note, also notes in sections M and N.

    12. Edward Keenan, "A Note on Marking Transparency and Opacity" *Linguistic Inquiry* 4 (1973) 421-24. Shaun Nichols gave me this reference.

    13. E.g., Michael Tye, "Belief (1): Metaphysics of," in Guttenplan, 140-146. See p. 145, noting that he uses *"de re"* for relational belief.

    14. Quine, *Word and Object*, §56. He applies the concept to attitudes on p. 274.

    15. Quine, "Five Milestones of Empiricism" (1975), reprinted as ch. 7 of his *Theories and Things*. R. Carnap, "Empiricism, Semantics, and Ontology," in the supplement to *Meaning and Necessity*, enlarged ed. (1956).

    16. Bertrand Russell, *My Philosophical Development* (1956) ch. 18, end of section I.

    17. Bertrand Russell, *Introduction to Mathematical Philosophy* (1919), ch. 16:

> But as long as we are using names *as* names, whether we say "Scott" or we say "Sir Walter" is as irrelevant to what we are asserting as whether we are speaking English or French. Thus so long as names are used *as* names [meaning that "Scott" does not abbreviate the description "the person called 'Scott'"], "Scott is Sir Walter" is the same trivial proposition as "Scott is Scott".

Quoted from p. 175 of the Simon and Schuster paperback edition.

    18. The distinction between descriptions that are the meanings of names and descriptions that are reference fixing for names was *named* by Saul Kripke in his "Naming and Necessity," first lecture, 274ff. Whether he or Ruth Barcan Marcus was the first to *make* the distinction is controverted. See Paul Humphreys and James Fetzer, eds., *The New Theory of Reference: Kripke, Marcus, and Its Origins* (1998), especially Quentin Smith, "Marcus and the New Theory of Reference: A Reply to Scott Soames," 40ff. Priority in the discovery of ideas is an important issue, but difficult because of the problems with sameness of meaning. If one person says something tersely and another says something elaborate ten years later, in the same vein and in such a way that many others come to understand it for the first time, did the first discover it and the second develop and promulgate it, or did the second discover it and the first only anticipate the discovery?

# B. All Attitudes are Propositional Attitudes.

Belief is one type of a more generic mental state that Russell called a **propositional attitude**.[1] Desire is another propositional attitude. In this section we make some claims about all the attitudes.

### §1. Generalizing to all propositional attitudes.

We'll define propositional attitudes a step at a time. First think of the word "attitude." Strictly, attitudes contrast with acts. For example, believing and judging contrast as attitude and act. Acts are things a person does, whereas attitudes are states of a person, among which are the reasons why she does what she does. (I'll say more about this contrast when we discuss dispositions at the end of this section.) We'll not be so strict in our use of the term "attitude"; we let it cover acts too. So folk psychology's basic category of entities is "attitudes." Other types of propositional attitude are these: desiring that something be so, fearing that something will be so, ordering that something be made true (this is really an act), thinking that something is so, wishing to know whether something is so. I'm sure that you could add indefinitely to the list. (That surety was another one!)

Beliefs and desires are the central attitudes, in that they are components of all the other attitudes. I suspect hatred, frustration, fear, loathing, shame, pride, expectation, surprise, disappointment, and the like could all be defined as beliefs of a certain sort coupled with desires of a certain sort. I'll not let us get sidetracked onto that project. Some of our attitudes are justified and others are quite unreasonable. The beliefs and desires that support and maintain them account for their differing in rationality; for the beliefs and desires may themselves be more or less reasonable.

Folk psychology countenances degrees of belief ranging from certainty of a proposition's truth to certainty of its falsity, and intensities of desire ranging from wanting its truth very much, through indifference, to wanting its falsity very much. That desire comes in degrees is often obvious from the discomfort we feel when it's unsatisfied or the pleasure we feel when it is satisfied, but degrees for belief? Why not just belief and nonbelief?

One argument for degrees of belief is based on the **preface paradox**, or in a parallel scenario, the lottery paradox. Here's the paradox: The author of a book believes each of the sentences she wrote, but confesses in the preface of her book that surely there's error in her book. Of course, if she knew what the error was she'd have corrected it. Convinced of her fallibility, she's ready to admit error even though she does not know what the errors are. Her position is reasonable. Yet it may seem that the author has contradicted herself, for as a matter of logic, if you believe that A and you believe that B, then you believe their conjunction, A and B. So if she believes each of the sentences in her book, she must believe their conjunction, which is her book. But to admit error is to deny that very conjunction. How then can she maintain her logical consistency and admit to error?[2]

There's a straightforward solution to this paradox, if we can believe our beliefs more or less and we do not believe all our beliefs with certitude. For if we believe A to some degree and believe B to some degree, then obviously we cannot be surer of the conjunction, A and B, than we are of the conjuncts, and in fact we might be less sure of the conjunction than we are of either of the conjuncts. Logic supports the gradual decrease in surety of a conjunction as we add more independent unsure conjuncts to it. Logic also supports believing to a high degree short of certitude *de re* about any randomly picked sentence in the book that it's true, and also believing to a high degree short of certitude *de dicto* that some sentence in the book is false. So let's admit that beliefs come in degrees. Our author then may admit to some error without inconsistency.

That still seems paradoxical if you think the author published a book she disbelieves. The corrective is her high opinion about how close her book is to the whole of the truth she aims for in her book, that is, how much verisimilitude^ it has, which refers to the fact that some falsehoods are closer to the whole of the truth than others. For instance, a conjunction with one false conjunct is closer to the truth than one with two false conjuncts. Indeed some falsehoods are closer to the whole of the truth than some truths are, for example, tautologies. (There's more on verisimilitude in section Z and the Glossary.) While the author's admission of likely falsehood is appropriate candor, it would be odd indeed if she were to add that it lacked verisimilitude. Why then would she publish her book? Why would anyone read it?

Certain results of the admission of some error may surprise you. Let our degrees of belief be modeled by the probabilities in probability theory. There are good reasons for thinking rational degrees of belief are so modeled, but we'll not tarry to discuss them. Rationality then requires people in one kind of circumstance to believe both sides of a contradiction equally, for when they believe one side 50-50, as we say, they must believe the other side 50-50 too. They believe the conjunction of the two propositions to degree 0, that is, not at all. For one of them must be false, and so the conjunction must be false, no matter which one is true. (Puzzled? The probability of a conjunction for you is the product of the probability you assign to one of them and the probability the other would have, if the first's probability were 1 for you. In the case we're considering, that's 0.5 multiplied by 0.)

You'll find the concept of **partial belief** (as a degree of belief less than certitude is customarily referred to) easier to understand, indeed it will be easier to understand belief as a state of mind admitting of gradations of confidence, if you don't equate believing with affirming or denying a sentence. Since typically sentences contain no adverb indicating unsureness (e.g., "perhaps"), you might think that one must have only extreme degrees of belief in order to express one's beliefs by affirming or denying sentences. Of course, that's not so. It may be that one expresses categorically only one's extreme beliefs; it need not be that one has only extreme beliefs. Resisting that equation of belief with assertion, you might still think that belief is a dichotomous state of mind—believing or not believing. If so, two ways out of the preface paradox are open to you. On the first, you transfer the gradation from the believing to the believed. That is, instead of the author's believing to degree *n* that the first sentence of her book is in error, she believes fully the statistical proposition that *n* is the chance that her first sentence is in error. On the second, you superimpose the dichotomous notion of belief right back on the gradated one, by defining one's dichotomous belief in a proposition as gradated-believing it more than one gradated-believes its denial. I don't recommend either of these alternatives, less fundamentally because I find their solutions to the preface paradox defective, more fundamentally because I see no argument that dichotomizing is essential to the notion of belief or important to any purpose beliefs serve. You are free to disagree, and you'll have lots of company if you do. We'll not tarry to examine this fuss.[3]

Another surprise from admitting partial belief is that degrees of belief and intensities of desire are not independent of one another. The relationship is this paraphrase of one of Richard Jeffrey's axioms for decision theory: The intensity of desire that a disjunction of incompatible propositions be true is a weighted average of the intensities of desire for each of the incompatible ways in which it can come true, the weights being one's degrees of belief in those ways. We should note two consequences. First, given a proposition whose truth one has a positive or negative desire for, the closer one's degree of belief in it is to certitude, the closer to indifference is one's intensity of desire for it or against it, where indifference means no difference in desire for it and for a tautology.^ One no more desires what he knows is or was the case than he desires that it either rain or not rain. The positive or negative feature of one's desire is replaced in the case of certitude by either excitement and enjoyment of it or dismay and suffering it. For a desiderative non-indifference is directed toward only that which is not for sure.[4] Of course, taking the proposition as a tensed proposition, *p now*, its being for sure is consistent with desiring its content *p* continuing hereafter to be the case. Indeed one wonders how much interpenetration of these fundamental and distinct attitudes there is. Can one believe anything without desiring the truth? Can one desire anything without believing something good?

The second consequence of the fact that desires are informed is that we cannot equate their intensities with the urgency of feelings, which do not vary with information. When one feels bowel or bladder pressure, the desire to relieve oneself varies with the degree of belief that the place is appropriate for doing so and no embarrassment will be incurred, despite the invariance of the felt pressure.

Degrees of belief and intensities of desire can be measured using the probability calculus and a utility calculus. Such measurements form the basis for an important interpretation of decision theory, which is the conceptual foundation for economics and the other social sciences, comparable to the foundational role that set^ theory occupies in mathematics. Some philosophers,[5] including me, think that decision theory is the transformation of folk psychology into a science. If so, it adds weight to the project we're pursuing (stated in the Introduction) of showing that the attitudes postulated by folk psychology are objective and worthy of scientific study. But decision theory is mathematical, and we won't get into that. And so we won't get into the phenomenon that decision theory elucidates, namely, the reasons that justify our having or changing our beliefs and desires.

Now to the second part of our definition of propositional attitudes: That belief is an attitude that's propositional means that it is directed toward a proposition. Other attitudes are also directed toward propositions. Our desires are desires that propositions be true. Our anger is our being affronted by the truth of a proposition. Our doing something is our acting, with the outcome being that something's so.

All the propositional attitudes have relational and notional varieties. For example, where there's the custom of arranged marriages, couples begin by desiring each other notionally and end, if all goes well, by desiring each other relationally. Russell may have been the first of the analytic philosophers to note the close connection of relational and notional attitudes, and their subtle difference, when he joked in 1905:[6]

> I have heard of a touchy owner of a yacht to whom a guest, on first seeing it, remarked, "I thought your yacht was larger than it is"; and the owner of the yacht replied, "No, my yacht is not larger than it is". What the guest meant was [relational and sensible], "The size that I thought your yacht was is greater than the size your yacht is"; the meaning attributed to him is [notional and nonsensical], "I thought the size of your yacht is greater than the size of your yacht".

How Russellian to introduce a major distinction by way of a witticism! You might try your hand at it too, like this: A bachelor, notorious for womanizing, decides to reform and tells his married friend, "I need a wife." The friend replies, "Not mine I hope." The friend imputes a relational meaning to his friend's words, suggesting skepticism about his reform. Russell gave another example, making use of the analysis of definite descriptions in their context in sentences, which I mentioned in section A:

> . . . when we say, "George IV wished to know whether Scott was the author of *Waverley*", we normally mean [the notional] "George IV wished to know whether one and only one man wrote *Waverley* and Scott was that man"; but we *may* also mean [the relational]: "One and only one man wrote *Waverley*, and George IV wished to know whether Scott was that man".

Russell had this distinction forced to his attention by his technique of paraphrasing sentences that contained definite descriptions (e.g., "the author of *Waverley*"), because two ways of paraphrasing are possible when the sentence to be paraphrased refers to someone's propositional attitude about the author of *Waverley*, as the quotation shows. He decided both ways are legitimate and mean different things. (Russell's analysis detects an ambiguity in the original sentence and in negative sentences also,[7] and it can disambiguate them. That fact is an argument for his thesis that definite descriptions are not genuine terms, for the alternative thesis seems helpless to do the same disambiguation. It is in addition to the argument we saw in section A, that it solved problems arising from singular terms that name nothing. We'll see another argument for Russell's thesis in section F. For now, however, we'll continue assuming definite descriptions are names.)

## §2. All attitudes are propositional, even though not all reports are.

A person's attitudes are interconnected, particularly by the practice of justifying an attitude by appeal to one's other attitudes. The everyday practice of justification, that is, the giving of reasons for one's actions and attitudes, makes human beings different from the other animals that have beliefs and desires. What is the nature of the difference in attitudes, which endows them with rational interconnections, and is it so great? We'll not stop to answer, but just note the extent of the interconnectedness in a human being. A big question, whose answer is affected by this interconnectedness, is whether propositional attitudes can be reduced to traits defined in the terms used by the physical sciences. If so, we'd achieve a great unification of the sciences of matter and mind, which so far must treat the mind differently from the way they treat matter. A major task is to do justice to the human difference within the reduction. These notes don't discuss the reduction of the mental to the physical. We don't define the attitudes reductively; that would be revisionary ontology.^ We discuss them in our customary mentalistic ways. Obviously, we must examine the variety of phenomena tied to the attitudes, including their interconnectedness, before we appraise any proposed reduction of them to states described purely in the terms of physical and chemical theory.

A reductionism of another sort may seem to be implied by the word "propositional" in the phrase, "propositional attitude," however. Are all attitudes reducible to propositional attitudes? This question, which requires a yes or no answer, confuses a psychological question with a linguistic question, and we must see what makes the confusion so seductive. We define **reductionism** generally as the consolidation of a variety of cases by equating all the varieties to just one of them. All are reduced to that one case. It's better to conduct a reduction at the level of semantic ascent, if it's feasible, for the precision it yields. In other words, the reduction should be a reduction of sentences about the reduced subject matter to sentences about the subject matter it's reduced to. The equating, which is at the heart of any reduction, is then showing the equivalence of the reduced sentences to the ones they're reduced to. Semantic ascent thus brings the clarity of logical structure and the detail of sentence-by-sentence equivalencies to the question of reductionism.

Many philosophers wish to foreclose the possibility of attitudes other than propositional attitudes. I'm one of them. All the attitudes should be seen as directed toward propositions, provided we allow incomplete propositions as well as complete ones. Your wanting a unicorn, despite the wanting's not being expressly toward a proposition, is at least implicitly directed toward one, namely, wanting that *you have a unicorn.* (Relational attitudes are directed toward incomplete propositions; the notional attitudes toward complete propositions, according to the preferred definition in section A. More on that soon.) This thesis is *not* at the level of semantic ascent; it's a claim in folk psychology. It would be a powerful argument for this thesis, however, if it could be shown that every report of an attitude is reducible to a report specifying the attitude's propositional object. Thus semantic ascent to a thesis about reductionism is distinct from the thesis in folk psychology, just as premises are distinct from the conclusion. The semantic ascent gathers linguistic evidence for the thesis in folk psychology.

I'll now defend the psychological thesis that all attitudes are propositional attitudes. But I'll admit that many of our ways of talking about our attitudes are not reducible to talk of attitudes directed toward propositions. These reports of seemingly nonpropositional attitudes are ways of communicating, which don't reflect the true structure of what they are communications about. How then is the psychological thesis of this section, that all attitudes are propositional attitudes, related to the linguistic thesis of reductionism, that all reports of attitudes are reducible to reports revelatory of the propositional object? If this reductionism had been true, it would've been a conclusive argument for the thesis. But, since many reports can be reduced, though not all can be, that still is an argument for the thesis, though not conclusive. Despite the fact that at the level of semantic ascent a reductionism of reports is false, the folk psychological thesis survives, since there are other arguments for the reduction of the attitudes reported on.

What I just warned against is excessive reliance on semantic ascent. It's only a tool, and sometimes philosophers, habituated to using it, let their habit warp their understanding of their problems. Philosophers are not primarily students of words!

I believe all attitudes are propositional attitudes, but I'm not a total reductionist in the sense just defined, because I don't think my folk psychological claim implies that all reports of attitudes must be equivalent to reports which display propositions as the content of the attitudes. Nor do I believe my admission of reports which display people, places, and things, and not propositions, as the attitude's objects requires that I give up my claim that all attitudes are propositional attitudes. For those reports need not be taken as displaying the structure of the attitudes they report. Let's now look at the evidence for the thesis, the partial reductive evidence and the evidence which is independent of the reductive evidence.

That the reduction sometimes works is our first evidence for the folk psychological thesis. If the thesis that all attitudes are propositional attitudes is correct, our grammar is misleading since we say things like "she wants a unicorn." Obviously, "a unicorn" is not a proposition, not even an incomplete one. What reasons have we for distrusting our grammar in such cases? It's an argument in favor of a reduction in this case that there's an analysis of this sentence which avoids committing to the existence of unicorns. Notice that to say someone shot a unicorn commits you to the existence of unicorns. For a unicorn-shooting to occur, there must be the unicorn shot. Is "wanting a unicorn" to be analyzed the way we analyze "shooting a unicorn"? Must there be the unicorn wanted? The analysis of "wanting a unicorn" as an attitude directed toward a proposition, namely, that one have a unicorn, avoids there having to be the wanted unicorn. First it avoids the analogy. For the words "a unicorn" occur in that analysis, not as the object of her wanting, but as the object of her having. That would not be the case if we analyzed "wanting a unicorn" in the same way as we analyze "shooting a unicorn." Secondly, it avoids the consequence of committing to the existence of unicorns. It will become clearer in section C how this second step of the argument works, after we discuss the notion of concurrence. The idea will be roughly this: To want that one have a unicorn includes to want the existence of a unicorn, which is a necessary condition for having it. But this existence is not a necessary condition for the wanting itself to occur.

Quine argued for a reduction of all attitudes to propositional attitudes on this ground of avoiding existence commitments. Quine also argued for it on the ground that the reduction helped us see how we could distinguish, for instance, two senses of the seemingly nonpropositional attitude of wanting a sloop. In the first sense the want is really directed toward a complete proposition, that I have a sloop, and represents the desire to be relieved of slooplessness in any way. The want is notional. In the second sense there is a particular sloop, and my want is directed toward the incomplete proposition, that I have *it*. Here the relief I desire must come from just one particular object. The want is relational. Both wants are propositional. Quine's two arguments for the reduction of attitudes to propositional attitudes would be conclusive, if there were no other way to avoid committing to the existence of nonexistent entities like unicorns or to draw this distinction (but there are other ways) and if all attitudes were subject to these two problems (but they aren't).[8]

Linguists adduce evidence that, when we utter something like, "Jim wants a wife," the sentence displays tell-tale signs that can only be explained by supposing that the mind, in the course of producing this sentence, had produced a preliminary version of the sentence, where the verb really was followed by a clause, which was then truncated. The idea is whimsically expressed in the title of McCawley's article, "On Identifying the Remains of Deceased Clauses."[9] One of several arguments he uses is to ask, what is the antecedent of the "it" in the following sentence?

●Jim wants a wife, but his mother won't allow it.

We can vary the gender and number of the noun phrase following the verb "wants," but the "it" properly remains singular and neuter. This constancy is right if the pronoun's antecedent is the clause, "that he have a wife," or another clause where "a wife" might be replaced by other noun phrases, like "some horses."

Nevertheless, we cannot construe every other report of a seemingly nonpropositional attitude similarly, that is, we cannot find a straightforwardly propositional attitude report it's identical to. So the *linguistic* thesis of reductionism is false. For example,

●Knowing Al and fearing him.

The attitudes underlying reports of knowledge and fear of Al are attitudes directed toward some propositions featuring Al such that you know some of them are true and fear others are true too. Let's distinguish the attitudes from the reports of the attitudes. I confess that I cannot find an identity between these reports of knowledge and fear of Al and reports that make explicit the propositional objects of the knowledge or the fear. Therefore I concede that this reductionism fails for the universal reduction of reports. For the requirements for reductionism are stringent: One must demonstrate the equivalence of the statement reduced to the statement to which it is reduced, and we cannot do that for reports like "she fears Al."

Nevertheless that a proposition is involved in her fear becomes obvious if we contrast "she fears Al" with "she fears for Al." The difference is in how Al figures in the propositions. In fearing Al, she must think of Al as responsible for harm to herself. In fearing for Al, however, the harm is to Al. She may fear that he'll propose marriage to her sister, thus causing himself great suffering, for she's engaged to another. Obviously, however, no such report of an explicit proposition will be logically equivalent to the original.

So I don't concede that the folk psychological thesis fails for the attitudes being reported. Her fear is directed toward something propositional about Al. Why not take such reports at face value and admit some attitudes are not propositional attitudes? Knowing Al is an instance of knowledge by acquaintance, the topic we began section A with. We noted there that philosophers postulate our acquaintance to be with complex things, like singular propositions, and also with simple things, which make up the complex things. Of the two kinds of acquaintance, with simples and with complexes, which comes first? The image of wholes assembled from preexisting parts may suggest the answer: acquaintance with simples. Simples would be subpropositional.

Not so fast! Why not the alternative image of an organismic whole, of understanding the parts only by their contribution to the whole? Then an acquaintance with the complexes would come first. My thesis requires the second image. The tradition in philosophy that prevails today prefers the first alternative, from parts to wholes. Traditional philosophers object to my analysis of the knowing of Al as a propositional knowing, for Al is a part of the make-up of the complex entities which are all the singular propositions about him. We know a complex by knowing its parts, they would say. Thus we must know him in a way independent of our knowing the propositions, since knowing him is a prerequisite to knowing them.

Against the tradition and its arbitrary image of construction, considerations in the theory of meaning require the **proposition** to be the *unit* of meaningfulness. The principle is often called the **context principle**, alluding to Frege's statement of it: ". . . it is only in the context of a proposition that words have any meaning . . ."[10] To put it another way, the primary semantic concepts are truth and falsity, which apply to propositions, not the concept of reference, which applies to names. Quine traces the initial realization of the truth of this principle to Bentham, and his practice of defining words only in the context of sentences, what we know today as contextual definition. A word is defined as it occurs in a sentence, by paraphrasing it with a sentence that does not contain the word.[11] The principle seems to have been a commonplace among jurists well before Bentham's time, however. Four hundred years ago, Francis Bacon said (in Karl Popper's translation of the Latin), "Out of all the words [of a sentence or paragraph] we have to extract the sense in whose light each single word is to be interpreted."[12]

This semantic primacy of the proposition seems to make the thesis that all attitudes are propositional attitudes a corollary, even while allowing reports of attitudes to escape reduction. I'm inclined to argue, any attitude is directed toward something understandable, that is, a meaningful something. Perhaps I should resist the inclination, for people have attitudes directed toward what seems meaningless, when they're perplexed, and they have attitudes toward nothing meaningful, even if they seem to have something in mind, when they're in a muddle. But the right way to deal with these cases is to say they are defective or counterfeit attitudes, precisely because they fail to be directed toward propositions. It's not that they are undefective attitudes directed toward things that are not propositions. What are the defective attitudes in their own right, if they're not intentional states? They'd be dispositional states, which I discuss later, or exercises of dispositions.

So attitudes are directed toward propositions, if the proposition is the minimal independently meaningful something, or, if you prefer, the primary thing meant by itself. (There you have another characterization of propositions, to add to those given in section A.) When people understand a sentence new to them, they already understand the words individually, but those understandings are just the understanding of other sentences in which the words occur, and some sentences consist of just one word, as we shall see in section T. This connection to the context principle, then, is a second argument for the thesis that all attitudes are directed toward propositions, if the argument for propositions being the minimal units of independent meaning can be made without begging the question. So I stick to my guns: The knowing of Al is derivative from the knowing of propositions in which he figures. The fact that some reports of attitudes resist reduction to reports that make explicit the proposition that the attitude is directed toward shows nothing about the underlying psychology. That's merely a linguistic phenomenon.

Here are more instances of attitudes which may seem like they are directed toward objects simpler than propositions:
●Thinking about unicorns
is having propositional attitudes, but just how being a unicorn figures in the propositions is so undetermined by the description "thinking about unicorns" that one cannot say which propositional attitudes one's thinking of unicorns is reduced to. So the reports of thinking about unicorns are not reducible to reports which have the form of reporting the proposition the attitude is directed toward. Big deal; the failure of the reduction does not prove there are attitudes that are not directed toward propositions.
●Loving or hating someone
may be more than just attitudes toward propositions,[13] but they're at least in part propositional attitudes.
●One can hear Turkish being spoken
without hearing that Turkish is being spoken. One can see 99 bottles, even

perceive them all, and not perceive that they number 99 or anything more specific than "many." But the recognition of something nonspecific would be propositional. In sections T and U we'll consider how perception can be a propositional attitude despite its seeming to be pre-propositional, so to speak.

●Having sensations
does not seem propositional, although perhaps we cannot have sensations without believing that we're having them, and perhaps pleasurable sensations are pleasurable by virtue of the person experiencing them having a propositional attitude of being pleased, for no ulterior reason, that he's having them.[14] Similarly for pain and suffering.

And there are some contentious cases:

●Suppose I just entertain in mind an object,
but think nothing about it. Berkeley asks us to think of a tree that nobody thinks of.[15] He's not asking us to think that nobody thinks of it; he's just asking us to think of *it*. Perhaps he asks too much. Frankly it's a powerful incentive to the thesis I espouse, a third argument for it, that it helps put Berkeley's "master argument" to rest. He requests of us anti-idealists, that we think the thing that's unthought of, which we postulate in opposition to his idealism,^ and realize the futility of the attempt and so the self-contradictory nature of our position. His argument depends for its force on taking the non-propositional mode of reporting attitudes as revealing a real psychological state. We must reject that! It's only a way of talking. People don't think the thing that's unthought of; they think the proposition, that there's a thing unthought of, and they think other propositions featuring that thing as their subject. No contradiction there.

The wily idealist has a come-back, exploiting our way of analyzing relational attitudes. He concedes people think of propositions, but notes they can think incomplete propositions about the thing that's unthought of. So he asks us to think something of it *de re*. Here's the proper reply, which I develop later in section T: Is not Berkeley asking us to imagine *that*, lo, tree? The "Lo, tree" is a proposition so simple it lacks division into subject and predicate. Thus one thinks of a tree in the sense needed to comply with his request without thinking of it in the sense he needs to derive a contradiction. Berkeley would not be happy with that analysis! Hmmmm ... Watch for the next installment of our debate with Berkeley. It comes in section J.

●Suppose Ctesias worships Zeus.
In neither this case nor the previous one does a proposition immediately suggest itself for the attitude to be directed towards. The difficulty here,

together with the availability of other ways to avoid unicorns and distinguish varieties of slooplessness, has led some to skepticism about this thesis.[16] But let's try. Looking more closely at Ctesias worshiping Zeus, is he not undertaking *that* Zeus recognize that Ctesias believes Zeus is his lord almighty? A better analysis has Ctesias undertaking to create a *de re* attitude in Zeus, that he recognize about Ctesias and himself, that the former believes the latter to be the former's lord almighty. Ctesias's worship is an attitude directed toward an attitude directed toward an attitude.

One more purported counterexample:

●David has a good idea of how the tune for "Happy Birthday to You" goes. If you ask him he'll hum it for you, but a hummed tune is not a proposition. Yet "having a good idea of" is an attitude. David's attitude is a propositional attitude. Although a hummed tune is not a proposition, it can be a term in one. The proposition that he has a good idea of is, "The tune goes like this: [here put the humming]."

Our thesis covers the contentious cases, after all. So there is a fourth argument for it: No purported counterexamples resist explanation in terms of propositional attitudes.

I reject two supposed examples of attitudes directed toward nothing whatsoever, neither propositional nor nonpropositional:

●So-called undirected anxiety.
It's rather omnidirected anxiety, and so has objects.

●One Buddhist thinker describes the trance state called cessation in a way that implies it "is, in essence, a consciousness with no intentional object, a consciousness that does nothing but provide a continual mental 'something' which ultimately will act as cause for the re-emergence of mental events (active consciousness, consciousnesses with intentional objects) from the attainment of cessation."[17] But that's mere assertion. Let's distinguish between the experience, which we should not deny, and the theory of what occurs in the experience, for example, aspects of it which might affect one's memory of the experience. Many Buddhist schools, while accepting the occurrence of a special trance state, reject the characterization of that state as contentless. I have no acquaintance with this state myself, but I wonder whether it might not be directed toward tautologous^ content without there being in mind any logically true sentence.

In any case, our analyses of beliefs are meant to carry over to all attitudes once their objects are expressed as complete or incomplete propositions. Thus if I desire an apple (a thing-object), we paraphrase this as, I desire *that* I have an apple (a proposition-object). If I see you (a thing-object), we paraphrase this as, I see *that* you are visually present to me (a proposition-object: "Lo, you!"), where "presence" is cashed out in some nonattitudinal way, perhaps causally. If I know you, there are several propositions distinctively true of you that I know. If the walrus hunts for a snark, the walrus endeavors that he himself find a snark. If I try to smile, I endeavor that I smile. Such propositional attitudes are the phenomena we analyze indirectly in these notes by concentrating on belief.

An important consequence of our thesis is that a person's attitudes are strongly interconnected, since propositions are strongly interconnected by relations of logic and probabilistic relevance. The consequence is so obviously a desirable one that it constitutes further support for the thesis. A person's attitudes, by virtue of their propositional content, are open to criticism to ensure that they are interconnected in the ways prescribed by logic and probability theory.

As an aside, it isn't merely accidental that many attitudes reported as about things, when expanded into attitudes toward propositions, take a peculiar sort of incomplete proposition as their contents, namely one that must include a pronoun that refers back to the person with the attitude, pronouns like "I" or "he himself." They are a special kind of relational attitude, which we begin exploring in section M. What Quine calls **egocentric propositional attitudes** are primitive instances of them, had by cats, for instance. The reference to propositions in the primitive egocentric attitudes can be eliminated by reducing the attitudes to behavioral dispositions under the control of a range of patterns of sensory stimulation.[18] (I explain dispositions in the next subsection.) Rather than stress a behavioristic analysis that eliminates their content, however, I'd say the content's referring to one's own action shows that these attitudes, when they're connected to behavioral dispositions, are the kind of desire that's called intending or choosing or deciding.[19] David Lewis argues from various considerations, including the fact that the egocentric attitudes of human beings are directed toward sophisticated contents that cannot be reduced to behavioral dispositions, that we should reduce all attitudes to attitudes directed toward incomplete propositions which refer back to oneself.[20] His approach to the contents of belief leads directly to an anti-Quinean view of relational belief: *All* belief would be relational. Notional belief would be just a variety of relational belief. We postpone pursuing this issue until section N, since most of the propositional attitudes we'll start with don't come from the attitudes reported with thing-objects.

## §3. Some mental states are not attitudes.

We use cognitive language for mental conditions that are not directed toward propositions at all, complete or incomplete, or at least not in any straight-forward way. We say we know how to drive a car or speak Italian. The analysis of know-how does not seem to posit that the person is directed toward any propositions. Know-how is skill, and skill is an acquired **disposition** to behave in certain ways under certain conditions. Thus we analyze it as we analyze dispositions in general. The generic way to analyze a disposition is in terms of stimulus and response. The form of analysis of dispositions, e.g., the disposition of salt to dissolve upon being put in liquid water, is a subjunctive^ conditional. Roughly thus:

Salt is soluble.

If salt were to be put in liquid water, then it would dissolve.

Generally: if the stimulus were to be, then the response would come about.[21] The logic of subjunctive conditionals is quite subtle and requires a course of its own to master.

Unfortunately for us who yearn for simplicity, dispositions form a polymorphous group. The simple formula for defining them in terms of stimulus and response falls short in two respects at least for mental dispositions, first, in the complexity of the possibilities of interchange between alternative stimuli and the connections between them and the responses, and second, in the relevance of meaningfulness to the identification of stimuli and responses. Consider first the complexity: A mental disposition, whether it's acquired by learning or by genetic inheritance, may involve so many stimuli and responses, which may be interconnected so complexly and so open-endedly, that it defeats an analysis of the disposition. Our moods and personality traits are just such complex dispositions. Your friend may be irritable (a disposition), but you might never be sure what stimulus will trigger his next expression of irritation. Other dispositions are so interlocked that they cannot be analyzed one by one, for instance, irritability and propensity to haste. Perhaps the interlocking is due to their being associated with attitudes, whose propositional contents then create the implicatory and probabilistic connections. Some mental dispositions come very close to being propositional attitudes, for example, perceptual skills in recognizing someone and intellectual skills like grasping the use of the word "or." One could not give a stimulus-response definition of this grammatical disposition atomistically, since it's interlocked with the dispositions to use other words, including "and" and "not." Some propositional attitudes include nonpropositional dispositions in their analysis, for example,

● your finding it hilarious that such and such is the case.

It would not be hilarious if, upon the stimulus of your thinking of it, you did not respond with involuntary contractions of certain facial muscles. It's probably a prerequisite to having propositional attitudes that one have acquired many of these interlocked cognitive dispositions. They too are part of having a mind.

The second shortcoming of the proposed definition concerns the involvement of meaning. Recall from the beginning of this section that we're using the word "attitude" loosely to cover acts as well as nonactive states. In the stricter sense of attitude, propositional attitudes also fall within the group of dispositions. For they are states of a person which mediate the causal connections between that person's stimuli and responses. Thus belief and desire are dispositions. These attitudinal dispositions seem to defy analysis in terms of stimuli and responses that are only described in the language of physical science. We must introduce meaningfulness and purpose as well in the very description of the stimuli and responses. Even the know-how mentioned earlier, knowing how to drive a car, may require reference to propositions. It's clear that no particular car is being referred to in this description of a skill. Just as reference to unicorns pushed us toward propositions earlier, so now these cars force us to look to a proposition as a whole, for example, that I drive cars. Surely the cars referred to here are not just those that I have driven or will drive. Just what is the relation to this proposition, which my car-driving skill invokes?

Perhaps some mental states might be analyzed equally well as propositional attitudes or as nonpropositional dispositions, a cat's for instance, as we noted a few paragraphs back. The thesis that all propositional attitudes are thus reducible to nonpropositional dispositions is the thesis of behavioristic **reductionism**. We won't discuss this reductionism either. From our standpoint within folk psychology there are mental nonpropositional dispositions, but they must not be so confused with the propositional attitudes that we don't even see the latter.

Dispositions contrast with actions and events. Thus mental actions are not dispositions, but rather the exercise of dispositions. For example, the act of judging something to be so is one of the ways we exercise the disposition of believing it to be so.

# Notes

1. Russell "The Philosophy of Logical Atomism" (1918), Lecture IV, part 4 (in Bertrand Russell, *Logic and Knowledge*, ed. Robert Marsh) calls verbs like "believe" propositional verbs, and considers whether what all such verbs "name" are attitudes—whence "propositional attitudes"—but he dislikes the psychologism.^ Later he embraced it and used the phrase "propositional attitudes," e.g., in his "On Propositions" (1919), republished in Marsh, 309, and in his Introduction to Wittgenstein's *Tractatus Logico-Philosophicus* (1922). Similar language, but expressing different ideas, occurs in work done in 1913, which he left unpublished. See volume 7 of *The Collected Papers of Bertrand Russell* (1984), e.g., p. 107.

2. Henry E. Kyburg, Jr., *Probability and Inductive Logic* (1970) 176, and for the early history of the paradox, 179. Kyburg tells us there that he introduced the lottery paradox in 1961: For all numbers N identifying the lottery tickets, you're virtually sure of each proposition that the lottery ticket bearing the number N will be a loser, but you disbelieve the conjunction of all such propositions. Many philosophers think that they can retain the dichotomous concept of total belief in a proposition or no belief in it and solve the paradox by the expedient of denying that people are committed to totally believing the consequences of their total beliefs. Understanding probability functions to model coherent degrees of belief in propositions, a theorem of probability theory, proofs of which were published by Patrick Suppes and Ernest Adams in 1966, requires coherent people to be so committed:

> If one or more premises together imply a conclusion, then the sum of the probabilities of each of the premises' denials must equal or exceed the probability of the conclusion's denial.
>
> Rephrasing this, let's say the probability of a proposition's denial is one's degree of uncertainty or dubiousness about the proposition. Then the theorem says there's a ceiling for your dubiousness about the conclusion; it's the sum of your dubiousnesses about the premises.

(The original proofs are in J. Hintikka and P. Suppes, editors, *Aspects of Inductive Logic* (1966), theorem 2 of Suppes's "Probabilistic Inference and the Concept of Total Evidence," 49-65, and theorem 10 of Adams's "Probability and the Logic of Conditionals," 265-316.)

If a coherent person totally believes each of the premises, then the sum of the probabilities of their denials will be 0 for her. No probability can be less than 0, so 0 is the probability of the conclusion's denial for her, and she therefore totally believes the conclusion. The commitment does hold for coherent people and is rendered paradox-free by admitting degrees of partial belief, for the theorem gives one wide latitude about how much to believe a conclusion, when one only partially believes the premises. For instance, to believe to degree 0.99 each of 100 propositions of the form "ticket $x$ will lose," where $x$ ranges from 1 to 100, and to believe in their conjunction to degree zero, is consistent with the theorem. The verisimilitude of the conjunction explains why a person should be willing to assert each of the propositions. Proponents of dichotomous belief may object to my modeling their idea of full belief as certitude, but even if the binary 1/0 approach models just full belief or absence of belief, not certitudes, a comparable theorem will hold for coherence of binary belief.

The equivalence of Kyburg's lottery paradox with the preface paradox is obvious. The only difference is trivial, that in the lottery the relevance^ between pairs of propositions is the same; in the preface, variable. The preface paradox was introduced by D. C. Makinson, "The Paradox of the Preface," *Analysis* 25 (1965) 205-207. Not seeing his paradox's solution in terms of probabilities, he overlooked the connection to the earlier lottery paradox.

3. I recommended avoiding the equation of believing and asserting, but Mark Kaplan defends it and dichotomous belief in general in his *Decision Theory as Philosophy* (1996), although he criticizes several alternative ways of superimposing dichotomous belief on the gradated notion. See chapters 3 and 4. As for transferring the gradation from the believing to the proposition believed, may I not be unsure whether the fifth digit in the decimal expansion of *pi* is 6, but be quite sure that either 0 or 1 is the chance of its being 6? Is not the theory refuted by anyone who has two states of mind simultaneously, one, her being convinced about the chance of its being 6, and another, her uncertainty to some degree about its being 6, and the chance in the first does not equal the degree in the second?

4. Richard Jeffrey, *The Logic of Decision*, 2nd ed. (1983). The 1990 paperback reprinting contains corrections and additions. The definition of indifference is on p. 82. The inverse connection between degree of belief and intensity of desire can be inferred from Jeffrey's equation 5-4. As the derivation of that equation from axiom 5-2 shows, the connection is proved only for the propositions that have mutually exclusive ways of being true. That's no limitation in practice, since every empirical proposition you're likely to think of has mutually exclusive ways of being true. Further connections can be inferred if one's set of desires changes according to the rule: If one's degree of belief in A changes to certitude, then one's consequent desire for any proposition X equals one's pre-change desire for X&A. While plausible as a description, this rule, Jeffrey's 5-7, is prescriptive exactly when it's also prescribed that one change one's degree of belief in X to equal $p(X|A)$ when one becomes certain of A (Jeffrey, 93).

5. E.g., David Lewis, section XI of his "Attitudes *De Dicto* and *De Se*," reprinted in his *Philosophical Papers*, vol. I (1983). He has in mind the decision theory developed by Jeffrey, cited in the previous note. More exactly I have that evidential decision theory in mind; he has in mind a correction of it, which he calls causal decision theory.

6. "On Denoting," 52. The joke is helped by the guest's use of the word "was," which is not misleadingly ambiguous about temporality here since yachts don't change size. People do, becoming taller, then shorter in advanced age. Suppose the guest had said to Bertrand Russell, upon first meeting him, "I thought you were taller than you are." Russell might take this temporally ambiguous statement in the other of its senses and reply, "True; when I was younger I was

taller than I am." But suppose the guest had said without temporal ambiguity, "I thought you *would be* taller than you are." Then Russell might have replied analogously to the yacht owner's reply, "No, I'm never taller than I am then." In short, tense can count.

7. For instance, "The king of France is not bald" may mean either that "one and only one is king of France but he's not bald," or "It's not the case that both one and only one is king of France and he's bald." The first asserts there is a king, but the second does not.

8. See the beginning of his "Quantifiers and Propositional Attitudes."

9. (1974); reprinted in James D. McCawley, *Adverbs, Vowels, and Other Objects of Wonder* (1979), ch. 10.

10. Gottlob Frege, *The Foundations of Arithmetic* (1884) §62. Also:

But we ought always to keep before our eyes a complete proposition. Only in a proposition have the words really a meaning. . . . It is enough if the proposition taken as a whole has a sense, it is this that confers on its parts also their content. §60.

Translation by J. L. Austin. An excellent presentation of this principle about meaning and the reasons for it, is in Michael Dummett, "The Context Principle: Centre of Frege's Philosophy," in Ingolf Max and Werner Stelzner, eds., *Logik und Mathematik: Frege-Kolloquium Jena 1993* (1995), 3-19.

11. W. V. Quine, "Five Milestones of Empiricism," in his *Theories and Things* (1981).

12. Karl Popper, *Objective Knowledge: An Evolutionary Approach* (1972) 187, note 39.

13. Robert Kraut, "Love *De Re*," in French, Uehling, and Wettstein, eds., *Midwest Studies in Philosophy*, 10 (1986) 413-430.

14. This view is defended by Fred Feldman, "Two Questions about Pleasure," in David F. Austin, ed., *Philosophical Analysis* (1988) 59-81.

15. George Berkeley, *Three Dialogues Between Hylas and Philonous* (1713), First Dialogue.

16. Richard Montague, "On the Nature of Philosophical Entities" (1969), reprinted in *Formal Philosophy*, 168. David Kaplan stresses the philosophical prejudicing involved in this reduction and his disbelief in it in his "Opacity," Appendix A, in L. Hahn and P. Schilpp, eds., *The Philosophy of W. V. Quine* (1986). See also Robert Kraut.

17. Paul J. Griffiths, *On Being Mindless* (1986) 68 and 106.

18. "Propositional Objects" (1965), reprinted in his *Ontological Relativity and Other Essays* (1969) 154f.

19. For discussion of analytical and empirical issues relating to intention in this sense see the articles in Bertram F. Malle, Louis J. Moses, and Dare A. Baldwin, editors, *Intentions and Intentionality: Foundations of Social Cognition* (2001).

20. David Lewis, "Attitudes *De Dicto* and *De Se*" in his *Philosophical*

*Papers*, vol. I (1983). By *"de se"* Lewis means what Quine means by egocentric propositional attitudes, attitudes that identify oneself and the present moment by singular terms like "I" and "now," not proper names or descriptions. We discuss them in sections M and N. They would be a special case of a *de re* attitude for Quine, or the other way round in Lewis's way of looking at the matter. Quine did not see how to extend his analyses of egocentric propositional attitudes to beliefs generally ("Intensions Revisited," 122), since his analyses depend on the primitiveness of the contents they are directed toward, whereas Lewis has made all attitudes instances of *de se* attitudes.

21. David Lewis, "Finkish Dispositions" (1997), reprinted in his *Papers in Metaphysics and Epistemology*. Lewis defends the analysis of dispositions in terms of a counterfactual conditional, but the simple version I give is vulnerable to counterexample, even apart from the problems that mental dispositions cause, and so Lewis proposes a more complex counterfactual conditional.

# C. A Standardized Language for Reporting Beliefs.

First I explain linguistic **regimentation**.[1] The idioms for reporting beliefs are insufficiently fixed for the philosopher, who must take care that we don't lose even our stronger intuitions about distinctions and implications because of our laxity in expression. So first, this section will explore these intuitions and, despite some controversy about its appropriateness, **regiment** their expression, that is, restate them in a standardized format. Regimentation is therefore a part of semantic ascent (introduced in section A).

## §1. The fundamental regimentation: about-positions and that-clauses.

Regimentation has two broad uses. One is in a theory of meaning, and we're not engaged in theory yet.[2] The other is part of a pre-theoretic preparation of the data. Insofar as regimentation is only pre-theoretic, it's not a necessary part of semantic ascent. Some philosophers who engage in semantic ascent are concerned to leave everyday idioms alone. But we're not as protective of the idioms for reporting beliefs because we're concerned with the beliefs reported on. If we gerrymander the reporting of beliefs to bring belief itself into higher relief, we're not tampering with the primary data of interest. So the regimentation (i.e., the gerrymandering) can be a legitimate part of semantic ascent.

The regimentation we engage in now is concerned with sharpening the distinction between notional belief (i.e., *de dicto*) and relational belief (i.e., *de re*) so that their difference is apparent from the way we report them. In the contrast between theory and data, regimentation is supposed to be on the side of the data, a mere tidying up. In effect it's an **intuition pump,** that is, an aid to seeing the data more precisely so that distinctions and implications come into sharper focus. Our competence in using our language is at least part of the prompter of our intuitions about meanings. So by sharpening our intuitions we hope to articulate what a competent user of the language must know.

Intuitions are—I would like to tell you—one's tacit knowledge brought to consciousness, not unfounded speculations. But honestly, they occur in response to more factors than our competence in using language, and so are not pure revelations of that competence. They're less than knowledge, since they can be deceptive and idiosyncratic, although they are more than speculations, since they point us approximately toward the truth. For better or worse, they are our starting point.

Philosophers use many kinds of intuition pumps. Russell's joke about the yacht (reported in section B) was one. Not regimentation, of course, his is a **thought experiment** that consists of elaborating a conversational scenario designed to elicit firm intuitions about what we would or would not say to our conversation partners. It pumps intuitions to the surface of our attention, intuitions that would not rise up simply by our contemplating the phenomena themselves. Regimentation is not a thought experiment, but it is an intuition pump. In this case our intuition expresses our competence with the language and our skill in telling when sentences are purpose-equivalent, that is, when they are just two ways for a speaker to accomplish the same purpose. We should be sensitive to whether regimentation falsifies the data and colors them to favor one theory over another. For now and until there's trouble, I'll assume our next regimentation won't distort the reports we'll consider. Actually we'll hedge that assumption: I'll state the common regimentation. Then, at the end of this section I'll state an alternative, which we'll call the Davidsonian regimentation, after the philosopher Donald Davidson who introduced it in 1968.

Let's consider two people with the odd names, Belia and Rep. (Belia doesn't care whether you pronounce her name Belleeya or Beelya.) Belia's the one who has belief or knowledge. All Rep does is talk to us about what Belia believes or knows. Rep *rep*orts on Belia's *bel*iefs:

> Belia believes that . . .
> Belia has the belief that . . .

Belia could report her own beliefs—

> "I believe that . . ." or
> "I know that . . ."

—but generally she just expresses their propositional content:

> " . . .".

The declarative mood of her sentence declares her belief in that which she says. When she says,

> "I don't believe that . . .,"

usually she means what she might have said this way:

> "It's not the case that . . .,"

which expresses disbelief.

The double purpose served by these sentences, namely, reporting a belief and asserting the content believed, shows us that to believe is to believe-true, but it also reveals a curious incapacity in Belia that she cannot tell us the whole truth about many of the beliefs she holds during the times when she reports on herself. She cannot specify the belief and tell us it's false, only that it may very well be. To know the actual situation we need the help of Rep.

When Rep reports that she doesn't believe something, he has to be careful to distinguish two meanings that his report might have, either that she lacks a belief, or that she believes the denial of that something. There's interplay between her expression and his reportage. Rep's reports are often based on Belia's expressions, since he understands her language; otherwise he bases them on inferences from her situation and behavior. (More about this soon.)

Consider now the matter of the reporter's **concurrence** with the truth of what he reports the believer to believe. Sometimes he reports Belia's beliefs, phrased to imply an expression of his own beliefs. For example, Belia thinks of each of her beliefs as true and as knowledge. Belia claims to know, for example, that all roses are red. Rep may or may not agree. If he agrees, Rep might report that Belia knows that all roses are red, or at least that she believes it correctly. In using the word "know" or "believes correctly," Rep is agreeing that Belia has the truth. Rep is telling us something *concerning himself*, namely, that he **concurs fully** with Belia on the matter reported. If he wants to remain **non-committal**, however, he only reports that

Belia believes that all roses are red.

(Imagine Rep saying this while sniffing a yellow rose.) I'll use the terms "belief" and "believe" in this same non-committal way. Belia, in reporting her own belief, might leave off the words, "I believe that . . ." on the grounds that they are redundant. I use them, not as Belia herself uses them in self-reporting, but as used by another who reports on her belief. In reporting a belief this way, the reporter does not imply that he believes it too.

Between the extremes of full concurrence and being non-committal, there are ways for Rep to show **partial concurrence**. Rep sees Belia sitting under a tree on her lawn, and suddenly an animal appears and scurries across the lawn. Belia says to Rep, "I saw a woodchuck. It ran into the bushes." Rep now must report what Belia believes. Since he saw the whole scene himself, he knows that Belia was acquainted with whereof she spoke, for she saw it. It was really there. So Rep says,

Belia has a belief *about* that animal we both saw, *that* it was a woodchuck and it ran into the bushes.

This report concurs with her belief partially. His wording conveys that he agrees, not that it was a woodchuck or that it ran into the bushes, but that the subject of her belief is indeed an animal. That concurrence, partial as it is, would be lacking if the report had been, "Belia believes a woodchuck ran into the bushes." When Rep **concurs partially** and is non-committal partially, he is making a *de re* report. We regiment his *de re* reports so that they have the form,

> "Belia believes *about* [here goes the material he accepts] . . . *that* [here goes the material on which he is non-committal] . . .".

We'll reserve the word "about" to introduce the objects of Belia's belief which Rep believes exist. That means Rep won't say, "Belia believes about Santa Claus . . ., or about unicorns . . ." since he disbelieves in them. Let's hereafter refer to the "**about-position**" and the "**that-clause**." All Rep's reports have that-clauses, but only his *de re* reports have about-positions.

Rep stands proxy for the truth about Belia's states of mind. We assume that Rep himself makes no mistake about the existence or nature of what he concurs with. If he did make a mistake, then his *de re* reports would be false by virtue of what was in their about-positions, and so of no interest to us. (If you'd rather not assume Rep infallible about Belia, assume I am and that I just don't record Rep's mistakes in these notes.)

To set up the arguments of sections H, I and J, let me introduce a distinction within the concept of Rep's partial concurrence. When I introduced the notion just now, I said:

> (1) Rep was concurring "that Belia was acquainted with whereof she spoke."

But thereafter I simplified that to:

> (2) Rep was concurring that the things that Belia's beliefs were about were real.

These two characterizations of partial concurrence are distinct; the first is a partial concurrence in two respects, the second of its characterizations is a concurrence in only one respect. The first adds, to the concurrence with the reality of the things that Belia's beliefs are about, a concurrence that she got her belief by acquaintance with them.

Let's start by defining partial concurrence in the simplified second way, in order to appreciate the later sections' arguments that show we must revert to the two-aspect definition of partial concurrence. In section J we'll start calling reports based on the simplified definition **fake *de re* reportage**.

Some attitudes, like knowing and perceiving, are called veridical attitudes for obvious reasons. On the simplified definition of partial concurrence, the *de dicto* report of these attitudes entails *de re* reports of the same attitudes. If Belia perceives or knows that her dog is barking, then she perceives or knows *about* her dog, *that* it is barking. This entailment is due to the fact that Rep cannot report a veridical attitude without his full concurrence in it, and so must admit about-positions. Since we'll eventually reject the simplified definition, consigning these entailments to being fake *de re*, let's not put much weight on this connection between veridical attitudes and relational ones.

### §2. The that-clause of a report: What the believer asserts governs the clause.

Let's consider next the aspects that complement the aspect of concurrence, that is, the aspects of reports which are the same for notional and relational reports, because Rep's concurrence is irrelevant to them. It seems right that, if Rep takes no responsibility for the material in the that-clause being true of the object of her belief, then Belia is a guarantor of the correctness of his choice of words. Do reports *entail* that Belia would guarantee that their that-clauses express her beliefs? Or is the connection something less than entailment, and if so what might that be? Let's put aside the question of alternatives to entailment until section E. Philosophers argue about the answers, as you might've guessed. In any case, Belia would guarantee the that-clause by way of either her word or her deed.

Consider first her word: If Belia assents to a sentence, Rep may use it to report what she believes, but only if he believes she understands what she assented to. If she does not understand it, then her assent to it shows merely she believes that the sentence is a true one, whatever it may say; her assent would not warrant reporting she believes what the sentence says. A child, a beginning student, or anyone with "blind faith" may be in this position, like so many of us who believe the sentence "$E=mc^2$" true without understanding it. So there's a context-insensitive implication to a *de dicto* belief ascription—"she believes that *p*"—from not less than two premises. One is the indirect discourse—"she says that *p*"—and the other is the claim that she understands "*p*." The conclusion comes only from both premises, and not from the first one alone. And, come to think of it, we should add that she's not lying in assenting to the proposition, and she has self-knowledge, that is, she's sane enough to know what she believes and use language rationally. Even the premise of indirect discourse should be taken as an inference from the more basic quotation of what she actually said (i.e., "she says, '*p*'"). So the inference to what she believes from what she says now looks quite complex:

> Her understanding of the proposition in the that-clause, her veracity, her self-awareness, and her assent to a sentence expressing it:—four premises together suffice^ for the truth of Rep's attribution to her of belief in that proposition.

(General claims like this one are sometimes referred to as **disquotation principles**, since we can imagine Rep reasoning from all these facts about Belia and the direct quotation,

> Belia assents to "*p*,"

to the conclusion

> Belia believes that *p*,

where the quotation marks around *p* in the premise are erased in the conclusion.[3]) Without the other premises, her assent's an insufficient basis for Rep's attribution of that belief to her.

Does her failure to assent to *p*, when asked, indicate that she does not believe it? Consider the question by contraposing^ the negative disquotation principle suggested by that question: If she is asked "*p*?," then, if she believes it, etc., she assents to it. That equivalent way of stating the principle makes clearer that more must be added to make it plausible.

> Her refusal to assert *p* or assent to "*p*?" when asked suffices for the truth of Rep's report of her not believing it, provided that, in addition to her other character traits, mentioned in the first disquotation principle, she is not shy, sworn to secrecy, in circumstances that lead her to have mental reservations, or the like.

This negative disquotation principle is more difficult to use than the first one we stated, since more restrictions would have to be met. It's an inference from her inaction, whereas the first principle was an inference from her action. Also, in untypical situations she may believe something without being aware that she believes it, in which case her sincere denial of belief is simply false. (We'll consider a failure of both disquotation principles in Part III.)

Beware of the name "disquotation." It contains a powerful suggestion that a that-clause duplicates what's in Belia's mind. Surely that's false. Rep cannot simply quote Belia, if Belia used words like "me" in what she asserts. For the word "me" coming out of Rep's mouth refers to Rep, not Belia, as it would if it were to come out of her mouth. Keep these *not*'s in mind:

> ●Rep's that-clause is not a direct quotation of Belia with the

quotation marks left off.

• If you recall the analogical stretching of primary and secondary qualities to cover intentionality, which I ventured in the Introduction, a that-clause is not an attempt to name a primary quality of Belia's mind. A that-clause may only give a secondary quality of her mind, as seen from Rep's mind.

• Just what a that-clause's relation is to what's in Belia's mind will be discussed partly in the next section, but mostly in Part III of the course. For now we know what it isn't: It's not a duplicate copy of what's in the believer's mind, the way a direct quotation of someone is supposed to be a duplicate copy of what that person said.

## §3. The that-clause of a report: What the believer does governs the clause.

The believer endorses the content of the report's that-clause. We've covered endorsement by word; now endorsement by deed. Her assent is not indispensable for the that-clause attributed to her in an affirmative report, i.e., one that says she does believe something. Her deeds may betray her beliefs. She may learn what she believes from her Freudian analyst, who is adept at ferreting out her subconscious beliefs. (It's possible that this is not mere suggestibility.) Belia can talk, but what of all those individuals who cannot talk but have beliefs? For example Rep may wish to report on the beliefs held by Belia's dog. In that case Belia's dog is the guarantor of the material in the that-clause by way of its deeds alone. For we can give a behavioral characterization of belief by the generic functions beliefs serve, the distinctive role they play in furthering the believer's goals.

In the following **schema connecting behavior to belief and desire**, take $s$ to be a state of affairs that may obtain (i.e., be actual) regardless of inadequacies in the believer's conceptual abilities to express it, and $p$ to be a state of affairs which the believer's conceptual abilities are adequate to express; furthermore $s$ is the actual state of affairs that $p$ most closely corresponds to. Though $p$ may lack truth, it can still have verisimilitude^ to actuality. (For God, in every case, $s = p$ and so $p$ is true; for us, we hope the identity is usually the case.) Then, for any $p$, if one *believes* that $p$, then

(i) one is in a state that, given optimal conditions, one is in

    (a) only if $s$ and

    (b) because of $s$, and

(ii) it's a state of being disposed to act in ways that would tend to satisfy one's desires, whatever they are, in a world in which $p$ together with one's other beliefs were true or (if $p$ is conceptually inadequate to the world) in a world in which $s$ and more conceptually adequate versions of one's other beliefs were true.[4]

Since this clause refers to desire, we also characterize desire behaviorally: For any $q$, if one *desires* that $q$, then

one is in a state of being disposed to act in ways that would tend to bring it about that $q$ in a world in which one's beliefs, whatever they are, were true.[5]

These behavioral characterizations of complexes of belief and desire provide a way for Rep to test the that-clauses of his attributions of belief to individuals who don't speak. So, despite their speechlessness, they're still the guarantors of those clauses by way of their deeds. For the beliefs and desires they have must be among the causes of the deeds they do, or the reasons for them, so that we can explain the deed by citing the beliefs and desires.

We won't dwell on the difference between explanation of someone's action by the citing of its causes and by the citing of the reasons the person has. The issue underlies there having to be two subparts of Part III of these notes. I believe we can finesse it here. Suppose Rep is considering some candidate for being the speechless individual's belief. If it can figure in no explanation of the individual's deeds, either by their reasons or their causes, then by the conditional schema above and the logical rule of inference, *modus tollens*, the individual does not believe it. But if it might explain the deeds and it's the best explanation available, then, by clause (ii) of the conditional schema and some plausible premises needed for applying **Bayes's theorem**, there's a likelihood the individual does believe it. Reasoning according to Bayes's theorem, strictly speaking, occurs within the probability calculus and requires exact numerical values for degrees of belief, which is often unrealistic. A verbal approximation of the use of the theorem, which works with only comparative values for degrees of belief, is the following two-stage argument form. Think of X as a hypothesis, theory, or explanation, and of O as a report of observations:

First stage:

(a) If X, then we would predict O; that is, there's positive relevance between them.

(b) The probability of X, independently of the success of the prediction, is not zero.

(c) The probability of O, antecedently to making the observation, is not zero.

(d) O is much more likely, hypothesizing X, than it would be on the disjunction of hypotheses contrary to X.

Second stage:

(concluded from (a)-(d)) X is more likely, given O, than it would be otherwise.

(e) By golly, we observe O, i.e., X predicts this successfully, and nothing else we learn along with O is adversely relevant to X.

Therefore, X is more probably true.[6]

The characterization of belief and desire, which was given earlier, is an instance of the first of these premises, where X stands for believing particular instances of *p* and desiring instances of *q*, and O stands for observable explanatory antecedents of those beliefs (as required by (i)) and the behavioral manifestations of the particular beliefs and desires (as required by (ii) and the clause for desire). The alternatives to X postulate other instances of *p* and *q*. Establishing the first four premises depends on background theoretical commitments.[7] The reasoning allows us to bypass Belia's words in getting at her attitudes.

Although we might ask her to confirm our inferences, no such confirmation is available for our inferences to the attitudes her dog has. This is not as big a difference between Belia and her dog as it may look at first sight. For her speech is itself behavior and so the schema connecting behavior to belief and desire applies to self-reportage. Earlier we connected this sort of behavior to belief by disquotation principles. The plausibility of the two disquotation principles comes directly from our unconscious application of the schema and Bayes's theorem to the behavior of assenting to *p*, and to the behavior of refraining from assenting to *p*.

Let's examine more closely the schema connecting behavior to belief and desire. Clause (i) connects a belief to what would be its explanation in optimal conditions. If we had omitted clause (i) of the characterization of belief, in terms of the best explanatory antecedents it could have, Rep could not've nailed down what in the world Belia's state of belief represented. Clause (ii) and the definition of desire are insufficient for distinguishing between two complex states of belief and desire, each of which might explain, let's say, Belia's behavior toward Rep. (She's being coquettish, and he smiles at her, which pleases her.) Does she have beliefs and desires about Rep that explain her behavior? That's the normal supposition. Perhaps, however, all the relevant beliefs and desires are really *about Jack*, whom Belia has confused with Rep in a global way.

Without clause (i) there's no way to settle which hypothesis rightly explains her behavior.

Let's convince ourselves of the indispensability of clause (i) to explain Belia's coquettishness.[8] Try leaving it out. Our explanation then must be by way of Bayes's theorem and clause (ii) alone and the characterization of desire. Note that, if two hypotheses are absolutely equal in predicting her coquettishness and differ in no other explanatory virtue, then Bayes's theorem won't decide between them for us. For we'll be lacking premise (d). Let hypothesis X be the normal supposition that her beliefs and desires are about Rep. To construct Y, the alternative hypothesis to the normal supposition, replace all Belia's supposed propositional attitudes about Rep with attitudes about Jack, including even her belief that Rep is named "Rep." She's now supposed to believe that Jack is named "Rep." We're not supposing an ordinary case of Belia's being confused, which she or we might uncover. It's not that Rep looks remarkably like Jack to nearsighted Belia, who has forgotten her eyeglasses, and Jack is around here somewhere. No. This is an absolutely perfect confusion.

Let's consider only her beliefs that can be reported as complete propositions, without any about-positions. Take $p$ to be

> either according to X "that Rep [meaning Rep] is attracted to me,"
>
> or according to Y "that Rep [meaning Jack] is attracted to me,"

and $q$ to be

> either according to X "that Rep [meaning Rep] increase his being attracted to me,"
>
> or according to Y "that Rep [meaning Jack] increase his being attracted to me."

The two hypotheses are in effect mirror images of each other and cannot make different predictions. So premise (d) is not established and neither X nor Y is rendered more probable than the other. Only a clause like (i) can help settle who her beliefs and desires are about: By (i) the name "Rep" can't mean Jack to her. For Jack is in none of the $s$ states that led to Belia's learning the name "Rep" and thereafter using it. So clause (i) tells us that we must take into account the influences on Belia, which rules Jack out of $p$. So premise (d) is now established; hypothesis X makes O far more probable than hypothesis Y does.

So far we've considered the insufficiency of verbal avowals of belief in settling the content of a that-clause, and also their dispensability for that purpose. Nevertheless we presume that we may infer from Rep's report something concerning what Belia does or says, and doesn't do and doesn't say. Let's now state a general principle of regimentation that captures that presumption: *The believer is in charge of the content of the that-clause.* This principle has four parts, in that the believer's control may be exercised to verify the reporter's that-clause or to falsify it, and she may exercise her control by her words or by her deeds:

|  | By her words: | By her deeds |
|---|---|---|
| Her way of verifying content of that-clause: | She assents to the that-clause. | The that-clause explains her deeds best. |
| Her way of falsifying content of that-clause: | She dissents from the that-clause. | The that-clause doesn't explain her deeds best. |

Table C-1. Four ways the believer exercises her control over the content of the report's that-clause. The columns are inclusive alternatives to each other, the rows exclusive of each other.

Belia, however, is quite verbose, and her words may indicate one set of beliefs and desires, and her deeds an opposite set. When they conflict, that is, when she activates the table's diagonal corners, is she then lying or unreflective? Perhaps so. We do tend to credit the deed over the word. Let's leave unsettled whether her persistent express dissent from a proposition, when her understanding, sincerity, and self-knowledge are granted, suffices to falsify Rep's attribution of that belief to her to explain her deeds. If Rep has proclivities to Freudian analysis of Belia, despite her embarrassed protestations, we'll not adjudicate.

Belia's attitudes might also be inchoate, partially formed, indeterminate, infected with a mix of understanding and confusion, which somehow Rep must be faithful to. For our regimentation of reports forces all of that into the content her belief is directed toward, which is to say, it's to be confined to the that-clause. Let's hope for Rep's sake that she is never in that mental condition which a recent President of the United States imputed to himself: "I have opinions of my own—strong opinions—but I don't always agree with them." Belia and the President are in charge of the reports' that-clauses, for better or worse. The about-positions are outside the realm of their mental murkiness, thank goodness.

## §4. Pronominal anaphora: what it is and who's in charge of it.

There's one tangle between about-positions and that-clauses that requires a word more on *dicta*. In one sense a *dictum* is a proposition whose expression is completely intelligible even if it were standing alone as expressed by a complete sentence, as the whole of what Belia is believing. A *dictum* in that sense is a complete proposition. Of course, there are that-clauses in *de re* reports too, but in them what follows the "that" usually contains an **anaphoric pronoun**, a "he," "she," or "it" that makes a cross-reference back to a thing named earlier in the discourse. The use of such pronouns we'll call "pronominal anaphora."[9] A sentence containing an anaphoric pronoun without also containing the singular term it refers back to is called an **open sentence**. An open sentence is one way of expressing an incomplete proposition. In *de re* reports the anaphoric pronoun refers back to a thing named in the about-position. Thus in the examples in the next paragraph, note the anaphoric pronouns and what they refer back to. Clauses with such anaphoric pronouns would not be completely intelligible if they were standing alone, since the "it" would not be identified. Such incomplete that-clauses are parts of reports *de re*. They're not the *dicta* of *de dicto*, which are propositions complete enough in themselves to determine their meaning.

How would Russell's original examples of relational propositional attitudes (in section B) be rephrased using our regimentation? The yacht example would go this way:

> The guest thinks, *about* the actual size of the yacht, *that* the size of the yacht is larger than it.

The authorship example would go this way, where "whether" substitutes for "that":

> George IV wished to know, *about* the author of *Waverley, whether* Scott was he.

Note the pronominal anaphora (i.e., the use of anaphoric pronouns) in each incomplete proposition that the attitudes are directed toward.

Who's in charge of the anaphoric pronoun; particularly, who determines what name may be put in the pronoun's place? Its antecedent is in the about-position in Rep's control, but the pronoun itself is in the that-clause in Belia's control. We rule in favor of Rep. This also solves one minor infelicity in our formulation of that-clause control. We don't want to allow Belia to quarrel with the pronouns in this report:

> Belia believes that I am in love with her.

If she does believe it, she would say, "Rep is in love with me." Obviously we don't want Belia's being in charge to entitle her to order Rep to change the word "her" to the word "me." We regiment this report as *de re*:

> Belia believes about me and herself, that the former is in love with the latter.

The original pronouns are now out of the that-clause, replaced by anaphoric pronouns, "the former" and "the latter." By our ruling, Belia's not in charge of them. In the next section we study a procedure called abstraction that solves the problem another way; it deletes all the anaphoric pronouns in that-clauses which refer back to about-positions.

To sum up the common regimentation, the one doing the wanting or the believing is the guarantor of the material in the that-clause.

Recall that in section B, when we considered the reasons for claiming all attitudes are propositional attitudes, we said that a reduction of "wanting a unicorn" to "wanting that one have a unicorn" had the desirable effect that the reporter of the want is not committed to the existence of unicorns. Now you can see why: Wanting *that* something be true introduces a that-clause into Rep's report on it, and Rep need not concur with the truth or reference of anything in a that-clause.

The opposite is true of the about-position. Suppose Rep reports correctly:

> (i) Belia believes *that* the woodchuck ran into the bushes.

I said we'll call a report like this, with no about-position, a report of belief *de dicto*. The inclusion of an about-position would've made the report one of belief *de re*. This is *de re*:

> (ii) Belia believes *about* the woodchuck *that* it ran into the bushes.

In section B we considered attitudes that seemed to be nonpropositional in that they seemed to be directed toward physical objects, for instance, imagining a duck. Belia conjures up in her mind an image of any old duck. I said attitudes like that are not really directed toward such things as any old duck, but rather toward propositions, even though ducks are real, an advantage they have over unicorns. In view of what we've been saying in this section, you may wonder why Belia's imagining is not *about* a duck. It's not; the imagining should be analyzed as taking only a that-clause. She's imagining that a duck is there. Why not about the duck? Because for a thing to be named in an about-position, it must make sense to ask for the details concerning it, and even if we don't know the answers, there must nevertheless be a truth of the matter. For example, does the duck Belia is imagining have a broken feather, a tick crawling underneath a feather? For a real duck there are answers to the questions, but for the imagined duck, there's no truth of the matter. Is the duck Belia is imagining in the water, on land, or in flight? Why, she says, that detail's been left indeterminate. Then her imagining is not about a duck in the regimented sense of "about." Ducks are real, but the one she's imagining is not; there's no particular duck her imagining is about. When she sees or remembers a duck, however, the seeing or remembering will be *about* a duck, but the attitude will be directed toward a proposition also.

To repeat myself, since "*de re*" means "about the thing" in the Latin language of the medieval logicians, it's an appropriate name for the relational kind of belief. The name "*de dicto*" will be appropriate for reports that contain no about-positions, if we think of the that-clause as naming a *dictum*. The idea is that, if you prefix the word "that" to a sentence, the resultant phrase is a name of what the sentence says, the *dictum*. The reporter's concurrence is not needed to the that-clauses of either his *de re* or *de dicto* reports, but concurrence is needed to the existence of the things mentioned in the about-positions.

### §5. An alternative to the standard regimentation: the Davidsonian regimentation.

I mentioned at the beginning of this section that I'd explain Donald Davidson's alternative way to regiment Rep's reports, thus the **Davidsonian regimentation**, which is sometimes called the paratactic regimentation (forming coordinate clauses) to contrast with the hypotactic format (making one clause subordinate to another) of the common regimentation. Here's the Davidsonian regimentation: Instead of thinking of the word "that" as a device for creating a name by prefixing it to a sentence, think of it as an ordinary demonstrative pronoun, a pointer-word. His suggestion is that we mispunctuated Rep's reports. They are actually pairs of sentences, not one:

(i) Belia believes *that*: The woodchuck ran into the bushes.

(ii) Belia believes *about* the woodchuck *that*: It ran into the bushes.[10]

English conveniently uses the word "that" in just the two ways Davidson wants to connect, and we might say the same of German's *dass* and *das*, except for their spelling. Not so in other languages, however; for example, in French the word introducing the complement sentence is *que*, but the pronoun is *là*. Fortunately, Davidson's regimentation does not depend on that convenient feature of English.

Another feature of the account as presented so far is more worrisome:

Rep points rather literally to his own words in his reports of what Belia believes. For example, if Belia believes that Rep is staring at her, Rep may report an hour later,

Belia believed that: I was staring at her.

The sentence "I was staring at her" must be Rep's since he determines the pronouns and tense. So the suggestion is odd in that it makes Rep say Belia has a relation of believing directed toward words of his own. If that's so, a report from him at the time of her believing, which would require the present tense, or another's report of Belia's belief, which would require the name "Rep" in place of the pronoun "I," would have her related to several different sentences, indeed as many as there are reports of her belief, although her belief is of only one thing. Davidson prevents this result by supposing reports say the believer believes something with the same content as the sentence pointed at. An alternative would be to follow instead Ian McFetridge's suggestion that Rep is pointing *through* his sentence *to* an internal state of Belia's with a structured content that's like his own sentence's.[11] Can we point to one thing by pointing at another thing? We can and do.[12] Point at a place on a map and tell me to meet you there. If I now sit on the map, rather than go to the place you pointed to, you would not have a good opinion of my grasp of the act of pointing. So also we can point to a *dictum* believed by another by uttering a sentence having the same content. (A fancy name for pointing is **ostension**.)

Yet, with the knowledge we've laid out so far, this regimentation looks appallingly misguided. For a sentence is either within quotation marks or not. We've seen reason not to put the reported sentence in quotation marks, since Rep is not quoting Belia. If the sentence is not in quotation marks, Davidson's regimentation seems to make Rep *assert* the second sentence, and he's only reporting on Belia, not himself asserting what the woodchuck did. Perhaps we have too simple minded an idea of the force to be given to the sentences Rep and we utter. Aren't there situations when someone will state what another person guarantees the truth of? Think of a government spokesperson or a person's press secretary. They don't have to believe what they "assert" on behalf of the one they speak for, even though they speak in their own person, using the pronouns and tenses appropriate to their own situation. McFetridge's suggestion, mentioned in the previous paragraph, is that we see those sentences as part of a device for pointing to the utterances of others. Perhaps we should think of Rep as using that device when he utters the reported sentence. There's the smiley punctuation mark that's become common, "":)"" or ☺, which means "don't think I assert that." If Davidson had invented a new punctuation mark to go with his regimentation of reports, perhaps it would be the common regimentation by now. But it isn't, although by the end of section E we'll come to see that there's much to recommend the Davidsonian regimentation.

Let's summarize all the disputes about how to regiment the data of *de re*, including one that won't be introduced until Part II:

1. Regiment them in the standard way.

    1-1. Their that-clauses take complete singular propositions.

    1-2. Their that-clauses take incomplete propositions.

        1-2-1. Their about-positions require the reporter's concurrence merely (fake *de re*).

        1-2-2. Their about-positions require more than the reporter's concurrence.

            1-2-2-1. The believer must fulfill the knowing-who-or-what criterion.

            1-2-2-2. The believer must relate to the object in a way that singles it out for her belief to be about it.

2. Regiment them in the Davidsonian way.

    2-1. The ostended sentence is a complete singular sentence.

    2-2. The ostended sentence is an incomplete sentence (Quine's amendment).

        2-2-1. Their about-positions require the reporter's concurrence merely (fake *de re*).

        2-2-2. Their about-positions require more than the reporter's concurrence.

            2-2-2-1. The believer must fulfill the knowing-who-or-what criterion.

            2-2-2-2. The believer must relate to the object in a way that singles it out for her belief to be about it.

The knowing-who-or-what criterion, like the notion of fake *de re*, will be introduced in Part II. I'll defend the position labeled 1-2-2-2 on this list against the alternatives, 1-1, 1-2-1, and 1-2-2-1. In Part II we'll end up calling position 1-2-2-2 the "dominance plus ellipsis" theory of the about-position. But there's a Davidsonian version of this theory, 2-2-2-2, an alternative I have no quarrel with.

# Notes

1. Quine, *Word and Object*, §33.

2. Quine, "Reply to Davidson," in Donald Davidson and Jaakko Hintikka, eds., *Words and Objections: Essays on the Work of W. V. Quine* (1969) 333-335. Quine notes that regimentation is necessary to the statement of a theory of meaning that implements the context principle, mentioned in the previous section.

3. The term appears in an influential article by Saul A. Kripke, "A Puzzle about Belief," in A. Margalit, ed., *Meaning and Use* (1979) 239-283, reprinted in Salmon and Soames.

4. Definitions or necessary conditions that omitted clause (i) have been common for decades. Clause (ii) is consistent with the claim in section B that belief comes in degrees, if we assume that we're disposed to act in ways that maximize expected value. The expected value of an act is the sum of the products of the degrees of desirability and probability of each of the alternative outcomes that an act may have. Thus, although action itself is binary—we act or we don't—the beliefs need not be, but may come in degrees. We do not act as if our beliefs were true, but rather in such a way that, if the beliefs we act on were true, we'd succeed.

5. Both necessary conditions are almost verbatim from Robert Stalnaker, *Inquiry* (1984) 15-18. The reference of each condition to the other is intended, and the circle is not vicious. Stalnaker would strengthen my conditionals to biconditionals, which simplifies his discussion of the indispensability of clause (i), in that he can bypass Bayes's theorem. For a counterexample to the sufficiency of these conditions for beliefs of necessary propositions, which would all turn out to be the same belief, see page 210 of Tim Crane, "The Efficacy of Content: A Functionalist Theory," in Jan Bransen and Stefaan E. Cuypers, eds., *Human Action, Deliberation and Causation* (1998) 199-223. Also I introduced into Stalnaker's conditions the relation of degree of correspondence between *s* and *p* to remedy the implication of Stalnaker's original statement that one is infallible in optimal conditions, a defect pointed out by Steven Schiffer, *Remnants of Meaning* (1989) 282, note 6. Even in optimal conditions one can have false beliefs, but they have some degree of correspondence to the truth, i. e., some verisimilitude.ˆ

6. For the curious, Bayes's theorem is an immediate consequence of Bayes's definition of conditional probability, symbolized $p(A|B)$, as $p(A\&B) / p(B)$, if $p(B)>0$, where the capital letters stand for propositions and you can read the "|" (pipe) as "if" or "given." The theorem, as applied to the case in the text, is:

If $p(O)>0$, then

$$p(X|O) = [p(X)p(O|X)] / [p(X)p(O|X)+p(not\text{-}X)p(O|not\text{-}X)]$$

We assume that Y is the only credible alternative to X, and so Y = not-X. Now suppose (premise b) that $p(X) = 0.2$ independently of any of its predictions coming true. Suppose we have an excellent crucial experiment (premise c): The $p(O|X) = 0.95$, while $p(O|Y) = 0.2$. Premise (a) claims the first of these numbers is higher than $p(O)$. We're interested in seeing what X's probability will rise to, if the observation O comes out as X predicts. For this probability we use the number $p(X|O)$. The new probability of X will be this number, if the new probability of O is 1 (i.e., certainty). O's new certainty is given by premise (e). You do the math. No? Ok; I'll do the math:

.5438 . . . = .2(.95) / [.2(.95) + .8(.2)]

In other words, observing O leads us to raise X, from being much less probable than Y, to being the more probable of the two hypotheses. This last step, which uses Bayes's theorem to recompute a new probability for X, given the new probability for O (premise e), is actually more comprehensive, recomputing new probabilities for all beliefs. The step is called conditionalizing on O, or Bayes's rule.

7. The background commitments don't have to be mentioned in the formalism of the previous note, since they're built into the probability function p(-), which assigns degrees of belief to each proposition in a whole field of propositions, representing the complete state of belief of a rational knowledgeable person at some time. We need only assume that it assigns high probability to the background commitments. For more, see the glossary entry, "absolute probability."

8. The case comes from Stalnaker, p. 18.

9. Anaphora is the rhetorical device of repeating words, like the "ask" in Kennedy's "Ask not what your country can do for you; ask what you can do for your country." Philosophers are interested in the repeating of a reference by way of pronouns, a semantic repetition, not just the repetition of words for rhetorical effect. Thus the adjective "pronominal."

10. Donald Davidson, "On Saying That" in Davidson and Hintikka, eds., *Words and Objections: Essays on the Work of W. V. Quine* (1969), reprinted with an added note as ch. 7 in his *Inquiries into Truth and Interpretation* (1984). Davidson discusses the reporting of sayings, not believings, but I am extending what he says to all attitudes. Davidson does not refer to *de re* regimentation. But Quine does in his "Reply to Davidson" on p. 335 in *Words and Objections*, and I've adopted his suggestion as part of what I call the Davidsonian regimentation.

11. Ian G. McFetridge, "Propositions and Davidson's Account of Indirect Discourse," *Proceedings of the Aristotelian Society*, 76 (1975) 131-45. See section IV. I'm not convinced that Davidson's original account has errors which require McFetridge's alternative of indirect pointing. But it's a viable alternative nonetheless. Furthermore, it has become popular. For example, it's adopted in the Davidsonian theory of Stephen Boër and William Lycan, *Knowing Who* (1986), ch. 3. My version of the entity pointed to is different still, in that I say the reporter is pointing indirectly to the contentful belief state within the believer who is reported on.

12. Quine called this "deferred ostension," as when we point to the gas gauge on our car's instrument panel and say, "It's almost empty." See his "Ontological Relativity," reprinted with corrections in his *Ontological Relativity and Other Essays* (1969) 39f. McFetridge's account of the thing pointed at indirectly is criticized by Ian Rumfitt, correctly I think, in section III of his "Content and Context: The Paratactic Theory Revisited and Revised," *Mind*, 102 (1993) 429-454. I've not adopted Rumfitt's correction, however.

# D. Pep Talk;
# Then The Adicity of Propositional Attitudes and their Contents.

This section begins with some motivation building, since the rest of the section is quite technical.

### §1. Pep Talk: Knowledge of relational attitudes can illuminate classical problems of philosophy.

How important is the distinction between relational and notional attitudes? Granted that, if they're distinguished in folk psychology, then the philosophers interested in folk psychology should study the distinction. But you may be having second thoughts about the point of *your* studying the ontology of folk psychology. Perhaps the distinctiveness of the mind is sufficiently captured in notional attitudes. Perhaps those interested in revisionary ontology, such as those who debate the materiality of the mind, may feel that notional attitudes present difficulty enough, that relational attitudes add nothing to the debate. Enough's enough! Why, then, should a philosopher like yourself make a fuss about the relational ones? Let's address this issue, since the next several sections are not going to be easy, and your endurance must be reinforced with added motivation.

I hinted in the Introduction that certain kinds of relational beliefs and desires are at the interface between the intentional and physical aspects of our human nature. To study relational attitudes is to study a kind of process that Descartes located in the pineal body of the brain. We need not concern ourselves with the location, but the manner of interconnection of body and mind is certainly important to understand. I also hinted that we'll learn something about the evolution of the mind, which began with relational attitudes. And in the course of our investigations we'll discover a new form of philosophical analysis that can interpret aspects of our thinking as signs of its evolution. These ideas will only begin to emerge in Part II and only reach explicitness by the very end, in Part IV.

In the meantime you might think of applying the distinction between the relational and notional attitudes in several other areas of philosophy. The distinction may impact several issues, some of which may especially interest you. Here's one from the history of philosophy:

●In section B I introduced Berkeley's so-called master argument for idealism^: Try to conceive of a thing that nobody ever conceives of. I showed that a resourceful idealist will exploit the distinction between the relational and the notional to counter the anti-idealist's replies.

We'll add to this debate in later sections. Here are some others that might puzzle you, first a group from the philosophy of religion:

● In Anselm's *Proslogion*, there's a difficulty in his second proof of God's existence, which argues for the inconceivability of the nonexistence of a being, than whom none greater can be thought (i.e., conceived to be). Its premises must be common ground with the atheist, who evidently does conceive of the nonexistence of this being. Anselm says, "in one sense a thing is thought, when the word signifying it is thought; in another sense when the very object, which the thing is, is understood."[1] Is Anselm distinguishing notional from relational conceiving?

●Even in his first proof, proving the actual existence of such a being, one of Anselm's premises is that it's greater for a thing to exist in reality and thought than for *it* to exist in thought alone. Could this premise be restated as the thing's superiority if it can be thought *de re* rather than merely *de dicto*?

●How do the proofs of God in natural theology connect up to religious faith in God, in view of the Christian doctrine that faith cannot be compelled by logic, but is entirely a gift from God? Could logic only prove *de dicto* beliefs, while faith is taken to be *de re* by the faithful?

●In the Introduction I mentioned conversion experiences, in which nothing the convert believes or desires changes in content, the change being only in the way the convert believes and desires them. I gave the example of Job's conversion and suggested that his beliefs about God changed from being *de dicto* to being *de re*. Might it be that Job himself came to take them to be *de re*, whether or not they became so actually?

●More generally, could it be that *de re* beliefs, when they're part of the grounding of desires, enhance the motivational force of those desires more than any corresponding *de dicto* beliefs would, because the desires they ground are locked with them in a *de re* cluster? If so, then I can quote Cardinal Newman's encomium to "real assent" as true of *de re* belief:

> [Real as opposed to notional assents] are sometimes called beliefs, convictions, certitudes, and, as given to moral objects, they are perhaps as

rare as they are powerful. Till we have them, in spite of a full apprehension and assent in the field of notions, we have no intellectual moorings, and are at the mercy of impulses, fancies, and wandering lights, whether as regards personal conduct, social and political action, or religion. These beliefs, be they true or false in the particular case, form the mind out of which they grow, and impart to it a seriousness and manliness which inspires in other minds a confidence in its views, and is one secret of persuasiveness and influence in the public stage of the world. They create, as the case may be, heroes and saints, great leaders, statesmen, preachers, and reformers, the pioneers of discovery in science, visionaries, fanatics, knight-errants, demagogues, and adventurers. They have given to the world men of one idea, of immense energy, of adamantine will, of revolutionary power. They kindle sympathies between man and man, and knit together the innumerable units which constitute a race and a nation. They become the principle of its political existence; they impart to it homogeneity of thought and fellowship of purpose.[2]

We'll explore some of these ideas briefly in section O. The quotation from Newman suggests more applications in the areas connecting psychology to ethics, for example:

●In Plato's *Symposium*, Socrates gives a speech which introduces the concept of sublimation of desire.[3] We fail to explain the dynamics of the sublimation, if we try to understand it merely as the replacement of one *dictum* by another in a merely *de dicto* desire, in the direction of ever more abstract *dicta,* under pressure from changing *de dicto* beliefs disclosing new *dicta.* It seems truer to the text to think of two complementary pressures driving the process. First, there's the desire for the true good, *de re*, present from the beginning, and a correlative "seeming good," also *de re*, of something that resembles the true good. The desire is disappointed by mere bonisimilitude (like verisimilitude^) of the two *res* even if the *dictum* of the seeming-good is fulfilled. Second, the objects the succeeding seemings-good are about become desensualized, and the *dicta* become dephysicalized or rationalized in reciprocal adjustments of aboutness and directed-towardness. With this conceptualization of sublimation, we may come to understand its Platonic mystical finale in a *de re* love for the form of the good. Our explorations in section O will be relevant to this matter.

●Aristotle thought weakness of will occurred when a person failed to believe actively or in the right way a singular proposition about the badness of the thing that is tempting her.[4] But is Aristotle's case for a doxastic defect made stronger, if the defective way the person has her belief is that it is a *de dicto* rather than a *de re* belief about the badness of that thing? Or it might just be a matter of degree of conviction: Convinced *de dicto* that cigarettes are bad for her, she nevertheless has a fairly strong belief, about this cigarette at hand, that it is good for her. This might be at least a sufficient condition of weakness of will, if not a full analysis.

●Another form of weakness of will may just be a matter of intensity of desires, which also may be a mixture of *de dicto* and *de re*. Although she desires *de dicto* to refrain from smoking cigarettes more strongly than she desires to smoke them, nevertheless, concerning this cigarette at hand, she desires *de re* to smoke it more strongly than she desires to refrain from smoking it. We might also consider mixing the beliefs with the desires, partnering the *de re* ones and pitting them against the *de dicto* ones.

●Aristotle says people don't deliberate about their ultimate and all-inclusive goal in life, that is, what constitutes their felicity. Suppose he's right; why then is it so? Could it be that people's desires are so structured that their desires for the ultimate things in life are established by a relation that underwrites their being *de re* desires? About felicity, everybody just wants it—that's all there is to say. We return to this speculation in section O.

●Bertrand Russell's lecture in Stockholm in 1950[5] on the occasion of his receiving the Nobel Prize for literature, points toward an application of folk psychology to politics: It does seem that some of our desires have no natural limits of satiation, typically the desires for power, fame, and fortune; also for having fun, so it seems. Russell identifies them as politically important desires and suggests that politics is the shaping of these desires. What *de re* and *de dicto* aspects of these desires account for their insatiability?

A final trio of possibilities in the theory of knowledge:

●The rationalists of the seventeenth century took knowledge to be certain. Is their case made stronger if the knowledge they mean is *de re* in view of the fact that the *res* are outside the scope of belief and so are, by default so to speak, certain? See my note 2 to section A for more speculation along this line.

●Did Aristotle anticipate the rationalists? Consider Ferejohn's argument that the first principles of scientific knowledge, according to Aristotle, are known *de re*.[6]

●In the theory of perception and memory, there's a position called "naive realism," which maintains the thesis that perception and memory are *de re*. The position was anything but naive as it was developed by realists at the beginning of the twentieth century. See for example, the New Realists.[7] When I remember my dog Smokey, he himself is the object that my memory is about, although he's been dead for fifty years. Suppose I see the star Sirius, which is eight and a half light years away. That very star as it was eight and a half years previously, not any image of it contemporaneous with my perception, is the object that my perception is about.

I don't know if these ideas will pan out, but they give you a model to explore on your own the possible applications of the relational-notional distinction as we progress. Clarifying concepts is a sterile endeavor, if the resulting clear concepts are not then applied to important issues. The clarifying takes time and the application seems forever postponed. So the more impatient fear utter futility. I hope these open questions stave off that fear, replacing it with eagerness.

## §2. One generic way, and two specific ways, to think of the that-clause.

I mentioned in section A that the *de re* believer relates to the incomplete proposition in a way quite different from the way she relates to the things in the about-position. Despite the difference, they both might be terms (in the sense of termini of a relation) relating to the believer in her relational belief. Rep can refer directly to the various contents of Belia's beliefs and generalize them. For example, he may say:

> I don't agree with everything Belia believes about the beast we saw.

To make sense of this quantification,^ one naturally assumes the incomplete proposition is just another one of the things related by the relation of believing. For logic assumes a domain^ of things which quantifiers range over, and Rep just quantified over Belia's beliefs.

But must we always assume this entity-interpretation of the terminus of the directed-toward relation? It might seem that we must, if we're to give an account of the validity of some arguments. These two arguments seem valid:

> Belia believes that an animal ran into the bushes.
> Therefore Belia believes something.

And

> Max believes everything Belia believes.
> Belia believes an animal ran into the bushes.

Therefore Max believes an animal ran into the bushes. These are *prima facie* valid inferences, whose validity is easy to account for if the terms of the directed-toward relation are entities. Perhaps, however, the less easy course is the truer one. There are organisms less sophisticated than human beings, whose repertory of contents of propositional attitudes is limited and never provokes steps of generalization like Rep's, which replace the that-clauses in his reports on Belia with quantifiers. Perhaps they have propositional attitudes whose contents are not separate terms in the belief-relation. Or, horror of horrors, we too may be such beasts. But if we take literally the "everything" in Rep's statement, then belief contents are themselves things.

Would semantic ascent help here? What part of speech is a that-clause? It might seem to be a singular term that names a proposition. For in locutions other than reports, that-clauses can occupy the position of subjects. For example,

That dinosaurs are extinct is a fact. So I believe it.

I recommend, however, that we begin with a more neutral grammatical characterization of the that-clause. In the regimentation we're working with, the word "that" simply introduces a complement of the attitude-verb. A complement of a verb is merely a completer of the verb's meaning. For example, suppose the people elect Joan president. Obviously, the people and Joan are the entities involved in this relation, but what of "president"? It would be foolish to look for another entity for this word to name. Rather it completes the meaning of the verb, which we understand as the unit, "electing president." Why not then at least open ourselves up to the possibility that similarly the that-clause of an attitude report names no entity at all, but rather the "that" introduces a sentence which completes the meaning of the attitude verb? We do so by describing the sentence introduced by the word "that" as a complement to the verb.

Now we can describe a debate within philosophy: Is the complement to the verb to be understood as standing for an entity or not? One view that it's not we'll call the **adverbial interpretation of the complement**. It understands the complement that-clause to complete the meaning of the verb rather like the way an adverb does. For example, Belia's believing *de dicto* that dinosaurs are extinct would be likened to this:

Belia believes [dinosaurs are extinct]-ly,

where the adverbial ending on the bracketed unit makes explicit, albeit strange, that no entity other than Belia is posited by the analysis. Despite the stuff inside the brackets, we're supposed to think that this idiom refers to neither complete nor incomplete propositions. *De re* beliefs would have this form,

Belia believes about Jack and Jill [the former loves the latter]-ly.

The adverb must show inner complexity. In particular, how could the adverbs for *de re* beliefs contain pronouns as constituents? Since Belia might believe *p*-ly in infinitely many ways of believing *p*-ly, because of the infinity of *p*'s, how can this infinity of ways be constructed from a finite number of component ways? By a grammar for adverb construction. Some who've proposed the adverbial interpretation of the that-clause have metaphysical axes to grind. We're not interested in revisionary metaphysics, and so we'll ignore them. Others, however, think an adverbial theory's the best way to describe the ontology^ implicit in folk psychology. The philosophers who hold views approximating this one include the early Wittgenstein, three of his interpreters, namely Peter Geach, Erik Stenius, and Wilfrid Sellars, and among our contemporaries, Kent Bach and Michael McKinsey.[8] We're quite unequipped to evaluate this theory now. We'll not discuss it any further until section Q.

The alternative to the adverbial interpretation of the complement is the nominative interpretation. It says the that-clause is a name for an entity. The evidence about quantification which we started with is a powerful incentive to treat the complement as a singular term naming the entity which is a term of the directed-toward relation. But it's hardly conclusive.[9] Until Part III, however, we'll talk provisionally as if the nominative interpretation were the correct view. We should also be mindful of the fact that some philosophers who take the nominative view posit a plurality of entities underlying every report. Let's keep our provisional talk down to just one entity. What entity will it be?

Here's a way to regiment reports to treat a belief's content as an entity: Quine[10] turns the incomplete that-clause of relational belief, which has the positions with the anaphoric pronouns in it, into a singular term for an attribute by an operation logicians call **abstraction**: applying an operator to a clause so that the result is a singular term. For example, the clause "they are divisible by 2" can be used to form the name of a set: the set of things which are divisible by 2. The operator in this case was the phrase "the set of things which are. . ." For our purposes we need attribute abstraction, however, not class abstraction. The incomplete sentences, which express the propositions that are believed about a thing, are convertible into names of the **attributes** which the believer attributes to the thing. Instead of a clause,

"it went into the bushes,"

we name a thing's attribute:

"the attribute of having gone into the bushes."

The rules of attribute abstraction we'll leave intuitive and informal; convert the incomplete proposition's verb to a gerund (ending in -ing), omit the pronoun, and prefix the phrase, "the attribute of" to the result. The abstraction creates a singular term, naming an attribute, out of a clause which is not a singular term. The phrase, "the attribute of having gone into the bushes" is a name. The reverse operation of converting an attribute name back into an incomplete sentence Quine calls **concretion**.

We adjust the idiom of belief to accommodate attributes as the entities that a belief is directed toward. Instead of saying Belia *believes*, with a that-clause giving the content of the belief, i.e., instead of saying:

> Belia believes about the animal we saw that it went into the bushes,

Rep will say Belia *believes-(. . .)-true*, with an attribute as that item which she believes to be true about the thing that Rep knows was the animal they saw, thus:

> Belia believes the attribute of having gone into the bushes to be true about the animal we saw.

Note also the disappearance of the problem (mentioned in section C) of who controls the anaphoric pronoun, because the pronouns have disappeared.

We could now drop reference to incomplete propositions, and declare all attitudes either propositional attitudes, if they're directed toward complete propositions, or else attributive attitudes, if they're directed toward attributes. Also, since a complete proposition can be interpreted as an extreme kind of attribute, we could say all the attitudes are attributive attitudes. But we won't. What would be gained by a switch from propositional to attributive? Rep could make general reference to Belia's belief contents with more patent justification:

> Belia believes *something* true about the animal we saw.

Other than this power to apply the full referential apparatus of logic (by which we refer to things) to the things that any propositional attitude is directed toward, not much is gained by switching to attributes, since we're already provisionally assuming the entity interpretation of that-clause complements. We'll continue to refer to all the attitudes as propositional attitudes. We'll also lapse into referring to attributes occasionally, and we'll have more to say about them in section G.

## §3. The adicity of attitudes.

We classify attributes and the predicates that express them, incomplete propositions and the open sentences that express them, and the attitudes themselves according to the number of things they connect to each other by their **adicity**: monadic (one-placed), dyadic (two-placed), triadic, tetradic, pentadic, and so on. (The word "adicity" is technical jargon, coined from the "-adic" suffix.[11]) For example, the predicate "gives" is triadic because it has three places for names: (1) gives (2) to (3).

A notional attitude relates a person to one or more complete propositions. Simply count the propositions and add one for the person, and you have the attitude's adicity. Thus notional belief and notional desire are dyadic. Preference is triadic, since it relates a person to two propositions: She prefers the truth of one of them to the truth of the other. Desiring or believing a proposition to a degree equidistant from the degrees to which one desires or believes two other propositions would be a tetradic attitude.

Relational and notional attitudes may be conditional as well as absolute. We've mentioned only the absolute relational and notional attitudes, "absolute" because people simply have them or not. A person may also have a **conditional attitude**, that is, an attitude only under the supposition of some proposition, for example, a conditional want, conditional belief, or conditional feeling of insult, all conditional on some proposition. For example, suppose you speak unkindly to someone, who responds, "If you mean what you just said, I take offense." He himself does not yet know if he takes offense, because the attitude's existence depends on your forthcoming clarification. It's taken philosophers a considerable time to realize that a conditional belief *de dicto* is not a belief directed toward one conditional proposition, "if X then Y." Nor is a conditional desire *de dicto* a desire for the truth of one conditional proposition. So a conditional attitude, if it's one thing, it's not by virtue of being directed toward one thing. We seem to have fallen into a dilemma, however. On the one hand, a conditional attitude's suppositions cannot be brought within the scope^ of the attitude, making the attitude be directed toward the condition for its own existence as well as toward its regular propositional object, the consequent, as it were, of the conditional. On the other hand, it would be mysterious in the extreme if the proposition's truth, which is the condition, brought into existence the attitude which is conditioned on it, as though free floating propositions had causal powers in virtue of their truth values.^

The solution seems to be to recognize the existence of a pair of attitudes, the first being a person's conditional attitude that establishes the conditionedness of a later attitude and the second being that later attitude. A conditional attitude, when it clusters with other attitudes to form the

premises of Bayes's theorem (discussed in the previous section), establishes what would be the person's reason for the later attitude and cause of
it, if she adopts the later attitude upon learning just the condition. We
model this situation in probability theory, when we interpret the dyadic
function,$^\wedge$ $p(X|Y)$, as a degree of belief in X, given Y. This is an attitude
directed toward *a pair* of propositions in such a way that, if the condition
Y is fulfilled, there comes into being the consequent monadic function
$p_Y(X)$, which implements the conditional attitude. (In mathematics, the
adicity of a function counts only the objects in the parentheses, without
adding in the person whose attitude it represents. Thus the potential for
great confusion, which we must guard against, because a dyadic function
represents a triadic attitude.) Don't think this latter function of X,
representing belief in X, is dyadic because of its being justified by the
condition Y being fulfilled. Since the condition is outside the scope of the
function and the attitude the function represents, it does not affect either's
adicity. But the condition did count in the adicity of the attitude that
*constituted* the conditional relationship. Reverting now from mathematics
to the method of counting adicity appropriate to attitudes, triadic are those
attitudes that establish for (i) a person the connection of an attitude she
might adopt (ii) toward X to (iii) Y, the reason she would have for
adopting it, were she to learn of Y's truth and nothing else pertinent to X.
Conditional attitudes are ripe for philosophical scrutiny, but we forbear
with regret.[12]

That applies to a *de dicto* conditional attitude. The adicities of the
relational versions of the attitudes, the absolute ones as well as the
conditional ones, are more complicated. Let's consider the adicity of the
predicate "believes," taken relationally. A *de re* report can have several
positions for singular terms after the "about." Suppose Belia believes
about Jack and Jill that the former loves the latter. The about-position has
two singular terms in it. There could be more. This is why Quine sometimes called relational beliefs "polyadic" or "multigrade." He had in mind
the expansion of the position after the "about" to include several singular
terms. The anaphoric pronouns, such as "former" and "latter," work a bit
harder to keep the cross referencing straight in these cases. To determine
the adicity of a *de re* belief, count the things mentioned in the about-
position and add one for the believer herself, even if we already counted
her among the terms her belief is about. If you accept the adverbial
interpretation of the complement to the attitude verb, you're done, but
believers in the entity interpretation add one more for the incomplete
proposition that is the content believed of the things in the about-position.

The sum is the belief's adicity. Thus Belia's belief about Jack and Jill, that the former loves the latter, is tetradic, relating her to two others by way of a fourth, an incomplete proposition, "(1) loves (2)." Suppose she loves Jack and is jealous. Her jealousy would be a tetradic relation of herself to Jack and herself (again) by way of a fourth thing, an incomplete proposition, "(1) belongs to (2)": Belia is jealous of the fact, about Jack and herself, that he belongs to her.

We distinguish the adicity of a belief from the adicity of the incomplete proposition that the belief is directed toward. If Belia believes about herself, that she's hard on herself, this is a triadic belief with herself counted once as the believer and only once more for being mentioned in the about-position, despite her being cross-referenced in both positions of the third element, the predicate of the incomplete proposition, "(1) is hard on (2)." (We discuss the adicity of these predicates next, once we're done with the adicity of belief.) Notional beliefs, in contrast to relational beliefs, are dyadic, having no about-position; they relate a complete proposition to one believer.

In section A I mentioned that around 1905 Russell thought knowledge was, in his words, a "dual relation," but changed his mind. During the years from 1910 to 1917, he thought it was a "multiple relation" instead. What Russell had changed his mind about was the adicity of knowledge, although he never used that word. When taken as a dual relation, knowledge was a dyadic relation between the knower and a complete proposition. It was what we're calling a notional attitude. When taken as a multiple relation, it was a polyadic relation between the knower and the several things that went into making his knowledge. It was what we're calling a relational attitude. The terms in the relation, besides the knower, included attributes and could include particular things. (Russell moved from a notional theory of knowledge to a relational one, because he wanted to avoid having to commit to the reality of such entities as false complete propositions, which his dual relation theory of belief committed him to. His multiple relation theory had an analogous consequence, namely, it committed him to the reality of uninstantiated attributes. Today we don't think of a multiple relation theory as superior to a dual relation theory. Rather there are two phenomena, and one theory accounts for both.)

In one respect our regimentation has not been faithful to Russell's distinction between knowledge by description and knowledge by acquaintance, a distinction which I described in section A to introduce the distinction between the relational and the notional. There I began by tying proper names to acquaintance and definite descriptions to knowledge by description. Then I bailed out. Now, according to our regimentation, the *dictum* of knowledge *de dicto* is any complete proposition, which can even be a singular proposition expressed using proper names, and the about-positions of reports of knowledge *de re* may be occupied by any name Rep concurs with, including definite descriptions as well as proper names. The two regimented formats, differing essentially in adicity (the count and the sort of things counted), carry the burden of the *de re / de dicto* distinction now, not the two kinds of singular terms.

In subsequent sections we'll constrain our regimentation more, making it more faithful to Russell's version of the distinction in one respect. But not exactly faithful, for in section I we'll decide that *de re* knowledge is transmissible as *de re* knowledge. It's just as well that we don't try for fidelity to Russell's conception of acquaintance, for by 1919 Russell gave it up because it depended on a concept of the self that he came to think untenable. (I told the story in note 4 of section A.)

I mentioned in section A that some philosophers subsume *de re* belief under *de dicto* belief by defining *de re* belief as a *de dicto* belief in a singular proposition. We're now in a position to state and evaluate one of their arguments for this view. They argue that the concept of belief is univocal,ˆ but that to analyze relational and notional beliefs so that they're structurally distinct is to mistakenly make the concept of belief equivocal. They think that having to mark different adicities of relational and notional belief is proof of the structural distinctness and so the equivocation. That all belief is *de dicto*, in their view, restores the univocity of belief, since all *de dicto* beliefs are dyadic. I find this argument weak, because I don't think that the marking of different adicities is a proof of equivocity. A univocal concept can be **multigrade**, that is, naturally have different adicities as context demands without compromising its univocity. An example of a multigrade concept is the relation "between."[13] If the context is a linear pattern, one naturally takes this relation to be triadic: *x* is between *a* and *b*. But suppose *x* stands in the center of a triangle, and *a, b,* and *c* stand at its vertices. Here it seems natural to me to treat betweenness as tetradic: *x* is between *a, b,* and *c*. If *a, b, c,* and *d* stood at the corners of a square, then if *x* danced around the center of the square, *x* would be between the four all the while, though not between any pair of them for long, and the enduring betweenness would be pentadic. If *x* were standing at the center of a pentagon, with five people standing at its vertices, this betweenness would be a hexadic relation. In all these situations betweenness is used univocally. The way we use "belief" is univocal analogously. In general, two expressions may differ in adicity without differing in meaning, when the meaning is multigrade. So, we'll have to see a better argument than this one for taking *de re* belief as *de dicto* belief in a singular proposition.

## §4. The adicity of attributes.

Just before digressing into historical and polemical considerations, I had noted that adicity applies not just to the attitudes but to their contents as well. Let's now turn to that matter. Consider the incomplete proposition in a *de re* belief's that-clause, or alternatively the attribute; it too has an adicity set by the several anaphoric pronouns in it. Corresponding to each of the singular terms in a list of names after the "about," there's at least one anaphoric pronoun in the that-clause cross-referencing back to that term, and the number of these anaphoric pronouns determines the adicity of the incomplete proposition in the that-clause. Thus, returning to the example of Belia's jealousy of Jack, Belia's belief-content about the couple is dyadic, but so is my belief-content about Belia alone, that she's hard on herself. The contents in the two cases are "(1) belongs to (2)" and "(1) is hard on (2)." A propositional content's adicity depends on the number of times it anaphorically cross-references the things in the about-position,[14] not how many things are listed in the about-position.

Attributes may have any adicity, as I use the term "attribute." But a monadic attribute is usually called a **property**, in contrast to an attribute of greater adicity, which is called a **relation**. Note that relations need not relate only different entities. Some relations only relate a thing to itself: It's provable by logic that identity is a relation that each thing has to itself and only itself. It's still dyadic. Just as self-relating are relations like "being as tall as," which we think of as relating distinct things. It relates things to themselves too, for not only is Belia as tall as Rep, she is as tall as herself. Other relations relate a thing to itself occasionally: Belia tripped herself.

Sometimes it's useful to form a property out of a relation, like the property of being a mother (obviously of someone). Let's see how this lowering of adicity works. Obviously, "(1) is the mother of (2)" is dyadic. If we fill in just one of the blanks with a name, we can think of the composite as having just one blank, and so the composite is monadic: "Joan is the mother of (1)," which by abstraction is the property of being mothered by Joan. We call such constructions relational properties, and they are monadic.

Can the adicity of a belief's content exceed the adicity of the belief it's the content of? Yes. Belia is at the races, and sees a horse set a record for the track for the third time. Belia believes about this horse that its third record exceeds its second one by more than its second one exceeded its first. The belief is triadic: her, the horse, and the incomplete proposition. But the incomplete proposition is tetradic, since it refers to the horse four times:

> (1) its third record exceeds (2) its second record by more than (3) its second record exceeded (4) its first.

(We'll keep matters simple in these notes by using only one singular term after the "about" and one pronoun in the that-clause cross-referencing back to it.)

In contrast, the belief-content of a *de dicto* belief is a complete proposition. It contains no anaphoric pronouns referencing names outside itself. Complete propositions are zero-adic attributes. Quine would say they're "medadic"; he follows Peirce's example in extending the use of Greek roots to the zero case.[15] To see why propositions are medadic attributes, just extend the concept I introduced for lowering the adicity of a relation to get a relational property. Start with the predicate of a proposition; it has several blanks to be filled in with names. As each name is inserted, the resultant composite has fewer blanks to be filled in, and, counting just them, the adicity is lowered. Filling in the last blank left brings us to an adicity of zero. We could even define a complete **proposition** as a medadic attribute, as I hinted earlier in this section when I suggested a proposition is an extreme form of attribute. But if I did define a proposition as a medadic attribute, I'd have to explain how to attribute an attribute that has no slot for a thing to which it is attributed! (Is it attributed to everything if it's true, to nothing if it's false? Then the complete truth about our world is an attribute of each of us. Since each of us bears all the medadic attributes that make up the world, each of us is Atlas!) Despite the embarrassment, it's a viable definition of proposition.

Names do not have adicity; predicates do. What predicates express have adicity too, but something that can only be named, never predicated, does not. Propositions, both complete and incomplete, or alternatively, attributes such as properties and relations, in general, things predicable have adicity. The name "Belia" has no adicity; this name is not predicable, but rather picks out a subject of predication. A name is not something that has blanks, either filled or unfilled; it's what goes into the blanks. The concept of adicity is not applicable to names.[16]

What makes predicates and sentences so different from names, that there's a difference between no adicity and zero adicity? Might not a complete sentence just name one of the truth values (truth or falsehood), or name a fact? No, despite the fact that Frege said as much. Similarly, isn't an attribute named by the predicate expressing it? No. The separation of names from predicates and sentences must be inviolate. A true sentence cannot name the truth value, true, or the fact in virtue of which it is true, for the simple reason that the world might have been such that the sentence, with no change in its significance, would have to name the value, false, instead, or the complement of the fact. Names don't operate this way. What sort of name would "Tweedledum" be if it named Tweedledum only if the world is one way, otherwise with no change in its significance, it has to name Tweedledee instead? Here's how Russell expressed this same point, (where Russell uses "proposition" to mean a sentence):

> It is very important to realize such things, for instance, as that *propositions are not names for facts.* It is quite obvious as soon as it is pointed out to you, but as a matter of fact I never had realized it until it was pointed out to me by a pupil of mine, Wittgenstein. It is perfectly evident as soon as you think of it, that a proposition is not a name for a fact, from the mere circumstance that there are two propositions corresponding to each fact. Suppose it is a fact that Socrates is dead. You have two propositions: "Socrates is dead" and "Socrates is not dead". And those two propositions corresponding to the same fact, there is one fact in the world which makes one true and one false. That is not accidental, and illustrates how the relation of proposition to fact is a totally different one from the relation of name to the thing named. . . .
>
> There are two different relations, as you see, that a proposition may have to a fact: the one the relation that you may call being true to a fact, and the other being false to the fact. Both are equally essentially logical relations which may subsist between the two, whereas in the case of a name, there is only one relation it can have to what it names. A name can just name a particular, or, if it does not, it is not a name at all, it is a noise.[17]

An attribute is a thing, and a predicate expresses it. The predicate, "has gone into the bushes," expresses but does not name the attribute of having gone into the bushes. If expressing an attribute is not the same as naming it, how do we name it? Easy: by a definite description of it. Now here's a trick question: What is the adicity of the name, "the attribute of having gone into the bushes"? If you answered monadic you're wrong, because names have no adicity even if they are the names of things that do have adicity. The attribute of having gone into the bushes is monadic, but the name of that attribute, "the attribute of having gone into the bushes" has no adicity. If you fell for the trick, you fell into the **use-mention confu-**

**sion**. This confusion consists of mistaking the name of the thing for the thing named. When one talks of the thing named, one uses the name; when one talks of the name itself, one mentions the name. When I asked the question about the adicity of the name, I mentioned the name. If you answered that it was monadic, you used the name. You answered a question I did not ask. You may think only simpletons would make this mistake, like one who prays to a statue instead of to the person it represents. Nevertheless, it has an uncanny way of showing up in smart people's thinking too.

### §5. Force is not an intrinsic property of propositions.

Let's now be more circumspect about the relation of sentences to propositions. For there's a discrepancy between the way predicates express attributes and the way sentences express propositions, which obscures the greater affinity of propositions to attributes than to what can only be named and never attributed. Let's isolate that discrepancy.

We must first notice an ambiguity. Surely the attitude of belie*ving* is directed toward the belie*ved*, desi*ring* toward the desi*red*, and in general the represent*ing* toward the represent*ed*. The -*ed* suffix is a mark of passivity here, not past time. The *ing/ed* distinction is blurry in our customary ways of speaking. We use the nouns, "belief" and "desire" (without the -*ing* or -*ed*), for either of these sides of the relation or for the relation itself. Worse than that, we use the noun "meaning" for either. Let's mind the *ing/ed* distinction as we think of the discrepancy between what predicates express and what sentences express.

The grammatical forms of sentences, together with the grammatical moods of their verbs, express the -*ing* aspect, the attitudes themselves. Grammatical sentence-forms and verb-moods are these: indicative (or assertoric), assumptive, interrogative, imperative, optative, and perhaps others (like the smiley sentences I mentioned when we considered David-sonian regimentation at the end of the previous section). Let's say that the sentence-form, the distinctive punctuation, intonation, and verb-moods show a sentence's **force**, and, following Wittgenstein, let's call what's left of a sentence, when its force is removed from it, the **sentence-radical**,[18] on analogy to a radical in chemistry, a core constituent of a compound. The sentence-radicals, abstracted as they are from their force, express the -*ed* aspect, the content, which is what we've been calling the proposition. A complete sentence-radical can be given a force, and so can an incomplete sentence-radical, if it's about enough things to complete it and we can list them. The sentence's force tells the audience how to take the content or proposition it's applied to, that is, what attitude to direct toward it. For the variety of forces corresponds to the variety of attitudes, attitudes being methods of projecting propositions, in Wittgenstein's terms. So alternatively, a sentence's force expresses the propositional attitude the speaker takes, or wishes the audience to take, toward the content. For example, the same content or proposition is expressed in all these sentences, and their forces' relation to the contents is made explicit in parentheses:

> Shut the door. (You make the content true)
> Would that the door were shut. (I desire the content to be true)
> The door is shut. (I believe the content true)
> Is the door shut? (You ease my wonder whether the content is true)
> Suppose the door were shut. (You assume the content true, despite its being false)

The proposition common to all of these sentences is the door's closure.

If a sentence expresses both a proposition and a force (or, as some prefer, the sentence means a proposition and the speaker's utterance of the sentence displays a force), then the **proposition** is in need of a way of being expressed by itself. It's time for more regimentation. The content should be expressed by a phrase built up from a verbal noun, like "closure," which is a noun built from the verb, "to close." Expressing content this way avoids conveying a force; conveying force belongs to the attitude toward the content. In practice, however, verbal nouns are awkward, and so we treat the that-clause as itself a name for the content. We treat the phrase, "that the door is shut," as naming the content, and prefixed to it is a force indicator. For example, the declarative sentence whose verb is in the indicative mood ("The door's shut") we would paraphrase as,

> It is the case that the door [is] shut.

The assertoric force is in that prefix, "it is the case . . ." and the brackets around the verb in the content, the that-clause, mean you should ignore its assertive force. What follows the "that," denuded of its force, is the sentence-radical. Expressions of the other attitudes attach different prefixes to that-clauses. We need not confine ourselves to paraphrasing the forces which syntax provides expressions for. We can branch out. For instance, philosophers often focus on one particular force, which is just mentally entertaining a content without regard to its truth or falsity. When we divide force from content as we do in our regimentation, we may adopt the attitude of mere entertainment toward the content, but the sentence-radical does not express this attitude. If it did, it would not be a sentence-radical; it would be a sentence with a force of its own. All the psychological stuff, the attitudinizing, is on the force side of this analysis. The propositional content, purified of all attitudes, is on the other side.

But is not mentally entertaining a content the fundamental attitude? No.[19] There might be a fundamental force and all other forces might be built up from that one, in any of several senses of "built up": analytically, computationally, ontogenetically, or phylogenetically. If there is, the fundamental attitude is more likely to be desiring, or both believing and desiring, than merely entertaining in thought. Or perhaps the indicative mood is the fundamental force, since it invokes the truth of the proposition. Then all other moods would be modalities of the indicative. Those speculations are meant as a tease; I'll say no more about them.

To return to the counting of the adicity of belief, let me summarize: An absolute notional belief is dyadic and it's directed toward a content that's medadic, a complete proposition. If an absolute relational belief mentions $n$ things in its about-position, its adicity is $n+2$ and its content's adicity is $n+m$, where $m$ stands for any extra anaphoric cross-referencings to the $n$ things. For conditional forms of the attitudes, add one more for the condition. If you find the concept of adicity hard to master, be consoled by the promise that counting procedures won't figure prominently in the rest of these notes. The concept of adicity, however, has already helped clarify the contrast I drew in section A between two ways of distinguishing relational from notional attitudes, and enabled us to answer the charge that my preferred way of drawing the distinction rendered verbs expressing attitudes equivocal. Furthermore, it's helped us see the greater affinity of propositions to attributes than to the kind of thing that can only be named, never attributed. That's to say, something with zero-adicity is more like things of higher adicity than like things with no adicity at all.

### §6. The adicity of iterated attitudes.

Before going on, I should prepare you for the eventuality that, when we look more closely at the relation of beliefs and their contents to time, we'll have to make room, in our counting of their adicity, for their relations to moments. Thank goodness that's not important yet; it comes up only in section M.

Even more complicated than accommodating time are relational beliefs about relational beliefs. Suppose Rep reports:

Belia believes *about* me that I believe *about* her that she believes *about* the animal that it ran into the bushes.

To determine the adicity of Belia's belief about what Rep believes, we note first that the whole report contains three about-positions. I recommend that we consolidate them into one in a step-by-step procedure, working from the innermost about-positions outward. So as a first step we consolidate the two inner about-positions this way:

> Belia believes *about* me that I believe *about* her and the animal that the former believes that the latter ran into the bushes.

Now the two remaining about-positions can be consolidated into one this way:

> Belia believes *about* me, her, and the animal that the first believes that the second believes that the third ran into the bushes.

The rules for adicity can now be applied to Belia's belief about Rep's belief: It's pentadic. The adicity of the propositional content which that belief is directed toward is triadic.

Can this iteration of relational beliefs within relational beliefs ever have philosophical interest? Yes. In section U we'll propose the primacy of empathy in the learning of language. Empathy is believing that another believes, perceives, or feels a certain way. So it is an iterative attitude. We have already tacitly appealed to it. For example,

> Rep empathizes with ( = about) Belia that she perceives about the woodchuck that it ran into the bushes.

Also, one theory of communication, due to the philosopher H. P. Grice, analyzes "a speaker's meaning something by what she says" in terms of just such a triple iteration. Grice proposes[20] that for Belia to mean something by her words is for this to be the case:

> Belia intends that she affect her audience by means of
> their recognizing that
> she intends that she affect them in that way by her words.

You might ask yourself if Grice has a chicken or egg problem. Which comes first, the attitudes that he thinks create meaning, or the meaningful propositions without which there can be no propositional attitudes?

Our discussion of iterated beliefs has been confined to the iteration of relational beliefs. What if we allow iteration of mixtures of relational and notional beliefs? Some complexities occur which reflect on the adequacy of concepts not yet introduced, and so we'll not pursue them here.[21]

# Notes

1. Anselm, *Proslogion*, M. J. Charlesworth, translator (1965), ch. 4. Avoid the often-reprinted translation of this chapter by Deane, which he made in 1856. It contains a sentence Anselm did not write; it was a marginal note made by a reader of the manuscript Dean translated..

2. John Henry Newman, *A Grammar of Assent* (1892 [first edition 1870]), ch. 4, §2. Michael Smith makes much of the fact that a value judgment and a desire must be locked together by their both being *de re* of the same thing. See his *The Moral Problem* (1994), esp. sections 3.5 and 3.7. He may not intend about-positions in the reporter's control, but only anaphoric pronouns with the same reference, and so not fully *de re* in our sense. I'll say more about these issues in section O.

3. Plato, *Symposium*, 210a-212c. The contrast between desire (or wishing for) and seeming-good is in *Gorgias*, starting at 466d.

4. Aristotle, *Nicomachean Ethics*, bk. 7, 1147a24-b19. Aristotle thinks that the singular belief is attached to four other attitudes: perception, the universal premise of a practical syllogism, the conclusion of the syllogism, which presumably accords with a rational desire, and finally to independent appetites. My thought is that *de re* and *de dicto* versions of the singular belief will be associated to those connections with different weights.

5. Bertrand Russell, *Human Society in Ethics and Politics* (1955), Part Two, ch. II.

6. Ferejohn, Michael, *The Origins of Aristotelian Science* (1991), ch. 2.

7. E. B. Holt *et al*, *The New Realism* (1912).

8. Kent Bach, "Do Belief Reports Report Beliefs?" *Pacific Philosophical Quarterly*, 78 (1997) 215-241. Michael McKinsey, "The Semantics of Belief Ascriptions," *Nous* 33-4 (1999) 519-557. The position I call the adverbial interpretation McKinsey calls the property theory, and my nominative interpretation he calls the relational theory. I've reserved the word "relational" for theories that postulate about-positions. So I avoid it when discussing theories of the directed-toward relation.

9. If I'm 6 feet tall, is there a height such that I have that one? If you and I are both the same height, is there a height we're both related to? These seem extravagant interpretations. See Robert J. Matthews, "The Measure of Mind," *Mind*, 103 (1994) 131-146.

10. In "Quantifiers and Propositional Attitudes," section II, and in *Word and Object*, Quine confines the word "attribute" to properties true of things taken individually, as distinct from relations, which are true of things taken in pairs, triples, etc. I use "attribute" to cover all adicities.

11. Alternatively, we might have gone with the Latin roots, unary, binary, ternary, etc. Then we'd've called adicity "arity."

12. For the richness of philosophical insights to be gleaned from the study of conditional attitudes, see two articles in Lou Goble, ed., *Blackwell Guide to Philosophical Logic* (2001). On conditional beliefs see Dorothy Edgington, "Conditionals," 385-414. See our glossary entry for "absolute probability" for the distinction between $p(X|Y)$ and $p_Y(X)$. The difference between $p_Y(X)$ and $p(X)$ is the difference between an absolute probability that's conditioned and an absolute probability that's unconditioned, which would be one's initial degrees of belief *a priori*.

On conditional desires see Risto Hilpinen, "Deontic Logic," 159-182. Perhaps, the distinction carries over to desires this way: Comparable to the absolute probability is a desire which has taken into account beliefs about the world, as was mentioned in section B, and comparable to a conditional probability is an "expected utility" of an action not yet done, which decision theory posits that we calculate in the course of deliberation.

13. In his "Intensions Revisited," Quine defines multigrade as having adicity *n* for each *n*. I relax that. Betweenness does not admit of adicities less than triadic, but I call it multigrade anyway. I'm not joking; my dictionary gives, as an instance of betweenness, a lion rampant between eight crosses, an enneadic relation.

14. Suppose one of the positions in the belief content is occupied, not by an anaphoric pronoun, but by a singular term. Suppose the statement of the belief is fully regimented, so that all singular terms that can go into the about-position are there, and this singular term remains in the belief content because the belief is not about the thing it names. Then I set it as part of the belief content, and the position it occupies is not to be counted in determining the content's adicity.

15. Charles Sanders Peirce, *Collected Papers* (1960), vol. 2, §272. See Quine, *Word and Object*, §34.

16. To apply the idea of adicity to singular terms is to take definite descriptions as real terms, contrary to Russell's recommendation. Or we accept Russell's idea and treat the adicity of singular terms as merely apparent adicity of apparent terms in apparent propositional structures. Then "the daughter of *x* and *y*" is a dyadic function, "the daughter of Henry VIII and *y*" is a monadic function, "the daughter of Henry VIII and Anne Boleyn" a medadic function, and proper names, e.g., Elizabeth I, are medadic functions by extrapolation. But they would have zero *referential* adicity, still different from the zero *attributive* adicity of a complete proposition.

17. Bertrand Russell, "The Philosophy of Logical Atomism," first lecture, reprinted in his *Logic and Knowledge*, edited by Robert C. Marsh (1956) 187f.

18. Ludwig Wittgenstein, *Philosophical Investigations* (1953) 11: "*Satzradikal.*" I follow Erik Stenius's account of this distinction in his *Wittgenstein's 'Tractatus'* (1960), ch. IX. Lloyd Morgan introduced in 1912 the -ing / -ed contrast in *Instinct and Experience*.

19. Descartes believed the answer was, Yes. Spinoza thought the fundamental attitude was belief. See his *Ethics* (1677), II, 49, scholium. Experiments by a cognitive psychologist suggest that Descartes was wrong. See Daniel Gilbert, "How Mental Systems Believe," *American Psychologist* (February, 1991) 107-30. Donald Davidson agrees with Spinoza. See his "Moods and Performances" (1979), reprinted with additional notes as ch. 8 in his *Inquiries into Truth and Interpretation* (1984). In that article he extends what I have called the Davidsonian regimentation to a theory of force.

20. In his "Meaning" (1957), reprinted in P. F. Strawson, *Philosophical Logic* (1967).

21. This subject is explored by Richard Holton, "Attitude Ascriptions and Intermediate Scope" *Mind* 103 (1994) 123-130. We introduce scope in the next section.

# E. A Standardized Logic for the Reports' Entailments.

Let's bring Belia and Rep back into our discussions. Belia believes, and Rep reports what Belia believes.

## §1. Regimenting conversational implicatures.

Belia has some control over what reports will be true reports of her relational beliefs, but it's incomplete control. Belia is not entitled to be a guarantor of the truth of the description of the thing (*res*) that Rep may employ in the about-position. To show this fits our intuitions, let's revise the story we told about them in section C, when we introduced the notion of partial concurrence. Belia saw an animal run into the bushes, as before, but in our new version she made a mistake. Rep sees the whole scene and knows the animal they see is a skunk. In this new story, Rep can't use the phrase "that woodchuck in the bushes" as a name for the object Belia has a belief about. Rep can't even report Belia's belief using in the about-position the name Belia would use. She would say "that woodchuck in the bushes." But that's not what it is; it's a skunk in the bushes. So Rep would report her belief as:

> Belia has a belief *about* that skunk in the bushes, and what she believes about it is *that* it is a woodchuck.

We have here another aspect of the about-position besides showing Rep's partial agreement with what Belia believes, a use of it according to which Belia (or the one whose belief is reported on) may *not* concur with Rep's report because of what he says in the about-position, without affecting the report's truth. Rep identifies what object the belief is about really, whether or not the believer has a correct understanding of the object of her belief.

> *First regimentation: Rep commands the about-position, not Belia.*

Rep is concurring with Belia's belief only to the extent of agreeing that it's somehow about a real thing.

Suppose that Belia believes about the skunk that it was returning to its baby woodchuck. The phrase "its baby woodchuck" is a singular term. Rep would not put it into an about-position, since skunks don't have woodchucks for babies. So he'll leave it in the that-clause. Who controls the use of singular terms in the that-clause? As we review unregimented examples, our intuitions tell us either the believer or the reporter may assert control over them. But the dual control comes at the price of ambiguity in the report. If Rep reports that "Belia believes that the skunk is a woodchuck," Belia may object to the singular term, "the skunk," as no part of any belief she has. Here Rep is asserting control within the that-clause, but the price he pays is that, although he's reporting a belief in the form of a belief *de dicto*, the *dictum* is not Belia's. If he cedes to Belia the control over singular terms in the that-clause, we can trust that the *dicta* of his notional reports are Belia's. We can sense the ambiguity of notional reports, which amounts to feeling that only the latter kind of notional report (Belia in full control of singular terms in the that-clause) reports notional *belief.*

As part of our regimentation of reports, let's say that when Rep leaves singular terms in his report's that-clause he's conceding to Belia exclusive control over those terms. (This decision departs from Quine's regimentation.)

> *Second regimentation: Belia controls the meaning of the that-clause, not Rep.*

This restriction of her control to control of the meaning allows Rep to choose the language and such matters of vocabulary as depend on the context of his reports, such as pronouns and tense, as noted in section C §2. Her control amounts to oversight of the precision of his translation of her belief. This regimentation is heavy-handed interference with the reporting, in order to get more resolution in the picture of the believing that's reported on. The believer's exclusive control over singular terms in the that-clause is report-regimentation, not belief-regimentation. And even then, it's no great handicap for the reporter. Rep has another way to say what he wanted to say: Instead of saying "Belia believes that the skunk is a woodchuck," he can say, "Belia believes about the skunk that it is a woodchuck." All this mitigates the heavy handedness.

To see more clearly what's involved in these two regimentations and the ones to follow, we must return to a point made at the beginning of section C about intuition pumps. Since we're about to make many thought experiments, we should be sensitive to their deficiencies as intuition pumps. David Lewis warned,

> if you hope to understand the folk psychology of belief by studying the
> linguistic phenomenology of ordinary belief sentences, you're in for big

trouble.[1]

For he believes it's altogether too easy to create contrary intuition pumps when the outcome of the thought experiment is supposed to be what you'd say to the other guy. Our speech is extraordinarily compliant to our speech partner's idiosyncracies. So it's unlikely that thought experiments of this variety will settle into any reflective^ equilibrium. We would affirm in one conversational setting what we'd be forbidden from affirming in another. In one conversational setting we might accept that one sentence implies another, but in another setting, we'd deny that very implication. Well, let's be on our guard, but also let's proceed. It's our hope that we can separate those implications which are impervious to conversational contexts from those which aren't, and rely on the former. In section K we'll face big trouble and begin to suspect limits on the value of semantic ascent.

Some implications of reports exist because of their conversational context while others exist willy nilly, impervious to variations in context. That's not a division of the implications just of reports; it divides implications in general. The implications willy nilly we'll call **entailment**s; a proposition that is entailed must be true, if the premises which entail it are true. We'll call those implications whose existence depends on their context **conversational implicature**s, a term coined by Grice to make the distinction.[2] They are conversational because the speaker depends on the listener to infer the speaker's intention from the oddness or insufficiency of the literal meaning of the words uttered, together with the rules of conversation and the conversational context. Implicatures include insinuations and the intended meanings of ironic and metaphorical remarks.

The chief mark of the difference between a speaker's reports' entailing some statement and their conversationally implicating a statement is that the speaker can block a conversational implicature, without incurring irrationality, by explicitly taking it back. Entailments exist by the laws of logic; implicatures exist by conversational courtesy. For example, suppose a logician's wife says jokingly to her husband's colleagues, "He made me pregnant, and he married me . . . but not in that order."[3] If she had not added the tag, the conversational implicature would've been that the events occurred in the order she'd stated them in (or it would've been an implicature, if her audience had not been logicians who automatically treat all conjunctions as commutative^). On the other hand, there's no conversational context where she could've added, ". . . but he did not make me pregnant," for the denial of such an addition is entailed by what she said, and it would be irrational to try to cancel the entailment.

Implicatures occur in the expression and reporting of beliefs. If Belia says of a margarine she just tasted, "I can't believe it isn't butter," she's implicating she does believe it isn't butter; she's exaggerating transparently to praise the quality of the imitation. Only one unskilled in conversation would conclude that she necessarily believes it is butter. As with ironic and metaphorical remarks, the implicature here corrects the literal meaning of what she says. In other circumstances implicatures add to the literal meaning of what was said. We'll see cases of adding in section L. Our second regimentation elevated an implicature to the status of an entailment. In 1981 Thomas McKay argued convincingly that it's a conversational implicature of a report, not an entailment, that the believer has veto-power over the report's that-clause.[4] Recall the negative disquotation principle, which was introduced in section C: Rep may infer from Belia's refusal to assent to the sentence, "*p*," that she does not believe that *p*. We realized back then that this principle is not logically valid in so bare a form. We tried to find an entailment by adding more premises to the one given, but we must now recognize that only a little ingenuity would be needed to justify rejecting the conclusion despite accepting all the premises we found. Our exercise of ingenuity would be demonstrating that the negative disquotation principle can be canceled and so has the status of an implicature only. McKay wanted to exploit the fact that implicatures can be canceled: Belia believes something despite her protestations that she doesn't. We're taking away from McKay and other philosophers this option by our regimenting the implicature into an entailment. That's too unscrupulous a way of winning an argument, even for sly me, and so I promise to revisit this issue in section X §6.

Since Grice's lectures in the late 1960's on conversational implicature, it's become necessary to examine all claims of entailment to see if they're only conversational implicatures. The examination can have devastating effects on some philosophical theses.[5] But it's very clarifying for those engaged in regimentation, which admittedly introduces artificiality. For we now see that **regimentation** is primarily legislating that some conversational implicatures of reports be elevated to the status of an entailment within our investigations, while others are to be dismissed altogether. We'll elevate an implicature (concerning whatever else besides existence Rep concurs in by his use of the about-position) to an entailment in section H. Which decision to make is guided by the purpose of highlighting the real features of belief itself. Regimentation cannot change the original, built-in entailments of reports, although the regimenting-in of some implicatures and not others is already incipient theorizing, despite our official position that we're just gussying up the data. We must be prepared, therefore, to defend our regimentation when it precludes certain theories, or else change our regimentations to accommodate the theories.

Perhaps you doubt that we can change the status of conversational implicatures as I suggested. I would argue that logic itself does this. For example, suppose we're talking of a pile of fruit. I say "some are ripe." You conclude "some are not ripe," for if that were not to be inferred, I should've said "all are ripe." On the other hand, suppose I had said "all are ripe." Now you'd have inferred "some are ripe," for surely some are if they all are. The sequence of the two inferences—from "all are" to "some are" to "some are not"—is incoherent; the last step contradicts the first. To resolve this we say that the second step in this series is only a conversational implicature, which is canceled if its premise is inferred from the universal statement. Is not the first step itself a conversational implicature? Elementary logic treats it as an entailment, because it requires that the domains^ of quantifiers not be empty. This makes it a law of logic that something exists! But logic could've been regimented without the requirement of nonempty domains for its quantifiers. Then we'd treat the inference from "all are" to "some are" as an implicature that could be canceled. Indeed, one development of logic, called free logic, allows us to do just that.[6] Moral of the story: If logic can legislate implicatures into entailments, so can we.

Applying the moral to our story, when Rep says, "Belia believes that it was a woodchuck . . .," the implicature is that she would assent to the that-clause. Ordinarily Rep could cancel that implicature by adding on, ". . . really, although she's quite unaware of that." Our regimentation has now forbidden him this freedom.

Next we must regiment three purported entailments of our two belief formats. They are (i) exportation and importation of singular terms, (ii) intersubstitution of singular terms, and (iii) generalization of singular terms. In the discussion of implication that follows, apply the test of explicit cancellability. If an implication is cancellable, it's only a conversational implicature, not an entailment, and we must decide the best way to regiment it. We'll conclude that reports of propositional attitudes are logically deviant from the norm; the three forms of normally valid entailments are invalid for reports.

We made much of the concept of a logically proper name, but in what follows I'll draw from a motley bunch of terms, including Santa Claus, Zeus, and various definite descriptions, counting them all as singular terms for the time being.

## §2. The exportation and importation of singular terms.

First I explain **exportation** and **importation** of singular terms back and
forth between their position after the word *about* and their position after
the word *that*. Suppose just for the moment that Rep felt he could've
reported Belia's belief in either a *de re* or a *de dicto* format. (As I've set it
up, anyone who has a *de re* belief will often have a corresponding *de dicto*
singular belief, but not always. So the contrast we want is one between a
belief state that's *de re*, which is paired with a *de dicto* state, and one that's
*de re* without being paired. Rep thinks it's the first case.) In this instance,
in making the *de dicto* report,
> (i) Belia believes *that* the animal ran into the bushes,

Rep happened to concur with Belia's having a given animal as the object
of her belief. Thus he could've regimented his report in the *de re* way of
reporting.
> (ii) Belia believes *about* the animal *that* it ran into the bushes.

From his original report (i), he **exports** her proper name for the object or
her description of it. That is, he takes it out of the that-clause in the *de
dicto* version, replacing it there with an anaphoric pronoun, and puts the
name into the about-position of the *de re* version (ii). **Importing** is the
reverse operation. We get report (ii) from report (i) by exportation; we get
report (i) from (ii) by importation.

The exported and ·imported formats thus strike us as options in
regimentation. Are the operations of exportation and importation also the
basis for implications? Should there be an implication from the *de dicto*
to the *de re* format, if the exported singular term is of something that
exists? In other words, given the existence of the thing named, should
exportation be a valid inference? For ordinary propositions it is valid:
> Jack loves Jill.

> Jill is such that Jack loves her.

> Jack is such that he loves Jill.

> Jack and Jill are such that the former loves the latter.

Names and anaphoric pronouns are supposed to work together in just this
way.

Then is exportation valid for reports? No, for the sentence resulting
from exportation of a singular term, even one naming an existent thing,
from a true *de dicto* report may not be true. For example,
> Belia believes that the oldest skunk is quite old,

but
> about this skunk here, who happens to be the oldest skunk,

unbeknownst to Belia, she does not believe it is so very old. That reversal of truth value is inconsistent with our taking the exportation of singular terms to be valid. In the converse direction, singular terms are not generally "importable" from about-positions into that-clauses, for the reason that names in about-positions need not be names Belia would agree to as expressing her belief. Thus, if it was a skunk that ran into the bushes,

> Belia believes *about* the skunk *that* it ran into the bushes.

But

> she does not believe *that* the skunk (or even a skunk) ran into the bushes.

Here the names and anaphoric pronouns are not working together as they did in the paraphrases of "Jack loves Jill." So reporters may neither export a name from a that-clause, nor import a name from an about-position into a that-clause, because it may turn the report false or ambiguous.[7] In some scenarios importation sounds valid when the name to be imported is a proper name of a nonfictional being or a demonstrative expression like "the skunk" (understood as "this recently visible skunk"). In that case we're recognizing a *de re* report, but it has a nonregimented form in that Belia's agreement is not required on what goes into the that-clause.

(Here I departed from Quine's positions; up to 1976 he had thought singular terms were always exportable and importable. He made this position more plausible than I have, since he does not recognize non-referring singular terms, nor does he recognize the ambiguity arising from dual control over the singular terms in the that-clauses of non-regimented formats. He had thought exportation was logically valid implication.[8] But problems with that thesis, namely, the seeming context-dependence of acceptable exportations, made him give up on making *de re* belief respectable enough for a science, and so the matter of the validity of exportation became unimportant for him. Although I favor his earlier theory of relational belief, I agree that this component of the earlier theory, the validity of exportation of singular terms, should be given up.)

> *Third regimentation: In attitude reports exportation and importation of singular terms are invalid.*

## §3. The intersubstitution of singular terms.

Next I explain entailments between statements by **intersubstitution** in them of names for the same thing. Different names of the same thing are **coreferential** singular terms, because **reference** is the relation of naming that holds between a name and the thing it names. Rep may use in the about-position of his report *any* of the names of the thing that happens to be the object about which Belia has a belief. The thing's names are intersubstitutable in the about-position in the report because the substitution there does not affect the truth of the report. (Note that intersubstitution involves an interchange of names in one position, whereas exportation and importation involve moving names from one position to another.) To emphasize that the truth is unaffected by the substitution, we may say they are intersubstitutable *salva veritate*, that is, preserving truth of the sentences: If the sentence to be substituted into is true, the sentence that results from the substituting is true also. For example, return to the first story about Belia (in C, where she makes no mistake). She was right after all; it was not a skunk they saw running into the bushes. Even so, if Rep reports her belief is about the woodchuck, then it's about the groundhog, another name for the same thing. It does not matter that Belia or Rep may reject one of those names due to ignorance or error. That substitutions should be *salva veritate* is simply a requirement for deductive implication: A sentence implies another sentence if it's impossible for the first to be true and the second false.

Underlying the substitution is the principle,

if *a* is the same thing as *b*, then whatever is true of *a* is true of *b*,

as Aristotle pointed out.[9] (And not even he has priority in stating the principle; Socrates seems to have been the first, using it when he criticized proposed definitions.) By semantic ascent from this principle, we see the names "a" and "b" are intersubstitutable *salva veritate* in truths where they occur and refer to *a*, that is, to *b*. Consequently, we call this the **principle of the substitutivity of identity**, for short, the principle of substitution. (I occasionally call it the principle of the intersubstitution of identicals. Of course, if you have the right idea, you should think the plural ending on "identicals" is wrong! It's short for "names of numerically^ the same thing." Use of the term "identicals" comes close to committing the use-mention confusion.) A consequence of this principle is its contrapositive^ form, favored by Socrates:

If something is true of *a* that's not true of *b*, then *a* is not the same thing as *b*.

Applying this form of the principle to reports of Belia's beliefs (putting "the groundhog" for *a* and "the woodchuck" for *b*), the groundhog is the same thing as the woodchuck, and so by *modus tollens^* everything true of the woodchuck should surely be true of the groundhog. Right?

It's easy to find sentences that suggest substitutivity fails, but sometimes it suffices to expose an equivocation to remove the suggestion. For example,

> ●The temperature = 20°. The temperature is rising, but 20° is not rising.

The example equivocates on "the temperature." It means "the temperature at present" in the first sentence and "the temperature[s] during a course of time including the present" in the second. In this second sense the temperature is not identical to 20°. Paraphrases suggest themselves that circumvent other purported counterexamples. (In the examples that follow I use the symbol "=" to express identity. Resist reading the symbol as "equals"; rather, when you see "=" read "is numerically identical to," or "is identical with," or "is one and the same thing as.") Consider some recalcitrant sentences:

> ●Suppose Belia = Harriet, so these names should be intersubstitutable in: Belia is so called because she is the believer (recall my introduction of the name in section C). Harriet is not so called for that reason. Solution: Replace "so called" by "called 'Belia'." Then the substitution works.
> ●Suppose the morning star = Venus, so these names should be intersubstitutable in: The morning star shines in the evening too. The word "too" sounds odd when "Venus" is substituted. Solution: Replace "too" by "as well as in the morning." The oddness after substitution disappears.
> ●Suppose Mark Twain = Samuel Clemens, so these names should be intersubstitutable in: Mark Twain's first name begins with "M" as you can see. But you can't see it after the substitution. Solution: Replace "first name" with "name, 'Mark'."
> ●Suppose three people are standing in line, Fred first, then Mary, then Bill. Fred leaves. So this is true: "The person behind Fred saw him leave." But although the person behind Fred = the person in front of Bill, this sentence is false: "The person in front of Bill saw him leave." And the sentence "Mary saw him leave" is incomplete. The solution is to replace the pronoun "him" by the name "Fred" before making the substitutions for "the person behind Fred."

These counterexamples show that the substitution of names may not just exchange names of the same thing. The substitution may also affect how some other part of the sentence works. Since this additional effect of the substitutions is an extraneous grammatical complication, our paraphrases rightly prevent it from occurring.[10]

Don't think the paraphrases are tampering with the data; rather they are cleaning up some messiness in our speech habits, so that we can extract genuine data.

Some apparent counterexamples exploit a conversational implicature, as occurs here:

●Groundhogs have the second day of February named after them.

The phrase "named after" invokes the implicature that the name used in the sentence is the name conferred (Groundhog Day in the U.S.A.), unless the implicature is canceled. We could just cancel it, or we might revise the ending to "named after their name 'groundhog'." It's not incongruous to say that woodchucks have a day in February named after their other name, "groundhog."

Some other proposed counterexamples to substitutivity cannot be disposed of so easily. In the next section, we'll consider contexts governed by the concepts of necessity and possibility (modalities) where substitutivity fails. Here's another example,

●L.B.J. = the 36th president of the U.S.A., although J.F.K.'s assassination caused L.B.J. to become the 36th president, it did not cause him to become L.B.J.

Here the true causal claim tacitly refers to a "causal law" of sorts, that the deaths of presidents cause their vice presidents to become the next president. So I propose that we understand the claim to be this: That J.F.K.'s assassination caused L.B.J. to become the 36th president *by virtue of that causal law governing succession to the presidency.* Perhaps in making the law explicit, a term in the definite description occurs again in the law, so that, when the substitution takes place in the term's original position, it seems to take place in both places. Then we might have a solution, for the falsity of the sentence would be the falsity of the claim of law once the substitution in it occurs. For example, suppose the relevant lawful consequence of the law is that, if the 35th president should die in office, the vice president shall become the 36th president. Then, when we substitute "L.B.J." for "the 36th president" we would seem to be substituting it both in the term's original position and in the law. One thing that would make the sentence false would be the substitution in the law. So we restrict the substitution to just the term's original position. Unfortunately, the resultant sentence still strikes us as false, although the law, made explicit and left unchanged, is still true. Making the law explicit is unlike the previous cases of making something explicit, in that the explication here does not show us how to save the substitutivity of identity. Furthermore, even if you could figure out a way to pin the blame for the falsity on the reference to laws, there are many examples of one thing making another to be the case even where there are no plausible candidates for laws to make explicit. That fact makes me *the more embarrassed of the two of us*. But it does not make me *Arthur*. So there are contexts in which substitutivity does not preserve truth, and I think one of them is the causal context. A related context where it fails is the counterfactual^ conditional.

Some philosophers defend substitutivity even in causal contexts, while others declare so much the worse for causal contexts. They are covertly modal, another context in which substitutivity fails, as I mentioned earlier. And science can do without modality! In other words, instead of admitting that substitutivity fails, we eliminate from serious discourse those contexts where it seems to fail. That's another strategy for saving substitutivity.

But most agree there's one indispensable context it fails in: *Within* the that-clause of a report of a propositional attitude, the situation is unconducive to substitutivity of identity. Generally we cannot be sure that we preserve the truth of the report if we intersubstitute same-referent names there. Belia may believe the groundhog hibernates, but does she believe the woodchuck hibernates? Perhaps not. Even if Belia would assent to the name-switch, we cannot be sure that we'd be reporting the same belief or a different one. On the other hand, we surely don't want to conclude that the groundhog is not the same thing as the woodchuck, simply because there's a truth about the groundhog, namely, Belia believes that it hibernates, which is not a truth about the woodchuck. So we should make an exception to the intersubstitutability of identicals, *a* and *b*:

> The principle does not apply to substitutions in statements concerning what a person thinks or feels, insofar as the that-clause, which expresses the thought or feeling, mentions *a* or *b*.

With this exception granted, we cannot use the contrapositive of the principle to prove a woodchuck is not a groundhog, merely because, let us suppose, Belia thinks she sees the one, but does not think she sees the other. A woodchuck is the same thing as a groundhog, despite all the ignorance and confusion that might exist in anyone's mind about this animal.

We can put the same point in terms of the attributes things have rather than in terms of intersubstituting their names in that-clauses. First, instead of using abstraction to form attributes exclusively from the that-clauses of propositional attitudes (as we did in section D), we can abstract from any proposition to form an attribute of its subject:

> Belia saw the woodchuck.

This proposition is the basis of two attributes:

> the attribute of having seen the woodchuck,

which abstracts from the proposition's subject position, and
        the attribute of having been seen by Belia,
which abstracts from the position of direct object of the verb, "saw." Belia
has the first of these attributes; the woodchuck the second.

Next, rephrase the principle of the substitutivity of identity in terms of
attributes:
        If $a=b$, then $b$ has exactly the same attributes as $a$ has.
In its contrapositive^ form,
        If $a$ has an attribute that $b$ does not have, then it's false that $a=b$.

All our points about substitution in propositions can be rephrased in
terms of the possession of attributes. When we use the principle in its
contrapositive form, we insert particular attributes into it in order to
demonstrate the nonidentity of two things. Thus Socrates in the dialogue
*Laches* demonstrated the nonidentity of courage and endurance, because
courage has the attribute of always being noble, but endurance does not
have that attribute; some of its instances are foolish.

Now the question before us is whether there are restrictions on the
kinds of attributes that can be inserted into the principle to prove
nonidentity. What about this attribute?
        The attribute of being what Belia believes $a$ is different from.
Of course Belia disbelieves $a$ has that attribute. She may believe that $b$ has
that attribute, even though $a$ and $b$ are the same thing. Wait! We just
proved they are not the same thing, or have we? If that attribute can be
inserted into the principle, then we have: $a$ does not have that attribute, but
$b$ does, so it's false that $a = b$. If you don't think we've proved the
nonidentity merely from Belia's state of mind, a confused state perhaps,
then we must not allow that attribute to be inserted in the principle. I am
recommending the latter course.
        In general, we should disallow inserting into the principle of
        substitutivity any attributes formed from reports of propositional
        attitudes by abstraction from positions in their that-clauses (for
        example, the attribute of being such that Belia believes that *it* is
        a woodchuck).
So whichever way you state the principle of substitutivity, its application
to propositional attitudes must be restricted to prevent spurious proofs of
nonidentity.
        *Fourth regimentation: The principle of substitution applies
        validly to the about-position, but not to any position in the
        that-clause.*

## §4. Generalization from singular terms.

Before proceeding to the next kind of entailment, I explain **generality** as distinct from singularity. So far we've considered singular sentences; they refer to individual things by name. Other sentences refer to things generally. Rep may use a pronoun in his about-position, namely an anaphoric "it" referring back to an expression like

"something is such that Belia believes about it that . . . it . . ."

that commits Rep to that something's existence. (That is, his sentence may be general **existentially**, which is to say that something exists about which Belia has the belief. Another way to be general is **universally**, which is for all of a class of things to be such that Belia has a belief about them.) Instead of using a proper name or description, Rep may report generally the existence of something about which Belia believes it ran into the bushes:

Something exists about which Belia has the belief that it ran into the bushes.

He can say this because existence is a characteristic of anything that may be named in an about-position.

When considering the distinction between singular and general, don't forget the distinction between beliefs and reports of beliefs. Rep's report is general, although he's reporting a singular belief *de re* of Belia's. Not only reports, but the beliefs *de re* can be general too. General ones would seem to be always paired to a correlative general belief *de dicto*. For when they are *de re*, the believer also has singular beliefs *de re* which imply the general *de dicto* one. That can happen if the general belief is existentially general, or if it's universally general but based on an exhaustive acquaintance with each of the instances of the universal generality. More dubiously, the universal generality can be *de re*, even if Belia's belief in it is grounded on its instances in some nonimplicative way. For example, if she bases her belief about all of a population on her having inspected a large representative sample from that population, her universally general belief could be viewed as *de re*. I'll mention problems with this view in sections H and I and solve them in L. In any case Rep can report Belia's general *de re beliefs* in a form different from the one he uses for his general *de re reports* of her singular beliefs. He reports her general *de re* belief thus:

Belia believes about $a$, $b$, $c$, and $d$, that all of them [or some of them] ran into the bushes.

Next I explain entailments by **generalization**, which is the inference of an existential generality from a singular sentence. To generalize a sentence one replaces the name of a thing in a sentence with the pronoun "it" and prefixes to the sentence the phrase "something is such that." For example,

> the dog barked;

so

> something is such that it barked.

The inference is valid according to elementary logic.                .

When the singular sentence reports propositional attitudes, however, there are two relevant kinds of place where singular terms occur, namely after the "about" and after the "that." Generalizing from about-positions is valid. Rep may put an anaphoric pronoun in place of the name in the about-position of his *de re* report, and prefix to the whole sentence the phrase, "something is such that . . ." The new pronoun and all those pronouns in the that-clause, which had referred back to the name in the about-position, now refer back to that quantifier.   The condition of pronouns within the that-clause referring back to a quantifier outside the that-clause is commonly called **quantifying in**. The quantifier outside reaches into the that-clause to provide an antecedent for the pronouns there. Obviously, when Rep generalizes the about-position, he quantifies into the that-clause from outside it. Quantifying in is valid when the generalization is made from a name in the about-position of a *de re* report, for the name had been serving as the pronouns' antecedent.

Generalizing directly from a name in a place after the "that," whether in *de re* or *de dicto* reports, covers two situations, which must be distinguished before we discuss its validity. So far we have tacitly restricted our discussions of generalization to **generalization with wide scope**, that is, the scope^ of the generalization was the whole report: Something is such that Belia believes about it that it ran into the bushes. Rep makes that generalization. He can generalize the reference in the about-position. There's another case to consider, however. Clearly, if

> Belia believes that a woodchuck ran into the bushes,

then

> Belia believes that something is such that it ran into the bushes.

Here the scope of the generalizing phrase, "something is such that . . ." is narrow, since its scope covers the words to its right, but the words "Belia believes that" are to its left, outside its scope. This is called **generalization with narrow scope**.

| Wide scope: | *something's such that . . .* | *. . . believes that . . .* | *. . . it . . .* |
|---|---|---|---|
| Narrow scope | *. . . believes that . . .* | *something's such that . . .* | *. . . it . . .* |

Table E-1. Two reports, showing the different order of three of their parts. (A quantifier's scope does not include what occurs to its left.)

We'll say more about narrow-scope generalization in section L. However, we're now concerned only with the validity of wide-scope generalization from names in the that-clause. Wide-scope generalization directly from names in the that-clause may not preserve truth and so fails to be valid. For example, within a that-clause the names of nonexistent things may be used to give true reports. Belia may still believe in Santa Claus, and Rep may report Belia's Santa-beliefs even though he no longer shares such beliefs.

(iii) Belia believes *that* Santa enters houses through chimneys. He won't say she has beliefs *about* Santa, however.

Rep may truthfully put in the positions Belia controls (after the "that") proper names and descriptions without his believing they refer to anything. Then he may not generalize: From his truthful *de dicto* report he may not deduce this:

(iv) Something exists about which Belia has the belief that it enters houses through chimneys.

The name "Santa" is ok within the that-clause, but we may not quantify in (as in the step from (iii) to (iv)) to the position occupied by that name inside the that-clause, replacing the name with an anaphoric pronoun cross-referencing back to a quantifier, as in the example above. To do that is in effect to illicitly convert a *de dicto* report into a *de re* report with respect to that name. In other words, in effect it creates an about-position where there was none, as the move from (iii) to (iv) shows. This stricture on generalization isn't in elementary logic, where we may generalize like this from any name. (Leaving aside what Belia believes, if there is no Santa, then it isn't true that he has eight reindeer. If it's true that Santa has eight reindeer, then it's got to be true that somebody does. The inference is valid.)

In section F, I'll explain how the logic of necessity and possibility (modal logic) violates the same logical principles as do propositional attitudes.

*Fifth regimentation: Wide scope generalization from names in that-clauses is invalid.*

## §5. The Davidsonian regimentation and the three entailments.

The conclusion *seems* inevitable: Reports of propositional attitudes are logically deviant in all three forms of implications involving singular terms. (We won't say anything about the matter until section G, but they're deviant in implications involving predicates also.) "Seems inevitable," I said, but *is* the conclusion inevitable? Every analysis in this section presupposed the common regimentation, in which Rep's reports are a single sentence with a single assertive force. In section C, however, where we introduced this common regimentation, I mentioned also the Davidsonian regimentation, which posits reports consisting of two sentences, only one of which has assertive force.

> Belia believes that.
> A woodchuck ran into the bushes

We're now in a position to see the value of this alternative regimentation. The failure of substitution to preserve truth is reconciled with logic! It's not that the substitution affects the truth of the sentence it occurs in, namely, the sentence corresponding to the common regimentation's that-clause. It need not, and in fact there's no reason to say it does. If a woodchuck ran into the bushes, a groundhog ran into the bushes. Nevertheless, a substitution in "a woodchuck ran into the bushes" may affect the truth of *the other sentence* which refers to it. This other sentence says Belia believes what Rep now says, and she may not believe what Rep now says, after the substitution is made. It has nothing to do with the truth of the sentence he now says; it has everything to do with his other claim that Belia believes that.

Recall that Quine extended Davidson's regimentation to *de re* attitudes thus:[11]

> Belia believes about the woodchuck that.
> It ran into the bushes.

He noted that generalization of the name in the about-position of the first sentence is in accord with logic, but it was already in accord with logic in the standard regimentation. More significantly, narrow scope generalization, that is, generalization confined to the open second sentence, is valid.

Even if Rep generalizes from the name "Santa Claus," it's within a sentence that has "smiley" force, ☺, and we may take that force to licence domains,^ "universes of discourse," different from the domain of the first sentence. Santa Claus exists in the second sentence's universe of discourse.

The inference's failure to preserve truth is again merely a failure of the first sentence of the pair: Suppose that Belia's dog also believes the same thing as Belia does about the woodchuck, but the dog's conceptual and logical aptitudes don't allow it to believe this: Some things are such that it ran into them. It is nevertheless a valid implication of what it does believe. Only the "that" in the first sentence now points to a sentence it does not believe, so it's false. Once again, Davidson's regimentation protects the logicality of reports.

You may wonder how giving a sentence smiley force differs from putting it in quotation marks. The difference is the difference between a sentence and a name. The smiley force is the force that a sentence has, but the **quotation** of a sentence is a name of the sentence quoted. Any nouns or pronouns inside the quotation marks no longer refer, or refer to themselves, not their normal referents. Consequently substitution and generalization from them, if the inferences are allowed at all, would not have the results you'd want. Davidson warned against confusing his approach with a quotational approach. We'll say more about quotation in section V.

Problems remain, however. Wide scope generalizations from names in the second sentence, in effect joining the two sentences since the quantifier will occur in the first sentence, still may not preserve the truth of the first sentence, since they create about-positions there. Furthermore, the universe of discourse associated with the second sentence may not be the domain^ associated with the first sentence. Consequently, exportation and importation of names in and out of the second sentence also may not preserve truth; such moves would also create and abolish about-positions undoing the distinction between *de re* and *de dicto*. Nevertheless, removing the embarrassment over substitution and narrow scope generalization is a relief.

Whoa! *Deja vu!* In section A, it seemed so neat at the beginning to distinguish knowledge by description from knowledge by acquaintance, and then, bam!, I had to mess it up by stating two alternative ways to distinguish the beliefs involved in the two, and promised the battle between the two would stalk our discussions. Now something similar has happened. Everything was going so smoothly, and now we have to face the fact that our common regimentation is not innocent data preparation after all. The common regimentation says that reports are suspect of violating logic. The Davidsonian regimentation says, on the contrary, that philosophers are suspect for not understanding how reports are to be regimented so that logic is not violated. That's philosophy.

For now we'll stick with the common regimentation, because in the
next two sections it's the commonest one used to make my points, and in
Part II of the course, which concerns the about-position, the two
regimentations don't differ. We'll have to face the question of the right
regimentation eventually, however, and it will be in Part III.

# Notes

1.  *A Companion to the Philosophy of Mind*, S. Guttenplan, ed. (1994), p.
427.
2.  H. P. Grice, "Logic and Conversation," published in part in Donald
Davidson and Gilbert Harman, eds., *The Logic of Grammar* (1975), and the whole
of it in Paul Grice, *Studies in the Way of Words* (1989), 22-40. Photocopies of
Grice's lectures circulated for years before they were ever published.
3.  Examples like this go back to Gilbert Ryle's *Dilemmas* (1954), pp. 117f:
"If you hear on good authority that she took arsenic and fell ill you will reject the
rumour that she fell ill and took arsenic. This familiar use of 'and' carries with it
the temporal notion expressed by 'and subsequently' and even the causal notion
expressed by 'and in consequence'." Also the second conjunct's meaning often
needs completing by information in the first conjunct: "I gave her the keys to my
car and she drove off." In which car? Mine. Was she at the wheel? Yes. Thus
commutation is prevented.
4. Thomas McKay, "On Proper Names in Belief Ascriptions," *Philosophical
Studies*, 39 (1981), 287-303.
5.  See W. T. Jones and R. J. Fogelin, *The Twentieth Century to Quine and
Derrida*, 3rd edition (1997), ch.12, for the story of the collapse of J. L. Austin's
analyses of our talk about perception once Grice's distinction was introduced into
the debate.
6.  Some think free logic is of little use, for who but a metaphysician would
want to cancel the implicature that something exists? It could only be to imagine
a contrary-to-fact situation. And if one did cancel the implicature, it becomes
trivial to state all truths under that assumption: Those formulas, in prenex^ form
with all universal quantifiers, are true vacuously, and so are all formulas
equivalent to them. Every other formula is false.
7.  This prohibition of importing any names from about-positions into
that-clauses constitutes a difference of the logic of belief from the logic of
modality (see section F). For in modal logic, if a name is exportable from a
necessary that-clause, e.g., [necessarily (that) 9>7, so about 9, necessarily (that)
*it*>7], then it is importable into the clause: [about 9, necessarily (that) *it*>7, so
necessarily (that) 9>7].
8.  "Quantifiers and Propositional Attitudes," section II (p. 190).
9.  Aristotle, *Topics*, VII.1; 152b25-29. His wording covers both forms of the
principle that I give in the text. Sometimes contemporary philosophers call one or
other or both forms "Leibniz's Law," which is erroneous since it misses priority

by about 2000 years! For Socrates's use of the principle, see Plato's *Euthyphro* and *Laches*. Leibniz enunciated a converse^ principle which we'll consider in section G.

10. This point and the last of the previous counterexamples, come from Kit Fine, "Quine on Quantifying In" in C. Anthony Anderson and Joseph Owens, eds., *Propositional Attitudes* (1990), 1-25. You now have the knowledge to unmask other apparent counterexamples. One from David Kaplan: "The rabbi was dismayed when Howie's mother spanked him." Howie's mother = Mrs. Wettstein. "The rabbi was dismayed when Mrs. Wettstein spanked him." The solution is the same as in Fine's example. Two more from John Ackrill: "The road from A to B is uphill." The road from A to B = the road from B to A. "The road from B to A is uphill." Again, "the baker was fired." The baker = the mayor. "The mayor was fired." The solution in each case is to impute ellipsis to the predicates. A much more challenging apparent counterexample comes from extending arithmetic operations to an infinity of terms, for example, adding an infinity of numbers. When you add an infinite number of zeros, just zeros and no positive integers, you would expect the sum to be zero. Might one not substitute for each zero in the summation the equivalent "$[(+1)+(-1)]$"? If so, by associativity for addition the summands can be re-expressed thus:

$$(+1)+[(-1)+(+1)]+[(-1) \ldots ,$$

where each of the bracketed terms is still equal to zero. For each zero in the original summation, we can assign exactly one bracketed expression, and all bracketed expressions will be matched to a zero. So they sum to zero if the original summation does. That leaves the first $(+1)$ in the new summation to make the whole summation equal to 1. So, if the original summation sums to zero, 1 = 0! Where's the error? Not that the sum is really 1/2 as Leibniz thought. I suggest this: What we substitute for zero in an infinite summation must be meaningful in that context. But negative integers are not always meaningful in such contexts. The mathematician Riemann suggested the test of meaningfulness should be that, if the negative signs were all changed to positive, then if the resulting series had a finite sum, then the negative integers are meaningful. Such is not the case in the series we're examining. See Bryan Bunch, *Mathematical Fallacies and Paradoxes* (1982) 68f. Therefore, despite the substitution's legitimacy in finite summations, in this context we substituted something meaningless, "$[(+1)+(-1)]$," for something meaningful, "0." The error's not in the principle of substitutivity, but in not noticing the context's rendering meaningless an identity that's ordinarily meaningful. (I almost said, render false an identity that's ordinarily true, but then I realized that would make the defense question-begging! I don't know if Riemann made the distinction.)

11. Quine, "Response to Davidson," in Davidson and Hintikka, eds., *Words and Objections: Essays on the Work of W. V. Quine* (1969), 333-335.

# F. Modalities and Propositional Attitudes: How Alike?

The propositional attitudes may not be alone in violating the rules of exportation and importation, intersubstitution of identicals, and generalization; it seems the propositions of modal logic do too. **Modal logic** is that add-on to ordinary logic that decides the valid propositions expressed with the modal phrases, "it is necessary that. . ." or "it's necessarily the case that . . .," and similar phrases with "contingent," "impossible," and "possible" in place of "necessary." Like ordinary logic, it has several parts: a part dealing with units no smaller than a complete proposition, which is its propositional part, and a part that looks within propositions to their subjects and the attributes (i.e., properties and relations) predicated of them, which is its quantificational part. For example, this proposition is valid in the propositional part of modal logic:

> If it's necessary that *if p then q*, then, if it's necessary that *p*, then it's necessary that *q*.

The next proposition is valid in the quantificational part of some modal logics.[1]

> If it's possible that everything has the property *F*, then about each thing, it's possible that *it* has the property *F*.

## §1. The superficial analogy between modal statements and reports of attitudes.

The propositions of quantified modal logic are like propositional attitudes in that they can have about-positions and that-clauses. So they are either *de re* or *de dicto*. For example, in the proposition of quantificational modal logic just cited, the antecedent is a *de dicto* proposition:

> it's possible that everything has the property *F*.

The consequent is *de re*:

> about each thing, it's possible that *it* has the property *F*.

In the *de dicto* case a complete proposition follows the "it's possible that." In the *de re* case, an incomplete proposition follows, containing an anaphoric pronoun referring back to the term in the about-position.

The analogy between modality and propositional attitudes goes further than that their propositions are *de re* or *de dicto*. There's also an analogy in that the failures we noted for propositional attitudes seem to afflict the propositions of modal logic when definite descriptions are taken to be singular terms. For example, suppose

> (i) 17 = the number of Jovian moons (i.e., moons of the planet Jupiter)

in fact, whether we know it or not. (It seemed true as of the year 2000, when the seventeenth one was found. More were found in 2001. Let's go with 17.) We know that

> (ii) It's necessarily the case that 17 > 7.

That's right. Now consider the substitution of the description, the number of Jovian moons, for the name, 17, in (ii). This is an attributive use of the description. Here's what you get:

> (iii) It's necessarily the case that *the number of Jovian moons* > 7.

Of course, the number of Jovian moons doesn't exceed 7 necessarily, if we, ignorant of the count of Jovian moons, mean by "the number of Jovian moons" whichever number it turns out to be. Thus substitutivity of identity is violated within the that-clauses of quantified modal logic.

The about-positions are well-behaved logically. Substitution of descriptions for names is valid there. For example, this is true:

> (iv) About 17 it's necessarily the case that *it* > 7.

The substitution of the description for "17" in the about-position in (iv) preserves truth:

> (v) About *the number of Jovian moons*, necessarily *it* > 7,

because which of the two names we use to refer to the number 17 makes no difference there. And this is still the attributive use of the description. The anaphoric pronoun *it* can be read as *that number*. And what number is that, if not 17?

Exportation and importation also seem violated in modal contexts. There is no importation from the true (v) to the false (iii), and it would be easy to concoct an example to show that the converse^ exportation is invalid, not always preserving truth.

Consider now failures of generalization with the proposition,

> (vi) It's possible that Santa Claus delivers gifts to all the world's children in a single night.

This seems true. If we were to generalize from Santa Claus, we would get,

> (vii) Someone is such that it's possible that *he* delivers gifts to all the world's children in a single night.

This seems false of every actual person in the world. So it looks like propositional attitudes are not alone in violating the laws of ordinary logic; part of logic does too!

Many philosophers have been beguiled by this similarity between modal statements and propositional attitudes to such an extent as to think they can give a unified treatment of the problems noted in the previous section and this one, and give a unified solution of them. I hope to convince you that this is hopeless. For the analogy between modal statements and reports of propositional attitudes is superficial. My answer to the question in the title of this section—how alike?—is, not very. I offer three arguments in the remainder of this section. For starters, there's a straightforward solution to modal logic's problems that does not work for propositional attitudes. It turns on Russell's distinction between definite descriptions and logically proper names. My second argument undermines attempts to reinstate the analogy by purging language of proper names, reducing them to definite descriptions. Lastly, I point out what I think is a *reductio ad absurdum*^ of the analogy: absurd "principles" for propositional attitudes analogous to modal principles. See table F-1 for a charting of the overall argumentative strategy of this section.

## §2. First argument: dissolution of the analogy between modal statements and reports of attitudes.

Let's explore the solution to modal logic's seeming violation of substitution and the other forms of inference. Although I've given counterexamples to the validity in modal contexts of otherwise acceptable inferences with singular terms, broadly understood to include definite descriptions, there remains the possibility that they are valid when the singular terms used are logically proper names. Recall from section A that a logically proper name is just a tag or mark on the thing named and is otherwise without conceptual meaning. Only existing things can have logically proper names, for how could you tag or mark what does not exist? Suppose it were to turn out that all the modal propositions' violations of logical rules depended on the use of definite descriptions, but when logically proper names were used, there were no violations: Logically proper names turned out to be exportable and importable, intersubstitutable and generalizable from within the that-clauses of quantified modal logic. If so, we found the culprit: the definite description and perhaps even our concept of a singular term.

Ever since section A we've acknowledged within the category of name or singular term both definite descriptions and logically proper names. I called your attention there to the controversial nature of this split in the category: According to Russell's technique of analyzing sentences that

| | tradi-tional account of sin-gular terms applied to: | Rus-sell's method of anal-ysis ap-plied to: | conse-quence for pur-ported analogy between MA & PA: | the rea-sons for that conse-quence: | what I argue for: |
|---|---|---|---|---|---|
| **stage I of the argu-ment** | proper names & definite descrip-tions | | they're analo-gous | both ML and PA violate substitu-tion & general-ization | As stage II ar-gues, ML's breaches of logic are illu-sory |
| **stage II of the argu-ment ("Argu-ment 1")** | logically proper names | definite descrip-tions | they're not anal-ogous | ML obeys the two rules; only PA doesn't | I agree with this defense of ML and its disana-logy with PL |
| **stage III ("Argu-ments 2 and 3")** | | proper names & definite descrip-tions | they're analo-gous | they both obey the two rules | I oppose the abo-lition of proper names |

Table F-1. The argumentative strategy in section F that modal logic (ML) is not, in the final analysis, analogous to the logic of propositional attitudes (PA). We already had stage I presented, and we're about to embark on stage II.

contain definite descriptions, the analysis's product is a sentence that does not contain definite descriptions. Russell concluded that definite descriptions are not terms at all in the logical structure of sentences, *a fortiori* not singular terms, but we decided to stay at the level of superficial structure where they are singular terms, *pace* Russell, until we found reason not to. We noted one reason in section A, not finding the King in either the list of bald persons or in the list of nonbald persons, then another reason in section B concerning the detection of ambiguities. It seems that now we are about to find a third reason: All the failures of exportation and importation, intersubstitution, and generalization in modal contexts have involved definite descriptions. If we had used logically proper names, perhaps the modal propositions would not have succumbed to the failures. If that's true (and it is), then the real trouble would not have been the illogicality of the modalities. The real trouble would seem to have been the treating as a name a kind of phrase that's not a name.

And it *is* true: Logically proper names cause no rule violations in modal contexts. Consider these pairs of logically proper names—there's nothing to prevent a thing from having more than one proper name:

●Hesper = Phosphor
(Russell's example[2] of proper names of the planet Venus, Hesper when seen after dusk, Phosphor when seen before dawn. The ancient Greeks used the two names before one of them—was it Pythagoras?—discovered the identity.)
●Cicero = Tully
(Peirce's names for the ancient Roman, Marcus Tullius Cicero[3]).
●1 = 0.99999...(nines forever)
(You may be skeptical, but the identity is proved without doubt.[4] Numerals are analogous to ordinary proper names; they're Carnap's **"individual expressions of standard form."** Unlike logically proper names, however, they admit of analytic^ truths relating them.[5] Consequently, if a system assigns one number two standard names, the identity will be provable. If you get into a predicament like the Greek astronomers' above and my new relative's at the end of section A, it's within your power to get out of it.)

Modal propositions, having in any position one of the names from a pair, allow substitution of the other; they allow exportation and importation, and generalization of the name, *salva veritate*. I leave the testing of cases to you.

Logically proper names are well behaved in modal that-clauses, because individuals continue to be referred to by those names even when we imagine them in possible but counterfactual conditions. John Stuart Mill has us perform this thought experiment with the proper name of an English city, "Dartmouth":

> But it is no part of the signification . . . of the word Dartmouth, to be situated at the mouth of the Dart. If sand should choke up the mouth of the river, or an earthquake change its course, and remove it to a distance from the town, the name of the town would not necessarily be changed. [We would say the town would still be Dartmouth; it would not be a different town.] That fact, therefore, can form no part of the signification of the word; for otherwise, when the fact confessedly ceased to be true, no one would any longer think of applying the name. Proper names are attached to the things themselves, and are not dependent on the continuance of any attribute of the object.[6]

We might even imagine its name being different! Then it would still be right for us to refer to it as Dartmouth, even if only to suppose Dartmouth were called "Fairview." One might even suppose Dartmouth was never founded, and in that scenario Dartmouth does not exist. Still, we know which city it is that would not exist, if it had not been founded. So, modal contexts, which include counterfactual ones, don't affect the reference of proper names. Kripke calls such names **rigid designators**.[7] They are modally rigid in that the entities they designate, sc., their referents, stay the same thing even as we vary the scenario for their referents from one possible but counterfactual situation to another. Numerals as names of numbers also have this trait, and so we've been taking them as analogs of proper names.[8] In contrast, definite descriptions lack this constancy of reference through variations in counterfactual scenarios. The definite description "the town located at the mouth of the Dart" does not refer to Dartmouth when it's used attributively in the scenarios Mill has us imagine. Although Dartmouth is the town located at the mouth of the Dart, if the river's course were different, Dartmouth would not be the town located at the mouth of the Dart, although it would still be Dartmouth. Such attributively used definite descriptions are not rigid designators, which is why they're not the meanings of rigid designators.

Yet the description might very well serve as a **reference fixing** definite description for the name for us, since in actuality the description applies to Dartmouth, England. A definite description, when used attributively in the context of introducing a proper name of the thing, which the description is true of, is said to be a reference fixing description for that name, but not the name's meaning. Why not the meaning? Because the name still names that thing in counterfactual scenarios which would falsify the description, as in the example I gave in the previous paragraph. So the name is modally rigid, but the description is not.

We have to admit, however, that this is not a conclusive argument against descriptions being the meanings of names. The description with the word "actually" or "in actuality" inserted so that it reads "the town that's actually [i.e., in actuality] located at the mouth of the Dart" does refer to Dartmouth in all those scenarios, since its reference is not determined by those scenarios, but by what's the case in actuality. So some descriptions of contingent things are rigid designators also. Might *they* be the meanings of proper names, if names are not mere labels? Since logically proper names either denote or are not terms at all, a modally rigid description is different from them in that it can fail to denote and still be a meaningful term. For example, the modally rigid description, "the person who in actuality won 25 gold medals in the 2000 Olympic games" denotes no one in actuality and so is rigidly nondenoting though meaningful. Aside from that distinguishing feature of logically proper names, there's precious little difference between using a contingent description as a reference fixer of a name, and using the same description with "in actuality" inserted as the name's meaning. Definite descriptions of abstract objects, numbers for example, also can be rigid descriptions: "the integer that is the immediate integral successor of zero." No consistent scenario makes this false of the number one.[9]

Setting aside the phenomenon of modally rigid definite descriptions, the elimination of definite descriptions from the category of singular terms would indeed save modal logic from the charge of illogicality. For then we'd've found no failures of intersubstitution of singular terms within the modal that-clauses, nor of their exportation, importation, and generalization. The reason is that all the purported counterexamples, which use the phrase, "the number of Jovian moons," evaporate upon being analyzed in the way Russell recommended for definite descriptions. For example, we saw that it's false to put "the number of Jovian moons" for "17" in "it's necessary that $17 > 7$," but it's ok in "about 17, it's necessary that $it > 7$." The first of these is,

[#1] it's necessary that $17 > 7$.

Supposing we're substituting a singular term for the singular term "17" in it, we get,

it's necessary that the number of Jovian moons $> 7$

The narrow scope Russellian analysis of this is:

It's necessary that something numbers the Jovian moons, nothing else numbers them, and *it* > 7.

This is false, and as analyzed it's not the result of a substitution in the first. Why? Only singular terms get substituted for singular terms, and the singular term just disappeared. The second one is:

[#2] About 17, it's necessary that *it* > 7.

Supposing we're substituting a singular term for the singular term "17" in it, we get,

About the number of Jovian moons, it's necessary that *it* > 7

The Russellian analysis of this is:

About something that numbers the Jovian moons, while nothing else does, it's necessary that *it* > 7.

This is true; after all, the number we're talking about is 17. (It's worth while to do the rest of the analyses.) These definitive results were published by Arthur Smullyan in 1947 and 1948.[10]

This defense of the logicality of modal logic has provided another argument that definite descriptions are not singular terms at all, for surely we don't want to say they are singular terms everywhere except inside the that-clauses of modal logic. Preferable to that adhockery is the view that they're not singular terms ever, but they mimic singular terms under the special conditions found in elementary logic.

Let's look further at the modal features of names to explore the disanalogy between singular terms and definite descriptions. Modal logic with identity contains the obvious validity (where *a* names something):

It's necessary that *a* = *a*,

since everything is identical with itself. It follows from this and the principle of the substitutivity of identity that:

If *a* = *b*, then it is necessary that *a* = *b*.

Call this the **principle of the necessity of identity**. We prove the principle thus: Recall that whatever is true of *a* is true of *b*, if *a* = *b*, or alternatively, whatever attribute *a* has, *b* has, if *a* = *b*. Suppose its antecedent true, *a* = *b*. Since

it's necessary that *a* is identical to *a*,

by abstraction we say that *a* has

the attribute of being necessarily identical to *a*.

So, by the principle of substitutivity, *b* must have that attribute too. Q.E.D. Ruth Barcan Marcus and Carnap introduced this principle in 1946. The contrapositive^ of this principle, (using "possible that not *p*" as equivalent to "not necessary that *p*") is:

If it's even possible that *a* is not *b*, then they are distinct things.

The derivation made use of an attribute formed from a modal statement by abstraction from a position in its that-clause, the one occupied by the first *a*. Recall that we disallowed inserting certain attributes into the principle of substitutivity, namely, when the abstraction of them was done on reports of propositional attitudes. Should abstraction also be disallowed from statements of modality, thereby undermining the proof of the principle? Before deciding, let's see if it gets us into any trouble.

Although

> the number of the sun's planets = the number of Jovian moons found before 1938,

the identity is not necessary. (The tenth and eleventh were found in that year, but surely they could've been found before then.) Ah, trouble so soon. Yet this is a counterexample only if we take definite descriptions to be singular terms. We could accept the argument I gave for the principle of the necessity of identity—that, if identical, then necessarily so—and avoid the trouble by knocking definite descriptions out of the category of singular terms. So again no counter-example, and the best explanation of the failure of definite descriptions to fit that principle seems to be that definite descriptions are not singular terms. That's a fourth argument against definite descriptions being singular terms, that in the principle of the necessity of identity, you cannot substitute definite descriptions for the *a* and *b*, preserving validity.

Generally, applying the Russellian analysis to a modal sentence containing definite descriptions in its that-clause will reveal that it's ambiguous, only one of the meanings being true. That true one will be a *de re* modal statement where the definite description no longer occurs. In its place is an anaphoric pronoun, referring back to a quantifier^ in the statement's about-position. Such is the case in this example: The sentence "17 = the number of Jovian moons" can be true without it being necessarily true that 17 = the number of Jovian moons, because the sentence really has this form in which no definite description occurs:

> Something numbers the Jovian moons, nothing else does, and 17 = *it*.

Alternatively, using our regimentation:

> About something that numbers the Jovian moons while nothing else does, 17 = *it*.

Applying the theorem of the necessity of identity to this can only mean applying it to its third conjunct: 17 = *it*:

> About something that numbers the Jovian moons while nothing else does, it's necessary that 17 = *it*.

True. In fact, the something which just happens to number the Jovian moons is the number 17. So all we're saying is that 17 is necessarily itself. We don't take back or contradict that it just happens to be the number that numbers the Jovian moons, and it might have turned out that 10 or 11 did that job instead of 17.

Our results have been favorable to allowing abstraction of attributes from modal propositions, and favorable to the whole project of a logic of modality. The Russellian way of interpreting these results—his thesis that definite descriptions should not be in the category of singular terms—is not the only way of getting the favorable results. It may be that definite descriptions are singular terms, but that modality has a strange effect on their meanings when they occur in that-clauses. Either singular terms include only the rigid designators, or the principle of the necessity of identity is restricted to rigid designators. We keep definite descriptions from giving us trouble one way or the other, besides Russell's way.

Where are we in the argument? I began this section with some examples of failures of inferences within the logic of necessity (modal logic) and drew analogies to the propositional attitudes. I then expressed my opinion that the analogies were superficial. We're now midway in stage II, in the midst of my argument for this opinion. I've shown how segregating definite descriptions from logically proper names solves the problems for modal logic. My next step must then be to convince you of the disanalogies, which I consider more revealing. Propositional attitudes are unlike modal contexts in just the respect of greatest importance to our studies. *The illogicality of propositional attitudes persists even when logically proper names are used in that-clauses.*

Things can have more than one logically proper name as we noted, and Belia may not be aware of both the names of the thing she has a belief about. Her ignorance suffices to create failures of substitution in that-clauses and of importation into them. (About-positions are fully referential, since Belia does not control them.)

We can use the pairs of proper names listed earlier to construct reports about Belia's beliefs whose that-clauses violate two of the forms of inference, substitution and importation, that is, the inferences don't preserve truth. We'll also further regiment the about-position in section H, so that exportation of proper names and wide-scope generalization from the that-clauses of *de dicto* reports are also invalid. We leave arguments until then, save for one remark: If the latter two rules don't seem to lead from truth to falsehood now, since we've built into the definition of a logically proper name that it names existent things, the appearance is merely the result of this definitional maneuver, which turns out not to be illuminating about Belia, since it means that, even if Belia thinks she's using a logically proper name, it must be a definite description in disguise if it names nothing existent. Rep would determine whether Belia uses logically proper names or not.

What are the failures with proper names? First, although, since it's necessary that $1 = 1$, it's necessary that $1 = 0.9999$ (9s forever), Belia may not have grasped the fact that the decimal system for naming numbers generates redundant names for all the numbers that terminating numerals name. (We understand terminating numerals in decimal notation to be continuable with zeroes forever. We could discard all the numerals that could thus have an unending series of zeroes starting somewhere to the right of the decimal point, and we'd still have names enough for all the numbers which the discarded numerals had named.) So, although Belia believed that $1 = 1$, unfortunately she believed that $1 > 0.9999$ (9s forever). This violates the rule of substitution, yet both reports of her mental state are true.[11] Another example is the young Pythagoras's conviction, which he later disproved, that Hesper is distinct from Phosphor. Since he believed that Hesper is Hesper, if substitution for either occurrence of "Hesper" were valid here, he'd have to have believed that Hesper is Phosphor before he discovered the identity.

The reason why these failures should perplex you is that the proper names of things should function simply as labels of the things. They're not descriptions, nor is cognitive content a part of their meaning. Two names of the same thing should therefore be the simplest form of redundancy, and yet in the that-clauses of attitudes they may not be intersubstituted. Why not, especially why not, since they can be intersubstituted in the that-clauses of modal statements?

Recall that I introduced this problem in section A with my own two names, Arthur and Sonny, and the beliefs of a new member of the family. She said she believed something complimentary of Uncle Arthur, but disbelieved it of Uncle Sonny. That situation should be impossible! I there listed four premises, any one of which could be rejected to remove the anomaly of the impossible happening. We could accept her self-reporting, but (*contra* premise iii) allow her to be in a state of self-contradiction, believing and disbelieving the same singular proposition. Alternatively, we could admit her consistency, but then (*contra* i) deny her beliefs are directed toward propositions, but rather toward sentences. Alternatively, we could (*contra* iv) reject the disquotation principle; even her sincere self-reporting would not be reliable concerning singular propositions.

Alternatively, something I omitted to mention in section A, we could weight her assentings over her dissentings, so that if she assents to a sentence expressing a proposition, we simply don't count her dissentings from other sentences which express the same proposition; dissentings would be less reliable than assentings. These last two alternatives reject features of our regimentation. Recall table C-1:

|  | By her words: | By her deeds |
|---|---|---|
| Her way of verifying content of that-clause: | She assents to the that-clause. | The that-clause explains her deeds best. |
| Her way of falsifying content of that-clause: | She dissents from the that-clause. | The that-clause doesn't explain her deeds best. |

Table F-2 (repeat of C-1). Four ways the believer exercises her control over the content of the report's that-clause. The columns are inclusive alternatives to each other, the rows exclusive of each other.

The two alternative ways of rejecting premise iv, which we just mentioned, demote the table's entries in the "by words" column from regimented entailments of the report's truth, or its falsity, back to conversational implicatures that can be canceled. The first of the two is a general demotion; the second only in the special case of Belia's attempted veto of singular terms.

## §3. Second argument: We should reject attempts to reinstate the analogy.

Finally, we may maintain that her beliefs are directed toward propositions, but (*contra* ii) reject the claim that she's using logically proper names in her sentences. This last has been a favorite ploy of those who rely on the analogy between modality and attitudes. Let's examine this last option in order to reject it. (We're now embarking on stage III of the argument in this section, as presented in table F-1.) The philosophers who see a deep similarity between propositional attitudes and modal statements can reinstate the similarity I've debunked by what I hope will look to you like an act of desperation. They declare the terms customarily deemed proper names are not logically proper names, that anything that looks like a proper name is in fact a definite description, and that the only occupants of referential positions in propositions are pronouns and logicians' artifices.[12] So the failures of logic that occur in propositional attitudes with proper names are really no different from the failures that occurred with definite descriptions. The cure's the same; use Russell's technique of analysis on them all, and the failures of logic disappear. We'll call this way of reinstating the analogy between modality and propositional attitudes *the purging of proper names from ordinary language*.

To see how a proper name could be a definite description, consider the individual Cicero. Something about Cicero makes him uniquely himself, which nobody else shares. Cicero obviously can be uniquely described as "the one with the attribute of being identical-to-Cicero," but to show the dispensability of the proper name better than this hyphenation gimmick does, describe him as "the one with the attribute of Ciceronizing." Instead of saying that Cicero was a Roman, say the one who Ciceronizes was a Roman. The definite description replaces the proper name.

To accommodate the greater tolerance of modal contexts for proper names, which is their modal rigidity, the purgers of proper names introduce **individual essences**. That is, they add that some parts of this attribute uniquely true of Cicero are essential to him, that he could not lack them and still be Cicero. I can only think of one such attribute, the attribute of being identical to Cicero. Treat the name "Cicero" as a definite description of him in terms of his unique and essential attribute. If Cicero has another proper name, say "Tully," then "the one who Tullynizes" will pick out the one who Ciceronizes in terms of a unique and essential attribute also, the attribute of being identical to Tully. (These are necessarily the same attribute, as I'll explain in the next section when we discuss the intensional identity conditions of attributes.) The two . descriptions pick the same person out in all the same counterfactual situations, just as the name "Dartmouth" picked out Dartmouth in all counterfactual situations. Thus these unique and essential attributes mimic rigid designation of an individual, although they're not designators of him; they are predicated of him.

The purgers give up two jobs of proper names. One thing that a proper name does, that this sort of description does not do, is guarantee the existence of the thing named, since you can't tag a nonexistent, but you can describe the essence of things that don't exist. This difference is acceptable to the purgers of proper names. So, before one can say it's necessary that the one who Ciceronizes is identical to the one who Tullynizes, one must be explicit that the one who Ciceronizes exists. Then this identity is true, and necessarily so because Ciceronizing picks out the essence of Cicero, as does Tullynizing. Another thing that a proper name does, that this sort of description does not do, is contribute to the meaning of a singular sentence in a way that makes it express a singular proposition. Names having been purged, ordinary language is left bereft of the means to express singular propositions, although logicians will supply an artificial technique for doing so in formal semantics to interpret unbound variables (logic's version of anaphoric pronouns without antecedents). The sentences of ordinary language will express general propositions. When one of a pair of sentences uses the word "Cicero" just where the other uses "Tully," the answer to the question whether they express the same proposition will depend on whether the words pick out the same unique and essential attribute. Since the purgers are legislating the purging, they're free to legislate here as well.

I said this purging of proper names from natural language is an act of desperation, because at least part of the difference between proper names and definite descriptions has had to be built into the definite description that replaces a proper name, in order to account for the difference in behavior of descriptions and proper names in modal that-clauses. That difference does not occur in propositional attitudes, however. So the trick to reinstate the similarity of modal propositions with reports of propositional attitudes has been this: On the one hand, make proper names into descriptions and we can regularize the logic of the propositional attitudes by Russell's technique of analysis of descriptions. That brings propositional attitudes back into line with modal propositions. On the other hand, make sure the descriptions that replace proper names describe the essences of things, and we can preserve the difference we observe between modal propositions and propositional attitudes in the behavior of proper names and ordinary descriptions in their respective that-clauses. Now we can say all this another way: The result is to make proper names into descriptions, which is no use whatsoever to modal logic, and we make those descriptions describe essences, which is no use whatsoever to propositional attitudes. Might not one suspect excess cleverness masquerading as real insight?

This concludes my first two arguments to convince you that the analogy between modality and propositional attitudes is superficial. The first one was positive, that in modal that-clauses proper names and definite descriptions behave differently while in the that-clauses of propositional attitudes they are equally misbehaved. Then followed a negative one, rebutting the purgers of proper names from ordinary language. Well, "rebuttal" is too strong a word; "gave cause for suspicion" is perhaps more accurate. So, I had better have another argument against the importance of the analogy between modality and propositional attitudes, and I do:

## §4. Third argument: An analogy between modal statements and reports of attitudes is absurd.

Here's more cause for suspicion about the parallelism between modality and propositional attitudes: a *reductio ad absurdum^* of the parallelism. Recall the contrapositive^ of the principle of the necessity of identity. I'll derive it directly from the principle of the substitutivity of identity in its contrapositive form, as restated for attributes, repeated here from section E:

> If $a = b$, then $b$ has exactly the same attributes as $a$ has.

In its contrapositive form,

> If $a$ lacks an attribute that $b$ has, then it's false that $a = b$, i.e., they're different.

We insert the attribute of "being such that it's possible that $a$ is different from (-)," where the blank (-) is filled in by the name of the thing that has the attribute, into the substitutivity principle thus:

> (M-viii) If it's not possible that $a$ is different from $a$, but it is possible that $a$ is different from $b$, then $a$ is different from $b$ in fact.

The next is a law of modal logic:

> (M-ix) It's not possible that $a$ is different from $a$.

So, by elementary logic, we conclude the contrapositive of the principle of the necessity of identity:

> (M-x) If it's possible that $a$ is different from $b$, then $a$ is different from $b$ in fact.

If the that-clauses of propositional attitudes behave like the that-clauses of modal logic, then we can ape this inference using "Belia believes" in place of "it's possible," starting with the contrapositive of the principle of the substitutivity of identity, as restated for attributes. We insert the attribute of "being such that Belia believes that $a$ is different from (-)" into it thus:

> (B-viii) If Belia doesn't believe that $a$ is different from $a$, but she does believe that $a$ is different from $b$, then $a$ is different from $b$ in fact.

Sounds weird, but the advocates of a complete parallelism between propositional attitudes and modal logic should accept it.

(B-ix) Belia doesn't believe that *a* is different from *a*.

That premise is true because Belia's no fool. So:

(B-x) If Belia believes that *a* is different from *b*, then *a* is different from *b* in fact.

Truly amazing. Is Belia divine? Your incredulity at this result completes my *reductio ad absurdum^* of the analogizing of propositional attitudes to modal logic.

The eminent logician Alonzo Church noted in the article cited earlier the parallelism between the Modal argument and the Belief argument, which we just stated. He suggested that anyone convinced of the significance of the overall parallelism between modality and propositional attitudes should accept both arguments as sound. Conjoin to this position the purging of proper names from ordinary language, and you eliminate the obvious counterexamples. For only variables are involved in the arguments, and no definite descriptions or proper names (which are both analyzed out of the category of singular terms in Russell's way) are substitutable for the variables, since the proper names along with the descriptions are not genuine singular terms. So you could not deduce that, if Belia believed 1 is different from 0.9999 . . . (nines forever), then 1 is different from 0.9999 . . . (9s forever) in fact.

Do you accept the first premise of the Belief argument, (B-viii), and consequently its conclusion? I don't. Consider the analogy between the Modal and Belief arguments: In M-viii, the substitution involves the attribute of

being such that it's possible that *a* is different from (-).

In B-viii, the substitution involves the attribute of

being such that Belia believes that *a* is different from (-).

I rejected the validity of inserting the latter attribute in the principle of substitutivity in section E. In that way I blocked the inferences from true premise to false conclusion that plagued us in E. And here I block the conclusion (B-x), which is intolerably paradoxical for someone who accepts relational beliefs.

However well motivated my rejection of the attribute's insertion is, however, you'd be right to feel my reasons for the rejection leave one thirsting for more. That's because I've only given you a *reason that* its insertability should be rejected. I've not given you a *reason why*. Reasons for believing that something is so seem to be merely provisional, until we find reasons for its being so and reasons why it must be so. In the case before us, the violation of rules of inference is only an indication that we'd better not insert this attribute into the principle of substitutivity. What's wrong with this attribute that makes it uninsertable? Perhaps it's not a real attribute or only real in the way brown is a real color, which is to say a secondary^ reality. (If that were the problem, however, brown shouldn't be insertable either.) We'll turn in the next section to the nature of attributes.

As for the modal attribute, it's not my concern here, but I could preserve a parallelism with modal logic by rejecting its insertion in the principle of substitutivity too. That would block the derivation of the principle of the necessity of identity. And some modal logics do without it.[13] But we don't even have a reason for believing modal attributes are not insertable into the principle of substitution. Modal logic has no paradoxes, once descriptions are analyzed out of the category of singular terms. I do agree with Church that those who believe in the parallelism should treat identically the insertion of modal attributes and propositional attitude attributes into the principle of substitutivity, either both allowed or both disallowed. The second of these alternatives is preferable to the first, but most preferable is to deny the point of any parallelism. As much parallelism as there happens to be is coincidence.

The moral of the reflections in this section is that, contrary to the trickery of the last proposals, the propositional attitudes are much more recalcitrant to being made logically respectable than are the idioms of modal logic. While Quine has been a critic of modal logic as well as of the propositional attitudes, and at a certain level of generality his criticism of each is the same, in the half century since Smullyan's defense of modal logic, the debates over the two have diverged. As far as the solution of modal logic's difficulties goes, definite descriptions may not fit in positions appropriate for singular terms in modal statements, either because they're not singular terms or because of the meanings associated with statements in the language of modal logic. Proper names, on the other hand, fit fine there. But the difference between definite descriptions and logically proper names makes no difference to the propositional attitudes. The problem with singular terms remains, since we aren't purging them. So, since it makes no difference to our project, we'll continue to use definite descriptions as singular terms also. (I've given four arguments, collectively close to conclusive, for Russell's eliminative analysis of descriptions, and you justifiably might wonder at my continuing to treat them as singular terms. The reason is that, once we know how to eliminate them, we also know the conditions for introducing them by definition. Even Russell introduced them back into his logic. Function^ notation in mathematics falls into the category of definite descriptions, and it's hard to imagine mathematics proceeding without such functions as (2+3) and $x^2$ appearing in positions reserved for singular terms.)

One loose end: I reminded you of my relative who believes contradictorily of me, but has only one proposition her beliefs can be directed toward. I refused to resolve the anomaly by purging proper names. Purging proper names could have given her two propositions to believe, neatly dispelling the anomaly, if I only had an Arthur-essence and a different Sonny-essence. But do I buy this solution? No; why should I! So the anomaly persists. Eventually we must face whether beliefs are directed toward sentences, which can differ even though they express the same proposition, or whether believers may have contradictory attitudes toward a singular proposition. We face the issue in Part III.

# Notes

1. For the curious: G. E. Hughes and M. J. Cresswell, *A New Introduction to Modal Logic*, 2nd or later printing (1996). The formula is on p. 246. It's valid in those logics that satisfy the inclusion requirement (p. 275). The reason for not recommending the book's 1st printing is that typographical errors occur, and one of the worst from our perspective occurs on p. 250 in the discussion of *de re* and *de dicto*, in effect reversing their meaning! Subsequent printings correct this.

2. Bertrand Russell, *Human Knowledge: Its Scope and Limits* (1948), Part VI, ch. VII.

3. Charles Sanders Peirce, *Collected Papers*, vol. 2, §271.

4. The simplest proof: 1/3 = 0.3333 (threes forever). Multiply both sides of the equation by 3: 3/3 = 0.9999 (nines forever). Of course 3/3 = 1. Some people don't connect the fact that there are infinitely many nines with the fact that there is no last nine. If there were a last nine, then the decimal would be less than 1. An antidote is reflection on Hilbert's hotel: It has an infinite number of rooms and all are occupied. A man comes in and asks for a room. The clerk says, "No problem." He presses a button, and a few minutes later he tells the man he has room 1. How is it possible? By pressing the button, he activated a message to each room that the occupant was to vacate it and proceed to the room with the next higher number. All occupants were accommodated, since there was *no last room*, but the first room was left empty. If you remain skeptical, you're guilty of the use-mention confusion: Two numerals, so two numbers. (Oh?) Some numeration systems create redundancy, that is, more than one name for the same number.

5. Rudolf Carnap, *Meaning and Necessity*, §18. As the quotation from Mill suggests, the idea is old. The numeration system for naming real numbers provides more than one name for each number that has a terminating decimal name, as the equation in the text shows. It may be that Carnap intended his category of expressions of standard form to exclude naming systems that provide more than one name for a thing. In that case, 1 is standard, but 0.999... is not; see §19, note

5. Carnap's nonredundancy condition may not be part of the definition of expressions of standard form, but a condition for defining a discrete coordinate language. He waives the condition in §19 for continuous coordinate languages. In that case all the expressions yielded by the numeration system for real numbers are in standard form.

6. John Stuart Mill, *A System of Logic*, Book I, ch. II, §5.

7. Saul Kripke, "Naming and Necessity," in Donald Davidson and Gilbert Harman, eds., *Semantics of Natural Language*, 2nd ed. (1972) 253-355; "Addenda" 763-769. The term is introduced on p. 269: "Let's call something a *rigid designator* if in any possible world it designates the same object, . . ." Kripke is careful to note that he is not saying the thing designated exists in every possible world. Although the name designates it when it does not exist there, what is the truth-value of sentences about it in that situation, either true or false, or neither true nor false? Either way is feasible. See Hughes and Cresswell, the first two sections of chapter 15 for the alternative ways of treating this situation. Kripke cites Mill's modal argument for the rigidity of proper names near the beginning of his first lecture. In his own restatements of it, he tends to use the formulation I put into the quotation in square brackets.

8. Consider the natural numbers, 0,1, 2, etc. Strictly only 0 is a proper name. The rest of the numerals are defined by descriptions that use that proper name, "the immediate successor of 0," "the immediate successor of the immediate successor of 0," etc. These descriptions are modally rigid. That and the hiding of the descriptions behind the numerals help the illusion that numerals are proper names.

9. Consider: "The town actually located at the mouth of the Dart might not have been the town actually located at the mouth of the Dart." Taking the descriptions that begin and end the sentence to be identical in meaning, the sentence is necessarily false. If you think the sentence true, your intuitions do not support my claim about "actually." In the face of such intuitions, I simply regiment in the adverb's rigidifying effect! Keith Donnellan notes the inconclusiveness of this argument from the modal rigidity of names to the conclusion that their meaning cannot be descriptions in his "The Contingent *A Priori* and Rigid Designators" in P. French, T. Uehling, and H. Wettstein, *Contemporary Perspectives in the Philosophy of Language* (1979) 45-60. He does not make the case in terms of the operator, "actually," however. It would be wrong to infer from his discussion that a description with sentence-wide scope is a rigid designator. For rigid designators are rigid even in sentences with insufficient complexity to force a distinction between wide and narrow scope of the descriptions in them.

10. Arthur F. Smullyan, Review of Quine's The Problem of Interpreting Modal Logic" *Journal of Symbolic Logic*, 12 (1947) 139-141; his "Modality and Description," *Journal of Symbolic Logic* 13 (1948) 31-37.

11. Belia corrected her mistake when she tried to find the difference by subtracting the latter from the former. She set out the subtraction problem by writing on the top line: 1.0000 (0s forever). Then she prepared this number for the subtraction by borrowing a 1 from the leftmost digit, and then continued the

borrowing until her top number turned into 0.9999 (9s forever), the very number she was going to subtract! Although Belia is now on the right track, her error, however momentary, sufficed to show that the distinction between proper names and definite descriptions does not help eliminate the logical deviancy of propositional attitudes.

12. E.g., Alonzo Church, "A Remark Concerning Quine's Paradox About Modality," in N. Salmon and S. Soames, eds, *Propositions and Attitudes* (1988) 58-65.

13. Hughes and Cresswell, 334ff.

# G. The Opacity and Hyperintensionality of That-Clauses.

Now I explain the distinction between referential and attributive positions in sentences. Concerning the referential positions I explain the referential opacity and transparency of their contexts in terms of the patterns of entailment already explained, namely, importation and exportation, intersubstitution, and generalization. We'll say the propositional attitudes are referentially opaque contexts for the referential positions in their that-clauses. Then concerning attributive positions I explain the extensionality, intensionality (with an *s*), and hyperintensionality of their contexts. Lots of big words to explain.

### §1. Referential and attributive positions in sentences.

Positions that names and pronouns occupy in sentences are called **referential positions**, in contrast to the positions that adjectives and verbs occupy, which are called **attributive positions** or predicative positions. The sentence, "Socrates | is human" consists of two positions, the referential followed by the attributive. In the notation common in quantificational logic, the difference between capital letters and small letters is exploited; the attributive position is occupied by the capital letter and the referential position by the small letter. Let "H" abbreviate "is human" and s = Socrates. Thus the sentence just given is reordered and abbreviated this way: "Hs." In many languages the order of the two positions does not identify the kind of position. Here's a way of testing independent of order: Whatever predicate occupies an attributive position could be occupied by its negation, but a name, the occupant of a referential position, does not admit of a negation. Thus we might say Socrates is not human, but it does not make sense to say that [not-Socrates] is human, where attaching the "not" is supposed to yield Socrates denied.

Attributive positions (or predicative positions) are also occupied by adjectival or verbal phrases, which are compounded of many words, some of which might be names. Thus "Plato loves" expresses a relational property (see section D) predicated of Socrates, and the phrase occupies an attributive position in the sentence "Plato loves | Socrates." This analysis stopped at an arbitrary point; we could've analyzed the sentence further as having two referential positions, with an intervening attributive position. The partial analysis illustrates my point, however, which is that complex predicative phrases, even those containing names, occupy attributive positions also. Every level of analysis, partial or complete, assigns contentful phrases to either referential positions or attributive positions. Finally, even the most superficial level of analysis does this: Since propositions are medadic attributes, we treat the positions occupied by the $p$ and $q$ in the formulas of elementary logic, such as *if p then q*, as attributive also.

So the best way to understand referential and attributive positions is relatively to a level of analysis. These four sentences go from least analyzed to most analyzed:

> Plato loves Socrates (one attributive position)
> Plato loves | Socrates (two positions: attributive | referential)
> Plato | loves Socrates (two positions: referential | attributive)
> Plato | loves | Socrates (three positions: referential | attributive | referential)

Russell's method of analyzing definite descriptions has the effect of removing the appearance that a definite description (in its attributive use) occupies a referential position in the sentence in which it occurs. The method does this by dispersing the description's component general terms into obviously attributive positions in the analyzed sentence.

With this distinction mastered, we can get down to business, first an affliction of the referential position called opacity, then an affliction of the attributive position called nonextensionality.

## §2. Referential positions: opacity and transparency.

The referential positions outside the that-clauses are open to generalization and open to intersubstitution of names with the same reference, in the sense that, if we perform these operations on a true proposition, a true proposition will be the result. Thus these linguistic contexts or modes of containment of referential positions are called **referentially transparent**.[1] In particular, the about-positions in *de re* attitudes are referentially transparent. We say the about-position belongs to the referentially transparent context to reflect the fact that a name there must function simply to refer to an object—existent objects only. It's as if one sees through the names to the things themselves. In the that-clauses of *de re* beliefs the positions of anaphoric pronouns cross-referencing to the about-positions are also open to substitution and generalization, and so they belong to the referentially transparent context.

The rest of a *de re* belief's that-clause would be the incomplete proposition predicated of these objects. There we find the opacity: Since the incomplete proposition may contain singular terms other than anaphoric pronouns, the proposition's occurrence within the context "believes that . . ." changes the positions of those singular terms to not purely referential positions. Thus "believes that . . ." is a **referentially opaque** context for the clause introduced by "that," because the reports will often turn from true to false if we perform the operations of intersubstitution and wide-scope generalization on the names within the incomplete proposition. A *de dicto* belief's that-clause has no purely referential positions in it. We say a linguistic context is referentially opaque to reflect the fact that a name that fails to refer (so fails to be generalizable) can be in it and the sentence still be true. "Opaque" seems a good description of this sort of construction, since it's open to doubt whether any name in such a construction is doing its customary job of disclosure, that is, referring to a thing.

If I dichotomize referential positions into purely referential and one grade of not purely referential, then I am supposing that, if a position is deviant with respect to one of the rules of inference, it is deviant with respect to all the others. There are theorems that go some way toward demonstrating that.[2] Our thesis that all attitudes are relational or notional propositional attitudes seems to undermine any counterexamples. If, for instance, you find a sentence that admits of generalization but not substitution in some referential position, the sentence probably is not in regimented form, and after being regimented the generalization will pertain to its about-position, while the failure of substitution will pertain to what's in its that-clause.

## §3. The ideal of extensionality.

We called the positions of singular terms in opaque constructions "not purely referential." To put it baldly, contexts that create the not-purely-referential positions are out-and-out illogical, since they violate two fundamental kinds of valid inference, generalization and intersubstitution. If importation and exportation of names between referential positions fail, one of the positions is not purely referential. Perhaps then, we ought to suspect the very intelligibility of locutions that make positions not purely referential. They fail to be intelligible to the fullest degree, the way mathematics and ordinary logic are intelligible. Logic and mathematics are paradigms of making intelligible the various contents to which they apply. This ideal of intelligibility, which Quine adheres to,[3] posits the necessary condition for it of **extensionality**: A subject matter's intelligibility depends on the extensionality of the discourse about it. Extensional contexts permit generalization and intersubstitution. Quine moderates his claim that extensionality is a necessary condition of intelligibility because intelligibility is not an all-or-none kind of thing. In the article just cited he says,

> There has long been discussion of revision of logic for the simplification and clarification of quantum theory, and I can conceive that extensionality might not remain immune.

But he hopes it does. For, although the clarification and simplification of our science have precedence over the preservation of extensionality, insofar as extensionality is compromised so is intelligibility.

However, extensionality is more multifarious than I indicated. Extensionality has two facets, (I) a facet applying to referential positions and (II) a facet applying to attributive positions. The referential facet (I) requires

(I-i) the applicability of standard logic (including substitution and generalization) to singular terms referring to things in domains^ of

(I-ii) well-defined entities that the subject matter is analyzed into.

The facet applying to the attributive position also has two parts

(II-i) the applicability of substitution to predicates expressing the same attribute, and

(II-ii) a restriction on abstraction to avoid commitment to modal attributes and attributes of being the objects of a directed-toward relation in propositional attitudes.

To the extent that logic is inapplicable to reports of belief, and their content cannot be analyzed into complexes of well-defined entities, they must fall short in crisp scientific intelligibility. Thus a failure of extensionality is a bad sign for propositional attitudes.

Item (I-ii) has priority in this definition, despite its second place. It is inspired by the axiom of set^ theory that specifies the identity condition for sets, namely, if a set $x$ has all the same members as a set $y$, then $x = y$. This axiom, (*Bestimmtheit*, translated into English somewhat retrospectively as extensionality), formulated in 1908 by Zermelo, settles many questions about sets, such as whether to count repetitive listing of membership (no, since the set {a,b,b} has all the same members as the set {a,b}), and how many null-sets there are (one, since { } has all the same members as { }). The converse^ of the axiom follows from the principle of the substitutivity of identity.

The requirement on sets, that they be well-defined, Quine generalizes to all entities susceptible to scientific examination: "*No entity without identity.*" That is to say, no reification, entification, or positing of entities without settling the identification or individuation of that which is supposed to be real. **Identity conditions** for a thing $x$ are procedures sufficient for settling the truth of statements of the form, $x = y$. They may also tell us how an individual is individuated and distinguished from other things, that's to say, they may be procedures that are also sufficient for settling the falsity of identity claims. They would be stronger than the one supplied by the contrapositive^ of the principle of the substitutivity of identity. A pair of attributes not consisting of an attribute and its negation, the only case covered by the substitutivity principle, may yet be such that if $x$ has one of them and $y$ has the other, then it's not the case that $x = y$. While difference conditions are dispensable, without conditions for the identity of a thing we may question whether it's a thing at all.

## §4. Attributive positions: extensional contexts.

Let's turn to the second facet of extensionality, (II), the facet that pertains to the attributive positions in sentences. Extensionality requires that phrases that express the same attribute be intersubstitutable *salva veritate* in attributive positions. At first blush, it's unclear why this facet should be indispensable for intelligibility. There are two alternative ways of justifying this facet of the ideal of extensionality. One is in the style of Frege; the other in the style of the early Wittgenstein.

Let's begin with the Fregean one: Facet (II) can be derived from facet (I) pertaining to the referential positions, if we extend the concept of identity conditions to cover attributive terms. In section D we noted that by abstraction we could convert the terms in attributive positions into singular terms, which would then occupy referential positions. So in effect we already reduced this second facet of extensionality to the first. Since the ideal of extensionality has its source of plausibility in the validity of the two rules of generalization and substitutivity of identity in referential positions, this reduction is important. Those who philosophize in the style of Frege think of extensionality as extending to attributive positions only because it applies to referential positions, and some of the terms in those positions can be converted by concretion to occupants of attributive positions. Otherwise the grounds for extending extensionality to attributive positions seem flimsy to them. For those positions are not for terms that stand for things.

Leibniz proposed a condition of identity applicable to anything. It's the converse^ of the principle of the substitutivity of identity:

> If every attribute (other than trivializing ones and irrelevant ones) that applies to *a* applies to *b* too, then *a* = *b*.

The trivializing attributes are those related to identity, such as the attribute of being identical to *a*. Obviously *a* has that attribute, and if *b* has it too, then of course *a* = *b*. If we allow that attribute as an instance of the antecedent of Leibniz's identity condition, the principle is a law of logic. For the purpose of formulating an informative identity condition, we omit that attribute as trivializing. The relevancy condition allows us to tailor the principle to particular cases. The axiom of extensionality in set theory is an instance of this principle tailored to sets. For the identity of ordinary objects, we omit the attributes that put *a* or *b* in the content of propositional attitudes. For consider the attribute of figuring in a dictum which Belia believes. The failure of *a* and *b* to share this attribute would not count against their identity. It's an empirical matter what's relevant to identity and difference. Does the occupation of distinct places at the same time suffice to differentiate two entities of the same kind? Look for the answer in the theory of that kind of entity; the theory may tolerate bilocation of numerically one entity.

We can perform semantic ascent on Leibniz's proposal with the result that we get a **principle of the identity of intersubstitutables**:

> If *a* and *b* are intersubstitutable in all relevant, nontrivializing contexts *salva veritate*, then *a* = *b*.

(In the good old days, these two versions were called "Leibniz's Law," and for good reason, since Leibniz often expressed pride in his discovery that there's no perfect similarity anywhere, it being impossible for two things to differ only numerically. Oh, how the terminology has become confused! So we'd better not use the name in our smug age, if we wish to be understood.)

In view of the processes of abstraction and concretion that move terms back and forth between attributive and referential positions, we can treat this principle of the identity of intersubstitutables as applying to any kind of position, not just referential positions. Thus if proposition *p* is intersubstitutable in all relevant contexts for proposition *q* *salva veritate*, then *p* = *q*. The only question is, what are the relevant contexts? (The answer we'll eventually settle on is modal contexts.)

Given the ideal of extensionality, a question of intersubstitutability arises concerning the things a relational belief is directed toward, namely the incomplete propositions or attributes, and not just concerning the things the belief is about. When is an incomplete proposition X, or attribute X, the same as a proposition or attribute Y, so that one can be put for the other without affecting the truth of the report? Let's introduce some terminology to help us think precisely about identities of this sort. We begin with the "extension" of a term.

Consider first the monadic terms. A monadic term's **extension** is the set of things it's true of. Its **antiextension** is the set of things it's false of. Ideally a term's extension and antiextension are mutually exclusive, and jointly exhaustive. But in ordinary speech inconsistent terms exist, whose extensions and antiextensions coincide. An example is the supposed attribute of some barber that he "shaves all those, and those only, who do not shave themselves."[4] It's best to say in such cases that no attribute corresponds to the linguistic expression. Partially defined terms also exist in ordinary speech, so that their extensions and antiextensions are not exhaustive. Given the extensions and antiextensions of terms, we can make comparisons. The attribute of having a heart (i.e., being cordate) and the attribute of having a kidney (i.e., being renate) are each monadic. Let's suppose they are true of exactly the same things. We then say they are **coextensive** attributes, because they have the same extension. Generalizing to cover polyadic terms, the extension of a polyadic term is a set of sequences^ of things.

A polyadic attribute's extension is the set of all the sequences it's true of. So the extension of "loves" is a set of pairs consisting of lover and then beloved. One and the same thing can occur nontrivially more than once in a sequence. In one pair I'm both lover and beloved. Extensions are always sets, and every consistent general term has an extension, even if it's the null^ set, which is the extension of "unicorn," since it's true of nothing, false of everything. The extension of the relation, "infinitely far away from," is the null set of pairs of things. Even complete propositions, which are medadic attributes, have extensions, although we don't naturally think of their extensions as sets of the things they're true *of*, for their medadicity precludes that. So we say all true propositions have the same extension, simply the true. The extension of true propositions can be thought of as that which they are true *to*, the actual world if you wish, rather than anything they are true of. All false propositions have the same extension, namely the false. By being false to the actual world, they all point away from it, so to speak.

We prove the extensions of propositions to be either truth or falsehood thus: By manipulating the terms of any true sentence in ways that don't affect the extension of the whole sentence, you can produce any other true sentence. Since the sentences' extension never changed but only truth is the same, the extension is truth. We use just two rules for producing one sentence from another while leaving the extension of the sentence unchanged: Substitute coextensive terms for one another in a sentence, and replace a sentence with a synonymous sentence. Substitution will leave the whole sentence's extension unchanged, because it does not change the extension of the sentence's parts. Synonymous paraphrase allows the extension of parts to change, but the synonymy guarantees that the whole sentence's extension did not change as a result of any changes in the extensions of its parts. For example, beginning with the truth, "Scott is the author of *Ivanhoe*," we can get to "29 is the number of counties in Utah in 1955" without changing the extensions of the whole sentences by making these substitutions and redistributions of content. First a substitution for "the author of *Ivanhoe*": "Scott is the author of 29 *Waverley* novels altogether"; next a synonymous paraphrase: "29 is the number of *Waverley* novels Scott wrote altogether"; finally another substitution, this time for "the number of *Waverley* novels Scott wrote altogether": "29 is the number of counties in Utah in 1955." It's true that Sir Walter was in the extension of one of the terms at the beginning, and somehow the number 29 displaced him, but that came from a paraphrase that preserved synonymy, and so the original sentence and the paraphrase must have had the same extension despite the different extensions of their component terms. It's intriguing that we cannot get away with just anything here; truths will only permute into truths, and falsehoods into falsehoods. This sort of argument, originally from Frege, was revived in 1943 by Alonzo Church and Kurt Gödel.[5] It's been dubbed "the slingshot argument."

Singular terms, on the other hand, don't have extensions, since they are neither true of anything nor false of anything; they simply name. (I recommend against collapsing naming into a kind of unit-set^ extension. For what then would it be to fail to name? That's to be no name at all, not a name with a null extension.) The singular term's failure to be either true or false of something is obvious in the case of logically proper names. Definite descriptions, such as "the largest satellite of the earth," are composed of the word "the" prefixed to a phrase that does have an extension, in our example, the unit set that contains the moon. You can think of the role of the prefix "the" as creating a thing's name from a phrase whose extension is a unit^ set containing the thing. (Since a unit set has properties its sole member may lack, for example, having just one member, I say they're not identical.)

Coextensive attributes are those that have identical extensions. Are they thereby identical attributes? One view of the identity of attributes, one consistent with the way we view the identity condition on sets in set^ theory,[6] would be that

> coextensive attributes are really the same attribute. Coextensivity is sufficient for identity. Call this the **extensional identity condition for attributes**.

On that view of the identity conditions of attributes, attributes reduce to classes. Consider monadic attributes: As with classes, we'd then expect intersubstitutability to work for the two singular terms, "the attribute of having a heart" and "the attribute of having a kidney," assuming that all and only those who have hearts have kidneys. In many propositions containing one of these singular terms we could make the substitution, and if the proposition were true to begin with, a true proposition would result.

Yes, in many sentences, but not in all. Belia may believe-true about the woodchuck the attribute of having a heart and demur on the matter of its having a kidney. Intersubstitution of coextensive attributes in a statement of her *de re* beliefs can change the report from true to false. It also fails in *de dicto* reports, where substitution *salva veritate,* as applied to complete propositions, would mean any truth may substitute for any other truth. So this kind of intersubstitution fails in the context of beliefs generally. Well, it's only one view of attributes that they have extensional identity conditions. Since the identity conditions for attributes aren't settled, it's not settled why intersubstitution of coextensive attributes fails here. We'd expect this change in truth-value, which results from the intersubstitution, if coextensive attributes can be different attributes, just as we'd expect truth-value to change if one were to substitute "John" for "Mary" in truths about Mary. But if coextensive attributes are the same attribute, then we have one more example of a failure of the substitutivity of identity in the that-clause, while it succeeds everywhere else.

Consider now the medadic attributes: By the extensional criterion there'd be just two of them, for all true complete propositions would have the same extension and all false complete propositions would have the same extension. It will follow that any truth can be substituted for any truth in a compound proposition, and the result will have the same truth value as the original. That consequence is welcome to the advocate of the ideal of extensionality. It's a commonplace of logic that sentences compounded by use of the connectives, "and," "or," "not," and quantifiers^, permit substitution of sentences for sentences based simply on the sameness of their truth-values, and the resulting compound sentences will have the same truth-value as the originals. According to the Fregean way of looking at this phenomenon, which we're examining now, namely, generalizing the concept of identity to apply to attributive positions, it's to be expected, since it's an instance of the substitutivity of identity. Furthermore, other connectives, like "because," which don't permit this truth-preserving substitutivity, definitely look misbehaved from this perspective, and so less intelligible. Extensionality requires such substitutivity.

Let's turn to the second way of justifying facet (II). Those who philosophize in the style of the early Wittgenstein don't account for the indispensability of extensionality's facet (II) for intelligibility by generalizing identity conditions. For example, most logic texts, including Quine's, don't interpret the sentential substitutivity of extensional logic as an instance of the substitutivity of identity, but rather as derived from the meaning-blindness of the connectives that logic analyzes; only the truth-values of the sentences they connect matter. The contrast between this approach and the one I've been developing is this: Does substitutivity work because the things substituted are really identical, or does it work because the context of logical connectives tolerates the substitutivity of nonidenticals because they're insensitive to the differences of the sentences they connect? If it's yes to the latter alternative, it's unclear to the Fregean why extensionality should be an ideal of intelligibility. Why should people find the connectives' insensitivity to difference a help to intelligibility? Another problem the Fregean would feel: Without the generalization of identity to attributive positions, the ideal of extensionality looks like a mere conglomeration of the four tidbits I numbered earlier in this section. What makes all the tidbits go together to form a single ideal? The Fregeans have given one answer. They don't claim that only the generalization of identity could serve to unify them. There may be another, less obvious unity to them all; all, as a group, may be jointly indispensable to account for the intelligibility of logic and mathematics, so that extensionality is not a disparate hodgepodge of ideals.

The other side has credible answers to these difficulties. Those who philosophize in the style of the early Wittgenstein[7] admit that the argument for the indispensability of facet II for intelligibility is distinct from the argument for facet I, in that facet II makes no appeal to identity conditions. Rather the argument is that to extricate logic from the content of discourse, we must strictly segregate the structural elements of our discourse from the contentful elements, and treat the structural elements autonomously. Thus all content is to be confined to atomic sentences, and all structuring of them into compounds is to be by way of contentless formal elements. The connectives such as "and," "or," and "not," rightly ignore differences in the content of the propositions they connect, and that's why the truth-value of compounds is unaffected by intersubstituting propositions of like truth-value or predicates true of the same things.

Once this segregation is completed, the analysis of logic can be pursued autonomously from the content by analyzing just the structural features of our discourse. All the great metatheorems^ about logic and mathematics, which have been proved in the past century, were tractable to proof only because of this autonomy of the structural from the contentful. For they often depend on mathematical^ induction on structural features which can recur to create unendingly complex structures. Thus the Wittgensteinians made a good alternative case for the indispensability of facet II to the intelligibility of discourse. And they did it without supposing attributes exist.

We'll not settle which is the better way to justify the ideal of extensionality. In the rest of these notes we'll assume the Fregean style of speaking about extensionality, because it will help us understand Carnap and Frege. The assumption is not intended to prejudice the case against the Wittgensteinian style.

### §5. Attributive positions: intensional contexts.

Carnap, after decades of accepting an extensional identity condition for attributes, reversed himself in the 1940's and offered an identity condition he called "intensional." William Hamilton, a nineteenth century logician, had coined a term "intension" (with an *s* instead of a *t*) to contrast with the word "extension." The extension of a term is, as we said, all the things it's true of. The **intension** of a term is the property or relation (i.e., the attribute) it expresses; alternatively, it's the attribute each of the things in the term's extension has that makes the term true of it. Whitehead and Russell popularized this coinage in chapter III of the Introduction to their *Principia Mathematica* of 1910.[8] Carnap followed their lead from the 1920's on.

Carnap wanted to describe the contexts that were sensitive precisely to the identity conditions of attributes, and he believed that factual information was irrelevant to their identity conditions.

> If, only as a matter of contingent fact, all and only those things
> that have one attribute have the other, the attributes are numeri-

cally distinct nevertheless. In contrast, coextensivity that's provable without appeal to contingent fact is sufficient for identity. Call this the **intensional identity condition for attributes.**

This condition distinguishes attributes from classes.

Carnap defined **intensional contexts** as those that conformed to the intersubstitutability of identical attributes strictly, that is, *only* identical attributes were intersubstitutable *salva veritate*, and **extensional contexts** were those that allowed intersubstitutability of nonidentical attributes too, if they happened to be coextensive. When factual information was needed to "equate" the things or attributes whose names were to be intersubstituted, that was not strictly an identity.[9] As so defined, extensional and intensional contexts are mutually exclusive.

An example of an intensional context is provided by modal logic,

it's necessary that Rep has a heart if and only if he has a heart.

But substitution for "he has a heart" of a factually identified coextensive term does not preserve truth:

it's not necessary that Rep has a heart if and only if he has a kidney.

So modal contexts are intensional. So, despite what the pair of sentences might suggest and despite the seeming opposition between intensional and extensional, modal sentences once again pass the test of logicality. For the substitution just performed was not a substitution of identicals. Therefore the resultant change in their truth value proves nothing.

Here's another example of coextensive attributes, in this case each having the null-extension.^ The first is embedded in a true modal sentence, the second in a false one. The attributes are enclosed in brackets for easy identification:

It's impossible for something to have the attribute of [being a barber who shaves all and only those who don't shave themselves].

That's demonstrably true, either because there is no such attribute, as we suggested earlier, or, if there is, nothing could possess it. This next is false, despite there being no planet with this description—they all do go round in the same direction:

It's impossible for something to have the attribute of [being a planet revolving around the sun in the reverse direction to all the other planets].

The first attribute applies to nothing, simply as a matter of logic; the second just happens to apply to nothing as a matter of fact. On the extensional identity condition of attributes they'd be one and the same attribute nevertheless. For they'd be identical to their extension, and their extension is the null-set. That seems counter-intuitive. So again, trusting our intuitions, the change in truth value proves nothing. What then of their intersubstitutability in extensional contexts? On Carnap's way of seeing things, extensional contexts are not very discriminating of identity, since they allow much intersubstitution of nonidenticals. Modal sentences are the better discriminators.

Modal sentences are also the key contexts for the identity conditions for propositions. If $p$ and $q$ are intersubstitutable in all modal contexts *salva veritate*, then $p = q$. Intuitively, propositions are possibility dividers, that is, a **proposition** partitions the range of possibilities into those consistent with its truth and those inconsistent with its truth. Modal contexts are just the right ones to test whether $p$ and $q$ create the same partition, in which case they're the same proposition. For, if there's a possibility consistent with one of them, but inconsistent with the other, there's a modal context in which their intersubstitution will fail. So propositions are intensions. Indeed they are the intensions of the sentence-radicals mentioned in section D.

The view that propositions, so understood, are suitable for being the objects of the attitudes' "directed-toward" relation, however, is just more of the thesis, that propositional attitudes are to be understood by analogy to the formulas of modal logic, which I objected to in the last section.

Definite descriptions are names composed of predicates. Since the predicates have intensions, so do the definite descriptions. If by logic alone one can prove two descriptions name the same thing, then the descriptions have the same intension and express the same attribute. Intensional contexts will allow their intersubstitution *salva veritate*. Otherwise definite descriptions are not intersubstitutable in such contexts. Those analogs of proper names, like numerals (expressions of standard form) which admit of logical derivation of statements of identity or nonidentity between them, also have intensions. Ordinary proper names, if they're not reducible to definite descriptions, seem not to have intensions. The fact that they are intersubstitutable in intensional contexts arises from the principle of the necessity of identity.

How does Carnap's distinction between intensional and extensional contexts relate to Quine's distinction between opaque and transparent contexts? On their face they're distinct, because Carnap's distinction refers to logical operations performed on attributive positions, whereas Quine's refers to operations on referential positions. Nevertheless, they are connected:

> A context is transparent in its referential positions if it is extensional in its attributive positions.

If, however, our previous section's solution to the modal paradoxes holds true, namely, that definite descriptions are not genuine occupants of referential positions, the converse is false:

> A context can be transparent in its referential positions even if it is intensional in its attributive positions.

Given the intensional identity condition for attributes, modal statements might even pass the test of extensionality! For, granting intensional identity conditions of attributes, statements having them as components conform to the laws of logic, and if an intensional identity condition makes attributes well-defined entities, that's all they need to conform to the ideal of extensionality. (It sounds odd, since modal contexts are intensional, and intensions contrast with extensions, but the definitions allow it.) Quine demurs, however. He's willing to concede the term "attribute" as meaning an entity having the intensional identity condition, but he objects to this identity condition, because it depends on there being a scientifically respectable distinction between matters of fact and of logic, and he does not believe the distinction is a sharp one except by sheer stipulation. This dispute between Carnap and Quine over the utility of the analytic-synthetic^ distinction in analysis is much too big for us to discuss in these notes, however. Let's play the game by Quine's rules, so that to accept intensional identity conditions is to reject the ideal of extensionality by virtue of the ill-definedness of the entities posited with intensional identity conditions.

Would that matters, complicated as they are, were so simple. Recall that I said the ideal of extensionality's facet dealing with the attributive position had two parts. We only considered the first of them. The second part restricted the process of abstraction (explained in section D). It turns out that, if you allow abstraction to such modal attributes as the attribute of being necessarily greater than seven or the attitudinal attribute of being such that Belia believes it to be a woodchuck, then these so-called "attributes" obey the extensional criterion of identity for attributes! If we let them in by abstraction, why fight to keep them out by disallowing intensional identity conditions? Keeping our minds within the pen of extensionality is turning out to be like herding cats. Well, no such abstractions, y'hear?

## §6. The irrelevance of intensionality to propositional attitudes.

We need not spend time on the subject of intensionality, since the chief lesson for us will be that the contexts generated by propositional attitudes are *not* intensional contexts, in the sense that Carnap defined. As he said,

> the whole belief-sentence ['John believes that . . .'] is neither extensional nor intensional with respect to the subsentence '. . .'. Consequently, an interpretation of belief-sentences as referring either to sentences or to propositions is not quite satisfactory.[10]

The contexts violate the principle of substitutivity of identity *even when the identities are provable without appeal to factual information.* For example, it's provable by logic and some definitions that $2^3 = 8$, and that $3^2 = 9$. Nevertheless, Belia's command of these necessary truths used to be poor, so that

> Belia believed that $8 < 9$,

but, given her denials and her pencil-and-paper calculations, it wasn't the case that

> Belia believed that $2^3 < 3^2$.

Another example concerns Belia's earlier studies of plane geometry. At one point in her studies:

> Belia believed the sides of any equilateral triangle were the same length.

But,

> Belia did not believe the sides of any equiangular triangle were the same length.

As we all know, it's provable that a triangle is equilateral if and only if it's equiangular. Well, her befuddlement was awhile ago. She's been studying set theory recently and has learned the definitions of a noninductive set and a reflexive set[11]:

> Belia's convinced that the set of natural numbers is noninductive.

But so far, it's not true that

> Belia is convinced that the set of natural numbers is reflexive.

But mathematics alone suffices to prove the equivalence, and so the identity:

> the attribute of being noninductive = the attribute of being reflexive.

The two reports would be necessarily equivalent if belief created an intensional context in its report after the "that." Carnap's exploitation of intensional identity conditions was great for rehabilitating modal logic. Nevertheless, once again we see that the problems with propositional attitudes are different and more obstinate. Carnap did define a relation of "intensional isomorphism" in terms of intensional contexts in order to capture the logical quirks of propositional attitudes.[12] I believe the example using groundhog and woodchuck (in section E, where truth changes to falsehood upon substitution, because of what Belia believes) shows his theory's untestability. For to make it work, you just postulate hidden structure where any counterexample supposes no structure. Thus the terms "groundhog" and "woodchuck," which I take to have unstructured meanings, would have to stand for structured meanings, like the meanings of phrases, to avoid the violations we encountered in section E. Even if that seemed to work, it would fall afoul of Benson Mates's criticism using iterated propositional attitudes. Suppose two sentences A and B are intensionally isomorphic, so that we could derive, *salva veritate*

   Whoever believes that A believes that B

from

   Whoever believes that A believes that A.

Nevertheless, when we enclose these sentences within the context "Nobody doubts that . . .," the substitution of B for the second occurrence of A changes the whole sentence from true to false, since philosophers doubt the adequacy of intensional isomorphism![13] So I'll ignore these convolutions of "intensionality with an *s*" as we study the attitudes. However, the Carnapian project of reducing intentionality to intensionality is alive and well.[14]

  We ignore intensionality with an *s*, as Carnap defined it. Others use the s-word differently, in particular Quine, who finds Carnap's definition of it indefensible. So he uses intensional to cover whatever is not extensional. In Quine's usage propositional attitudes are intensional contexts. Many others follow his example, even though they accept Carnap's sharp distinction between analytic and synthetic. They think Carnapian thoughts, but express them in Quinean language; why I don't know. More careful thinkers have recognized that, if they use the term "intensional" to talk about propositional attitudes, they need to introduce degrees of intensionality.[15] Instead of that, however, I prefer Carnap's own usage, according to which propositional attitudes are neither extensional nor intensional, not because I am Carnapian, but because I want to stress the difference between modal locutions, which are intensional, and reports of propositional attitudes, which are not: Let's call them **hyperintensional contexts**, although we must not assume that one needs identity conditions more stringent than intensional ones. The term was introduced by Maxwell

Cresswell in 1975.[16] Hyperintensional contexts are contexts that are neither extensional nor intensional. They turn out to be contexts whose content is governed by the person being reported on. However close in meaning two reports may be, the person reported on settles whether they're both true, and if they are both true, whether they report the same belief.

I don't endorse the thought that there are entities meeting identity conditions more stringent than intensional ones. And I certainly don't wish my use of the term "hyperintensional" to imply that there are hyper-intensions to go along with the extensions and intensions of general terms. The Davidsonian regimentation is very good at depriving hyperintensional contexts of their apparent ontological^ import. Recall that in the Davidsonian regimentation, the proposition Belia believes stands as a distinct sentence in Rep's report. Then the issue is simply whether Rep has said the same thing as what Belia believes. What looks like a problem of substitution for the standard regimentation looks more like a problem of translation in the Davidsonian regimentation: How should Rep translate into his own words what Belia believed in hers? If the problem of hyper-intensionality is not a matter of finding even more stringent identity conditions, and I don't think it is, then perhaps it's best not to conflate that problem with the problems associated with intensionality at all. The conflation would send us off on a goose chase to catch entities meeting even more stringent identity conditions. Another reason to keep the Davidsonian regimentation alive in our thoughts, then, is that it breaks the grip of a bad analogy on our minds. (Since translation ideally puts exact synonyms for synonyms, it yields intuitively correct results even in opaque and hyperintensional contexts. Can we exploit the concept of translation between languages to create other "*salva veritate*" problems even for the Davidsonian regimentation? Yes! But I'm saving that difficulty until section V, since there are bigger fish to fry with it than just a variant style of regimentation.)

Since we define hyperintensional contexts in terms of Carnap's two other kinds of contexts, i.e., contexts that are neither extensional nor inten sional, they concern attributive positions. So the question arises how a hyperintensional context relates to an opaque context. It seems we can say that

> a context is opaque in its referential positions, if it's hyperin-
> tensional in its attributive positions.

This is another difference between intensional and hyperintensional contexts.

We can summarize our discussion of contexts with a table:

|                 | **Extensional**                      | **Intensional** | **Hyper-intensional**                   |
|-----------------|--------------------------------------|-----------------|-----------------------------------------|
| **Transparent** | logic, math, & physical science      | modal logic     | [empty]                                 |
| **Opaque**      | [empty]                              | ?               | that-clauses of propositional attitudes |

Table G-1. The contexts of referential positions (the rows), related to the contexts of attributive positions (the columns).

## §7. What was Brentano's thesis really?

Quine rejected modal logic because it violated extensionality for no good reason. He'd've rejected propositional attitudes for the same reason, if they had not been so indispensable in people's thinking about each other. So this ideal of extensionality is at the heart of all our difficulties. If you feel the ideal of extensionality uncompelling, you're not alone. Two major figures who agree with you are Frege and Carnap. In 1892 Frege noted the failure of extensionality in propositional attitudes,[17] but he did not blame opaque constructions, i.e., modes of containment of referential positions that caused them to be not purely referential. Instead he postulated that a singular term occupying that sort of position did refer to something, but not to what it customarily refers to. This something had different identity conditions from the customary referents. In effect he was anticipating Carnap, looking to nonstandard identity conditions for the solution.

In 1957, Roderick Chisholm associated the thesis of the nonextensionality of reports with a definition of the mental which Franz Brentano had defended in 1874. The association was anachronistic. For it attributed to Brentano the idea of semantic ascent, which he seems to have been innocent of, and also the view that attitudes are directed toward propositions, which he seems to have been innocent of also. Although part of Brentano's explication of intentionality implied the opaqueness of reports, he never proposed a one-to-one correspondence of intentionality of attitudes at the level of the phenomenon to the nonextensionality of reports at the level of semantic ascent. Nevertheless, Chisholm defended this recommendation and even dubbed it "Brentano's thesis."[18] Although it is *Chisholm's* thesis and at one point he was careful to call it only "a thesis resembling that of Brentano," the name "Brentano's thesis" unfortunately stuck to this linguistic thesis. I'll not use the name. Chisholm's linguistic thesis is false; the failure of extensionality is only a generic trait of the reports of attitudes, since many nonmental idioms fail to be extensional. Examples are·". . . lacks . . ." (the landscape lacks unicorns), ". . . resembles . . ." (she resembles a mermaid), and ". . . prevents..." (atmospheric conditions prevent class 10 hurricanes, the idea being there are no class 10 hurricanes any more than there are mermaids or unicorns). Even "*p* because *q*" seems not fully extensional, in that substitution of truths for truths fails to be *salva veritate*.

What is the real Brentano's thesis? I referred obliquely to it in the Introduction when I explained the term, "intentionality," a term whose currency is traceable to Brentano. I demurred then from the real **Brentano's thesis**, that intentionality is uniquely mental, although I agreed that minds are the only things to display spectacular intentionality.

In favor of the other side of the dispute, you ought to feel the value of constraining your philosophizing to conform to the ideal of extensionality. Those who do feel it, yet think propositional attitudes are logically respectable, have looked for another way to avoid the charge that the propositional attitudes are illogical, a way that does not reject the ideal. Perhaps we'll find it.

We've now completed the regimentation of formats and their entailments. It's been a long haul from A to G only to prepare our data. The standardizing of our ways of reporting beliefs should not strike you as tampering with our data, but rather as rendering our idioms less ambiguous. Perhaps our motive of sharpening a distinction between relational and notional attitudes could be reversed, and someone might regiment the distinction so that it's less sharp. Perhaps it could be regimented so as not to seem to violate the extensional ideal of intelligibility. Setting that possibility aside until section L, however, so far we've just been preparing our data for study, mindful of the fact that we may have prejudiced the data against some theories. If so, we'll have to reconsider the regimentation.

Let's now take up *a theory* of the about-position. It will be a component of a general theory of the attitudes. Sections H through O concern this component of the general theory. Later sections will be devoted to the other component of the general theory, namely, the theory of the directed-towardness.

# Notes

1. Quine introduced the concept in his "Reference and Modality," in his *From a Logical Point of View* (1953) 142. A formal statement of the concept is in *Word and Object*, 144.

2. Kaplan lays out a proof of one theorem: if substitution fails, then generalization must fail. See his "Opacity" in L. Hahn and P. Schilpp, *The Philosophy of W. V. Quine* (1986; second, expanded edition 1998) 234. Quine, claiming the proof fails, offers a repair in his "Reply to David Kaplan," 291. Quine does concede, however, that one can stipulate a new sense to generalization where substitution fails, if one wishes to allow such generalization.

3. W. V. Quine, "Promoting Extensionality," *Synthese* 98 (1994) 143-151.

4. Bertrand Russell thought up this barber, in his 1918, "Philosophy of Logical Atomism," lecture VII (p. 261 of *Logic and Knowledge*). To prove *a priori* there's no such barber, ask whether he shaves himself. Show that either answer leads to contradiction.

5. Alonzo Church, "Review of Carnap's *Introduction to Semantics*," *Philosophical Review*, 52 (1943) 298-304. Kurt Gödel, "Russell's Mathematical Logic" in Paul Arthur Schilpp, *The Philosophy of Bertrand Russell* (1944). See his note 5. The argument there is spelled out by Kenneth Olson, *An Essay on Facts* (1987) 94.

6. An application of Leibniz's general identity condition, where the only relevant attributes describe a set's membership.

7. Ludwig Wittgenstein, *Tractatus Logico-Philosophicus* (1922). §5.54 states facet II of extensionality, and §5.55 states facet I. I state in the text an interpretation of the sections that are between these two. In the Introduction to the second edition of *Principia Mathematica* (1927), Whitehead and Russell note a use of extensionality which points to this way of justifying extensionality (xiv), and in Appendix C of the second edition, they announce the principle of extensionality. See ch. 10 of Russell's *My Philosophical Development* (1959) about this use.

8. Subsequent volumes of the first edition appeared in 1913.

9. Rudolf Carnap, *Meaning and Necessity*, 2nd ed. (1956), §§4-5, 11-13.

10. *Meaning and Necessity*, §13.

11. For the curious: Abraham Fraenkel, *Abstract Set Theory*, 2nd ed. (1961), pp. 28ff. A nonempty set I is noninductive if there's no positive integer $n$ such that I has just $n$ members. A nonempty set is reflexive if it has a proper subset that's equivalent to it, that is, there's a one-to-one mapping from all and only the things in the set to all and only the things in the subset. For the purposes of the equivalence, we leave the empty set out of consideration. A note in the previous section referred to Hilbert's hotel. The set of its rooms was described as noninductive. But the trick of providing for more occupants without adding rooms depended on the set being reflexive.

12. *Meaning and Necessity*, §§14-15.

13. Benson Mates, "Synonymity" (1950), reprinted in Leonard Linsky, ed.,

*Semantics and the Philosophy of Language* (1952) 125.
14. Particularly in the work of Cresswell, D. Lewis, and J. Katz.
15. Ruth Barcan Marcus, "Modalities and Intensional Languages," *Synthese*, 27 (1962) 303-322.
16. M. J. Cresswell, "Hyperintensional Logic," *Studia Logica*, vol. 34 (1975) 25-38.
17. Frege, "On Sense and Reference" in P. Geach and M. Black, *Translations from the Philosophical Writings of Gottlob Frege* (1960). Quine contrasts his approach with Frege's in *Word and Object*, 151.
18. Roderick Chisholm, *Perceiving: A Philosophical Study* (1957) ch. 11, "'Intentional Inexistence".' Brentano's thesis, as Chisholm states it:

> Let us say (1) that we do not need to use intentional sentences when we describe nonpsychological phenomena; we can express all of our beliefs about what is merely "physical" in sentences which are not intentional. . . . But (2) when we wish to describe perceiving, assuming, believing, knowing, wanting, hoping, and other such attitudes, then (a) we must use sentences which are intentional or (b) we must use terms we do not need to use when we describe nonpsychological phenomena. (172)

By "intentional sentence" Chisholm means an opaque construction exhibiting all the failures of extensionality. For some examples of opaque constructions used of nonmental things, see Stalnaker's *Inquiry* (1984) 11f. Chisholm offers those I cite in the text in his article, "Intentionality" in Paul Edwards, ed., *Encyclopedia of Philosophy* (1967). Chisholm would have to say they're all idioms we could give up without loss of power to express physical truth. For Franz Brentano's own words, see his *Psychology From an Empirical Standpoint* (1874) p. 88 of the English edition.

# Part II: Theories of the Aboutness, from H to O

The second part of these notes, consisting of eight sections, develops one aspect of any theory of propositional attitudes, the aspect that deals specifically with the relational attitudes. Why do the reports of such attitudes have the properties they do have, sometimes seemingly illogical properties? We consider several theories.

Since this little introduction functions as a package for the next sections, a warning label would seem appropriate. In 1986 the following paragraph appeared in the book *Knowing Who* by Boër and Lycan. If it was true then, it probably is still true today:

> In case any reader is not already aware of the fact, we should mention that philosophers' treatment of belief *de re* over the past decade is a disgusting mess. We doubt that any two contributors to the literature have used the expression *"de re"* in just the same way; between terminological confusion and substantive divergence of theoretical goals and interests, writers on this topic have spent most of their time and ink talking past each other. For this reason one might want to urge a total moratorium on the use of the term *"de re"* and its apparent antonym *"de dicto,"* the moratorium perhaps backed by the death penalty or at least mutilation followed by transportation to Yazoo City, Mississippi. We have considerable sympathy with this proposal, ourselves. (111)

But it didn't stop Boër and Lycan from writing on the subject, and it won't stop me. They and I think the subject leads us to something important, however messy the way. Will you join us?

# H. The Sufficiency-of-Concurrence Theory of Relational Reports Refuted.

Belia saw an animal run into the bushes, and Rep reports her belief by saying, "Belia believes *about* that animal we both saw, *that* it's a wood-chuck." Rep's telling us what he observed, but there's also theory in that report. It's a bit of Rep's theory of Belia, of her state of mind. Let's consider some constraints which folk psychology puts on Rep's theorizing about Belia.

### §1. If people observe that something's so, why say they're theorizing about it?

Is folk psychology a theory? The claim has become, since 1986, contro-versial.[1] Despite the hubbub, I claim that **folk psychology** is the folks' toolbag for creating theories about one another. When I talk to you, I'm continually creating a theory of your mental state. It includes what interests you, what you know and don't know, what your mood is, how sympathetic you are toward me, what you understand of what I've said to you, and on and on. My theorizing about you is constrained not only by what I observe of you, but by principles such as that you're a thinking thing, that you think like me, and that you're rational, or irrational if the evidence warrants it. This theory—my theory of you at the moment—guides me in conversing with you and interacting with you. People take for granted theories being applied in technology to make medicines, planes, bridges, and computers. The most basic technology people have is for dealing successfully with one another, and that too is an application of theory. It provides not only for mentalistic description of others but also for normative judgment of them.

I also create theories of my own mental states. Indeed, all that I believe of my own mental states is my theory of my mind. My theory of myself is not merely descriptive of me, but also normative in that it guides my actions. It's unlike contemporary scientific theories in other respects as well: Since people tend to think of theories on the model of the great theories of physics, like the atomic theory of matter, they're not accustomed to the idea that a theory might be used to formulate what they learn by introspection about themselves. For they don't observe atoms directly. So they tend to think to be mutually exclusive that which they observe and that which they theorize about. But the theory-observation dichotomy does not hold in folk psychology in the way it seems to in atomic physics. People do seem to report their observations of themselves directly, without any steps of inference, in the terms provided by folk psychology. Thus they *observe theoretic* entities, their mental states. But this may be less a case of direct awareness than a case of expert diagnostics, as psychologist Gopnik suggests.[2] For example, someone expert in chemistry can just look and see things in the terms that chemistry provides. Perhaps introspection is like that.

To understand how theory can inform perception, including introspection, we must understand what a theory is. What is a **theory**? Traditionally, a theory is taken to be a syntactic thing, namely, a group of sentences or propositions that systematize, by means of enhanced inferential connections among the propositions, an otherwise diverse and disconnected body of facts, which they describe. An empirical theory systematizes a diverse range of empirical facts. Scientific laws also collect a range of facts into a unity, but theory goes further in collecting the laws themselves into a unity. The subjective payoff of theory is this: The systematization embodies the theorizer's understanding of those facts; it explains why they are facts and enables the theorizer to predict further facts within that range and to influence which facts come into existence.

In this definition of theory there's no restriction against theories providing the very concepts in terms of which the theorizers state the facts which they observe and which the theory explains. But philosophers of science have a model of the testing of a theory that suggests that people must test a theory against observations which don't presuppose the truth of the theory. If they observe the theoretic entities which their theories of themselves posit, how do their observations provide non-circular evidence for the theory? Before answering, let's remember we're not doing epistemology in these notes; we're doing descriptive ontology. We shall later (in sections T and U) examine Quine's account of observation. It has the consequence that sentences reporting observations can both have an analysis in the terms of some theory and yet also support (or not support) the theory without presupposing the analysis. With that caveat in mind, here's an answer: Since people not only observe things in the terms which folk psychology provides, but also act on their desires, also formulated in folk psychological terms, the continuing utility of a theory for achieving their purposes is the evidence of its truth or of its verisimilitude^ at least. The technological application of the theory provides the evidence. In seeming contradiction to this answer, contemporary science separates the confirmation of a theory from its application, but that's only because of people's aversion to the risks in applying a science that might be false. The folk who developed folk psychology had to take the risk and learn the hard way. Granted the wholly generic tools which folk psychology supplies to the folk for creating the specific theories of themselves and each other, these theories are testable and correctable, and often pass the tests. But how stringent are the tests of application? Might not mediocre approximations of the truth be good enough for successful application, if the applications don't require exactitude? Yes, we must admit this.

We may also think the testing of the theory against evidence to have been done by natural selection itself. Persons with brains more predisposed to theorize in the folk psychological way outcompeted persons whose brains were less predisposed. The fact that this theory is ingrained in human beings, even to the extent of permeating their very perceptions of each other, indicates that human beings may be built to facilitate their learning the theory. There's evidence that children come to think of themselves and each other in the terms of this theory by the age of three and a half years on average. Before that, they make mistakes about their own mind in the same way they make mistakes about others'. When they learn the full theory, it's simply learned as part of the process of their maturation.[3] The situation is similar to the way they learn their language. Failure to acquire the skill of theorizing in the folk psychological way leads to poor language skills and even autism.[4]

If human brains are adapted to working specifically with this theory, then we should ask how it would be possible for the theory's origin to predate or at best be contemporaneous with the origin of speech. If the theory's origin predates the origin of speech, we must not conceive of the theory as a linguistic object, something composed of sentences, as the traditional account of theories says. And indeed we need not think of any theories this way. A **theory** may be a semantic (or model-theoretic) thing, namely, a family of **structures**, a technical term in formal semantics (i.e., in model theory). The structures collectively characterize the propositions of the theory without the mediation of any linguistic expression of them.[5] In Part III, sections Q and R, we'll see how the folk might have brought theory to mind without bringing sentences to mind.

So far we've been discussing theory in the sense of theories of particular people at particular times, for example, Rep's theory of Belia.

Folk psychology itself, if we abstract from all the specific theories people construct of each other, is merely generic theory, a set of constraints on the development of the specific theories and the conceptual tools for stating them. These notes are concerned with the scientific respectability of those tools. And even concerning that I'm only doing part of the job, for there's much to a generic theory that I leave out. I suggested in the Introduction to these notes that we're doing only the preliminaries, like the way anatomy is preliminary to physiology. I'm concerned with the entities which folk psychology tells the folk their mental states consist of, namely, propositional attitudes. That's the ontology of folk psychology. My generic theorizing, as distinct from Rep's specific theorizing about Belia, is confined to understanding the coherence of such an ontology and its susceptibility to scientific understanding. How propositional attitudes interact, leading to purposive behavior, is an investigation that goes beyond ontology and so is left out.

Some philosophers will object to my characterizing folk psychology as generic theory. They claim that I thereby commit myself to the correctability of even the generic tools it provides for specific theorizing, even the ontology of propositional attitudes, if some competing theory promises to do the work better. For these generic aspects would be empirical theory, if they are theory, and all empirical theory is correctable. Thus I'm opening the door to the revisionary metaphysics I mentioned in the Introduction.[6] Yes, I'm guilty as charged. (I indulged in some of that revisionary speculation myself in the Introduction, speculating that features posited by the folk psychological framework may have the status of secondary^ qualities.) Beyond my so-called error of strategy in polemics, however, they say I'm wrong in fact. For folk psychology has features that make it different from empirical theorizing. We already saw one, that people report their own mental states in its terms without the need for inference. Another is that folk psychological theory has features that physical theory lacks. For example, when people describe each other's voluntary motions, they don't do it in terms of the motions' physical properties such as speed and trajectory. They say what purposes the motions are for. Another example is that they don't just predict where they'll end up; they predict the realization of the goals they aim for that fit standards of rationality. Thirdly, folk psychological theory lacks features that physical theory has. For example, folk psychology is unconcerned with filling the gap in causal statements connecting outcomes to causes. Physical theory seeks the mechanism that makes the connection. I accept these differences of folk psychological theorizing from the ways that physical science theorizes. Folk psychology fits the definition of theory nonetheless. So, let's now turn to our preliminary bit of generic theorizing.

## §2. Constraints on Rep's theorizing about Belia's relational beliefs.

When Rep reports that Belia believes about the animal that it's a woodchuck, he's theorizing that she has a relational belief. So far I have given the impression that Rep was free to introduce an about-phrase into his reports of Belia's beliefs whenever he agreed that Belia's belief was about something real. Some philosophers, including me, believe that it would be a mistake for Rep to take that liberty. The mistake is fostered by the weak analogy between *de re* belief reports and *de re* propositions in modal quantified logic. In modal logic it may not be a mistake to export genuine singular terms from modal that-clauses. But modal logic's a different subject!

Suppose the reporter concurs merely in the reality of what a belief is about. I'll now prove (to my satisfaction, at least) that this simple concurrence is *insufficient* justification for his using an about-position in his report. Concurrence here means only Rep's agreeing to the reality of the things Belia's belief refers to. See the distinction between the alternative conditions for partial concurrence (sentences (1) and (2)) at the point in section C where the notion of partial concurrence was introduced. Since then we've been assuming provisionally the simpler of the two (sentence (2)). Now we're going to prove that it's not a sufficient^ condition for introducing an about-position. The argument against the idea of the sufficiency-of-concurrence for a relational report will proceed in four steps, considering first those generalizations that are existentially general, then those that are universally general, and thirdly those pseudo-singular generalizations that use definite descriptions—we'll see that Russell's analysis of definite descriptions is appropriate in this case, and finally a genuine singular proposition.

*Step 1.* Some beliefs cannot be expressed by naming individuals; they are beliefs of generalizations. Belia, for example, believes there are Swedes, although she doesn't have anyone in mind as the Swedes of her belief. Rep can report Belia's belief in a natural way thus:

Belia believes that one or more persons are Swedes.
The phrase "one or more persons" does not name anyone in particular, but it does occupy the position of subject term, i.e., the referential position. Does Rep's agreeing the words refer to an existent person suffice for his putting them in an about-phrase, regardless of Belia's situation?

No. Rep also believes there are Swedes; he agrees also in using the

same indefinite subject term as Belia would use: "one or more persons."
The suspect idea is that his concurrence entitles him to appropriate this
subject term for use in front of the that-clause.

> Belia believes *about* one or more people *that* they are Swedes.

This report is no different in meaning from:

> One or more people are such that Belia believes that they are
> Swedes,

and:

> There are people whom Belia believes to be Swedes.

Our intuitions about the meaning of this last version tell us that it's a false
report. Its clear import is that Belia has certain people in mind as the ones
she thinks are Swedes. But she doesn't. So the report is false. So it cannot
be implied by a true report of what she believes. Nor is a reporter of
Belia's beliefs entitled to report Belia's belief of a generalization in this
way merely because he concurs in the belief. He's not entitled to, even if
he concurred totally and reported that Belia *knows* there are Swedes. For
Belia could know there are Swedes, yet have *no* belief about any particular
person, that he or she is a Swede. These beliefs are *de dicto* merely.

*Step 2.* We can make this same point about beliefs that have all of a
class as their subjects. Suppose Belia believed all apples have white
interiors. Rep reports the fact in this way:

> Belia believes that all apples have white interiors.

Suppose Rep agrees totally and would say that Belia knows or at least
believes correctly that all apples have white interiors. His concurrence
would *not* entitle him to format his report of her belief this way:

> Belia believes *about* all apples *that* they have white interiors.

For that means the same as:

> Each apple is such that Belia believes about it that it has a white
> interior.

Belia need not believe any such thing. There may be an apple she mistakes
for a tomato and believes about it that it has a red interior. She still
believes that all apples have white interiors. So, however much Rep agrees
with Belia, he should not format his report to suggest Belia is somehow
acquainted with the subjects that make her belief true.

(When I explained generality in section E, I suggested that Belia could
have a *de re* belief about all of a population based on a sampling of the
population. Note that, if so, we might generate a contradiction by adding
that view to the considerations just given: Belia looks casually at an apple.
About this particular apple not in her sample, Belia both is and is not a
believer in the whiteness of its interior, for she's not a believer in its white-

ness because of a mistaken perception of it—she thinks it's a tomato—and she is a believer in its whiteness by an inductive generalization about all apples, and so her general belief about apples applies to this one. I have contradicted myself! More about that sort of problem and its solution in the next sections. The sophists of old traded on this contradiction. They said, "Do you know that every pair of things is even in number?" After you say yes, they contradict you. "No, you don't, for here's a pair of things you would've denied to be a pair. So you couldn't have known that it was even in number. *A fortiori*, you could not have known about every pair that it's even in number." And let's admit that they come up with a surprising pair.[7])

*Step 3.* First a recap: We're evaluating the theory that these two kinds of reports (with and without about-positions) differ only on the reporter's concurrence in some aspects of the belief reported on. The theory is implausible when applied to beliefs of generalizations, as the previous steps showed. At most it applies to beliefs about individuals named by proper names or descriptive phrases that purport to pick out a unique object, like "the fountain of youth."

Yet it fails even here. The critical next step in the refutation of this theory is a *reductio ad absurdum*.^ If the theory were true of reports of beliefs about named individuals, then it would have to be true of reports of existentially general beliefs, for the former kind implies the latter kind. We've just seen, however, that it cannot be true of reports of the general beliefs. Therefore, neither can it be true of reports of beliefs about named individuals. Here is the argument. Belia has two purely general beliefs:

Belia believes that there are finitely many Swedes.

Belia believes that no two are tied for the rank of tallest Swede.

Belia is a clever logician who knows that these two generalities are sufficient grounds for introducing the article "the" into her belief. That is, she knows that, if the predicate "tallest Swede" is true of one thing only, then she's entitled to put the article "the" in front of it to refer to *the* tallest Swede. In effect, in believing these two generalities, Belia believes that the tallest Swede exists. Belia now infers an innocuous third belief which she expresses this way, meaning by it nothing but a truism:

The tallest Swede is a Swede.

Rep reports Belia's truistic belief thus:

Belia believes that the tallest Swede is a Swede.

To test the sufficiency-of-concurrence hypothesis, let's say Rep agrees fully with Belia's first two purely general beliefs. In that case he might've reported them combined in this way:

Belia knows that the tallest Swede exists.

Rep appropriates Belia's term "the tallest Swede" as his own. Perhaps neither Rep nor Belia have in mind anyone in particular. Or Rep does, although Belia doesn't. Perhaps Rep is acquainted with the tallest Swede. None of that should matter on the sufficiency-of-concurrence theory we're refuting. No matter what may be the basis of Rep's concurrence, his concurring that the singular term "the tallest Swede" denotes something entitles Rep (according to the wrong theory) to export the singular term and report Belia's belief in this way:

Belia believes *about* the tallest Swede, *that* he or she is a Swede.

And Rep would be entitled to generalize from the about-position to:

There is a certain one whom Belia believes to be a Swede.

The last two statements say that Belia has someone in mind. But she doesn't. Something has gone wrong.[8]

Perhaps the last two statements don't say to the ordinary person, who hasn't been subjected to all my brain-washing, that Belia has someone in mind. Perhaps there's only a conversational implicature of Belia's having someone in mind, which we should cancel. When the implicature is canceled, the statements are true, and nothing's gone wrong. Ok, but when that implicature is canceled, so is our regimentation. What's left is loose talk about a phenomenon. I admitted in section E that regimentation involves elevating some implicatures to entailments. If this is just such a case, so be it. (But if you want a locution to capture the correct entailment, which explicitly cancels the implicature, in section J I'll regiment the passive voice form, "the tallest Swede is believed by Belia to be a Swede," to serve this purpose. It's fake *de re* reportage.)

We argued from the true premise that Belia knows there are Swedes to the false conclusion that Belia has one or more persons in mind as Swedes. Some of our subsidiary premises must therefore be false. One such premise was that Belia believes that no two Swedes are tied for tallest. Surely Belia can know that sort of thing, if she's thinking of very fine measurements that in effect rule out ties within a finite population. Another subsidiary premise was that Belia was entitled to paraphrase her two general beliefs as "The tallest Swede exists." Again surely that's one legitimate use of the definite article "the," the attributive use we mentioned in section A. False, therefore, is the only other subsidiary premise, the theory of the sufficiency-of-concurrence for reports to have about-positions. Rep's concurrence with a belief is not sufficient grounds for using an about-phrase in reporting it. At least we demonstrated that it's insufficient if applied to beliefs expressed with singular terms that begin with the definite article used attributively.

*Step 4*, for those unhappy with my choice of a singular proposition: We've not said much about singular propositions, except to postpone the question whether a belief in a singular proposition is identical to a belief *de re*. We're now in a position to deny the identity and see why they're not the same.[9] Suppose that Belia could introduce a proper name for the tallest Swede, perhaps using that very description as a *reference fixing* device in lieu of her actually learning his real name. She calls him "Sven." Now Rep can say she believes a singular proposition,

     Belia believes that Sven is a Swede.

By sheer coincidence the tallest Swede is Sven Svenson, but even if he'd been Jussi, he'd've acquired the second name, "Sven," from Belia's naming him that. Rep tells him,

     Belia believes that you're a Swede.

Note that Rep violated our rule that no substitutions are allowed in that-clauses. That includes substituting the word "you" for Belia's newly introduced name of "Sven." But Rep may be off duty, and we don't pay him much anyway. Now Sven might say,

     She believes that about me!

Let's not quibble about these reports; after all we're trying to evoke intuitions about the nature of Belia's belief, not about Rep's reportage. Months later Belia is introduced to Sven. Here's the question you must answer: When they reminisce, would Belia agree that she had had that belief about Sven before being introduced to him? She should know whether her belief in that singular proposition, "Sven is a Swede," using the proper name she just introduced with a reference fixing description, was a relational belief or a notional one. Quine tells us, if she had spoken Latin or a romance language, she'd have to decide which it is in order to know what verb mood to use in expressing subordinate clauses. To quote Quine's Spanish,

> thus '*Procuro un perro que habla*' has the relational sense . . . as against the notional '*Procuro un perro que hable*' . . .[10]

I don't know if this linguistic distinction can be made where the proper name "Sven" replaces the indefinite "un perro." In any case, I'm asking you to engage in an empathic intuition into her state of mind; how would she classify the belief she had formed before meeting Sven? How would she classify it at the time of her coming to believe it, and later on? Do you really think that, when Sven and Belia meet for the first time, and he tells her that he's a Swede, she could say this?

You're simply confirming what I've believed all along about you.

Since she fixed the reference of the name "Sven" by the definite description, "the tallest Swede," if she believes the truth that Sven is a Swede, she must also know it, and know it *a priori*. Yet, since "Sven" does not mean "the tallest Swede"—that's how reference fixing differs from defining—Sven might not've been the tallest Swede, not even a Swede. So it's a contingent truth she knows *a priori*.[11] The fact that she came by this knowledge all too easily I suspect would lead Belia to say her belief was notional merely.

Only our regimented forms of reportage capture the distinction in kinds of belief. Especially in this thought experiment, Sven's "about" in his reply to Rep—"about me"—is not the "about" of our regimented form. For by this stage in our analyses surely you don't think—note my browbeating tactics here—you don't think that Belia has a *de re* belief about Sven Svenson, one directed toward an incomplete proposition denoting his nationality. At most we might concede to her a *de dicto* belief in a singular proposition that Sven is a Swede. After all, suppose she had fixed the reference of the name "Sven" by the description, "the tallest Swede ever." Then who would Sven have been? Probably, no one has brought, or ever will bring, that person to mind by way of that description.

Proponents of the view that singular complete propositions are what relational attitudes are directed toward won't be so easily thwarted. Robin Jeshion concedes the result we got from our thought experiment: She concedes that Belia does not have a relational belief, and also concedes that the reason Belia doesn't is that she used the device of reference fixing all too unseriously. Nevertheless, Jeshion defends the view that, if certain conditions of serious use of the device were fulfilled, Belia could've had a relational belief about Sven Svenson before ever meeting him, by way of fixing the reference of a name for him.[12] In particular, Belia must really intend to think about the guy she named "Sven," opening a file folder on him in her mind, so to speak, to file there all the things she comes to believe about him, and she must want to label the folder with some name that does not import any restrictive information, which would belong inside the folder and not on the label. If that's her purpose, then she does indeed, according to Jeshion, acquire a *de re* belief about Sven Svenson by reference fixing, prior to meeting him.

Do your intuitions accord with Jeshion's? Mine do not. I still don't think Belia would've had a *de re* belief about Sven. However serious her purpose for the reference fixing, it does not transfer Belia's psychological condition from being *de dicto* to being *de re*. To see this, notice that she might meet Jeshion's conditions by opening a mental folder for Sherlock Holmes or Santa Claus, knowing they are fictions. Jeshion bites the bullet and says that even then Belia's beliefs are *de re*. With her thereby denying the necessity of a referentially transparent about-position, I begin to wonder whether she and I are talking about the same phenomenon. Jeshion's gambit is instructive despite being unsuccessful, for she ends up conceding so much to the side I favor that it's reassuring! And it does seem right that Belia's seriousness has something to do with her having *de re* beliefs. Perhaps Jeshion hasn't quite put her hands on the right conditions. In my opinion, the right condition is stated by the dominance theory of partial concurrence, which I introduce in the next section.

I admit that I've yet to prove that the content-term of the directed-toward relation is an incomplete proposition rather than a complete singular proposition. My first argument for that will come in sections M and N. In view of this promissory note, from now on Rep must obey the rules of our regimentation. So in the case of Belia's fixing the reference of a name solely by a description, as she did the name "Sven," he will *not* report that

Belia believes about Sven, that he is a Swede.

Even if she has a *de dicto* belief in a singular proposition whose subject is Sven Svenson, she does not thereby have a *de re* belief about him. To keep this division sharp, we must reaffirm section E's third and fifth regimentations, that exportation and generalization of proper names are not valid from *de dicto* reports of belief in a singular proposition. For here we saw a case where the operations may not preserve truth.

Sufficiency-of-concurrence has now failed in all four scenarios.

### §3. What are the missing ingredients? In some cases it's extensive causal rapport.

The rules of our regimentation depart from the model of modal logic, but we rejected that model. Many philosophers accept the model and don't comply with this regimentation, and so the distinction between belief *de re* and belief in a complete singular proposition is lost. I must admit, however, that many of the best contemporary philosophers, e.g., David Kaplan and John Perry, are glad to lose this distinction. I'll address some of their concerns in the next section. My reply to them in a nutshell will be Donnellan's, that Belia's belief *de dicto* in a singular proposition, by way of a reference-fixing description and without any causal rapport with the thing so named, is only something she could say, not think. We want Rep to report what Belia thinks. (So the disquotation principles of section C will come under increased suspicion, since they assume people can think whatever they can say.) People are often in the condition of being able to believe that sentences express truths without knowing the truths expressed. Everyone knows that $E = mc^2$, or more exactly most only know the sentence expresses a truth. In the case of using attributively a description to fix the reference of a proper name, people's powers for meaningful and true statement are outstripping their capacities for belief.

I'd say the same of another linguistic trick invented by David Kaplan, namely the **demonstrative use** of a description, by means of which people utter a singular proposition directly, or they may exploit it to introduce names.[13] The content of a description used demonstratively is not a component in the proposition that's being stated. What may be the case in this respect with the referential use of a description (see section A) is the case with a demonstrative use of it. The main difference between the demonstrative use of a description and a referential use is that the referential use calls upon various contextual cues to reveal the speaker's intended reference, while the demonstrative use exploits an explicit demonstrative (Kaplan coined "dthat . . ."), so that the language's semantic rule for its use selects its direct referent in accord with the description it precedes, a referent which may or may not be the one the speaker intended. For example, Belia may think of the first child to be born in the twenty-second century. She may then use that description demonstratively to refer to "dthat very child." Having so "demonstrated" it, i.e., referred to it directly with the linguistic equivalent of pointing to it, namely, by way of a demonstrative use of a description, she may then utter a singular proposition about the child or give the child a name, let's say "Newman II," and state truly the singular statement, "Newman II will be the first child born in the twenty-second century."

My response to this new-found linguistic power is that it renders semantics autonomous from psychology. Semanticists will welcome the emancipation, but there's a price of irrelevance, for once again human powers for statement are outstripping human capacities for belief. When people use purely linguistic devices to ensure the singular reference of their words, where there's no possibility of pointing or animadversion to the entity referred to, then they're opening a linguistic access to propositions but without a cognitive access to them. In these cases people believe that the propositions their singular statements express are true; they don't believe anything *about* the things which are the subjects of those propositions. People can express in words what they cannot think.

What then is missing in these cases, which is not missing in genuine *de re* belief? I hypothesize about the believer herself: Belia herself supplies another necessary^ condition; more exactly, some property of her state of belief is another necessary condition for Rep's use of an about-position, along with Rep's concurrence, which is now only one necessary condition, not a sufficient condition. There *is* a phenomenon of relational belief.

But what is that necessary condition that Belia surely supplies? More arguments are needed to settle that, especially since it's a matter of controversy. Here I'll simply state the alternative I prefer for relational beliefs about the ordinary things people deal with:

> For Belia to have some definite concrete individual in mind is for her to be affected by that individual in a way that leaves her with information about the individual.

Clearly that sort of information is absent from the examples we've been studying, and its absence accounts for the intuitions we have about those examples.

Applying this suggestion to our regimentation of a major class of belief reports, Rep can only introduce about-phrases in those cases where Belia has knowledge by acquaintance with that something. More generally, if her belief is about something perceptible other than herself, she must be in **extensive causal rapport** with that something, even if it be indirectly. This is the relation referred to in the phrase "relational belief," when her belief is about something perceptible. The about-phrase is reporting on that rapport as much as it is expressing the reporter's concurring with aspects of the belief. In other words, the believer's causal rapport and the reporter's agreement are both necessary for the report to have an about-position. (In later sections we'll consider how to relax a causal account of the about-position to cover beliefs about oneself and imperceptible objects.)

Philosophers today do broaden the notion of perceptual acquaintance to a kind of "causal rapport" between the believer and the thing she has a belief about. David Lewis defined the phrase, *"my being acquainted with someone"* in this way:

> I and the one I am acquainted with "are so related that there is an extensive causal dependence of my states upon his, and this causal dependence is of a sort apt for the reliable transmission of information" about him to me.[14]

This information is down-to-earth and up-to-the-minute, of the sort William James alludes to in his own generalized definition of acquaintance:

> We are acquainted with a thing as soon as we have learned how to behave
> towards it, or how to meet the behavior we expect from it. Up to that point
> it is still 'strange' to us.[15]

An assumption, implicit in these characterizations of rapport, is that the
information transmitted from the scene to the seer carves up the scene into
the bodies, persons, and the other things she sees and has beliefs about. I'll
question this assumption of ontology^ in Part III, section T. We can be
more noncommittal about ontology. Lewis defines one's "seeing" as a
particular kind of extensive causal dependence of one's state on scenes
before one's eyes,[16] however which way one carves the scene up. This
definition avoids unnecessary ontological assumptions. The definition of
rapport should simply generalize what we say of perception.

We already adduced one consideration, and will adduce several more,
to show that Belia's causal rapport, or lack of any, must affect the way in
which Rep reports her belief, *regardless* of the context he finds *himself* in
when he makes his report. If Belia is in causal rapport with the thing she
has a belief about, but Rep is too ignorant to concur in the existence of the
thing, then he'll not report a *de re* belief, *but she'll have one anyway*. Her
causal rapport is only a necessary condition for the relational report, because the reporter supplies another necessary condition for the report. But
her rapport's sufficient as well as necessary for her belief to be relational.

Here we see one of the pitfalls of semantic ascent: Belief is one phenomenon; reportage is another. Suppose her rapport suffices for her having
a *de re* belief; her rapport plus Rep's concurrence suffice for Rep's stating
a *de re* report of her *de re* belief. Or more simply, given that her belief is
*de re* by virtue of her causal rapport, Rep's concurrence is then sufficient
for a *de re* report of that belief. That's my theory of reports. I separate the
conditions for the phenomenon of relational belief from the conditions for
reporting the phenomenon. I replace an unconditional sufficiency-of-
concurrence theory of reportage with a conditional one. The condition is
rather simple: Only the objectively *de re* beliefs may be reported *de re*.

# Notes

1. For the original articles, see Martin Davies and Tony Stone, editors, *Folk
Psychology: The Theory of Mind Debate*, (1995). See also their follow-up
anthology, *Mental Simulation: Evaluations and Applications* (1995). Their
Introduction to the latter anthology notes the tendency of the "theory theory" to

hybridize with the "simulation theory" of the nature of folk psychology, a tendency I share.

2. Alison Gopnik, "How we know our minds: The illusion of first-person knowledge of intentionality," *Behavioral and Brain Sciences*, 16 (1993) 1-14.

3. Gopnik does not agree that the child's last stages of learning folk psychology are part of the maturation of the brain. See note 8 to the article just cited. She thinks children all do just happen to be little scientists who come up with the same theory. For a defense of the natural selection of folk psychology as a biological adaptation in human beings, see George Graham, "The Origin of Folk Psychology" *Inquiry*, 30 (1987) 357-79. Graham notes that, for folk psychology to provide adaptive advantages to its adherents, it must constrain their theorizing to imputations not only of rationality, but also of similarity to the theorizers.

4. Peter Mitchell, *Introduction to Theory of Mind: Children, Autism, and Apes* (1997).

5. This note is only for those who studied formal semantics: A structure is an ordered sequence, consisting first of a set of objects, followed by a set of extensions of the properties and relations taken to be real and of interest. Of course, given a set of objects, set theory guarantees the existence of all subsets of them, all sets of pairs of them, all sets of triples of them, and so on. But only some of these are extensions of the properties and relations that define the structure. A model is a structure plus an interpretation of a language as meaning elements of the structure. The syntactic account of theories said that a theory is a set of sentences which are theorems in a particular theoretic language, and this language is interpreted in a model that identifies truths consistently, such that all the theorems are true and all the theory's rules of inference preserve truth. If all the truths of the model are expressed in theorems, the theory is complete relatively to that model. The semantic account eliminates the middle man of a language and its theorems and rules, and identifies a theory directly with a set of structures, i.e., the models minus the rules for interpreting the terms in a language. The structures in the set together "characterize," i.e., identify, the set of truths of the theory. The semantic account leaves open what form theories take in people's minds; it needn't be sentences.

Using the terminology in Hughes and Cresswell, *A New Introduction to Modal Logic* (1996) 40, the relation of a frame to a model in the semantics of modalities is analogous to the relation of a structure to a model. Frames contain elements not found in structures so that they can characterize the modalities. If theories are not extensional, the semantic characterization of them would refer to frames, not structures.

6. The position that I and many others take on the status of folk psychology as theory is criticized by Lynne Rudder Baker, *Explaining Attitudes: A Practical Approach to the Mind* (1995), ch. 3. She defines theory as that from which we can elicit "a reasonably comprehensive set of statements that meet the following conditions: (1) Sentences in the set purport to describe, explain, and predict phenomena in a certain domain and (2) they are subject to replacement in the relevant community—typically a disciplinary community that certifies the

epistemic credentials of the sentences" (p. 72). Her argument against the status of folk psychology as a generic theory targets her opponents' failure to prove that it meets the second condition. However, she concedes that it does! She then targets any attempt to extrapolate from its revisability to its wholesale replaceability (pp. 79f). We may wish her success in that polemic, but her case against folk psychology being a theory collapses with her own admissions on p. 79.

7. Aristotle, *Posterior Analytics*, I.1 (71a31ff). Since this trick could be played even against people's knowledge of axioms, Aristotle rightly notes that knowledge of axioms is to be taken in the *de dicto* sense.

8. R. C. Sleigh, "On a Proposed System of Epistemic Logic," *Nous* 2 (1968) 391-398, esp. 397n. Sleigh attributes the insight to J. Hintikka; see section XII of "Semantics for Propositional Attitudes," reprinted in Hintikka's *Models for Modalities* (1969). Kaplan also warns against this move in his article, "Quantifying In," in Davidson and Hintikka, eds., *Words and Objections.*

9. The thought experiment about to be developed is based on Keith Donnellan's reanalyses of Kripke's example of Leverrier, an astronomer, fixing the reference of the as-yet-undiscovered planet's name "Neptune" by way of an attributively used description, and of Kaplan's example of fixing the reference of the name "Newman I" by way of a demonstratively used description. The reanalyses occur in part III of his "The Contingent *A Priori* and Rigid Designators" (1977), reprinted in French, Uehling, and Wettstein, eds., *Contemporary Perspectives in the Philosophy of Language* (1979), 45-60. Donnellan tries to evoke the intuition that these ways of introducing names can generate beliefs that certain sentences using them express truths, but not *de re* beliefs about the things named. The Big Felix thought experiment, created by Stephen Schiffer, "Naming and Knowing," also in French *et al.*, 61-74, seeks to evoke the very opposite intuitions, but they're about the appropriateness of reports, whereas Donnellan's evokes intuitions about the beliefs reported on.

10. W. V. Quine, "Quantifiers and Propositional Attitudes" (1956), reprinted in his *The Ways of Paradox and Other Essays*, revised and enlarged edition (1976) 186.

11. This consequence was noted by Kripke in his "Naming and Necessity." He also claims that some necessary truths people can only know *a posteriori*, for example that Hesper is Phosphor. The necessary *a posteriori* can be *de re* knowledge, but the contingent *a priori*, being known only *a priori*, can only be *de dicto*. The thought is implicit in Russell's insistence on the identity of the propositions "Scott is Scott" and "Scott is Sir Walter," which we quoted in a note to section A. I return to the issue of which sort of entities the relational attitudes are directed toward, incomplete propositions versus complete singular propositions, in several of the following sections and especially in Part III, second subpart. Here I only note that the identification of a belief as relational depends partly on features of Belia's mind, not solely on the singular form of that which her belief is directed toward. Thus my call here for your intuition when you empathize with her.

12. Jeshion, R., "Acquaintanceless *De Re* Belief," in Campbell, J. K.,

O'Rourke, M., and Shier, D., eds., *Meaning and Truth: Investigations in Philosophical Semantics* (2001). For Jeshion's idea to work, she must deny the cogency of Donnellan's and our argument, which purports to show that never do proper names so introduced give one *de re* attitudes about the thing so named. In §3 of another article, "Donnellan on Neptune," *Philosophy and Phenomenological Research*, 63 (2001) 111-135, she makes the case for its noncogency this way: Donnellan did not exclude an analogy between stipulative reference fixing and the kind of case we imagined in section A, where a new relative of mine comes to have beliefs about me under two names. If she were to learn that Arthur and Sonny were the same person, she might say to me, "I did believe some awful things about you," thereby claiming *de re*-ness for her original belief. Jeshion claims, and I deny, that beliefs with names introduced by reference fixing stipulations can be similar enough to that situation to warrant a similar claim of *de re*-ness. Jeshion says

> there is no reason why [the structure of the Arthur-Sonny case] should fail to seem to be present [in the Sven case] unless one is antecedently committed to the idea that via the stipulative act, the stipulator attains no non-meta-linguistic *de re* belief at all. (p. 121).

Alas, what to me is simply the deliverance of a datum of intuition that the cases are disanalogous is to her a question-begging refusal of a datum of intuition that the cases are analogous. Put aside the analogy between her statement and the charge that we are either self-deceived or liars, which I hope she'd deny. Granted the flimsiness of any one intuition and its susceptibility to attack in this way, philosophical theories must look for many independent bases for support. Thus the case for our theory of *de re*-ness must collect those bases over the course of the next seven sections.

13. David Kaplan, "Dthat" (1978), reprinted in French, Uehling, and Wettstein, eds., *Contemporary Perspectives in the Philosophy of Language* (1979) 383-400. "Demonstrative use" of a description is defined on p. 389.

14. The quotation is from David Lewis, "Attitudes *De Dicto* and *De Se*," p. 155. I do not endorse all aspects of his theory of *de re* belief.

15. William James, "The Sentiment of Rationality" in his *The Will to Believe and Other Essays in Popular Philosophy* (1897).

16. David Lewis, "Veridical Hallucination and Prosthetic Vision," in his *Philosophical Papers* (1986), vol. 2, ch. 24.

# I. The Indispensability of Causal Rapport for Some Relational Attitudes

In the previous section we concluded that Rep's concurrence that a belief's about a real thing was not sufficient grounds for his introducing an about-position into his report of it. I asserted that, in the case of beliefs about things of the sort a person perceives, causal rapport with them is not just sufficient, but also indispensable, for her having a belief *de re* about them. I don't mean that all her relational beliefs require causal rapport with the things they are about. Over the course of the next six sections we'll survey her relational beliefs about a variety of things:

- concrete particular things (sections I-L).
  - those the believer perceives
  - those the believer does not perceive
- oneself and the present moment (sections M-N).
- abstract objects (section O).
- valued nonexistents (section O).
- God (section O).

A person's relational beliefs about at least three of the last four items won't depend on causal rapport with them. Therefore, when we define partial concurrence for the general case, causal rapport won't be indispensable. But causal rapport must be a consequence of the definition in the particular cases where causal rapport applies. So let's begin by defending its indispensability in the cases to which it applies.

## §1. Arguments for causal rapport as indispensable in a class of cases.

For relational beliefs about the concrete particulars, causal rapport with them is indispensable. What arguments can be given for this assertion? There are some, but they are what are called "inferences to the best explanation." That is, our argument points to phenomena that seem best explained by supposing the causal rapport. But inferences to the best explanation are instances of Bayes's theorem, which we used in section C, and so are only probabilistic arguments, in that the phenomena we consider might be explained by alternative hypotheses. Then the issue comes down to this: Which of the hypotheses is the least strained and most plausible account of the phenomena?

We must pit the causal rapport hypothesis against some competitors. To start with, consider any theory that says it's sufficient for having a *de re* belief about a thing that the believer express her belief with a singular term that denotes that thing. This theory amounts to saying that belief *de re* is nothing more than belief *de dicto* in a complete singular proposition. In contrast I've been claiming that a belief *de re* is belief directed toward an incomplete proposition, that's believed about things which (in a major case) the believer is in extensive causal rapport with.

The first argument to refute the complete singular proposition theory is this: There's the fact we noted in the last section, that Belia's belief, that the tallest Swede is a Swede, is not in the least a *de re* belief because she hasn't a clue who the tallest Swede is, even though she expresses her belief in terms of a singular term denoting him. She simply does not believe about him (or her!) the attribute of being the tallest Swede. She's only noting that since all Swedes are Swedes, the tallest one is too. The absence of her causal rapport with the tallest Swede can account for her belief not being *de re* about the one who happens to be the tallest Swede, but a theory that takes any singular term at all to generate a singular proposition and a belief *de re* about the thing denoted cannot. This failure refutes it.

A defender of the sufficiency of singular terms alone for *de re* belief might complain that "the tallest Swede" gets introduced in a way that belies its claim to being a singular term. It can be analyzed away in the manner that Russell recommended. (See section A.) The propositions it entered into are therefore not singular but general. Ok, but here's a second argument: In the previous section, there was our fourth step, Belia's belief that Sven is a Swede. This is a singular proposition, albeit one whose proper name was introduced solely by a reference fixing description. I suggested she could not think it, although she could believe true the sentence expressing it.

Here's the argument: Let's consider a singular term that the proponent of this theory will admit is a singular term: "Rep." We considered behavioral characterizations of belief and desire in section C, and discussed the reason why the characterization of belief should tie a person's belief state, belief in $p$, to the person's being in the state only if $p$ and because of $p$, at least in optimal conditions. In retrospect we see the characterizations stated in that section are not of *de re* beliefs or desires as we've been understanding them. But they do apply to *de dicto* beliefs and desires of singular propositions, if the sentence expressing $p$ contains a genuine singular term. Therefore, let the sentence contain the name "Rep." Recall that we were unable to specify behaviorally which of two singular propositions was the content of the belief because we could not also refer to an explanation why Belia was in the belief state she was in. We imagined her using the one sentence in two situations which are the same except for Belia's meaning for her terms. In one, her use of the name referred to Rep, but in the other her use of it referred to Jack. If we had not specified that she was in the belief state that *p* because of *p*, we could not've told which proposition her sentence expressed. So we've already seen an argument for causal rapport on the grounds that content is indeterminate without reference being made to the content's "because." And causal rapport is one kind of "because."

Other phenomena call for the indispensability of causal rapport for beliefs *de re* about the things people perceive, forcing the insufficiency of just the use of a singular term. Here's a third argument, one constructed by Thomas McKay.[1] Suppose Belia sees the woodchuck enter the bushes, and it is indeed a woodchuck. She believes *about* it that it's female. More than that *de re* belief, however, she believes *de dicto that* the woodchuck in the bushes is female. The phrase, "the woodchuck in the bushes" is a genuine singular term not open to the suspicions "the tallest Swede" aroused, and it denotes uniquely. Is the *de re* belief identical to that *de dicto* belief in a singular proposition? The story continues: Alas, the animal she saw run into the bushes was male, and it ran right out the other side of the bushes and is not in the bushes. But another woodchuck, which Belia never saw, is the only woodchuck in those bushes, and it is female. She tells Rep the woodchuck is female; he thinks not. To prove her point she hires an unemployed philosopher to photograph it if it comes out. She then leaves the scene. After a while she has a photograph of the woodchuck coming out, and it is female, but as we noted it's not the woodchuck that went in. Belia thinks she has confirmed her original and abiding belief in the femaleness of the woodchuck that was in the bushes. She has the evidence of a picture of a female woodchuck.

First let's be clear what the issue is. The issue is not the belief *de dicto*. We can concede that Belia out of sheer luck had a true belief *de dicto*, for the thing denoted in fact by the singular term is in fact female. Rep reports:

> Belia believes *that* the woodchuck that was in the bushes is female.

He also says, after seeing the photo,

> Belia's belief is true.

Our intuitions tell us that the original *de re* belief is false. Before the

woodchuck emerges for her portrait, Rep reports, to the intense irritation
of Belia:

> Belia believes *about* the woodchuck she mistakenly thinks is still
> in the bushes, that it is female.

He also says of this belief he's just reported,

> Belia's belief is false.

The falsity he's calling attention to is not the mistake referred to in the
about-position. It's an error in the that-clause. So it cannot be identical to
the *de dicto* belief of a true singular proposition. We say that what made
her *de re* belief false, independently of her *de dicto* belief being true, is
that her causal rapport was with the first of the two woodchucks, the male
one, and that was the one her *de re* belief was about.

Consider what our competitor theory says: Such a belief in a singular
proposition, the woodchuck in the bushes is female, suffices for having a
*de re* belief. (To mark this sense of *de re* belief, defined as belief in a
singular proposition, I put quotation marks around the term thus: "belief
*de re*.") Is the "belief *de re*" the one she formed when she saw the first
woodchuck run into the bushes? Is it a "belief *de re*" about the woodchuck
that ran in, and so false of it, or is it a "belief *de re*" about the woodchuck
that was photographed running out, and so true of it? We examined the
second alternative and found it not to be the *de re* belief, which is false.
Does Belia have, during the time before the female woodchuck's portrait
session, another "belief *de re*" besides the false one, a true one about the
female while it's still hidden in the bushes? The theory we're considering
suggests so, and the form of words used to express the "belief *de re*"
would mean that proposition, but what psychological motive is there to
think so? Perhaps these theorists will reply that such another "belief *de
re*" is needed to explain Belia's action of having a photograph taken of it.
The proximate reasons for, or causes of, her action are localized in her
mind, namely, the beliefs and desires residing there. The explanation of
her action begins with her intention in performing it: She intends to have
a photograph taken of the female woodchuck in the bushes. She'll tell us
as much. A sufficient condition for having that intention includes that she
believe the singular proposition that (according to this theory) the "belief
*de re*" would be directed toward, namely, the one expressed by "the
female woodchuck is in the bushes." *Voilà*; her action is explained . . .

Poorly explained. This theory wrongly says Belia's action carried out
her intention successfully. It supports Belia in her misconception of what
her intention was, and her misassessment of her success. Although she did
intend to photograph *a* female woodchuck, she did not intend to photo-

graph *that* female woodchuck; she intended to photograph the woodchuck she saw, which happened to be male, and she wanted it to turn out to be female. She did not succeed in photographing that one, but another one instead, one which would have fulfilled her wants of its being a female woodchuck, if it had been the one she intended to photograph. There are two conditions for success of her intention, getting the right individual and getting the right property. This competitor theory misses the condition that gets the right individual, the *de re* part. The obvious way to be consistent with the intuitions about Belia's mistakes is to establish the object that Belia intended to photograph, the *res*, by the causal rapport she had with it. That was just the first of the two animals.

In his defense, the theorist may charge that our criticism confuses causal explanation with appraisal, confuses a descriptive project with an evaluative one. He is noting the states of Belia's mind that cause her to do what she is doing. When it comes to assessing the success of various aspects of her actions, he can appeal to the false things Belia believes, such as "the animal that ran into the bushes is the woodchuck that's in there still." Indeed he can refer to the things she fails to believe, which therefore could not enter into a causal account of her actions but which are relevant for appraising their success or failure. He can extend the reach of his causal investigations outside the locality of Belia's mind to include the causal rapport she had with the first woodchuck and did not have with the second. The theorist thinks it a virtue of his theory that it cleanly separates description from evaluation. And we must admit that the very form we attribute to a *de re* attitude lends itself to the idea that there's an internal^ relation between causal explanation by way of the that-clause and appraisal of success by way of the about-position. In particular, there's no way to lock perceptions, beliefs, desires, and intentions into a cluster, not just in the sense of their operating together to effect the same action, but also their each being about the same particular objects, which the action is to act upon, if we don't take into account the less proximate causal factors that are not localized in the mind. The causal rapport is just such an unlocalized factor which identifies a cluster as being *de re* about the same particular objects. When we say an action's cause was such a *de re* cluster, we're describing it, and also setting up an evaluation of its success. Let's leave this matter unadjudicated for now; we return to it in section O.

A similar argument for showing the indispensability of relational propositional attitudes for explaining intentional action was developed by Steven Boër and Sean Crawford.[2] Crawford argues that relational attitudes are necessary to explain a person's deliberate interactions with things, as distinct from her accidental interactions with things. Let's review this fourth argument.

The reason Belia hired someone to wait for the woodchuck to emerge and photograph it, rather than photograph it herself, was that she was thirsty and couldn't wait around. So she went inside, and there on the table was a pitcher of lemonade. She poured herself a glass and drank it. Now Crawford alters the scenario: Suppose Belia was so thirsty that by the time she got to the house she was hallucinating. She hallucinated a pitcher of lemonade and a glass so vividly that she went through the motions of pouring lemonade from the pitcher to the glass, lifting it to her lips, drinking it, and uttering a long sigh of hallucinatory relief. The first scenario was Belia the perceiver. The second scenario was Belia the hallucinator. We might say the perceiver and the hallucinator went through the same motions.

To explain those motions, we look to Belia's beliefs and desires. Crawford is anxious to answer the following challenge from those who have no use for relational propositional attitudes: Since the motions are the same in the two scenarios, we may suppose the beliefs and desires are the same, which explain the motions. If so, since the beliefs and desires that explain the hallucination case can only be *de dicto*, there being no pitcher, lemonade, or glass for them to be about, then the beliefs and desires that explain the perceptual case must also be *de dicto* merely. The whole difference between the two cases is simply the presence of the pitcher, lemonade, and glass in the perceptual case and their absence in the hallu-cinatory case.

Boër and Crawford respond to this challenge by having us suppose another scenario, that the items were in fact present in the hallucinatory case, and Belia was just extraordinarily lucky with the hallucination she was having. This is the scenario of Belia the lucky hallucinator. There are still intuitive differences between what Belia does when she perceives the lemonade and what she does when she is a lucky hallucinator of lemonade. One is that as a perceiver she's justified in believing her action will succeed; as lucky hallucinator she believes she will succeed and indeed does, but is unjustified in her belief. A second difference is that as a perceiver she intentionally pours *that* lemonade from *that* pitcher into *that* glass, whereas as lucky hallucinator, although she actually pours *that* lemonade from *that* pitcher into *that* glass, she intended to pour the hallucinated lemonade from the hallucinated pitcher into the hallucinated glass. She only accidentally poured real lemonade from a real pitcher into a real glass. Boër focused on the first difference, Crawford on the second.

Perhaps the first difference can be accounted for without appeal to relational attitudes. But can the person who has no use for relational attitudes explain the second difference without resorting to relational attitudes? It seems not. Yet the difference can be explained. The lucky hallucinator simply does not have the relational attitudes which the perceiver has. The perceiver's beliefs, desires, and intentions are *about* the very things she acts upon; the lucky hallucinator's are not; she's simply lucky. Notional attitudes plus the presence of the objects referred to by the notional attitudes don't distinguish the intention of the perceiver and the absence of that intention in the lucky hallucinator and so cannot explain the difference. We revisit the issue in section O.

Again, however, the suspicion arises that the *de re* format posits an internal relation between causal explanations of actions and appraisals of whether or not they count as successes, and if successes whether they are accidental or predictable successes.

Despite its fending off challenges at least to respectable stand-offs, clearly more must be adduced in favor of the causal rapport hypothesis. The theory that *de re* belief is simply *de dicto* belief in a complete singular proposition, without regard to causal rapport on the occasion of belief-formation, can be amended: *De re* belief could be belief *de dicto* in a complete singular proposition, a belief prompted by causal rapport with its subject. That gives us a different *de dicto* belief in the first scenario we described, about Belia's mistaken identification of the sex of the animal she saw. It would be a belief in a false singular proposition, getting around our criticism and making us find another one. At this point I would ask the holder of the theory to prove that Belia has in mind a singular term for the animal. For nothing in our theory of *de re* belief as belief in incomplete propositions commits us to that—yet. This thought experiment is still open.

## §2. Extending the range of causal rapport.

Not only are there other competing theories, but the causal rapport theory needs further elaboration. For one thing, to attribute relational belief to Belia, it seems unmotivated to require the causal rapport to be direct and immediate, as it was when she saw the woodchuck, and as it would be if she had seen with her own eyes the Swede. If the underlying idea is the causal propagation of information about a thing from that thing, then surely direct perception is only one way that happens. It's time to look for other ways, and one of them will be testimony, so that *de re*-ness is transmissible by testimony. Let's then delineate our theory in this direction by pitting it against a second theory, this one requiring an excessively strict understanding of causal rapport as current direct unrestricted perceptual acquaintance. We may identify this theory with Russell's concept of knowledge by acquaintance with concrete particulars (section A).

The main argument against the Russellian view is to force all three of the adjectives, "current," "direct," and "unrestricted" to bloat until they explode. For would not a child who has a relational belief directly about an uncle have had it by listening to the man over a telephone, seeing him in a movie? Indirectness can bring people closer to something as well as allow greater remoteness. They can use magnifying glasses; they can use x-rays to see inside. Would not a child who has unrestricted acquaintance with her father have had it nonetheless if she were blind or deaf? Russell avoids the bloating of the adjectives by shrinking them: People can only be acquainted with those concrete particulars which are sense data. Many would take this extreme constriction as a *reductio ad absurdum*^ of this position. A similar attack can be launched against the adjective "current." Does not a person who currently has relational belief about something retain it while blinking, and in immediate memory? and in episodic memory an hour later? If not, when the person meets the thing again and learns something new of it, she cannot form a *de re* belief consisting of a conjunction of that which she's believed and that which she learns.

The proponent of the strict theory can bite the bullet and insist on the strictness, but I sense a doctrinaire and polemic motive. My intuitions in these cases support leniency. The proponent may concede the intuitions and yet draw the line at communication: The person who has *de re* beliefs by acquaintance cannot communicate the *de re*-ness of a belief which she communicates to someone who lacks the acquaintance. This we can say is the sensible weakening of Russell's position which leaves it in opposition to the position I advocate. Since I'm admitting that *de dicto* beliefs can be directed toward singular propositions, to parry with the point that people obviously communicate singular propositions inflicts no wound, for that's not to show they communicate *de re*-ness. So first let me elaborate what my theory would say. If it makes good sense, we'll see the thesis of *de re* incommunicability to be unmotivated.

If it's too much to require (*pace* Russell) perceptual acquaintance, how indirect may the causal rapport be? Very. Suppose Belia is convinced there's a tiny country on the Italian peninsula called San Marino. Belia reads in the newspaper—indirect causal rapport—that the chief of state of San Marino is bald. Belia is not perceptually acquainted with this man. Or is it a woman? She doesn't know, but she believes that the chief of state of

San Marino is bald. She tells everyone. Eventually the chief of state of San
Marino learns what Belia has been saying. He reports:

> Belia believes I am bald.

The ministers around him all mutter among themselves:

> Belia believes *about* that one there, the chief of state, *that* he is
> bald.

A logician present infers:

> There is someone whom Belia believes to be bald.

We are to interpret these reports, not as *de dicto* reports of belief in a
singular proposition, in the manner of Rep's report of Belia's belief about
Sven, the tallest Swede (at the end of the previous section), but rather as
*de re* reports.

If you think only *direct* causal rapport warrants this *de re* locution, the
ministers and the logician will seem to be formatting their report of Belia's
belief as if she were perceptually acquainted with the one about whom she
has this belief. But she isn't. They are the ones acquainted with the chief.
Did they misrepresent Belia's beliefs?

Whether the ministers were mistaken does not depend on whether
Belia's phrase "the chief of state of San Marino" is formed with the
attributive use of the definite article (a use described in section A and
referred to again in step 3 of my argument against the simple sufficiency-
of-concurrence theory in section H). It does depend on how disconnected
she was from the referent of the definite description when she formed it.
Belia believes there is *a* chief of state and no two are chiefs. If that general
belief were the sole basis for her use of the phrase "*the* chief of state," the
italicized article's use would be, yes, attributive, not creating a phrase
occupying a referential position in the fully analyzed proposition, but that's
not the central failure in failing to be *de re*; it's rather the lack of community she'd have with the referent. And the ministers' report would be
mistaken since they treat the phrase, yes, as if it should occupy a referential position, but again their more central mistake would be attributing to
her a community with the referent.

But in fact that's *not* how she acquired the phrase. She did not
construct it from beliefs about the existence and uniqueness of a chief. She
read it in a newspaper. That's how this belief differs from her belief about
Sven. In this case she was accepting the testimony of an eye witness to the
chief's baldness, let's say. The eye witness had a *de re* belief, which was
transmitted to Belia. We can call the underlying principle the **principle of
transmissibility of *de re* belief** about perceptible objects.[3] If you accept
another's *de re* belief, your belief is *de re* too, even if your new belief is

the first *de re* attitude you have about that perceptible particular which the other's belief is about. The principle's ground is simply intuition, and unfortunately one that Russell did not share. However much he changed his views on acquaintance, one view he seems never to have changed is the incommunicability of the propositions one believes based directly on acquaintance. At most you could get another to believe that your sentence expressed a truth, although the other's attitude would not be directed toward that true proposition. Militating against this view of Russell's, the causal rapport is the operative feature of acquaintance, and that feature is communicable, if you think of the communicator as continuing the causal propagation of the rapport by the act of communicating. The communicator is *ipso facto* a conduit for the causal rapport. So the receiver of the information believes an incomplete proposition about the same thing that the communicator believes the proposition about.

The same operative feature, the causality, underlies a principle of intrapersonal transmissibility of *de re* belief, a principle that's so obvious it goes without saying, namely the transmission of a person's *de re* belief from herself in the original perceptual situation to herself at later times, by way of her recalling it. Transmission through memory is just the continuation of the causal propagation of the rapport. The cross-person transmission is just the lengthening of the memory channel of propagation, which is just a within-person transmission. We should also admit that in both cases there is loss in the extensiveness of the causal rapport. Sometimes the loss can be severe enough to destroy the transmission of *de re*-ness. The process can be corrupted in humdrum ways, such as misstatement and misunderstanding in the interpersonal case and memory loss in the intrapersonal case.

We must admit disanalogy between the case of memory and the case of interpersonal transmission. In this latter case the transmission of *de re*-ness is not automatic even when there would be insignificant loss in the extensiveness of the causal rapport transmitted. Voluntary control enters into interpersonal transmission, once when the speaker decides to communicate and again when the listener decides to accept. The belief does not spread like a contagion from speaker to listener. The loss of *de re*-ness can be due to the choices by the parties to the transmission. The speaker, for example, may choose to utter a general sentence that fails to convey the *de re*-ness of the information. It seems that the speaker must use a singular sentence, one where the singular term is either a proper name, or a description used referentially, or a demonstrative term.

How then is *de re*-ness transmitted, when it is, considering that the vehicle of transmission is a complete singular sentence? Minimally the listener need only accept the sentence as true. If the sentence-acceptance is not merely a simple sort of credulity, then it's accompanied by a *de dicto* belief of the complete proposition which the singular sentence expresses. May not it be *de re* too, since the two formats are not mutually exclusive? One indication of the further transmission of *de re*-ness would be if the parties to the communication agree that there is something about which they share a belief. Again, it would indicate that there are two beliefs, the *de re* as well as the *de dicto*, if there's a behavior change in the believer consequent upon acquiring the *de re* belief, although the belief in the form of a complete singular proposition had been believed all along. Perhaps an example of what I mean is in the Bible, Job's conversion. Job believed all the complete singular propositions God had earlier communicated to him by scripture without God's appearing to him in person. Let's suppose these propositions included references to the behemoth and leviathan. We can imagine that his acceptance extended only to the *de dicto* versions. Then God appeared to him in person and communicated the same propositions, adding a touch of drama and severity. We can imagine that Job acquired from God the corresponding *de re* beliefs about the two animals, directed toward incomplete propositions with the same contents as the predicates of his earlier *de dicto* beliefs concerning them. For, if Job did acquire new beliefs, the change in his beliefs would explain this change in his behavior: Job tells God, "now my eye seeth thee. Therefore I reprehend myself, and do penance in dust and ashes" (42:5- 6). Those who don't believe the story should consider whether it suffices for our explanations that the change in Job was merely his taking himself to have acquired *de re* beliefs.

Incidentally, the story of Job's conversion also bears on the alternative analysis of relational belief, that it's just belief in complete singular propositions. Anyone inclined to that view will have no need of a principle of transmissibility of *de re* beliefs, since causal rapport enters their account only as relevant to how a belief is acquired and not at all relevant to the structure of the belief. My appeal to a principle of transmissibility will seem to them like damage control on behalf of a weaker theory. To counter this criticism, I look for a case of behavior-change without change of any of the beliefs or desires directed toward complete singular propositions. What then accounts for the change? None of the beliefs and desires countenanced in their theory, for those attitudes did not change. Suppose Job has many such *de dicto* beliefs and desires in which God and his creations are subjects, and yet he just whines and whines. Upon seeing God, he says, "With the hearing of the ear, I have heard thee: but now my eye seeth thee. Therefore I reprehend myself, and do penance in dust and ashes." In other words he acquires *de re* beliefs and desires directed toward incomplete propositions with content identical to that of the predicates of the complete propositions he already believes and desires, and they are *about* the one he's now in causal rapport with and about the things that one transmits causal rapport with via His testimony. These new attitudes are what account for his change of heart and behavior.

I conclude that, as long as the causal propagation of the speaker's rapport with the object of her belief keeps its integrity through the process of communication, the listener ends up with a *de re* belief. Part of what preserves the integrity of the process may be that the speaker and listener believe they are observing the canons for transmission of *knowledge*, whose preservation through communication requires that much more stringent standards be met.[4] But let's remind ourselves that the issue here is the transmission merely of belief, not knowledge. Even if the that-clause in a report of the transmitted belief were false of the object the belief is about, a *de re* belief would've been transmitted, albeit a false one.

We must deal with the objection that transmission of *de re*-ness does not depend on preservation of causal rapport. Let's give ourselves a choice at this point in the way we develop the story of Belia's San Marinoan beliefs, since some philosophers believe the importance of what's believed is relevant to classifying it as *de re*, not just the nature of its source. Consider importance to Belia: (I) She might be studying the connection of presidency and baldness. If the newspaper reporter had gotten the bald one's *title* wrong, Belia might admit error in her *de dicto* belief, that the chief of state is bald, negating the utility of her *de re* belief to her study. Although she no longer believes that the chief of state is bald, she persists in thinking she learned about someone's baldness, though no longer relevant or important to her study. Belia would say, "Well, whoever he was, he's bald." She'd have a true *de re* belief about the one the reporter saw but misidentified as San Marino's president. So Belia would be treating the newspaper's use of the description "the chief of state of San Marino" as referential (see section A, for the contrast between attributive and referential uses of descriptions). Nor was she using her definite article attributively, but referentially in her "the chief of state of San Marino" to refer to the bald one. The loss of the information's importance to her didn't change that. (II) Alternatively, presidency may be entirely incidental to Belia's belief. So the falsity of her *de dicto* belief may leave the importance of her *de re* belief unaffected. Our considerations of cases I and II concerning importance have not proven that considerations of importance affect whether the ministers were mistaken in the *de re* way they reported her belief when she based it on another's testimony.

Summing up the San Marino thought experiment: Belia can be acquainted with not only what she herself perceives, but others can acquaint Belia with what they perceive. In other words, Belia can become acquainted with an object through perceiving it or receiving the testimony of others who perceived it. Since eye witness testimony did lead Belia to believe in the baldness of San Marino's chief of state, the ministers correctly formatted their report with an about-position. The definition of acquaintance in terms of extensive causal rapport (in section H) is broader in just the way needed to include hearing the testimony of other seers.

Perhaps we need to broaden even further the concept of a *"de re"*-warranting transmission of information about *res* by way of an intermediary to include some inferences from random samples to properties of the population sampled. If Belia elicits information from many citizens, chosen randomly from the citizenry of San Marino, she has *de re* beliefs about each and about the sample group as a whole. The latter beliefs she generalizes to the entire citizenry of San Marino. If she believes *about* the sample as a whole, that a majority of them think their chief of state is bald, then does she, by inference, believe *about* the citizenry as a whole, that a majority of them think their chief of state is bald? Or does she only have a *de dicto* belief about the citizenry as a whole? More generally, Belia often projects from her present experience to what will be true in the future. Does that inference warrant *de re* beliefs about future beings? If by her San Marino generalization she gets *de re* beliefs but not by a generalization to future beings, is it only because Rep concurs in the existence of the citizenry of San Marino, but does not concur in the existence of the future beings? Whether Rep has anything to do with Belia's belief being relational is the subject of the next section. (I'm not now settling the relationality of beliefs by induction, but in step 2 of the argument in section H I noted that contradiction threatens us if we admit *de re* beliefs generated by inductive generalization. See section L for a solution to the threatening contradiction which gives me more reason not to extend *de re* beliefs to include inductive generalizations.)

### §3. Consequences of the stricter definition of partial concurrence for reports.

I take it that I've now motivated our acceptance of section C's first definition of partial concurrence, which requires of Rep, before he attributes a *de re* attitude to Belia about concrete particular things, that he concur that she is in causal rapport with them. The next question is whether *he* must be in causal rapport with them in order to report Belia's attitudes.

He need not be. Whether or not he is in rapport with them might affect how he refers to them in the about-position of his reports. He might be in rapport with them, and in all the woodchuck scenarios we considered he has been perceptually in rapport with the animals. His rapport was independent of Belia's. Alternatively, he might be put into rapport with a concrete thing by Belia herself transmitting her *de re* beliefs to him. Rep may accept, and be right to accept, that she sees something he doesn't see. The believer-reporter relation is no exception to the principle of the transmissibility of *de re* belief. The concurrence might just be an instance of transmission, although it need not be. Rep might engage in a round-about inferential process that blocks Belia's transmissions, on the basis of which he concurs that Belia's in rapport with something or other. But he demurs on the truth of just about everything else in her belief about it. In that case he has no rapport with the object of her belief. He must use a general phrase in his about-position. For example:

Belia believes about some animal hereabout that it's female.
Despite the fact that Rep's about-position refers generally to something he's not in rapport with, he's attributing a *de re* belief to Belia in accord with our first definition of partial concurrence, which requires him to attribute causal rapport to her.

### §4. Another alternative to the causal rapport theory: Socrates's dominance theory.

The logic of our argument in this section has been Bayes's theorem, which pits alternative hypotheses against each other. You'd rightly criticize the argument for causal rapport so far as weak, due to a dearth of competing hypotheses about the nature of *de re* attitudes. We only considered two, something weaker (complete singular propositions) and something stronger (Russellian acquaintance). Here's another, which is different in a creative way. It's a development of Donnellan's idea of a referential use of a description, something we just referred to in treating of Belia's use of the description, "the chief of state of San Marino."

One could characterize the kind of theory I've presented so far as "separationist." Surely I could not've posited a sharper cleavage between the about-position in Rep's control and the that-clause in Belia's control. They're not so separable that there can be an about-position without a that-clause; we precluded that possibility in section B, by arguing that all attitudes are propositional. Nevertheless, might there not be a more integrative approach than mine? Perhaps Rep controls the about-position only because Belia grants him permission to control it, in the way that a person who uses a definite description referentially expects the listener to disregard incidental error in the description, so that the intended referent is picked out. For example, perhaps the bald person was not the chief of state after all. Well, whatever he is, he's bald. In section A we introduced referential uses with the example of Belia telling Rep at a party that the guy with the water glass was rude to her. Rep knows that the guy is well into a triple martini on the rocks and disregards Belia's error about what he's drinking. That's the guy she believes she was insulted by. Rep has interpreted her exactly as she intended. The **dominance theory of partial concurrence** generalizes this situation. It's that the believer can have intentions that her own conceptions of the things she has beliefs about can be *overridden, dominated* in her attitudes by the truth, if her conceptions of them contain error, with the effect that her attitudes still succeed in being about them, despite herself. These intentions, which may be explicit and *ad hoc* or tacit and standing intentions, are a necessary^ condition for any rapport she has to count as the relationality of her attitudes, and the intentions, along with the rapport, warrant the report's about-positions, which are transparent.[5] If the intention were made explicit, it would be a *de dicto* declaration (*de dicto* except for the reference to herself) that her beliefs are about whatever is real, as distinct from what seems real, and her desires are about whatever is good, as distinct from what seems good. That kind of *de dicto* declaration of intention by Belia warrants Rep to report her beliefs and desires in a *de re* format. The link, forged by the appearance-reality distinction, is surprising. (In two paragraphs I'll weaken the theory's reliance on intentions, whether declared or tacit.)

If the dominance theory is correct, much of my theory of relational attitudes can be conformed to it. In particular, our procedure of regimentation still works in its entirety. The central point that the that-clause of a relational belief is an incomplete sentence holds; the beliefs would be directed toward incomplete propositions. Our characterization of Rep's partial concurrence would change, however. To report a relational attitude Rep would concur in the reality of the thing Belia's attitude was about and would note that *his concurrence is made relevant by the fact that she cedes the dominance in her attitude of the way the thing actually is over her conceptions of that thing.* Acquaintance and causal rapport would not be part of the definition of partial concurrence. The scenario of causal rapport might have less to do with Belia than it would with Rep, contrary to what I just said in the previous subsection. For when Belia gives Rep permission to control the about-position, she licences him to use *any* information concerning her to decide what thing is the referent to be named in the report's about-position, but he's otherwise free to name it any way he thinks to be in accord with the facts. *It just happens that her causal rapport with objects is often good information for Rep to use*, both to determine her referent and to determine the facts of the situation.

We owe the dominance theory to the classicist, Terry Penner, who found it in Plato's early "Socratic" dialogues. He attributes the dominance theory to Socrates. Although Socrates was concerned with identifying the object of any desire, claiming it's something actually good, his and Penner's theory generalizes to all the attitudes. It's as if, when Belia cedes control of the about-position of an attitude, that is, when she acknowledges the relationality of her attitude, then, if the attitude's a belief, she cedes control to the truth and, if the attitude's a desire, she cedes control to the good. Rep is merely the viceroy of truth and goodness. Just as he would report her seeing rather than looking, if her visual state met a success condition, so he reports her attitudes relationally rather than notionally, if her attitude meets a success condition for aboutness.

Although Plato reported Socrates's theory, he came to reject it,[6] and Aristotle surely did, thus ensuring its eclipse.  We're going to try to salvage it. First, we finagle by specifying that the dominance theory is about the concurrence governing an about-position. (I cannot say that Penner or Socrates acknowledge any distinction between aboutness and directed-towardness, which my version of their theory presupposes.) Then we generalize it not only to other attitudes besides desire but to more primitive attitudes along lines suggested by Naomi Reshotko.[7] Perhaps, instead of positing intentions, however tacit, we should consider Belia's concession to the true and the good to be her default position, which she must countermand in order to be taken as having purely *de dicto* attitudes. One consequence of taking this concession as the default position of any organism with attitudes is that the relational attitudes are more primitive than the notional ones, since only the more developed minds can counter-mand the concession. It's not that the world takes charge of ensuring the referential success by the believer's leave, as we suggested when we introduced the theory by analogy to descriptions used referentially. Rather the world *is* in charge of the referential success of all attitudes until minds wrest control from it. The first lingual members of the human species, and each child since, had to take command of the subject positions of their beliefs by deploying some sophisticated referential weapons. Even when people bravely assert control, they often fall back on the earlier ways, as in the referential use of description, like insecure adolescents, which is what human beings are in the objective order of things. I'll postpone further discussion of this insight into evolution until section N, where I introduce the concept of "concerning-positions."

The idea that belief has success conditions, namely, being about something and being true of that thing, is obvious. Failing the second it's false, and failing the first it's not even relational. The idea that desire also has success conditions is controversial. Failing one the desire's not fulfilled, and failing the other it's not even about that which is actually good. We already noted that explanation of action pushes us to the idea of locking beliefs and desires into a cluster having the same referents. The same dynamic will push us to the idea of desires being about the actual good. I'll postpone further discussion of this interesting application of dominance theory to desire until section O.

I already conceded at the beginning of this section that causal rapport won't explain the relationality of several areas of relational beliefs. So perhaps the dominance theory is not so much a competitor as a useful generalization. Before deciding whether that's so, we must eliminate an unfortunate feature of this theory, one that threatens even causal rapport theory. If Belia is ceding control to truth, not just to the empirical mode of reaching the truth (which is what causal rapport is), then might she not also countenance referential uses of descriptions that cannot be cashed out in terms of perceptual acquaintance or more extended forms of causal rapport? Might she not even countenance Kaplan's demonstrative use of a description, mentioned in section H? Indeed, does anything constrain what can count as a relational attitude according to the dominance theory? Quine thinks that's a problem even with the constraint of causal rapport.

# Notes

1. Thomas McKay presented the form for this scenario in his "Actions and *De Re* Beliefs," *Canadian Journal of Philosophy* 14 (1984) 631-635. My "female woodchuck" substitutes for "F" and "saltshaker" in his examples.

2. Steven E. Boër, "Neo-Fregean Thoughts," in James Tomberlin, ed., *Philosophical Perspectives*, vol. 3 (1989), and Sean Crawford, "In Defence of Object-Dependent Thoughts," *Proceedings of the Aristotelian Society*, vol. 98 (1998) 201-210. Crawford writes in response to Harold W. Noonan, who wrote in response to Boër among others. See Noonan's "Object-dependent Thoughts and Psychological Redundancy," *Analysis*, 51 (1991) 1-9.

3. Kent Bach develops a principle of transmission of *de re*-ness that does not depend on the descriptions transmitted in his *Thought and Reference* (1987) 31ff. Thomas McKay also states the principle in his "Names, Causal Chains, and *De Re* at Beliefs" in James Tomberlin, ed., *Philosophical Perspectives*, vol. 8, Logic and Language (1994) 293-302. The name of the principle is mine.

4. See Peter J. Graham, "Conveying Information," *Synthese*, 123 (2000) 365-392, for a discussion of conveying knowledge, as distinct from merely conveying belief. His term, "Information-based belief" is close to my use of "*de re* belief."

5. Terry Penner and C. J. Rowe, "The Desire for Good: Is the *Meno* Inconsistent with the *Gorgias*?" *Phronesis* 39 (1994) 1-25.

6. Plato rejects it for appetitive desires in the *Republic*, bk. 4 (438a-439a) but accepts it for rational desires in bk. 6 (505d).

7. Naomi Reshotko, "A Reply to Penner and Rowe" *Phronesis* 40 (1995) 336-341.

# J. If Reports of Relational Belief are Context-sensitive, Are They Unscientific?

I announced in section H a sufficiency-of-rapport theory of *de re* beliefs about ordinary objects, and a sufficiency-of-concurrence theory of *de re* reports of the beliefs conditional on their being already *de re* beliefs. In the previous section we stated the whole extent of Rep's concurrence in the case of beliefs about perceptible objects: He must concur in two respects. (Recall the distinction made in section C between two definitions of partial concurrence.) My theory implies he not only must concur that what Belia believes refers to real things, but also must concur, in the case of ordinary things, that the causal dependence of her belief-states on the things is such as to constitute extensive causal rapport with them. For Rep must make a judgment about that rapport, namely, whether her belief state is *de re* or not, depending on her causal rapport, before he can report *de re* her belief or only report it *de dicto*. Let's henceforth accept the more complex definition (1) of partial concurrence stated in section C:

> In making *de re* reports of beliefs about ordinary things Rep concurs not only in the reality of the things Belia's beliefs were about, but also that she was in causal rapport (i.e., acquainted) with them.

## §1. The indexicality of relational reports.

Rapport must figure in concurrence. Rapport was somewhat loosely defined, using vague words like "extensive" and "reliable" in section H, and we've been making it looser by allowing forms of indirect rapport. Are the standards of extensiveness and reliability in the definition of causal rapport absolute enough to yield a notion of extensive causal rapport that's objective enough for science to find useful? If so, we'd expect that any reporter of *de re* beliefs would use the standards to determine his concurrence in the fact that they do hold. If we find instead that reporters vary their standards to suit the demands of their purposes in communicating, that would be evidence that there's no objective notion of extensive causal rapport.

Quine suggests that rapport is simply an **indexical** notion. Indexical notions, including verb tenses and the words "I," "now," and "here," get their referents on any occasion of their use from the very context of their use, by way of a rule of reference fixing. An utterance of the word "I" refers to the utterer; an utterance of "now" refers to the time when it's uttered; an utterance of "here" refers to the place where it's uttered. The demonstratives "this" and "that" are pointer words whose reference on any occasion is the thing then pointed to, relatively to the purposes of the communication which disambiguate the pointing. Distinguish the reference fixer of a particular use of an indexical pronoun from the pronoun's meaning. One cannot substitute for an utterance of "I" the phrase which fixed its referent, namely, "the utterer of this utterance of 'I'," as one should be able to, if the two were the same in meaning. For the pronoun is a rigid designator, whereas the description is not. Thus it's false that

        I might not have been me,

but true that

        I might not have been the utterer of that utterance of "me."

We noted the difference between a meaning and a reference fixer in section A.

The term "indexical" comes from C. S. Peirce's theory of signs.[1] We use the term more restrictedly than he did. Peirce contrasted the indexical pronouns with the anaphoric ones, calling the latter degenerate indices, in that the fully functional indexicals are tied to their referents directly by the rules for the fixing of their reference, whereas anaphoric pronouns are tied to their referents only indirectly by first referring back to another sign. It's better, however, to see anaphoric and indexical pronouns as fundamentally different types of signs, and we won't restrict our use of the term "indexical" to just pronouns. Any concept, which the language associates with a rule that assigns it a definite referent or extension *by reference to the occasion of its use*, is indexical. An example of an indexical relation, which Peirce gives, is one thing's being to the right of another. The spatial perspective of the speaker fixes the extension of the property of being to the right of something. The tenses of verbs are also indexical, depending as they do on the temporal perspective of the speaker.

Indexical concepts are not *ipso facto* vague or ambiguous ones. The pronoun "I" is not ambiguous just because both you and I can use it. When you use it, it cannot mean me. Nor is the word "now" ambiguous because you can use it today, tomorrow, and a year from now. On any one use it refers to the time of its use. The appeals to context in the case of indexicals are built into the language as rules; in contrast, in the case of reducing ambiguity and vagueness, the appeals to context are made at our discretion as part of our skill as conversationalists. For instance, how extensive a duration is intended when people use the word "now"? The word is vague to the extent that the question is left unanswered. We see that its vagueness is separate from its indexicality. Is now to be this hour or this minute? The rule associated with its indexicality forbids any unit of time other than those that include the time of its utterance. Other features of the context of its use help cut down on the remaining vagueness somewhat. Is the distinction between the two appeals to context as sharp as I've drawn it, or is it itself vague? To the extent that it is vague, to that extent the border between indexical notions and vague notions is vague. My impression is that Quine exploits *this* vagueness in his argument against relational belief.

Let's apply the notion of indexicality to relational belief. Back when we discussed regimenting thing-attitudes as propositional attitudes, we noticed (at the end of section B) that the propositions we came up with in those regimentations always had indexical components. "Belia wants a sloop" became "Belia wants that *she herself* have a sloop." She'd say, "I want a sloop." Like the pronoun in her sentence, her attitude's an indexical one, although we did not use the word "indexical" then. We used "egocentric." Sections M and N are devoted to the indexical attitudes.

But Quine now calls our attention to a different indexicality present in the relational attitudes: Although "extensive causal rapport" is not a word we use in reports of belief, that concept underlies the use of the phrase "believes *about*." So the question is whether the phrase "believes *about*" is also indexical. Is the correct use of this phrase indexed to features of the circumstance of its use, so that it would be correct in one context to report Belia's belief relationally, but not correct in another context to report that same belief relationally? If so, what does that show about the belief reported on? Presumably, that it's not intrinsically one or the other. Such a result would be bad news for my defense of the scientific utility of relational attitudes.

In looking at reports to discern something about beliefs, we're back to the technique of semantic ascent. In subsection §2 I'll consider an apparently proper case of a *de re* report of a belief that could itself be a *de re* belief only by the wildest stretch (Burdick's police report). The case purports to refute the principle I laid down at the end of section H, which was that only the objectively *de re* beliefs may be reported *de re*. Bad news for my project, if I cannot undermine it.

An alternative but equivalent expression of the indexicality problem is this: The problem with belief is whether the opacity or transparency of different parts of a relational report is a **context-dependent** feature or an invariant one. (For example, the meanings of "small" and "large" are not invariant, but depend on their context, namely, the words they modify: Small whales are large animals, but large mice are small animals.) Extrapolating beyond verbal context, Rep makes his report in a certain social context. By "context" in this context I mean the whole environment in which Rep makes his report, his purposes and beliefs, and those of the ones he reports to. A context-dependent property of anything is not an objective property of it but rather one that exists by social conventions associated with speech. I'll not quibble with Quine over the difference between indexicality and context-dependency. Indexical words are associated with rules of the language that fix the words' meanings. Context-dependent words are associated with conversational rules for fixing their meanings. Thus the difference between the two is like the difference between entailment and conversational implicature, which we noted in section E. Since we there ran the two together in our regimentation, it gains me nothing to insist on Quine's not running indexicality and context-dependency together here.

If the referential transparency of some parts of a *de re* report is a context-dependent property of the report, so are exportation and generalization in relational reports. Then the distinction between the two kinds of belief is not a matter that logic can settle by examining a report's logical form alone, for that would be determined by the report's context, not the belief. If we did manage to regiment the relational reports, we'd be stuck with saying of a logical rule that it sometimes applies validly to these reports and sometimes not. But that's illogical.

This indexicalization of a believer's causal rapport to the context of the reporter's report is the problem that led Quine in 1977 to give up his theory of the about-position in reports of relational belief and the whole project of making *de re* belief respectable for science.[2] He decided that relational belief was too sensitive to the context of reporting the belief for the purpose of determining the reporter's concurrence with the believer. It was so sensitive that no universal procedure could be stated for deciding whether a belief is to be regimented as a relational belief, no way of dichotomizing precisely on formal grounds, and thus relational belief was beyond salvaging for any scientific purpose. Philosophers just have to rest content with notional belief as the only kind of belief that might be scientifically valuable. He extended his new view to all attitudes, so that even perceiving and remembering are notional only.[3] I explain this in section T.

I think Quine's post-1977 reason for giving up relational attitudes was insufficient, and I'll defend his theory of 1956-1977 against him. It's odd enough that perceiving and remembering *de re* are done away with for the serious purposes of science. Concerning belief in particular, he and we must do justice to its features. We saw in section H the inappropriateness of Rep using the *de re* format for Belia's "tallest Swede" beliefs. The inappropriateness of Rep's using an about-position cannot be blamed on features of the context of his reporting, such as what purpose his report is going to be used for. If it could be, in some context of reporting Rep would be justified in reporting, of Belia just as she was described in section H, that there's a certain person whom Belia believes to be a Swede. Can you describe such a context? I've tried, but it always turns into a joke. Quine need not be supposing that the concept of extensive causal rapport is so malleable, however. It need not stretch to fit this limiting case in some extreme context of communication and so erase the very distinction between the two kinds of belief. No.

For Quine, the distinction remains, but stays vague, to be made precise, now one way now another, only by speakers depending on the context of their discourse about people's mental states. As he says, (understanding his phrasing "knowing who or what" as doing roughly the work of our extensive causal rapport people have with the person or thing they know):

> I conclude that the requirement that distinguishes de re from de dicto, namely knowing who or what, is a function of the contextual situation and not a general distinction. This classifies it with the indexicals; also with necessity and possibility, according to my view of them. The indexicals and necessity and possibility are convenient in daily discourse, to the point of virtual indispensability; and we may say the same of propositional attitudes de re, notably [the format exhibited by the sentence, "There are some whom Ralph believes to be spies,"] while admitting none of these idioms to absolute or nonindexical scientific discourse.[4]

Quine is not saying that there's no phenomenon of belief *de re*; that it's a chimaera, an artifact of our ways of talking. Rather, it's altogether too many phenomena, or a range of phenomena so ill defined that we may pick and choose among alternative ways of rendering it precise, depending on what our purposes are in talking.

Quine and others have said that the importance of the informational content of Belia's belief, to Rep and the ones he reports to, is what Rep must attend to in order to judge whether the causal rapport is extensive enough. If it's extensive enough by the criterion of importance, that all by itself entitles him to use the *de re* reporting format. Since importance to the reporter and his audience varies with the context of reporting, of course no principled division between the two kinds of reports of belief could be drawn then. So the method of semantic ascent would yield no sharp distinction between two kinds of beliefs, except perhaps clear-cut extreme cases of each kind.

Quine underwrites his intuitions about individual cases by adopting the **knowing-who-or-what** criterion for the *de re* format:

> A reporter may refer to an object of someone's belief in an about-position if and only if the believer knows who (or what) it is.

The criterion embodies a powerful prejudice that whether a belief is relational or not depends more on the knowledge that's in the believer's mind than on the events that occur in the world, as the criterion of causal rapport would have it. What counts as such knowledge is sensitive to the contexts of reporting; therefore, according to the criterion, so is the *de re* form of reporting. To defend the alternative criterion of causal rapport from excessive sensitivity to the context of reporting, we'll have to dissociate it from the knowing-who-or-what criterion and weaken the cognitivist prejudices that support the latter. We'll do that in the last two sections of this Part.

## §2. A defense of the fixity of meaning of the concept of relational attitudes.

There's a semantical importance and a psychological importance. We can put the contrast in kinds of importance in this way: What's the more important aspect of Belia's belief state in a context of reportage? Is it its semantic aspect, namely its referential success, or is it its aspect that enables the report's hearers to explain, predict and influence Belia's behavior? There seems to be a trade-off between these two aspects. The more we emphasize the one, the less is left in the report for the other purpose.[5] For when we emphasize the about-position we are deemphasizing what's in her mind that refers to the things named in the about-position. In other words, the context of reportage determines the primacy of the semantical or the primacy of the psychological in the report.

Quine's critique depends on the primacy of the psychological, for context-sensitivity seems most plausible there. Other philosophers agree with Quine more or less. Burdick agrees that the precising conditions are contextual; he does not agree that there are two reporting formats, at least not two such that one obeys the laws of logic and one does not.[6] Stich also has argued that the distinction in types of reports does not reveal two kinds of belief. It reveals only ways reporters have of weighting the respects and degrees of resemblance between the belief states they are reporting on and what their own belief states would be if they were in the believer's shoes (that is, if they were on the same avenues of causal rapport).[7] He thinks this weighting is determined solely and vaguely by the context of the reporting and not by reference to the believing reported on. On the side of less agreement with Quine, despite a legitimate expectation created by Quine's citing Boër and Lycan's study in depth of the knowing-who-or-what criterion, they don't use the criterion to make the distinction between *de dicto* and *de re* beliefs, for they think that would make the beliefs more context-sensitive than the facts would warrant![8] They don't use causal rapport either, and for the same reason that it's too sensitive to contexts of reporting. Although they deploy a distinction like my distinction of semantical versus psychological, they don't see that the contexts that force the semantical considerations to be primary might cut down the excess sensitivity of causal rapport to contexts or deliver a concept of a serious context.

Are the post-1977 Quine, Burdick, and Stich right in supposing Rep provides a condition for Belia's *de re* belief, simply because he provides a necessary condition for a *de re* report? Let's try one more case, this from Burdick.[9] In this case Belia has causal rapport that's not only indirect but also *merely potential* rapport. By potential rapport I mean the rapport does not exist, but Belia and Rep know in advance that the rapport could be established easily. How easily, like how directly, must it be establishable, in order for the report to be *de re*, and for the belief itself to be *de re*? Consider: Belia's a bank executive who opens the bank in the morning and notes a robbery occurred. She knows that the hidden cameras are working and they survey the whole area of the bank; surely the robbers have been photographed. Rep is a policeman taking down her statement. May he report that Belia believes *de re* about individuals whose pictures are on the as-yet-undeveloped film, that they robbed the bank?

I doubt the sufficiency of potential rapport. After all, getting a library card or a club membership increases one's potential rapport without automatically increasing one's *de re* beliefs. On the other hand, suppose the bank hires Sherlock Holmes to crack the case. Two days later at 8 a.m. near the lockers in the railway station, a cleverly disguised Holmes expects the robbers to make their drop within the next 3 minutes. Of course he's right. Does he have a *de re* expectation, albeit one based only on potential rapport? Watson thinks it must be so. If so in Holmes's case, why not in Belia's?

But that's not the question most at issue, when we ask whether Rep may report that Belia believes *de re* about the individuals whose pictures are on the film, that they robbed the bank. The issue is rather this one: Is the answer to that question determined more by Rep's being a policeman trying to solve a robbery than by Belia's state of mind? The issue is whether there's an objective distinction between cases involving causal rapport and those not involving it, or whether the borderline cases vindicate Quine's position that the whole distinction is context-dependent and not objective.

It may seem reasonable to you to suppose that the policeman, Rep, does use the *de re* format to report Belia's belief even though her rapport is potential merely:

> Belia believes *about* the photographed individuals *that* they robbed the bank.

If Rep's relational report is legitimate, and relational reports may only be given of relational beliefs (as we concluded at the end of section H), Belia's belief is relational too. It seems, however, that the conditions of the reporting are more determinative of this result than the conditions Belia herself was in. To see this, change the reporting conditions somewhat: Belia is on the witness stand in the trial of the robbers. Let's grant that the accused are the ones photographed by the bank cameras and the jury receives the evidence for this before Belia takes the stand, and let's grant that her testimony does not count as eye-witness testimony against the robbers, since she did not perceive them. Nevertheless, may the account of the trial record the beliefs she testifies to as being *about* the accused (as an eye-witness's testimony would)? No; potential or indirect rapport *does not count* toward a report's being relational in this juridical context of reporting. So one and the same event of believing may be reported relationally in one context and in another context must not be so reported.

What can we say about this argument from semantic ascent against the scientific status of relational belief? I think all it shows is a failure of the technique of semantic ascent to reveal the phenomenon *in this case*. From the fact that semantic ascent in this case does not indicate a sharp and context-free distinction between the two kinds of belief, to conclude there is none—that's the fallacy of arguing from ignorance. Recall the remark of David Lewis that I quoted in section E; it's most apt at this point:

> if you hope to understand the folk psychology of belief by studying the linguistic phenomenology of ordinary belief sentences, you're in for big trouble.

If we keep semantic ascent subservient to our overall examination of evidence, we can stay out of trouble. We must look at *serious contexts*. In particular, I think the courtroom context does introduce strict proprieties for reporting *de re*; it's as if the jurors were the first non-eye-witnesses allowed to come to believe relationally about the accused individuals that they did or did not do the things they are accused of. For example, the jury in the trial of Timothy McVeigh for bombing the federal office building in Oklahoma in 1995 converted their beliefs about the perpetrator from *de dicto* to *de re* about him upon reaching their verdict. The judge, addressing the accused, reports *de re*, "the jury found *you* guilty." I think that the serious consequences of trials have forced even on common usage a greater fidelity to the phenomenon itself of relational belief. Thus I do think the technique of semantic ascent has more to show us about the phenomenon of relational belief, if we distinguish serious from nonserious contexts of reporting, and the next two sections are devoted to extracting that extra.

I'd like to define a serious context for reporting as one in which a *de re* report is appropriate only if the belief reported is *de re*. Nevertheless, a point on the other side of the debate is that the seriousness of the courtroom is not decisive. Rather, it happens to be a context of reportage which establishes the primacy of the semantic (i.e., referential success) over the psychological (explanation of Belia's behavior). Other serious contexts could weight the psychological over the semantic. Very well; we must look for semantically serious contexts, such as the courtroom example. It has a dynamic feature: At the beginning the *de re* form of report is simply not allowed. Then later, as a result of evidence, the jurors may come to such beliefs. They don't cease to have *de dicto* beliefs when they come to have *de re* ones. That's simply a datum a theory of relational belief must explain. We'll develop a theory that does that in the next two sections. The psychological and the semantical may be contemporaneous concerns, and the psychological may not diminish in importance as the semantical grows. Any rebuttal of my position is weak, if not just fallacious, that would move from the susceptibility of reports for serving the psychological purposes of audiences to the conclusion that the phenomenon of relational belief cannot be pinned down. That would be another case where semantic ascent would be overplayed in philosophical arguments.

A second issue is whether indexical elements are legitimately part of an objective science of psychology. Quine sees strictures against indexicality in science: Indexical sentences figure only in a science's statements of its evidence, measurements, and its technological applications, not in its statements of theory or in its atlas of the world or chronicle of the world's history except as an eliminable convenience. The strictures are appropriate for physical science. What about the special sciences of the human way of life? These sciences may have for their goals theorizing about indexical phenomena, including the delineation of the range of values of the indices, so that their theories may be applied to social policy. That which is about indexicals need not require indexicals for its expression, however. In particular, the kind of psychology we're about to develop need not. It can mention them without using them. Thus we may accept the strictures Quine sees and still maintain the scientific respectability of *de re* attitudes.

## §3. Fake *de re* reportage.

In view of these results it seems reasonable for us to assume we can distinguish genuine from the fake *de re* reportage that occurs in unserious contexts. We may do this by reserving another mode of reporting for the generic case of superficial *de re* reportage, where only the simpler definition (2) of partial concurrence applies, which is less specific than definition (1), referred to at the beginning of this section. The generic mode of reporting will be the passive voice format:

> *x* is believed by Belia to be F.

Ordinary speech treats this passive voice as equivalent to the active voice with an about-position. But let's reserve it for Rep to make evident which definition of partial concurrence he's following. When he uses this passive voice form, he registers nothing about Belia's rapport, and he does not imply the active voice form. His report is generically *de re*, whether or not Belia's belief is, since the subject position is purely referential. Rep could've reported Belia's *de dicto* belief directed toward the singular proposition that Sven's a Swede, using this superficial *de re* format, since Rep believes Sven exists, and he'd be obeying our rules of regimentation:

> Sven Svenson is believed by Belia to be a Swede.

Since we're regimenting a distinction where ordinary speech recognizes no distinction, it's easy to confuse this superficial *de re* reportage with the genuine report where Rep avails himself of the fact that the about-position is purely referential, and he uses a name there that Belia would object to.[10] For example, at the beginning of section E we supposed Belia made a mistake about the animal she saw run into the bushes:

Belia believes about the skunk that it's a woodchuck.

Rep's report is still genuinely *de re*, in the sense of conforming to definition (1) of concurrence, because it conveys that she's in rapport with that object, whether or not she would recognize it so named. Since in this story definition (1) for concurrence did apply, according to our new regimentation he would *not* say something so weak as,

The skunk is believed by Belia to be a woodchuck.

Consequently let's call this regimented form his **fake *de re* reportage**. For anyone who could not say something stronger than this is simply not in a position to make a genuine *de re* report. There are two ways of being in the position of having to use the fake format: not knowing whether Belia is in rapport with an object and knowing that she's not in rapport. Strictly, because of the way I introduced the fake format, an active voice report entails the truth of the passive voice report, in the sense that anything more specific entails the less specific. And so my naming the less specific format "fake" creates the awkward result that to be genuine entails to be fake. That's just mischief, easily stopped at the cost of some clutter in our regimentation. I call the reportage fake because to use it is to conversationally implicate that one cannot give a report in the active voice, the genuine *de re* format. (Similarly, to refer to someone's putative father is, by implicature, to raise a doubt about parentage.) Rep won't have much recourse to this form, however, for we'll focus on cases of rapport, conveyed by the active voice with an about-position.

We should also allow for mixed cases of *de re* reports, fake with respect to one position, but genuine with respect to another position, when the adicity of the incomplete proposition is greater than one. The regimentation required to express these cases is baroque, requiring both an about-position and the subject position of the passive form of "believe." For example, since Belia has no rapport with Sven, but imagines him to believe a woman she sees is his long-lost daughter, Rep reports,

About this woman, Sven is believed by Belia to believe [about her?] that she is his long-lost daughter.

The phrase in square brackets indicates a point of vagueness. Kent Bach and Richard Holton have considered whether there's a philosophical payoff in just these mixed cases for having two formats for *de re* reporting.[11] Perhaps the formats allow the reporter to make useful distinctions about the relational or notional character of the attitudes of the intermediate parties he reports on. In Rep's report, Belia herself is a reporter of Sven's beliefs. What sort of belief, relational or notional, is she attributing to Sven? If she thinks she's located the daughter whom Sven only surmises must exist, then the belief she attributes to Sven is notional merely, and the phrase in square brackets should be omitted. Alternatively, if she thinks Sven has identified this woman and thinks of her as his daughter, then the phrase in square brackets should be inserted.

Although I'll continue to call this reportage fake *de re*, some philosophers think it fulfills all the roles one would want fulfilled by *de re* reports in a theory of communication. Think of Rep, not just as a hired hand for our philosophical digging, but as a person learning things about his own environment from Belia for his own benefit. From that perspective it's incidental whether Belia is in causal rapport with the things her beliefs are about. Philosophers of language study Rep's reports for their own sake. We need not quarrel with these philosophers; their investigations are legitimate, but they simply are not disputing or contributing to ours, which uses reports as an entry point into the ontology of folk psychology.[12]

### §4. *De re* reportage applied to Bishop Berkeley's challenge.

The concept of fake *de re* reportage has another philosophical payoff. In section B I argued that my claim that all attitudes are propositional attitudes helped put to rest Bishop Berkeley's "master argument" for idealism,^ namely, that the believers in matter could not conceive without contradiction the very thing their (and my) position declares to be conceivable, namely, the thing that is never conceived of. Berkeley challenges us to conceive of it. If the attitude of conceiving takes *a thing* like a tree as its object, then Berkeley wins the challenge; we contradict ourselves. But if all attitudes are propositional attitudes, then we conceive *the proposition*, there's a tree that nobody ever conceives of.

The recess in the debate is over, and Berkeley responds that he wants us to have a *de re* conception of the tree. If there's a tree that nobody ever conceives of, there's a tallest such. Conceive, about the tallest of the trees that nobody ever conceives of, that it's quite tall. I think we should tell the Bishop that he's berking up the wrong tree. That definite description can only be used in fake *de re* reportage:

> The tallest of the trees nobody ever conceived of is conceived by
> us to be tall.

Still no contradiction, since this sentence is only a manner of speaking about the reality of our conceiving a proposition. Not convinced? Behind this form of reportage is only a *de dicto* attitude. We were only conceiving *that* the tallest of the trees nobody ever conceived of is tall. No contradiction there. The first conceiving reported in the sentence is of a proposition, the second one reported in the definite description is of a thing, in the fake mode of reporting. The Bishop will ask for the reality behind the fake mode: What proposition is everyone failing to conceive in failing to conceive of the tree? I'll say more about that kind of proposition and about the Bishop's master argument in section T.

The fake *de re* has ramifications for the debate we inaugurated in section A with the friends of complete singular propositions. I suggested in section H that people's linguistic resources may give them the means to express in words propositions that they cannot think. The format for fake *de re* reportage is just the way to report such expressions of the unthinkable. In this way Rep can report propositions that Belia may express but cannot think. He may have to use this form, even when he's basing his report on what Belia herself says, relying on a disquotation principle. For, despite what she says, she may not be up to believing it.

The reporting of *de dicto* beliefs directed toward complete singular propositions as if they were *de re* I classify under fake *de re* reportage. The intuitions we evoked in sections I and H showed the beliefs are not genuinely *de re*. It should be noted, however, that the theory of *de re* attitudes that claims their defining attribute is that they are directed toward complete singular propositions has some praiseworthy features, which emboldens its advocates to work around those intuitions. It would not, for instance, have to resort to the expressible but unthinkable, as I just did. The virtue most in contrast to my own theory, in the eyes of my critics, is the implication that the phenomenon of *de re*-ness is immune to variations in context of reporting. That virtue, coupled with its potential for overcoming the divide, not only between the two kinds of attitudes, but also between modal logic and the attitudes, encourages its partisans to refine it and reject the theory that posits incomplete propositions and causal rapport. We incompleters have not by any means polished off the complete singular crowd, who may include some of you. I only expect to finish the job by section W.

### §5. Referring to intensional entities in the about-position.

I also classify under fake *de re* reportage a clever way of regimenting reports, developed by Robert Kraut,[13] whose effect is that *all* belief turns out to be *de re*. It makes use of formal techniques developed originally for modal logic and requires mastery of that subject. We cannot develop it fully, therefore, and for some it may be better to skip this subsection. The main idea is that the domains of the quantifiers in reports can be functions^

from possible scenarios to individuals, rather than the individuals themselves as we've been supposing all along. The function has its own unity, and so we can think of it as representing an individual composed of its values in each of the possible scenarios. We may think of such a function as an integrator.

The idea of an integrating function is familiar from outside modal logic. For example, we can think of definite descriptions as referring in different scenarios to the different values^ in the range of such functions. Thus in different scenarios different persons are picked out by the description, "the first emperor of Rome." Mark Antony is picked out in one scenario, not the actual one. In this nonactual scenario things don't go so badly for Antony, and he somehow outmaneuvers Octavian and becomes emperor; he might even have assumed the name Augustus. The tricky part for thought is to think of *the one* individual who is composed of Mark Antony in one situation and Octavian in another situation, the actual one, and *that* individual is the first emperor of Rome in *each* of those situations. The function is to be thought of as introducing a sense of "numerically^ the same individual."

When a function's values are the same individual in each possible scenario, not only in the sense of "numerically the same" which the function introduces, but also according to our intuitive sense of numerical sameness, it's called a constant function. For example, a modally rigid description means a constant function: "The first emperor of Rome in actuality" picks out Octavian in all possible scenarios, since Octavian actually did become the emperor Augustus.

We cannot complain that this constructed sameness is phony, for it may turn out that then our intuitive sense of sameness is phony too. Kraut exploits the fact that ordinary things, which endure through time, might be composed of a succession of brief temporal stages strung together along a space-time line. If so, that construction is represented by functions from times to the stages of the constructed things at those times. Then the sense of sameness which the function introduces is just our intuitive sense of sameness of ordinary things![14] It's a small step—or is it?—from functions whose domains are times to functions whose domains are possible situations. (In sections M and N we'll explore further the analogy between time and modality.)

Kraut shows that all belief can be analyzed as *de re*, when the *res* are these sorts of functions, constant or nonconstant, and their domains are the alternative scenarios consistent with all the believer believes (or, if her beliefs are inconsistent, with a largest consistent subset of what she believes). For example, Belia's command of Roman history is a bit fuzzy. She knows civil war broke out after Julius Caesar's assassination, and the side known as the triumvirate won. The triumvirate consisted of Mark Antony, Lepidus, and Octavian, but she doesn't know which one of them became the first emperor under the name Augustus. Nevertheless, she believes he was not assassinated. According to our own regimentation we'd say she has a *de dicto* belief that the first emperor of Rome was not assassinated. Kraut would have us say instead that her belief is about *the* single individual who is Antony in one scenario, Lepidus in another, and Octavian in another. The *res* her belief is about is not any one of them, but the single individual constructed by the function, someone who turns out to be the one in one scenario, the other in another scenario, and another in another scenario. Thus Rep may report, using our format for fake *de re* reportage,

The first emperor of Rome is believed by Belia not to have been assassinated.

Be careful. Kraut has us assign an unusual referent to the definite description when it supplies the subject for an incomplete proposition following "believed." A strange individual this emperor, Belia's mental concoction. With individuals like that, all *de dicto* reports could be recast as *de re*.

Kraut thinks his regimentation answers Quine's misgivings about the scientific respectability of *de re* idioms. In fact, however, he's only showing that formal techniques are flexible and powerful enough to accommodate even the most intricately byzantine context-sensitivity. Quine's objection to *de re* idioms is not answered, but simply transformed into worries about these functions. For example, a nonconstant function from possible scenarios can be thought of as defining an individual according to some nonextensional criterion of numerical^ identity. It's nonextensional, because it identifies inhabitants of different nonactual scenarios as being the same individual. In our example, the scenarios are all those consistent with what Belia believes about Roman history. They represent what might've been, for all that she believes. The scenarios are not consistent with each other in the way they fill out what Belia's unsure about. For her in her state of unsureness, "first emperor of Rome" specifies a kind of identity between Mark Antony, Lepidus, and Octavian in the alternative scenarios in which one of them becomes emperor, namely *the* individual who is Mark Antony in one scenario, Lepidus in another, and Octavian in another. If she were to learn more Roman history, this individual would lose a limb or two, the Antony limb and the Lepidus limb, so to speak, simply by her coming to believe that Octavian was the first emperor.

We already rehearsed (in section G) Quine's difficulties with nonextensionality in the realm of attributes. His qualms are just as strong in the realm of nonextensional individuals. The nonextensional is an undisciplined and lawless realm. Might not some unfortunate Czech wake up to find he's turned into an oversized cockroach one morning? I don't have a problem with that. Hey, it's better than an English doctor turning into a werewolf or a Transylvanian count turning into a vampire bat. Here's one qualm that's relevant to context-sensitivity, the theme of this section: Kraut admits that his regimentation generates a gradation of nonextensional criteria of identity for individuals across possible scenarios, depending on how many constraints must be fulfilled for there to be numerical identity of an individual inhabiting the scenarios. Selecting a criterion is determined by context, but which context? The selection may be equivalent to fixing the extent of Belia's beliefs about Roman history, if I'm right, or equivalent to fixing the purposes of Rep and his audience, if Quine's right. Is Belia's mind the context which settles whether her beliefs are *de re*, or is the occasion of Rep's reporting her mind the context? Kraut's technique does not settle this detail, and thus his analysis does not address the question of context-sensitivity at issue in this section. Kraut himself ends up siding with Quine on the matter,[15] and so his claim to have made relational belief suited for scientific theorizing is unwarranted.

Quine would have another objection: According to Kraut the referents of rigid designators are constant functions. The very idea of a constant function depends on an already given notion of numerically^ the same individual from one possible scenario to another. Presumably this prior notion uses an extensional criterion of identity, which Quine prefers, and so constant functions add nothing but complication. By this extensional criterion, Octavian = Augustus, and Belia's belief fails to be about him or any other extensionally identified individual, and so is not *de re*. Kraut might reply by simply giving up the notion of a constant function. Instead he may refer to a maximally constrained function. I doubt this alternative is coherent, because if the individual so identified inhabits alternative scenarios, the scenarios themselves may supply enough differentiation to allow one to deny the identity. Maximally constrained function is no substitute for constant function.

In conclusion, it seems that Kraut's techniques reformulate the issues, casting them in a new light, but the new light does not illuminate them.

## §6. Tu quoque, Quine.

We may, however, draw a positive lesson from all that. Quine cannot object to my search for privileged contexts in which relational belief works as a scientifically respectable notion. For he too does the same for the concept of numerical^ identity. In the context of identity of things over time, Quine defends the notion that we can make scientific sense of successive events being stages of numerically the same enduring object. Yet this notion is very context sensitive. I'd like Quine to confront none other than the wily Bishop Berkeley on this point:

> Or suppose a house, whose walls or outward shell remained unaltered, the chambers are all pulled down, and new ones built in their place; and that you should call this the *same*, and I should say it was not the *same* house: would we not for all this perfectly agree in our thoughts of the house, considered in itself? And would not all the difference consist in a sound?[16]

I can hear Quine explaining to the Bishop (as he explained to Hintikka[17]) that there are serious contexts which settle the criteria for numerical identity. And I say the same to Quine concerning relational belief. And what do I hear Quine replying? "You're bluffing. Let's see you do it." Well, then, it's off to work we go!

# Notes

1. Charles Sanders Peirce, *Collected Papers*, vol. 2, Book II, ch. 3.

2. Quine, "Intensions Revisited." For a clearer statement of the objectionable feature of indexicality, see his "Reactions" in P. Leonardi and M. Santambrogio, eds., *On Quine* (1995), section VI.

3. Quine, *Pursuit of Truth*, section 26.

4. Quine, "Reactions," 358. Quine gets the "knowing who" criterion for *de re* attitudes from Jaakko Hintikka, who introduced it in chapter 6 of his *Knowledge and Belief: An Introduction to the Logic of the Two Notions* (1962). In the text I say that the knowing-who criterion does roughly the same work as the causal rapport criterion. There are several differences, however. The knowing-who criterion will work for abstract objects, unlike the causal rapport criterion. The knowing-who criterion does not need supplementation by a transmission principle, as does the causal rapport criterion.

5. Jerry A. Fodor, "Methodological solipsism considered as a research strategy in cognitive psychology" (1980), reprinted in his *Representations* (1981). The point is made on pages 235f.

6. Howard Burdick, "A Logical Form for the Propositional Attitudes,"

*Synthese* 52 (1982) 185-230. See 193-195.

7. Stephen Stich, *From Folk Psychology to Cognitive Science* (1984) ch. 5. Compare Quine's point in *Word and Object,* 218.

8. Boër, S. E., and Lycan, W. G., *Knowing Who* (1986), ch. 5, sections 3.6 and 4. However they shilly shally on the reality of *de re* belief (see note 25 of ch. 5).

9. Howard Burdick, "A Logical Form for the Propositional Attitudes."

10. Michael Corrado is the first one I know of, who called attention to the confusion of genuine *de re* with the fake version. He called the fake version "accidentally referential belief propositions," in his "What *De Re* Belief is Not," *Analysis* 35 (1975) 188-192. Thomas McKay notes correctly in "Actions and *De Re* Beliefs," *Canadian Journal of Philosophy,* 14 (1984) 631-35, that David Kaplan mistook a genuine *de re* report for fake reportage simply because the genuine report took advantage of the purely referential character of an about-position. I suspect that Kaplan was groping for the sense of fake reportage embodied in the fulfillment of condition (2) of partial concurrence, but not condition (1), the distinction that Corrado had singled out.

11. Kent Bach, *Thought and Reference* (1987). See ch. 10, 200ff., for his discussion of "multiple attitude sentences." (My fake *de re* reportage is like Bach's "de re [belief reports] that are not [de re belief] reports.") Richard Holton, "Attitude Ascriptions and Intermediate Scope," *Mind* 103 (1994) 123-130. Holton, however, opts not to introduce a second idiom, thinking that our definition (1) of concurrence suffices. Our differing assessments on this matter are due I think to his contrasting causal rapport with the knowing-who criterion, whereas I'm contrasting causal rapport with the mere existence criterion.

12. Robert Brandom's analyses in terms of the commitments and entitlements of communicators apply to the common elements of genuine and fake *de re* reports. For a positive account of the value of fake *de re,* see his *Making It Explicit: Reasoning, Representing, and Discursive Commitment* (1994). Brandom, however, attacks three positions, all of which I defend in succeeding sections:

> . . . the point of view adopted here nonetheless differs from that typical of the boosters of strong *de re* beliefs [I'm one!] in its assessment of their theoretical significance. First, these beliefs do not form an autonomously intelligible sort or stratum of beliefs; one cannot coherently describe a situation in which this is the first or only kind of belief that is in play. [I'll describe that situation in section N. It's the boiler room analogy.] Second, although essentially indexical beliefs have a special sort of object-involving content that other beliefs do not, that object-involvingness should not be thought of as a *nonconceptual* element in their content; rather, the special sort of access to the objects their contents are about that the use of indexicals makes possible is the special kind of *conceptually* articulated access (though it is not correct to think of the role of the conceptual as *mediating* mind and its objects). [He contradicts here my kinetic theory of core indexical reference, to be defended also in section N.] Finally, important as essentially indexical beliefs are for our empirical

knowledge and practical activity, what is of primary significance for understanding the representational dimension of thought and talk—its intentionality or aboutness in general—is the combination of doxastic perspectives expressed by (weak) *de re* specifications of the conceptual contents of beliefs of any sort [i.e., what I call fake *de re*], *not* the special sort of content possessed by strong *de re* beliefs, nor the special sort of rapport with objects they embody (pp. 551f.). [He precludes naturalizing aboutness by way of an understanding its evolution in the language of thought, a project implicit in folk psychology, as I try to show over the course of these notes.]

One could not wish for a clearer challenge. I accept.

13.  Robert Kraut, "There are no *De Dicto* Attitudes," *Synthese* 54 (1983) 275-294. He works within a framework, which Jaakko Hintikka developed by extending the conceptual tools of modal logic to the logic of attitudes. In section F, I rejected an analogy between modal logic and the logic of attitudes. That should not be confused with rejecting the stretching of the logical tools for systematizing modal logic to cover the logic of attitudes. That's a separate issue.

14.  Robert Kraut, "Worlds Regained," *Philosophical Studies*, 35 (1979) 239-255.

15.  "Worlds Regained," 254.

16.  George Berkeley, *Three Dialogues between Hylas and Philonous*, Third Dialogue.

17.  Quine, "Reply to Jaakko Hintikka" in Hahn and Schilpp, eds., *The Philosophy of W. V. Quine*, 228.

# K. Paradoxes in the Concurrence+Rapport Theory of Relational Reports

Instead of producing more evidence against the post-1977 skepticisms, Quine's and others', which I admit needs doing, I'll develop Quine's pre-1977 theory to correct certain internal problems uncovered by David Kaplan. Kaplan was the first to deduce paradoxes from the theory. I take Quine's earlier theory to have been like the theory I've been defending: a rapport theory of relational beliefs, and a concurrence-plus-rapport theory of relational reports, where the reporter's concurrence counted as a precising condition of the dichotomy between rapport and lack of rapport. In the next section we'll look at two ways of developing the theory to avoid the paradoxes, one by Kaplan, the other by Burdick.

## §1. Must Rep contradict himself to report Belia's beliefs accurately?

Let's carry on the story of the skunk running into the bushes. Belia makes a mistake. She has a belief about it that it's a woodchuck. Now let the skunk run out again. Belia sees it and this time recognizes it as a skunk. She says, "Oh, there's a skunk here too." Belia believes that skunks differ from woodchucks. Therefore she believes it's not a woodchuck. Now Rep reports both her beliefs:

> First, Belia believes *about* the one and only animal she saw, the skunk, *that* it's a woodchuck.
> Secondly, Belia believes *about* the one and only animal she saw, the skunk, *that* it's not a woodchuck.

The question is, has Rep attributed a self-contradictory belief to Belia?

It's true that Rep has said Belia believes about the skunk

> (i) both *that* it's a woodchuck and *that* it's not a woodchuck.

But Rep has *not* said that Belia believes about the skunk

> (ii) *that* it's both a woodchuck and not a woodchuck.

Note the placement of the word "both" in those two incomplete propositions. If Belia were aware that the object of her two beliefs was one and the same thing, then she'd be thinking it's both a woodchuck and not a woodchuck. What's conjoined by the words "both . . . and . . ." is different in case (ii) from what's conjoined in case (i); only in case (ii) would a conjunction be part of what's in her mind, for the conjunction would be within the that-clause. She'd be guilty of a contradiction. For, the conjunction in case (ii) is tighter than it is in case (i); it ties two predicates to the same thing. But case (i) need not be interpreted that way, for nothing Rep tells us about Belia requires that we interpret the two anaphoric pronouns in the first as referring to the same thing. We could form an attribute from the first conjunction by abstraction, but it would be the attribute of something $x$ and something $y$, which may or may not be identical to $x$, such that $x$ is a woodchuck and $y$ is not. At most Rep's two reports say Belia attributes that attribute. Rep's actual reports of her beliefs do *not* assign her a contradictory belief, because his reports do not say how she identifies the object or even whether she thinks of it as one or two. Rep knows that only one animal ran into the bushes and back out again. Rep made that plain in his reports of Belia's beliefs about it. But his reports didn't assign that knowledge to Belia, nor did they deny it to her.

Rep could avoid raising a suspicion of Belia's consistency by leaving the about-position out of his report:

> Belia believes that the animal which ran into the bushes is a woodchuck and that the animal which ran out of the bushes is a skunk.

But Rep might then go on to say that, since the animal-into-the-bush is identical to the animal-out-of-the-bush,

> Belia believes that the skunk is a woodchuck.

Rep must come to appreciate how uncharitable he's being to Belia. Certainly Belia would not agree to any such assertion as "the skunk is a woodchuck." We see the wisdom of our decision (in section C) to let the test of the correctness of what Rep puts in the that-clause in his reports be what Belia would affirm. (Recall, if Belia is unaware that another name for a woodchuck is "groundhog," Rep would be wrong to report that Belia believes about the skunk *that* it is a groundhog. Belia commands the that-clause.) Rep can snicker that Belia believes *about* the skunk *that* it is a woodchuck, but he may not report she believes *that* the skunk she saw is a woodchuck. For that would imply she's confused over the natures of skunks and woodchucks, and she's not that confused. She just didn't get a good enough look.

The distinction between about-positions and that-clauses has now paid a handsome dividend in letting Rep separate Belia's superficial errors of perception from deeper conceptual errors. That's evidence favoring the distinction. Although simple concurrence theory is wrong, concurrence-plus-rapport yields a theory of reports that gives us a purely referential about-position, and thus we have hope of sharply distinguishing a rapport theory of relational belief by means of a semantic ascent to their reports. On the other hand, is there evidence not in favor of a purely referential about-position? Yes.

Rep is the more likely candidate for contradicting himself! Belia has two beliefs about the skunk as a result of her misperceiving it the first time when it ran into the bushes.

(1) Belia believes about the skunk that it is a woodchuck.

(2) Also Belia believes about the skunk that it's not a woodchuck.

I already noted that the two reports don't imply that Belia believes a contradiction.[1] In fact she'd deny that (1) reports her belief. Does Rep now believe a contradiction? He believes these two things are true of that skunk:

Belia believes it to be a woodchuck.

Belia believes it not to be a woodchuck.

Logically, stating the contradictory of a clause requires denying it by putting "it's not the case that . . ." in front of it. So we have not found Rep to be contradicting himself yet, for we've not yet shown him committed to:

(3) It's not the case about the skunk that Belia believes it to be a woodchuck.

(3) is equivalent to (1)'s denial: "Belia does not believe about the skunk that it is a woodchuck."

We can derive Rep's commitment to (3), however: If Belia's consistent in her beliefs and is logical and she believes about the skunk that it's *not* a woodchuck, then it's not the case that Belia believes about the skunk that it *is* a woodchuck. For, considering reports with no about-position in them, a consistent and logical person's believing *that* something is not true implies her not believing *that* it is true. We extend this implication pattern to reports with about-positions in this way: Given one's consistency, one's believing a denial *about* something, conceiving of that thing in a certain way, implies one's not believing the predicate denied also true *about* that same thing, conceiving of it in the same way. For (by way of a *reductio ad absurdum^*),

(a) if anyone did, she'd be committed to believing about that thing the conjunction of the denial and the predicate denied. That's absurd.

(b) If she didn't commit herself to that conjunction in this circumstance, that would be a logical defect in her as great as the defect of inconsistency.

The defect in alternative (b) is failure to obey a psychological version of the rule of **closure under conjunction**. A language has this property if the conjunctions of all propositions are propositions too. Extrapolating to psychology, a person's set of beliefs is like a language's set of sentences in this respect. We say the field of propositions which a person's attitudes are directed towards contains the conjunctions of all the propositions it contains. Thus, if it contains $p$ and it contains $q$, then it contains $p\&q$. Assuming your logicality in other respects, nonclosure occurs when you believe $p$ and you believe $q$, but you fail to believe $p\&q$. It can be logical not to believe the conjunction as much as either of the conjuncts, when your beliefs in them fall short of full conviction. We noted this fact in section B when we discussed the preface paradox to motivate the idea of partial belief.[2] We even noted there that it's logical sometimes for a person to have equal partial belief in the two arms of a contradiction, but no belief at all in their conjunction. But if you believe $p$ and you also believe $q$, each fully and without reservation, then you must fully believe $p\&q$. Now we want to put the squeeze on Rep, don't we? He has to find out Belia's degrees of belief. Too bad, Rep, her strength of conviction in each of her beliefs couldn't be higher. Logic now forces the issue. Either way, that is, alternatives (a) or (b) listed above, we get an *absurdum*. For the *reductio* argument to force Rep to assert (3), he must be assured that Belia's error is not a mistake of logic. She fits the description of the logical and consistent person which the *reductio* argument assumed. So Rep must assert (3).

When Rep reports Belia's belief (2), indicating how he thinks it's tied to reality by the way he fills in an about-position, he must still be able to give Belia her due as a consistent person, committed to closure, and report her disbelief, (3), as well. In reporting the disbelief, he's not using the negative disquotation principle mentioned in section C, which is itself suspect. The report of disbelief follows from two premises, the positive disquotation principle that yielded (2) and a commitment to Belia's logicality. These two things—conceding Belia's consistency and basic logicality, and letting us know what her belief's about—seem independent of each other. So Rep is committed by (2) to (3), and his (3) contradicts his (1). Let the reporter beware of his about-positions! Perhaps they're not so purely referential after all!

Belia is perfectly consistent, if somewhat mistaken. But Rep cannot report her mistake without contradicting himself. True, Belia has two ways of thinking of the animal she saw, and she doesn't connect them. It's no use pointing to the divorce of (1) from (2) and (3) in Belia's mind in order to save Rep from self-contradiction. You must find that divorce in Rep's mind, but he knows perfectly well there's no divorce; the skunk featured in (1) is the very skunk featured in (3).

It's even worse for Rep than we said. Belia has a dog well trained to stay away from skunks. This dog chases after the animal that runs into the bush, but when the animal reappears, the dog runs away. If animals also obey the rule of closure, Belia's dog was guilty of the same confusion as Belia was, as his behavior shows. Rep should be able to report without contradicting himself that the dog is confused, but he can't without contradicting himself. What a predicament! Rep is less rational than the dog.[3]

Well, shall we just sacrifice Rep's rationality? The guy's expendable in the interest of science, right? No, it's no help to be so cold-hearted. Rep's self-contradiction can also be viewed as a problem for the about-position. For, if both (1) and (3) are true, it follows that the skunk does not exist. Nothing exists with contradictory properties. (1) assigns it the property of Belia's believing it to be a woodchuck, and (3) denies that very property of it. If (1) and (3) are both true, then the about-position is being used to refer to a nonexistent. (Recall from section G the barber who shaves all and only those who don't shave themselves. He does not exist, since he both does and does not shave himself.) Whoa! We must not allow both (1) and (3) to be true reports as they stand.

I hope the knowing reader has been amused to rework the example of Belia, changing her name to Ralph. Instead of an animal running into and then out of the bushes, you will have a man (Bernard J. Ortcutt, to give him a name) be seen in two sorts of circumstances, once at a beach under respectable circumstances and several glimpses of him wearing a brown hat under questionable circumstances on which we need not enter here. Rep is you, and you know that one and the same person was seen. Instead of Belia's belief about having seen a woodchuck, put Ralph's belief about having seen a spy. This rework of the example yields the main case considered in Quine's "Quantifiers and Propositional Attitudes." The last five paragraphs above will also have amused the knowing reader, who'll see it as reworking David Kaplan's extension of Quine's case (in "Quantifying In"[4]). So will the solution in section L. (You can compare this section also to Guttenplan's discussion of Monique's beliefs about the British Museum, in the second part of his "An Essay on Mind."[5]) Ever since Quine proposed this puzzle, philosophers have been very creative in making slight variations on it, to highlight different features of the puzzle. We'll examine some of them in later sections, but we'll dispose of all of them by the solution proposed in the next section.

## §2. Variations of the paradox.

Since the 1970's, Rep's rationality has been impugned by making him use
the dyadic attribute of identity in his reports, thereby alluding to Frege's
quest for a theory of meaning that would allow one's learning the identity
of the morning star with the evening star to be informative, given that they
are one and the same. For learning that $a = a$ is not informative.[6] Rep's
predicament, reformulated in terms of identity, parallels his predicament
with such monadic attributes as *being a woodchuck*. Belia does not believe
that woodchucks are skunks. So she'd deny that the animal that ran into the
bushes is identical to the animal that ran out. But Rep knows their identity.
So he reports:

Belia believes about the animal that it's not identical to it.
That's unfair, Belia protests. She's in charge of the that-clause, and she
believes of each animal, that *it's identical to it*! She just doesn't believe of
the skunk that *it's identical to the woodchuck*, nor of the woodchuck that
*it's identical to the skunk*. There are three identity predicates in play here.
The first is dyadic, but the other two are monadic. The latter two express
relative properties, a concept that was explained in section D. Concerning
the dyadic relation of identity, we must separate a restricted dyadic predicate for expressing it, $x = x$, from an unrestricted predicate for expressing the same relation, $x = y$. The two pronouns (the $x$ and $y$) in the unrestricted relational predicate are not forced to refer to the same thing. Belia
uses this unrestricted form when she says truly of two things, that they're
not identical to each other. Restrictedly, the two pronouns refer to the
same thing. It would be more perspicuous if we used the pronouns
"former" and "latter" for stating the unrestricted predicate, and two "it's"
for expressing the restricted predicate.

Rep may see little difference between the restricted dyadic predicate
he used to report the relation Belia's belief was directed toward and the
monadic relative predicates he's entitled to use by virtue of her protestations and her control of the that-clause. For his control of the about-
position allows him to say that there's just one thing her belief is about.
Nevertheless, for him to ignore the difference between the two that-clauses
is to disregard the instructions we gave him about letting Belia have
control over the that-clause's content, and he pays a price of self-contradiction by disregarding it. He may think this way: Since she has a belief
directed toward nonidentity, either the relation of nonidentity or a relative
property of nonidentity with the woodchuck, and there is only one thing
her belief is about, then the nonidentity is applied to just one thing:

Belia believes about the animal that it's identical to the woodchuck and that it's not identical to the woodchuck.

Then by the reasoning we noted earlier about negative beliefs, he infers

Belia does not believe about the animal that it is identical to the
woodchuck.

But Belia insists she believes the animal that went in is identical to the
woodchuck. Rep dutifully reports the same of the one and only animal,
and guess who just contradicted himself, as he would also have if he had
used the dyadic identity predicate:

Belia believes about the animal that it is identical to it, and she
does not believe that about it.

Nor is it so obvious how Rep could formulate an accurate report giving
Belia her rights over the that-clause without giving up his own rights over
the about-position. Perhaps we've uncovered a flaw in our regimentation.
We earlier noted that Rep's reports of Belia's beliefs entail that she also
believes the conjunctive incomplete proposition, "it's a woodchuck and it's
not a woodchuck." We noted that Belia would not think the two pronouns
refer to the same thing, and she would put it this way:

"the former's a woodchuck and the latter's not a woodchuck."

*But Rep does know their identity.* Just how would Rep report *de re* that
relational belief of Belia's? How could he be faithful to the unrestricted
form in the that-clause, when his about-position mentions just one thing,
forcing a restricted interpretation?

### §3. The proper-name version of the paradox.

Again with identity, the problem has not been with Belia. We're dissing
Rep, and if he doesn't stop contradicting himself we'll have to rename him
Disrep. Things would get much trickier for him if Belia were to introduce
two proper names, say Woody and Pepe LePew, for the animal. So far
she's been content to use the definite descriptions, the woodchuck and the
skunk. The difference is that the definite descriptions are not modally
rigid, but the proper names are. It will turn out that, despite the seeming
complexity for the sake of complexity, this version of the paradox based
on proper names will supply a crucial argument for my theory of *de re*
attitudes, which I'll state in the next section. So let's develop the story, or
rather develop another story, since Rep has called a time-out. Recall from
section F the tradition that the Greeks gave the morning star the logically
proper name Phosphor and the evening star Hesper, and that Pythagoras
was the one to discover their identity. Let's say he discovered this fact only

late in his life. The young Pythagoras had *de re* knowledge about Hesper and about Phosphor, but, until he discovered their identity, he believed that they were distinct. We control the about-position, and we use our name for the planet there:

> The young Pythagoras believed about Venus that it is identical to it.

For surely he believed Hesper is Hesper. We now become as high-handed in our dealings with young Pythy as Rep was with Belia. In virtue of his denial of the identity of Hesper with Phosphor, and brushing aside his control of the that-clause and his vociferous rejection of the specific form of the dyadic predicate we use there,

> The young Pythagoras believed about Venus that it's not identical to it.

So:

> The young Pythagoras did not believe about Venus that it is identical to it.

We are as irrational as Rep.

If we pay attention to the distinction between predicates, which are linguistic, and attributes, which are not, we'll see that we get to choose from four predicates to use in the that-clauses of our reports on the young Pythagoras to express either of just two attributes which his *de re* attitudes are directed toward. The dyadic attribute of identity can be expressed either by the restricted predicate, $x = x$, or unrestricted predicate for expressing the same relation, $x = y$. Attributes are individuated by intensional identity conditions (section F), and these two predicates pick out the same intension. The other two predicates are the monadic relative predicates, "= Hesper" and "= Phosphor." Unlike Belia's "= the wood-chuck" and "= the skunk," which expressed different attributes, because the definite descriptions are not modally rigid, the two monadic predicates we have for reporting on Pythagoras do express the same intension, despite the verbal difference. The one monadic attribute is distinct from the one dyadic attribute of identity, for everything bears that relation to itself, but only one thing has that monadic attribute of identity with the planet. Nevertheless there's an internal^ relation between the two attributes: By the substitutivity of identity, if Hesper's identical to Phosphor, then whatever property Hesper has Phosphor has too, and vice versa. Also if Hesper has the property, "= Phosphor," then, since Phosphor does too, by virtue of their identity to the same thing they're identical to each other.

These are our tools: one planet, two attributes, four predicates; how shall we deploy them to describe the mind of the young Pythagoras? The planet's referred to in the about-position, the predicates go in the that-clauses, but they only express one or other of two attributes for Pythagoras's beliefs to be directed toward. Nevertheless, since the that-clauses are hyperintensional contexts, we expect failures of substitutivity between the predicates expressing the same intension. And now our own consistency is threatened: The young Pythagoras both affirms and denies each of the attributes and all four of the predicates of Venus, when he tells us that Phosphor is not Hesper. If we try to reinstate his consistency, we'll lose the ability to describe his discovery, when he was old, that Phosphor is Hesper. For surely that transition was his giving up his belief in the nonidentity of Phosphor and Hesper.[7] Finally, if we attribute a modicum of logicality to him, even our own reports on him will contradict each other.

Recall my new relative, introduced in section A—yes, Belia married into my family—who has not learned Sonny is Arthur. Her refusal to believe of Arthur what she believed of Sonny raised problems for the idea that her beliefs were directed toward singular propositions. For the difference in the names makes no difference in the singular propositions expressed by sentences differing only in which one of the names occurs in them. We still have the problem of singular propositions, but now it turns into a dilemma: My relative's beliefs are directed toward complete singular propositions or incomplete propositions. If the former, we get the paradox stated in section A. If the latter, then she did believe and disbelieve the same incomplete proposition about me and it might as well have been "being Arthur" which she both did and did not believe of me. I just contradicted myself, but I'm getting used to it.

We approved a principle of the transmissibility of *de re* belief from one believer to another in section I. It's no objection to this principle that it can lead to conflicting beliefs about the same thing, if perception itself can lead to that condition. But it does lead to analogous conflicts: My new relative believed, by transmission from some of my nephews, complimentary things about me, which it's not the case that she believed about me, because of the uncomplimentary things she believed about me by transmission from other nephews of mine. Whoops; I contradicted myself, or I don't exist!

Before proceeding to solutions, here's an example using another propositional attitude, namely wanting. If Rep sticks to wants *de dicto*, Rep can say that Oedipus wanted to marry Jocasta, but did not want to marry his mother, and neither Rep nor Oedipus would be guilty of inconsistency despite Jocasta being Oedipus's mother. If, however, Rep reports Oedipus's wants *de re*, Rep becomes inconsistent. For, *about* that woman there, who is Jocasta, Oedipus wants to marry her, and *about* the same woman, who is also his mother, he does not want to marry her. So it's not the case that he wants to marry her. Rep just committed himself to an inconsistency, *p&not-p*, never mind Oedipus. The guy who does the talking takes the rap.

# Notes

1. Consider **partial beliefs**, that is, beliefs held with less than full conviction. On a scale from 0 to 1, full conviction we say is belief to degree 1. Again we can defend Belia. According to probability theory, if her two beliefs were contradictory, Belia's degrees of belief in them severally must sum to 1. Here they sum to almost 2. Therefore, they're not contradictory.

2. When we think of beliefs as coming in degrees and modeled in probability theory, then nonclosure is only a defect of rationality for one's certitudes. But if one believes two propositions only somewhat, then one may believe their conjunction even less or not at all, as we noted in section B. Recall from there the paradox, usually called the lottery paradox, but which is easily grasped as the preface paradox: I believe each sentence in a book I've written, but I'm equally convinced that I've made at least one mistake, and I confess this in the preface. Where my mistake is I don't know, or I'd've erased it. This belief in my fallibility implies that I don't believe the conjunction of all the sentences in my book. Obviously, I'm not irrational. The solution to the paradox is easy in probability theory, if one admits the beliefs in the sentences are mostly partial beliefs.

3. Quine treated attribution of beliefs to other animals as mostly unscientific dramatization of animal behavior, in the mode of Walt Disney, insofar as it goes beyond stimulus meaning, *Word and Object*, 219. See also "Propositional Objects" (1968), reprinted in *Ontological Relativity and Other Essays*, 146ff, and "Intensions Revisited" (1979) 274 for qualifications. As his philosophy matured, he gave greater importance to empathy and with it more scientific status to the results of its use. But it's still only "vague science."

4. Quine's "Quantifiers and Propositional Attitudes" (1956) is reprinted in his *The Ways of Paradox and Other Essays*. Kaplan's "Quantifying In" is in *Synthese* (1968), reprinted in D. Davidson and J. Hintikka, eds., *Words and Objections: Essays on the Work of W. V. Quine* (1969).

5. Guttenplan's "An Essay on Mind" is in S. Guttenplan, ed., *A Companion to the Philosophy of Mind* (1994). For Monique see section 2.1.2.1. Guttenplan develops a new paradox, which I say nothing about here. In quantum mechanics scientists believe probabilities distribute according to type, not instances of the type, as if it were right to believe, of the state of two coins coming up different sides, that it has a probability of 1/3, rather than the normally correct 1/2. It seems like this situation in quantum mechanics might be a serious version of Guttenplan's problem of Richard and the café chairs. What counts really is the chair type and not the chair individuals.

6. "On Sense and Reference" (1892), in P. Geach and M. Black, *Translations from the Philosophical Writings of Gottlob Frege* (1960) 56-78.

7. Michael Tye, "The Puzzle of Hesperus and Phosphorus," *Australasian Journal of Philosophy*, 56 (1978) 219-224, argues for the equivalence between a *de re* attitude and an attitude directed toward a singular proposition, and he bites the bullet on this puzzle, namely, that to believe Hesper is Hesper is to believe Hesper is Phosphor, for there's only one singular proposition here. So Pythagoras's discovery of the identity cannot be his coming to believe another proposition. This is the problem of hyperintensionality, not the problem I'm addressing in this Part II.

# L. The 1968 Solution to the Paradoxes and Its Aftermath.

The scenario that gives rise to the paradoxes is the one where Belia sees a skunk go into the bushes, but she mistakes it for a woodchuck. When it scurries out, she recognizes it as a skunk, but does not realize it's the same animal that she saw go in. Rep makes two reports, which imply the paradox. The reports were, recall from the previous section,

> (1) Belia believes about the skunk that it's a woodchuck.
>
> (2) Also Belia believes about the skunk that it's not a wood-chuck.

Recall the previous section's derivation, from report (2) and plausible assumptions, of a contradiction to report (1). For (2) implied, given reasonable assumptions about Belia's complexity and logicality,

> (3) It's not the case about the skunk that Belia believes it to be a woodchuck.

It strikes us that, if we're to save Rep's consistency and our characterization of the about-position as purely referential, Rep has to bring Belia's mind into his reports' about-positions. One way is for him to mean his reports to be elliptical.

Ordinary **ellipsis** is the leaving out of words too obvious to everyone to need saying. Often there's a grammatical sign of the omission, as when I say that Jack fell down and broke his crown, and Jill did too. The "did" is a grammatical marker that Jill fell down and broke her crown. Not all ellipses have such grammatical markers to aid listeners, however. Listeners have other ways of uncovering an ellipsis. Sometimes a speaker means something, although he does not intend any of his words, spoken or merely thought, to indicate the meaning; the context does the work. In that case, Crimmins and Perry recommend that we not invoke ellipsis, but rather "unarticulated constituents" of the content of what he says.[1] We'll not worry about their distinction, since we're frankly regimenting.

We here postulate an ellipsis as part of a technique of regimentation; we hypothesize ellipsis to remove nonsensical implications from the words said. If Rep intends the reports to be elliptical, we can block the derivation of (3), the contradiction of (1). In this section I present two ways to solve the paradoxes, the first discovered by David Kaplan, the second by Burdick. Both discover ellipses in reports, but different ones. I will prefer the first because it can be incorporated into the dominance theory I introduced in section H. According to that theory people wrest control from the world of the ensuring of their attitudes' referential success. The ellipsis theory provides an account of how they do that and how they incur risks in doing so.

## §1. The Kaplan solution: The reporter does not contradict himself.

According to the first solution, due to Kaplan, when Rep's reports (1) and (2) are fully spelled out, they refer to the private names Belia uses in her thoughts. The reports with their ellipses made whole, i.e., the italicized material made explicit, are:

> (1´) Belia *has adopted a name for the skunk* and she believes about the skunk *with that name* that it's a woodchuck.

> (2´) Belia *has adopted a name for the skunk* and she believes about the skunk *with that name* that it's not a woodchuck.

(1´) and (2´) need not be referring to the same name. Let's be given the name that Belia uses for the animal at her first sighting of it: "*a*." The name for it at her second sighting is "*b*." In her mind there are *dicta*, which we may express this way:

> *a* is a woodchuck, and
> *b* is not a woodchuck, and
> *a* is not *b*.

Although these don't constitute a contradictory set of sentences, there's still a question whether together they express an inconsistent^ proposition, and whether Belia believes that proposition. I'll reserve the issue of Belia's consistency to the next subsection. We're tackling now only the simpler issue of Rep's consistency.

Postulating the ellipsis, we can dispel the appearance of Rep's self-contradiction. Report (2´) implies, given Belia's basic logicality, this version of (3):

> (3´) Belia has adopted a name for the skunk and she does *not* believe about the skunk with that name that it's a woodchuck.

Note that this new version of (3) does not contradict our new version of (1). The negation in it has narrow scope.^ The sentence is a conjunction, but only its second conjunct is negated. It's to be distinguished from the following wide scope negation, which does contradict (1´):

(4) It's *not* the case that both Belia has adopted a name for the skunk and she believes about the skunk with that name that it's a woodchuck.

The adding of a reference to names to the report rendered it possible to distinguish two ways of introducing a negation in Rep's reports, with narrow scope and with wide scope. The narrow scope way that (3´) illustrates is clearly the negation that Rep needs in order to defend his consistency, when he reports Belia's both believing and failing to believe about the animal that it's a woodchuck.

Rep does not want us to understand him as deliberately contradicting himself. So he wants us to draw a conversational implicature about Belia's inner names, and our theory regiments into his reports this implicature by supposing an ellipsis and making it explicit, which elevates the implicatures to the status of entailments. (Recall section E on the connection of regimentation to conversational implicature.) What had been missing from our setup of the paradox was Rep's reference to the names that Belia adopted for making her own reference.

The suggestion of mind-reading may seem odd. Does Belia have names for things, and Rep have names for Belia's names for things? Why not? She *uses* her names, and he *mentions* them. (Recall that distinction from the end of section D.) If he does not have proper names for each of her names, at least he can quantify over them, saying "some name."

## §2. The Kaplan solution: The believer does not contradict herself.

The question arises whether we have here in the postulate of inner **nonce names** (i.e., something's name for the nonce, that is, for the time being) a genuine phenomenon of the belief or just an artifact of Rep's concurrence with Belia, something he attributes to her to save himself, which would make it only a phenomenon of reportage. We decided earlier (in section H) that Belia's state of knowledge by causal rapport was a necessary condition for Rep's right to use the *de re* mode of reporting. Recall Belia's knowledge of the baldness of San Marino's president, but lack of knowledge of Sven Svenson's tallness. We defended this account in sections I and J. Now to resolve the paradox presented in section K we resort to causal rapport again and assert that the nonce name "*a*" is a product of that causal rapport. Since Belia's dog got caught up in the paradox, there'll have to be nonce names for the woodchuck even in the dog's mind, if this solution is to work.

So the nonce name is not just an artifact of Rep's concurrence. The report predicts that, if Belia were to express her belief, the name she'd use to publish her belief would be a surrogate for a mental nonce name for her, most likely but not necessarily, since publication to her conversation partner is constrained by what the partner will understand. Perhaps the prediction is that, if we were to have Belia record her belief for herself, she'd use a name that expressed her mental nonce name. Here I assume that names occurring mentally are not sounds, but that when they are phoneticized for speech, their identity is transmitted to the name's phonetic version.

The causal rapport not only gives Belia descriptive information, but the rapport is **reference fixing** for the nonce name in a way that reflects how Belia grasps that information. I think only reference fixing is going on here, not defining, because the causal rapport that fixed the referent of the name in actuality might itself have been different, in the sense that the same information might have been conveyed via a different causal route, preserving the identity of the two termini, the naming event and the thing named, and so the rapport is not part of the meaning of the name. Furthermore, the rapport fixes the name's referent in a way independent of the descriptive information conveyed by the causal rapport, for she grasps that information as contingently true of the thing named. Thus the negations of these descriptions must be possibly true of the thing named. Thus the descriptions are not part of the meaning of the name either.

We introduced reference fixing in sections A and F, and the concept has undergone some stretching. Perhaps we should note the ways it has stretched. In section A, we made the idea represented in the upper left-hand quadrant of the following chart definitive of the notion, although we noted the ideas in all the other quadrants except the lower right, which we introduce now.

|  | By description: | By nondescriptive means: |
|---|---|---|
| *Ad hoc*: | Arthur, Sonny, Dartmouth | Referential uses of descriptions |
| By linguistic rule: | Jack the Ripper | Names introduced by causal rapport |

Table L-1. Examples of four types of reference fixing of singular terms.

The two rows indicate that reference fixing may occur, either because someone decides on the spot to make use of it for the terms she's about to utter, or because there's a rule of the language that fixes the term's reference. The nonce name, in the lower right quadrant, is free to be a rigid designator, since it's introduced by reference fixing, not definition. The causal rapport, then, is another form of nondescriptive reference fixing, like the nods and gestures underlying the referential uses of definite descriptions, noted in section A. But even if it's a rigid designator, it does not follow that it's a logically proper name, for some descriptions are also modally rigid designators.

Several reasons suggest that in fact a nonce name can have descriptive content as part of its meaning. One cogent reason is that we must account for those of Belia's beliefs which are not about real things, because, let's say, she formed them as a result of hallucination, or something like that. So we cannot take causal rapport to be indispensable to all inner names; they can be definite descriptions. Not all inner names are rigid designators; not all that Belia may think to be proper names are even names in fact. Nevertheless, we can accommodate these concerns while reserving the notion of nonce name for the names of the things Belia's in causal rapport with.

Another reason for descriptive names, not so cogent, is that otherwise Belia falls into the predicament we noted in section A of someone who had two logically proper names of me and believed contrary things of me. Belia's current situation is similar: To repeat, Belia believes something which she might express with this sentence:

*a* is a woodchuck, and *b* is not a woodchuck, and *a* is not *b*.

If the two names are logically proper, and the singular sentence expresses a complete singular proposition, the proposition is an inconsistent^ one. If Belia's belief is directed toward the proposition and not the sentence, then she believes something no rational person should. Some philosophers would say, better to suppose that the names are not logically proper. Thus Russell, who, as we saw in section A, insisted that, if the sentence "Scott is Sir Walter" does not express the triviality that Scott is Scott, it must be because it means "The person called 'Scott' is Sir Walter." I say this reason for thinking of the inner names as descriptive is not so cogent. First, it presumes that attitudes are directed toward intensional entities like propositions, and descriptive names help that assumption. But it does not help the assumption enough, because there are still problems of hyperintensionality it does not resolve. Furthermore, the thesis gratuitously rules out examples like the one about Arthur and Sonny in section A as well as the Hesper and Phosphor case I introduced in the previous section. We'll see soon that we can alleviate Rep's embarrassment in reporting these beliefs, provided that the inner names he refers to in his reports are logically proper names whose referents were fixed in ways he can also refer to. Finally, it opens the way for a disfiguring "correction" of the ellipsis theory to avoid reference to names at all, replacing them with concepts, "modes of presentation," or intensions themselves as the items the ellipsis refers to. If we allow for reference to proper names, as I think we must, then none of these substitutes will work, because there's nothing to the meaning of a logically proper name but the thing meant. We're stuck with the name itself. But if only the name will make the ellipsis work in the case of beliefs with logically proper names, parsimony recommends reference to names in all the cases. (This is the argument I referred to in the previous section, to motivate my extending the paradox to cover logically proper names.)

Conceding some descriptive content to some mental names and the status of logically proper name to others, however, in what role might the name itself function in *de re* reportage? Rep may use it and comment on it. In *de dicto* reportage, Rep may say, if he knew the phonetic version of the name Belia used,

Belia believes that *a* is a woodchuck.

A name that's been used more than once for the same thing may accumulate associations with descriptive content, in addition to its tie to the thing named, a tie established by the causal rapport between the thing and the believer. If Rep knew the name and if, when the descriptive content was part of the meaning of the name, he agreed with it, then he could report,

Belia believes about *a* that it's a woodchuck.

There may still be reason to postulate ellipsis in this report if he wants us to know he's adopting Belia's own name; it may be the claim that such a name is a *vivid* designator, that is, a nonce name rich in descriptive associations for the person who introduced it as a name for a real thing. An inner name is commonly, but not always (e.g., in hallucinations), based on its creator's extensive causal rapport with the object designated. The richness of the descriptive content makes the name vivid for its creator. We call this approach to the content of Rep's ellipsis the **vivid names** approach. In the main it was created by David Kaplan, but it's implicit in Russell's 1940 theory of noticing.[2]

When Kaplan introduced the idea of vividness, he did not make a distinction between descriptions being the meanings of names and descriptions merely fixing the referents of names. Consequently it's unclear how vivid names would be rigid designators, as I suspect he would've wanted them to be (so they'd behave right in counterfactual^

reasoning with them). Also causal rapport with a name's referent is not a necessary part of what makes a name vivid for a person, according to Kaplan. Thus my introducing "nonce name" to make that connection, a connection that Kaplan captured with his term, "name *of.*" We'll understand vivid names, like nonce names, to be proper names, with all descriptive accretions consigned to being reference fixers.

Still, however, there's a residual mystery. Usually the reporter doesn't know the name in the believer's mind, so he refers to some name being there and reports that the believer believes "with that name." What is it to believe with a name? We need to replace the phrase "with a name" in the explication of the ellipsis with something clearer. The problem is urgent since the name's playing havoc with the assigning of an antecedent to the pronouns in the that-clause. If Belia believes about the skunk with a name that it's a woodchuck, is the antecedent of the "it" the skunk or the name? It seems the pronoun wants to refer back to both. Well, Belia doesn't believe the name is a woodchuck. So it must be the skunk. But then we're back to attributing to her the belief that the skunk is a woodchuck, and the mystery returns, how does she believe that with a name? Just how do we exonerate Belia of the inconsistency of believing about the skunk that it is a skunk and that it's not a skunk? We'll now elaborate a theory of the phrase "with a name," to wit, that the name introduces a further element of the ellipsis, namely a reflexive content of the report.

To introduce and motivate a report's having reflexive content, let's return to the issue of Belia believing an inconsistent proposition and apply the ellipsis theory to the reports of her believing an identity and a non-identity. We'll also consider the young Pythagoras, before he discovered that Hesper was identical to Phosphor. The fact of there being more than one anaphoric pronoun in a predicate of identity creates complexity, not to mention the further perplexity when their antecedents are only logically proper names. The more complex ellipsis affects the adicity of relational belief. A belief *de re* is multigrade in two ways:

(1) believes about $(2_1)$, $(2_2)$, etc., with names $(3_{11})$, $(3_{12})$, etc. for $(2_1)$, names $(3_{21})$, $(3_{22})$, etc., for $(2_2)$, etc., that (4).

The first step toward a solution of these cases that are multigrade because of the multiplicity of names is not to void any points we already made. In particular, we cannot let Rep override the believer's control over the substance of the that-clause. To illustrate the problem, we and Rep may try to report that there's a name with which Belia believes about the skunk that it's not identical to it, and there's a name with which the young Pythagoras believes about Venus that it's not identical to it. They insist on their rights over the that-clause and deny that they affirm the clause asserting nonselfidentity of anything whatsoever. After all, they know that it's a law of logic that $x = x$. Thus they force us to use the unrestricted predicate for expressing the same intensional entity, the relation of identity: $x = y$. In other words, hyperintensionality will arise even with the ellipsis theory, for the theory concerns the about-position, and hyperintensionality concerns the that-clause. Despite the separateness of the problem of contradiction developed in section K from the problem of hyperintensionality, the resurrection of hyperintensionality in the form of the believers' insistence that the that-clause use the unrestricted predicate of identity forces the reporters to make reference twice to antecedents for the pronouns. Only once in our reports on Belia and Pythagoras did we and Rep make reference to a name of the thing, but each of them named it twice when they denied an identity.

There's a right way and a wrong way of making reference to names twice, however. We should not refer to their multiple namings in these ways:

- Belia has adopted names for the skunk, and she believes about it with a pair of distinct ones, that it's not identical to it.
- Belia has adopted names for the skunk, and she believes about it with a pair consisting of the same one twice, that it is identical to it.
- The young Pythagoras adopted names for Venus, and he believed about it with a pair of distinct ones, that it's not identical to it.
- The young Pythagoras adopted names for Venus, and he believed about it with a pair consisting of the same one twice, that it is identical to it.

Even though none contradicts any other anymore, the two pairs provide no solution, because the first and third of the sentences are false. For the believers deny their that-clauses. (The reports say the believers affirm a logically invalid formula, not-$(x = x)$.) Nor should we report the conjunctive incomplete proposition, which Belia believes, in this way:

- Belia has adopted names for the skunk, and she believes about it with a pair of distinct ones, that both it is a woodchuck and it's not a woodchuck.

How then should we proceed? The two pronouns in the that-clause are not to be tied to a single referent. To indicate that they're not, it's more perspicuous to use the pronouns, "the former" and "the latter" to indicate the difference of antecedents. That forces the reporters not to bunch the names together in a plural, "there are names," but rather:

> There's a name$_1$ which Belia adopted for the skunk such that she believes about it with that name that it is a woodchuck, and there's a name$_2$ which she adopted for the skunk such that she believes about it with that name that it's not a woodchuck.

When it's the identity relation in the that-clause, the report will look like this:

> There's a name$_1$ which Pythagoras adopted for Venus such that there's a name$_2$ which he adopted for Venus such that he believes about it that the former is not identical to the latter.

The that-clause is wrong, however, since Pythagoras should not be reported as believing the nonidentity of the names.

Once again, the names are wreaking havoc with the pronouns in our that-clauses. Appeal to names seems inevitably to call for an additional clause as part of the ellipsis: a **reflexive content of a report**, for Rep must specify whatever conditions make his report true which the rules of the language leave unspecified. According to this development of the ellipsis theory, the full expression of a report of Pythagoras's belief is

> There's a name$_1$ which Pythagoras adopted for Venus such that there's a name$_2$ which he adopted for Venus such that he believes about it that it's not identical to it, by virtue of his having fixed the referents of the two names in ways that made it unlikely for him that they named the same thing.

In the case of Belia's belief about the skunk, that it's a woodchuck, the full report would be,

> (1´) Belia has adopted a name for the skunk and she believes about the skunk that it's a woodchuck by virtue of her having fixed the referent of the name in a way that made it unlikely for her that it named a skunk.

The added content is called reflexive because it refers to the name, whatever one Belia adopted. Note please, the added content does not report something reflexive going on in Belia's mind. The phrase "the name" is a variable as it occurs in the definite description, "the referent of the name," whose antecedent is the quantifier at the beginning of the report. This clause does work for the reporter. Yet its occurrence in the that-clause requires that the believer verify it. To see how she does it without herself entertaining reflexive content, recall from section C that the verification may be by her words or by her behavior. The clause explains her behavior without attributing reflexive thoughts to her by saying something about how her inner names came to have the referents they do have.

Suppose the reporter knows the believer's inner proper names, as we do Pythagoras's two names for Venus. The reporter can skip the generalized reference to names in his report and go directly to specifying the belief's content in terms of the actual names. Thus he reports,

> Pythagoras does not believe about Venus that it is identical to it, by virtue of his using "Hesper" in place of the former "it" and "Phosphor" in place of the latter, and his having fixed their referents in ways that made it unlikely for him that they named the same thing.

The reflexive content, instead of reporting something additional about Pythagoras, is merely machinery of reportage. Suppose we rework the reflexive content so that the reporter mentions the monadic relative predicates, "is Hesper" and "is Phosphor" in his statement of it:

> Pythagoras does not believe about Venus that it is identical to it, by virtue of his not believing that the predicate "is Hesper" is true of all and only things that the predicate "is Phosphor" is true of.

Since the two predicates express the same monadic attribute, the reflexive content is simply stating the problem of hyperintensionality. That's an issue concerning directed-towardness, expressed by the that-clause, to be discussed in Part III. So let's leave the matter of reflexivity. In section N we'll reconsider whether there is a reflexive content of belief which must be reported, and not just reflexive machinery for reportage.

It should be clear enough now that the attribution of ellipsis to the reports and the making it explicit in our regimentation will immunize the reporter from self-contradiction when he reports on Belia's and Pythagoras's beliefs. The reports' "by virtue of" clauses introducing the reflexive content also exonerate Belia and Pythagoras of illogicality.

## §3. Additional merits of Kaplan's theory.

Let's examine four excellences of this theory, in addition to its saving face for Rep. The first excellence: If the concept of a vivid name can be made precise enough to be scientifically useful, the vivid names approach can explain the validity of a form of generalization that we've ignored until now, namely **generalization with narrow scope**. Ever since section E, where we introduced the distinction, we've tacitly restricted our discussions of generalization to **generalization with wide scope**, that is, the scope^ of the generalization was the whole report:

Something is such that Belia believes about it that it ran into the bushes.

Rep makes that generalization. He can generalize the reference in the about-position. And if the vivid names approach is right, he also generalizes the reference to Belia's vivid name for the thing he names in the about-position:

*Some* name and *some* animal, such that the former designates the latter, are such that . . .

Belia generalizes too: Clearly, if

Belia believes that a woodchuck ran into the bushes, or as she'd say, "*the* woodchuck,"

then

Belia believes that something is such that it ran into the bushes. Here the scope of the generalizing phrase "something is such that . . ." is narrow, since its scope covers the words to its right, and the words "Belia believes that" are to its left, outside its scope. We can explain this narrow scope generalization as valid within Belia's inner logic, a generalization from her inner singular sentences, which use nonce names, to her inner general sentences.

Although we understand the operation of generalization from a name to be an operation on sentences, it need not be restricted to sentences, and it may not be so restricted in the mind. In section Q, we'll discuss the unity of propositions, the so-called problem of the propositional bond, and there we'll open up new ways of thinking about names. In the meantime don't assume that mental names can only occur in mental sentences, which might support the theory that directs beliefs toward the complete singular propositions such sentences would express. Names might very well just be the entities in a mental model of a state of affairs. Models are more holistic^ than propositions. So the occurrence of names in models need not support the theory either. Models defined in terms of proper names can be generalized.

The second excellence of the theory: The vivid names approach can solve a problem concerning pronominal anaphora, namely, how some pronouns are bound to an antecedent while others are left unbound. Relatively to any episode of causal rapport there'll be the original naming (a "dubbing") and one or more anaphoric reoccurrences of that name. Namings are distinct from anaphoric uses of the names, which are events parasitical on the namings. Anaphoric uses of names are not quantified-over separately from the namings that provide their antecedents. Even if the anaphoric names differ qualitatively as well as numerically from the names introduced in their antecedents, we collect them as instances of the same name analogously to the way a quantifier collects same-design variables within its scope. For example,

>    Al [the naming] is interested, but he [anaphoric name] is sleepy.

is analogous to:

>    Someone $x$ [quantifier] is such that $x$ is interested, but $x$ is sleepy.

The disanalogy between the mind's way and logic's way is that the mind does not require same design. Indeed, two namings may use physically exactly similar names in her brain, but the mind somehow treats them as independent and can detect which of the two an anaphoric occurrence is to be assigned to. So a naming comes with some indication of scope for the purposes of memory, but not quite like the linear system of scope indication that symbolic logic popularized.

The solution to the problem of Rep's contradictions is evident. The only way Belia can contradict herself in what she believes about what she saw is by using the same name twice. The same name twice can occur in two ways, either once in a nam*ing* and then anaphorically evoking that naming, or twice anaphorically, each evoking the same naming. For example, either:

>    I dub you "thing that's a woodchuck," and you're not a wood-chuck,

or:

>    I dub you "thing that ran into the bushes"; you are a woodchuck and you're not a woodchuck.

These are contradictions, but *two namings* don't generate a contradiction, even if physically identical names occur in those incidents. That's why you don't contradict yourself when you use the pronoun "this" twice, once to deny of the wall that it's a book, and once to affirm of the book that it's a book. Two namings can generate sentences which express an inconsistent proposition, if they happen to be namings of the same thing. And Belia has done just that. Where $a$ and $b$ name the animal that went into the bushes and back out again, then to deny $a = b$ is to deny a necessary proposition and affirm an inconsistent^ one, as we proved in section F. The *sentence* is not provable from logic alone, however, and so a sentence which is its denial is not a contradiction.

The third excellence of the theory: We noted in section E that failures of substitution for proper names occur in that-clauses. Like Pythagoras, Belia may believe that Phosphor is Phosphor but not believe that Hesper is Phosphor, since she does not know that both the names name the same thing. Suppose Rep not only knows that Belia is using some name; he knows which names. Rep can now use the theory that there's ellipsis of nonce names to evade the contradictions:

> Belia has adopted the name "Phosphor" for Venus and she believes about the latter with that name that it is identical to Phosphor.

Also,

> Belia has adopted the name "Hesper" for Venus and she believes about the latter with that name that it's not identical to Phosphor.

Although each name simply picks out Venus, each is vivid in different ways for Belia. In particular, the causal rapports with Venus that fixed the referent of each name are different. Rep adds reflexive content to that effect, cashing out the phrase, "with that name."

Fourth excellence: The vivid names approach also settles a question we wondered about in sections H and I. If the identity of vivid names is determined by their creator's causal rapport with the things named, is it reasonable to suppose, if Belia has a *de re* belief about *all* of a class of things, that she has a name for each and every one of them? Not if the belief arises by inductive generalization, since she's not in causal rapport with each of them. This is another reason to deny that such universally generalized beliefs are *de re*. Recall this table from section A, to which we add one thing in the upper right box:

|  | singular beliefs | general beliefs |
|---|---|---|
| relational beliefs (*de re*) | singular & relational | *No inductions here.* |
| notional beliefs (*de dicto*) | singular & notional | general & notional |

Table L-2 (A-1, revised). A cross-classification of two dichotomies, implying their independence. (Instances in the lower left box come under suspicion in section W.)

We're not finished entertaining the possibility of general relational belief, however. It comes up again in Part III. In the meantime, Belia wishes Rep to report to us how she solves a problem she confronted while reading Descartes. She was quite impressed with the evil genie's ability to deceive her, so much so that, although she's sure she now exists, she's not sure of her memories of having existed before now, even the most recent ones. On the other hand, she's a thinking thing, and thought takes time. So she cannot've begun to exist just at this present instant. Is she sure or unsure about having existed before now? Somehow the answer seems to be both . . . She considers a domain consisting of past times she'd assign a nonzero probability of her existing at. "Aha!" she exclaims. Rep reports her solution consisting of three beliefs, the first *de re*, capturing the unsureness, the second *de dicto*, capturing the sureness, and the third is comparative of the sureties of the two types:

> ●Belia is unsure to varying degrees about each time before now that she existed then.
>
> ●Belia is quite sure that she has existed from some time before now.
>
> ●Belia is at least as unsure that she existed at all those times before now as she is of having existed at a least likely one of them.

The invalidity of importation and exportation ensures the distinctness of the *de dicto* beliefs from the *de re* belief and the consistency of Belia's solution to her puzzle. The three beliefs each contain elements of generality, although by the definition of "general belief" given in section A, they're singular, because they also refer to her and to the present moment. Nevertheless, the puzzle indicates how general *de re* beliefs can be consistently less sure than their *de dicto* general counterparts, and so it's useful for the table's upper right-hand compartment not to be empty.

### §4. Identity conditions for vivid names.

Perhaps the vivid names approach is insufficiently substantiated, both in respect of whether they exist and what they are if they exist. Whether they exist is an empirical question. This is several questions: whether they exist at all; whether they exist in each species capable of attitudes; and whether in at least human beings, they always occur when a person is in causal rapport with an object. It's evidence that they exist in Belia on the occasion we studied, that their existence would solve the problems we've noted. But might a human being be in rapport with an object and the rapport not create names? Might there be species so primitive that rapport never creates names in them? Perhaps a paramecium classifies the things it comes into rapport with only as nutritious or noxious, but never bothers with individuating them. The ellipsis theory calling for vivid names is not refuted by any of these cases, unless Belia-style confusions can occur even when we know that no mental names are occurring. I can think of no clear-cut case where the confusion occurs but no mental names occur. It's hard to put a paramecium in this condition, for example.

Let's look at Quine's criticism of our account of what they are, if they are, and in the next subsection his preferred alternative treatment of the paradoxes. The theory of vivid names refers to names themselves as entities. "No entity without identity," says Quine. Recall section G, that the ideal of extensionality required well-defined entities. When logicians refer to names, they're the public names in the language specified by the logic, and their spelling identifies them. What are the identity conditions for the vivid names that exist only in someone's head? For each name on these pages it's just the sameness of its graphic design, but the brain's not a writing tablet. The problem of identity conditions is pressing, for the intelligibility of the theory depends on solving it. The vivid names approach has not solved the paradox until it solves the problem of individuating these terms, since its solution of the paradox requires mentioning names and quantifying over them. Sometimes two occurrences of the same name, judged to be the same purely phonically or graphically, mean different things, sometimes different names mean the same thing.

Let's embellish our story to demonstrate the residual problem of identity conditions for names. Belia, let's say, doesn't use either definite descriptions or proper names to identify what she saw on each occasion; she uses a demonstrative pronoun, the same one on each occasion. (**Demonstrative pronouns**, e.g., "this" and "that," are not anaphoric pronouns; they get their reference usually by gestures toward things.) Although she names what she saw run into the bushes "this," and what she saw run out she names also "this," she does not know that the former this is the latter this. Here she's used the same singular term twice. Intuitively, she has not contradicted herself even so. You can verify it for yourself in the way we suggested when we pointed out the second excellence of the nonce name theory. Point to the wall and say, "This is not a book." Now point to the book and say, "This is a book." You've not contradicted yourself. Neither has Belia contradicted herself in using the demonstrative "this" twice. Yet the vivid names approach would seem to imply that she does, since it only plays on graphic or phonic or some such design difference to ward off contradiction. And Rep's bringing in Belia's mind would be of no avail in keeping his reports also from being self-contradictory, if Belia's mind were just a tablet where names, mere designs, get recorded. We have to go beyond mere phonic, graphic, or any other physical identity conditions for sameness of names, so that we can distinguish Belia's first "this" from her second.

At least part of the solution to this problem is causal rapport. The vivid names approach calls for vivid names to be caused by episodes of causal rapport. This yields a component of the identity conditions for vivid names:

> Name $x$ is identical to name $y$, if the episode of causal rapport that caused the one caused the other.

This is a sufficient^ condition for identity; perhaps we can raise it to being a necessary^ condition also (i.e., reading the "if" as "if and only if"). Even so, names are only as well individuated as the episodes of causal rapport are. Quine will remind us that the episodes are individuated contextually. Thus one and the same episode may count as a vivid name and also as not one, just by varying the context of the report it enters into. That makes the approach unsuited for science.

But can we mount a defense? Perhaps we can cite the case discussed in section J, that the law concerning juries promises a privileged context; this context reveals the essence of relational belief because it prioritizes referential success. Further, the ultimate identity conditions for these nonce names must refer to their instantiation in the brain. Here their identity may be fixed not only by an isolated structure, but may depend also on the context of brain structures to individuate names. Perhaps there's a correlation between the brain's context-providing structures that individuate mental nonce names and the social contexts for serious *de re* attributions, as in a jury's deliberations, so that the inner one instances a name if and only if the social one ensures its referential success. Then an outer and an inner approach would converge to the same answer. We're deep into utopian science at this point, since we cannot observe that such identity conditions hold true in any particular case. We must distinguish between specifying identity conditions and specifying conditions for feasible testing of an identity. Logic and analysis requires the former; the latter is good to have but not required.

### §5. The Burdick solution: The believer and reporter do not contradict themselves.

As you might've guessed, the vivid names approach is not Quine's favorite alternative to his own surrender on *de re* belief. Vivid names and episodes of causal rapport stand or fall together. If the concept of the one is context-dependent, the concept of the other is also, because the identity conditions for names connect the names to the episodes. My view is that vivid names are to be expected in psychological theory. That gives us a second reason (after the reason provided by the law governing a jury's reaching a verdict) to look for a context-invariant characterization of naming episodes. That's repugnant to Quine. After his preference for being resigned to the illogicality of *de re* reports, as evidenced by the paradoxes of the last section, and banishing them from science, Quine's second in order of preference is a theory developed by Howard Burdick,[3] which resolves the paradoxes but nevertheless leaves *de re* reports without value to science.

Burdick also resorts to ellipsis to solve the paradoxes. He postulates that *all* referential positions in *all* sentences are filled in with **ordered pairs**, consisting of, first, the ordinary subject of the sentence's predicate and, secondly, a mode of presenting that subject in words which need not be true uniquely of that subject. So the words in the second position aren't naming the thing in the first position; they're describing it. We symbolize the pair thus: $<\_,\_>$, where the underlinings indicate the positions of the paired groups of words. Rep is in command of the first position in the ordered pair, and Belia commands the second position. In ordinary sentences the reporter and the believer are the same person. Only in reports of another's beliefs do they separate into two persons.

Both positions in the ordered pair can be quantified into. For example,

some $x$ is such that . . . $<\_,x>$ . . . , and

every $y$ is such that . . . $<y,\_>$ . . . .

People don't think of ordinary sentences as having a pair for a subject. The reason, according to this theory, is that the second term is quantified in just that way and need not be expressed. Thus a simple statement like "candy is sweet" is analyzed as implicitly generalized:

Some mode $x$ of presentation is such that $<$ candy, $x >$ is sweet. The situation is like my saying of someone that she is a mother; she is a mother of someone, but I leave that reference unexpressed.

To make reading the analysis of beliefs easier, we'll capitalize variables occupying the second place in a pair. Rep's *de re* report that

Belia believes *about* the skunk that it ran into the bushes will look like this:

Some mode of presentation $S$ is such that Belia believes "ran into the bushes" true of (i.e., *about*) $<$ the skunk, $S >$.

$S$ is, of course, the words "is the woodchuck." But Rep ignores that detail in his reports *de re* by the expedient of generalizing over the words.

Rep could report Belia's erroneous *de dicto* belief that, as she would say, the woodchuck ran into the bushes this way:

Something $s$ is such that Belia believes "ran into the bushes" is true of <*s*, "is the woodchuck">.

The *s* in this case is the skunk, but he ignores what it is by generalizing over it in this report *de dicto*. If Belia were to be deluded and have a belief about what happens to be nothing at all, the first position of the ordered pair would be filled by the null set. One of many virtues Burdick claims for his approach is that exportation of singular terms out of that-clauses is now a valid implication. They occur in first position in the pairs, and Rep controls the first position.

The paradox of the previous section is avoided, as the vivid names approach avoids it, namely, by blocking the derivation of a negation corresponding to sentence (3) of the previous section. From these two *de re* reports,

> (1´´) Some mode of presentation *S* is such that Belia believes "is a woodchuck" true of < the skunk, *S* >.

> (2´´) Some mode of presentation *S* is such that Belia believes "is not a woodchuck" true of < the skunk, *S* >.

The fact that (1´´) and (2´´) need not be referring to the same mode of presentation prevents us from deriving any self-contradiction in Belia. Let's be given the mode of presentation of the animal at Belia's first sighting of it: "*A*." The mode of presentation of it at her second sighting is "*B*." Combining the truth with Belia's beliefs yields this *dictum*:

> Something *x* is such that <*x*,*A*> is a woodchuck, and <*x*,*B*> is not a woodchuck.

Since *A* is not *B*, neither are the pairs <*x*,*A*> and <*x*,*B*>. So no contradiction there. As for Rep's contradicting himself, we cannot deduce the denial of (1´´) from (2´´), but only

> (3´´) Some mode of presentation *S* is such that Belia does *not* believe "is a woodchuck" true of < the skunk, *S* >.

Burdick does not take attitudes to be directed toward complete singular propositions or complete sentences, but rather toward predicates. He can therefore make a distinction between predicates which is analogous to that between a dyadic relation and a monadic relative property. Consequently our argument for the superiority of the view that *de re* attitudes are directed toward incomplete propositions rather than toward complete singular ones cannot be deployed against Burdick. On that score his theory is as good as mine.

The consistency of Rep is preserved, and so is Belia's without having to resort to speculations about inner names. At most we postulate inner predicates. Furthermore, there's no mystery about identity conditions for these subjects, since only things and words are terms in the pairs. With equal success in evading the paradoxes and greater success in conforming to the ideal of extensional identity conditions, the pairs approach wins the first round against the vivid names approach.

According to Burdick, reports of relational belief quantify over the second position in the pair, and reports of notional belief quantify over the first. We've assumed from the very beginning that there really are two formats for reporting beliefs. That assumption lay at the heart of our regimentations in section C. If Burdick is right, the difference between the formats is trivial at best; there's no formal kind of difference, no great battle between the extensionalist ideals of intelligibility and the dark miasma of referential opacity. For Burdick, the decision which of the two positions in a pair is to be quantified over is left to the context of reporting to determine, a totally context-dependent matter. The extent to which causal rapport affects this decision is also totally a context-dependent matter. On that issue he adds nothing to Quine, agreeing that the *de re - de dicto* distinction is too relative to the context of reporting to be of value to psychological theory.

For our part, we might concede Burdick's blending of the two formats for reporting beliefs. Indeed it makes the job of defending a context-invariance of relational belief easier, because the case for context-invariance exploited a particular regimentation of the distinction between relational and notional attitudes mainly for heuristic purposes, not for indispensable evidence. The heuristic purposes are perhaps better served by Burdick's reformulation of the distinction in terms of which one of the two positions is quantified over, for he neutralizes logic itself; logicality is no longer at issue. The extensionalist ideal is still the issue, but the point of contention is narrowed to the matter of a domain of well-defined entities (see section G). Quine and Burdick see only context-dependency, so no well-defined entities. Believers in the context-invariance of relational belief won't look just to the context of reporting to determine which position is quantified over in a report. We look to the things themselves, or in other words, that which is reported on, to detect the differences between relational and notional beliefs.

# Notes

1. Mark Crimmins and John Perry, "The Prince and the Phone Booth: Reporting Puzzling Beliefs," (1989), reprinted with postscript in Perry's, *The Essential Indexical and Other Essays* (1993). See section IV. Barbara L. Davidson describes her solution to these puzzles as completing an ellipsis in her "Belief *De*

*Re* and *De Se,*" *Australasian Journal of Philosophy,* 63 (1985) 389-406. Although she has priority in the use of the name "elliptical," the earlier theories are also properly described thus.

2. David Kaplan, "Quantifying In," (1968) reprinted in D. Davidson and J. Hintikka, eds., *Words and Objections: Essays on the Work of W.V. Quine* (1969) 206-242, section IX. Bertrand Russell, *An Inquiry into Meaning and Truth,* chs. 3 and 24, where he connects the noticing to proper naming. Kaplan includes descriptive components in a vivid name (p. 229), so that the believer can bring the name to mind. He also admits the concept "is to some degree relative to special interests," thereby giving Quine an opening to reject this approach as unsuitable for science.

3. Quine, "Burdick's Attitudes," *Synthese* 52 (1982) 231-233; also *From Stimulus to Science* (1995) 98. Burdick's first paper was cited in a note in section J, "A Logical Form for the Propositional Attitudes," *Synthese,* 52 (1982) 185-230. Another paper of his is "A Notorious Affair Called *Exportation,*" *Synthese* 87 (1991) 363-377.

# M. Beliefs About Oneself and About the Present Moment: the Data.

At the end of section B we noted the phenomenon of "egocentric propositional attitudes" and deferred discussion of them. They are beliefs and other attitudes about oneself, and we'll examine the data on them in this section. Attitudes about the moment at which the attitude occurs, i.e., an attitude's present moment, are analogous to attitudes about oneself; so we'll cover them too.

If there's a kind of relational belief that escapes the vagaries of causal rapport, it would seem to be beliefs about oneself and beliefs about the time of believing. For a believer can get no closer to that which her belief is about than this: believing something about herself at her present moment—"me now." If we can establish the scientific respectability of this kind of relational belief, perhaps a way opens for saving the other relational beliefs, which do depend on causal rapport. Here we pass beyond Quine's investigations; he says little about this kind of belief. The little he does say he subsumes under the heading of egocentric attitudes. Such attitudes, as Quine characterizes them, are not any and all attitudes whatsoever that are about oneself; they are just those that predicate very primitive attributes of oneself, of the sort a cat might entertain of itself. Let's set aside for now Quine's assumption of simplicity of predicate; that's not the point to focus on.

## §1. The indispensability of beliefs in the first person for actions.

Before expanding our theory of the about-position to cover beliefs about oneself and the present moment, let's examine the data. Let's begin with the connection of belief to action. A nontrivial necessary^ condition for a change in Belia's behavior is a change in one of her attitudes toward contents—that much is trivial—specifically and nontrivially, a change to one that she'd express to others indexically. The argument for this thesis consists of simple thought experiments involving no semantic ascent.

There are four kinds of belief about oneself, three of which are irrelevant for understanding the direct connection of belief to action:

(i) Irrelevant is the one where Belia has a belief that just happens to apply to herself. If Belia had a belief about the girl Jack's in love with, but didn't know that Jack's in love with Belia, then her belief would be *de dicto* with respect to that girl. The subject referred to in its that-clause would be Belia, but she would not be aware of that fact. The reason we set this belief aside as irrelevant is this thought experiment. It's insufficient by itself, without her being aware of her identity with the one Jack loves, to motivate her acting in her interests on this matter. Without the awareness of, as she might say, "I am the one," she cannot act on her belief in ways that suit her purposes.

King David (in the Old Testament[1]) had a belief about himself that was purely *de dicto* after listening to the prophet Nathan. Nathan told David about a man who misbehaved. David accused the man in Nathan's story of injustice and ordered punishment for him. Only then did Nathan point out, "You are the man." Until the moment David realized "I am the man," he had no idea that he believed of himself that he was unjust; his belief had been simply *de dicto*. Nathan had arranged to create first the wrath that the behavior itself warranted, and then the self-recognition in the story, so that the wrath was turned toward David, *de re*. It worked: David replied, "I have sinned against the Lord." So *de dicto* beliefs directed toward propositions expressed with definite descriptions are irrelevant, even when the descriptions apply to the believer.

(ii) Also irrelevant for us is a *de re* belief that Belia may have about herself *qua* Belia, where "Belia" is the mental proper name that figures in her belief's content. For that use of a name raises the separate matter of her knowing that "Belia" is her own name. If she's become confused about that and cannot affirm "I am Belia," her belief is still relational, and it's about herself, although she doesn't know it. She may believe about Belia that she's dehydrated, but if she doesn't know that she herself is Belia, her belief would not prompt her to get a drink. (You say, she'll get a drink anyway, but I say it wasn't *that* belief that prompted her to.) Since such a belief about herself cannot affect her behavior as a belief about oneself should, without the help of another belief about herself, namely that "Belia" is her own name, it's not about herself in the sense I intend. It's that helper belief that's of interest. You may think it impossible not to believe that helper belief, but it is reported. In 1890, William James wrote:[2]

> In half-stunned states self-consciousness may lapse. A friend writes me: "We were driving back again—in a wagonette. The door flew open and

X, alias 'Baldy,' fell out on the road. We pulled up at once, and then he said, 'Did anybody fall out?' or 'Who fell out?'—I don't exactly remember the words. When told that Baldy fell out, he said, 'Did Baldy fall out? Poor Baldy!'"

(iii) Even a *de re* belief about herself expressed with a demonstrative pronoun, such as "this," is irrelevant for us. Belia may see herself in a mirror but not recognize herself or the mirror, and form a belief about "this person." In an extreme case she may even use her finger to point back at her own body and say "this person." Yet it's still possible that she may be unaware that this person is herself. The result of that ignorance is that the beliefs she forms about this person don't affect her behavior to suit her purposes as they otherwise might have. Ernst Mach supplied another example of the irrelevancy:[3]

> Not long ago, after a trying railway journey by night, and much fatigued, I got into an omnibus, just as another gentleman appeared at the other end. "What shabby pedagogue is that, that has just entered?" thought I. It was myself; opposite me hung a large mirror. The physiognomy of my class, accordingly, was better known to me than my own [physiognomy].

We can imagine Belia to be in such predicaments. Novelists like Charles Dickens[4] and Dorothy Sayers have put their own heroines into them, where the heroines know someone's in pain, but don't know they themselves are: Thus Sayers's Harriet receives a blow to the head in *Gaudy Night* and is knocked unconscious. She wakes up in hospital, thinking:

> Somebody had a headache—a quite unbearably awful headache. The white bright light in the infirmary would have been very pleasant, if it hadn't been for the oppressive neighborhood of the person with the headache, who was, moreover, groaning very disagreeably. It was an effort to pull one's self together and find out what the tiresome person wanted. With an effort like that of a hippopotamus climbing out of a swamp, Harriet pulled herself together and discovered that the headache and the groans were her own, and that the Infirmarian had realized what she was about and was coming to lend a hand.
> "What in the world—?" said Harriet.
> "Ah," said the Infirmarian, "that's better. No —don't try to sit up. You've had a nasty knock on the head, and the quieter you keep, the better."

Harriet goes from being annoyed to being concerned, once she acquires the belief that's expressible by her using the pronoun "I." All along she's been having other beliefs expressible in the first person, like "I'm annoyed with the moaner." But she lacked the belief, "I am the moaner." Baldy also continued to have indexical beliefs, just not the one that he himself fell out of the wagonette.

(iv) The key insight here for us is that one's beliefs, which one would express to others using the pronoun "I," are the ones that affect directly one's behavior and dispositions to behave, whereas beliefs directed toward the same content, but not expressible with that pronoun, don't by themselves affect behavior. When we see Belia getting a drink and we ask her why, she replies, "*I am* dehydrated." Let's call the relevant fourth kind of belief about oneself "indexical belief." The thesis our intuitions support is that *one's indexical beliefs are indispensable to one's action.* For whenever our thought experiments postulated that Belia was unaware of a crucial indexical identity belief, she lost an ability to act in her own interest.

By now you've seen identity statements in so many thought experiments, it's almost a reflex to think substitution arguments are involved. Not here. We're not engaged in any semantic ascent. We're simply noting the incapacitating effect on Belia of her unawareness of indexical identities.

Similar intuitions can be evoked concerning the time. "Now-beliefs," that is, beliefs that are indexical with respect to time, are also indispensable for action. "Now" is the indexical pronoun for the time of speaking, as "I" is of the speaker. Beliefs about now also share the special connection to action. Arthur Prior noted that a patient's mother's feelings of relief come, not when she realizes that her child's operation is over at 4 o'clock, but when she realizes 4 o'clock is now. Then she'll say, "Thank goodness that's over." A more obvious example of the connection is her departing for the operation at noon. She may know that she and her child must leave at noon, but noon may come and go without her departing, if she does not realize that noon is now.

Propositions have intensional identity conditions, and so the question arises, how do the complete singular propositions expressed by indexical sentences differ from the complete singular propositions expressed with proper names and demonstrative expressions. What distinguishes the singular proposition Belia expresses (in case iv) with "I am dehydrated" from the singular proposition she expresses in case (ii) with "Belia is dehydrated" or in case (iii) with "This person is dehydrated"? Nothing; no case of the one can possibly fail to be a case of the other two. Belia is expressing the same complete singular proposition in all three cases. Yet the indexical belief has different effects on Belia. This is bad news for those who think all belief is directed toward complete propositions and the *de re* beliefs are directed toward singular propositions. (We'll parlay this intuition into an argument for relational attitudes being directed toward incomplete propositions at the beginning of the next section.) We must be mindful that we don't say the indexical belief's content contains indexicals. Indexicals are words. We call the belief indexical, because there are indexicals in the sentence which the believer uses to express it to others.

## §2. The intensive pronoun as distinctive of reports of beliefs in the first person.

Time now for some semantic ascent. Let's turn to a datum about reports. To capture this fourth type of belief one can have about oneself, Rep might distinguish his report of it from his reports of the believer's first three kinds of belief. The first three beliefs he'd report this way:

> 1. Belia believes that the one Jack loves is on holiday. (Like: David believes that the one Nathan described is unjust.)
> 2. Belia believes about Belia (or herself *qua* Belia), that she is dehydrated.
> 3. Belia believes about the person she notices and points to, that she is dehydrated.

But Rep describes Belia's fourth belief about herself with an **intensive anaphoric pronoun**:

> 4. Belia believes about herself, that she *herself* is dehydrated.

The second instance of "herself" intensifies the anaphoric pronoun "she." The two together constitute an intensive anaphoric pronoun. (Unfortunately, the reflexive form, which is the first instance of "herself," is the same as the intensive form in English. We're not concerned with that reflexive form here.) From his using intensive pronominal anaphora in the that-clause, we understand that the kind of confusion and misdirection of reference, which may infect the *de re* beliefs that Rep reported second and third, cannot infect this belief. His intensive pronoun is telling us something about the way Belia would express the belief to Rep. She'd use the pronoun, "I":

> I am dehydrated.

(I'm not saying it's Rep's intention to tell us this by his use of the intensive pronoun. What his intention is we leave to theory. We're still canvassing the data.)

In this expression of her belief, Belia uses the first person pronoun. Grammar classifies the personal pronouns by their person. The pronoun,

"I" (or "me" or "myself") is called the **first person pronoun,** "you" is called the second person pronoun, and the pronouns, "he," "she," and "it" are called third person pronouns. When people use the first person pronoun, they're talking "in the first person" of themselves. We'll treat the adverb, "now," as a pronoun *pointing* to present time, not naming or describing it. Now-beliefs, which are otherwise analogous to beliefs expressed with the first person pronoun, don't share this second datum, the reporter's use of an intensified pronoun, although perhaps "that very moment" would correspond to "she herself."

Consider the several cases of confused people that I've quoted, and notice that, prior to the removal of their confusion, you could not report what the people believed about themselves using the third person intensive pronoun in the that-clause. In the cases of Mach and Harriet, however, after they discover the truth, you do report their discoveries by using the intensive form:

Mach discovered that he himself was the shabby pedagogue.

Harriet discovered that she herself was the one with the head-ache.

Their discoveries correspond to the moments when they became disposed to express their beliefs about themselves in the first person. *In general, the reporter's use of the intensive third person pronoun in his report corresponds with the fact that the person whose belief he's reporting would use the first person pronoun to express that belief to others.*

## §3. The indispensability of beliefs in the first person for complete knowledge.

To appreciate the first two data about "me-now"-beliefs, let's consider a third datum. The first person pronoun is a rigid designator, in the sense that any particular utterance of it rigidly designates the person uttering it. The rigidity of its reference is proved this way: One can express any counterfactual using it, without the referent of the pronoun changing:

If I had been . . ., then . . .

No matter how you fill in the blanks, the reference of the pronoun does not change. Even outlandish supposals—if I had been twins, there'd have been me and me, and the two would've been distinct—still refer to just me. That's not the case with a counterfactual like,

If *the tallest mountain* had been in Alaska, then Sal would've climbed it.

A sentence like that is not supposing Mount Everest's in Alaska, but that a different mountain was the tallest one. The name in italics is not a rigid designator of Mount Everest.

The fact that different people's utterances of the first person pronoun make it mean the different people does not undermine this point about individual utterances of it. The uttered pronoun designates rigidly whomever it designates. In that respect it's unlike the reference fixing description, "the utterer of this utterance of "I," as we noted in section J when we introduced the concept of indexicality. For I am the utterer of that utterance of "I" contingently; it could've been that someone else uttered that very utterance.

An argument created by Arthur Burks explains the indispensability of rigidity for full knowledge.[5] Descriptive knowledge is consistent with the reduplication of that which is being described, so that there may be indefinitely many scenarios fitting the same description. Suppose the universe is like wallpaper, with repeating patterns. We describe the universe's unit of pattern. Surely description's not enough to locate ourselves in such a universe, since what's described repeats. We're like the itsy bitsy spider who climbs up one section of the wallpaper. Which section? Only a demonstrative, "*this* section" fixes it, or a proper name, e.g., "Terra-sector," because they are rigid designators. Of course it might still feel lost, and quite rightly. But with a few more demonstratives, for instance "the section over there is Mars-sector," it could get its bearings.

We can push the reduplication argument further to establish the indispensability of indexicals for full knowledge. David Lewis presents a variant of Burks's scenario, which emphasizes the indexical "I" over the demonstratives, which Burks had emphasized. Lewis imagines two beings (gods, let's say) who know all that can be expressed with proper names, quantifiers, and descriptive predicates, but lack all knowledge that would explicitly connect what they can express to indexical and demonstrative information. Thus they know all complete propositions, general and singular, all that science aspires to, all history, even of the future, all that identifies the actual world, and all subjective propositions such as what it's like to the bat to be a bat. But they don't know such identities as are expressed by the sentences, "noon is now" or "this unique scene is my location." Or rather, they know the propositions, that a certain time is noon and that a certain sector is the location of a certain god, but not the nowness of the time or the hereness of the location, for this is extra to the propositional information. It's worth repeating that words like "now," "this," and "my" have different referents on different occasions of their use in sentences, and it's those referents that figure in the propositions expressed on those occasions. Keep the indexicals in the sentences; the propositions are abstract entities, intensions, medadic attributes. Yet if the indexical information were redundant, the gods should still know all there is to know. But they don't.

> Still I can imagine them to suffer ignorance: neither one knows which of the two he is. They are not exactly alike. One lives on top of the tallest mountain and throws down manna; the other lives on top of the coldest mountain and throws down thunderbolts. Neither one knows whether he lives on the tallest mountain or on the coldest mountain; nor whether he throws manna or thunderbolts.
> Surely their predicament is possible. (The trouble might perhaps be that they have an equally perfect view of every part of their world, and hence cannot identify the perspectives from which they view it.)[6]

First, let's understand the last sentence. One's perceptual perspective can locate one, although Burks's reduplication argument suggests it might not suffice alone. In the normal case, one's sense of one's location shows itself in one's indexical beliefs. So to deprive the gods of indexical beliefs is to deprive them of a unique perspective from within the world. We think of them as perceiving all at once from everywhere! Spiders have three pairs of eyes; do they see from three perspectives? The gods have more perspectives.

Even if each god has a distinct proper name, neither knows which name is his own. Although the descriptive knowledge which they have is not self-locating knowledge, clearly there is such knowledge as self-locating knowledge. Indexicals and demonstratives express precisely that self-locating knowledge when it's in one's fund of knowledge.

It's not the whole thrust of this thought experiment that indexicals and demonstratives must be rigid designators. When I point to myself or to this thing in front of me, that fixes who and where I am, whether or not there are qualitatively identical replicas of this scenario elsewhere in the universe. So they are rigid designators. Yet such pointing does not make it register in my beliefs in the way that makes a difference to my action. What more then is required besides rigid designation? The answer is more variety of contents for beliefs to be directed toward. As we've been suggesting all along, for a belief to be directed toward an incomplete proposition is something more, different from and in addition to belief being directed toward complete singular propositions. Lewis's thought experiment complements the thought experiments we started this section with. His shows the indispensability of indexical beliefs to full knowledge whereas our earlier thought experiments showed their indispensability to purposeful action.

So far in this section we've examined three phenomena concerning indexical and demonstrative pronouns in reports, phenomena first discerned in 1949 by Burks (concerning "this"), in 1957 by Geach (concerning "I") and in 1959 by Prior (concerning "now"). With complementary arguments, Burks, Geach, and Prior established the indispensability of these pronouns for expressing the whole of what a person believes. They're indispensable in accounts of one's reference to single things and one's knowledge of singular facts (Burks's duplication argument), in accounts of the use of intensive pronouns in reports (Geach's argument[7]), and in accounts of the connection of one's knowledge to one's purposive action (Prior's argument).[8] Their indispensability is known today as the **thesis of the essential indexical**. But these pioneers' arguments for the truth of the thesis of the essential indexical were not appreciated at the time and had to be rediscovered. In 1959, Strawson rediscovered Burks's argument, in 1966 Castañeda rediscovered Geach's argument; and in 1977-1979 Kaplan and Perry rediscovered Prior's. In the fifteen years following Castañeda's paper, a flurry of articles appeared by Anscombe, Castañeda, Chisholm, Kaplan, D. Lewis, and Perry, which ensured that the insight would not be lost again.

The pioneers had to swim against the current of philosophical opinion. Russell and Quine had proposed the opposite view of indexical pronouns and tenses, namely, that they are replaceable in all sentences by names for the things they indicate without any loss of information. (We'll develop Quine's procedure in the second subpart of Part III of these notes. We'll expand it to accommodate rather than supplant the essential indexical.)

## §4. The diverse proofs of the essential indexical are mutually compatible.

The indexical was proved essential in different ways, and we should worry a bit whether the proofs are indeed complementary. The proof that indexical attitudes are indispensable to purposive action might seem to tell us that the attitudes are only dispositions, of the acquired type we call know-how in contrast to knowing-that. If we take it as a proof that they're only forms of know-how, it seems to be contradicted by the proof that the indexical states of mind are a form of knowledge that some proposition is true, additional to the common forms of propositional knowing-that. The suspicion of incompatibility is buttressed by this observation: Proponents of the proof that the states are knowing-that tend to ignore the proof of their indispensability for action. Witness Lewis's saying his two gods do things although they lack indexical beliefs; that's impossible according to the proof that having them is indispensable for action. And proponents of the proof of their indispensability for action leave unacknowledged, if they don't deny outright, that indexical beliefs are a form of knowledge additional to the common forms of propositional knowledge. They don't distinguish the content of indexical states from other forms of knowledge, only the way they establish reference. We can put the suspicion in the form of a dilemma: There are only two mutually exclusive categories to assign indexical states to, knowing-how and knowing-that of the ordinary propositional kind.

I recommend denying the dilemma and the incompatibility of the two proofs. It's true that the informational input to dispositions must be indexical in format. To say that is just to restate the conclusion of our proof, but it goes beyond our proof illegitimately to say that all indexically formatted states are inputs to dispositions. I have many states that are never such inputs, for instance, memories concerned with the distant past.

Here's an example of a purely intellectual use of an indexical belief. It's another argument that indexical beliefs have content. It can persuade those familiar with the calculation of probabilities. Belia volunteers to participate in the Sleeping Beauty experiment, not knowing quite what to expect, but hoping for the best.[9] It involves putting her to sleep and waking her up and administering a memory blocking pill, so that she does not remember the awakening. She's told that she'll be put to sleep and awakened either once or twice, depending on whether a fair coin comes up heads or tails, respectively, upon being tossed in a fair way outside her view. Before the experiment begins, she quite properly believes that the chance of heads on the toss is 1/2.

In what seems like no time at all, Belia finds herself awakened, but alas, not by Prince Charming. Well, maybe next time, but what's the chance of a next time? She's aware that she cannot know whether this is a first or a second awakening, because of the action of the memory-blocking drug. Given that she's just awakened, what does she believe the chance of heads on that toss to have been? It's 1/3.

And she still has a chance of being awakened by Prince Charming, the chance of the second of the three cases she considers. She reasons this way,

> Either I'm waking up for the first time and the coin came up heads,
> or I'm waking up for the first time and the coin came up tails,

or I'm waking up a second time and the coin came up tails.
If the experimenters were to tell her that the coin had come up tails, her probability would be redistributed equally over the second and third of those disjuncts. She'd be equally in doubt whether she's waking up for the first or second time. If the experimenters were to tell her, not that the coin came up tails, but that she is waking up for the first time, then her probability would be redistributed equally over the first and second of the disjuncts. She would be equally in doubt whether the coin came up heads or tails. What then must be the probability distribution over the three disjuncts given that she's just awakened and is told nothing? Each is 1/3.

There's no contradiction in her changing her mind about the chance of heads from her previous estimate of 1/2, because she's learned something since awakening. You guessed it, something indexical: "I've just awakened." If the memory drug had blocked her recall of names, the experimenters could've told her that the coin came up tails in the experiment on Belia and that Belia's been awakened for the second time, and she'd be none the wiser. Her estimate of the probability concerning what happened to the coin would still change, because it's conditioned on her indexical information. There's a negative relevance^ between awakening without memory of prior awakenings and the coin having come up heads.

The argument depends on indexical information being information; if it's not information, then her change of estimate is simply irrational. But it's not. Furthermore, if the indexical state were merely a disposition to action, it would be unavailable as the given in a conditional probability equation. Section N will address how indexical information can be information and yet differ from ordinary propositional information.

## §5. The referential specialness of indexical beliefs.

Anscombe[10] contributes a fourth argument: In addition to being a rigid designator, the uttered first person pronoun has special features pertaining to reference:

> •Its referent on any occasion of its use is not subject to variation by the speaker's intention to refer, as the word "this" is; it's user-proof. Even if I pretend to be someone else, it's me I refer to.
> •It's fail-safe in that on any occasion of its use it succeeds in referring, no matter how uninformed or misinformed its utterer happens to be about the referent. It refers without the speaker needing to identify the referent.
> •It's infallible in that its reference always goes right, no matter

how totally wrong its utterer may be about the referent when
using it. If I go crazy and believe Arthur does not exist, and that
I am Elvis Presley, the one I refer to is still me.

• It's incommunicable in the sense that no one else can refer by
using the word "I" to the same person as Belia does by using the
word "I." If Rep used it in reporting Belia's first person beliefs,
he'd only succeed in referring to himself.

(The second item says ignorance and error don't make the pronoun a
partial function`; the third says ignorance and error don't make it the
wrong total function.) All these data can be summarized as the
Specialness of First Person Reference. As a datum it's a referential
specialness, worthy of singling out by a special name. Lewis suggests
attitudes *de se*. Theory will have to explain the referential specialness.

Quentin Smith gives examples of the use of the first person which cast
doubt on its referential specialness.[11] It's instructive to defend the specialness against them. Suppose Belia's teaching history to a class of young-
sters and says,

Ok, who am I? It's now 1815. I'm short, I'm looking at my horse
that's just been shot, I'm looking at the Prussians arriving on my
flank, and I'm watching the English beat my army in the valley
below. Who am I?

Of course all the students say she's Miss Belia, to make her cross in the
expectation that then she'll become really amusing, except for one who
says, "You're Napoleon, and the language we're both speaking is French."
Has Belia used the pronoun "I" not to refer to herself, but to Napoleon
instead? There are two ways of analyzing the case's abnormality, which
is generated by the pretense. One is to say all the attributions "short,"
"looking at a horse," are normal, outside the scope of the pretense, so to
speak, but that the referential behavior of the "I" is abnormal. The other
is to treat the referential behavior of the pronoun as normal, and so
referring to Belia, and take the attributions to her to be abnormal, such
that, taking them as true, Belia has the further attribute of being Napoleon.
This second analysis preserves the referential specialness of the pronoun.

But now Belia pretends to see her armies vanquished and moans:

I've been annihilated. I don't exist anymore!

If you think of your armies as you would your hands, then, just as you
say, "I'm hurt" when your hands are hurt, so you'd say it if your armies are
hurt. Perhaps only a Stoic would quibble about the "I" when only the
body is hurt, whereas we all are somewhat awed by the Napoleonic
presumption. Then there's the melodramatic egotizing of the defeat.

Clearly, the abnormality is with the predication of nonexistence. If so, the usage of the pronoun is still consistent with its referential specialness.

## §6. Digression on the difference between the now and the present tense.

There's an analogous referential Specialness of the Now. Before reviewing that, we must distinguish the reference of the now from the reference of sentences whose verb is in the present tense. Past and future tensed sentences can be interpreted as referring to times by their position in relation to the now; the past is times before now, the future is times after now. But, although the present is now, the times referred to by present tensed sentences may not be now. To understand this, we must examine tenses.

All tenses are parasitical on the present tense in the sense that all tensed sentences contain a constituent present-tensed sentence. Obviously sentences in the present tense do. Other sentences, having verbs in the other tenses, can be regimented into containing the present tense by the device of tense operators:

It will be the case that . . .

and

It was the case that . . .

where the triple dots are filled in by tensed sentences, ultimately by present tensed sentences. The present tense is not an operator, as we shall see. **Operators** are not referring devices, nor are they general terms. They're familiar to you, since logical words like "and" and "not" are operators; so are the modal operators like "it's necessarily the case that." An operator is just a device we attach to a sentence to make another sentence. Although we paraphrase the modal operator in English with a sentence, like "it's necessary that" we might've been pithier: "necessarily." Treating operators as adverbial prefixes helps reinforce the idea that they do mean properties, which is also wrong; they're just devices for making new sentences out of old ones.

It's harder to find pithy expressions of the tense operators so that we don't treat them as referring devices. Perhaps just "hereafter" and "heretofore" will work to express the tense operators, provided that we cancel the implicature that "hereafter" means *all* the appropriate times hereafter. We cancel it by adding "at least once," yielding these paraphrases:

Jack will be happy ~ Hereafter (at least once) Jack is happy.
Jack was happy ~ Heretofore (at least once) Jack is happy.

But always hereafter, I'll intend the implicature-canceling phrase in the parentheses without saying it.

The idea in the two paraphrases is that the embedded sentence that Jack *is* happy, in all its present-tensedness, is true at sometime after now in the first case, or in the second example at some time before now. Note that present tense in this usage does not refer to present time, unlike the now, which is only the present time. The present tense in a sentence simply indicates that the sentence *is true at a time if what it says happens to be the case at that time*; it doesn't tell which time, the way "now" does. This condition of truth for present tensed sentences implies that the present tense, unlike the other tenses, is not an operator on sentences. If it were, then either the sentences it operated on would be tensed or they would not be. If not, then they'd express timeless truth, and it would be pointless to attach to them an operator that only has point if it's attached to something that is sometimes true and sometimes not. So it's attached to a tensed sentence. Which tense? It must be the present tense. Either we generate an infinite regress or we generate redundancy, for "it's the case that it's the case that . . ." is equivalent to "it's the case that . . ." So we must admit that the distinction between the operator and the sentence operated on collapses in the case of the present tense.

Truth itself is *a relation* between a tensed sentence and a time, truth-at-a-time. The truth of interest about whole sentences is their truth at the time of utterance, truth-now. For the future-tensed sentence, "Jack will be happy," to be true-now is for the embedded present-tensed sentence inside it to be true at a time after now. Similarly, for the truth of the past-tensed sentence. Confining ourselves to tensed sentences, all truth is true in virtue of present-tensed truth being true sometime.

Which utterance, you may ask, is the one that's true at some other time than now, and how is it shown to be true then? It would be wrong to think of oneself as engaged in time travel to the other time, and then uttering a present-tensed duplicate of the one embedded in your original sentence, and then seeing if that one is true then. Science fiction is quite unnecessary. The truth evaluation of embedded present-tensed sentences is evaluation of the very concrete and time-bound instance embedded in the past-tensed or future-tensed sentence you uttered actually, not some duplicate. And we do absolutely nothing at all with ourselves or with that present-tensed component of the utterance. We and it both stay put, and still it has a valuation as either true at the other time or false then. Truth elsewhen is like truth elsewhere. You know it's cold at the top of Mt. Everest. You don't dream that an evaluation of that sentence requires transport of you and the sentence "it's cold" to the top. Likewise no time transport.

A consequence of these considerations concerning embedded sentences is that truth, even when conceived of as relative, as we just did, should be an attribute of instances of sentences, the utterances of them, rather than the sentences themselves. An absolute truth may work for non-embedded utterances, because the time and place that defines them would only be repeated redundantly if we say their truth is at that time and place. But absolute truth does not work for the utterance of embedded sentences, since we must often think of their truth at times and places other than those that define those utterances.[12]

Thus, that there were dinosaurs is true now in virtue of the truth in the past of the sentence that there are dinosaurs. Of course, no one expressed the truth at that time, not Fred Flintstone nor the jolly Semanticist in her time machine. That the sun will be a supernova is true now in virtue of the truth in the future of the present tensed sentence-instance inside this: Hereafter, the sun is a supernova. Again, even if human beings survive to observe the initial stages of this event several thousand million years hence, it's unlikely that any of them will survive the event and utter the present-tensed truth. Nevertheless, the present-tensed sentences are true then. Indeed, the present-tensed sentences expressing the propositions that are true at those times are the ones contained implicitly in our own sentences, that there were dinosaurs and that the sun will be a supernova. These present-tensed sentences don't have to be uttered then for them to be evaluated as true then. One may find this separation of the context of utterance (now) from the context of evaluation (then) confusing if one confuses the conditions for the truth of a past-tensed or future-tensed sentence with the tests or evidence for their truth. What constitutes the truth of a past-tensed or future-tensed sentence is distinct from the present evidence for their truth.

We allow iterated tense operators:

it was the case that it will be the case that . . .,

and the like. In the case of iterated operators, only the outermost one, or the one with the widest scope,ˆ is read as "hereafter" or "heretofore." The inner ones are read as "thereafter"or "theretofore." Thus

Jack shall have been happy ~ Hereafter theretofore Jack is happy.

In other words,

it will be the case that it was already the case that Jack is happy.

Imagine a horizontal line representing time, the future being to the right.

Select a point on the line to represent the now. You want to know if the sentence is true now. To find out, take direction from the first operator in the sentence and move to a point to the right and ask if the sentence, "it was already the case that Jack is happy" is true at that point. To find that out, take direction from the operator in that sentence and move to a point to the left and ask if the sentence, "Jack is happy," is true then. If there are two points for which the answer is yes, your original question is answered yes. If there are not, it's answered no.

With iterated tense operators we have considerable power to express various tensed truths. But it's known that there are only fifteen nonequivalent forms, if time is linear, and to express all fifteen, we never need more than a pair of tense operators, and even some of the pairs are equivalent to a simple tense.[13] For example, the iteration "it was the case that it was the case that p" entails "it was the case that p," and if between any two times there's a third, then the converse entailment holds also, so they're equivalent on that natural assumption.

Another sort of iteration, where the scopes^ of the tense operators don't cover the same sentences, leads to potentially infinite complexity, however. For example,

Tweedledum arrived at noon, but Tweedledee had gone by then. To express the pastness of the conjunction, one past-tense operator has the conjunction within its scope, but the "had gone" of the second conjunct requires a second past-tense operator, thus:

It was the case that {both [Dum arrives] and it was the case that [Dee goes]}

Evaluating the truth of this compound involves five evaluations of its components thus:

For the whole to be true at the time of its utterance,
- the conjunction in {...} must have been true before then, which by the rule for "and" means
- both conjuncts were true before then;
- the first of its conjuncts was true when the conjunction was true, because it's present-tensed, and
- the second of its conjuncts was also true then, but it's in past tense and so
- its present-tensed component was true even earlier.

The rules for interpreting the operators refer us from the time of utterance to a time before then to a time before that time. In all cases the evaluation process comes back to the truth at some time of a contained present-tensed sentence.

Let's now order Rep to formulate his reports of Belia's tensed beliefs in the way we described. More regimentation of data. We regiment tenses using operators, because most natural languages seem to treat tense the way they treat modality. There's a strong analogy between tense operators and the modal notions of possibility and contingency. The now is like the modal concept of actuality, and other times are like alternatives to actuality, that is, like other possibilities. **Tense logic** is a thriving branch of modal logic, which explores these analogies. Thus you'll find evaluating a present-tensed sentence for *truth at* another time than now easier to comprehend if you think of it the way you evaluate the indicative mood sentence that's inside the modal sentence, "it's possible that all world records are broken in the next Olympic Games." As we say, we find the possibility true in actuality, because, in addition to actuality there are alternatives to it, and the contained indicative-mood sentence is *true at* one of these, actuality or its alternatives: All the records *are* broken there.

Modal logic countenances restricting the domain^ of possible scenarios, to explain restricted senses of possibility. Tense logic can do the same, restricting times to recent ones, for example. There's no need to think "it was the case that" ranges over all past times back to the Big Bang. A conversational implicature sets the relevant domain of times. Modal operators and tense operators are also alike in that they can affect the domain of entities we quantify over. Thus we can say "there could be more things than there actually are" and "there will be more things than there now are," which bring in domains of possible things and future things.

Although we regiment tensed sentences analogously to the way we regimented modal sentences, we need not let that dictate how we think about time. Russell once commented that people's idioms of speech represent the "fossilized ignorance of our cave-man ancestors," and Berkeley made the useful distinction that, although we will continue to say such things as that the sun rises, "in such things we ought to 'think with the learned and speak with the vulgar.'"[14] (Understand the word "vulgar" nonpejoratively from the Latin, *vulgus*, meaning the people.) That discrepancy between thought and speech entails, of course, that we have two conditions of truth, not just the learned's, according to which the earth, not the sun, does the moving that accounts for dawn, but the common folk's, according to which it's true once a day that the sun rises from below the horizon. In the case at hand, our philosophy of time itself is not at issue, but I'll tell you mine anyway: My own view is that the "modalizing of time" is indeed an instance of the fossilized ignorance of our cave-man ancestors, and that the "spatializing of time" is the better course to take in the philosophy of time. That is to say, "the now" is more like "here" than like "actuality." But I recognize that my view of time is not built into people's customary ways of speaking.

## §7. The referential specialness of the now.

We noticed that tensed declarative sentences are true or false about the now. In that case we reinterpret the propositions they express, which up to now we've assumed to be complete propositions, as incomplete. Tensed declarative sentences express monadic attributes of the now.

So Rep reports tensed beliefs as *de re* beliefs. If Belia believes that Jack will be happy, then Rep reports concurrently in regimented form:

Belia believes about now, that hereafter Jack is happy.
Rep reports concurrently with Belia's belief that Belia believes that there were dinosaurs thus:

Belia believes about now, that heretofore there are dinosaurs.
(In nonconcurrent reportage, Rep couldn't use the word "now.") The whole that-clause represents an attribute of the now despite its lacking an anaphoric pronoun. We could always make a pronoun explicit by reading "hereafter" as "hereafter it," where the "it" refers back to the "now" in the about-position.

We're now in position to affirm that the pronoun "now" has the same special referential features as the first person pronoun:

- Its referent on any occasion of its use is not subject to variation by the speaker's intention to refer, as the word "this" is; it's user-proof.
- It's fail-safe in that on any occasion of its use it succeeds in referring, no matter how uninformed or misinformed its utterer happens to be about the referent.
- It's infallible in that its reference always goes right, no matter how totally wrong its utterer may be about the referent.
- It's incommunicable in the sense that people speaking at other times cannot refer by using the word "now" to the same time as Belia does by using the word "now." If Rep used it in reporting Belia's beliefs about her time of believing, he'd only succeed in referring to the time of his reporting.

We earlier noted that indexicality of time has the same indispensability for action and full knowledge as indexicality of the first person. So in all respects we have an analogous Specialness of the Now.

# Notes

1.  Second book of Samuel, ch.12. Bertrand Russell refers to this episode toward the end of his 1905 article "On Denoting."

2.  *Principles of Psychology* vol. I, 273, fn.

3.  *Analysis of Sensations* (1897) 4, fn.

4.  *Hard Times*, part II, chapter 9. Mrs. Gradgrind's daughter, Louisa, asks her, "Are you in pain, dear mother?" She answers, "I think there's a pain somewhere in the room, but I couldn't positively say that I have got it." Mrs. Gradgrind has been saying strange things throughout the novel, however, like "If only I had never been a mother, then wouldn't you kids be in a pretty pickle" (not an exact quote, see part I, chapter 4). And in the scene where there's a pain in the room, we're conscious of Louisa's own pain. Are we to suppose her mother preternaturally sensitive to her pain, or hers and her mother's pain merging? This is hardly a story to cite as empirical evidence. Dickens is rather satirizing theories that leave out the first person point of view. Mrs. Gradgrind, ever in awe of her husband's devotion to such impersonal knowledge, "Ologies" as she calls them, has finally lost hers altogether. But her last words are: "But there is something—not an Ology at all—that your father has missed, or forgotten, Louisa. I don't know what it is." We're discovering what it is in this section.

5.  Arthur Burks, "Icon, Index, and Symbol," *Philosophy and Phenomenological Research*, 10 (1949) 673-89.

6.  David Lewis, "Attitudes *De Dicto* and *De Se*" (1979) reprinted with an addendum in his *Philosophical Papers* (1983) 139. The two gods have a perspective-neutral kind of knowledge, which precludes the human kind of perception of space and time. Lewis suppresses the neutrality of temporal perspective for the sake of his main point. Nevertheless, it's highly relevant to discussions of the nature of time and how we perceive it. So I've focused on the temporal perspective-neutrality in my thought experiment of "the scheduler" in chapter 5 of my *Darwinism and Philosophical Analysis*, Utkal Studies in Philosophy, vol. 9 (2003) and at greater length in my "Time Plus the Whoosh and Whiz" in Q. Smith and A. Jokic, eds., *Time, Tense and Reference* (2003). I also question whether the gods could act coordinately with events in the world, contrary to Lewis's description of them throwing stuff at us.

7.  Peter Geach, "On Beliefs About Oneself" (1957-8), reprinted in his *Logic Matters* (1972), section 4.1.

8.  Priority in conceptual innovation is a tricky business, since one must infer the total thought from its partial and fuzzy expression. Does, for example, Arthur N. Prior deserve credit for this argument? Here is the total evidence upon which I credit him. Note that it says nothing about action or the now explicitly:

> . . . half the time I personally have forgotten what the date *is*, . . .; yet even in this perpetual dateless haze one somehow communicates, one makes oneself understood, and with time-references too. One says, e.g., "Thank

goodness that's over!", and not only is this, when said, quite clear without any date appended, but it says something which it is impossible that any use of the tenseless copula with a date should convey. It certainly doesn't mean the same as, e.g., "Thank goodness the date of the conclusion of that thing is Friday, June 15, 1954", even if it be said then. (Nor, for that matter, does it mean "Thank goodness the conclusion of that thing is contemporaneous with this utterance". Why should anyone thank goodness for that?) 17.

"Thank Goodness That's Over," *Philosophy*, 34 (1959) 12-17.

9.   Adam Elga, "Self-locating belief and the Sleeping Beauty problem," *Analysis* 60 (2000) 143-147.

10.   G. E. M. Anscombe, "The First Person" (1975), reprinted in her *Metaphysics and the Philosophy of Mind* (1981), ch. 2. A previous note mentions the difficulty of crediting priority for ideas. Here's an ironic instance. Anscombe attributes priority for discovering the meaning of the intensive pronoun in reports to Castañeda (22, fn). I attributed it to Geach on the basis of a publication a decade earlier than Castañeda's. Geach is Anscombe's husband.

11.   Quentin Smith, "The Multiple Uses of Indexicals," *Synthese*, 78 (1989) 167-191. I dealt with his example of "I" referring to what's mine in my "Consciousness and Self-Reference," *Erkenntnis*, 43 (1995) 155.

12.   W. V. Quine, "Response to Gibson," *Inquiry* 37 (1994) 501-502. Quine does not say here truth is relative, but he's not thinking of the problem of evaluating embedded sentences, which I think forces the relativity.

13.   Ørstrøm, P., and Hasle, P., *Temporal Logic* (1995) 178.

14. George Berkeley, *The Principles of Human Knowledge* (1710), section 51. I don't know who he's quoting.

# N. Beliefs About Oneself and About the Present Moment: the Theories.

The previous section presented data concerning "I" and "now," albeit slightly regimented. Here I present theories.

## §1. A criterion connecting change of behavior to change of contents believed.

The main theories agree in accepting a criterion of the identity and difference of individual believed contents that's based on their effects on the believer's behavior. Without that criterion, our previous section's main argument for the distinctness of beliefs expressed in the first person would be undermined. The criterion is:

> Suppose a person's believing, in a particular context, about $x$ that X and her believing to the same degree in that same context about $y$ that Y would have different effects on the believer's behavior, when all else that's independent is held constant. Then they are different believings, and since their difference is not a difference of location, mood, or any other difference besides a content that would account for the difference in ensuing behavior, it must lie in their contents. So it's not the case that both $x = y$ and X = Y.

Our conclusions from the two gods thought experiment in the previous section depended on this assumption. The gods knew all the facts that could be captured in descriptions. They knew all the information contained in singular propositions. They knew that the god Thor sat on such and such mountain. Yet Thor did not know the indexical fact, that he himself was Thor and that here was that mountain. Well, he could've remedied that in a twinkle, you think. He could just look and see which place is closer to him, or decide to stand up, and he'll see which god stands up. That one will be him. The thought experiment of course does not let him know anything except by description and perhaps by the referential use of descriptions and proper names, even if we did suppose (paradoxically, it would seem) he has perception and the ability to act. So these strategies are of no avail. He's descriptively omniscient, but otherwise ignorant. We relent and give him the knowledge he lacks. Instead of merely believing that the god on the mountain stood up, he believes that he himself stood up. His discovery opens new avenues of thought and action. Now the criterion comes in to support our conclusion, that this knowledge is a new content, not just a new way of believing the same old thing he's been believing all along. Since $x = y$, X is not the same as Y. So if X is the complete proposition,

   that the god on the mountain stood up,
then Y is the incomplete proposition,

   that . . . stood up.

The situations of David, Baldy, Mach, and Harriet are similar. A change in their beliefs brings on the change in their behavior. But the relevant complete singular propositions are already believed. They all believe complete singular propositions featuring themselves as the subjects. What then is the new belief that accounts for the new behavior? Belief in an incomplete proposition.

The criterion implies that, if there's a change in action, there's a change in content believed. John Perry seemed to reject this criterion, which depends on connecting states of believing with believed contents, at least during the early 1980s. Consider his alternative criterion, that if there's a change in action, there's a change in *sentence accepted*, not necessarily a change in content believed. If Belia's believing, formatted in the first person, could be the very same believing as one she could express only with a proper name or a demonstrative, despite the behavioral difference that we noticed would ensue, then the incapacity to use the first person due to ignorance, and the behavioral disconnection that accompanies that incapacity, would have an explanation quite different from the one we've been assuming, which has been that the removal of the incapacity and the disconnection is due to her acquiring another belief. Perry associated the difference in behavior to the accepting of the indexical sentences themselves, in the examples of how Baldy, Harriet, Ernst Mach, David, etc., change from rejecting a first-person sentence to accepting it, which for Perry does not signify any change in the propositions they believed, which in each case is a singular complete proposition. The change in their acceptance of sentences has the behavioral significance it does only because they were taught indexical sentences in contexts which called for them to act in accord with information to reach their goals. According to Perry, believing complete propositions and accepting sentences can vary independently, so that the sentences one accepts may change without the proposition believed changing. The change in sentence-acceptance exposes a change in the mental state that causes behavior, without exposing a change in the proposition believed.

We postpone further consideration of this theory until Part III, second subpart. Note, however, that it points to an alternative to our criterion, one that explains the change in behavior, not by positing a replacement of the content, but by positing an addition to it. Not something else, but something more. Perry's recent work[1] suggests that this extra need not be a sentence that's accepted. It may be an add-on content, which he calls the belief's reflexive content because it refers to the belief and perhaps also to its primary content. Instead of positing incomplete propositions as contents, he posits an extra complete propositional content that says that the belief, in addition to the truth condition for its original complete propositional content, has a reflexive truth condition. For example, in the case of the gods, we find the god to lack a belief in a proposition such that

> the belief *(but not the primary proposition)* is true only if the one who believes *it* is the god on the mountain.

This latter would be the belief's reflexive content. If the gods knew all complete propositions, however, how could they have missed this one? Perhaps we should address Harriet's change:

> the belief *(but not the primary proposition)* is true only if the one who believes *it* has a headache and is moaning.

We'll return to this theory later in the section.

## §2. The no-name theory of reports of indexical beliefs.

We'll examine two theories that accept the first criterion. In other words, they acknowledge that a change of behavior implies a change in the content believed. My names for the theories are the no-name-for-oneself theory and the special-name-for-oneself theory. I advocate the no-name theory, and will attempt to refute the special-name theory.

The no-name theory (anticipated by Anscombe in 1975, originated by David Lewis and Roderick Chisholm in 1979, apparently independently of each other[2]) says that, in the reports in which Rep uses the intensive personal pronoun, he suggests something more than just that Belia might express herself in the first person. In fact, he's not at all suggesting how she'd self-report. Belia's first person mode of expression just happens to be a concomitant phenomenon to the more basic phenomenon. Rep's tacitly suggesting something about the belief underlying her first person form of expression. Namely, he's suggesting that the aboutness of Belia's belief *de re* does not depend on any name of the *res* occurring in Belia's mind. She does not use in her inner belief any inner name equivalent to the "I" she uses to publish her belief to others. She simply makes attributions to herself and her now directly. Thus it's the "no name" theory of belief in the first person.

The no-name theory is really a subtheory of the ellipsis theory of *de re* belief. We simply allow for more versions of ellipsis. According to the ellipsis theory as presented in section L, Belia can have *de re* beliefs about herself, using names for herself:

>Elliptical: Belia believes about herself that she is dehydrated.

>Analyzed: Belia has adopted a name for herself on the basis of a causal rapport with herself, and she believes with that name that she is dehydrated.

Several of the unusual examples we cited in the previous section turned on the fact that the believer did not know the name was a name for herself. She may see a thirsty-looking person in a mirror, as Ernst Mach saw himself in a mirror. She may think the name refers to someone else. Let's not over-generalize from these examples. In particular we may not claim to have discovered a universal truth about *de re* beliefs. The no-name theory appeals to ellipsis also, but in another way:

>Elliptical: Belia believes about herself, that she *herself* is dehydrated.

>Analyzed: Belia believes about herself, *without the aid of any name for herself*, that she *herself* is dehydrated.

The complete no-name theory consists of four components, which together explain the phenomena of the previous section. Only the first of the four has been introduced so far:

>●The reporter's ellipsis says the believer uses no name to make the belief be about herself and the present time, and consequently needs no reflexive content concerning them.

>●The content of the that-clause is an incomplete proposition directly attributed to herself and the present time. Direct attribution is yet to be explained.

>●The believer herself and the present time are established as the subjects of the direct attribution by two facts, first that she is moved by the attribution, and secondly the time is the time at which she is moved by the attribution, in accordance with a kinetic theory of core indexical reference, to be explained.

>●If she has a language for communication and she's capable of awareness of her agency insofar as it's affected by direct attribu-

tions, then she can express her beliefs using "I" and "now."
Awareness of one's agency is yet to be explained.

We'll explain each of these theses in this section.

The no-name theory can account for the referential specialness of indexicals. It's plausible to hypothesize that the fallibility of reference in the belief reported in the first pair of reports is due to the use of a name, whereas a reference to herself would be infallible, were Belia to use the first person pronoun in an expression of her belief, as in the belief reported by the second pair. If that hypothesis is true, then perhaps that contrast in fallibility is due to her using no name to refer to herself in the belief itself. For with a name, one can always be mistaken about its reference. If her infallibility of belief about herself of the type we're now considering is simply due to her *not having the opportunity to be fallible*, then the analysis of the report of this type of belief (where the reference by Belia, which is indicated by the report's intensive pronoun, is infallible and fail-safe) also reveals an ellipsis, but one which says she does not have the opportunity to go wrong in the use of a name, because she doesn't use a name.

In other words, Rep's use of the intensive anaphoric pronoun, "she herself," tips us off to his theorizing about Belia's belief state and the nature of the referring going on in it. That's what he did, according to the ellipsis account of *de re* belief presented in section L, and here we're only showing more of the richness of his theorizing. *Our* theory of the about-position is that the reporter who uses it is theorizing about the believer's state of mind, and expects his listeners to understand as much by inferring the conversational implicatures of the ellipses containing the theory.

We theorize similarly in the case of reports where time is important: Belia believes that Jack will be happy. Rep reports this in regimented form as a *de re* belief about now:

> Belia believes about now *without any name for this time*, that thereafter Jack is happy.

The about-position is still extensional. So we might replace the word "now" with the date. But the that-clause is tensed, and not only because Rep speaks a language with obligatory tense. (If Rep had reported in Chinese, it would not've had to be tensed.) It's tensed also because Belia's indexical beliefs about time must have tensed content by virtue of their indexicality, and she controls Rep's that-clause. We'll return to indexical beliefs about time later.

So far the theory accounts for two of our four data, namely the referential specialness of first person reference and reference to now, and the intensive pronoun in reports of beliefs. How does the theory help explain the indispensability of self-ascription to action and the unique reference of self-ascription despite reduplication? First, concerning action, it shows how there are two beliefs and not just one with two ways of being expressed. Recall Harriet from the previous section; she may believe (about herself, as it turns out) that that moaner is a bother, but not believe that she herself is a bother. The former, which identifies its subject by means of a name, does not affect her behavior, whereas the second does. The no-name beliefs are the ones that affect behavior, because the referential specialness of the first person and present time is best accounted for by there being no name, and beliefs in the first person and present tense are the ones that affect behavior. Second, concerning knowledge, the duplication argument shows that there is more knowledge than knowledge of complete propositions. Self-locating knowledge is distinct from the descriptive knowledge contained in complete propositions, as our propositionally omniscient beings demonstrated for us in the previous section. They each have knowledge of complete general and singular propositions, replete with definite descriptions of themselves and proper names of themselves. Nevertheless, neither knows what's expressed by a sentence in the first person, "I am that one." Self-locating knowledge is clearly more knowledge than propositional knowledge. Furthermore it's the sort of knowledge needed for guiding action.

A major consequence of this no-name theory concerns the sort of confusion between beliefs that led us to postulate vivid names in the minds of those with *de re* beliefs. It predicts the confusion cannot arise in the case of indexical attitudes. For if such a confusion could arise between two indexical beliefs, a no-name theory obviously could not appeal to different names to resolve the contradictions that would arise in reporting it. For the reporting of indexical beliefs contains an ellipsis saying there are no pertinent names in the believer's mind. So Belia may aver indexically in English that she herself is thirsty. Now there's no possible situation in which she also believes in the first person present tense that she's not thirsty. Of course, she may say that, but she could not believe it. If she says it in a different language, say Latin: *Nunc ego non sitiens sum,* disguising the contradiction behind differences in sentence and language, she still cannot believe it if she believes she's thirsty. I take our intuitions to confirm the prediction, and that's a sign the no-name theory is on the right track. Our intuitions prevent us from over-generalizing the vivid-name theory. Rather the vivid-name theory and the no-name theory each fall within the ellipsis theory and account for different types of belief.

Another consequence of the no-name theory is that it prevents the reduction of *de re* attitudes to *de dicto* ones. One might suppose a reduction possible on the grounds that the ellipsis theory suggests that Belia has complete singular sentences in mind when she believes *de re*, because she has names in mind, and what else are names good for except to express sentences with? The complete singular sentences can only express complete singular propositions, which would be what her attitudes are directed toward. Our account is not so easily destroyed, because now, given what the new ellipsis says, sc. no name, there's no way to complete the incomplete propositions and make the completed ones the only objects of the directed-toward relation. We must allow incomplete propositions as objects of the directed-toward relation. Once the reduction is stopped for some *de re* attitudes, there's less pressure from considerations of simplicity to reduce the others. So the vivid names we hypothesized for the other *de re* attitudes need not be taken to be subjects of complete singular propositions, even though they could be. I suggested in section L §3 another role they might play, items in mental models. Models are more holistic^ than propositions.

### §3. The principle of transmission applied to indexical beliefs.

This no-name theory of indexical belief requires no limitation on the principle of the transmissibility of *de re* beliefs. Indexical beliefs are a variety of *de re* beliefs. These *de re* beliefs' contents are incomplete propositions in Belia's mind and remain so in Rep's mind and in ours when we learn from Rep about Belia's indexical beliefs. The difference is that, whereas she had no name for herself, Rep does have one for her in his about-position. He also has one in any belief he himself has about her. So the indexicality of beliefs in the first person is not transmissible, only their *de re*-ness is.

   In contrast, the indexicality of beliefs about the now is transmissible. You tell me it's cloudy; I believe it's cloudy. Both beliefs are about the now. Indeed, in the case of Belia's beliefs about now, their contents can be transmitted to herself at a later time without loss of indexicality. The belief-content gets modified, but the indexicality persists. This arises from the way tenses work. All tensed sentences are about the now, whether they be past or future or present tensed. Let's review how they work. In the previous section, I explained them in terms of sentences and words which operate on sentences to make different sentences. Now I'll rework that explanation in terms of propositions and functions^ operating on propositions to make different propositions.

Corresponding to a present-tensed sentence is an incomplete proposition completable by a time. It may be incomposite; for example, Belia may say, "It's cloudy." When she believes that by itself, she believes it indexically about the now. When it's a component of a composite proposition, ("It's cloudy or there's a dust storm coming or maybe a scourge of locusts") the construction requires propositional functors, which are abstract entities that correspond to the operators on sentences. They operate on the component propositions to yield the composite proposition. Among such functors are the past and future tenses, which only operate on incomplete propositions that are completable by times: "It will be cloudy." That we analyzed as the composite "Hereafter it's cloudy." In terms of propositions, the past and future tenses operate on an incomplete proposition corresponding to a present-tensed sentence, and create another incomplete proposition, a composite one which is attributable to the now if the component incomplete proposition is attributable *at* some other time *to* that time, either a time before the now in the case of the past tense or one after the now in the case of the future tense. So, as Belia changes from believing it's cloudy to believing it was cloudy, she continues to believe something indexically of the now, although what she believes of it gets modified.

But is her belief that it was cloudy a *de re* belief about the earlier time? We only said her former belief, "it's cloudy" was an indexical belief about that earlier time, and her current belief, "it was cloudy," is an indexical belief about her current time. Is this latter belief also a *de re* belief about that earlier time as well as an indexical belief about her current time? If it is, it's due to the special nature of episodic memory. That gets us into fascinating material, but we must resist the distraction.

## §4. The special-name theory of indexicals refuted.

D. H. Mellor and I accept the no-name theory. Perry does also for what he calls agent-relative knowledge, but not for the reasons Mellor and I have.[3] Do you accept it? Perhaps you think Rep's use of the intensive anaphoric pronoun to refer to Belia tells us not only that Belia would express her belief with a first person pronoun, but that the Specialness of First Person Reference is due to a special sort of self-knowledge, which gives her a private and incommunicable vivid name of herself, whose reference she cannot fail to understand, however confused she might otherwise be. For, you may think, the no-name account makes it mysterious how any reference to the self is established, and so only a special self-acquaintance can account for the referential specialness of the I and the now. You may think she expresses herself with these pronouns because they correlate with inner names that have *the same specialness* that they do. For Rep to report that Belia believes that she herself is in need is to bring in an ellipsis more like the original one. There's a special I-ish name with which she believes about herself that she is in need.

Some may wish to add that with this name Belia's belief is directed toward an incommunicable complete singular proposition not otherwise accessible. The subject of this proposition is none other than Belia Herself, not to be confused with mere Belia, the subject of communicable versions of those propositions. But this is extravagant in that it's a patent *non sequitur* from the data of the previous section, which can be explained by more parsimonious hypotheses. The gratuitousness of it should make us suspect that wishful thinking is here straining to find support. The phenomenon of the essential indexical adds new knowledge over and above scientific knowledge, but not new ontology, and we'll not pause to say any more in refutation of the claim that it does, since wishful thinking is endlessly resourceful in prolonging fruitless arguments. If Death could be put off until He won a debate on the reality of death with the one dying, no one would ever die.

We'll consider a more modest alternative to the no-name theory, which assumes no new things or types of propositions, but only new names that people sometimes use to direct their attitudes toward complete singular propositions about themselves. This we'll call the special-name theory of belief in the first person.

I admit that most philosophers have gone this route. I believe they overgeneralized the lesson of sections K and L. Despite the peer pressure, give the no-name account a hearing: To see that this type of *de re* belief does not depend on any representation of oneself occurring in one's mind, we must first distinguish having the belief from having the linguistic capability for self-reporting. We already noted there's a distinctive way for Belia to self-report this sort of belief. She'd express the content of the that-clause directly:

(I believe that) I am dehydrated.

The first-person pronoun, however essential it is to this sort of self-report-age, is not essential to *the having* of a belief of this kind. Obviously, cats and dogs don't use first person pronouns in their egocentric attitudes. To see this also in the case of persons, we can imagine a person who is an exact duplicate of Belia internally and externally. We can call her Trixy.[4] Suppose Rep reports that

Trixy believes about herself, that she herself is dehydrated.
Belia's and Trixy's beliefs are not just different acts of believing, they're
about different people. Yet their beliefs' incomplete propositional content
is identical, as we required when we made Trixy a duplicate of Belia.
Their minds are qualitatively indistinguishable.

Consider a second belief:

Belia does believe about herself, that she herself is Belia,

and she is right. Since Trixy is a duplicate of Belia down to the last detail,
she too believes about herself that she herself is Belia, but she is wrong.
If their beliefs were complete propositions, they'd be believing the very
same proposition, and they'd either be both right or both wrong, since one
and the same proposition cannot be both true and false. So here's how to
resolve the conundrum: Their beliefs both have identical incomplete
propositional content, namely,

that . . . is Belia.

And it's directly attributed, without the use of any mental names. So their
mental states or the realizations of those states in their brains are exactly
similar. Yet Belia's belief is true, and Trixy's is false.

Might not the difference in the truth value^ of their beliefs depend on
different instances of the same mental name occurring in their minds? The
idea is of a sort of name that only one person can produce instances of to
identify a subject of predication and the predication come out true of the
one so identified. This is the special name. To exclude this possibility,
consider that we've supposed Belia cannot fail to understand the reference
of this name. How come, then, that her duplicate *has to misunderstand* it
as applying to herself rather than to Belia? Special names were supposed
to be user-proof and fail-safe, sharing the specialness of the indexical, "I."

According to Perry-style version of the special name theory, Belia's
and Trixy's beliefs have a reflexive content associated with the special
name they use. It should identify Trixy's misunderstanding. They both
believe what they believe by virtue of their believing the truth that the
referent of the special name is Belia. That's the first candidate for the
reflexive content, but it won't do the job. The reflexive content must be not
only that the referent of the special name, but also the only possible utterer
of it, is Belia. If so, it contravenes the supposition of the case, because
Trixy can no longer be a duplicate of Belia. For the reflexive contents of
their two beliefs must differ. For Belia:

Some special name-instance is such that Belia believes about
herself that she herself is Belia by virtue of believing that the
referent of the name is Belia and the only possible utterer of that

name-instance is Belia.

For Trixy:

> Some special name-instance is such that Trixy believes about herself that she herself is Belia by virtue of believing that the referent of the name is Belia and the only possible utterer of that name-instance is Belia.

The name-instances referred to are distinct. If no one but Belia can instance the name, then Trixy's instance is not an instance of it, but of some other. Perhaps everytime she tries to utter Belia's secret name, she utters her own and doesn't notice the slip. Ockham's˄ razor should suffice against such necessarily secret names. One might justify them on the ground that they're just the first-person pronouns adapted for private beliefs, but would one attribute such pronouns to cats and dogs, who never had the communicative use of such pronouns?

To complete the picture, we must now develop the three remaining features of the no-name theory, of the four alluded to earlier. First, to explain the difference in truth value between reports of superficially similar beliefs, we no-name theorists postulate **direct attribution or self-ascription**:[5] In beliefs about oneself, the believer attributes (or ascribes) an incomplete proposition to herself directly, that is, without the mediation of a proper name or demonstrative to guide the attribution to the right subject. This then explains the reporter's way of reporting the belief, that avoids any suggestion of covert names. This is how Trixy could be ascribing falsely by ascribing being Belia to herself and all the while being qualitatively identical to Belia. Beliefs about the now also directly attribute properties to the moment that the believing occurs in.

One of the great obstacles to understanding direct attribution is the seeming platitude that, in order to think a complete thought, the mind must be directed toward a complete proposition. Not so. Its seeming so platitudinous just reflects a lack of imagination. The word "complete" means in our discussion "evaluable by itself as either true or false." A thinking can be complete in this sense even if its content is not complete. That's the insight embedded in the concept of direct attribution. In directly attributing an incomplete content one thinks a complete thought without a complete proposition. Recall the **context principle** from section B: Terms have meaning only in the context of a proposition. Clarify that now to say that terms have meaning only in the context of truth-evaluable units. Directly attributed incomplete propositions are truth-evaluable units. If a language were so primitive as to have only predication by direct attribution of incomplete propositions, it would be meaningful by the context principle.

As "no name" is to the subject-about-which, so "direct" is to the predicate-toward-which; the one if and only if the other. The phrases "direct attribution" and "self-ascription" are appropriate only for describing the attitude of belief, however. To directly attribute to oneself is to directly *believe* true of oneself. We should generalize directness so that it's not tied to just the declarative force, which the word "attribution" suggests. Predicates and incomplete propositions occur in other forces, as in desires for example, and they may be predicated directly with these other forces without benefit of a name for the subject of predication. We'll continue to refer to direct attribution, however, with the understanding that directness should be generalized to all the other forces.

Imagine a foot race near the finish, and the runner in front glimpses her competitors gaining on her—a desire, a belief, and now an order to herself: Faster! This is direct attribution in the imperative mood. Is this not the intentional content of a volition, that is, an act of will? When she wins, she reports her final spurt in the first person: "I gave it all I had."

## §5. The kinetic theory of self-reference fits well with the no-name theory.

Direct attribution sounds like a name for a mystery. For how can Belia refer to herself if she uses no name or representation of herself? An answer was proposed by Falk, Shoemaker, and Mellor, independently of each other.[6] Put briefly, in order to feel this mystery, you have to be in the grips of a cognitive model of reference, namely, that to refer to something is to know enough about it so that what you know can serve to distinguish it from other things. Such a theory of reference leads the theorist immediately into a vicious circle, since to know something one must first refer to it. One might try to distinguish two kinds of knowing to get out of the circle, perhaps knowledge by acquaintance establishes reference, while knowledge by description is the knowledge true of the referent. Alternatively, you might come to see that postulation as an act of desperation, if you consider instead a noncognitive account of reference: First in the order of definition of concepts comes the fact that the believer's direct attributions affect her purposeful actions directly. If she believes that she herself is dehydrated, you can expect that she'll do something to quench her thirst. Given that connection, we can simply identify the referent of her belief as that which drinks because of the belief. More generally, we define the reference of a belief in the first person and present tense as being about that which is moved by the belief. Falk calls this the kinetic theory of core instances of indexical reference. If indexical reference is indispensable for purposeful action, then purposeful action is sufficient for indexical reference; it's that simple.

The kinetic theory breaks with the knowing-who-or-what criterion of *de re*-ness, which is clearly cognitivist.^ It was a headache for us anyway, extremely sensitive to context for what counted as knowing-who, as we noted in section J. Good riddance. Those who hanker after some cognitive way the believer identifies herself as referent of her belief may take the line that reporters should distinguish two forms of *de re*-ness. The first is reported with about-positions, when the believer employs explicit naming in accord with the knowing-who-or-what criterion. The second is reported with **concerning-positions**, when the believer has no name to identify the thing mentioned in the concerning-position and engages in direct attribution. Perry recommends this course. He writes of it as if he had a dominance theory in mind, such that a concerning-position is for the world, determining reference on behalf of the believer, to fill in, and an about-position is for those believers who have wrested control of their referring from the world. Too strong a bifurcation, however, could interfere with detecting the continuity between the two situations, even their mutuality. Furthermore we should keep in mind that what holds in speech may not hold in thought. The main evidence, other than cognitivist prejudice, for a concerning-position comes from people's speech, for sentences can be complete sentences without referring to the things they concern. (It seems a *non sequitur* to me, however, to reason from the lack of a name in one's public utterance to the lack of a name in one's mind. The absence of names in sentences is not the rationale for any no-mental-name theory that I'd propose.) Perry's example is "There's an apple," whose analysis has me and the present time referred to in the concerning-position because it reports a perception of an apple in front of me now. Such a sentence does not call for any theory of the believer's reference to herself and the present, according to Perry, either in speech or in thought. Location of utterance does the work for the believer. In response, I'd say the kinetic theory of indexical reference adds insight to this superficial description of the situation, namely, the insight of the sufficiency of purposeful action for indexical reference. I bring up the device of a concerning-position here to caution that the motive for introducing a second sort of referentially transparent position should not be to enforce the knowing-who-or-what criterion on the about-position. A concerning-position may have its uses, however, for even if we stay with causal rapport, ought we not to admit the possibility that causal rapport exists and it does not result in the creation of a mental name? Might the provision of a way of reporting that pays attention to this distinction be a good reason for introducing a concerning-position? We return to this issue in section T, where we envision a pre-ontological stage of mentality.

Core instances of indexical self-reference are beliefs in the indicative mood and the other attitudes expressed in the first person and present tense. These are the beliefs and desires that tie directly to one's agency at the moment. The kinetic theory has a corollary concerning self-reportage, the fourth item covered by the complete no-name theory. Most animals are capable of indexical beliefs but not of communicating them to others. Nevertheless the theory would be incomplete without a theory of human self-reportage. Falk proposed that when a person is aware that her beliefs and desires interface directly with her muscles and glands—her machinery for action, if you will—that direct awareness of something about the state of her own agency leads her to choose to publish those attitudes in language using the first person pronoun and present tense and indicative mood.[7] We may call such awareness of states of her own agency her volitive consciousness. Not that a volition is always involved; a belief's being ready for a role at the interface does not entail actually acting on the belief. I'll leave unresolved any perplexity over how one might introspect what often is an inactive state. The main point is to resist the idea that, to use the pronouns "I" or "now," we need to introspect something I-ish or Now-ish. Once a person has many standing and recurrent beliefs in the first-person, there's some point to introducing a self-concept to label the dossier, so to speak, for mental house-keeping purposes. Only extensive self-reportage creates the need for such a self-concept; it's not that the self-concept comes first and makes self-reportage possible.

Each of us is like a great ship plying the ocean. Its parts must communicate with each other, and so must ours. It must also communicate with other ships. The prerequisites of the two types of communication should not be confused. On the deck is our communication officer, using the full resources of our language with other ships. When commands go down to the boiler room, however, the niceties of speech don't count. When the boiler room gets word from above, "Full steam ahead," no one down there acts perplexed and wonders "When?" or "Which one?" This is direct attribution. Only the one subject can be intended and only the one time. Worries about the boiler room crew not knowing how to identify the intended subject and the intended time are unwarranted. This **boiler room analogy** provides a connection to Part III, where it recurs in sections P §5, Q §6, and S §1. In section Y of Part IV we return to the boiler room for a closer look at what goes on down there.

I mentioned in the Introduction that we would find the real nexus between the intentional and the physical, which Descartes located in the brain's pineal gland. Well, we just found its real location. This discovery should now make many of my earlier comments easier to understand. I recommend looking back to my allusions to Job's conversion, first in the Introduction and more elaborately in section I. Doesn't it make more sense now how his coming to have relational beliefs might have been the mechanism of his conversion? Also review Cardinal Newman's encomium to action-reinforcing virtues of relational attitudes quoted in section D. It too should make more sense now.

If this kinetic approach accounts for the phenomena of indexical reference, Ockham's razor recommends it over the cognitive approaches. For its parsimony on the matter of knowledge makes it cover the simplest cases of egocentric attitudes, such as a cat's, as well as the most complex cases, such as our own. Furthermore, it can exist independently of the rest of intentionality. I promised in the Introduction to present a technique of analysis which can reveal the evolution of mentality. Here has been one instance of it. For if we've located the interface between the intentional and the physical, it must be the first thing to evolve in the evolution of mentality. All further evolution depends on it.

Grasping this idea requires that we think of relational attitudes as the more primitive of the two kinds of attitudes. The relational, in turn, divide into those that involve mental names and those that don't, and the latter are the most primitive. To understand this sequencing of the attitudes may require a shift in your perspective on them. I suspect that many philosophers are impressed by the fact that relational beliefs are immune to certain kinds of error that afflict notional beliefs, and they assume that immunity from error is a sign of greater sophistication rather than greater primitiveness. The particular kind of immunity from error which relational beliefs have, namely, that they cannot fail to be about something, is not due to more circumspection by the person with the attitude, but less. They cannot err merely because they don't claim to know. The sort of error that can make an attitude fail to be about something requires sophisticated referential devices which only notional attitudes deploy. So, practice thinking of relational attitudes as more primitive than notional ones, and of indexical attitudes as the most primitive of the relational attitudes.

If the kinetic theory of reference for core indexicals is true, then it can be extended to other forms of reference as well. For if core indexical reference is the primordial reference, all other reference most likely evolved from it. Falk wrote a paragraph on how reference to things other than oneself may have originated; it's near the end of his "Reference to Myself." Years earlier, even before the work on the essential indexical, Adam Morton suggested a similar line of thought. He suggested

> that a belief refers to a particular object, in the context of a psychological explanation, when the belief is sustained by [feedback] processes that normally can guide actions of the kind being explained to objects situated as the object is—if such processes were not operating the agent would not continue to hold the belief.[8]

More recently the psychologist Nicholas Humphrey developed a kinetic theory of reference to one's sensations:

> Indeed let's suppose, for the sake of argument, that what it is for someone to *feel* a particular sensation is just for him to engage in the *appropriate form of sentition*—and to issue whatever instructions are required to create the relevant outgoing signal from the brain.[9]

In section B, I suggested that having sensations could involve entertaining propositions. I cited Fred Feldman's suggestion that pleasure and pain may contain propositional content. Now I add that, in the feeling of any normal pleasure or pain—I exclude Harriet's headache and states produced by some analgesics—animals directly attribute an incomplete proposition about the realization of their good. For surely, nothing changes behavior so immediately as the feeling of pleasure or pain. If this is correct, then Plato was right to suggest there are such things as false pleasures.[10] These are but hints at how the kinetic theory might be developed, and that's where matters stand today.

### §6. Adicity and direct attribution.

One last issue concerns the **adicity** of the incomplete propositions. Our conclusion points out a vagueness in our account of adicity in section D. Up to now, we could speak equally of a monadic attribute as true of things taken one at a time, or as something whose expression in a predicate is completed by any one of the available names. The former is a propositional characterization of adicity, the latter is a sentential one. In the case of direct attribution, however, the two characterizations fall apart, for the sentential one itself bifurcates between the sentences of a public language, which Rep must use, and the sentences of a language of thought (to be discussed in Part III), which Belia uses. In the language of thought, the sentential characterization of a monadic incomplete sentence does not apply to predicates directly attributed. No names are in use there in beliefs about oneself and the present. Even the propositional characterization needs clarification: Insofar as attributes are the things that are attributed, they are monadic, but the attribution of them results in a medadic condition, a completeness of the state which is believing of oneself. We have a noninferential volitive consciousness of them in that medadic form there at the interface of the intentional (orders to carry out an action) with the postintentional (the muscles' response to the orders), if you will. So we self-report, using indexically formatted sentences.

The problem with direct attribution and adicity is the problem noted earlier of having a complete thought without a complete proposition. How can it be that a complete thought is medadic though its content remains monadic? Earlier I just bit that bullet, but here I offer an alternative interpretation of my kinetic theory. Instead of direct attribution, there is assertion without attribution; truth-or-falsity without reference. Suppose that in the boiler room of the ship that is me, "full steam ahead" is a complete order, and "steaming forward at full throttle" is a complete assertion, which is true not because it's of me at the present moment, as though truth depended on reference. It's simply true to, not "of" but "to," the immediate spatial and temporal vicinity of its utterance. Then the kinetic theory simply amounts to a way of attaching that sort of prereferential utterance to the relevant vicinity, without being a theory of implicit reference. I'll explore this option more thoroughly in section T, when we introduce Quine's concept of a holophrastic sentence.

# Notes

1. John Perry, *Knowledge, Possibility, and Consciousness* (2001) and his *Reference and Reflexivity* (2001).

2. David Lewis, "Attitudes *De Dicto* and *De Se*," (1979), reprinted in his *Philosophical Papers*; Roderick Chisholm, "The Indirect Reflexive" in C. Diamond and J. Teichman, eds., *Intention and Intentionality: Essays in Honour of G. E. M. Anscombe* (1979), ch. 4. Chisholm develops the idea in his *The First Person* (1981).

3. John Perry, "Myself and I" (1998), reprinted in his *The Essential Indexical and Other Essays*, expanded edition (2000) 329.

4. The case of Trixy is the case of Heimson, who thinks he's Hume, which is discussed in the literature, e.g., by Lewis in his "Attitudes *De Dicto* and *De Se*." We look at it again in section W.

5. Chisholm uses "direct attribution"; Lewis uses "self-ascription." I omit

slight differences in the way they characterize this concept. I shall not use "self-ascription" because it can be confused with uttering a report about one's belief: "I believe that . . ." can be called self-ascription.

6. Arthur Falk, "Knowledge of Myself," *Prajna*, Journal of Utkal University, India, 6 (March, 1986) 1-26, and "Reference to Myself" *Behaviorism*, 15 (1987) 89-105; "Consciousness and Self-Reference," *Erkenntnis*, 43 (1995) 151-180. A brief statement of the idea appears in Sydney Shoemaker's "Introspection and the Self," *Midwest Studies in Philosophy: Studies in the Philosophy of Mind*, 10 (1986),101-120. See p. 112. D. H. Mellor presented a kinetic theory of reference for core indexicals in his paper, "I and Now" (1989), reprinted in his *Matters of Metaphysics* (1991). His argument for the theory presupposes the truth of analytic behaviorism, which he gets from Frank Plumpton Ramsey. My argument, in contrast, depends only on the strong intuitions evoked in section M for the indispensability of indexical beliefs for action.

7. Arthur Falk, "Consciousness and Self-Reference," 174f.

8. Adam Morton, "Because He Thought He Had Insulted Him," *Journal of Philosophy*, 72 (1975) 5-15. The quotation is from p. 9.

9. Nicholas Humphrey, *A Natural History of the Mind* (1992) 162. He elaborates on p. 184:

> to have a sensation is not, after all, just to issue an instruction, but rather 'to issue a potential instruction and to receive a confirmatory answering signal within the scope of the subjective present.' The intentionality would have been established . . . ., for the anticipated outcome and the actual outcome would be rolled in one.

Humphrey believes the intentionality implied in the word "instruction" can emerge from the recurrent feedback loop. We discuss feedback loops in section Y.

10. Plato, *Philebus* 36c ff. In conditions of scarcity most pleasures and pains are true, but in conditions of extreme abundance, such as for the upper classes in ancient cities like Sybaris and in much of today's world, they're mostly false. For example, the pleasure of the third scoop of ice cream is false, and the pain of an addict's withdrawal symptoms is false also.

# O. The General, Unified Theory of Relational Beliefs: Ellipsis + Dominance

In this section we unify the ellipsis theory of sections L and N with the dominance theory of partial concurrence of section I. (Recall that the dominance theory says that the person who has a relational attitude has a tacit default intention that the truth dominate the referential aspects of her attitude. This intention entitles the reporter of her attitude to treat it as transparently about a real thing she's related to.) The two theories together help us zero in on the relationality of relational attitudes. The general theory's dominance component constrains what the objective terminus of the relation can be, and its ellipsis component constrains what the subjective terminus can be. The theory will unify all the subtheories we've been exploring; it will subsume the no-name theory of section N and the causal rapport theory of section I as special cases of relational beliefs, namely, as beliefs about oneself, one's present, and perceptible objects. In addition the general theory will allow for relational beliefs about abstract objects, values, and God, which are the topics that this section is mostly devoted to.

Let's begin with the question of relational attitudes about abstract objects and afterwards consider the valued nonexistents and God.

## §1. Problems of hyperintensionality with beliefs about abstract objects.

We skirted whether Belia has relational beliefs about abstract objects, although we did note that her interest in mathematics led her to beliefs about the number nine, the empty set, and such. Are they *de dicto* beliefs merely? Well, let's not make Belia herself an issue here. Consider the mathematician Srinivasa Ramanujan. In a memoir, the mathematician G. H. Hardy wrote of him,[1]

> He had, of course, an extraordinary memory. He could remember the idiosyncrasies of numbers in an almost uncanny way. It was Mr. Littlewood (I believe) who remarked that "every positive integer was one of his personal friends." I remember once going to see him when he was

lying ill at Putney. I had ridden in taxi-cab No. 1729, and remarked that
the number seemed to me rather a dull one, and that I hoped it was not an
unfavourable omen. "No," he replied, "it is a very interesting number; it
is the smallest number expressible as a sum of two cubes in two different
ways."

Perhaps Ramanujan had an extraordinary memory as Hardy says, and was
merely recalling a calculation he'd made. It might've been more than that,
however, as it seems to be in my case. I know that 83 is a prime. If you
asked me out of the blue, I would've answered immediately. The reason is
that I memorized the multiplication tables when I was very young, and
throughout my life I've recalled them innumerable times. I now know
intuitively (*de re?*) which numbers are not in the tables, and 83 is one of
the missing ones. Among the missing ones are some that are not primes,
e.g., 51. An early curiosity led me to identify their factors, and 83 isn't one
of the interlopers. So 83's prime. This is more than a recall of a calculation, and similarly for Ramanujan at a fantastically more advanced level.
So perhaps he had a *de re* knowledge of the number 1729.

   If there is such knowledge, it would circumvent some of the substitution problems that have plagued us. Let's first recall the problem: It's a
consequence of modal logic that mathematical sentences like "1+1=2" and
"2+2=4" and "83 is prime" express the same intension, since they're all
necessarily true, and so, necessarily, each is true if and only if the others
are true. Using the intensional criterion of identity (section G), these are
all the same proposition. A theory of belief that makes all beliefs about
numbers really beliefs directed toward complete mathematical propositions faces the problem of hyperintensionality in a particularly desperate
form. For Belia might believe any one of these sentences without believing
the others, and so substitution of one for the other in Rep's report,

           Belia believes that *p*,

would change it from true to false, despite their expressing the same
intension, that is, the same proposition.

   *De re* belief is not belief in complete propositions, however. Belia may
believe *about* the number 1, that it has the property of its sum with itself
equaling 2. That *de re* belief is distinct from another *de re* belief she may
have *about* the number 2, that it has the property of its sum with itself
equaling 4. The property that 1 has is not the same intension as the
property that 2 has, and of course 1 is not the same thing as 2. So, if we
accept *de re* beliefs about numbers, then we're not forced so immediately
into embarrassing failures of substitutivity. For, although the sentences
constructed from names of numbers and predicates of numbers may

express the same intension, the numbers and the properties taken separately are not the same intension. So their failures to be intersubstitutable prove nothing.

Alas, although we get some respite, it's not enough. Already in section G, we saw two expressions of a property of sets, "being noninductive" and "being reflexive," which express one and the same intension, since their definitions are provably equivalent. Even if Belia's beliefs about sets are *de re*, she may believe a set is noninductive without believing it's reflexive. Now if the supposition that there are *de re* beliefs about numbers and sets had solved all the problems of intersubstitutivity, we'd be tempted sorely to concede there are such beliefs. But if the supposition just reduces the problems without eliminating them entirely, then we'd better find other grounds for the supposition.

## §2. Problems with being in causal rapport with abstract objects.

There are reasons to be suspicious of the supposition of *de re* beliefs about numbers and sets. First of all, it's a matter of controversy whether abstract objects exist. If they don't, there are no *de re* attitudes about them. If they do, people cannot be in causal rapport with anything abstract, which raises the question what relation between abstract entities and people establishes the possibility of *de re* attitudes toward them.

Let's begin then by considering what abstract entities are. Later we'll consider whether they exist. Numbers and sets are instances of abstract entities. An **abstract entity** is defined as the kind of being that's not directly a term in a causal relation, neither a causer of anything, nor an effect. Indirectly yes, by an agent thinking of it, but directly no. One may criticize the definition: What of fear of the number 13 (triskaidekaphobia)? Isn't the number directly scaring people? No. The thought of it scares them, or they see instances of the numerals. What of people's becoming acquainted with natural kinds, like gold, water, the tiger? That would be causal rapport with kinds. In reply, I could just say people become acquainted with instances of them, but I'll say more about natural kinds later in this section.

So far I've only given a negative characterization of abstract entities, and it's enough to eliminate causal rapport with them. What are they positively? To ask that question is to ask for identity conditions. I don't know any identity conditions that fit all and only abstract objects; we'll have to be content with piecemeal coverage. Abstract entities may have either extensional or intensional identity conditions. Sets have the one, attributes the other; both are abstract entities. Characterized either way, many but *not all* abstract entities are **universals**, defined as a kind of object that's multiply instantiable. That is to say, instances, representations, or expressions of one universal can exist in space and time and have causal properties, without compromising the numerical unity of that abstract entity, which itself has neither spatial nor temporal location. Thus the abstract entity, humanity, has billions of instances on earth at this time, but it itself is not split into bits. I'm fully human, and so are you; we don't divide up humanity and share it out to all the human beings. Thus the abstract entity is not to be confused with the mass of human flesh, of which you have a little bit and I have a little bit. The mass of human flesh is a concrete entity. I said not all abstract entities are universals. In contrast to attributes, sets are not thought of as having instances, although they are abstract objects too. Numbers can be thought of as either attributes or sets. None of these things seems to have location in space or time. Some things that are located in space at a time have no direct causal efficacy, and so fit the definition of abstract entities. I think of the Tropic of Capricorn and the International Date Line.

A **concrete entity**, on the other hand, is defined as the kind of entity that enters into causal relations directly. Usually that requires they be located at a place during a time. Negatively characterized, they are not multiply realizable as some abstract entities are. Concrete entities are the instances, not that which is instanced.

My preferred contrast between abstract and concrete in terms of entering directly into causal relations—concrete yes, abstract no—is not the only way philosophers make the contrast. Some prefer location in space and time—concrete yes, abstract no. By my contrast God is concrete and the equator is abstract. The alternative contrast makes God abstract and the equator concrete. And what would spacetime itself be, abstract or concrete? To avoid digression here, let's remind ourselves that our topic is propositional attitudes!

Do abstract objects exist? Most people come to philosophy not believing abstract objects are real. Certainly they are right about some of those I mentioned, like the Tropic of Capricorn. It's an imaginary line around the earth. Is a disbelief in the totality of them correct? The view that *no* abstract objects are real is called **nominalism**. According to nominalism, all things, mental and physical, natural and supernatural, are concrete particulars. The name was inherited from the medieval version of the view, which claimed there's nothing to abstract objects but the names. If nominalism is true, there are no *de re* attitudes toward abstract objects.

We'll not get into the debate, save only to remark on where the burden of proof lies. Since most people assume that abstract objects are not real, the burden of proof first falls on those few who claim they're real. The obligation has been fulfilled: Arguments for their reality have accumulated starting with Plato's and Aristotle's arguments for the reality of universals from the nature of knowledge. The twentieth century added new arguments for the reality of at least the extensional abstract objects, such as sets and numbers. Among philosophers, therefore, the burden of proof has now shifted to the nominalists to prove that sets and numbers don't exist. For mathematics refers to sets and numbers, and one cannot just chuck all mathematics as fiction. No philosopher would respond to a nominalist's demand for proof that mathematics is not fiction; on the contrary, the nominalists must reconstruct the concepts of number and set so that mathematics stays true while referring to just the things they think do exist.

In the meantime, how has our understanding of existence evolved to accommodate the very idea of the existence of abstract objects? There are not two concepts of existence, one for existing concretely and another for existing abstractly ("subsisting"?). The concept is univocal; the adjectives "abstract" and "concrete" don't distinguish modes of existing, only modes of existents. Quine gave to philosophy an utterly emancipating proclamation, a **criterion of ontic commitment** that's fully general. He encapsulated it in the mnemonic:

to be is to be the value^ of a variable.[2]

The words whimsically allude to Bishop Berkeley's "to be is to be perceived." And indeed, one way to read them is that existence is just a matter of being thought about. Egads! That's not what they're supposed to mean. It's not a criterion of things' existence; it's a criterion of people's ontic commitment. (We may think we get a criterion of things' existence by expanding the slogan this way: To be is to be the value of a variable of a true theory. In fact, however, it cannot function as a criterion of existence, for we can only know what we *take to be* a true theory, and so we're back to a criterion for a person's ontic commitment.) To avoid misunderstanding this slogan, Quine expanded it:

> We look to bound variables in connection with ontology not in order to know what there is, but in order to know what a given remark or doctrine, ours or someone else's, *says* there is; and this much is quite properly a problem involving language. But what there is is another question.

More elaborately and less misleadingly, he states his criterion thus:

The variables of quantification, 'something', 'nothing', 'everything', range over our whole ontology, whatever it may be; and we are convicted of a particular ontological presupposition if, and only if, the alleged presuppositum has to be reckoned among the entities over which our variables range in order to render one of our affirmations true.

The variables referred to are bound to quantifiers. The import of existential quantifiers,^ which we read not only as "something is such that . . .," but also as affirming existence: "there exists an entity such that . . . ," is obvious. Universal quantifiers also have existential import, for, as we noted in section E, the inference is valid from "everything is . . ." to "something is . . . ." The inference is valid even from a premise with the quantifier, "nothing," for the sentence "nothing is . . ." is equivalent to "everything fails to be . . ."

The liberating effect of the criterion is that thinkers are free to accept as existing whatever domain^ of entities the anaphoric pronouns (i.e., variables) in their theories need to refer to for the theories to have application and be determined to be true. The theories may be formal, as mathematics is, or empirical as are physics and folk psychology. So if set theory says there is an infinite set, and I accept set theory as true, I'm committed to the existence of an infinite set. To accept a theory as true is to commit to the reality of the things it refers to. That's one's "ontic commitment." Don't be afraid to accept the criterion of ontic commitment in its full generality; you have nothing to lose but your mental chains; you have the world to win. The criterion also confirms our intuitions that the Tropic of Capricorn is imaginary. Its existence is not needed for any theory science accepts to be true. We have the same reason for denying existence to *possibilia*^ and intensional objects, such as the top card of the deck of playing cards, considered simply as the top card, or the National Anthem, apart from singings of it.

### §3. Extending the ellipsis theory to cover relational beliefs about abstract entities.

So far we considered *de re* attitudes toward concrete objects, oneself, and the things people are in causal rapport with. We also considered *de re* attitudes toward the present moment, which we can particularize as a temporal cross-section of the universe, that is, the present moment consists of the whole universe at that moment. Now the question is, can people have *de re* beliefs about sets and numbers? If so, causal rapport would have nothing to do with it, nor would the guidance of the believer's behavior as postulated by the kinetic theory of indexical reference. For abstract entities are causally inert.

Nevertheless, some philosophers believe that people can have *de re* beliefs about abstract entities. Bertrand Russell defined knowledge by acquaintance in a way that implied people can be acquainted with them and so have *de re* knowledge of them (see section A). Let's just consider the natural numbers. Diana Ackerman thinks a person can have *de re* beliefs about them, believing anything at all about them, true or false, just so long as the person uses a common numeral to name the number.[3] The numeral presumably forces one to believe some truths, like the position of the number in the number series. Starkly contrasting with this universal access to the abstract, one might imagine Descartes requiring that a person have a clear and distinct idea of the entity. His claim that all clear and distinct ideas are true might entail that they are *de re*. In that vein, David Lewis conjectures a person might have *de re* beliefs about the numbers, only if the person knows their essences.[4] That entails knowing a bundle of necessary truths about them. Ramanujan could be said to know the number 1729 and most of its neighbors in their essences, and so he had knowledge *de re* about each of them.

In section J we noted in passing a criterion for *de re* belief, due to Jaakko Hintikka, which we called the **knowing-who-or-what** criterion. According to that criterion, one's attitude is *de re* if one knows enough about the thing to identify it, regardless of causal rapport with it. Both Ackerman's and Descartes's criteria are instances of the knowing-who-or-what criterion. It's a candidate for being the unified theory of relational beliefs, in competition with the dominance theory, which I'll propose. On the face of it, it looks as if the knowing-who-or-what criterion accommodates better the possibility of *de re* attitudes toward abstract objects.

How transmissible is *de re* belief about abstract entities? If the beliefs must be knowledge, simple communication won't suffice for transmission. The auditor must fulfill conditions of knowledge. How much knowledge would be enough depends on who's theory of *de re*-ness is true. Ackerman's is fairly lax. If Descartes's is the right one, only those who master a true theory of the objects have *de re* beliefs about the abstract objects. Transmission would not be the issue; mastery would be. Mastery is extremely sensitive to context, and puts us back into the problems dealt with in section J. Let's hold out for a unified theory that's less context sensitive.

If there are relational beliefs about numbers and other abstract objects, we must extend the ellipsis theory of relational reports to cover them. For paradoxes can arise for Belia's beliefs about them and Rep's reporting of those beliefs, similar to those which led us to accept the ellipsis theory. He must attribute to Belia mental names of the objects and add reflexive contents that refer to the names. In the case of the natural numbers, if we follow Ackerman, their names must be in standard form, that is, numerals. The concept of a standard name Carnap developed, as we saw in section F when we discussed the identity of the number 1 with the number 0.99999(forever). Curiously, Ackerman refuses to discuss this case!

What if Belia were to believe about the number 1 and the number 0.9999(forever), that the former is greater than the latter, the latter less than the former? Since the two numerals in the about-position are intersubstitutable, exchanging positions as the former and the latter, i.e., as antecedents of those pronouns, Belia's belief would be a self-contradiction and any report of it would imply a contradiction in the reporter, as we demonstrated in section K, unless the theory of reports allows an ellipsis which tacitly refers to the two names she uses for the one number and a reflexive content which embodies her confusion about them. Alternatively, we could follow Descartes and say that confusion of this sort is sufficient to demonstrate that the belief is not *de re*. A cartesian view is likely to load theorems into the reflexive content of a belief *de re* about abstract objects.

### §4. Extending the ellipsis theory to cover relational beliefs about the essences of concrete entities.

What is it to know what a certain concrete object must be, to be the thing it is? Concrete objects also have their individual essences. Might people also know *de re* concrete things this way? Might Mendeleev, for example, have had *de re* beliefs about the elements, gallium, scandium, and germanium, before they were discovered, because they were predicted and described by his periodic table of elements? With concrete objects, however, existence is sharply separated from essence, and *de re* knowledge is at least knowledge *de the re*'s existence, which is not contained in the knowledge of its essence. So knowledge of a concrete thing's individual essence does not seem sufficient to give *de re* belief about it. Nor is it likely anyone would ever come to know the individual essences even of the concrete objects that are existent, unless they were quite simple.

The chief argument for the view that knowledge of essences yields *de re* knowledge of objects is the analogy between the *de re* forms in modal logic and those of propositional attitudes. Names expressive of essences can be used in modal logic to express *de re* necessities. So far, however, we've found little reason to be impressed by that analogy.

To dismiss the chief argument for an idea may not be to dismiss the idea itself, and it's not dismissal here. For the idea that people can have *de re* beliefs by knowing the essence of the *res* has the intriguing consequence that knowledge of scientific laws might be knowledge *de re* of all those things sharing a species essence. For the laws can be thought of as relations of species essences. We excluded (in section L) relational beliefs about *all* of a kind, but only if the beliefs were based merely on an inspection of some of the kind. We noted there (§3) how Belia solved a dilemma relating temporality with the Cartesian *cogito* by means of a *de re* claim about all past times. Now we note that insight into a species essence, the kind itself, may underlie the human ability to theorize about nature.

But how are the vivid names of species essences introduced into Belia's mind? Surprisingly, causal rapport may have something to do with their introduction. People use the names of species essences or natural kinds in sentences, for example, "gold" when they say that atoms of gold have 79 protons in their nuclei, and that gold is yellow. These can be relational beliefs. Belia can believe *about* gold that it's yellow and has 79 protons in each atom of it. This report will be elliptical, with the ellipsis referring to the fact that Belia has a name for gold. Many philosophers today believe that causal rapport underlies these names too. Are people in rapport with abstract objects after all, since essences and kinds are abstract?

Although people are not in causal rapport with abstract objects, they are in rapport with stuff, with gold in the example. The result of the rapport is a name very much like the proper name of an individual. We can think of gold as a single scattered object, nuggets of it here, veins of it there, false teeth of it in my mouth, and so on. We can discount the parceling of it into bits and just think of the totality of it as the individual entity, gold. Similarly for human flesh, as I suggested earlier. Animals, unlike gold as we ordinarily think of it, necessarily come in units. Counting units of human flesh is not arbitrary; counting perceivable units of gold seems arbitrary. Otherwise there's no ontologically^ significant difference between them.

We can think of a language's names for the stuff being introduced on the basis of its speakers' causal rapport with the single distributed object —with a bit of it, *a fortiori* with it. So their names for stuffs are really proper names, and Belia has a vivid mental name for gold. For her the word "gold" means

> "that stuff, consisting of the bit of stuff I first learned to call 'gold' and all the rest that's identical in nature to that bit."

Note the lack of descriptive content in this meaning of the name. She does not need to know the nature of gold. She's just stating a criterion of individuation of the stuff gold, namely, it has a homogeneous nature, whatever it is and however that nature is separated out from the accidents of gold, such as isotopes of gold. Water is named in the same way, as are tigers and human beings. There are three isotopes of water, one of them radioactive, but all water has the nature of two hydrogen atoms combining with an oxygen atom. Belia does not have to know that fact when she names water:

> "the stuff that consists of this bit and all the other bits with the same nature as this bit."

Similarly, tigers can all be parts of the individual entity, which is tiger stuff.

The most popular argument for one feature of this account, namely that Belia's name for the stuff can be proper-name-like in its lack of descriptive content and dependency on causal rapport, is called "the twin earth thought experiment," created by Hilary Putnam in 1975.[5] We shall not tarry over this argument, since we'll visit twin earth in section S. The argument for taking biological kinds to be individuals was presented by David Hull in 1976.[6] Hull's arguments are for the thesis that biological species are the individuals required by biological theory. Aside from the requirements of theory, species-individuals also make good sense in an account of *de re* attitudes about species and natural kinds, insofar as causal rapport underwrites them.

Our discussion of this subject is misplaced in a section about attitudes toward abstract objects, because the import of our discussion is that a person's relational attitudes toward kinds and species are attitudes toward distributed concrete stuffs, and therefore they are to be understood exactly the way we understand relational attitudes toward concrete things. I discuss it here because these beliefs are usually classified as about abstract entities, such as species essences.

### §5. The dominance theory unifies *de re* attitudes, despite the diversity of what they are about.

The ellipsis theory posits either no names or vivid names and associated reflexive content in Belia's mind. Some of the names are proper names, the names of natural kinds, and standard names. All these can lack defining descriptive content. That lack allows the merger of the ellipsis theory of mental names and the dominance theory of partial concurrence in this way: When the believer concedes dominance to the world in determining what her attitudes are about, she's conceding to the world the determination of the referents of her mental names. With descriptive names, in contrast, the believer asserts her own dominance. The ellipsis theory constrains the dominance theory in just the right way: The world exercises its dominance in the way specified by the definitions of these three kinds of names. Causal rapport defines logically *proper names*; the schema stated above defines *names of natural kinds* in a way that builds on causal rapport; and the definition of *standard names* in section F fixes what the world can say about numbers. Furthermore, the aboriginal reference relation, described in the kinetic theory of *indexical reference* in section N, fits the dominance theory perfectly in that the person with the attitude refers to herself and her present moment simply by acting on her belief-desire complex.

Way back in the Introduction I said that what characterizes relational attitudes is a "distinctive relation" between the person having the attitude and the thing the attitude is about. Can we now say what is distinctive of all the relations that make relational attitudes possible? Let's try: The person and the thing, the two terms of the relation, must be in the world together, with the person acquiescing to a subordination to the world in the fixing of that thing as the referent of her attitude, and the world does fix it in one of the various ways it can do that. The most primitive way is described in the kinetic theory of indexical reference to the self and the present, and another one, important because it underlies perception, is causal rapport. Both relations of subordination occur at a prevolitional level, at the interface of the body and mind. The extension of the subordination to the realm of abstract objects is an acknowledgment that they too are part of the world. Here a believer's volition in mastering a theory may enter as a factor establishing the right relation of the believer to the objects of her belief. But when the person forces the matter of reference by descriptional means, the resultant attitude is notional merely.

Human beings' self-subordination and deference to the world for establishing the referential aspects of their attitudes is a survival of a primitive kind of mentality, an inheritance from prehuman ancestors who had no alternative for establishing reference. Yet, although people do have alternatives, they continue to defer to the world partly in recognition of their communal way of life. *De re* attitudes have central roles in coordinative behavior including learning from each other's testimony. We should observe Belia in a community. Belia expects those she cooperates with to pick up useful information from her about their common environment, within which they all succeed or fail in their joint efforts. It pays her to preserve primitive ways when they can be corrective of her unwarranted referential presumption.

One may wonder whether fake *de re*, which we discussed in section J, suffices for communication about a common environment. If communication were all that dominance theory is concerned with, it would make the distinction drawn in section J between fake and genuine *de re* superfluous. On the contrary, however, dominance theory is primarily about the establishing of reference in attitudes, and insofar as it applies to communication, it sharpens the distinction between the two modes of *de re* reportage. Fake *de re* would work in societies that attached "let the buyer beware" labels to all communications. There the audience, not the speaker, would be taken to determine whether the communication was *de re*. We'd be back to the simple concurrence theory of the about-position, according to which Rep does not take Belia to acquiesce to the dominance of the actual over her attitude nor to get into the relation to the actual by which its dominance takes hold. The dominance theory, in contrast, assigns to Belia the propensity to fulfill a condition, the condition that makes her attitudes be about something. When that's the prevailing condition among believers, the practice in effect attaches a seal of certification to their communications of their beliefs. So dominance theory entails the distinction between fake and genuine *de re*, since it acknowledges the believer's possibilities of achieving the right relation to the objects of her attitudes or failing to. Furthermore, when we extend *de re* attitudes to include being about abstract objects, there's still point to having two *de re* modes of reportage, when Rep wishes to distinguish cases where she is trustworthy and fulfills her intention in a reliable way from cases where she only fulfills it serendipitously and is still untrustworthy.

The dominance theory has another possible payoff in recapturing an insight we discarded in section D. At the end of the section, I mentioned Grice's attempt to derive propositional meaning from iterative attitudes: The speaker of a proposition intends to affect the hearer by means of the hearer's recognition of the fact that the speaker intends the effect. I suggested the analysis of propositional meaning suffered from chicken-or-egg disease, since it seemed that even these intentions presupposed the conveyance of propositional content. The dominance theory as Penner and Rowe present it is an attitude about attitudes and offers no cure.[7] In the form developed here, however, it extends down to primitive states and offers to ground the analysis on an attitude that has no such presupposition. The speaker's primordial attitude of deference to the world in the matter of reference does not require a proposition as its content and is something the hearer may assume. The iteration of attitudes back and forth between conversation partners can build from there.

The question of the *de re*-ness of beliefs about abstract objects seems to produce a clincher argument for the dominance theory, for dominance tells us how beliefs in abstract objects can be *de re* in a univocal sense, along with the *de re* beliefs about such a variety of concrete things. I should say it's a clincher if knowledge itself can be treated as a univocal concept. If so, the world dominates in the case of abstract objects in the sense that, since no one is in causal rapport with abstract objects, the master of theoretic knowledge of them is in a position to have *de re* attitudes toward them, if anybody is. For theoretic knowledge is, in this case as in the case of empirical theory, objective knowledge of denizens of the world. So Quine's criterion of ontic commitment would have us believe (and I do). I can now give Quine's extensionalist ideal a nod. The abstract entities that humanity has theoretic knowledge of are those with extensional identity conditions. Intensional theories, that is, theories of abstract entities meeting intensional identity conditions, are unknown except to a few logicians. Therefore the case for *de re* attitudes toward extensional abstract objects is far better supported.

Is there another reason to prefer the dominance plus ellipsis theory to the knowing-who-or-what criterion as the general unified theory of relational belief? The merger of the dominance and ellipsis theories is not as susceptible to the vagaries of contexts of reporting as that criterion is, and that's a good reason for preferring our theory. Not that dominance is impervious to relativity to context. The matter of mastery of theory is susceptible. Its susceptibility is far less than that of the knowing-who-or-what criterion, however.

## §6. *De re* desires and evaluative beliefs about the nonexistent.

So far we've skirted the issue of Belia having relational beliefs about what she values, which are the beliefs most closely joined to her desires. In section D's pep talk I hinted at the possibility that value judgments *de dicto* might morph into *de re* judgments with powerful effects on her motivation, but I've not said much more since. It's about time to break the silence, don't you think? The dominance theory of concurrence can help us. Socrates, we were told in section I, invented the dominance theory and applied it foremost to desires. In the case of desires, according to Socrates, the person with the desire has a tacit default intention that *the good* dominate her attitude's references to worth. This intention entitles the reporter of her desires to treat them as relational, transparently about that which is actually good, whether or not actually in existence, and about the actually bad. There'd also be beliefs *de re* about the good *qua* good and the bad *qua* bad.

It seems Socrates's claim forces us into a dilemma: What do terms in the about-position of reports of desires and value judgments refer to, the really existent or the really good? On behalf of the really existent, two situations are to be noted: (i) People make value judgments about things and events, about themselves and others and their actions. Insofar as these concrete things existed or occurred, the judgments about them may be *de re* by virtue of causal rapport with them just as any other belief may be. It makes no difference to the relationality of the belief whether being big or being bad is predicated of the thing. (ii) Insofar as people's desires and valuations pertain to themselves, in the first-person, they're about themselves. These indexical desires and valuations enter into indexical belief-desire clusters, *a fortiori de re* clusters, to cause and justify their actions.

On the other hand, value judgments naturally extend beyond the concretely existent, whether it be a past, present, or future concrete state, for the value judgments are of the goals of our desires, which are about what might never exist concretely. Belia's valuations of the situations that have no concrete existence justify her attempting to bring them into existence, though she may fail, or her thwarting their ever coming into existence. What applies to her value judgments applies *a fortiori* to her desires. Surely she has desires with respect to these nonconcretes; can they be *de re* desires in that respect, and if so, can the value judgments associated with the desires be also *de re* beliefs, so that the beliefs and desires are locked into a *de re* cluster?

There are two ways for desires and valuational beliefs to be *de re* about the good. First, one might format a desire in a way that refers to a state of the desirer which does not yet exist nor may ever exist (for she may prevent it or fail to achieve it). Then that desire, understood as referring to such a state, may be equivalent to a desire directed toward attributes of the desirer. In other words, there's an equivalence between an attitude *about* a state of oneself and a veridical attitude *directed toward* attributes of oneself. (Recall veridical attitudes from section C.) For example, I know I will die. Therefore I can have beliefs *de re* about my death. The *de re* attitude would be about the state if and only if the veridical attitude is directed toward the attribute defining the state. The point of this procedure is that we may expand the range of *de re* valuational attitudes if we can help ourselves to valuational attitudes that are veridical in what they are directed toward. It's not clear how we go on to explain their *de re*-ness by the dominance theory, however.

A second and perhaps preferable way of achieving the same expansion appeals to theory. For us to impute *de re*-ness in this respect to these attitudes, in support of Socrates's position, we steal a page from our discussion of relational beliefs about abstract objects. As in that case, so in this; we must assert that a true theory of worth has the really good as the values^ of its variables, regardless of whether the really good situations are concrete and exist in our neighborhood of possibilities or are not concrete and exist nowhere nearby. Then, granted the true theory of worth, to have *de re* attitudes about the things which are the values of its variables is to be master of the theory, just as in the case of abstract objects. This may sound more elitist than Socrates intended, unless a case can be made that the more ultimate the good, the more instinctively everyone knows it, and so the more widely and better known it is. If so, then everyone could have *de re* attitudes toward the most ultimate good for any human being. And most people do think they do, since after all they're living their lives in accord with the theory. Perhaps what we're calling theory is instinctive theory, welling up from another interface between mind and body, from where a person's sense of achievement and well-being arises. However inconclusive that sense is, it's an important test of our conception of felicity. If this is right, then the proper comparison is not to a person's theoretical *de re* beliefs with names and reflexive content, but rather to her core indexical beliefs, with no names and no reflexive content, utterly basic.

Let's say we've made sense, one way or the other, of attitudes *de re* of unrealized worth. We go on to consider a possible flaw in the way philosophers conceptualize the distinction between means and ends, which can interfere with our appreciating the theory of attitudes *de re* of worth.

A theory of worth looks like a hierarchical structure with the good at the top. We tend to think of the hierarchy of values top-down, with the real good at the top and seeping down the hierarchy of means to endow them with goodness. (Might we not think of an inverted hierarchy, the bottom-most point being the pits? In that scenario a person's goals would be evaluated in terms of how much better than the pits their achievement would make things. Let's put this alternative aside.) Because of the inclusiveness of ultimate goals, or goal if it's just one, e.g., felicity, no single action ever suffices to achieve a pure ends-desire; in fact it may take a course of actions over a lifetime to achieve it. So the success of any one action is simply the achievement of a means.

People's desires consist of their desires directed toward ends, that is, goals. Are there desires directed toward the means to the goals? If so, some of their means-desires are directed toward states that are means to their goals merely. Example: desire to have an aching tooth pulled. Others are for means which happen also to be ends desired for their own sakes. These subdivide into those directed toward a means instrumental in bringing about the end and those directed toward means to an end in the sense of being ingredients in the end. Example of the former: desire to date one's intended spouse, which is enjoyable but also furthers one's goal of consummating the relationship. Example of the latter: desire to hear a joke, which is an ingredient in having a good time. In contrast to all these, a person's pure ends-desires are for things desired simply for their own sakes and not for the sake of anything else, not even for the sake of being an ingredient of a more inclusive state.

For all the support this view of the matter has in the philosophical tradition, it's not the only view. It's unclear that such means-desires would do any work in the theory that could not be done by the beliefs about means and the standing desires for goals, indeed just one standing desire for the goal of felicity.[8] Decision theory makes no distinction between means-desires and goal-desires; it takes all a person's desires to be directed toward total states of the world as it would be after the person acts. Nor does the evidence of introspection support the traditional acceptance of means-desires unequivocally. The evidence consists of facts such as people's continuing to feel what they take to be a desire for a means even when they've forgotten their end. Such is hardly the case for a desire for an instrumental means merely, like desiring to have a tooth pulled. If I forgot my goal I'd quickly shelve plans for extracting the tooth. The evidence could only be cases where the means is an ingredient of felicity. Even in such cases, the operative desire may still be the desire for felicity, operating in conjunction with beliefs about the ingredients of felicity.

According to either view, the ordering of means to ends generates a hierarchy of the states which either my value judgments or my desires are directed toward, with the components of felicity, my final ultimate goal, at the top, and the instrumental and ingredient means to them below, and the means to the means even further below, and so on, until we come to the base of the hierarchy, consisting of the most basic components of my actions, like putting one foot in front of the other to walk. The more elaborate the structure, the more places there are at which my beliefs about the means to my good may go wrong, or my desires may go astray. But above the point where I go wrong, my desires and value judgments are directed toward the actual good. It's part of the dominance thesis that error always occurs somewhere down the line concerning the means. Therefore the real good always heads the hierarchy.

Here's another support for the alternative view that people's real desires are only the standing ones they have for their ultimate goals: It's rarely noted that the appearance-reality distinction can apply just as well to desires as to the goods desired. It's a commonplace among philosophers today that people's desires are directed toward the apparent goods. Appearance in this context is generic and skeptical, neutral between true appearance, things seeming to be the way they in fact are, and false appearance, things seeming to be otherwise than they are. But the dominance theory, as Socrates introduced it to analyze desire, proposes that there are *de re* desires, transparently about the good, regardless of appearances. The good, so desired, is extensional. Socrates challenges today's philosophers' commonplace. What philosophers call a real desire for a merely apparent good may only be an apparent desire, one's real desires being only for real goods. The mental state is real enough, but it's a mistake of some sort.

On the other hand, supporting only *de dicto* attitudes toward a final good, everyone has an extraordinary talent for self-deception. The scatter-shot results of people's efforts may also indicate that only the "fake *de re*" reports of their successes are warranted. An analogy between desire and belief undermines the whole Socratic project, it seems. People desire that each of their desires be directed toward the actual good, just as they believe that each of their beliefs is directed toward the actual truth. These are not just general beliefs. Each of their beliefs is such that they have another singular belief (second-order) that the first belief is a belief in something true. Each of their desires is such that they have another singular desire (second-order) that the first desire is a desire for something good. But we have ample evidence that the second-order desire, like the second-order belief, is unrealized. It seems like an awkward self-deception to declare that, when the second-order desire seems unfulfilled, the first-order desire responsible for the mishap had only been an apparent desire, and so it did not count against the second-order desire being fulfilled. The analogy with belief would seem to show the hollowness of the maneuver. Would we save a person's second-order *belief* when it seems unfulfilled by declaring of the offending first-order belief that it had only been an apparent belief? Are beliefs in apparent truths, which are actually false, only apparent beliefs? That's not at all plausible, nor should we suppose the analogous move plausible in the case of desires. Another way of putting the objection: It's flagrant wish fulfillment to declare that, when events thwart one's second-order desire that one's first-order desire be for the good, the latter desire was only apparently, not really, for that bad thing.

What can the defender of the Socratic theory say to undermine the criticism implicit in the analogy, that the theory confuses a desire with a second-order desire to have a desire for the good? The defense is to present an alternative analysis that's at least as adequate to the facts. For starters, one cannot have a second-order desire about a desire unless one initially has a second-order belief about that first-order desire, perhaps a belief that it's a desire for a bad thing. The desire not to have that desire is consequent on that belief. In other words, it should be common ground that people must first have singular beliefs about the contents of each of their first-order desires, before they can form desires about those desires. Indeed, Socrates distinguished what one desires from what seems best to one. I take the latter to be the belief about the content of one's desire.

Might those beliefs be false, just as other beliefs may be? False about what—the desiring or the content desired? Socrates prefers the latter, a choice we can make sense of this way: Suppose that I'm conscious of my desiring, but the contents I desire are not immediately disclosed to consciousness; suppose that I have to theorize about them. (For example, am I just thirsty, or is it specifically a beer that I want?) Suppose further that the theory I come up with directs my actions' implementation of my desire. (I believe my desire is just to quench thirst; I have a glass of water.) If I find myself disappointed by the results, well then, my theory of the content of my desire must've been wrong. (I guess I really did want a beer.) To say I had an apparent desire for water is just to say that I believed my desire to be a desire for water. If I describe this scenario correctly, it seems wrong to say that, since I acted on the desire by drinking a glass of water, that's what I must've really wanted. No, it's only what I believed I wanted. I acted on the desire, by drinking a glass of water, but it was not a desire for a glass of water.

The next step is to argue that what I really wanted was the good. Perhaps I didn't even want the beer, if it's not good for me. In that case, the test of the real object of a want cannot be restricted to the satisfaction ensuing upon the action, but a much more elusive satisfaction over all and in the long term. In view of these difficulties, we must argue the case more positively. One argument for such *de re* desires, veridically directed toward the real good, I'll now present in four steps:[9]

1. Belia's just driven onto a congested highway, with Rep in the passenger seat and the woodchuck in the back. Her goal is to have the vet cure the woodchuck whose condition is deteriorating quickly, and so she's

on her way to the vet and she's in a hurry. The highway gives her a choice of three lanes, all of them slowed down from the heavy traffic. She wants the quickest lane. She thinks it the middle lane. So she turns onto the middle lane. Will she get to the vet on time?

2. Dominance theory clearly applies to desires for means. Whatever Belia may think the appropriate means to her own ends are, she and we can concede that people's desires for means are really for what are actually the means to their ends. Rep must tell us what Belia desires, and so he judges whether some means are good really or merely apparently good by reference to Belia's more ultimate goal, which the means are supposed to serve.

Returning to our suspenseful story, as the woodchuck hyperventilates noisily, Rep tells Belia,

You really want to be in the left lane.

Clearly, there's a sense in which Belia wants the middle lane, since that's the lane she chose to be in. She also wants to be in the fastest lane, and if the left lane is the fastest lane, what she really wants is to be in the left lane. It's not our purpose to deny the sense in which she wants to be in the middle lane. Our purpose is to establish there is a sense in which she wants to be in the left lane. That one is her *de re* desire-for-means, which is dominated by her desire-for-end. The desire to be in the middle lane is a *de dicto* desire, even though it is associated with *de re* beliefs about the middle lane.

The Catholic church distinguishes between the divorce of people married to each other and the annulment of a marriage. In the case of divorce, a marriage exists and then it's dissolved. In the case of annulment, the marriage never existed in the first place. One ground for annulment is lack of consummation. But marriages may be annulled, even when the parties went through the ceremony of wedding and had children. When the church grants the annulment, the parties are delighted to admit that all those years they thought they were married, they never were! Often the grounds for the annulment are defects in the intention of one of the parties to marry, which prevented the marriage from occurring, despite appearances to the contrary. Now the analogy to Belia's situation is this: In switching to the left lane, is she divorcing herself from the want to be in the middle lane, in which case it was her real want, or is she admitting an annulment of her ever having wanted to be in the middle lane? Let's see. Belia does not quarrel with Rep's remark. Instead she examines the traffic patterns ahead of her, and announces:

You're right. This is not the lane I wanted.

She turns onto the left lane. The middle lane was an apparent good merely. In the *de re* format of desires apparent goods are irrelevant; they're not what the desires are about. Ok, but was it divorce or annulment? If the latter, what was the defect in her mental state which prevented her wanting to be in the middle lane, despite appearances to the contrary?

3. In order for this concession of dominance (of the good-as-end over one's desires for means) to work, the assumption must be that the goal itself is really good. For something other than the goal is really good if it serves as a means to the really good. If someone takes that thing or action for being a means to the real good, but it's not really a means to it or it is really a means but not to a goal that's really good, then it's an apparent good merely. Consider the second of these two ways of being an apparent good, namely, it's really a means, but only to an apparently good end: If the ultimate end could not be supposed to be really good, then all we could conclude are conditionals of this sort:

> If the ultimate goal is really good, then this action is really good, if it's a means to that goal; if the ultimate goal is not really good, this action is merely an apparent good, even if it really is a means to that goal.

If we're to avoid the skepticism of not admitting any categorical value judgments, it had better be that, for anything to be an apparent good, something must be a real good, and that'll be what people's ultimate desires are about. If the apex of the hierarchy of means and ends is the goal of felicity, then felicity is a real good, and this real goodness infuses the rest of the hierarchy with real goodness.

Actually there are alternative forms of skepticism:

- Given that I know my ultimate final goal, is it really good?
- Given that my ultimate final goal is the really good, do I know my goal?

Which of these skepticisms is the one more in accord with my actual states of uncertainty? According to the first, I ask, what if felicity is not really good? Odd, although some philosophers have asked that question. Rather than admit that the ultimate goal is not really good, I'd rather say that the ultimate goal is really good, but I don't know well enough what it is to aim for it. That's an argument for Socrates's version.

Suppose that Belia gets to the vet, but the vet tells her that it would be better to let the animal die, for if it could be saved it would suffer terribly. Now Rep tells her what her desire-for-end really was:

> You really want to let the animal die now.

And she replies:

Yes, that's what I want.

Is there a sense of wanting that would entitle them to put the verb "want" in the past tense? Surely she wanted the animal's felicity all along. Only now she sees the means-want which her goal-want entailed all along. She wanted all along the means to the goal she wanted all along. This supports the annullment account of her conscious apparent desires.

4. In short, people's ultimate and final desires, toward which all their other desires are ordered, are for the real good. Belia may be mistaken even about her more ultimate goals. Rep may tell her,

> Oh Belia, if you had known what you really wanted for the woodchuck, you would not've made the trip. For you wanted the best thing for the woodchuck, and the best thing was for it to die quickly.

What people really want is the really good. Are their wants then *de re* about the values^ of the variables of a true theory of goodness?

Being mistaken about what's really better would not change the fact that people's wants are about the really better. So, instead of talking about apparent goods, we should talk of apparent *de re* wants in the case of mistaken wants. Once we put the real good in charge of the hierarchy of means and ends, then we may, if we wish, continue with the *de re* idiom in stating people's proximate desires. For example, if we know another's ultimate desires, when we see the proximate means she desires and judge them to be inadequate, we may say to her, "You don't really want that."

Needless to say, I hope, we should not understand the theory to mitigate the blameworthiness of someone who does wrong intentionally, providing him with a novel excuse that he didn't do what he really desired. Our conceptualization of culpability may have to be reorganized to justify people's practices, however. We're now face to face with one of the Socratic paradoxes, that no one intentionally harms himself.

Assuming that we can circumvent Socratic paradox, we can support and give some operational detail to this proposal. In the case of animals, biological science tells us what this ultimate good is, that all animals desire. It is their inclusive^ fitness. Even in the case of human beings, this is their ultimate good, for the most part, although a philosopher like Schopenhauer might say we just identified the pits. People do think values of human excellence and ethics may override inclusive fitness. A biologist can observe an animal community and appraise its success in achieving its ultimate goals. Why not think ethics, even the ethics and ideals of human excellence that override inclusive fitness, are just part of the true biological theory of the human species, a theory still in its nascent stages?[10] Then human beings, along with all other animals capable of the indexical level of mentality, would have belief-desire clusters about the actual good for themselves, without benefit of mental names for it. The world dominates all the basic referential aspects of people's attitudes, both with respect to the good and to the real.

## §7. *De re* attitudes about God, directed toward God's attitudes.

Assume that God should be classified with concrete entities. People cannot have relational beliefs about God unless God exists. That follows from the transparency of the about-position. We need not determine whether God exists, however, to see how folk psychology deals with attitudes about God.

Can people have relational beliefs about God, if God does exist? Surely that's what everyone believes, for how else account for the phenomenon of praying? Prayers to deities are to "you, God." Consequently, many people take themselves to have beliefs *de re* about God. Faith is the conviction that one is in a relation to God that establishes one's attitudes as being about God, that is, as *de re*. It's common today to say having faith is consistent with having less than certitude that God exists,[11] and this raises an issue we've not so far faced: When the believer has less than certitude of the existence of the being her belief is about, what is her belief's probability when she believes about the being that, for example, he is our father in heaven? Actually, that's not our question, but rather this: What probability enters into her calculation of whether to pray and proclaim to him that he's our father in heaven? (Belief is usually not a matter of choice, but praying's an action which is a matter of choice. So it's appropriate to think of calculating whether to pray.) I suggest that, in acting on what she takes to be her *de re* belief, it's the probability she assigns to the content it's directed toward, conditional on the existence of God. In the standard case of one's certitude of the existence of the entity one's belief is about, this conditional probability equals the absolute^ probability of the belief's content. But when there's less than certitude about that entity's existence, even if there's only a low degree of belief, the conditional probability of the content can be high. I'm generalizing to the case where the absolute and conditional probabilities differ. Also in the normal case, to have a degree of belief in a proposition equal to its probability conditional on another proposition's being true is to have learned and accepted that other proposition without having learned anything else of relevance. We say the learner conditionalized on the proposition. To conditionalize on that proposition is to be sure of it forever after. Here I'm supposing a reversible and context-dependent way for different degrees of belief in a proposition to be appropriate for use in deciding what to do.[12] When one thinks a thought, temporarily giving it a probability conditional on something uncertain, the conviction does not last, and the person of faith slips back and forth between the two degrees of belief in a proposition $A$ as circumstances call for one or the other, sometimes equal to $p(A|\text{God exists})$ and other times just $p(A)$. The fluctuation is analogous to that occurring in reasoning about temporal relations, which D. Lewis described.[13]

What relation is this, which makes people's attitudes *de re* and yet makes room for the believer's uncertainty? Considering God to be the source of all the being there is that might not have been, God is extraordinarily remote from human experience. It seems likely that physical science will account for the Big Bang of 13.7 billion years ago, from which evolved the observable universe, as an event arising from a background scalar field, which also gives rise to myriads of other universes. If so, then we must push the Creator back to being the source of that background scalar field and of all the other universes arising from it. Now that's very remote from the here and now! But religions posit revelations by which God circumvents the remoteness. In Christianity it's the doctrine of the trinity, whereby God becomes manifest in the God-man Jesus, "the Word," and through the ever-present Holy Spirit. Given God's existence and self-revelation, not only can people have relational attitudes about God, via causal rapport, but they could have attitudes toward God, whether or not they were aware of the fact, and even if they denied it. Such is the nature of *de re* beliefs.

Such a revelation as religion posits would validate not only relational attitudes about God, but also the attribution to God of the attitudes posited by folk psychology. Let's turn then to the peculiar nature of the content you might direct such beliefs toward. God himself has propositional attitudes, and your relational attitudes would be directed toward God's attitudes. For example, God loves you, promises you victory over death, and the like. Perhaps we can make use of the concept of a secondary quality, as Locke thought of it. God's attitudes would be secondary qualities as much of God as people's attitudes are of their own minds, containing objective information about God, although not the same objective information as people's attitudes contain about themselves, which I assume pertains to their central nervous systems. I think it fairly obvious that God would not have one of those. Nevertheless, the folk psychological ontology^ of attitudes would be just as indispensable in both cases.

Some people have faith that God has been revealed to human beings in the form of a being with intentional states, about whom they can have *de re* attitudes. Needless to say, it's not the job of folk psychology to settle the truth of their faith. It's internally consistent, if folk psychology is. Surprisingly, their faith is not even inconsistent with their pursuing the metaphysical project of naturalizing the human mind, the subject of Part IV of these notes. The naturalization project has two forms, one the synchronic^ reduction of the intentional states of animals to physical states of their bodies and the other the diachronic story of the evolution of the intentional states from conditions in which intentional states did not exist. If the synchronic reduction succeeds, it need not follow that all beings with intentional states are physical. For the same intentional state can be instantiated in different ways. The diachronic story is not so simply integrated with theology: If the situating of intentionality within evolution succeeds and intentional states reveal their being the products of natural selection operating on the accidents of history, then that would complicate the issue of applying intentional categories to God, because they carry historical baggage, often rightly appraised as truly screwball effects. For example, vertebrate eyes have blind spots; the two branches of the bilateral vertebrate nervous system switch sides below the cranium. The reason? Accidents of history. In section R I'll even suggest that the essence of intentionality is a design flaw. The fact that intentionality can be directed toward the false and the nonexistent suggests this, in my opinion. Is God also flawed in just the way that natural selection happened to create flawed minds?

In defense of faith, perhaps human beings can be material beings evolving by natural selection and evolving to apply an ontology of intentional states to themselves, and the ontology turns out not only to be secondary qualities of themselves in one way, but secondary qualities of God in another way. One's faith may include such a remarkable coincidence. One might reduce the appearance of coincidence by noting that the secondariness of qualities is a matter of degree, yellow being more secondary than red, brown more secondary than yellow, in terms of the greater involvement of the subjective components in people's perception of yellow than red, of brown than yellow. Applying intentional categories to God might be an extreme form of secondariness.

### §8. Summary of the dominance plus ellipsis theory of aboutness.

Our theory of intentionality has two parts, of which we've now completed the first. Here's an outline of what we've concluded, within the context of the whole theory:

- ■The theory of intentionality.
  - ●The theory of aboutness.
    - ○First type of ellipsis: no name.
      - •attitudes about oneself and the now. Kinetic theory of indexical reference.
      - •attitudes about other things without benefit of a name. (the good for oneself?)
    - ○Second type of ellipsis: vivid name.
      - •names due to extensive causal rapport. (perceptibles)
      - •names based on expert theoretical knowledge. (abstract objects)
  - ●The theory of directed-towardness. To be examined in the next part.

The dominance of the world in controlling what an attitude is about is strongest in the first cases listed, and least in the last case listed.

# Notes

1. Quoted by James R. Newman, *The World of Mathematics* (1956) vol. I, Part II, ch. 13.

2. W. V. Quine, "On What There Is" in *From a Logical Point of View* (1953, 1961 revised second edition) 15.

3. Diana Ackerman, "*De Re* Propositional Attitudes Toward Integers" in R. W. Shahan and C. Swoyer, eds., *Essays on the Philosophy of V. W. Quine* (1979).

4. David K. Lewis, "Attitudes *De Dicto* and *De Se*," 154f. Lewis only uses noncommittal words, "might" and "may."

5. For Putnam's original article and many responses to it, see Andrew Pessin and Sanford Goldberg, *The Twin Earth Chronicles: Twenty Years of Reflection on Hilary Putnam's 'The Meaning of "Meaning"'* (1996).

6. David L. Hull, "Are Species Really Individuals?" *Systematic Zoology*, 25 (1976) 174-91; and "A Matter of Individuality," *Philosophy of Science*, 45 (1978) 335-360.

7. Terry Penner and Rowe, C. J., "The Desire for Good: Is the *Meno* Inconsistent with the *Gorgias*?" *Phronesis*, 39 (1994) 1-25.

8. Mark C. Murphy, "The Simple Desire-Fulfillment Theory" *Nous* 33 (1999) 247-272.

9. The rush to the vet is based on Naomi Reshotko's scenario in her "Do Explanatory Desire Attributions Generate Opaque Contexts?" *Ratio (New Series)*, 9 (1996) 153-170.

10. I develop this thought in the last two chapters of my *Darwinism and Philosophical Analysis; Utkal Studies in Philosophy* (2003).

11. For the combination of faith as the taking of one's beliefs to be *de re* of a being whose existence one is uncertain of, see Joshua L. Golding, "Toward a Pragmatic Conception of Religious Faith," *Faith and Philosophy* 7 (1990) 486-503; and my "A Decision-Theoretic Analysis of Faith" *Philo* 5 (2002) 174-195, which is also chapter 9 of my *Darwinism and Philosophical Analysis*.

12. John C. Harsanyi, "Acceptance of Empirical Statements: A Bayesian Theory Without Cognitive Utilities," *Theory and Decision* 18 (1985) 1-30, defends the use of probabilities conditional on a certain proposition, rather than the actual probability of that proposition, when calculating the expected payoffs of an action, in certain circumstances. The issue for us would be whether religious circumstances fit his criteria.

13. David Lewis, "Counterfactual Dependence and Time's Arrow," republished with an addendum in his *Philosophical Papers*, vol. II (1986). See its sixth paragraph. Note the irrelevance of so-called Dutch book arguments (arguments to the effect that it's irrational for you to have degrees of belief in mutually exclusive and jointly exhaustive alternatives such that a bookie could offer you a "book" of bets on them, each of which you'd consider fair or advantageous, and yet it would guarantee the bookie an advantage no matter what happened): The bets would have to be over propositions whose truth values could not be settled. The arguments would prove the irrationality of such fluctuation if they were relevant.

# Part III: Theories of the Directed-Towardness, from P to X

The third part of these notes, consisting of nine sections, develops another aspect of any theory of propositional attitudes, the aspect that is common to relational and notional attitudes, namely that of being directed toward something propositional. But what is directed-towardness? And what is the object our attitudes are directed toward really? We divide this Part into two subparts, depending on whether we conceptualize that thing, which an attitude is directed toward, as a representation or as something represented. We consider several theories.

I've been taking the occasion of these introductions to the Parts to issue notices of hazards to one's health from pursuing these investigations. You would not think introspection would be hazardous; think again. Consider the plight of John Perry, as he worked on his book *Knowledge, Possibility, and Consciousness*:

> Humans, we might think, are always aware of their experiences; not only are experiences epistemically accessible for us, but we know of them in some way; we are at the very least aware of them. This view does not strike me as correct, even for humans. In the case of an adult human in a contemplative mood, say someone working on a philosophy essay, it is hard to imagine having an experience with a distinctive subjective character without being aware of it. But in fact this happens all the time. Right now I am refocusing on the feelings I have as my fingers hit the keys—something I don't usually do. I notice that my left forefinger is just slightly more sensitive than the others, perhaps even a bit sore. This act of attending to the experience is quite different from the experience itself. I've been having these experiences all along, but just now began attending to them, in order to find a good example of a hitherto unattended-to experience.
>
> It is often the state of being aware of or knowing about an experience that is causally crucial to subsequent events. As I continue to focus on my left forefinger, I begin to worry. Perhaps that feeling is an early sign of repetitive stress injury. Perhaps I have some kind of tissue rot that is going to start with my left forefinger and quickly spread throughout my body. Perhaps this is the result of my cracking my knuckles, and for that reason insurance won't cover it. And so forth. The sensation in my finger is really

very minor and transitory and wouldn't have caused a problem at all if I hadn't noticed it while searching for hitherto unattended-to sensations. But the awareness of it has led to a whole series of further mental events, worries, fears, indignation (at the insurance company) and the like. I am so wrought up I may have to quit for the day. (p. 49)

You too can quit right here. You no doubt have already noticed a subtle deterioration in your mental health. Will your insurance cover such self-abuse? What's this, you're willing to incur all the risks of going on? I admire your fortitude and courage and your intemperate desire for wisdom.

# First Subpart of Part III, from P to U.
# Mind is Directed Toward Representations.

Is the mind directed toward that which represents something, according to folk psychology, or is the mind directed toward that something? One view is that there's a mind-dependent entity, something "in" the mind, which depends on the mind for its existence in that the mind creates it or captures it from the environment and sustains it in existence. This would be the representation. In contrast, that which the mind represents must exist prior to being represented, and so is a mind-independent being, existing "without" the mind, as Berkeley would say. Which sort of entity are the attitudes directed towards?

The things the mind makes are instances of representations. So the thesis that the attitudes are directed toward instances of representations is called "representationalism." The first subpart examines this alternative. The second subpart will examine theories that suppose the mind directed toward mind-independent things. We'll call them "nonrepresentationalisms."

You should know the author's position on all this. While I think that instances of representations play an important role in any theory of directed-towardness—that's my syncretist^ side—they're not what attitudes are directed towards. Therefore, I'm a nonrepresentationalist.

Let's reflect on our motivations before proceeding. Are you content with a change of subject, perhaps even overjoyed? Yes? Read on. No? A word for those of you whom the pep talk in section D on *de re* attitudes excited or whom the problems of Part II challenged: Anytime you find the next four sections distracting you from your preferred train of thought on the *de re*, you can skip to sections T and U for more food for thought on the *de re*. But please return; there's good stuff here, and not wholly unrelated. All the sections of this subpart help establish and flesh out the boiler room analogy we noticed in section N §5, which therefore connects all the sections to the *de re*.

# P. Do We Believe Predicates and Sentences?

The last eight sections concerned primarily the theory of the about-position in reports of attitudes. By semantic descent, so to speak, from the reports to the attitudes reported on, they concerned that part of the intentionality of attitudes which is their aboutness. This is only a part of a general theory of the attitudes. We must now broaden the scope of our theorizing to include a theory of the that-clause in reports. The that-clause of a report brings us closer to the belief itself, since the believer herself is in charge of its content. By semantic descent, it's a theory of the other aspect of the intentionality of attitudes, their directed-towardness.

## §1. Are representations the objects of the directed-toward relation?

Are attitudes directed toward things the mind itself makes, things which exist only insofar as they are the contents of attitudes? Or are they directed toward things the mind finds, things which would exist even if they were not the contents of attitudes? If you're skeptical of that contrast, good for you. For another possibility is that the mind makes what it finds. In other words, I may have set up a false dichotomy. For example, consider the number *pi*, which is the ratio of a circle's circumference to its diameter. Philosophers argue about whether it and other numbers are mind-made things or mind-found things. If they're made by the mind, we must modify the definition of abstract objects (stated in section O) as things that are not terms in causal relations, for if the mind did create them, they're effects of mental causality. Other problems will have to be addressed, such as how circles, abstract objects created by the mind, could be created before the mind created the real numbers, one of which is the ratio of their circumferences to their diameters, namely *pi*. Let's resist the temptation to join this issue.

However issues such as this one may divide philosophers, no one denies that the names of this number are things the mind made up. They include the decimal expansion of it, an infinite sequence of digits in the decimal numeration system. If God made the numbers, still the mind gets the credit for the numerals. Now the dichotomy of "made versus found" crumbles: For mathematicians have to find, discover, whether the digits occur within the decimal expansion in a way that mimics a random sequence. They have to discover, for example, whether a sequence of six "9"s appears within the first thousand digits. Similarly then, that which attitudes are directed toward may be both made by the mind, and yet be subject to discovery by the mind. Nevertheless, the contrast is good enough to get us started on our map of the intellectual territory we're to cover.

Once we perform some semantic ascent, the main question about the object of the directed-toward relation becomes: What do the that-clauses in reports name? For they name the object of the directed-toward relation. Perhaps they name attributes, which are less obviously things made by the mind than predicative words are. We've had evidence since section G, however, that attributes, including propositions, are insufficient as objects of the directed-toward relation in propositional attitudes. For they have intensional identity conditions, which suit them for being the contents of the that-clauses of modal logic, but not the contents of the that-clauses of propositional attitude reports, since in them even intensions fail the substitutivity test. We may extend the results about this failure, which we obtained in Part I, to include the beliefs about oneself that use no name for oneself. Recall from sections M and N that such beliefs cannot be directed toward complete propositions. They cannot be directed toward attributes either: Abbott's old book, *Flatland*,[1] has us imagine that space has an indefinitely large number of equally real dimensions, only three of which organize people's perceptions. What would it be like if their perceptions could be organized by fewer dimensions? Abbott has us imagine creatures who only need two, breadth and depth. Thus Abbott calls their world "Flatland." Perhaps we human beings have analogous limitations, the threeness of our perceptual space being just as much a secondary^ quality as the twoness of theirs. I bring the story up only to note the detail that all male members of the middle class in Flatland are equilateral triangles. Might not one of them believe himself to be equilateral without believing himself to be equiangular? It seems he could believe *de se* the one and disbelieve *de se* the other, and so, although the names "equilateral triangle" and "equiangular triangle" name the same intension, they're not intersubstitutable *salva veritate* in reports of beliefs about oneself. In fact, *all* the attitude contexts are hyperintensional in the predicate positions of their that-clauses and opaque in the subject positions of their that-clauses, whereas modal contexts are intensional and transparent, once definite descriptions are eliminated by Russell's paraphrase, as described in section A.

What then could be the object of the directed-toward relation in hyperintensional and opaque contexts? One answer sticks out as just so obvious: words themselves. "Equiangular triangle" and "equilateral triangle" may have the same intension, but they surely are different words. Buddha and Siddhartha Gautama are one and the same, but those names surely are different. Pegasus may never have existed, but the name surely does. Does it not seem premature to go on an ontological safari to hunt for hyperintensions, opacity-resistant entities, and other metaphysical beasts, to solve our problems with the directed-toward relation? We may end up going on that safari, but not until we convince ourselves that words are not the solution. If they are, the objects of the directed-toward relation are the homely things which the mind makes to represent other things: its representations.

## §2. Mapping the intellectual terrain ahead.

Part III, which we just began, is subdivided in two. The first subpart is devoted to **representationalism**, which is also called the representational theory of the mind. It's the thesis that an attitude exists in an organism insofar as a representation occurs in that organism and the representation, *in situ* thus, has the role of object which the attitude is directed toward. The most common representationalism is **sententialism**, the thesis that the representations which attitudes are directed toward are the sentences *in situ*, whose occurrence in an organism gives existence to the organism's attitude. I state this view in this section and subject it to criticism in sections Q and R. In section R I consider the most popular representationalist alternative to sententialism, connectionism. I don't consider the several views to be mutually exclusive. The mind could use all kinds of representations.

Not all theories of directed-towardness which posit sentences as its object are sententialisms. Sententialism is a representationalism. It posits a concrete occurrence of a sentence in an organism as constitutive of its attitude, and the object of the attitude is not a sentence in the abstract, but that very sentence *in situ*, because only in its time and place of occurrence is a sentence fully interpretable. When we get to nonrepresentationalism in section V, we'll see a theory that appeals to sentences in quite another way (eternal sentence nonrepresentationalism). It won't be a sententialism, because it won't be a representationalism.

The second subpart of Part III will consider nonrepresentationalisms. In denying that the attitudes are directed toward representations, those nonrepresentationalisms that accept the folk psychological framework affirm that the attitudes are directed toward what the representations represent. The representationalist and nonrepresentationalist positions are mutually exclusive, if there's only one thing which the mind is directed toward in propositional attitudes. Suppose, however, that there's two, and the mind finds the one only by means of making the other. One finds the fish only by making the net. Then attitudes are directed simultaneously toward both the representation and the represented. This position is a kind of syncretism^ that I'll criticize in section X. But finding room for both in an analysis of attitudes, even if not as simultaneous objects of directed-towardness, would be a legitimate syncretism.

There are two mutually exclusive strategies by which the word-theorists (as we may call sententialists) use the words themselves to answer the question about the object of the directed-toward relation: Some theorists replace attributes and propositions with words, and other theorists supplement them with words. Note the contrast between replacement and supplementation. According to the first type of answer, words are a sufficient object of the directed-toward relation. Nothing else is needed. According to the second, words are only part of the object, in which case we must complicate the directed-toward relation so that it connects the believer not only to words, but to extensions or intensions as well as to words. According to the supplementation type of answer, the directed-toward relation might be this: The believer is directed toward a sentence which makes a proposition accessible to the believer. Not just sentential-ists, but the theorists who prefer entities other than people's words to be the object of the directed-toward relation, i.e., the nonrepresentationalists, must also choose between these two strategies. Those who opt for sup-plementation might say, for example, the believer is directed toward a proposition *by way of* her assenting to a sentence which expresses it.

The supplementation strategies of both the representationalists and nonrepresentationalists seem to merge, differing in terminology merely. To avoid the blurring and to capitalize on the parsimony of replacement, this third Part explores the replacement strategy versions of the two camps, that is, the strategy of eliminating reference to what the other side says is the object of the directed-toward relation. For representationalists, that means eliminating reference to attributes and propositions and replacing them with reference to words. In particular, we'll consider replacing propositions and attributes with the sentences and predicates that a believer uses to, as we've been saying, express the propositions and attributes. Many distinct sentences may express the same proposition. If a person's attitudes are directed toward sentences, not the propositions they express, that will account for the hyperintensionality and opaqueness of that-clauses. Since the sentences are concretized *in situ* they're fully interpretable. Sententialism confines propositions to their natural home in modal logic. (However, despite our developing a sentential model of the attitudes, we'll continue to call them propositional attitudes, rather than sentential attitudes. Also, although I'll talk of sentences, I wish you to understand me to mean sentence-radicals. Alternatively, understand the sentences as introduced by the word "that," which is supposed to drain them of their assertoric force, thereby rendering them suitable objects for attitudes other than belief.)

According to sententialism, Belia's *de dicto* beliefs are directed toward complete sentences. Whether her *de re* beliefs are directed toward complete sentences or incomplete ones, that is, toward predicates, depends on our ellipsis theories of her mind. If the theory attributes to her the possession of mental names for the thing, then sententialism presumes they're part of an inner complete sentence, which her *de re* belief is directed toward. Alternatively, if we're attributing to her the no-name mode, i.e., direct attribution of a predicate to herself and the present moment, then her *de re* belief is directed only toward the incomplete sentence. Later on we'll consider how Rep reports beliefs that are directed toward sentences.

Since we're officially only explicating the theories implicit in folk psychology, sententialism is the thesis that folk psychology identifies and distinguishes attitudes by the sentences they're directed towards. Many representationalists think that folk psychology does not put all its eggs into the one basket of sententialism, but rather is noncommittal on the nature of the representations named by that-clauses. That's a cautious generic representationalism. According to generic representationalism, folk psychology identifies and distinguishes attitudes by the representations they're directed towards without restrictions on the nature of the representations.

We define generic representationalism by contrast with specific representationalisms. Specific representationalisms all agree that the objects of the directed-toward relation are representations in the mind. Thus sententialism is one kind of representationalism, since the sentences occurring in the mind are representations. But there are other kinds of representations, to wit, maps and visual and auditory images. Specific representationalisms agree that people's attitudes are individuated and concretized by the representations they instantiate. They don't all agree, however, that the representations which do this are sentences. Connectionism, another form of representationalism we'll consider in section R, rejects the model of sentences in favor of another form of representation, which should serve to explain the hyperintensionality and opaqueness of attitudes as well as sentences do. Generic representationalism, in contrast to these specific representationalisms, says that, as far as folk psychology tells us anything, it tells us only that some species of representationalism is true, but not which one. According to the generic account, folk psychology is only generically a representational theory of the mind. Science is therefore free to make discoveries about the nature of representations without contradicting folk psychology.

That last sentence is full of demons! Don't let them out yet! We must remind ourselves of a lesson stated in the Introduction: We're mainly engaged in descriptive metaphysics in these notes, namely the metaphysics implied by folk psychology. We leave the prescriptive metaphysics to the end in Part IV. The distinction between description and prescription becomes critical for your understanding of Part III of these notes, since so much of the literature we'll be referring to disregards it or is explicitly prescriptive. In particular, the main prescriptive metaphysics entangled in all the "-isms" introduced so far in Part III is the **naturalization project**. The naturalization project seeks to prove that the mind is nothing more than a physical thing, operating in accord with the laws of physics and chemistry. More particularly, the mind achieves all its intentionality by virtue of the organization of its material parts. Some would say because it's a computer. The naturalization project is therefore the core of a materialist metaphysics. Notice how neatly sententialism, when taken as a replacement strategy, fits into the naturalization project, since standard computers manipulate sentence-like symbols. Connectionism, another form of representationalism, comes directly from the design of nonstandard computers. Young bloods will rush into these battles over revisionary or prescriptive metaphysics, but I, an old man, remind you that the descriptive task is not yet complete. Come back to school!

Since we're still in the school of folk psychology, learning what it has to say about intentionality, but some of you are eager to join one or other of the armies in the great metaphysical war over the true nature of the mind, I offer you this much: I'll pay attention to whether or not folk psychology says anything which takes sides in this war, or whether it's noncommittal. Note for starters that I introduced the various representationalisms only by reference to their ability to account for the hyperintensionality and opacity of that-clauses. That's a very folk-psychological way of legitimating these positions, regardless of their suitability to the naturalization project. Looking ahead, generic representationalism promises a favorable assessment of folk psychology within science. In the next subsection I present a concept of a representation that opens the way to naturalization.

So back to our lessons. The term "representationalism" unfortunately has more than one meaning for us, in that it stands for either a replacement strategy or a supplementation strategy. Worse still, it has even more meanings in philosophy. As I use the term, it stands for a position in the philosophy of mind analogous to the position called formalism^ in the philosophy of mathematics. Formalism was the view that mathematics is simply the manipulation of symbols, without regard to their meaning. According to formalism, people add numerals, not numbers. In other words, the representation and not the represented is the object of mathematical operations. That's like saying the representation and not the represented is the object of the directed-toward relation, which is my definition of representationalism. Although my definition accords with the usage of many philosophers, still others make the word mean a thesis in the philosophy of language about how representations represent. It's enough that you be on your guard when you read others.[2]

### §3. A conception of representations open to the naturalization project.

All attitudes, by virtue of being directed toward something, are acts of representing. "Between" the represent*ing* and the represent*ed* there's the representation. **Representations** are information. **Information** is just facts that happen also to represent—pardon my circularity—other facts. For example, the occurrence of images on the retinas of your eyes is information about the scene in front of your eyes. The images are representations of that scene. So are the reflections on the surface of a still lake, seen from one side, representations of the shoreline opposite. I tend to use the word "representation" broadly to cover not just the exploited information, but the available information, whether or not any mind has yet found a method of interpreting it and exploited it. So the word does not connote something sentence-like, dependent on a mind for its existence.

Representations have their own intrinsic nature which physical science describes, but it's an extrinsic property of a fact that it represents another fact. Part of the extrinsic nature of representations is their negative entropy,^ or the complement of entropy. To understand this, imagine a square standing for the space of all logical possibilities. Each point or pixel within it stands for one possible way the totality of fully determinate facts may be, and just one of these pixels is the actual way they all are.

Call it the actual pixel. (I say pixel rather than point to make the illustration finite.) To represent a person's knowledge, mentally draw a circle in the square so that the actual pixel is inside it along with some others. The circle stands for the person's representation of the truth, the truth she knows. What she knows is, in effect, that the whole truth does not lie outside the circle. The truth she knows can be more or less informative. The smaller the circle the more informative the truth she knows. The informativeness of the representation is an extrinsic property of the representation because it requires reference to the way things are actually.

The circle in the square depicts the complementarity of information and entropy. The more the person knows, the greater the area outside the circle, which therefore measures the information. The area inside the circle is the entropy. Entropy in this sense is a measure of the residual uncertainty given what the person knows. For example, consider an urn with four marbles, each one colored either red or blue. The truth about them is one of sixteen possible microstates. See table P-1.

Think of general statements about the urn as describing its macrostates. We can compare the informational content of macrostates by referring to the possible microstates, any one of which might underlie the macrostate. For example, there's more information and less entropy in telling you that all are red, which is consistent with only one microstate of the urn, than in telling you that all are of the same color, which is consistent with two alternative microstates. A macrostate of a system may contain information as well as uncertainty about its own microstate, as in this case. Another example is water's macrostates: When water boils, the fact conveys information about the agitation of its molecules, but also much entropy since the underlying microstate may be any of very many.

| | Marble-1 | Marble-2 | Marble-3 | Marble-4 |
|---|---|---|---|---|
| 1 | R | R | R | R |
| 2 | R | R | R | B |
| 3 | R | R | B | R |
| 4 | R | R | B | B |
| 5 | R | B | R | R |
| 6 | R | B | R | B |
| 7 | R | B | B | R |
| 8 | R | B | B | B |
| 9 | B | R | R | R |

| 10 | B | R | R | B |
| 11 | B | R | B | R |
| 12 | B | R | B | B |
| 13 | B | B | R | R |
| 14 | B | B | R | B |
| 15 | B | B | B | R |
| 16 | B | B | B | B |

Table P-1. Sixteen possible microstates of an urn with four marbles, each either red or blue.

A system's state can also tell us about its prior states. Only orderly states can be high-fidelity representations of prior states. Physicists demonstrate a connection between measures of disorder and measures of uncertainty with a quaint being called Maxwell's demon, which we'll not go into.[3] The consequence of the connection is that we can apply the second law of thermodynamics to entropy in the sense of uncertainty. The second law says that the entropy of a system does not decrease, order can only come from order, usually greater order. We may suppose this property of a state to be connected to its property of being information, so that *all the orderliness in the universe at a time is information about the prior orderliness from which it came.* For example, slight variations in the cosmic microwave background radiation represent the uneven distribution of matter in the universe 300,000 years after the big bang, and physicists have measured the variations. The universe is full of this sort of naturally occurring aboutness. Almost all of it is uninterpretable by human beings, and even if they could understand it, they'd ignore most of it anyway. They pick up on just the few bits they find useful.

We noted earlier that representations have both intrinsic and extrinsic properties. Concerning the extrinsic properties of the representations of prior states, between the representation and the fact represented is the channel of transmission. Ideally the channel has no effect on the information transmitted over it. In actuality, however, we expect information to be degraded in two ways during transmission through any channel. First, it loses detail and becomes less specific. For example, the reflection from a lake's surface of the opposite shore contains less information about the opposite shore than you could receive by direct sight of it. A signal is maximally degraded in this respect when it represents any possible state; it becomes tautologous. Second, information becomes infected with extraneous information, which is called noise. For example, the cosmic background radiation enters all radio channels that include its frequency, where it's considered to be noise infecting the information transmitted. A signal is maximally degraded in this second respect when it represents no possible state; it becomes inconsistent. Channels differ in the amount of protection they provide against each kind of degradation.

A simplifying assumption we've been making is that all signs are in the declarative mood, signifying what is the case about the microstates of a system or what used to be the case about the system. Only ignorance of the true theory of nature and the distribution of events over the world keeps people from seeing that the information is about the future as well. When the future's overdetermined, that is, when something will occur despite a gazillion quantum mechanical indeterminacies in the meantime, there's information in the world about the future. The genetic code is information in this way. With the invention of life, however, it seems to us that another mood for signs was invented, namely, the imperative mood. For the signs that we call the genetic code seem to be instructions for the synthesizing of proteins. In fact they're signs of what will become the case, only given the conditions for carrying out the instructions. They don't cease to be signs also of what is or was the case, but the new directionality in signifying comes to overlay the old, since the signs don't cease to point to the future merely because the conditions for their fulfillment are not occurring. Is this sort of increase in information an increase in order? It need not be thought so, and in any case order comes at the price of increased entropy elsewhere. (Desires are signs in a similar way.)

The declarative representations have two sorts of extrinsic properties. One of them is necessary and the other is accidental. If the representation is found in nature, like reflections on lakes, then its necessary property is its relation to the thing represented, and its accidental relation is to the organism which interprets it and exploits it purposefully. When the representation is artificial, as a sentence is, then its necessary relation is its relation to its interpreter, without whom it would not exist, and its accidental relation is to the thing represented, since it's founded on convention. In sections R §4 and Y §6 we'll address the issue of false found representations, whose connection to what they represent is natural although accidental. Natural imperative representations signify only in virtue of their accidental relations, since they depend on their contexts for their implementation.

Consider found representations. There must be representations that minds don't make but rather find in nature. Because there was already information ready for the taking about earthly environments, minds first came to exist when the processes of variation and natural selection lucked upon methods of interpretation of pre-existent information, which led to the purposeful exploitation of this information. If information in that mind-independent sense were not just about everywhere, we'd not understand why the first minds evolved on a mindless earth, or how they evolved. Animal senses work with found representations. For example, a few inches to your right there's unused information about the scene in front of you. Do you need to see the scene from a different angle? Move over and intercept that information. You put your eyes in the places where the information is.

Since representations have their own intrinsic nature, one can observe a representation and miss the information it contains. Thus the need for methods of interpretation to evolve. The simplest method is to respond to the representation exactly as if it were the thing represented. In the simplest cases, which would've been among the first to evolve and among the first a child uses, this method works! For example, the touch of the nipple to a new-born's lips evokes the sucking response that's rewarded with mother's milk. With the evolution of exploitation came misexploitation. What it took for this to evolve is a matter of controversy, which we skip over until sections R and Y.

I hope this discussion has made clear that representationalism can account for attitudes in other species, even very primitive ones. Words and the things made of words are of course representations, made by the most advanced mind in nature. A language is a system for creating the particular kind of representation we call sentences. Artificial representations are only possible for beings who are already masters of interpreting natural representations. But simpler organisms have representations too. The moral of the story seems to be that we should expect a continuum from primitive to advanced attitudes, not an all-or-none dichotomy between those capable of attitudes and those incapable. And that bodes well for the naturalization project.

### §4. The synergy between syntax and semantics.

Let's explore sententialism. Several matters pertaining to the identity conditions for sentences must be addressed. First of all, sentences are in a language. One and the same string of sounds might be one sentence if it's in one language, but a different sentence if it's in another. Donald Davidson notes that the German "liebt" (loved) and the English "leaped" sound the same, so that if you heard the sentence "Empedokles liebt" pronounced, you might mistake it for an English sentence that Empedocles leaped, as he's reported to have done, into the caldera of the volcano, Etna. So for a belief to be directed toward a sentence is to believe within a language.

That language's **syntax** defines what strings of words constitute grammatical sentences. So, if Belia's beliefs are not directed toward propositions and attributes, which are not in a language, but rather toward complete sentences and predicates, they must be grammatical, that is, entities constructed from words according to the syntax of some language. This is the **syntactical criterion of identity for thought-objects**. The thought-objects are syntactic structures, as defined by a language. Sententialism is committed to this criterion, and other representationalisms are committed to something analogous to it.

Syntax does not define what a sentence means—that's the job of semantics—syntax settles just whether it's properly constructed. The first sentence of Lewis Carroll's nonsense poem, *Jabberwocky*, "'Twas brillig, and the slithy toves did gyre and gimble in the wabe:" is syntactically correct English, although it expresses no proposition.[4] We can tell that "toves" is a plural noun and that the verbs, "gyre and gimble," follow the subject and are in syntactic agreement with it. Syntax is just the study of structure; complementing the syntax, **semantics** is the study of the meaning the structures have. The two together form the subject of grammar. Be warned, however; this contrast, though correct, is deeply misleading about their relationship. Let me digress to explain why.

We accept the theory that the structure of sentences can be described in the particular way which we call syntactic. That is, a sentence's structure is susceptible to description by a branching tree, with the root node standing for the category of "sentence." It branches to nodes standing for categories like "noun phrase" (or "nominal," which includes noun phrases) and "verb phrase" which are the immediate constituents of a sentence. These nodes branch to further nodes. Thus the "verb phrase" branches to nodes standing for categories like "intransitive verb" plus an optional node for "prepositional phrase" or "adverbial phrase." The "nominal" category branches to nodes for "determiner" and "noun." The "noun phrase" can branch to nodes for "adjective" and "noun." At the end of the branches are lexical nodes, putting words for the last categories.

In the old days this was called parsing a sentence. I just mentioned the categories for parsing another of *Jabberwocky*'s sentences:

"The mome raths outgrabe."

Determiner+adjective+noun+intransitive verb (?+prepositional phrase).

The second and third words are consolidated into a noun phrase. It and the determiner are then consolidated into the noun phrase that precedes the verb phrase, and those two phrases are the immediate constituents of the sentence. Perhaps the mome raths outgrabe in the wabe, if they were where the slithy toves were, as seems likely. If that's what Lewis Carroll intended us to understand, there's an ellipsis, and the prepositional phrase is part of the complete sentence.

The tree diagrams can show structural differences, which are not apparent simply by looking at the categories of words and their order. Here are two sentences which are superficially similar in structure.

The children are drawing lions in the fourth grade.

The children are drawing lions in their cages.

Their tree diagrams bring out the difference:

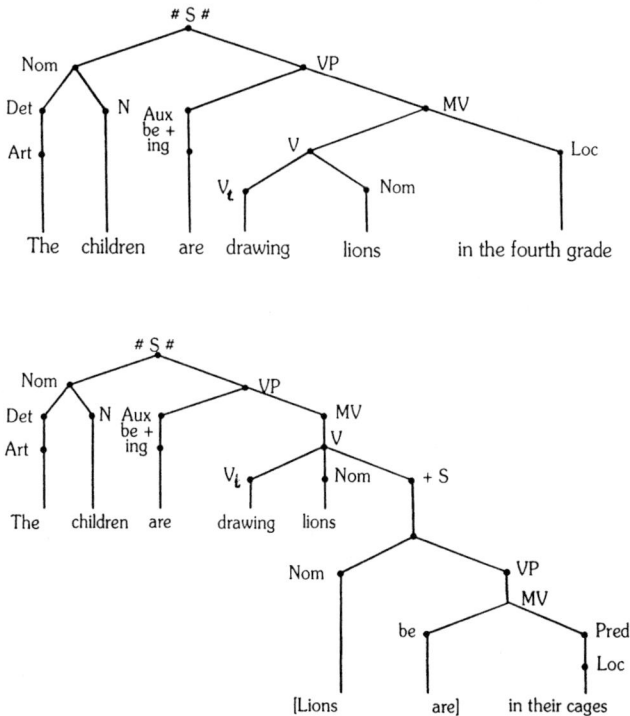

Figure P-1. Sorry, we always draw the trees upside down, their roots at the top and their tips at the bottom. "MV" means "main verb"; subscripts on V mean "transitive." From Owen Thomas, *Transformational Grammar and the Teacher of English* (Holt, Rinehart, and Winston, 1965) 167.

The rules for constructing the parsing trees are called phrase structure rules. An example of such a rule is that a simple sentence is composed of a noun phrase and a verb phrase. Traditionally linguists worked to find the complete set of these rules for each language. The rules can be recursive, that is, they provide nodes which allow the rule to be used over again. For example, a sentence may be composed of two sentences conjoined by the word "and." There's no prohibition against the sentences conjoined being themselves the products of that very rule thus:

(*p* and *q*) and (*r* and *s*)

Thus a small set of such rules, plus a lexicon (i.e., a list of words), generates a potentially infinite class of syntactically well formed sentences. We need only this cursory idea of the procedures of syntax for our current purposes.[5]

Here's what we do really need to know: Syntactic structure is not just the construction of sentences from constituent expressions constrained according to their categories. Syntax is a means to an end: Syntactic categories are supposed to provide semantics with all that's needed for it to supply meanings. Thus syntax is a precursor to semantics, and subservient to it. For example, once we comprehend the structure of the sentences of *Jabberwocky*, we feel ready to assign meaning to them. Of course, we cannot, but we can for the two sentences about drawing lions. We'd assign their component terms meanings by starting with a sentence's smallest units on their syntactic tree diagram, and finding the meaning assigned to them, by meaning assignment rules, also called semantic valuation rules— "valuation" in the mathematical sense of assigning a value^ to a variable. (In the case of *Jabberwocky*, those rules are missing.) Then semantics tells us how to assign meanings to each of the more inclusive categories, based on the meanings assigned to their immediate constituents, proceeding right up to and including the category of "sentence," i.e., "#S#." Syntax builds the tree diagram from the initial node #S# downwards; semantics interprets the tree upwards ending with an assignment to #S#. Semantic trees have the things meant at the nodes, not the words.

It's difficult to see how semantic valuation rules might proceed to the meaning of the whole from the meaning of its parts, if the whole did not have a syntactic structure for semantics to hang the meaning assignments on. For there are infinitely many possible sentences, all of which must be assigned meanings, given the meanings of a finite vocabulary. Although in my exposition of the distinction between syntax and semantics, I began by separating them, that was only to show how they do go together. So the moral of this digression is not their independence of one another, but rather the assistance they give each other. Let's give this moral a name, the **thesis of the synergy of syntax and semantics.** The thesis is most obviously true of the formal languages created by logicians, but it's also true of natural languages, although less obviously so.[6]

The synergy of syntax and semantics works out in two different ways, depending on whether the semantics is the semantics of expressions composed of simple expressions or the semantics of the simple expressions themselves. We'll save the semantics of simple expressions for section S. The semantics of compound expressions is based on a principle called **semantic compositionality**: The meaning of compound expressions is determined by the meanings of its simple components in ways that track the syntactic construction of the compound up the tree from the vocabulary elements at the tree's tips. End of digression on the synergy of syntax and semantics.

Syntax is also tied to **phonetics**, that is, the theory of the attachment of sounds to sentences. English phonetics is obviously different from French and Chinese phonetics. Because of the synergy between syntax and semantics on the one hand, and on the other between it and phonetics, we get the thesis that syntax links meaning to sound. Syntax seems indispensable to the vocal realization of meanings. It's difficult to see what else but syntactic structure could provide this link.

## §5. Speculating about an unvocalized language of thought.

Despite the synergy, it remains true that the syntax of a sentence identifies which language it belongs to. Which language are Belia's beliefs in? The one she speaks of course! (Belia speaks Italian and English, as we know.) But might we be wrong, and is there more to say here? Let's speculate: Besides the thousands of public languages which human beings use for communicating with one another, there may be a language that is natural to all human minds, which we all use for thinking and internal control. This hypothetical inner language is called Mentalese or **LOT**, (abbreviating the "language of thought").[7] It does not depend for its original existence on spoken language. If anything, the priority in evolution and individual maturation goes to LOT.

Presumably, if other animals have propositional attitudes, then, since they don't use public languages, their beliefs must be directed toward predicates in their own species's LOT. The hypothesis of LOT thus solves one problem for the view that attitudes are directed toward sentences, namely, that of nonlingual believers. Some philosophers reject sentences as objects of the directed toward relation on the ground that deaf-mutes clearly have beliefs but no language, as was the case for Helen Keller until the famous episode at the pump with her teacher, which she described in her autobiography, *The Story of My Life.* The sententialist's answer is that she and other deaf-mutes always had the language LOT and its sentences. At least a core component of it is part of everyone's original equipment.

A wrong way to differentiate LOT from communication language is to think of LOT simply as that very communication language, but the communicants are reduced to one; the speaker is the whole audience. If you think of the difference this way, you've not distinguished languages, but uses of language. People do talk to themselves, but usually in their communication language, as Hamlet did in his soliloquy. What they're mentally aware of, like the words Hamlet utters to himself, is not in LOT. The philosophers who introduced the concept of a language of thought did think of it as simply the soliloquizing use of a communication language. But developments in linguistics, particularly Noam Chomsky's theorizing, suggest that the truth is the exact reverse, that language is primarily an inner language, which gets externalized in a hodgepodge of ways.[8]

But may it not be that LOT is merely ordinary language stripped of its phonetic embodiment? According to this way of thinking of it, phonetics is an add-on to semantically interpreted sentence structures. For internal thinking, these syntactic structures suffice without embodiment in sounds or letters or anything else. And it does seem to introspection that we think directly in meanings, without anything like the concretization that phonetics gives to people's outer speech. One might almost say that people have direct conscious access to meanings in their minds, without the benefit of concrete symbols. Contrary to this view, however, there's a thesis that underlies much of representationalism, whether conceived as a replacement strategy or a supplementation strategy. It's this:

Despite the introspective appearances to the contrary, we have no direct access to meanings unmediated by representations with their own intrinsic formal nature. However unconscious people may be of them, concretized symbols provide theirr only access to meanings. It doesn't matter whether the symbols are concretized in preconscious or subconscious mental stuff or in physical stuff.

Thus the **central thesis of representationalism**: Attitudes are directed toward concretized symbols with their own formal natures as well as meanings.

The argument for this principle can take two tacks: that it's true, or that it's implied by folk psychology. One argument for it covers both: Harman argues that it's true simply by definition. Let a particular attitude be directed toward some content. For example, Belia believes the woodchuck was in the bushes. It's consistent with folk psychology that *simply by definition* an instance of the symbol for the woodchuck being in the bushes *is identical to* her concrete state of having a propositional attitude. If the content is believed, the symbol for it in the language of thought is "stored as a belief"; if the content is desired then the symbol is "stored as an end."[9]

We must acknowledge immediately that not all propositional attitudes can be characterized this way. There are attitudes that occur simply through the nonoccurrence of other attitudes. One's blind trust that something is so is the expectation that it's so and the absence of any suspicion that it's not so. Expectation can also be an absence of an attitude, as when people unconsciously presuppose that something is so, that is, have a belief in some other content that implies it or is positively relevant^ to it without their being aware of the connection. Yet these attitudes-by-absence are parasitical on those to which the definition would apply, namely, attitudes by virtue of the presence of something. If the definition is part of folk psychology, we might imagine Belia saying to herself about her attitude of belief, "There's this thing in me, an instance of a sentence, in virtue of the truth or falsity of which the success or failure of my attitude depends." The argument is important, since without it the thesis might seem to be just a piece of dogmatic stipulation on behalf of the naturalization project.

Indeed several philosophers think it just that, the attribution of the definition to folk psychology being mere window-dressing. They think folk psychology defines belief and the other propositional attitudes as social states, not inner states, that is to say, in a way that makes them depend on normative relations between people. Thus belief in a proposition is a commitment to other people to defend its truth. Attitudes connect to actions as reasons, not as causes. Well-argued expositions of this position can be found in the work of Arthur Collins and Frederick Stoutland.[10] To rebut the criticism, the representationalist would distinguish two kinds of normative relations that seem to encumber people by virtue of their having propositional attitudes. Some, such as the commitment to the truth of what one believes, are surely definitive of belief and must be part of any explication of what it is to store a representation-instance as a belief. But others, such as the commitment to defend the truth of what one believes, can only apply to believers who happen also to be communicators; these norms belong rather to the province of conversational implicatures about belief. Such implicatures are canceled when people attribute beliefs to their pets, for instance. In the case of pets, the commitment to the truth of what they believe may imply no more than that they attempt to get it right, and pets do display some inquisitiveness and self-correction of that sort. The rebuttal continues: More central than normativity to the definition of the whole class of attitudes is their status as causes and effects—recall the criterion of identity we stated in section N—which they can have only by their being concretized, and reasons for acting can affect people only if they are causes. We'll not tarry to develop the ensuing debate. We'll see more of this kind of thinking in the second subpart, which is devoted to nonrepresentationalism.

A less harsh judgment on the central thesis of representationalism teases apart two of its aspects. The first is that any attitude is concretized by the instancing of a representation, and the second is that the attitude is directed toward this instance. The causal powers of an attitude can ride on the first part alone; the appeal of the second part is that, if no objections can be raised against it, Ockham's^ razor endorses it. To be a representationalist one must accept both parts. Critics could argue that folk psychology only offers us the first part, and the second part is indeed objectionable. Some nonrepresentationalists do argue that way; I for one will argue thus when we come to the sections on nonrepresentationalism. So the first part could be common ground; I'll call it **Harman's thesis** when it comes up in our discussions of nonrepresentationalism, although Harman's a representationalist, committed to both parts.

Even if we do accept one or both parts of the central thesis, however, factual matters cannot be discovered by definition. So several matters are left unsettled by Harman's argument. Foremost is the location of the concretizing, which surely is inside the person. Second is the question of the way the representations are individuated. As mental acts are, but how are mental acts individuated? It's possible that representations are so integrated into systems of representations that it's bogus to say a person has several distinct beliefs. When Rep reports Belia to believe a particular sentence, it may only be the case that she has an integrated belief system according to which that sentence, among many other sentences, has some degree of credence.[11] That the plurality of beliefs is not bogus is therefore a further matter to be settled by empirical evidence. Such integration (holism^) may also hold of desires, which are tightly organized into a system of mere means, means which are also ends, and ends which are not means. Are they a plurality of desires, or only a single hugely complex desire? Furthermore, that the symbols in a language of thought are *sentences* cannot be a matter of definition. It follows rather from the belief states having the properties of sentences: They proliferate as sentences do, by syntactic construction, and they are interrelated by consistency relations.

With so much left open, what *is* settled by the central thesis? The internal syntactic structures have some intrinsic nature, not phonetic but phonetic-like in that it concretizes and particularizes them. Since we're exploring sentententialism, we'll continue to think of LOT as consisting of sentences occurring in the mind.

A stricture one might impose on LOT is that sentence structures are in LOT, if and only if they're in the communication language. Though the embodiments may differ, the structure's the same. We need not be too strict about a parity between structures as thought and structures as vocalized. A popular move among linguists today is to associate some of the peculiarities of the syntaxes of communication languages to the phoneticizing, so that the linguists can hold that all human beings think in the same LOT, and linguistic diversity enters only with the phoneticizing, for instance, German speakers putting the verb at the end of a sentence, English speakers in the middle.

If the phoneticizing tampers with structure, we should suspect other differences between LOT and communication languages. And there are at least two major differences not due to phoneticizing. The first concerns **conditional attitudes**, which we introduced in section D. These attitudes are essentially dyadic; so in accord with Harman's thesis, in LOT there are two sentences joined only by their being contents of the one dyadic attitude. Yet in public communication they're expressed by a single compound sentence, an indicative conditional sentence, causing no end of confusion in philosophy. To end it, we should suppose that LOT contains no unitary indicative conditional sentences.[12] The second was introduced in section N, where we speculated about direct attribution. Direct attributions seem to be at the heart of any language for guidance and control of oneself. The expression of those beliefs by the use of the indexical pronouns, "I" and "now," seems to be purely a phenomenon of the communication language. That part of LOT which is the language of self guidance and control is basic and primitive in the sense that it's part of the animal heritage of human beings. Section N's **boiler room analogy** is worth recalling here: If you were a big ship and your parts communicated with each other analogously to the internal communications system of a big ship, much of the LOT of direct attribution would be the language of your boiler room: "Full steam ahead!" and the like. We human beings share this part of LOT with other animals.

There are other reasons for thinking it simplistic to say LOT is converted into speech by shuffling and phoneticizing LOT's elements. For one thing, human LOT is an extendible language. Thus it has a bottom end, common perhaps to all primates, and a top end, where the most creative thinkers think thoughts in top-end LOT that may have no expression in current communication languages. Here LOT would be out ahead of the communication languages, pressuring them to grow to express original thoughts.

In the case of human thought, along with shuffling and phoneticizing, there's another process, compression, which complicates the linguist's claim to know the structure of sentences in LOT. For example, English may be related to LOT somewhat like the way languages for programming computers, e.g., FORTRAN, Basic, and C, are related to **machine language**. In fact LOT itself may have this layered structure. Machine language is the most basic code in terms of which you can program a computer. It may only consist of strings of 1's and 0's. The letter A, for instance, translates into a distinctive sequence of them, eight digits long. The computer's built to respond directly to sentences in this language when the computer receives them as input. Sentences in higher level programming languages cannot control a computer directly. They have to be run through another program called a **compiler**, which translates the higher level program into sentences of the machine language, which the computer then responds to. Programmers use the higher level programming languages because they bundle lots of operations into units represented by simple code. The compiler then unbundles the code into all the complex multiplicity of simple instructions needed to make the computer respond. So a machine language is just a direct-response language of the sort we speculated about in section N, the language of the boiler room.

We flesh and blood things may be computer-like in that we also operate with the help of a direct-response language, which would be LOT or at least an indispensable component of it. A direct-response language, in order to be one for human beings would have to be encoded in their genes and be the same language for each of them. If the suggestions about direct attribution in section N are right, at least some of the sentences in their machine language are incomplete, since the subjects of the sentences are always the self and the present moment and so need not be expressed to be effective. Furthermore, human brains come equipped at birth with compiling procedures, which enable people to learn public languages by bootstrapping from the human LOT. The procedures enable them to tell which sentences in their LOT are to be expressed by which sentences in their public languages.

The point of drawing this speculative analogy between human beings and computers is to suggest that for Belia to believe a sentence is for her to believe at least something in LOT, or something in English which the compiler in her brain compiles into a sentence in LOT. However, the analogy between LOT and a machine language may be much better than the analogy between FORTRAN and English. For English enables its speakers to speak about anything, whereas FORTRAN is just for programming a computer, a design feature it shares with the machine language. Consequently, it's reasonable to think of the compiler translating sentences of FORTRAN into sentences of the machine language. If LOT is just a language for the inner control procedures used by human brains, then—I'm sorry—English will have an infinity of sentences and a great deal of vocabulary that have no equivalents in LOT. So it would be inaccurate to describe an English speaker's inner compiler as translating English into LOT. The solution seems to be that the LOT is more than a control language. In fact it may be more than one language. Perhaps the L is plural, and LOT should stand for the languages of thought.

## §6. The individuation of sentences.

Speculation's fun, but back to the problem of identity conditions for sentences. Let's recall the syntactic criterion of identity of thought-objects and note that it provides for the concretization, that is, the particularization or individualization, of the objects. The sentences of public languages are concretized by the connection to phonetics. Something in thought is phonetics-like in that it concretizes our thoughts.

Let me put some flesh on this analogy. In public languages syntactic characteristics are marked phonetically. Thus plural nouns have typical ways of being pronounced. Past tensed verbs are usually marked by pronouncing the -ed ending. If the physical particularity does not come from its being voiced, then it's in the writing. The particularization of the syntax of LOT is in *events* of attitudinizing. Those events are somehow like phoneticizing sentences but are otherwise unknown. So we let the physicality of utterances in public languages stand as a surrogate for the particularization.

The connection between syntax and public physicality is people's entry into the meanings of their public languages. They get the syntax and vocabulary from the sound, and the meaning from the syntax and vocabulary. This process is sometimes obscured by the fact that they disambiguate the syntax of a sentence by first noting its context in a conversation they've understood so far and from that context they infer what it must mean, and so back to what its syntax is. For example, the sentence "flying planes can be dangerous" has a syntax in which the subject of the sentence is "planes," if it occurs in a discussion of the effect of speed on the impact of crashes. If the context is about piloting, then the syntax makes "flying" the subject of the sentence. Nevertheless, the first and central way into the meaning of a sentence is by way of its physical characteristics' disclosing its syntactic structure. This is true for LOT too, if our analogy to a machine language is right. We postpone to section S any further discussion of meaning.

Let's return to the subject of mental causality. How could a sentence be a nexus in a cause-effect connection? The answer depends on a distinction: Sentences have a dual mode of existence, as abstract entities and as concrete entities. Sentences exist as abstract entities in the sense that all the sentences exist that can be constructed from a language's lexicon, applying that language's rules of syntax. There are infinitely many of them (at least!), since there's no requirement that anyone actually do the construction. The situation is analogous to numbers, abstract entities also. Most of the numbers nobody will ever think of individually. Similarly, most of the sentences nobody will ever think of individually.

Abstract entities are not causes; causes are concrete. Thinking of a sentence is one way of **instantiating** it, just as speaking it and writing it are other ways. The abstract entity is multiply instantiable: A sentence has concrete existence when it's uttered, inscribed, made the focus of conscious attention, or constructed by the brain's compiler. For all these acts have a locus in the web of cause-and-effect. They have a place and time of occurrence, even if we may not notice it, as in that last speculation about the compiler. Instantiation is any of these ways of concretizing, particularizing, or giving a thing a definite location in space and time. Instantiation is a precondition for being a cause or effect, at least in the usual kinds of cases. (There are unusual kinds, for example, causing the nonexistence of something. Then its nonexistence is an effect, but to be nonexistent is just this: to be not instantiated!)

In the sense in which you and another can believe the same thing, or share a belief, the beliefs are abstract entities, even if they're directed toward sentences. (More on this in section V.) You and the other person may have the same beliefs, but clearly there is your believing it and there's a distinct believing it that's the other person's. The two believings are located in different places and times and are causally active events. The abstract belief, which is your belief *and* the other's too, is, like any abstract entity, nowhere and causally inert. What's numerically the same is the abstract entity. What differ are the instantiations of that one entity. The same point applies to one person's believing the same thing on different occasions. When I want to call your attention to the belief-instantiation, I'll hereafter speak of believ*ings*. I'll speak of beliefs when the distinction's irrelevant. Belief-types I'll call belief-types.

(Adapting Peirce's terminology, philosophers today use "**types**" to refer to the universals that are the most determinate relatively to some theory. Comparison of universals for determinateness amounts to placing them on a scale of genericness, from the most generic ("thing") to most specific (relative to English grammar, the sentence "snow is white"). Those at the determinate end are types. Instances of types are frequently called "tokens," and instantiation is called "tokening." I'll steer clear of this jargon. Where no theory is involved, the concept of type is inherently vague. A particular symphonic performance could be an instance of the type "Eroica," although, because of their distinctive conducting styles, Toscanini Eroicas and Bruno Walter Eroicas are more determinate types. The vagueness leaves some clarity at the extremes. For example, although the performance is also an instance of the generic "symphony," it would be odd to call that universal a type.)

Applying the lesson now to sentences, note that the distinction between the abstract entity and its instance is syntactic, not semantic. Two inscriptions or utterances of sentences count as believings which are instances of the same type provided that they're derived from the same lexicon entries by the same syntactic operations. Syntactic sameness is in the first instance a qualitative sameness of a formal sort, the sort of sameness that a dumb computer could react to as being the same. In LOT there's a strong formal similarity between instances of the same type, if LOT is like a machine language. In communication languages we have to allow for different voices, different fonts, the difference between spoken and written sentences. In the end, however, all syntactic sameness is identified by the formal features of the instances, be they physical or not.

If beliefs are directed toward sentences, it's desirable that the type/instance distinction cut beliefs and sentences in parallel: that the belief-types be directed toward sentence types, and believings toward instances of sentences. Is that parallel what we find? Are believings directed toward types of sentences, or toward their instances? If we say toward the particular occurrences that instantiate a sentence by uttering it or internally rehearsing it, we get two benefits. First, we have something that can individuate beliefs from one another in a way that accounts for their having distinctive causal properties. For two beliefs directed toward the same sentence-type may be quite distinct in their spatial, temporal, and causal properties, and so the sentence-type cannot account for this difference in causal properties, but the location of a believed sentence-instantiation can, because it's causally connected to the location of the believing; indeed, the believing and the sentence-instance that's believed may be at the same location. Secondly, we can still say that two believings, directed toward two instances of the same type of sentence, are in a derivative sense directed also to the type.

## §7. Problems for sententialism.

Let's recap the advantages we've noticed in theorizing that beliefs are directed toward sentences.

> ● First of all, sentences and words are individuated finely enough to solve the hyperintensionality and opacity problems. The Flatlander can believe he is equilaterally triangular without believing he is equiangularly triangular, because his beliefs are directed to one but not the other of those two predicates. Also you are free to want to ride Pegasus and believe you can. For you want a predicate true of yourself.

> ● Secondly, the syntactically characterized instances of sentences say something about their concretization, whether it be physical embodiment or not, for concretization is a prerequisite for their having any causal efficacy.

> ● Thirdly, that believings may be distinct instances of the same syntactic type provides a way to make sense of the idea of shared beliefs.

Ah, sweetness and light, but not for long. It's time for havoc.

We'll consider three arguments for LOT providing the contents of our attitudes, which Jerry Fodor used, and three arguments against LOT providing them, which Andy Clark used.[13] When we compare their arguments pro and con, it's striking that the very features, which Fodor's pro arguments point to as excellences of LOT, Clark's con arguments point to as its defects.

Recall that syntactic structure is something that the sentences of LOT have, and that it is construction from constituents. So the argument over LOT is over the indispensability of syntax, that is, of a particular kind of construction of meaningful units which yields sentences, for the existence of the things which our attitudes are directed toward.

The arguments for LOT:

> •The need for constituent structures so that semantics may generate all the variety of meanings we are capable of believing. The parsing trees of sentences are indispensable to the operation of semantic valuation^ rules. This entails that the things with meaning are sentences.

> •The need for constituent structures for any theory of consequential thinking, since logics only generate inference patterns by referring to the constituent structures of the items related by inference. More generally, mechanisms for the production of thinking require items that fall into types and can recur, as classical computer languages suggest.

> •The need for constituent structures to explain human linguistic competence in the recognizing of grammatical sentences and producing them. This is often called the **systematicity** of human capacities: The human ability to understand a sentence implies the ability to understand many more structurally and lexically analogous sentences, i.e., they use the same parts analogously. Systematicity is characteristic of the contents of human attitudes.

The arguments against LOT:

> •Syntactic structure presumes *as simply given* the lexical rules that apply at the last nodes of a parsing tree. Also given are the semantic valuation rules that apply to the lexical items. Thus LOT does not help us understand how people come to new concepts of a basic sort. It only allows newness in the sense of recombinations of old ideas.

> •Any theory of consequential thinking and its mechanisms must take into account two features we observe to be true of people's thinking, particularly their theorizing: The semantic holism^ of their theorizing has two components:

>> ○When people theorize, they assign probabilities or degrees of belief to any sentence, with sensitivity to properties of the entire belief system. Anyone familiar with the operations of conditionalizing or updating one's degrees of belief in all the items in one's field of beliefs, as described in Bayesian decision theory, has a good comprehension of this feature.

>> ○When people theorize, any part of their theory can affect decisions about what to include in any other part

of the theory. Recognizing this isotropism is a corrective to too rigid a foundationalism,^ be it deductive,
aping Euclid's geometry, or inductive, granting infallibility to sense experience.

A result of these two characteristics of our thinking is an
"interanimation of sentences" (Quine's expression), which
characterizes our thinking and belief fixation, and which is
unaccounted for by LOT.

● The way LOT explains the systematicity of human competence
has people manipulating syntactic atoms of meaningfulness into
different compounds. It says nothing about how these atoms are
internally related to one another. Such relations between the
atoms are best pictured as the atoms located in a common
multidimensional logical space.

I am myself convinced that the interrelation of meanings is holistic,^
although Fodor is not.[14] At best the LOT hypothesis is seriously incomplete about meaningfulness. The incompleteness could even be that it gets
wrong what attitudes are directed toward. But if not sentences and
predicates, or not just them, what else could attitudes be directed toward?
A representationalist answer is forthcoming from the next two sections.

# Notes

1. Edwin A. Abbott, *Flatland: A Romance of Many Dimensions* (2nd ed., 1884).
2. My usage of "representationalism" and "sententialism" accords with that of
J. Christopher Maloney, in his article in *A Companion to the Philosophy of Mind*,
"language of thought (1)." But Devitt and Sterelney, *Language and Reality*,
second edition (1999), ch. 9, use "representationalism" to mean a thesis about how
representations represent.
3. The curious should consult Harvey S. Leff and Andrew F. Rex, eds.,
*Maxwell's Demon: Entropy, Information, Computing* (1990).
4. Curious about this nonsense poem? Lewis Carroll wrote it, and it appears
in his *Through the Looking-Glass*, ch. 1. The first stanza is:

> 'Twas brillig, and the slithy toves
> Did gyre and gimble in the wabe:
> All mimsy were the borogoves,
> And the mome raths outgrabe.

5. Steven Pinker, *The Language Instinct: How the Mind Creates Language*
(1994) is both instructive and amusing. See ch. 7 for a presentation of syntax.
6. To see how linguists work out the synergy of syntax and semantics, see

Gennaro Chierchia and Sally McConnell-Ginet, *Meaning and Grammar: An Introduction to Semantics* (1990).

7. Gilbert Harman, *Thought* (1973), ch. 4. Jerry Fodor coined the acronym LOT for the language of thought around 1975. Wilfrid Sellars coined the term Mentalese no later than 1968 in his John Locke Lectures, published as *Science and Metaphysics: Variations on Kantian Themes* (1968), e.g., 35 (also a Robotese and a Jumblese for the verbless language of thought to be suggested in section Q. See his *Science, Perception, and Reality* (1963) 55 and 226). He coined Behaviorese by 1956 for the language Ryle would use to talk about minds (p. 527 of "The Chisholm-Sellars Correspondence on Intentionality," *Minnesota Studies in the Philosophy of Science*, vol. 2 (1958). Steven Pinker (ch. 3 of *The Language Instinct*) and Fodor himself use "Mentalese" as a synonym for LOT. "Mentalese" has always meant a language minds think in, *not* a language for theorizing about the uniqueness of minds, as though mentalese contrasted with physicalese.

8. Noam Chomsky, *New Horizons in the Study of Language and Mind* (2000). See also Neil Smith's "Forward."

9. Gilbert Harman, *Thought*, 58f.

10. Arthur Collins, *The Nature of Mental Things* (1987); F. Stoutland, "Real Reasons" in J. Bransen and S. E. Kuypers, editors, *Human Action, Deliberation and Causation* (1998) 43-66. Collins would object to the thought I just put into Belia's mind; see ch. 7, sect. 5. I confess to not seeing the force of his argument, which amounts to the observation, either that Belia need not ever have that thought, which is something one might say about any thought, or that for Belia to have that thought would lead to her incoherence, a charge that supposes the whole belief, all of what it is, is just this sentence instance, which is not so. The instancing of the sentence we associated with the genus, having a propositional attitude.

11. This suggested paraphrase is from David Lewis, who does believe people's beliefs are that thoroughly integrated. See *A Companion to the Philosophy of Mind*, 422f.

12. For an accessible introduction to the problems with indicative conditional sentences and a proposal for solving them, which I believe supports my assertion that unitary indicative conditionals don't occur in LOT and are not the contents of monadic mental states, see Ernest W. Adams, *A Primer of Probability Logic* (1998). There may be unitary subjunctive, i.e., counterfactual,^ conditionals in LOT, however, and also conditionals within the scope of a quantifier, e.g., "Johnny will do it, if anyone does."

13. Jerry Fodor, *Psychosemantics* (1987), Appendix, "Why There Still Has to Be a Language of Thought." Andy Clark, "language of thought (2)" in Guttenplan, *A Companion to the Philosophy of Mind*, 408-412.

14. Jerry Fodor and Ernest Lepore, *Holism: A Shopper's Guide* (1992).

# Q. The Adverbial Theory of Directed-Towardness.

This section and the next consider representationalisms that are different from sententialism. The first one we consider is the adverbial theory of the directed-toward relation, briefly introduced in section D. It rejects the thesis we've been assuming all along, that there's an entity which attitudes are directed toward, whether it be a proposition or a sentence. We'll examine the major criticism the adverbial theory makes of all entity theories, which is that such theories cannot account for the unity of the complex entities they posit as the object-terms of the directed-toward relation.

### §1. The problem of the unity of a proposition or sentence.

A that-clause, if it's a singular term as some think, names an entity. To be an entity is to be either simple, that is, without parts, or complex, with parts. If a proposition is the thing named and it's a complex entity, what makes its parts cohere so that they're not just a collection? And if they do cohere, are they one only as an amalgam or conglomerate is one, or is there more unity than that?

The problem of unity also afflicts sententialists. If an attitude is directed toward a sentence, or more exactly, a sentence-radical, as the sententialists maintain, the sentence-radical either has no parts or it does have parts. It seems that most of them must have parts. What then makes the parts of a sentence-radical cohere, so that they're not just a collection? What constitutes their unity?

Historically this problem led to philosophers focusing on explaining the role of the verb in a proposition, where by the word "proposition" they meant either a sentence or something in the mind like a sentence. (I'll call this entity a subjective proposition to remind us that we're not referring to medadic intensions.) Russell asked this question in 1903, and concluded the unity of the proposition had something to do with its verb:

> A proposition, in fact, is essentially a unity, and when analysis has destroyed the unity, no enumeration of constituents will restore the

proposition. The verb, when used as a verb, embodies the unity of the proposition, and is thus distinguishable from the verb considered as a term, though I do not know how to give a clear account of the precise nature of the distinction.[1]

Why did he say, "when analysis has destroyed the unity, no enumeration of constituents will restore the proposition"? Comparison of a proposition to a Christmas stollen could've told him that the unifying factor must be temporally first in the act of judging a proposition to be true. Imagine someone pulling apart a stollen and collecting all the bits of candied fruit (analogous to names and verbs) and crumbs (analogous to relations, since they come from what held the words together). He wonders how someone stuck the fruit together with those crumbs! The answer is, of course, that first came the dough providing the unity; the fruit bits came later and were folded into the dough. Analogously, the *propositional bond*, by which any proposition hangs together internally, comes from some dough, and the words are folded into it. Does the verb seem like the dough, or is it the crumbs, or is it just a bit of candied fruit, like the names? It will turn out that the verb does not unify the proposition. But to know what does unify a proposition is to know why verbs occur in our speech.

Russell never makes this discovery. During the next decade, Russell directed his attention away from the proposition that consists of terms in the way a sentence consists of words, and toward the mental act of judgment as the source of the unity. Corresponding to a sentence, for example, "Desdemona loves Cassio," which Othello might utter, there's his judgment (mistaken judgment, as we know from the play) that Desdemona loves Cassio. The question of what makes this mental act of judging a unity is just as pressing as is the question of the unity of the proposition. Again something like a verb is involved. But like which verb? There are two: There's the verb of the proposition judged, "loves," and there's the verb of the report of the judging, "judge," which introduces the proposition judged.

Othello judges that Desdemona loves Cassio.
Russell inclined to the verb "judge" as pointing to the unifying factor.[2]

Just when Russell was thinking of these matters, a twenty-something showed up at his door and asked to be his student: the young Wittgenstein. Russell showed him the manuscript he was working on. Thus began an exchange between the old geezer (well, Russell was in his forties) and the young whippersnapper, which would change philosophy.

Wittgenstein convinced Russell to give up the theory of judgment he held between 1910 and 1912. For Wittgenstein saw that Russell had not solved the problem of the unity of the judgment any more than he had solved the problem of the unity of the proposition a decade earlier. I tell this story in all its argumentative detail in a publication in the journal *Russell*.[3]

Wittgenstein was himself perplexed about the issue of unity. He formulated the problem in his notebook on 20 September 1914:

> . . . to say how propositions hang together internally. How the *propositional bond* comes into existence.[4]

Wittgenstein had convinced himself that the judging relation cannot bind elements into the proposition judged. Therefore, the proposition must have unity independently of the judging. For it has its own existence. As he says in another place in his notebooks, with my insertions in square brackets:

> This shows that a proposition itself [a subjective proposition, something in the mind] must occur [= reference to it must not be analyzed away] in the statement to the effect that it is judged.[5]

If we extrude the verb of propositional attitude from the bonding problem, and yet admit that a subjective proposition would not exist without some attitude or mood directed toward either it or a proposition it's part of, we can see our one problem bifurcating. There's the accounting for the propositional bond independently of the attitude, and there's the accounting for the role of the attitude as internally^ related to the proposition. There are two aspects of the problem: content-unity and mood-essentiality. So Russell stated the one (pre-bifurcated) vexing problem as Wittgenstein's discovery of a non-natural kind of unitary fact, one with two verbs, a verb of propositional attitude such as "judges," "believes," "wishes," or the like, and a verb of the proposition that is believed or wished for.[6] Russell made public these debates over his theory of belief a decade later in his Introduction to Wittgenstein's *Tractatus Logico-Philosophicus*.[7]

To understand Wittgenstein's own solution, we must distinguish two modes of representation: roughly, facts representing facts and things representing things. Now forget the things; we'll focus on the representational kind of facts. I trace this distinction to an idealist philosopher enormously influential at the turn of the twentieth century: Francis Herbert Bradley. Despite Russell's later disavowal of monistic idealism,^

his sense of the unity of judgment as an ever-present issue developed under Bradley's influence. Bradley had himself made an issue of the unity of judgment against associationist^ accounts of judgment. Bradley had also said that meaning is what a certain sort of fact had; such facts he called signs.[8] Facts. What are they? They, like propositions, seem complex unities. So what unifies them?

Both Russell and Wittgenstein agreed with Bradley that the fundamental sign was a fact-sign. So propositions should be seen as facts, not as objects. Wittgenstein stated this in his 1913 notes thus, with my insertion of the square brackets:

> In "aRb" "R" looks like a substantive but it is not one. What symbolizes in "aRb" is [the fact] that "R" occurs between "a" and "b". Hence "R" is *not* the indefinable in "aRb".[9] [Rather the signifying relation relating the three of them is the indefinably basic thing.]

He restated it in 1922 in his *Tractatus*, 3.1432:

> We must not say, "The complex sign '*aRb*' says '*a* stands in relation *R* to *b*'"; but we must say, "[the fact] *That* '*a*' stands in a certain relation to '*b*' says *that aRb*."

Russell's appeal to fact-signs had a different slant from Wittgenstein's. Russell reduced the problem of accounting for the propositional bond to the proposition's representing or misrepresenting something already well-consolidated, namely a fact. Since facts are to be represented only by facts, some facticity of a subjective proposition does the representing and unifies the representing entity as well. Here I think Russell never quite saw what Wittgenstein was driving at. For Russell, as for Bradley, this signifying facticity is just the occurrence of the whole propositional complex. Russell says in 1919:

> Propositions are facts in exactly the same sense in which their objectives [i.e., what they stand for] are facts. The relation of a proposition to its objective is . . . a relation between two equally solid and equally actual facts.[10]

For Wittgenstein, calling a proposition a fact does not explain its unity because the unity of a fact needs explaining. The unity does not come through the fact's own verb, but rather through the proposition's component names occurring in a special relation to each other *unassisted by any verb*. The names' relation to each other constitutes the signifying facticity, and this was the special facticity that unified the proposition in the judger's mind. The verb has nothing to do with it. That's what he said in his 1913 notes and repeated in 1922 in *Tractatus* 3.1432.

Russell even parrots this remark of Wittgenstein's, which I quoted above, in his Introduction to the *Tractatus* (correcting the typo "the person's name" to "the persons named" on page 10. Square brackets contain my comments, although I think they'd be Wittgenstein's also):

> If we say "Plato loves Socrates," the word "loves" which occurs between the word "Plato" and the word "Socrates" establishes [*wrong; he should have said "is established by"*] a certain relation between these two words [*actually a pre-English-language relation between their mental counterparts in the subjective proposition*], and it is owing to this fact that our sentence is able to assert a relation between the persons named by the words "Plato" and "Socrates."

He missed seeing how the verb-containing sentence derives from the verbless proposition. Whenever Russell says in his own voice something to the effect that, *that* the symbols in a proposition occur as they do signifies *that* such and such is the case, he means only to reaffirm that facts signify facts. He sees the correspondence of fact to fact as replacing the relation of self to objects, which underwrote his 1910/1912 theory of judgment, the one Wittgenstein had savaged.[11] He does not solve the problem of the propositional bond. Wittgenstein's solution turns on supposing that verbs are artifacts designed for the publication of judgments in speech. As judgments exist in the mind, there are no verbs, just nouns configured in relation to one another so as to represent a relation between the things they name.

Just as a verb is a type, and particular occurrences of it are instances of the type, so the relation among names in a mental judgment is a type, and particular occurrences of the relation are instances of the type. But unlike instances of verbs, which may occur outside statements, in lists for example, particular instances of a relation cannot occur except as relating things. Thus for a relation to *occur* is for a complex unity to occur, namely, the things being in that relationship. At least this is the case for the special relations we'll explain in the next subsection. Some relations are relations of disunity, like "(_) is unrelated to (_)"; we're not referring to them! So let the things related be names, and let the relation that relates them be one that represents a relation that might hold between the things the names name. This positing of a relation between names solves the problem of the propositional bond. Along with the solution comes a picture of a level of thought structured in a more primitive way than sentences are: thoughts that are complete without verbs.

In 1954, Stenius provided the needed clarification of Wittgenstein's account of the verb in the construction of sentences that express verbless subjective propositions in people's thoughts,[12] and in 1957 Geach provided the correlative correction to Russell's account of judgment as Wittgenstein would have corrected it.[13] We'll now explore this account.

## §2. The adverbial theory's solution to the problem of the unity of a proposition.

I call this theory the **adverbial theory of directed-towardness**. I mentioned this theory way back in section D as the theory that took the that-clause as an adverbial complement to the verb expressing the propositional attitude. To believe *de dicto* that a woodchuck ran into the bushes is to believe [woodchuck-ran-into-the-bushes]-ly. (That's supposed to be an adverb!) To believe *de re* about the woodchuck is to believe [ran-into-the-bushes]-ly about it. In other words there's this concrete mental event and whatever things it's about. The rest is just a property of that event, expressed by an adverb.

Why not reverse the roles of the event and the adverbial property? That would be to take the occurrence of the proposition as the concrete event and to treat belief as a modifier of it: That the woodchuck ran into the bushes is in the mind believingly. Notice, there's that complex unity assumed without any explanation of how it came to be unified. Part of the motivation of the adverbial theory is to not assume any such thing, but to explain it.

The adverbial theory capitalizes on Harman's definitional maneuver, which I mentioned in section P. For an attitude to occur is nothing but for a sentence or subjective proposition to occur in the mind in the mood appropriate to that attitude. Now we ask two questions: First, how does a subjective proposition manage to occur in the mind as one thing, something with parts, yet with its own unity? Secondly, how does this unity manifest a mood, making it one attitude rather than another? The whole picture of directed-towardness as a relation between a thing supplying mood and a thing supplying content—notice the picture disappears, morphing into a mere way of speaking. First we posit the subjective proposition's parts: Singular terms occur in the mind. Then we posit that they instantiate a special relation constituting them into the unity of a subjective proposition. Then we posit a property of that unity, that it function a certain way in the mind's workings, establishing it to be a believing or a desiring.

I contrasted the adverbial theory with the entity theory in section D, but never said any more about the former. Now we have the background we need to proceed. A result of Part II is that we have reason to think the minds of believers contain names. The adverbial theory's adverb may now be better thought of as expressing the manner in which the names are in the mind, rather than the manner of the believing that goes on by means of them. That mood will be a further property of the mental state. I associate this theory with the early Wittgenstein, the two philosophers I referred to earlier, namely Erik Stenius and Peter Geach, and the philosopher Wilfrid Sellars. Let's now see if we can understand the adverbial theory.

To put the theory in its starkest light, it undermines the sententialist position about the nature of LOT by asserting three things:

- There are no verbs or other predicate symbols in LOT. The only concrete symbols in LOT are names occurring in minds.
- The content of thought arises simply by instances of the names being in significant relations to one another. These arrangements—in their representational role they're in many dimensions—are not sentences; they're presentential picture-like states of mind. (We'll call them subjective propositions, although the term disguises the adverbial nature of this thesis, that the attitudes just are states of mind consisting of instances of names in significant relations to one another, i.e., in a structure.)
- Our minds create verbs and other predicates only for the purpose of expressing our presentential thoughts in public speech, where the predicate symbol has a role most like a subscript's. Since public speech is unidimensional (i.e., just a sequence of sounds), the verbs are subscripts on the unidimensional concatenations of names, individuating the otherwise generic concatenation (i.e., linking together as in a chain).

These theses attack some central features of sententialism, whereas the three criticisms that concluded the last section conceded much to sententialism.

The all-important complexing of the singular term symbols in a subjective proposition, so that they become parts of one thing, just is Geach's twiddle construction ("twiddle" being his name for "§"; the movement of your thumbs as you twiddle them will remind you of this symbol). With the symbol Geach constructed a reference to a property that represents another property. The construction is by way of the property it represented. That is to say, he put the name of the property represented within the scope of the typographic symbol §, and the result was a name of the representing property. A property which represents the property of being green, I call a twiddler of green, because its name is "§(green)." This name is a general term; many other properties may be called by this name, for instance, the property of something's appearing black when red light shines on it. The thing's property represents to me its being green. Another example: There's the property of being a French word consisting of these four letters in this order: V, E, R, T. Here's another name for that property: §(green), because it represents being green.

Geach discovered the universals that are **"twiddlers"** of other universals, that is, universals instantiated by entities in minds, where they stand proxy for other universals. Thus §(green) is a property, a non-color property to be sure, of a symbol in a person's mind for a thing, a symbol like a demonstrative or proper name, and this property of a symbol goes proxy for the greenness of things. When a symbol for something is §(green), meaning it has the property of being §(green), that's a proxy for the thing symbolized being green. We have two properties here: the twiddler, being §(green), and the twiddled, being green. Can we give a more intrinsic description of the twiddler, being §(green), one that tells us what property the symbol has rather than just what the symbol's having that property stands for? Perhaps someday we'll be able to. Maybe it will be the symbol's being a brain circuit, and its twiddler property will be an activation of a neural route to the occipital lobe. Folk psychology itself leaves open the specification of the intrinsic properties of twiddlers. So while we're students of folk psychology, we should not allow the question to distract us.

A twiddler universal is not itself a symbol, that is, it's not a concrete entity with a function. To suppose otherwise would return us to unillumi-nating accounts of the difference between names and verbs. The symbol "§(green)" is a symbol in Geach's theory, not one in the mind of the judger; the property that "§(green)" symbolizes is instantiated by some-thing in the judger's mind; it would be a *singular term* symbol only. By the judger's symbol simply *having* the twiddler property, without her symbolizing the property, she's predicating greenness of the thing her symbol refers to. That's the subjective proposition in a judgment or other mental act. The only symbols it contains are names; the twiddler provides the propositional bond. The twiddler just is the special relation between names that I mentioned at the end of the previous subsection. For this just is the bond among the names that composes them into a subjective proposition.

As a unifier, a twiddler is just like the structural relationship between the parts of chairs or brooms, which make the parts one chair or one broom. Actually, and somewhat paradoxically, twiddlers are greater unifiers, since §(constitute a disunity), when applied to the names of the disunited things, creates a unity, and it's true if and only if the things named do not constitute a unity. Twiddlers, because they're twiddlers as well as relations, do more than unify their *relata*.^ That complex, which is the unity they create, represents something truly, or falsely with some degree of verisimilitude.^ So we can call the complexes which they create directional, that is, they tend toward a fact if they're true to it, or away from the fact if they're false to it by their twiddling something else instead. In contrast, chairs and brooms are non-directional complexes because the relation holding among their parts is not a twiddler.

Twiddler universals come in a variety of adicities; §(green) is monadic while §(loves) is a dyadic relation of symbols. When two singular term symbols stand in that relation in Othello's mind, he's predicating the love relation of the things that they symbolize. Othello's symbol for Desdemona stands to his symbol for Cassio in the relation of §(loves), and so he's judging that Desdemona loves Cassio. Note that I attribute predication to the person judging. No symbol yet has that function in our exposition of the nature of thinking in LOT. LOT lacks predicate symbols.

Twiddler universals are indispensable in any account of judgment, even the most sophisticated sort of judgments. For twiddler polyadic universals are *the glue that holds the name-symbols of a judgment together* as something more than a list, as something representational. Twiddlers do their work without verb symbols. For a subjective proposition with §(green) for its glue is true or false as the thing named in the subjective proposition is green or not. A subjective proposition with §(loves) for its glue is true or false as the pair of things named in the subjective proposition are, or are not, such that the first loves the second. With twiddler glue Geach solves the two difficulties that troubled Russell's 1910/1912 relational theory of judgment, namely, what can be within the judger that could represent a relational fact, and how the thing within could be structured so as to represent it.

The account in the last four paragraphs is the theory of the propositional bond I wish to defend as coherent within folk psychology. The twiddler's instantiation is a fact that *signifies* a fact. The twiddler is a sign. It's a universal, whereas symbols are particulars. So it's a non-symbolic sign. Since its instantiation by symbols and its going uninstantiated by symbols are both significant, a twiddler has two-to-one reference, whereas symbols have one-to-one reference, if I may adopt Quine's perceptive phrasing.[14] Symbols must be embedded in the instantiation of twiddler signs for the symbols and sign to work in judgments. The connection between the problem of the propositional bond and the twiddler theory is such that the latter accounts for the former in a fairly obvious way. Less obvious is the connection of the third thesis, that this is an adverbial theory of directed-towardness. It seems that the twiddler solution to the problem of the propositional bond could be adopted by an entity theory of directed-towardness. It would maintain that the entities are just the instances of names in a twiddler relation, constituting a compound entity, the content of presentential judgment. I must admit this possibility, so that the argument for the adverbial interpretation of the presentential scenario just depicted will be its accord with Ockham's razor.^ The scenario forces everything to be particular and concrete; the entity theory, as conceived originally, allowed for the object of the directed-towardness to be abstract. With that option eliminated, the adverbial theory is properly parsimonious. My own preference for the adverbial theory is indirect, since I'll end up supporting a nonrepresentationalist account of the directed-toward relation, with the consequence that, of the two representationalisms, more of the adverbial theory can be salvaged and incorporated into a syncretist theory of attitudes.

### §3. The adverbial theory's account of how the dominance principle works.

The judgment, in an attitude of judging something to be the case, is a representation in the sense in which we used the term in section P. In the present section we're looking at the internal constitution of a mental representation. Since it exhibits order as any representation must, it will have an internal constitution. The parts of the representation can be found or made, so that the representation itself is either found, made, or a hybrid of the two. Othello's judgment is wholly a made thing, since the twiddler represents love by convention and it holds between entities that are names by convention. But a mental representation can be wholly found. We can, if we wish, build a proposition by applying twiddlers to images. We may think of images as natural singular terms related in natural ways. Russell's idea of an image-proposition was that it's the mind's product, consisting of images and preceding the mind's forming of sentences.

When the twiddler is one that's found, but the names related by the twiddler are made, we have a hybrid mental representation. We know from sections L and M that we have beliefs and desires that are relational and *de re* without being indexical. Many philosophers think their distinctiveness comes from the occurrence of singular terms in them. I'd like to suggest that the distinctiveness has more to do with the occurrence of a twiddler in them which enters the mind naturally and does not depend on conventions for its representational powers. I think the representational content of these *de re* or relational beliefs is a hybrid form, conventional names and natural twiddler. The twiddler, following a causal path into the mind that was not laid out by conventions, finds names there to relate. The names are related in a way that models the way the things named are related. Perhaps this analogy will help: Spread iron filings randomly on a piece of paper, and then bring a magnet close to the underside of the paper. The iron filings will arrange themselves into a picture of the magnet's lines of force. Let the magnetic field as it occurs on the upper side of the paper's surface be a twiddler of the magnet's orientation underneath the paper. Let the iron filings be the names available for the twiddler to arrange into a proposition.

The payoff of this suggestion is an account of the semantical properties of relational beliefs. What if one of the names related by the twiddler is not the right one? No matter. The twiddler dominates in this situation, generating the phenomenon we know as the referential transparency of *de re* attitudes. There's a dominance principle in play here: The environment dominates over people's intentions in settling the semantical properties of their mental states. Since dominance is a generalization of the concept of a referential use of a definite description, it applies to the correcting of the misuse of names.

It's tempting to speculate about the evolutionary advantages among hominids just beginning to experiment with mental names so that the naturally occurring twiddlers may relate the names' instances in their minds. Surely the technique of building mental models in this way was prone to error. A dominance principle was simply a way for limiting the bad consequences of a certain kind of error. We find it operating in our own thinking still as a survival of those times. (I admit these paragraphs on dominance theory's application to twiddlers are sketchy.)

There are some constraints on the signs we're calling twiddlers:

> When the twiddler is instantiated in a judgment, it must convey information about the twiddled.

Informativeness is no more than positive relevance^ in the probabilistic sense. It suffices for the twiddler-twiddled relation that the probability of occurrence of the twiddled, given the occurrence of the twiddler, is greater than the absolute^ probability of the occurrence of the twiddled.

Equivalently, the probability of the absence of the twiddled, given the absence of the twiddler, is greater than the absolute probability of the absence of the twiddled. Since we're not interested in the occurrence of twiddled universals at just any old time or place in the cosmos, we recognize the relation of positive relevance may be itself indexical. Giving a frequency^ interpretation to the relevance condition for being a twiddler and combining that with the truth conditions for subjective propositions, we get something like a principle of charity in translating and interpreting propositions: Truth is not uncommon; expect others to have found it.

> Secondly, the twiddler must play a role in the guidance of
> purposive activity.

Since the twiddling relation will often follow lines of causation, as in perception, the twiddler is the more proximate of the causes of action, when both it and the twiddled are causes.

### §4. How the adverbial theory accounts for the origin of verbs and sentences.

I'll now show that this embedding of symbols in an instantiation of a twiddler is the origin of syntax. We derive sentence structures from subjective propositions, which consist of singular terms in twiddler relations. Let's grant for the moment that the speaker produces names in her public language to match the names in her subjective propositions. Minimally this involves phoneticizing her inner names, and there may be more to coordinating one's inner names to the names which her language supplies for communication. How that happens is a major topic reserved for sections T and U. Suppose she can do it.

Her sentences must consist of phonetic symbols in a linear or unidimensional order of concatenation. Sequentiality is the bottleneck that subjective propositions must be squeezed through before they can go public. Some don't make it into the strict linearity of quantification, as the theory of branched quantifiers shows.[15] And mere sequentiality of names does not by itself create enough differences to express all the propositions we wish to express. Think of all the propositions featuring Desdemona and Cassio. We could link the two names to mean that Desdemona sees Cassio by pausing one second after saying "Desdemona" before saying "Cassio." A pause of two seconds could mean she avoids him; a pause of three seconds could mean she detests him; a pause of four seconds means she colors when she sees him looking at her. Not a promising procedure.

But the trick of deriving linear concatenations from subjective propositions is simple for the speaker of loosey-goosey natural languages. ("Loosey-goosey" alludes to the point made at note 8 of the previous section, that communication languages are hodgepodges.) The speaker introduces a verb symbol in response to the proposition's twiddler universal. Thus Othello creates *another concrete individual.* Such symbols are verbs, while the original symbols in subjective propositions were names only. The name symbols are now concatenated with each other, with a verb symbol thrown in to individuate the concatenation. The multiplicity of twiddler relationships that can exist between name symbols in subjective propositions is reduced in speech to a single non-twiddling relation of concatenation of symbols in all sentences in this way: The speech community introduces a new category of symbol, one concrete verb per original twiddler universal, and then lets the concatenation of the phoneticizations of the original name symbols with the new verb symbol stand proxy for the original subjective proposition consisting solely of names unified by the twiddler universal.

Verb symbols come with rules for interpreting the orderings of the name symbols alongside them, so that asymmetric relations can be symbolized. Syntax is an adjunct to verb symbols. Thus do we derive sentence structures from subjective propositions. A subjective proposition, a semantic **structure** consisting of $n$ name symbols in a twiddler relation with each other, turns into a sentence with $n+1$ symbols, the extra one being a verb symbol, concatenated in series with each other.[16] Recall the directly attributed subjective proposition of section N and the no-name theory developed there. In preparing a direct attribution for presentation in a sentence we go from none to two symbols. The first person pronoun is introduced along with a verb.

The relation of the verb to the twiddler universal is that of a word to the thought it expresses. If the verb has a lower adicity than the twiddler it expresses, as for example the verb, "is grandparent of" (or "to be grandparent of"), we're entitled to understand the verb as overlaying a more complex thought. There's also notational redundancy. Geach at first denied, but later acceded to the claim that §(sharper than) = §(blunter than), and in general the active and passive voices of a verb express one and the same relation, e.g., §(hits) = §(is hit). This result is desirable because it corrects for a defect of sententialism, namely, that it provides too much difference and thus overcorrects for hyperintensionality. Can a person believe that this thing is sharper than that one, without also believing that that one is blunter than this one? Can a person believe that Jack hit Joe without believing that Joe was hit by Jack? It seems not, and these identities, expressed in terms of twiddlers, yield precisely what's needed to cut back on the proliferation of differences.

On the other hand, it does not undercorrect for hyperintensionality. One drawback of Geach's notation is that it disguises the fortunate fact that there's no bar against distinct twiddler universals representing the same twiddled universal. Thus a property of a candle flame, that it's hot, can be twiddled by the symbol for a thermometer reading a high temperature, by an image of the candle flame being blue, and by a symbol for one's hand having the twiddlers of being close and being hot. In the realm of analytic knowledge, §(is noninductive) and §(is reflexive) are two twiddlers for the same property of sets. If each of these twiddler universals gets its own verb, then this adverbial theory can account for failures of extensionality as well as sententialism does. If two distinct twiddler universals manage to be expressed by the same verb, we get ambiguity.

I've not connected the verb symbol to the twiddled universal, but to that universal's twiddler. Since it would be a blunder to say the verb predicates the twiddler of the names, we've not yet introduced any predication by verbs. Of course, by introducing verbs for creating a sentence to express the subjective proposition, what we've done is to duplicate the proposition's twiddling. Thus, in the sentence, "Desdemona loves Cassio," there's the relation between names, namely, of one name's *being before the symbol "loves" which is followed by* another name. The "loves" symbol enables us to individuate the otherwise generic concatenation, and generally verbs are for making concatenations distinctive, the way different subscripts on a variable $x$ make different variables. I italicized the verb "loves" along with the rest of the relation to show that it's a bit of what goes to make up the twiddler relation; it's not one of the relation's *relata*. In determining the adicity of the sentence's twiddler, the verb's not counted, only the names. Contrast that claim with the claim that verbs predicate; my claim is that verbs' first job is *syncategorematic^ merely*, working to compress a shapely proposition into a sentential line. A verb is a device for creating a one-dimensional substitute for a multidimensional thing. I mean by that what Wittgenstein meant when he wrote in 1913 that a verb "looks like a substantive but it is not one."[17]  I mean what Stenius meant when he called a verb the "characteristic" of the real logical predicate which is the relation between the names.[18] I mean what Sellars meant when he said "that predicate expressions are ancillary expressions and are dispensable in a way in which referring expressions are not."[19] When at the start I attributed the argument that I would make to Wittgenstein, I had this point in mind. It is what Russell never grasped, that *LOT does not need verbs.* We saw in section N that LOT does not need the pronouns "I" or "now"; it does not need verbs either.

Verbs, or verb-like devices, are needed in the sentences of public languages. The directionally complexing relation, i.e., the twin roles of a twiddler, being the unifier of words into a sentence and the representer of a subjective proposition, cannot be just concatenation, since the concatenation relation cannot be the twiddler of *every* other relation, and it serves as much to create non-directional complexes like names as it does to create directional complexes like sentences. So it cannot illuminate the distinction between directional and non-directional. But verbs, as known to speakers of Indo-European languages, are not essential as long as there's some device for creating the directionality. Indeed, in Chinese the syntax governing word order makes unnecessary any special symbols for verbs, although combining some terms with the term for "hand" will make them verb-like; position alone can make words verb-like. The variety's to be expected in the loosey-goosey realm of communication languages.

Derivatively, verbs do predicate. The individuated relation between the public names, a certain way of their concatenating with each other by means of a certain verb, is a twiddler of the twiddler in thought, §(loves), that is, it is §(§(loves)), which by the truth conditions for § reduces to another §(loves). That is to say, if a sentential §(§(loves)) twiddles a true propositional §(loves), it will twiddle (_loves_) truly also and thus be a §(loves). This second §(loves), which is in a sentence, introduces predication into the sentence, just as the first one introduced predication into the judgment, because it twiddled (_loves_). We conventionally assign the verb this predicative function in sentences. For the verb is the only part of the twiddler relation that interpreters can sense individuating it enough to reveal the universal being twiddled. But the verb "to love" all by itself is no twiddler of love. The verb is also a term called "general" only because the twiddler, which is no term but shows through with the help of the verb, has many alternative sets of *relata*. We conventionally assign the adicity of the twiddler to the verb. Although I can account for our inclination to treat verbs as general terms that predicate, my point is that it's more illuminating to resist the inclination and treat them as syncategorematic, like subscripts.

Although a mental twiddler of some relation has its own intrinsic properties, we don't know what they are. Because we only know the twiddler from the fact that it twiddles another universal, we can only name it by using the twiddle symbol. In contrast, another twiddler of that same relation, one occurring in a sentence, is obviously a temporal concatenation of physical events. Here we can name it by its intrinsic properties. This obscures the fact that it too can be named in the same way the mental twiddler was, as a twiddler.

A picture will help illustrate the basic points I wish to make. See figure Q-1.

THEORY SAYS:

Just two people, and the relation, LOVES is not true of them

The Fact of the Matter

Just two images (i.e, names) and the relation §(LOVES) is true of them. So the thought is false.

Othello's Thought of the Matter

Three symbols, two names concatenated distinctively by the addition of the third. The relation §(§(LOVES)) is true of the names. So the statement is false

Desdemona loves Cassio

Othello's Expression of His Thought

Figure Q-1. A triptych of (i) the cause of, (ii) the occurrence of, and (iii) the effect in speech of twiddlers in Othello's mind.

Speakers of languages may have in their minds subjective propositions with twiddlers containing verbs or presupposing verbs, by virtue of the fact that they are speakers. They can sing, "Whatever you can do I can do better," in effect quantifying over verbs. They think in their LOT with subjective propositions more like sentences than they need to. But some thinking precedes public language, so thinking must be able to occur independently of public language.

Subjective propositions as I described them can be attributed to infants and other species of animals. None need manufacture verbs to think. They also don't have as full a repertory of names as a speaker of a language has. The names in their elementary subjective propositions are not rigid designators by virtue of what human adults have: a culture that's cohesive across time and space. Their subjective propositions cannot name Cicero, but they do have singular terms. Surprisingly, they arise from twiddlers! But that's a story for sections U and W to tell.

### §5. What's in the mind of the reporter of another's mind?

I can now account for our reportings on another's beliefs as *de re*. If all one's sentences are in effect twiddlings of subjective propositions in one's own mind, then the same technique can be adapted for representing in one's mind the subjective propositions in another's mind, and then forming a report of them. Geach said as much, but he did not say clearly that we can capture the distinction between relational and notional forms of reports with the twiddle construction, depending on whether nominal symbols in the report fall outside or inside the scope of the twiddler. Consider this example, which we used in section K: Suppose Rep and Belia both saw an animal run into the bushes. Rep believes that Belia believes that the animal is a woodchuck. In Rep's mind is the subjective proposition concerning Belia's relational belief: There's a **nonce name**, ®, denoting the animal they both saw. It's endowed with vividness for Belia by her seeing the animal, and Belia believes about the animal, using ® for its name, that it's a woodchuck. Thus, according to Rep, in *her* mind is a subjective proposition of the form,

"®§(is a woodchuck)"

for some ® vivid by perception.[20] Let Rep name that occurrence of a subjective proposition ©. Rep is committing himself to ® actually denoting some animal vividly for Belia. That's a triadic semantic relation. The proxy in Rep's mind of this relation between her, the name, and the animal, the twiddler of this relation, holds between three things: (1) Rep's name for Belia, (2) a variable ranging over Belia's vivid names, as indicated in the analysis just given, or his meta-name for Belia's vivid name, and (3) his own name for the skunk (for that's what it was in section K). Let the variable or metaname be a capital R. Then in *Rep's* mind is a subjective proposition of the form,

"R §(vividly names for) 'Belia' 'the animal that ran into the

bushes' & R §(occurs in) © & 'Belia' §(believes) ©."
Rep's own vivid name for the thing that Belia calls ® is "the animal that ran into the bushes." In these subjective propositions about subjective propositions are names of particulars. If subjective propositions and their parts are what we refer to when we report one another's *singular* beliefs, then the names in them must rigidly designate for the reporter, vividness being a requirement only for the believer. They entitle the reporter to export them out of the scope of the belief operator, that is, transfer them from his copy of the subjective proposition reported on to the subjective proposition reporting.

## §6. The verbless language has a name: Jumblese.

Well, is the theory presented in this section true? The evidence I've presented is simply that it solves the problem of the propositional bond and is in other respects adequate for thought. I've not explained truth functional compounds of basic subjective propositions. Wittgenstein did elaborate an account of that in his *Tractatus*. Though sketchy still, the theory is testable. There might be evidence from cognitive science that verbs exist in the mentalese of everyone and not just in the competence of those who publish their thoughts in spoken languages. I'm not aware of any such evidence. The fact that people introspect themselves talking to themselves, using verbs, is not a refutation of the theory, because the theory does not say that they cannot do that. It only says they need not do that, and in much of their thinking they don't.

Recall the boiler room analogy from section N. Down in our boiler room, no names are used. Only direct attribution occurs there. Now we find no verbs are used either. Nothing is left to use in direct attribution! Yes there are: medadic twiddlers, incomposite propositions. It's beginning to look a lot like the Cartesian locus where intentional states fit brain states, something I alluded to in the Introduction.

Just one more thing: We need a name for this type of mentalese. Let me quote Wilfrid Sellars[21]:

> [Wittgenstein's *Tractatus*] is telling us that it is philosophically clarifying to recognize that instead of expressing the proposition that a is next to b by writing 'is next to' between 'a' and 'b', we could write 'a' in some relation to 'b' using only these signs. In a perspicuous language this is what we would do. Suppose that the Jumblies have such a language. It contains no relation words, but has the same name expressions as our tidied up English. Then we could translate Jumblese into English by

making such statements as

    'a

       (in Jumblese)    means *a is next to b*

    b'

and be on our way to philosophical clarification.

Well, there you have it. Suppose we're the Jumblies, and Jumblese is our language of thought! Sellars's single quotation marks before the "a" and after the "b" indicate that we're to interpret the "a [above] b" as a unit, two names arranged vertically to make one verbless sentence in Jumblese.

# Notes

1. Bertrand Russell, *The Principles of Mathematics* (1903) sect. 54.

2. Bertrand Russell, *The Problems of Philosophy* (1912). Ch. 12, "Truth and Falsehood."

3. "The Judger in Russell's Theories of Judgments," *Russell: the Journal of the Bertrand Russell Archives*, new series, vol 17, no. 2 (Winter, 1997-98) 101-122. I quote several of its sentences in the remarks I make in the next few paragraphs, but without quotation marks. The article was expanded from a section of my "Singular Knowledge" in *Realism: Responses and Reactions (Essays in Honour of Pranab Kumar Sen)*, ed. D.P. Chattopadhyaya, S. Basu, M. N. Mitra, and R. Mukhopadhyaya (2000) 382-404. The positive adverbial theory in this section is also an expansion of a section in that article.

4. *Notebooks, 1914-1916*, 2nd edition, revised (1979) Appendix I. p. 5e. Compare *Tractatus* 4.221.

5. "Notes on Logic, September 1913" in Ludwig Wittgenstein *Notebooks, 1914-1916*.

6. *The Philosophy of Logical Atomism*, in Marsh, ed., *Logic and Knowledge: Essays 1901-1950*, 226.

7. "Introduction" to Ludwig Wittgenstein, *Tractatus Logico-Philosophicus* (1922) 19-22. With the publication in 1967 of his *Autobiography*, we learned more about these debates from his letters. See also Elizabeth R. Eames, *Bertrand Russell's Dialogue with his Contemporaries* (1989). I think that the criticisms that Peter Geach levels against Russell's 1910 theory of judgment (in his book, *Mental Acts* (1957, 2nd edition, 1971) are just the sort Wittgenstein was making in 1913. The *Tractatus* is not cited in the book, despite the theories being so similar.

8. F. H. Bradley, *The Principles of Logic* (1883), Book I, ch. I.

9. See p. 99.

10. "On Propositions: What They Are and How They Mean," in Marsh, 315.

11. "Introduction" to the *Tractatus*, 20.

12. Erik Stenius, "Linguistic Structure and the Structure of Experience" *Theoria* 20 (1954) 153-172. See p. 170 for verbs as characteristics. See also his *Wittgenstein's 'Tractatus'* (1960), ch. 7.

13. *Mental Acts*, ch. 14 and the preface to the 1971 edition.

14. W. V. Quine, "Russell's Ontological Development" *Journal of Philosophy* 63 (1966), reprinted in his *Theories and Things* (1981) . See p. 82.

15. W. V. Quine, *The Philosophy of Logic* (1970) 89.

16. In note 5 to section H, I alluded to the semantic account of theories. It does not make sentences the carriers of theory, but rather, in the language of formal semantics, structures are the carriers. What I just described as being in the mind prior to the act of publishing it in sentences is just a structure. The additional component needed to turn a structure into a model is the interpretation of linguistic units. Now we see the mind does exactly that when it devises verbs or something verblike to create sentences.

17. *Notebooks, 1914-1916*. Appendix I, 99.

18. *Wittgenstein's 'Tractatus'*, 138.

19. Wilfrid Sellars, *Science and Metaphysics* (1968) 109. Compare Wilfrid Sellars, "Naming and Saying" (1961).

20. This account is based on Kaplan's analysis in his "Quantifying In."

21. Wilfrid Sellars, "Naming and Saying" (1961), reprinted in his *Science, Perception and Reality* (1963) 226.

# R. Do We Believe Connectionist Representations?

In section P we considered the thesis that Belia's attitudes are directed toward predicates and sentences. More exactly, we divided a sentence into its mood indication and content indication. Her attitude is directed toward this sentence content. This is the thesis of **sentientialism**. The LOT hypothesis is an instance of sentientialism. In section Q we began whittling away at this hypothesis, while staying within a representationalist framework, and we'll whittle some more in this section.

## §1. What connectionism is.

Still another alternative thesis is that Belia's attitudes are directed toward nonlinguistic representations, which are concrete, physical, causally active entities. Neurons in her central nervous system interact in a network, and states of the network are the representations. Attitudes are directed toward them. This thesis is called **connectionism**.[1] It contrasts with sentientialism because the stable states of networks don't constitute a language, since they're not structured syntactically like sentence contents.

Sentientialism and connectionism dispute over the indispensability of syntax for giving physical shape to meaning. According to the connectionist, syntactic constructions are only indispensable to a particular way of giving physical shape to meaning, namely their vocalization in a linear stream of sound, but not to the more general need of giving meaning some physical shape or other, which need not be linear. Since beliefs are internal, they're not constrained by the needs of vocalization, and so may not have syntactic shape. Network structures are a nonlinear, i.e. multidimensional, alternative to syntactic structures, and they have obvious affinities to brain structures.

When we discussed twiddler relations between vivid names in Belia's mind in section Q, we had to forgo any description of how those relations were instantiated. We could not describe the configuration of the names or their interconnections. Instead we just used the twiddler prefix to say that the relation between the names represented the twiddled relation relating the things named. In this section, however, we describe a network relating nodes—a net, for short—which could very well model the way the twiddler relation is instantiated by a sequence of names. If so, we can combine connectionism with Jumblese.

It would be hard to maintain that folk psychology implies connectionism. Connectionism is a theory that arose from the study of computers. But if folk psychology only implies a generic representationalism, then connectionism is compatible with folk psychology. So a study of connectionism is relevant to assessing the thesis that folk psychology only implies a generic representationalism.

This section's devoted to giving you a hands-on feel for what a net is and how it can solve problems of opacity and hyperintensionality. But, you say, you get queasy sticking electrodes into Belia's living brain tissue? Okay, we'll skip the hands-on, and just work with schematic diagrams. I'll describe how opacity and hyperintensionality arise, relying on an artificial example presented by Tank and Hopfield.[2] It's a **Hopfield net**.

### §2. Setting the stage: recognizing someone familiar.

The net will represent something going on in Belia's brain as she looks at someone. According to connectionism, Rep may report that

Belia recognizes person A and believes that there he is.
But we find no inner words composing the sentence, "there A is" in Belia. What's to be found instead is an inarticulate recognition event, "Lo, A!" which expresses the fact that a neural net in her central nervous system has reached a stable state. The stable state of her neural net is the representation which her belief is directed toward. If Belia's coming to recognize someone she sees *is simply* an internal neural net reaching a condition of stability, then our task is to show it will exhibit such features as failure of generalization and substitution, and other marks of the mental such as having a sense. If we can do that, we'll vindicate my belief that connectionism has many of the virtues of sententialism. Lacking sententialism's defects, it emerges as a viable hypothesis about what things the attitudes are directed towards.[3]

Belia cannot recognize A without relying on her memory of previous encounters with A. Memories of that sort are called episodic memory. There's evidence that people form a memory of an object by retaining a record *of features* of that object.[4] The method of recognizing an object by means of activating a network, consisting of a *distribution* of records of features, is not only realized now in computers, but also there's experimental evidence that memory of objects by features is characteristic of the memory possessed by birds and perhaps of all vertebrates. So Belia has this feature-based sort of memory by which she recognizes people and comes to believe in their presence.

Suppose within Belia there are six units that specialize in storing records of one or other feature of a person such as these:

- responds to the call "Rep,"
- short in height,
- young in appearance,
- fat in weight,
- blond in hair color, and
- brown in eye color.

The units are quite complex in themselves, but we won't analyze them. Suppose that none of these features require episodic memory in order to be recognized, so that my account could be used to explain even Belia's first memory. All there is *a priori* is a "feature space." It has six dimensions, and each dimension has only two units: present and absent. The feature space has a place for all possible combinations of features. Each place is identified by its six coordinates, for example,

< present, present, present, absent, absent, absent >.

Some of the combinations are singled out as the constituents of a memory of someone. That is to say, the features overlap in physical space and time.

### §3. How a Hopfield net yields recognition.

Here's how the net works: Each of the six units in the feature space falls into a + or a - state, depending on the presence of the feature in the memory-forming perception or the presence of a contrary feature. A unit may also stay inactive or indeterminate. If Belia is to remember Rep, who is short and young, but thin with brown hair and blue eyes, then her perception must give these six units the values, +, +, +, -, -, -.

Suppose she senses these traits together often enough to form an associative bond between them. This bond is the excitatory and inhibitory connections between the nodes. (Since the units are connected by associative bonds, we'll call them nodes.) We need four concepts: nodes, bonds, paths, and signals.

- Nodes may be in either of two states of activity, positive and negative.
- Bonds between nodes are either excitatory or inhibitory.
- Paths between nodes are the outcomes of bonds, when memo-

ries are superimposed, and are either excitatory or inhibitory.
●Signals along paths are either positive or negative.

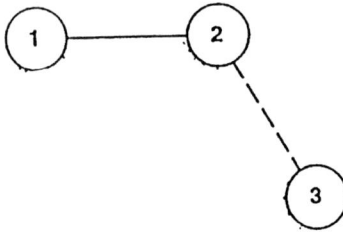

Figure R-0. The solid line between the nodes represents an excitatory path;
the broken line represents an inhibitory path.

A node sends a signal of the same sign as itself along an excitatory path.
It sends a signal of the sign opposite to its sign along an inhibitory path.
Suppose in Figure 0, node 2 is positive; then a positive signal goes to 1
and a negative signal goes to 3. Suppose node 2 is negative; then a negative signal goes to 1 and a positive signal goes to 3. I'll not concern myself
with how a network acts to set in place these connections, though there
may be a role in this training for short-lived images replicated from sense.
     Consider now how we might store *three* memories superimposed on
one another in these six nodes.

| Nodes: | 1. Responds to "Rep" | 2. Height short | 3. Appearance young | 4. Weight fat | 5. Hair blond | 6. Eyes brown |
|---|---|---|---|---|---|---|
| Memory of A | + | + | + | − | − | − |
| Memory of B | + | − | + | + | − | + |
| Memory of C | + | + | − | + | − | − |

Table R-1. Three memories in a space of six features.

Three memories are superimposed on the same six nodes through the permanent bonds left by the formation of the memories. The mechanics of the associative bonds between the six nodes are thus: The nodes send signals to one another to influence the state of the recipients. For the moment consider the memories separately. The bond between any two units, due to one of the memories, is either excitatory or inhibitory. If the two units are of the same sign for that memory, their bond is excitatory; if they are of opposite signs, the bond is inhibitory. Signal-exchanges are determined by the nature of the bonds. Signals are either positive or negative. A positive node sends a positive signal to excite any neighbor who is also supposed to be positive for that memory, but a negative node sends a negative signal to excite a neighbor who's supposed to be negative. Thus what counts as an excitatory signal depends on the sign of the sender. For example, for memory A, when considered just by itself, the first three nodes would all be exciting each other by exchanging positive signals, and the last three nodes would all be exciting each other by exchanging negative signals. But each of the first three is inhibiting each of the last three with signals opposite to the senders' signs and the same as the receivers' signs.

The result of all this activity is the implementation of a consistency principle: The incoming signals always add up to have the same sign as the node itself. Thus, to conform to the consistency principle, a change in the incoming signals may force a change in the node's sign. If they sum to 0, the receiving node stays in the state it was in.[5]

Surprisingly, the three memories can be superimposed by letting them share the same feature space. We can accommodate the need of each memory to make the bond between two nodes be either excitatory or inhibitory, and when they prescribe oppositely, the net design out-solomons Solomon in its wisdom. The kind of path between two nodes gets settled even when their bonds are opposite for the different memories. Find the net-sum value (excitatory or inhibitory or sometimes neutral when the number of memories is even) for the bonds between any two nodes and let the final associative path between the nodes, all memories combined, just reflect that net-sum.[6] Thus the bonds between node 1 (responds to "Rep") and node 2 (height short) is excitatory for memories A and C, but inhibitory for memory B. The principle of majority rule: The path between nodes 1 and 2 will be excitatory.

The boxes in the next table represent the relations between the nodes; since the relations are irreflexive and symmetric, only some boxes are filled in. (The empty diagonal boxes don't represent possible exchanges because the relation is irreflexive, and the other empty boxes are redundant because the relation is symmetrical.) The left side of the equation in a box lists the excitatory (e) or inhibitory (i) nature of each memory's bond between the pair of nodes. The right side is the sum value for the path with memories superimposed.

| Nodes | 1 | 2 | 3 | 4 | 5 | 6 |
|-------|---|---|---|---|---|---|
| 1 | | e,i,e=e | e,e,i=e | i,e,e=e | i,i,i=3i | i,e,i=i |
| 2 | | | e,i,i=i | i,i,e=i | i,e,i=i | i,i,i=3i |
| 3 | | | | i,e,i=i | i,i,e=i | i,e,e=e |
| 4 | | | | | e,i,i=i | e,e,i=e |
| 5 | | | | | | e,i,e=e |
| 6 | | | | | | |

Table R-2. Computation of the final associative paths between the nodes. For example, the entry in row 1, column 2, shows how it comes to be that the path between nodes 1 and 2 is excitatory. The three terms on the equation's left side express three comparisons of the signs in each row of columns 1 and 2 of table R-1. Where the two signs are the same in the same row of the two columns in table R-1, there's an e here in R-2; where they're different in table R-1, there's an i here in R-2.

Thus once the memories are superimposed on one another, the net-sum of the associative bonds between the six nodes create these paths, with solid lines being excitatory and broken lines inhibitory.

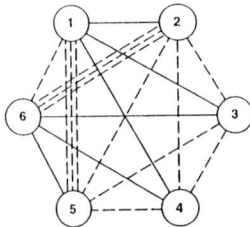

Figure R-1. An associative memory with six nodes. The figure is from *Scientific American*, 257 (Dec., 1987) 112, but it's been corrected, and the paragraph that follows is adapted from there.

The nodes are linked by excitatory (*solid line*) and inhibitory (*broken line*) connections. The number of lines in each link represents the strength of the connection; each solid line represents a connection strength of $+1$ and each broken line represents a strength of $-1$. Each node might represent a characteristic of a person, as shown on table R-1. Suppose one wants to store three memories, or sets of characteristics. The nodes that are supposed to be in the $+1$ state are given an excitatory link to the other $+1$ nodes and an inhibitory link to the $-1$ nodes. To store information about all three memories one simply adds up the connections. For example, the link between nodes 2 and 4 is $(-1)+(-1)+(+1)$, or $-1$.

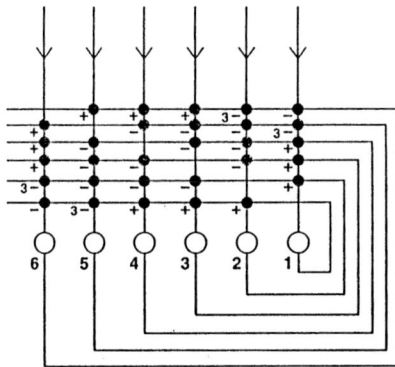

Figure R-2. The same network that the hexagon of figure R-1 represents is here redrawn as a crossbar network with the excitatory or inhibitory nature of the connections indicated by the signs at the crossings. Some readers with programming skills may find this representation more revealing; other readers will miss nothing if they ignore it.

The first thing to note is that we can achieve stable networks, that is, states in which the nodes already in one or other state don't get changed by the signals they receive. Thus if one evokes one of the memories in its entirety, say memory A, by putting the first three nodes into a positive state and the last three in a negative state, the network is stable despite the fact that the second and third nodes are sending each other inhibitory signals although they're in the same positive state. For what maintains them both in a positive state is the net-sum of received signals.

| Receiving node & Current state for memory A: | Vector of inputs<1,2,3,4,5,6>, numbers naming nodes, and the result: |
|---|---|
| 1 (+) receives: | <0,+,+,-,+++,+>, which sums to +. |
| 2 (+) receives: | <+,0,-,+,+,+++>, which sums to +. |
| 3 (+) receives: | <+,-,0,+,+,->,  which sums to +. |
| 4 (-) receives: | <+,-,-,0,+,->,  which sums to -. |
| 5 (-) receives: | <---,-,-,+,0,->,  which sums to -. |
| 6 (-) receives: | <-,---,+,-,-,0>,  which sums to -. |

Table R-3. Memory A is a stable state of the network.

Node 2 is receiving six signals enforcing its positivity and only one pushing it to negativity. Node 3 is receiving three positive signals against two for negativity. The same thing happens between nodes 5 and 4, which would be sending negative signals to each other for memory A, were it not for the other two memories sharing the network. Despite their inhibiting each other, they take on the same value, negativity, because each is receiving from the other four nodes enough negative signals to offset the positive ones they send each other. Somehow, what brown hair and thinness can't do for each other, namely, evoke each other, the other four traits, the Rep name and being short and youthful but not brown-eyed, can compensate for. Not only do the stored bonds allow memory A to be evoked stably, but also memories B and C, using the same set of bonds.

We can suppose, if we want, that once the network is in a stable state of activity, the person who is remembering constructs a phantasm of the combined features and thus remembers the person. But it would be a phantasm constructed with only six features for sure; the rest of the image would have to be blurry, giving rise to the phenomenon of images being less determinate upon inspection than we would've expected of replicas that simply persist and are not in need of reconstruction. Of course, stability of a network is not sufficient for an imaging or a recognizing, only just as indispensable for remembering as an image was formerly thought to be.

## §4. How the Hopfield net yields opacity and hyperintensionality.

This network is supremely simple in order to introduce the concepts by which we can understand misrecognition in a way that does not introduce the **homunculus** (Latin for the little guy inside Belia's brain who interprets what's going on in there—a form of vicious regress, since one would have to explain the brain of the homunculus). But its simplicity has its seeming drawbacks: Explorations of the model will reveal that, for various combinations of values for the nodes, the system will stabilize not only on the *bona fide* memories of A, B, or C, but also in one of two other configurations, which are mere pseudo-memories. They are -, +, -, -, +, - and -, -, -, +, +, +. If all the node values resulted from original external stimuli, then the net's stability generates a false sense of familiarity with the person who was the source of the stimuli. But the first of these two nets can come about as a result of just node 3 being stimulated to be negative. The net stabilizes in the six values after two rounds of signaling. If that single stimulation were the source of the net, it would generate a sense of familiarity with a being who may not exist, for nothing may possess that configuration of properties. Also there are many ways of assigning values to some or all the nodes that lead to perpetual oscillations. The net cannot make up its mind. For example, if nodes 2 and 6 are made +, the system vacillates between two states, neither of which are memories. Tank and Hopfield suggest that a more realistic model in which three memories are embedded would have 20 or even 30 nodes,[7] not just 6.[8]

But even the more realistic nets succumb to these sorts of aberration, and so I should find something psychologically interesting in the flaws. I do: The two pseudo-memories are exactly what we expect in intentional systems; names occur that don't have referents. Were it not for this feature of nets, names that don't have referents would not occur.[9] Further, since memories are mutually exclusively actualized, and person C might very well be person A, despite appearances, we have failure of intersub-stitutability, since remembering A when C should be remembered is clearly an error even given A = C. I'll demonstrate this later. Were it not for the facts that nets like this one are based on a few features and cannot actuate more than a single memory at a time, intersubstitution of names would not fail. If we are generating intentional phenomena, then we are generating two marks of the intentionality of singular terms.[10] For we can also interpret the net's states in terms of linguistic entities. For one thing, they are assentings to observation sentences, "Lo, B!" (We discuss these in section T.) The net's the place where several alternative observation sentences compete for realization. More speculatively, imagine ways of activating the net independently of perceptual stimuli, and ways of feeding our net's output into nets for generating language. Then our net assumes the role of vivid proper names.[11] I leave the details of that to another occasion.[12]

Now Belia can recall one of the first two memories from a *partial* perception, say by picking just three of the memories' characteristics.

Suppose in seeing someone, she notices just three of the relevant features. Note from Table R-1 that frequently, but not always, just three features will distinguish a memory from its co-tenants in the network. When she notices distinguishing traits which assign values to the nodes for those traits, the stored bonds will cause the remaining ones to take on the values that are correct for that memory. See Figure R-3. Thus, in memory A, even if the last three nodes are not stimulated by perception, let's say, to go to negative values, the first three send them inhibitory signals, except from node 1 to node 4. Even then, the negative signals from nodes 2 and 3 overcome that, and node 4 goes negative. After the first exchange of signals, node 1 is positive along with nodes 2 and 3, which stay positive because the sum of 0 for their inputs leaves them in the state they were in, and nodes 4, 5 and 6 are negative. No further changes occur as a result of signal exchanges.

initial values:

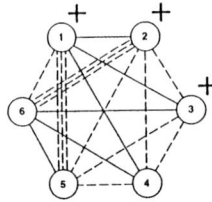

values after first exchange:

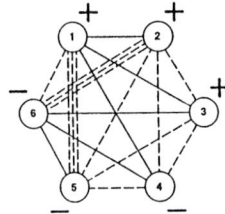

Figure R-3. This activation of just three of the six nodes stabilizes in memory A.

How might we replace the homunculus with an informative indispensable condition for false recognition? Let's say perception causes one node of the circuit to be given a value. Belia sees someone young. Thus perception makes node 3 positive. See Figure R-4. This is consistent with either memory A or B. Now come two rounds of signal-exchanges, after which the network becomes stable on memory B. So Belia suffers a possible misrecognition, if the perception is really of A. (When I first figured this model out, I explained it to a student while walking to my car.

We stood and talked by the car for some ten minutes. When he left, I tried opening the car door. It wasn't my car.)

We must inspect the two rounds of signal exchanges that end in a stable memory B, if we're to be truly convinced that the homunculus is absent. After the first round of associations is complete, all the other nodes have been assigned values.[13] But although in the first round all nodes receive values, node 4 is not at its final value, and after the second round of exchanges, which switches node 4 from a negative to a positive value, the network is stable. Given conditions that would become sufficient for recognition once the net stabilizes, the stability triggers recognition. Belia is recognizing the person she sees, perhaps someone seated and so his height is not evident to her, as a tall, fat person of her acquaintance. That's the memory that becomes stable, given the single initial input. It's a memory of B; see table R-1. Perhaps some phantasm of B is evoked for her consciousness. But of course, the identification may be erroneous; it may be A before Belia, not B. The error then derives from the way the associative bonds were overlaid, making the recall of A from just the sight of youth impossible, although the recall of A from other configurations is possible from the same network.

initial values:

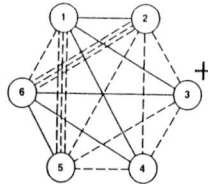

values after first exchange:

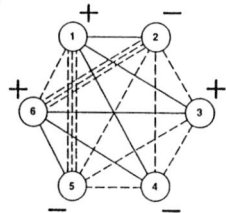

values after second exchange:

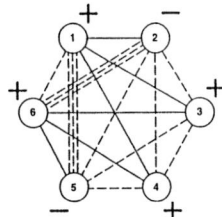

Figure R-4. This activation of just one of the six nodes stabilizes in memory B.

Although the initial values were consistent with either memory A or memory B, the system selected memory B. This could be a misrecognition. If Belia is looking at A in fact, and he stands up revealing to her someone short and thin, then her perception resets nodes 2, 3, and 4, and the new rounds of exchanges result in her recognizing A, correcting her first impression. That first impression, the sight of youth, was a limited mode of presentation; we see in the overlapping of memories the origin of the **intension** or sense of a representation. The sense of a representation of a thing is the way a representation presents that thing, a mode of presentation of that thing. Sense is connected to intension, defined in section G, because a representation may present a thing by way of some of its properties (intensions). *The sense of a particular occurrence of a stable state of a network is the set of original activations of the network that stabilized in that state. The sense of a stable state, taken as a type, is the set of all the sets of partial activations that will stabilize in that state.*[14] Two stable states are guaranteed to have distinct senses, even when they are memories of the same individual.

An engineer might see certain features of nets as imperfections according to her standards of network performance. Curiously, these very imperfections endow the nets with the marks of intentionality. The more inevitable these imperfections are, the more reassured are we who seek the mind. It does not disconcert us to find these exalted marks of mind in the imperfections of nets. After all, we already knew that these marks are imperfections when measured against the standards of extensional logic; they are failures of the laws of existential generalization and substitutivity of identity.

The Hopfield net is a counter-example to the thesis that representations are representations by virtue of their being used for certain purposes, in other words, by virtue of their having use-functions, and in consequence they're capable of misrepresenting only by virtue of their being used to achieve certain purposes. The net, I claim to the contrary, is capable of representing nonextensionally and representing the nonexistent quite apart from its being put to use. The thesis I reject is stated well by Fred Dretske:[15]

> [Function] captures the normative element in the idea of a representation. . . . There is information without functions, but there is no representation without functions.
>
> . . .
>
> The senses, and the states they produce by way of performing their function, are thus evaluable in terms of how well they do their job.

Dretske's thesis does allow for naturally occurring misrepresentations, as for instance sensory illusions, since it allows for naturally occurring use-functions. For use-functions can be given to things not only by people, as when workers manufacture tools, but also they can be assigned to systems naturally, according to Dretske, by being shaped by natural selection acting on a lineage of organisms. Dretske distinguishes the use-functions of naturally occurring systems, which accrue to them by virtue of their being the products of natural selection, from the use-functions of states of those systems, which accrue to some of them by virtue of their being shaped by conditioning:

> . . . natural functions are always acquired through some historical process like natural selection (for systems) and learning (for states). (p. 170)

As the first quotation shows, however, the thesis imports evaluative notions, i.e., notions of right and wrong means, into evolutionary biology. The proponents of this thesis are driven to this vestige of anthropomorphism by the intuition that misrepresentation is a species of malfunction. No malfunction without function. Ergo, use-functions are found in nature. The Hopfield net shows us a way out of this conceptual dead-end.

Might not **misrepresentation** and falsity come with the net's sheer complexity and not with its functionality? I think so. The net had six feature detectors. For our purposes they were simple on-off devices. Dretske would call them indicators or information collectors. They're not capable of misrepresentation; their states are either information or not information. The net itself is complex and capable of misrepresentation. Many of the stable states of the net are representations, as I hope Dretske would admit. There's nothing internal to the system that would single out the states that represent nonexistent persons and separate them from the acknowledged representative states. We can put it this way: *In all the intrinsic respects in which the truly informative representative states are like each other, the misrepresentative states are also like them.* Therefore, if the former are representations, so are the latter, and anyone who happened to make use of the net would so take them. That grouping of states is not a fact derived from the functionality of the states but only from their complexity. We don't need to bring in norms at this point. Norms come in after the fact, namely when the representations, including the misrepresentations, come to be exploited by an organism to achieve its purposes.

The falsity of a stable state may be either positive, representing what is not there, or negative, not representing what is there. Therefore, the occurrence of that which is represented is neither necessary nor sufficient for the representation to occur. But if it's a found representation, must there not be a natural connection of one or the other sort to that which is represented? Otherwise, there could only be a connection established by convention. There's a way between the horns of this dilemma: The individual nodes of the net are such that there's a causal connection of their states to the occurrence of the features that trigger them in the initial stage of a net's activation. That suffices to make the representation a found one. The autonomous interaction of the nodes thereafter generates the representation that is the net's stable state. The naturalness of that interaction keeps the representation's relation to that which is represented from being established merely by convention, although it's neither a necessary^ nor sufficient^ natural relation. In this way the net is both a found representation, representing naturally, but capable of falsity.

Although Dretske would have to concede that the net's stable states are not the result of any conditioning, he'd no doubt argue that my separating complexity from functionality and normativity is artificial, for such a net exists only by being shaped by natural selection to service an organism, or by genes controlling the maturation of the brains in which they occur. These processes import functionality and normativity. I'd reply this way: Granted that Hopfield nets are unlikely to exist in nature without natural selection, it is nevertheless a possibility, and it's a valid thought experiment to suppose that, separately from any evolution, Hopfield nets were part of the environment along with photons and compression waves in the air, and that after some time, during which the nets were just hanging around, organisms evolved to exploit the informational value of the photons, the sound waves and the nets. What do your intuitions tell you about the nets before they were exploited? Were all their states representations, some of them being misrepresentations? My intuitions prompt me to say yes, because of the point made earlier: In all the intrinsic respects in which the informative representative states are like each other, the misrepresentative states are also like them. Therefore, if the former are representations, so are the latter. Dretske asks you to see some of their states as representations and others as not representations. Even if you cannot decide, your indecision's enough to make Dretske's stance suspect.

If your intuitions agree with mine, we can reverse the conceptual order that Dretske requires, that functions and norms must exist before representations can come into existence. The truth seems to be that sheer complexity gives rise to misrepresentations of the nonexistent. Norms become important only because beings who use such complex representational systems benefit by steering clear of the false ones. We need only concede one asymmetry to Dretske: Because of the way falsity gets into nature, it's logically possible for all nature's representations to be true, but not for all of them to be false.

## §5. Some conclusions and some cautions.

The net illustrated how the signs of the features are distributed over a network and are interconnected in a way that allows several memories to be superimposed on one another. We're freed from thinking that, to each inactive memory there's a distinct sign in storage. We conceptualize how to have not only distributed representations instead of localized ones,[16] but also a multiplicity of signs that can be non-discrete in storage and mutually exclusive in activation without total confusion.[17] The ancient analogy between thought processes and speaking is eroding, and will erode further if I can make good on the connectionist promise to replace images (and singular names). Ultimately, I'd like to show how all the basic meaningful units acquire their meaning from the way their unmeaning parts interact, but not in this section, which assumes records *of* features. Paul Churchland gives a clear example of a net that discriminates features without there being any node meaning any of the features, and I need not repeat his work.[18] Whereas his network discriminates a rock from a metallic object, the networks providing input to Belia's inner network would discriminate between a short and a tall person, for example, and feed the result to one of the nodes in the network we're supposing to be in Belia. Each of the six nodes in her network stands for a whole net of the sort Churchland describes. Nevertheless, I do derive a corollary not to be sneezed at: I created two marks of the intentionality of singular terms,[19] namely, failures of existential generalization and of intersubstitutability of co-referential terms. They indicate intentionality, for **intentionality** is the "aboutness" of signs. Since my model depends on the presence or absence of six features, the features define a space of $2^6$, or 64, possibilities, most of them unrealized possibilities. The marks of intentionality become evident when signs are about these unrealized possibilities.

  Although Belia's inner net only captures two features of intentionality associated with one kind of term, the demonstration of that is a part of a broader project based on the idea that the features that philosophers see as marks of intentionality, and are happy to discover, are features that the computer scientists see as design flaws and are unhappy to discover. We've known since Quine pointed it out, that the two marks of intentionality I mentioned are violations of laws of extensional logic; it's not surprising, therefore, that the computer scientists who observe these violations in their systems declare the systems flawed. And philosophers have been reluctant to praise connectionist networks for virtues not recognized by computer scientists. So one hears from philosophers much about things like connectionist systems "degrading gracefully" and little about the emergence of intentionality in them from a non-intentional substrate. I propose that philosophers look at the design flaws in connectionist systems to find intentionality.

("Wait a minute. Hey, you who wrote this! Are you saying that to understand the distinctive features of the mind, the glory of creation, is to understand them as screw-ups?" Yes; that's exactly what I'm saying.)

Stabilized nets are not sufficient for recognition. Stability is a physical property of nets, while recognition belongs to the family of semantic concepts. Consider a computer program sufficiently advanced to pass the **Turing test** or to make a robot act purposefully and appropriately. (In 1950, Alan Turing proposed a behavioral test for computer understanding: Program it to receive a text and answer questions about it. Put a human being in the same situation, reading the text and answering questions. Have a third person in another room ask questions of the two, not knowing in advance which is which. If that person cannot come to tell which is the human and which the computer after a thorough questioning of the two, the machine has passed the Turing test for understanding. Turing called his test the imitation game.[20]) Despite passing the behavioral test, however, the syntax of even such a powerful program is not sufficient for semantics. Suppose the program is serial coding, as many sententialists suppose the human brain's to be; that is, unlike connectionist systems, it consists of a sequence of imperative sentences, which the machine executes one at a time in a set order. **Serial programming** of this sort could sustain the illusion that sufficiently powerful syntax is sufficient for understanding, since serial syntax that's complex enough to pass the Turing test manipulates a bit of code *if and only if* (near enough for illusion) semantics interprets it.

But it's only illusion, and connectionism dissipates it. Connectionist programming of this complexity obviously manipulates entities not subject to semantic interpretation, and what is subject to interpretation is sometimes not manipulated by the program. Thus the programs connecting Belia's retinal signals to feature detectors and then to her six nodes operate at the beginning with uninterpretable signals. So there goes the "only if." The memory of A, B, or C is the configuration of six nodes together, and that's not an entity any program manipulates. So there goes the "if."[21] I don't know any illuminating sufficient condition for remembering, but stable nets are as significant a chunk of one as images were thought to be.

The Hopfield net we studied sufficed to capture some of the essential features of intentionality. But obviously it's simplistic. More adequate nets require additional features, such as intermediate stages of processing called "hidden layers," weighting of connections, and "backpropagation" whereby the results of the system's acting on a net's stable state can affect the weights of the connections leading to a stable state. Such nets learn from the consequences experienced.

It's an open question how much of mentality the nets can capture. Steven Pinker lists five problem areas for nets such as we've studied (which he calls "autoassociative nets"), which are not problems for sententialism:[22]

> ●Knowledge of individuals in their individuality. Only a part of Belia's knowledge of persons A, B, and C, was represented in our net, namely, their distinctive appearance whereby they might be recognized. But our concept of individuality allows for numerical diversity despite exact similarity. How capture that sort of knowledge?
> ●The compositional knowledge of meanings, whereby with comparatively few building blocks of meanings we can compose a super-astronomical number of propositional meanings.
> ●Knowledge of generalizations with quantified variables, a kind of knowledge that depends on the previous two types of knowledge.
> ●Knowledge based on recursive procedures, such as knowledge of propositional attitudes, which is expressed as a proposition inside a proposition.
> ●Theoretical knowledge based on exact logic and precise definition, in contrast to fuzzy logic for reasoning about stereotypes.

If nets are to overcome these problems, they'll have to incorporate special purpose devices of a sententialist stripe to do it, which amounts to a concession that connectionist nets are not the whole story. Pinker thinks some mix of sententialism and connectionism will prove to be the most adequate theory of the mind, and surely a mix of the two is more adequate than either alone. Which one will occupy the central territory and be the senior one in the partnership?

# Notes

1. Neuroscientists coined the term, and it was appearing in their writings at least as early as 1981 (e.g., Robert Miller, *Meaning and Purpose in the Intact Brain* (1981) 48ff, and J. A. Feldman, "A Connectionist Model of Visual Memory," in G. E. Hinton and J. A. Anderson, eds., *Parallel Models of Associative Memory* (1981) 49-81). For Miller the term stood for the testable working hypothesis that brain structures are omniconnected, each neuron being able to influence the state of each other neuron via sequences of synaptic connections. The alternative would be that the interconnectivity within a structure is sparse. Another term used for connectionist ideas is "parallel distributed processing."

2. David W. Tank and John J. Hopfield, "Collective Computation in Neuronlike Circuits" *Scientific American* 257 (Dec. 1987) 104-114. I use their model from p. 112. Their diagram misrepresents the connections between nodes 4 and 5 and between 5 and 6. Daniel Roe pointed this out to me.

3. What follows is almost verbatim from my "A Connectionist Solution to Problems Posed by Plato and Aristotle," *Behavior and Philosophy*, 23, no 3/24, no 1 (Winter 1995/1996) 1-12.

4. Steven Rose, *The Making of Memory* (1992) 157; fn 7 on 287, and 287-9.

5. An alternative rule would let the receiving node change to a neutral or 0-state, if its inputs sum to 0. This alternative prolongs the computations of the net before it settles down to a stable state. The rule for the case of sum = 0 which we have adopted is espoused in D. Rumelhart and J. McClelland, *Handbook on Parallel Distributed Processing* (1988), 70, and Philip D. Wasserman, *Neural Computing: Theory and Practice* (1989) 95.

6. Wasserman, 98.

7. Alan Gelperin, J. J. Hopfield and D. W. Tank, "The Logic of *Limax* Learning" in Allen Selverston, ed., *Model Neural Networks and Behavior* (1985) 258.

8. Tank and Hopfield, "Collective Computation in Neuronlike Circuits," 113. I am indebted to my student Daniel Roe for writing a program for exploring this net, which uncovered its deficiencies and my own as a calculator.

9. The system fulfills a prediction made by William Bechtel, "Connectionism and Intentionality," *Program of the Eleventh Annual Conference of the Cognitive Science Society* (1989) 553-560.

> It is conceivable that activation patterns could be induced that do not correspond to anything normally caused by input patterns. These would be representations of non-existent objects. We know they are *about* these objects, and not others, because they are the representations that would be produced if the system ever did confront such an object. (559)

10. Roderick Chisholm, *Perceiving: A Philosophical Study* (1957),

"Intentional Inexistence."

11. The concept of a vivid name is from David Kaplan, "Quantifying In," in D. Davidson and J. Hintikka, eds, *Words and Objections* (1969), section IX.

12. Not to be too mysterious, I believe Quine develops several concepts in his *The Roots of Reference* (1974), especially in Part II, which enable us to understand how vivid names could have evolved from the mental equivalents of observation sentences.

13. If we had adopted the alternative rule mentioned in note 5, our original node 3 for youthful appearance would have lapsed into neutrality. Why? A truly mindless application of the consistency principle: All its inputs sum to 0; of course it has no inputs, but rules are rules. A smart homunculus may have wondered if this was an exceptional case and allowed node 3 to keep its value. But nothing in our model is smart. In the second round nodes 1 and 2 would go neutral because they receive as many negative inputs as positive.

14. Strictly this is a component of a term's sense. For a more complete characterization of sense, see my "Essay on Nature's Semeiosis," *Philosophy Research Archives*, 20 (1995) 297-348. See the second to last subsection.

15. Fred Dretske, *Naturalizing the Mind* (1995) 4-5.

16. G. E. Hinton, J. L. McClelland, and D. E. Rumelhart, "Distributed Representations" in D. Rumelhart, J. McClelland and the PDP Research Group, *Parallel Distributed Processing: Explorations in the Microstructure of Cognition* (1986) vol I, ch. 3.

17. Plato envisioned the non-discreteness, but not the possibility of its not causing confusion. *Theaetetus*, 195a.

18. Paul Churchland's *A Neurocomputational Perspective* (1989), ch. 9.4.

19. Roderick Chisholm, *Perceiving: A Philosophical Study*, ch. 11 "Intentional Inexistence." First, existential generalization: Ordinarily we may generalize from, for example, "Newton discovered the law of gravitation" to "Someone discovered the law of gravitation" because singular proper names do indeed name. Not so, however, if we allowed names like "Santa Claus" so that we could say such truths as "Virginia believed in Santa Claus." Second, substitution of co-referential names: If the morning star = Venus, then, ordinarily, whatever is true of the morning star is true of Venus. Not so, however, if we allow among those truths "Pythagoras discovered that the morning star = Venus." For it's not true that he discovered that Venus = Venus. Ordinary logic fails in each case because of the intrusion of talk about people's intentional states.

20. A. M. Turing, "Computing Machinery and Intelligence" *Mind* 59 (1950) 433-460.

21. In the case of serial programs, the **Chinese room argument** dispels the illusion. In Guttenplan, see Searle's "Searle, John R." for a statement of the thought experiment that purports to show that one's intelligent and purposeful manipulation of symbols is not sufficient for one's understanding their meaning. We'll explore it in section Y. In "Is the Brain's Mind a Computer Program?" *Scientific American*, (Jan. 1990), Searle extends the argument to connectionist programs (28f). But the condition from which the illusion arises, i.e, that syntax

manipulates an entity if and only if semantics interprets it, does not hold for connectionism, and so no extension is called for.

22. Steven Pinker, *How the Mind Works* (1997), "Connectoplasm" 112-131.

# S. Do We Believe Semantically Narrowly Individuated Contents?

Almost everything in our discussion of representationalisms has been about the syntactic and phonetic, as in the case of sententialism, or otherwise concretely symbolic. What about meaning? In section P we reviewed the semantics of compound expressions, which inherit meaning from their simple components, but we said nothing of the semantics of these simple components. If representationalism is to succeed in replacing propositions and attributes with words or other representations as the things a person's attitudes are directed towards, it must acknowledge that they have meaning. Recall the distinction made in section P between replacement strategies and supplement strategies. Supplement strategies make it easy to deal with meaning: They supplement representations with meanings. But we're considering representationalism as a replacement strategy. If the replaced entities are the represented propositions and the sentences are the representations, how can we explain a representation's meaning without appeal to any proposition represented?

### §1. The nature of the directed-toward relation according to replacement strategies.

The sententialist replacement strategy answers by analyzing the **understanding** of a sentence, for to understand it is just to grasp its meaning. Almost all propositional attitudes entail that the person with the attitude understands that which the attitude is directed toward. Understanding is then a component in all attitudes, and indeed is at the heart of the directed-toward relation.

A caveat is in order: In section A we distinguished between a believer assenting to a sentence as merely a true sentence, and her understanding it. Now it's a pressing matter to distinguish believing a sentence from merely assenting to its truth whether one understands it or not. In the latter case, the sentence one understands and believes is "The sentence, 'blah blah,' is true." That's what gets compiled into LOT. The part in single quotation marks remains mere "blah blah" in LOT; it's uncompiled.

Nevertheless, whenever you hear "blah blah" you say, "How true!" In contrast, the sentences people understand are wholly compiled.

If LOT is a single uniform system within each person, the three previous sections give conflicting accounts of it. If LOT is a conglomeration of ways of thinking, however, then all three may be true of it as it exists within a person. People who have public languages may think in those languages, or think in a LOT with verbs. They may also think in Jumblese, with names but no verbs. And the instances of names may just be activated Hopfield nets. We could no doubt add more tools to LOT. This is a syncretist's way of thinking of LOT. After all, who can say that thinking is just one thing? Nevertheless, for our purposes in this section, we'll take LOT to be that part of a person's thinking apparatus which exists independently of public language.

Dividing sentences into those in public languages and those in LOT, the sententialist divides the account of understanding sentences into two parts: understanding them in a public language and understanding them in LOT. Generally, a person understands a sentence of her public language if and only if she translates it into her LOT, which she understands directly. It would seem pointless to have a language of thought if one could not understand it directly! Nor can one misunderstand one's LOT, although one might understand it idiosyncratically, compared to how others understand theirs. So if a person can translate the public sentence into her LOT, she'll grasp its meaning.

The problem of meaning narrows down to the question, what is understanding a sentence of LOT? Understanding a sentence is knowing its meaning, and in the case of an indicative sentence that includes knowing how to settle at least in principle whether it's true or false. This makes a dilemma for sententialism: Settling the truth of a sentence requires that one identify the referents of the names in the sentence and settle whether the referents are in the extensions of the predicate words. That purely extensional procedure does not solve the problem of the nonextensionality of that-clauses in modal statements or in reports of propositional attitudes. So philosophers who opt for the extensionalist path will adopt the Davidsonian regimentation of propositional attitudes and cast aspersions on modality. A popular alternative path is to appeal to propositions and attributes, but that's not in accord with sententialism as a replacement strategy. Is there another way to get at understanding that a replacement strategist can follow? To avoid the dilemma we must find a third thing for the understanding of LOT to consist of, without having to hypostatize that third thing. It will be the roles that sentences play; their roles will be constitutive of their meaning.

Recall section N and the analogy of direct attribution to the language of the boiler room. Since human beings all understand the no-name present-tensed sentences of LOT that are the content of their boiler room attitudes of belief and desire, and they implement the attitudes innately, in the sense that they're built to respond directly to these most basic parts of LOT, computer-like, with behavior appropriate to their purposes and circumstances, perhaps there we have at least a necessary^ condition for understanding that avoids the dilemma just posed, because it preserves the data of opacity and hyperintensionality and is compatible with a replacement strategy. A computer understands its machine language in just this sense of acting appropriately, given its program and data. It's a peculiar sense, in that it's an understanding that finesses the semantics of reference, extension, and truth-value. Obviously these semantical matters, as well as consciousness which no machine yet has, do play a role in people's understanding. Nevertheless, let's play along with the replacement strategy. Suppose that, for any language to be understood, *some* of its sentences must be such that their prompting one's appropriate action is both necessary and sufficient for one's understanding them. The idea is that every understandable language must have a boiler room component, alluding once again to the analogy in section N §5. The reason is that people understand nothing unless they have propositional attitudes toward some things, believing some and desiring others. Recall from section C the **schema connecting behavior to belief and desire**: To believe and to desire entail having one's actions guided by some of the things believed and desired. The understanding that's a component of those guiding attitudes is the core understanding, on which all understanding is built. If this is so, the compilation into LOT being a necessary condition for understanding a communication language is not a trivial one, since only LOT will be that language that contains the boiler room component. (And what if people understand something in LOT for which the compiler gives them no translation into their communication language? They must then create more communication language.)

So for understanding the boiler room class of LOT's sentences, perhaps responses at a preconscious level that are prompted by them and that are appropriate to the circumstances are both necessary and sufficient^ for understanding them. Because we think of the appropriate responses as identifying the sentence's terms' referents and extensions in one's environment and as interacting with the referents in appropriate ways, the appropriateness may just be what the replacement strategy needs to avoid appealing to propositions and attributes.

But most sentences are not tailored for use in the boiler room. What's their connection to the sentences that are? For instance, people understand works of fiction, ancient history, and the pure math which has no application to engineering or any other field of action. People invent artificial languages with no sentences that can be translated into their own boiler room sentences. Why should their understanding of all these sentences depend on the sentences occurring in a language with a boiler room component or being translatable into such a language? And even if they do depend on such a component, what's the nature of the dependence? Nobody knows. If the boiler room prerequisite is right, however, we must speculate that one's understanding of all sentences has something to do with one's being able to extract information from them for guiding one's actions, and be suspicious of any appearances to the contrary.

If this speculative account of understanding in terms of appropriate purposive action is correct, we're led to a sententialist conjecture about the directed-toward relation. Up to now we've avoided the issue of what the directed-toward relation was really. Sententialism supposes it's a relation between believers and their words. What relation is that? Here's a conjecture that accords with the replacement strategy:

> A belief is **directed toward** a sentence (strictly, a sentence-radical) in all cases if, and in some cases if and only if, a concrete instance of the sentence or its compiled version is a part of what's in control of the believer's behavior, however mediated or conditional the part's control may be, and the behavior is on purpose and appropriate.

The "if and only if" condition applies to beliefs used in the boiler room. The conjecture, not quite a definition in form, was implicit in our discussion in section P of LOT containing an analog of a computer's machine language, which it responds directly to. Also the principle which we stated at the beginning of section N, about what makes beliefs distinct from one another in content, is a corollary of this conjecture. For one's actions to be guided appropriately by sentences in LOT is *ipso facto* to understand them. The particular role a sentence of LOT plays in the control of behavior is connected to its meaning. *Indeed it's identical to one aspect of its meaning.* That identification is the subject of this section. In section V we'll state the nonrepresentationalist alternative account of the directed-towardness relation. Then we'll have to decide which of them is wrong. For now, we explore this version.

We can explain other features of understanding public language by appeal to an already understood LOT: To understand that two sentences are *synonymous* is for them to be compiled to the same sentence in LOT. Of course, two sentences may be synonymous, but a person's compiler might not compile them to the same sentence. Then the person will fail to see the synonymy. This result is exactly what we need to account for the opacity and hyperintensional failures of substitutivity.

Other mental states concerning public language also can be described: To produce an *ambiguous* sentence from an unambiguous sentence in LOT is for the compiler, working conversely from its usual mode, to produce a public sentence that it could have produced from another sentence in LOT. To understand a sentence as ambiguous is for a person's compiler to find two nonequivalent sentences in LOT or it specifies different sets of instructions for verifying it. To understand a sentence as *deficient in meaning* is for a person's compiler to be unable to complete the construction of its verification conditions. To *come tardily to an understanding* of what one hears only after a lapse of some time, appreciating a joke for example, is due to the lapse of time before the success of its compilation enters consciousness. For people who speak different languages to *believe the same thing*, despite their speech differences, is for each of them to construct the same LOT sentence.

## §2. Defining the issue between the replacement strategy and its representationalist alternatives.

Placing the conjecture about the nature of the directed-toward relation in a more general context than in just the sententialist replacement strategy, any representationalism must take stands on the nature of the relation and the attaching of meanings to representations. Here's the question that's emerged as the central one to answer: Is that which attaches meaning to symbols something internal to the person (along with the symbol that's the vehicle of the meaning) or not? In other words, do the properties intrinsic to a person determine the contents of her attitudes? The conjecture stated above suggests they do.

Intrinsic properties of an object don't involve other things, are not relational properties of the object. For example, I'm characterized intrinsically by such traits as my height and my shape, for height and shape are intrinsic properties. I'm also characterized extrinsically in relation to other things, as an uncle and a computer-literate person, for example. A person's intrinsic properties are those of its properties that are not relational—see section D for relational properties.

The thesis of **semantic internalism** is that certain of a person's intrinsic properties suffice to determine the semantic content of the person's attitudes, or at least that part of their content that accounts for opacity and hyperintensionality. (This thesis is not to be confused with epistemic internalism, a thesis in epistemology, which is of no concern to us here, about what it is to have knowledge.) One motive for the semantic thesis of internalism is that folk psychology makes the causal efficacy of a person's attitudes depend on their contents. Moreover, the causal properties of things depend ultimately on their intrinsic properties. An attitude's content affects its efficacy, but its efficacy is only affected by an individual's intrinsic properties. So content is an intrinsic property. Semantic internalism is a way of articulating how the causally efficacious and the contentful are the same thing. A conjecture I stated earlier was that a person's responding appropriately to some sentences attaches meaning to all the sentences connected to them in one way or another. The conjecture suggests semantic internalism is true: When people understand what their attitudes are directed toward, that which they understand is internal to them.

We should not use the phrase "in the mind" to define the internality proposed by semantic internalism. It's not the thesis that meanings are "in the mind." That phrase has a traditional meaning in philosophy. Something's "in the mind" if its existence depends on its being an object of thoughts. That's the way Berkeley used it. In contrast, something's internal to a person if its existence depends on the person's nonrelational properties, which can be of any sort, including nonsemantical and nonmental.

Although semantic internalism has been a common accompaniment to sentimentalism, and so it's our focus of interest, we'll get a better sense of what's at stake by first looking at its opposite: To say a person's meanings are *not* determined by her intrinsic properties, is to adopt the thesis of **semantic externalism**: Thus Hilary Putnam's remark, "'meanings' just ain't in the head." But what then would meanings be, if they're determined by a person's extrinsic or relational properties? What, in other words, is the positive thesis of semantic externalism? Semantic externalism is a thesis about the meanings of the words and sentences that occur in minds: The words' meanings are external to the minds.

Beware of trivializing the thesis. Externalism's not a thesis that the meanings of terms are their extensions, any more than internalism is a thesis that extensions are not meanings in any sense of the word. Nor is it a thesis concerning the about-position of *de re* reports, which everyone agrees is not for stating what's in the mind of the person reported on. Semantic externalism would be true by definition of the names in the

about-position.[1] Semantic externalism becomes interesting only because
> •it's applied to the nonce names in the mind of the person who
> has the *de re* attitude and to what the that-clauses of reports
> express, and because
> •it seeks to put even the meanings of that-clauses outside the
> head, depending on extrinsic properties of persons, and yet
> •preserves the data of the opacity and hyperintensionality of
> those that-clauses, features that are not features of about-posi-
> tions.

In other words the externalist will put meanings outside the person but
have them conform to nonextensional identity conditions.

As applied to the meanings of that-clauses, semantic externalism is the
thesis that to specify the meaning of a vivid name or a that-clause, i.e., of
that which an attitude is directed toward, one must specify features of the
environment of the person who has that attitude. Those features are an
indispensable part of the meaning. When we defined representationalism
in section P, we noted that the object of the directed-toward relation was
a representation *in situ*. Semantic externalism directly contradicts the
internalist over whether this site extends beyond the person and moment.
If that's right, then externalism is a kind of representationalism, since it has
not given up on that inner representation, but is only disputing the way to
assign meaning to it.

### §3. The evidence that a person's intrinsic properties do not fix meanings.

Hilary Putnam argued for semantic externalism in lectures beginning in
1968, publishing his "twin earth" thought experiment in 1973 and again
in 1975, greatly expanded. His argument was clarified and extended by
Tyler Burge in 1982, and Putnam accepted the clarification.[2] Since the
thought experiment which Burge develops makes it clearer that the
internal or external nature of the nonextensional meaning of that-clauses
is at issue, I'll state Burge's version first.

The thought experiment has three steps:
> •First step: We imagine that Belia has *our* concept of arthritis,
> but gets a bit of it wrong. For instance she thinks arthritis is
> identical to rheumatism, and so can occur in muscle and bone as
> well as in the joints. Defined strictly, arthritis is a disease only of
> joints. Despite getting a bit of the concept wrong, we know she
> does have our concept, if the identity is established by the fact

that she intends to have the community's concept, intends us to understand her as having that one, and when we correct her she accepts our correction. Rep will report that Belia believes that arthritis can be in the bone. He rightly identifies her belief as employing the concept of arthritis.[3] Note that, because of her erroneous application of the idea of arthritis to disease that's not in a joint, her concept cannot have quite the same role in her thinking that a correct concept would've had.

●Second step: We imagine a situation, where Belia is exactly the same as she is in the first step, but counterfactually^ the people in her community all agree with her that arthritis covers rheumatism of the bone as well as of the joints.

●Third step: We're invited to agree that, in the counterfactual situation, despite the concept, which the counterfactual Belia has, being similar to our own concept of arthritis, it's *not our own*. Rep should *not* report that Belia believes that arthritis is in the bone. She believes some other disease is in the bone, despite the fact that she uses the word "arthritis" to name it.

The conclusion of semantic externalism about arthritis follows: Since Belia's intrinsic states are the same in steps one and two, and only her environment and her community differ from step one to step two, the meaning of "arthritis," which changed from step one to step two, is not determined by what is actually intrinsic to Belia. Externalism in general follows to the extent that the concept "arthritis" is typical of concepts.

Although we must bring in Belia's community to identify the meaning of her word "arthritis," we don't cede to the community control over the that-clauses of reports of her beliefs, which would make them referentially transparent contexts. Rep's report, true in the first instance, that Belia believes that arthritis can occur in the bone, might turn to false in the same scenario with a coextensive term replacing the term "arthritis," even though externalism must mention something external to Belia's mind in specifying the meaning each term has for her. For she remains in charge of the that-clause, and she might reject that substitution in it.

A meaning of "arthritis" that depends thus on a community is customarily called "**wide content**" or "broad content" since, to specify it, one must mention things in the person's environment. It contrasts with "narrow content," which would be a meaning specifiable without such reference. We must be careful not to beg some questions here. When Putnam introduced the distinction between narrow and wide (or broad), he was thinking of two ways of individuating *psychological states*, narrowly in terms of their intrinsic qualities only or broadly in terms of their relations to environments. According to externalism, only broad psychological states are states directed toward something and only broad states can be contentful. The term "narrow content" would be an oxymoron.

It would be wrong to think that people might describe their psychological states as directed toward contents in both these ways, the broad way being extensional and the narrow way nonextensional. That identification of the broad with the extensional is one of the things Burge corrected. The broad is nonextensional meaning, since it's the content that people's attitudes are directed toward. And since the broad is nonextensional, the narrow is superfluous for semantics.

Nevertheless, both the terms, "narrow" and "wide" or "broad," came to be applied to the contents as well as to psychological states, despite the externalists' claim that content was only wide. By 1985 their opponents managed to stick the adjective "narrow" to content also. The phrase appeared that year in an article by Brian Loar. However, one of narrow content's chief defenders in the years following, Jerry Fodor, abandoned it as superfluous in 1993.[4] The status of narrow content is still unsettled. It's still in question whether people's attitudes do have as content something at all semantical in the narrow sense. Maybe in the narrow sense there are only psychological states which are instances of syntactic objects. Let's use the term "narrow psych-states" for the time being until we're presented with an argument that these states of mind are contentful in some narrow sense of content.

Here's such an argument: The relation of narrow psych-states to wide contents could be this:

> If one person in a constant environment has states of mind that don't differ in their intrinsic properties, and so are the same psych-states, then they don't differ in wide content either.

More generally, in the mathematical sense of function,^ narrow psych-states within the confines of a single person have the prerequisite feature to be a function from some or all of that person's environmental contexts to the wide contents for that person. (I'll say more about that "some or all" in a moment.) Contrary to the suggestion implicit in their names, a narrow psych-state is not *a part* of wide content. Forget parts; think functions. Narrow psych-states and wide contents are related like the way the mass of an object is related to its weight: Given the object's context, namely, given a gravitational field and the object's position in that field, its mass determines its weight. Similarly, given a person's environment, her psych-state determines her wide content. The structure you should have in mind is $f(x)=y$, where $x$ covers all the external stuff and $y$ is the meaning. The psych-state is the f. Nothing in the counterfactual situation just considered in Burge's thought experiment, or in the next thought experiment involving twins, undermines this purely intrapersonal relationship between the narrow and the wide. For the experiments involve varying the $x$. This functional relation is consistent with the narrow psych-state being the instantiation of a syntactic state merely. Perhaps, however, the state's determining this sort of function may endow it with enough semanticity to be a content also.

Reference to a community of speakers is not the only way that wide content can invoke the person's environment. It may bring in also the things that are being talked about or things like those things, which the person experienced before. For example, Hilary Putnam's **twin earth thought experiment** in favor of wide content has us imagine:

> a duplicate (in German, *Doppelgänger*) of Belia, varying in no way in her internal states from our familiar Belia, but living on Twin Earth where everything is much the same as here, except there's a clear liquid in the lakes which can be used to quench thirst, can boil and freeze, and in general replaces water in the everyday life of Twin Belia. But it's not water, for it's not made of two hydrogen atoms connected to an oxygen atom. Since Twin Belia is a duplicate of Belia, we imagine some ignorance to protect the duplication: Belia does not know that water is $H_2O$ and Twin Belia doesn't know her liquid is, let's say, XYZ. What Twin Belia says sounds very much like English, and she calls that liquid "water." She uses that word very much the way Belia uses it, although the meaning of "water" for Twin Belia is not water; it's that other stuff, water's twin. Our conclusion must be the same as it was in the case of arthritis. Since Belia and Twin Belia are alike in all their intrinsic properties, but the sound "water" as it comes out of their mouths does not have the same meaning, the meaning of "water" is not in their intrinsic properties.

Generalizing, if "water" is a typical word, a word's meaning is wide content, that is, it's the $y$ value of a function when applied to an $x$ covering the word-user's world of referents, extensions, and truth values as well as her community of other users of the word.

A third experiment will help refine externalism. Gareth Evans presented another thought experiment involving one person at two times, which we can derive from the twin earth experiment simply by dismissing

Twin Belia. Instead let Belia herself be transported during her sleep to Twin Earth. Upon waking up she notices no difference at all. She drinks water's twin and is refreshed. She says to herself,

"That was good water."

Did she say something true? Evans suggests that at least on the morning of her waking, she said something false. For it was water's twin, not water, that she found so good.

This result might seem to suggest that a narrow psych-state is something semantical after all, a narrow content. For she carried her meaning with her to the new context. But the falsity of her remark is explained by an extrinsic property of Belia, something in her history, namely, how she learned the word "water." To see this, let's return to the account of a narrow psych-state as a function from contexts to wide contents. I hedged by saying it was a function from "some or all" contexts. The Evans experiment suggests that in order to state this function correctly we must separate genuine demonstrative words from words like "water" and "arthritis." Belia's word "that" is a genuine demonstrative and it's associated with a function from contexts to meanings, just as a psych-state is associated with a function from contexts to meanings, so that her word "that" does indeed refer to the twin water she drank. In contrast, words such as "water" have the property of being modally rigid designators, like proper names. That seems to be the way to interpret the Putnam and Burge thought experiments. The terms "arthritis" and "water" are modally rigid designators, because their referents won't change with change to a counter-factual scenario. Their meaning is fixed once and for all in the learning of them. So rigid designators have broad content as their meaning, with the original context of reference-fixing being the controlling context. The narrow psych-states underlying their use cannot be functions from any and all the contexts, which Belia may find herself in, to their extensions or referents. For if they were, Belia's use of the word "water" on Twin Earth would have referred to water's twin, and she'd have said something true. But what she said was false. So it looks like the function must be stated for modally rigid designators this way instead:

> The psych-state associated with a person's use of a modally rigid designator is a function from *the contexts in which she learned the word* to their referents in those contexts, such that the extension of the word consists of those referents and all the other things essentially the same as them.

In other words, the $x$ in $f(x)=y$ includes a person's history. I believe Putnam intended this historical dimension of externalism to be an outcome of his experiment too. In section O, when we discussed the meaning of kind-terms, we built this reference to history into their meaning.

Evans goes on to suggest that if Belia stayed for a very long time on Twin Earth, say the rest of a very long life, gradually her beliefs about what she drinks there would come to be true ones. So even the principle we just stated is not quite right, in that some factors can outweigh the control of the learning environment over the extension of a term. Perhaps her intention to conform to the language practices of her community (as in the first of our thought experiments) takes precedence. Let this pass for now; we return to it in section Y.

### §4. A person's intrinsic properties suffice to identify that which she understands.

Our three thought experiments can be interpreted to support the thesis that there's no use for narrow content in a theory of meaning. Semantic internalists tend to be more accommodating in their interpretations of the thought experiments, i.e., more syncretist^: For internalists the experiments only show a theory of meaning must invoke both narrow and wide contents. A statement of the identity conditions for **narrow content** is given by internalist David Lewis:

> if [persons] X and Y are intrinsic duplicates, and if they live under the same laws of nature, and if they are the same in kind, then they must be exactly alike in narrow content.[5]

By restricting the duplication to what's intrinsic to X and Y, we allow their environments to be different. Lewis refers to the laws of nature and so his internalism has let a bit of extrinsicness into the characterization of narrow content. Belia and the counterfactual Belia (or Twin Belia or Belia after transport to Twin Earth) do fulfill the conditions which Lewis specifies, so that the pairs share narrow content. According to the externalist interpretation of the thought experiments we just performed, however, they don't share a meaning, and so narrow content is a useless notion. They only share a nonsemantical psychological state. According to the externalist, a narrow psychological state, being what Belia and Twin Belia have in common, will explain the common features of their behavior. Since they're duplicates for the purpose of understanding the causation of their behavior, the narrowly individuated states of their thoughts will be the causes of their behavior, and also the explanation of why they behave similarly. That causal similarity leaves content undetermined. Causation's one thing, semantics quite another.

Lewis objects to this separateness on several grounds. One is that it's a hasty generalization from an experiment based on a few ideas, arthritis, water, and a few dozen others. The thought experiment would have to work on every concept in order for this separateness to be concluded, and there are beliefs for which it cannot be made to work. For example, Belia believes that *the disease her community calls "arthritis"* can occur in bone. The concept she uses in this sentence is not her concept of arthritis (which is identical to the community's concept), but this one: disease her community calls "arthritis." This concept is not affected by the change to the counterfactual situation in the thought experiment because the reference of "community" changes with the change in situation. Rep reports truly in the first scenario, Belia believes that the disease her community calls "arthritis" includes inflammation of bone. And he still reports the same truly in the second scenario. Belia's belief was false in the first scenario, and true in the second scenario, but the meaning of the words believed was unchanged from one scenario to the next, despite the difference of the communities referred to. (Recall, these experiments are supposed to show the externality of an aspect of meaning other than extensions, namely that aspect of meaning which is prior to extensions and determinative of them.) The case is similar, if Belia and Twin Belia conceptualize *liquid my community calls "water,"* because, although both the community and the extension of "liquid" changes, what their words mean is the same when they both believe the words, "the liquid my community calls 'water' is potable." Lewis thinks there are many such concepts that resist the intuitions evoked by the Putnam-Burge type thought experiments.

Just what is the narrow content of LOT, stated more informatively than in terms of its mere locale? A good first approximation is that *concepts* are narrow content. What are concepts? A common internalist answer refers to **conceptual role semantics**. Mental acts are not just differentiated intrinsically by their syntactic differences and extrinsically by what they refer to. A person's mental acts are differentiated from one another in a third way that's both intrinsic and semantic. So much is a matter of agreement between conceptual role semantics and the traditional accounts of concepts associated with Aristotle and the early modern period. In contrast to the earlier accounts, however, conceptual role semantics differentiates a person's concepts in a holistic way, whereas the traditional theories differentiated them in a more atomistic way. Conceptual role semantics differentiates them by invoking their interactions with other concepts, and that leads to holism.^ The semantic individuation of one concept invokes a role a symbol plays in a person's thought, which connects it with other symbols, and they in turn invoke still others, until one has a grand network of many of them, if not the totality of them.

According to the conceptual role semantics attached to sententialism, the **concept** associated with a word is a role which the word plays in a person's inner life. Don't say that a concept plays a role. The concept *is* the role played by a symbol. Symbols in different languages may play the same role and so express the same concept. In consequence they are translations of one another. The role is a hybrid of a logical role and a causal role. A word's logical role is its place in a syntactic pattern of implication and probabilistic relevance relations; its causal role is its place in a pattern of causes and effects.

Note how conceptual role semantics is a natural addition to the representationalisms employing the replacement strategy: Sentialism provides us with the internal entities that play the internal causal role. Even the verbless language, Jumblese (section Q), provides names. Conceptual role semantics seeks to derive many of the aspects of meaningfulness from the causal and logical roles that words and sentences play in mediating the causal connections between a person's senses and her muscular and glandular reactions, i.e., her behavior. For example, two concepts may happen to have the same extensions and even intensions, but differ in role, and so we get hyperintensionality immediately. Another good consequence is an account of conceptual creativity: New concepts are just symbols in new patterns of causality and logic. The causal role here envisioned contrasts with the causal rapport we discussed in Part II, for causal rapport connects a person to her environment. Causal role is therefore a specification of narrow content, inner causes and effects, whereas causal rapport goes with wide content.

I introduced the principle of semantic compositionality in section P to account for the meaning of compound expressions in terms of the meanings of their simple components, but I left open how to think of the meaning of simple expressions. Conceptual role semantics repairs that hiatus. It invokes the synergy between syntax and semantics in a way that complements semantic compositionality. For a noncompound symbol's meaning comes from the syntactical constructions it enters into and from the syntactic transformations, e.g., implications, permitted because of its presence in them. In other words, syntax and formal logic make the meanings of the symbols in LOT's lexicon. They then combine to make the meanings of the constructions by compositionality.

One of the originators of conceptual role semantics was Wilfrid

Sellars, who attributed it to Kant! Sellars contrasted conceptual role semantics with pre-Kantian theories of concepts.[6] One of them is an Aristotelian theory about how people form their concepts of things by "abstraction" (not the same as the attribute-abstraction defined in section D), which has lost popularity because abstractionism misconstrues the way perception is necessary to knowledge. Contrary to abstractionism, the human intellect cannot perceive and then abstract its concepts from its perception. Nor does the early modern philosophers' weakening of abstractionism (to a matter of an idea's copying one of the things it's an idea of) fare any better. Contrary to their resemblance theory of ideas, concepts do not have to be related to what they are concepts of by any relation of resemblance. Rather the intellect is preprogrammed to apply some of its concepts to extract the useful information inherent in perception, and is free to create other concepts, in terms of which it formulates the hypotheses it tests against experience. We'll leave the discussion of perception to the next two sections. Let it suffice for now (*pace* Fodor[7]) that conceptual role semantics provides a more defensible account of concepts to replace the theory of abstraction and its equally slavish successors.

(There's nothing inevitable about the association of sententialism with conceptual role semantics. Arch sententialist Jerry Fodor is the most vehement of critics of conceptual role semantics. He accepts an internalist causal thesis, which he calls individualism, asserting the causal sufficiency of internally individuated psychological states, but rejects the semantic thesis of internalism, that meaning is narrow content. Concepts for him can be defined atomistically in terms of broad content.)

Let's put some flesh on the bones of conceptual role semantics. Roles are roles in logical networks and roles in causal networks. Let's look first at causality. Lots of internal events have causal roles, but they aren't all therefore meaningful. A hiccup can have powerful ramifications, but that does not make it a word. So conceptual role theory must delimit what constitutes a meaning-making causal role. We can form a rough idea of what that might be from the roles of the thoughts in the following rational process:

> Belia feels thirsty.
> She desires to quench her thirst.
> She believes drinking water quenches thirst.
> She perceives water over there.
> She knows she can get the water.
> So she decides to drink that water.
> She notices us watching her and

is tempted to mischievously and counterpredictively pour the water over her head.

She resists temptation and drinks the water.

Belia smiles with satisfaction and winks at us.

This pattern is the same for Twin Belia, despite what she calls "water" not being water. Identity of their narrow content implies by Lewis's criterion identity of their behavior and identity of explanations of their behavior. The identity of narrow content is not just a matter of transitions from thought to thought, such as occurred when Belia made her decision, was tempted and resisted temptation; there are also transitions into thought from inner sensations such as in the first and last steps in the sequence and from the senses as in the fourth step, and there are transitions out of thought to behavior as in the second to last step. So I would not favor calling a concept just the inferential role of a word; it's a more inclusive role than that. It includes causal connections to sensory input and motor output. Obviously, the role of the word "water" must include the fact that visual and tactile sensations of a certain type can induce one to assent to the word if queried whether one is sensing water. Similarly for all other names of perceptible things. (The externalist exerts pressure at precisely this point.)

As most philosophers develop it, conceptual role semantics is not innocent metaphysically. In stating the conceptual roles, they try not to make use of any notions that presuppose meaningfulness, like purpose and the semantics of logic. With this motivation, conceptual role semantics is often called "causal role semantics." I put off to section Y any discussion of this application of conceptual role semantics to the naturalization project. At best, folk psychology is noncommittal on such a project. If we need to bring in mentalistic notions to delimit the conceptual or meaning-making causal roles, there's nothing wrong with doing so, since we're not engaged in naturalization here. Notice that I referred to logic as well as causality in stating the conceptual-role-semantical definition of a concept. A naturalizer would consider that redundant, since he'd say logic is inference from premise to conclusion, and inferring, when treated merely syntactically, is simply cause and effect. Later in this section we'll have reason to back off from so swift an equation of logic with causality.

The obstacle to any simple reduction of conceptual role semantics to causal role semantics is the fact that each type of mental event or state is the intersection^ of two types at least. One type consists of the acts and attitudes, for example, wanting or recalling; the other is what the attitude is directed toward, say, to be a movie-star, to be in pictures. An attitude is the conjunction of a causal state and a contentful state. Wanting to be in pictures, then, is one conjunctive type, the attitude plus what the attitude is directed toward. Recalling being in pictures is another conjunctive mental event. A simplistic causal role semantics would say the meanings of *what the attitudes are directed toward* are determined by the causal roles *the attitudes* play in a person's mental life. Let me say that again: The meaning of one thing, the sentence, is given by the causal role of another thing, the attitude. How peculiar! Perhaps Harman's identification of the sentence with the mental act, mentioned in section P, will overcome this obstacle. In the meantime let's savor the difficulty.

It's not problematic to connect the kinds of attitudes to causal roles. If we leave out the content of an attitude and consider only the kind of attitude, say a believing or a wanting, one's being in that very generic kind of state implies one has the very generic causal features of a purposive being. The generic attitudes would be defined and distinguished from one another by the generic functions they serve, their goals. In the following conditionals, which I repeat from section C, take $s$ to be a state of affairs that may obtain regardless of the believer's conceptual abilities to express it, and $p$ is a state of affairs which the believer's conceptual abilities are adequate to capture; furthermore $s$ is the state of affairs that $p$ is most verisimilar$^$ to. Then, for any $p$, if one *believes* that $p$, then (i) one is in a state that, given optimal conditions, one is in (a) only if $s$ and (b) because of $s$, and (ii) it's a state of being disposed to act in ways that would tend to satisfy one's desires, whatever they are, in a world in which $s$ (together with one's other beliefs) were true. For any $q$, if one *desires* that $q$, then one is in a state of being disposed to act in ways that would tend to bring it about that $q$ in a world in which one's beliefs, whatever they are, were true.[8] The conditionals identifying each attitude refer to their causal roles.

The contents collect attitudes into mental types differently. A belief and a desire can have the same content, despite their different roles in causation. The contents themselves are individuated by their implication and relevance$^$ relations[9] to other contents. When the implication and relevance relations of two terms are the same, their content's the same. These relations are important for psychology to study, because they enhance a mind's adaptive plasticity of response to the extent that it exploits those relations. For example the belief that one is in pictures and the desire that one be in pictures are grouped together by virtue of their identical content. This ensures that they interact. In particular, in a rational person their interaction ensures that the desire is eliminated, since one does not desire what one has; rather one enjoys it. On the other hand, if the belief were that one was not in pictures, then the two would interact to yield a disposition to act to bring it about. Logical relations between contents are not functions in the sense of goal-directed dispositions, nor can any causal process simulate them completely since any content has an infinity of implicative connections. For any finite subset of them, there will be distinct propositions whose implications contain that subset. So nothing less than an infinite set of implications has a chance of characterizing an attitude's propositional content uniquely.

Logical relations exist between sentences, complete or incomplete, but many terms have content although they cannot stand as sentences, for example, "average," "swiftly," and "with." Nevertheless, they too have logical roles, which is the difference their presence in sentences makes to the sentences' logical relations. Thus propositional content is determined first, and then content is assigned to the sub-propositional parts of propositions.

How relate the causal role of an attitude to the logical role of a content? The logical role of a content constrains what states can co-occur with it and how the causality prompted by an attitude having that content will flow. Just how the constraint works is unclear; physics and chemistry recognize no constraints on the flow of causality in the brain other than physical and chemical ones. That's a problem for the naturalization project, which we're not engaged in. We must think in folk psychological terms, that cause and effect here connect mental states as reasons to the states they're reasons for. Even granted this, the constraint is contingent on the rationality of persons. The constraint can also be idiosyncratic, depending on a person's intelligence, personality, and character. Nevertheless, we say that it's in virtue of their contents that beliefs and desires have the effects they have.

Belia will exploit the logical roles of the contents of her attitudes to make decisions and inferences. The inferences she makes are a minuscule sample of all the inferences the logical roles of her contents warrant. Therefore reference to her actual inferences is not going to define conceptual roles, although reference to the infinite totality of logical relations does define them. So for now we leave logical roles coordinate with causal roles and not reduced to them.

## §5. Difficulties with conceptual role semantics.

Here are some criticisms of conceptual role theory in terms of logical and causal roles (offered by Fodor and Lepore[10]) along with some replies:

1. It does not define meanings in a way that allows them to combine in

the manner that compositionality requires. So it does not fit with sententialism too well after all. The conceptual role theorist can reply that compositionality is the pattern of operations on the simple syntactic items to yield the meanings of compound syntactic items; conceptual role semantics operates on the compound syntactic items to yield the meanings of the simple syntactic items. There's no circle here, since conceptual role semantics moves from *uninterpreted* syntactic structures to their roles and thence to assigning interpretations to the simple elements. Then semantic compositionality moves from the interpreted simple elements to assigning interpretions to the structures. Several other criticisms pertaining to the relation of compositionality to holistic semantics, of which conceptual role semantics is the chief instance, are also answered by Peter Pagin.[11]

2. It does not make anything but a contingent and seemingly arbitrary connection between a concept and what it's a concept of, as the Twin Earth thought experiments show, but this is counter-intuitive. The answer to this criticism is a fact we already mentioned, that in the intrapersonal and noncounterfactual case it's not a mere contingent connection. Within the person herself there cannot be two concepts identical in role but distinct in reference. We should ask why this is so. What is it about the individuation of roles of a term that, for that person, time, and environment, makes a term's role uniquely determine its extension? Somehow the roles of terms in people's thought model the roles of things in their world.

3. It is holistic, and that has bad consequences for the rest of philosophy. Peter Pagin defends semantic holism against this objection with great success. So here I'll only say that holism comes in degrees, and conceptual role semantics may be less holistic than Fodor portrays it as. First of all, the need for some approximation to atomism in a conceptual scheme may be satisfied, not by an atomism in the semantics of concepts, but in the epistemological role of observation sentences. These are discussed in section U.

Furthermore, even concerning the semantics of concepts, some implications are more central to concepts than others. We'll need to distinguish noun concepts from predicate concepts, because the central implications for nouns are different from those for predicates.

Take the case of nouns. Belia's concept of water, when she was a child living by the Atlantic, was most centrally defined by such facts as that

water is a kind of fluid, and
water divides into two subkinds, fresh water and salt water.
The parts of water are themselves water,
but water is a part of all living things.

The implications most central to a concept concern relations between more inclusive and less inclusive kinds and between parts and wholes. A recent proponent of this idea is Paul Thagard.[12] Here's a map of part of the concept of a primate's body. The solid lines represent part-whole relations. Read them as "[upper noun] has a [lower noun]." The broken lines represent kind-subkind relations. Read them as "[right noun] is a [left noun]."

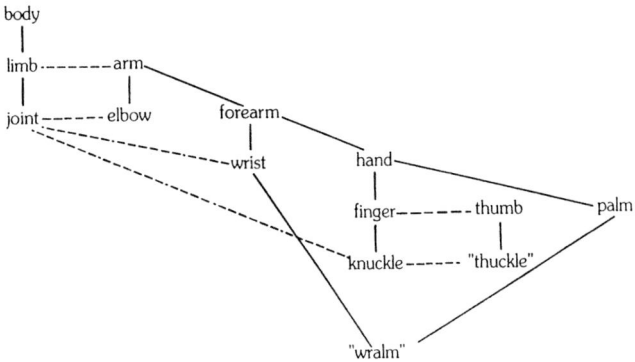

Figure S-1. Map of part of the concept of a primate's body, taken from Thomas Bever and Peter Rosenbaum, "Some Lexical Structures and Their Empirical Validity," in R. Jacobs and P. Rosenbaum, eds., *Readings in Transformational Grammar* (Ginn and Co., 1970) 7. The two items in quotation marks are not in the ordinary person's scheme of concepts, and Bever and Rosenbaum predict much greater resistance to adding "wralm" than "thuckle."

Less central, but still important characterizers of a concept are the universal generalizations it figures in, such as, to continue with the example of water, that fresh water quenches thirst, salt water does not. The most central implications for verbal and other predicative concepts, in contrast, are synonym and antonym relations, as well as universal generalizations.

This qualification, that implications vary in their centrality to the individuation of the concepts that occur in them, is still semantic holism, but not so holistic that no two people ever share the same concept. They do share the same concept if they accept the same relationships of kinds and parts that are at *the core* of the concept. Fodor and Lepore think that conceptual role semantics must either accept the incommensurability of the meanings of any two minds or buy into the idea that there's a class of truths besides logical truths which people cannot change their minds about. Contrary to the latter alternative, however, people can change their minds about the truth of the central implications. Two examples from the history of science: People can decide that whales are mammals, not fish. That's a change in their concept of whale. Or they may decide that the air in which things burn intensely is not air that lacks a part called "phlogiston," but is rather itself a part of normal air, namely, oxygen. That change in their conception of parts eliminated the concept of phlogiston from their repertory of concepts.

4. A criticism of my own: Conceptual role semantics seems well adapted to sententialism, but incompletely adapted to Jumblese, the verb-less language, and not well adapted to connectionistic representations. For neither of them seem to provide the formal entities which will be assigned a role. Jumblese can use the conceptual role account for its names but not for the predicates. Furthermore if Jumblese is combined with the no-name theory of beliefs in the first person and present tense, there are no names involved at all. Connectionism contrives to get to complete thoughts without recourse to any symbols. To account for all these beliefs we need a semantics that does not hang on the provision of syntactic or formal entities to play the roles. Thus conceptual role semantics is only part of the story of narrow content.

## §6. State-space semantics complements conceptual role semantics.

The idea of a state-space, however, does provide an account of the predicative concepts of Jumblese, and of the no-name and connectionist beliefs. A state-space is an abstract space with any number of dimensions which represent the independent parameters of a concept. Recall the six-dimensional space for recognition, which we used in the previous section. Similarly, the concept of color can be thought of as a space, this one of three dimensions: hue, saturation, and brightness. The dimension of hue is circular, being the familiar color wheel, showing the familiar color oppositions, red-green, blue-yellow, and the intermediate colors. Black and white are zero-hue, but occupy the polar positions in the brightness dimension, which can be thought of as poking through the center of the color wheel. The saturation dimension is the plane of the wheel, with colors most saturated at the extremes and becoming paler and more greyish as one approaches the center. In this way we envision a space where each position in the space represents a distinct color. Experiments on what colors are discriminable by the human eye made it feasible for psychologists to construct the Munsell color spheroid, bulging in places where people can discriminate more colors, puckered in places where they discriminate less.[13]

Suppose those who think in Jumblese can think that ripe strawberries are bright red. They do not have the predicates "ripe" or "are bright red." But they do have the name "strawberries." And they have the concept of being bright red in the sense that something in their minds has the structure of a Munsell color spheroid. We can add a dimension that stands for degree of ripeness. Then they think that ripe strawberries are bright red by simply placing the name into that spheroid in the region that represents bright red at the right place along the ripeness dimension. In fact, this way of thinking of predication yields an account of tacit knowledge. The tacitly known principle, "the riper the redder," for example, represents a trajectory down from white through pink to red with increasing ripeness. Other obvious truths are implicit in the very structure of the color spheroid, such as that blue is different from red. The generic truths, e.g., red is a color, require that the color spheroid be itself located in a higher dimensional space, of which color is just a region. That might be the space of sensory qualities.

Now imagine that *all* predicative concepts can be represented by abstract spaces like this one. For instance, the concept of loving/being loved will have dimensions defining lover or beloved, the kind of love (parental, filial, friend, spousal, etc.), intensity of love, and so on. For Othello to think that Desdemona loves Cassio is for him to have the structural equivalent of such a space in his mind and he places the two names "Desdemona" and "Cassio" in the appropriate places in that space.

A totally comprehensive state-space, with as many dimensions as there are possibilities for description, is called a **logical space**. If we think of the dimensions as corresponding to all the logically independent atomic propositions, and the values on each dimension as just two, true or false, then we get the logical space of contemporary modal logic: The occupants of points in this space are complete worlds, in the sense of alternative total universes. The idea of a logical space goes back to the early Wittgenstein.[14]

Beliefs in the present tense and first person, to which the no-name theory applies, still exploit concepts in the sense in which concepts are state-spaces, even though no names are located in them. The spaces have to be thought of as having origin points, as in geometry: When imposing a scale on a space, you decide on a place with the zero coordinates. The best model for this case is a map of your actual space. If you're in a building, you can imagine the building from a bird's eye view and your place in the building. That way you think of yourself in the third person. Now to convert that to a map with yourself as the point of origin, just describe the building not as the bird sees it, but as you would if you were to travel from where you are to each of its rooms. In other words, the building is mapped from your perspective. If we imagine that state-spaces do not have to have a constant scaling, but that there's a space for which oneself at the present moment always provides the point with the zero coordinates, so that it's always a perspectival map, then one can have thoughts without any names at all.

State-space semantics is an application of connectionism to semantics, and today is most closely associated with Paul Churchland, who defends it very well against its critics.[15] The Churchlands (Patricia as well as Paul) are even better known as critics of folk psychology. They espouse an extreme form of revisionary metaphysics,^ which claims that propositional attitudes are as unreal as phlogiston and other constructs of false theories. In a true theory, they will be replaced by brain structures, and people's current semantics will be replaced by something that does not depend on the concepts of truth and reference. Contrary to the Churchlands' intent, however, here I'm proposing state-space semantics as one of the ways a folk psychologist can envision the content of attitudes. I see no reason to think that folk psychology is locked into just one way of thinking of content. Nor does the folk psychologist need to give up the semantics of truth and reference but only to generalize it; indeed folk semantics is already broader than the logician's in that it countenances verisimilitude.^ As I've been saying, I'm a syncretist. One need not choose between concepts as roles that words play, and concepts as state-spaces. Folk psychology can have both, and indeed one who thinks in Jumblese needs both.

# Notes

1. This misunderstanding of semantic externalism is embodied in Jerry Fodor's early discussion of it in his critique of Putnam, "Methodological Solipsism Considered as a Research Strategy in Cognitive Psychology," reprinted in his *Representations* (1981) 246. His own version of semantic externalism, however, embraces extensionality. See his *The Elm and the Expert: Mentalese and Its Semantics* (1994), ch. 2.

2. Many of the important papers are collected in Andrew Pessin and Sanford Goldberg, eds., *The Twin Earth Chronicles* (1996). Although Putnam's 1975 paper, "The Meaning of 'Meaning'" is in this collection, his 1973 paper,

"Meaning and Reference," *Journal of Philosophy*, (70) 699-711, is not. The 1982 Burge paper I refer to is his "Other Bodies," reprinted in the Pessin and Goldberg collection, where Putnam states his agreement with the criticism on p. xxi. Putnam stakes his claim to priority in footnote 7 of his "The Meaning of 'Meaning,'" which refers to his 1968 lectures. But Gareth Evans, "The Causal Theory of Names" *Proceedings of the Aristotelian Society*, supplementary volume 47 (1973) 187-208, develops a thought experiment with many of the same externalist implications as Putnam's twin earth experiment and was published contemporaneously with Putnam's "Meaning and Reference."

3. And, for an ironic example, we rightly report, using the common concept of gold, that Hilary Putnam has the following ridiculous beliefs: ". . . chemically pure gold is nearly white. But the gold we see in jewelry is typically yellow (due to the presence of copper) . . ." "The Meaning of 'Meaning,'" p. 33 in Pessin and Goldberg. Don't believe a word of it.

4. Brian Loar, "Social Content and Psychological Content," reprinted in the Pessin and Goldberg collection. "Narrow content" appears on p. 187. Loar attributes the term's use to "many." Jerry Fodor's abandonment of the notion is in his book, *The Elm and the Expert: Mentalese and Its Semantics* (1994).

5. In his article in *A Companion to the Philosophy of Mind*, 425.

6. Wilfrid Sellars, "Being and Being Known," ch. 2 in his *Science, Perception, and Reality* (1963).

7. Jerry Fodor, *In Critical Condition: Polemical Essays on Cognitive Science and the Philosophy of Mind* (1998). The chapters of Part II attack conceptual role semantics in detail, but he chiefly objects to its holism.

8. Both necessary conditions are almost verbatim from Robert Stalnaker, *Inquiry* (1984) 15-18. He cites Daniel Dennett, "Intentional Systems," *Journal of Philosophy* 68 (1971) 3-22.

9. Relevance^ relations are probabilistic dependencies, explicated in probability theory. This way of developing conceptual role semantics was presented by Hartry Field in his "Logic, Meaning, and Conceptual Role," *Journal of Philosophy*, 74 (1977) 379-409.

10. Jerry Fodor and Ernest Lepore, *Holism: A Shopper's Guide* (1992).

11. Peter Pagin, "Is Compositionality Compatible with Holism?" *Mind and Language*, 12 (1997) 11-33. Perhaps difficulties found in formalism^ are difficulties for representationalism in general. Formalism, due to the mathematician David Hilbert, was shown to be inadequate by the work of Kurt Gödel in the 1930s. An analogous defect will occur in representationalism, when it's taken as a replacement strategy, only if all representations are like mathematical representations.

12. Paul Thagard, *Conceptual Revolutions* (1992), sections 2.5f. The distinction between noun concepts and predicate or verb concepts is on p. 28.

13. Unabridged Merriam-Webster dictionaries have a picture of the spheroid under "color." For the story of this space see C. L. Hardin, *Color for Philosophers* (1986) 159ff. My use of the sphere is meant only to illustrate a conceptual space, not to immerse us in controversies about color.

14. An exposition of Wittgenstein's concept of logical space is ch. 3 of Eric Stenius, *Wittgenstein's 'Tractatus'* (1960).

15. "Conceptual Similarity across Sensory and Neural Diversity: The Fodor-Lepore Challenge Answered" in Paul M. Churchland and Patricia S. Churchland, *On the Contrary: Critical Essays 1987-1997* (1998). See also "To Transform the Phenomena: Feyerabend, Proliferation, and Recurrent Neural Networks" in the same volume.

# T. Quine's Arguments against Non-notional Perception.

We can divide the sentences of the language of thought, or its subjective propositions, if the language of thought is Jumblese and sentences come only in speech, into three general categories: those formulating the mind's intake from the senses, those formulating the mind's output to the muscles and glands, and the intermediary subjective propositions or sentences. Let's examine more closely the first of these categories, which covers the items that formulate our perceptions.

## §1. Sentences that express our perceptions without referring to anything.

Concerning a subjective proposition's concrete embodiment, might it be a medadic twiddler? If it's medadic, it contains no names. That would be another blow to sententialism, because of its reliance on syntax. Quine's theory of perception delivers this blow. More importantly concerning the subjective propositions' semantics, might perception be insufficient to settle questions of reference? In other words, might perception underdetermine semantics? That would be a shocker, and Quine's theory of perception delivers this shock.

In section J we discussed Quine's favoring of the notional propositional attitudes over the relational ones. This favoring of complete propositional contents extends even to his analysis of perception. In his *Pursuit of Truth* he says:

> [O]bservation terms, retrospectively seen as designating objects, are best viewed at their inception rather as one-word observation sentences. The same attitude best befits the ascription of perceptions: think of '*x* perceives *y*' in the image rather of '*x* perceives that *p*'. We say 'Tom perceives the bowl' because . . . we fancy ourselves volunteering the observation sentence 'Bowl' . . . (p. 65)

On its face, it's quite counter-intuitive to say: The report, "Tom sees a bowl," should be analyzed as *de dicto* with a that-clause:

"Tom sees that Bowl,"
where "Bowl" is a complete sentence, not an ellipsis. For perception, which is seemingly paradigmatically relational, is here dressed up as notional. Really now! Why not instead regiment perception as something relational, like
"About the bowl, Tom sees that it's present"?
Quine rejects this alternative.

Perhaps you don't think Quine is being so radical. You may think that, although Tom's public utterance prompted by his perception was a one-word exclamation, the sentence which he thinks in his LOT is more complex. Don't suppose that Quine supposes that. Suppose instead that even in his LOT Tom formulates his perception first in a one-word sentence. Or at least he did for the first weeks of his life, or at least the early mammalian ancestors of the human species did.

I can reconcile Quine's notional understanding of perception with the obvious fact that it's relational. Rephrasing Quine's claim about reports as a claim about perception itself, to perceive is simply to discriminate the true from the false. People discriminate the two directly from the condition of their senses without constructing the truth-value from perceived referents and their perceived predicates. Indeed, discrimination of truth-values, not discrimination of referents by acts of pointing, is the primordial semantic ability. In the case of the primordial semantics of the one-word sentence, "Bowl!" ask not what it's true about; ask what it's true to. (A complete proposition has truth-to; an attribute has truth-about.) At least some truth-to comes before any truth-about. The truth-to that comes before any truth-about is the truth that comes to people by way of their causal rapport with the world around them. People justify their truths-about only after they acquire these truths-to. That reversal of logical and genetic dependency is counter-intuitive^ to many, and this section addresses that counter-intuition in order to weaken it. For Quine's right. Quine attacks the counter-intuition with a syntactic point and a semantic point. We begin with the semantics.

Perhaps, since truth is as obviously relational as reference is, while the true sentence is the notion—the notion is true to the world—we have here an insight that the relational and notional need not be mutually exclusive in all cases, as we've been assuming since we introduced this contrast in section A. One and the same mental state can be both. Whether there's exclusion of the notional from the relational, so that a mental state cannot be both at once, depends on the object-relata^ of the relational. According to most philosophizing about perception, the object-relata have been things, the relata of the relation of reference, named in the about-position. Let's pause to reflect: What if that which an attitude is true-or-false to is not anything it's about, but just the object-relatum of the relation of truth, namely, the world? In that case the folk psychologist can leave for later the imputing of acts of referring to perceivers and an ontology of referents for them to refer to.

You may protest: An **ontology** is a theory of the most general kinds of existents. For instance, our perception is not ontologically neutral; it's impregnated with the theory that we perceive bodies and persons. So a folk psychologist imputes an ontology of bodies and persons to perceivers. For bodies and persons are what the perceivers refer to. Ontology also concerns the number of things that exist, one (monism), two (dualism), many (pluralism). People's perceptions entail a pluralistic ontology, which the folk psychologist therefore imputes to them. The imputing of an ontology is the imputing of a semantics of reference. I reply: Quine is forcing us to pay more attention to the roots of reference and consequently of ontology.

The folk psychologist theorizes about the origin of semantics in five settings:

- ●Procedure: The mind processes the information it receives from the senses, deliberates and eventually decides on a course of action. In the flow of such thoughts, sentences expressing observations occur upstream. Sentences expressing intentions to act occur downstream.
- ●Ontogenesis: The newly born mind develops its most primitive skills and eventually comes to possess the full panoply of adult abilities.
- ●Phylogenesis: Since the human mind has many innate skills, which other primates possess some of, and other mammals possess still less of, the story of the human mind's origin from a common ancestor with very little mind is a story of the progressive accretion of mental abilities.
- ●Methodology in science: The problem of showing the evidential basis for our scientific theories is also a story of what comes first in a sense, and again this first thing is perception.
- ●Methodology in anthropology and linguistics: How does a linguist justify theories about an alien language when there's no one yet bilingual in it and his own?

In all these five settings for folk psychological theorizing about people's minds and minds other than people's, Quine's thesis is that there's a pre-ontological stage and we should make an issue of when reference comes in and what ontology of referents to impute to the person at the stage where ontology enters. We should not begin by simply assuming that reference occurs and we know which ontology to impute to a person (it would be our own, of course). It does not matter that the first three settings are directly about what's first in temporal order whereas the last two are directly about what's first in the order of justification. Quine's problematizing of ontology holds in both types of scenario.

Let's think primarily of the first of these five settings. Belia will represent the first scenario, and Rep will be in a position analogous to the linguist's in the fifth scenario as he speculates about Belia's LOT. Bypassing any imputing of ontology to a mind at the setting's beginning point has this consequence, that it removes the mutual exclusion of the relational mental state and the notional mental state, if we think that the initial mental state is relational but need not be described with an about-position. Also we must back off from tying the definition of causal rapport, presented in section H, to an assumption that the ontology of Belia's propositional attitudes *de re* is the ontology of true causal theories. The reporter reveals his own ontology in the way he fills in the about-position in his reports, but we can avoid committing the perceiver herself to any ontology by our definition of rapport. Lewis's definition of seeing, also presented in section H, is sufficiently noncommittal about ontology.

Let's explore the bypassing of ontology. Semantic ascent is our tool. Even with perception we can employ semantic ascent: To perceive is, in the usual case of an adult human being, to be ready to assent to an **observation sentence**. For one's sentence to be an observation sentence in Quine's sense, requires, first, that one's sensory neurons be stimulated appropriately during the period within which one would assent to it or dissent from it, the stimulation being the prompter of the assent or dissent, and secondly, that all members of a community agree on when it's correct to assent to it or dissent from it, so that a particular assent is to an observation sentence if all competent witnesses concur.[1] Let's go observe Belia again. With us is Rep, reporting Belia's attitudes as usual. Belia sees an animal run into the bushes. Thus, "Lo, woodchuck!" is the *dictum* that she'd utter or assent to upon perceiving what she took to be a woodchuck. Since Rep (and the rest of us) concur, Belia's "Lo, woodchuck!" is an observation sentence.

If the second of the two conditions does not hold, the sentence will at least be **observational for** the person who assents to it because of the stimulation.[2] Some upstream sentences in a person's LOT would be observational for her. We may also extend the first clause of the definition of an observation sentence for the sentences which are observational for her, so that the sensory neurons whose stimulation prompts the assent include a person's interoceptors (e.g., toothache) and proprioceptors (e.g., dizzy).

An ambiguity threatens the second clause of the definition of an observation sentence. Quine says that "all linguistically competent witnesses of the occasion" concur in assenting to the sentence. What if there are no witnesses other than Belia? Then it's true vacuously that all witnesses concur. Does that entail no difference between an observation sentence and a sentence that's observational for Belia in such cases? This is not what Quine means. Quine defines the notion of a sentence being "observational for a group" in this way:

> . . . [I] account a sentence observational for a group if it is observational for each member *and* if each would agree in assenting to it, or dissenting, on witnessing the occasion of utterance. (p. 43)

The second clause applies whether or not there are actually witnesses, for it's to be understood as a counterfactual conditional: All members of the group are such that, if they *were* to witness the occasion of Belia's assent to the sentence, they *would* assent too.[3] Let's take this to be a statement of what it is to be an observation sentence.

The first part of the definition of an observation sentence mentions sensory stimulation rather than the objects that caused the stimulation. That allows us to separate the actual assent to the sentence from any assent to the ontology seemingly implied by the sentence. In the example I gave a few paragraphs back about Belia and the woodchuck, I got ahead of Quine. I attributed an ontology of substances and bodies to Belia, since I said that she took herself to be perceiving *a woodchuck*, namely, a thing which belongs to the category of substance or body. If instead I only talk of her sensory stimulation, as Quine suggests, we leave Belia's ontology out of account at the start. So Quine's semantic point is that, although the sensory stimulation establishes something relational between Belia and some aspect of the world, it does not relate her to a *res* that's a part of the content of her belief, since a person's assent upon prompting by a pattern of stimulation could be non-ontological or pre-ontological in the most upstream stages of mental processing and probably is so for the initial stages of the other four settings.

Quine reinforces this semantical defense of notional perception with some reflections on syntax. The content of the belief is a sentence that's not divided up into subject and predicate; it's a **holophrastic sentence**, like "It's raining" or "Fire!" which have no semantically significant subjects, so no ontology. Neither does the sentence we began with, "Bowl." Neither does a baby's utterance, "Momma" or "Milk." (Quine coined the term "holophrastic" from the Greek adjective, *holon*, coupling it to "phrase," to describe sentences that are complete despite not being divided into subject and predicate.) The contrast to a holophrastic sentence is an **analyzed sentence**, one which displays its subject and predicate because it's analyzed into words. It would be convenient to say that holophrastic sentences lack syntax, whereas analyzed sentences are syntactically complex. But this would not be quite right. If a child utters "Milk!" when there's none near her, we understand it to be a command. When she utters, soothingly, "Ah, milk," she's making a statement, her command having been fulfilled. Near the end of section D, we made the distinction within sentences between mood indicators and sentence-radicals, and this distinction applies to holophrastic utterances. For the holophrastic command and the holophrastic statement shared a common sentence-radical expressing the same proposition. So there's that much syntactic complexity in a holophrastic utterance. But the sentence-radical in each is holophrastic, that is to say, lacking distinction of subject from attribute. Nevertheless, we can say this much: Holophrastic utterances offer no way for a syntactic analysis to take hold of them that posits in them subjects and predicates and quantification.^ Analyzed sentences do allow for that.

Rep's reports of perceptions are to be thought of as reporting holophrastic observation sentences:

> The content clause [of a report of someone's perception] purports to reflect the subject's state of mind rather than the state of things. From the ascriber's [e.g., Rep's] point of view it figures holophrastically; its component terms do not necessarily refer, here, as he means them to when he speaks for himself. (p. 68)

Quine also extends the concept of a holophrastic sentence to some sentences which do have subjects and predicates, namely the sentences used in reporting perceptions. For the purpose of understanding the truth they convey by virtue of the fact that one's assent to them is prompted by perception, their semantics can be described adequately as holophrastic, even though they can also be described as analyzed into subject and predicate. Semantics describes the meaning of sentences, not their word structure. Quine says of such an analyzed observation sentence,

As a response to neural intake, the sentence is holophrastic: the neural intake is keyed to the sentence as a monolithic whole, no matter whether the sentence was first acquired by simple ostension or by excursion through theory in the manner [in which we might learn 'There's some copper in the solution.']⁴

With the adjective "holophrastic" so extended to all observation sentences, let's refer to a sentence's **holophrastic sense**, as Quine once did,⁵ that is, a holistic^ mode of access to the sentence's truth-value, which is not meant to preclude analyzed modes of access. Actually, it's misleading to invoke holism to describe the absence of a division of subjects from predicates. For holism contrasts with atomism, and holophrastic observation sentences come as close to being isolatable and independent atoms of assent or dissent as anything does in our conceptual scheme. (That's qualified in section U.) In contrast, the assent to the analyzed sentences, if they do not have a holophrastic sense, is much more holistic in the sense of depending on the assent to other sentences.

Although we assumed at the outset in section A that notional and relational were mutually exclusive categories, we just faced up to the existence of a form of belief which looks like a mixture of both. So be it.

Let's return to a defense of a pre-ontological stage in each of the five settings. In the first three, where temporal order is paramount, perhaps it's easier to accept such a stage:

●In the phylogenetic setting, there would be animals so limited that their use of information simply does not get to a stage of ontology.

●Similarly for a newborn human being. Perhaps its first sensing is just of a "blooming buzzing confusion." Then ontological analysis kicks in.

●In the procedural setting, which covers even adult human perception, clearly people are conscious of their visual world as organized into bodies and persons, and so their perception is not ontologically innocent. Between the initial intake of sensory stimulation and their visual consciousness of their surroundings, there's two-tenths of a second of processing, in accordance with innate and learned procedures that are not innocent of theory. It's reasonable to suppose this processing begins with holophrastic formulations of the sensory intake.

The two settings where justification of our theories is paramount are more a matter of the theorist's analyzing the evidence so that it's pre-ontological, in order to avoid question-begging and vacuous justifications. In particular, in the fifth setting, of the linguist theorizing about another language, we see that the language's ontology is not delivered to him, take it or leave it, by an authoritative external source.

A critic of pre-ontological stages may think that, although a holophrastic utterance to a global stimulus, like "It's muggy" or "It's dusk," can be described correctly as pre-ontological, an utterance prompted by a focused overlap of certain kinds of stimulation is committed ontologically. But that's not so. For example, describe Belia's "Lo, woodchuck" like that, as a monolithic whole. Belia's observation sentence, described holophrastically, is prompted by just such a focused overlap of different kinds of stimulation. Nevertheless her utterance leaves it indeterminate whether Belia's assent commits her to reference, let alone to an ontology. In the justificatory scenarios, to call a sentence a holophrase is to say that the conditions of assent to it ignore its analysis, i.e., holophrase in these contexts is not a syntactic notion, but rather a way of describing the sentence by the speaker's relation to it.

### §2. Introduction of reference and an ontology of referents.

Let's now go to the next stage of complexity. The sentences require analysis into subject and predicate because there's inference going on that recombines subjects and predicates to form the inferred sentences. Subject terms give us reference. What referents are being referred to? If Belia uses the term "woodchuck" as a subject term, not merely as a holophrastic sentence, then what's the ontology of referents for that term? It could be any of:

> bodies, or
> universals, or
> events, or
> parts, or
> fusions, or
> cosmic complements of bodies, or even
> the stimulation, which she may be unaware of.[6]

These alternatives amount to our saying that her utterance of "I see the woodchuck" (where "woodchuck" is no longer a holophrastic sentence, but a term within a subject-predicate sentence) translates into our ontologically committed language as one of these sentences arbitrarily:

> I see the woodchuck body!
> I see woodchuckhood instantiated!
> I see one of a sequence of woodchuck-stages!

I see a bunch of undetached woodchuck parts!
I see a segment of the fused mass of woodchucky stuff!
I see the cosmic complement of a woodchuck!
I see woodchucky stimulation at my sensors!

Or Belia may be committed to no ontology at all:

I see being woodchucky going on there.

In fact, stimulation does underdetermine one's ontology, no matter how complex and focused the stimulation may be. As prompted simply by stimulation, any one of these ontologies will do equally well.

Do you think not? Try to imagine stimulation that distinguishes them. You will fail. For example, consider an ontology which recognizes only the **cosmic complement** of a body. The way we'd think of it, it's the entire universe, minus that body. So for each body, there's exactly one cosmic complement of it. A person who is stimulated by the body to say "Lo, body!" might be referring to its cosmic complement. There's no necessity that says the person must refer to the occupant of the space from which the stimulus comes. There's no necessity that, in pointing your finger, the object you intend must be at the target point; it may be all around that target point. The pointing will work just as well. You might object, when Othello suspected Desdemona of loving Cassio, surely he could not've meant Desdemona's cosmic complement loves Cassio's cosmic complement! Right. But who said his word "loves" means what our word means? Notice that the cosmic complement of the cosmic complement of body $x$ is identical to body $x$. With that it mind, perhaps Othello's word "(1) loves (2)" means "(1) is the cosmic complement of that which loves the cosmic complement of (2)." This predicate is true of the cosmic complements of $x$ and $y$ if and only if, as we'd say, $x$ loves $y$. Therefore, if Othello's word "Desdemona" means what we mean by the cosmic complement of Desdemona, and his word "Othello" is similarly construed, then there's nothing to choose between in the two readings.

It's the same with an ontology of **universals** as with cosmic complements. There's a woodchuck if and only if there's woodchuckhood instantiated. Perhaps for each thing there's a most salient universal it instantiates. A person stimulated by a body to say "Lo, body!" may be referring to the most salient universal the body instantiates. Think of how you point to a certain shade of blue; you find a particular thing that instantiates it. So, if a speaker might be pointing to a universal by pointing at a particular, then, despite our best efforts, we'll fail to show that sensory stimulation is determinative of the perceiver's ontological commitments.

The other ontologies are distinguished from each other by principles of theory. For example, an ontology of bodies or substances entails the thesis that time does not divide an object into parts. A substance is whole and entire in each of the moments of its existence, so that what there is of me today is identical to what there was of me yesterday. Such is not the case in an ontology of events. If I am reconceived to be an event, then I'm stretched in the time dimension, and time divides me just as space does, and rather more so, since I turn into a spacetime worm segmented by time. A substance ontology provides naturally countable units, unlike a mass ontology, which is the thesis that any part of mass X is also mass X, for example, all the parts of water are water. This ontology is rejected by atomic theory, since the parts of one water molecule are not water. Since all mass of a kind is part of the totality of the mass of that kind, it does not come in readily countable units. We could add countable units to a mass ontology, and get the ontology of fusions or undetached parts.

If perception does not determine one's ontology and the semantics of one's terms, then what does? In section O on abstract objects, I floated the idea that a species of organism is itself an individual. That was an exercise in theory determining ontology. Now we face the full force of this idea. In section S, we noted that a concept can be defined by its logical role. Now we fill in some details about the logic that must be involved. The full determination of one's ontology depends on a sophisticated conceptual scheme, with its theoretical apparatus for expressing numerical identities and differences, that one applies to one's stimulation. For instance, I can point twice and say that, although this is *numerically the same* body as that, this part or stage of it is *numerically distinct* from that part or stage of it. Nothing physical about our pointings to this and to that distinguishes the identity affirmed from the identity denied, if I mean by "body" either a unity that persists whole and entire through time, or a collection of undetached body parts, or a set of body stages sequenced continuously through spacetime. What one must have in one's conceptual scheme to have a determinate ontology is, in the terms of logic, quantification and the identity relation.

Some philosophers have argued against Quine, but not that we can get a person's ontology from her holophrastic assents and dissents prompted by stimulation. Rather they argue that there's a superficial level of analysis of sentences which allows one to infer a person's ontology from patterns of her inferences, short of an analysis invoking the full panoply of linguistic devices of individuation, which I referred to in the previous paragraph. We can query her inferences and so discover empirically her ontology. Perhaps just an analysis of her speech into subject and predicate and allowing for the connectives "and" and "not" will do the trick.[7] Here's an example. Suppose the issue for us to decide is whether Belia has an ontology of bodies or one of conglomerations of connected parts. When she says "woodchuck" does she mean a woodchuck substance or a bunch of undetached woodchucky parts? If the former, "woodchuck" is predicated of one thing and the sentence is singular; if the latter "woodchuck" is predicated of each member of the bunch and the sentence is universally general. In the latter case, one can have a singular sentence by predicating "woodchuck" of just one of the parts. The ontology of conglomerations of undetached parts can be thought of as an ontology of masses with the added condition of attachment. For example flesh is an entity in an ontology of masses; so is gold and water, in that all the stuff which one can call "flesh" or "gold" or "water" is taken to be a part of the masses of flesh, gold or water, each distributed through the universe. The ontology of conglomerations divides the mass into things according to the breaks in it. A conglomeration is not attached to any other part of its mass. Thus flesh here and flesh where you are will count as two things, because there's no bridge of flesh connecting us.

That's the setting; now for the test that will decide if we can detect a person's ontology relying on just the superficial features of Belia's conceptual scheme. The superficial method for distinguishing the two ways of imputing ontology to her is to find a pair of woodchucks joined as Siamese twins, and have her distinguish the two as A and B. We have a decisive experiment if there's a predicate which she'll deny of their common part if she thinks A and B are substances but affirm of it if she thinks they're bunches of undetached body parts that share a predicate. The predicate we need is "is woodchucky A and woodchucky B," where the term "woodchucky" is ontologically neutral. If A and B are woodchuck substances, then the common part is not a woodchuck (i.e., not woodchucky) and *a fortiori* not either woodchuck A or woodchuck B. Belia will deny the predicate of that part. If however, A and B are for her conglomerations of undetached parts *sharing the woodchuck predicate* (i.e., woodchucky), as is the case with any part of a mass, then the common part is both woodchucky A and woodchucky B. She will affirm the predicate of it. So we can decide from Belia's assents and dissents to our queries which of the two ontologies she accepts, and we use nothing more sophisticated than conjunction. We don't rely on the logical apparatus of individuation, quantification and the identity predicate. So Gareth Evans has been interpreted as saying and so others do say.[8]

First note that this argument concedes one of Quine's major points, that the jump to analyzing sentences into subject and predicate at the stage where some reference is to be imputed is not itself determined by stimulation. For the argument requires that the analysis into predicates be already completed. It's a weak argument against Quine's claim that sophisticated logical devices are indispensable for having an ontology, for at several points in the elaboration of the scenario Belia must make use of the concept of numerical identity and difference, just as Quine said. The very detection of a common part of distinct entities involves that concept. The weakest thing about the argument, however, is that at most it uncovers a weakness in using a particular ontology as an example, but leaves the point intact for other examples.

Before Evans made this criticism, Quine had already been forced to distinguish two kinds of indeterminacy, only one of which is at issue in Evans's criticism. Here's the indeterminacy that Evans is *not* denying: Quine had found a perfectly general argument within set theory for the indeterminacy of reference, which he calls the **proxy function argument**.[9] A proxy function is a function^ which takes all singular terms and all general terms as its domain, and permutes the referents of the former and extensions of the latter, even to the extent of moving from one ontology to another, so that all the true sentences using those terms stay true and all the false sentences stay false under the permutation. The trick we used earlier to read Othello's sentence, "Desdemona loves Cassio," to be about cosmic complements was an application of a proxy function. Because the trick is applicable generally, it's impossible to detect which of the two ontologies a person accepts simply from her assents and dissents to sentences, obviously if they are holophrastic, and even if they're analyzed but not to a depth which reveals quantification and identity in them. And even if they are analyzed to reveal quantification and identity, which may show the person has a multi-type ontology, the proxy function can switch the types which the person's various vocabularies refer to. Quine calls that thesis the **indeterminacy of reference**.

Belia's a fine logician, as we know, and she tells us that she understands the proxy function applied to her statements. Furthermore, her ontology is extensive enough to include the ontology of the terms in the function's domain^ and the ontology of the terms in its range, and she takes the entities referred to by the terms in the function's domain to be numerically distinct from the entities which the function pairs them with via the terms in its range. Furthermore, the terms do have the first ontology for their referents, namely, the one the function imputes to the terms in its domain. Quine is happy to allow Belia to say all that, because it's rife with the full panoply of sophisticated logical devices which he says are needed to have a determinate ontology. Belia continues, when she says "Johnny is good" she does not mean the cosmic complement of Johnny is a cosmic complement of a good person. If she had meant that, she would've said that in just those words! But now Quine applies a proxy function to her sentences which permutes the referents of the terms for one part of her ontology (e.g., "Johnny") and the terms for another part of her ontology (e.g., "cosmic complement of Johnny") so that their referents are switched. She protests. How can we tell which reading of her words is the one she's protesting against? Indeed, how can she herself tell which interpretation of the proxy function she's denying?

If Evans concedes the indeterminacy of reference, what indeterminacy is he denying? Quine calls it the **indeterminacy of translation**. It's the thesis that two claims, on behalf of two translation manuals, that each correlates all the sentences of another language to sentences in one's own, compatibly with the behavior of all concerned, might *both be true* and yet

> the two translation relations might not be usable in alteration, from sentence to sentence, without issuing in incoherent sequences. Or, to put it another way, the English sentences prescribed as translation of . . . [the target language's] sentence by two rival manuals might not be inter-changeable in English contexts.[10]

The thesis allows for wider discrepancy between the translation manuals than just what follows from the indeterminacy of reference. A conversion of the meanings of terms by a proxy function would allow the alternative sentences being interleaved without incoherence and the sentences would be interchangeable in English contexts. The indeterminacy of translation is therefore the more radical claim.

The argument for the indeterminacy of translation is that observation of another's assents and dissents to whole sentences is the ultimate evidence for deciphering another's language, and it's insufficient for identifying which of her linguistic devices are the devices of quantification and identity. The linguist's identification of them is part of a theory of the grammar of a person's language, and the theory's truth is underdetermined by observational tests. Another theory of the language's grammar might parcel out the work of quantification among the language's terms differently and still make the same predictions about assents and dissents to whole sentences. Evans is denying this empirical equivalence of any grammatical theory with some other theory incompatible with it, and it's as so interpreted that I judged his argument weak.

### §3. Application of the indeterminacies of reference and translation to Rep's reports of Belia's perceptions.

In view of the underdetermination of a person's conceptual scheme's ontology by the stimulation of her senses and her response to it, if we were to extend the regimen of an about-position to reports of Belia's perceptions, it might not be revelatory of something objective and perceived; the entities Rep's utterance might be about may not be the entities hers is about, even though they use the same words. Thus, if Rep is to avoid commitment to an ontology unwarranted by Belia's assent, consider Belia's assent to be to the truth of a holophrastic meaning-content. Quine's counter-intuitive idea is beginning to make sense after all. We should not regiment the sentence "Tom perceives the bowl" as "About the bowl, Tom perceives that it's present."

Furthermore, in view of this sidelining of ontology, we must revisit the matter of the reporter's concurrence with the perceiver in his reports of her perception. (See sections C and J.) For, up to now, the reporter's concurrence has been to the believer's ontology. When Rep reports Belia's perception, he may adopt any of three modes of reporting, indicating three degrees of his concurrence. First, he may not require her assent:

"Belia perceives a skunk, whatever she may think she perceives."
Secondly, he may report what Belia would assent to, but omit his concurrence:

"Belia is experiencing in a perception-like way what she takes to be a woodchuck, whether or not it really is perception."
Thirdly, he may report in a way that requires both their assents to what he reports her to perceive:

"Belia is aware of seeing a woodchuck."
Consider only the latter two reports. Rep can be justified in making these reports, even if Belia says nothing, by projecting himself into her situation and frame of mind and realizing that he'd assent to that observation sentence himself: "Lo, woodchuck!" This sentence is observational for Belia, and she would utter it or assent to it on this occasion; it's observational for Rep too, although he may not himself utter it or assent to it on this occasion. Suppose, however, Rep gives the third report where he too would utter it. What are the prerequisites for such a concurrence?

Nothing ontological. According to the post-1977 Quine, not even the same stimulus-pattern prompts the two of them to assent to it. This is in addition to the fact, noted in a recent paragraph, that their assents do not indicate their ontologies. Sameness in stimulation could only be qualitative sameness (i.e., exact similarity), since they don't share one nervous system, and even qualitative sameness of stimulus-pattern would require a similarity in the organization of their nervous systems. An exactly similar neural organization goes beyond the neurological evidence, and exactly similar stimulation is hardly to be expected in any case. We also want to account for reporting the perceptions had by an animal of another species. So we must give up the idea that concurrence is based on a "constancy of stimulus meaning from speaker to speaker,"[11] that is, a shared **stimulus meaning**, an idea Quine used to use. Minus the bit about being shared, however, the concept is useful. The stimulus meaning of a sentence for one person is just the set of stimulations that prompt her assent to it and the set of stimulations that prompt her dissent from it.

The upshot of all this is that there's no hope of divvying up the concurrence bit by bit. Rep's concurrence need be only to her *whole sentence's* being based on acquaintance, which makes his report notional, *de dicto*, only, despite his reference to her acquaintance or perceptual causal rapport. Up to now we've pretended all acquaintance is thing-acquaintance. Now we recognize an acquaintance which is not thing-acquaintance; it's *holo-acquaintance*, that is, acquaintance with the undivided prompting stimulus of a holophrastic observation sentence, a state of affairs. Holo-acquaintance extends the idea of causal rapport, so that it is rapport with the object-relatum of the truth relation, not just the object-relatum of the reference relation, that is, the rapport, if true, is true-to, not true-about.[12]

Concurrence in such holo-acquaintance does not support the common theory that perception is automatically not *de dicto*. On the other hand perception is clearly more than notional. Mustn't it be one or the other? No. Let a sentence whose truth is known by holo-acquaintance be as much a bit of relational knowledge as of notional knowledge, albeit pre-onto-logical knowledge, because it is founded on causal rapport.

### §4. Sparring with Bishop Berkeley again.

Returning to our logic-boxing with Bishop Berkeley, the most recent round of which took place in section J, we now deploy this concept of a holophrase based on holo-acquaintance against his request that we supply a *de re* conceiving of the unconceived. Let's give him a holophrastic *de re* conception. This is our way between the horns of the dilemma the Bishop would like to set for us: It evades his criticism that we're only giving him general propositions, without forcing us to give him a singular proposition that's analyzed. So we let the Bishop put us into a treeish scene, and we mutter holophrastically, "Lo, tree!" Although we're in causal rapport with that which we are conceiving, what we're conceiving is a proposition still, not a tree. Section J's solution still stands, despite the added rapport.

The matter of ontology must be faced in our sparring with the Bishop, for it may seem that having an ontology is indispensable to having *de re* beliefs. Could a person be in extensive causal rapport with a scene and be left bereft of any ontological theory, so that the resulting belief state were at best related to nothing that could be put in the about-position other than "out-there" or even just "this"? Or worse than pre-ontological, how about anontological (like anencephalic)? Yes, but we must be careful. The resulting belief state might be notional merely, as if our believer were a pure **Pyrrhonist**, a skeptic who only believes that she's appeared to in this way or that way, without reference to anything doing the appearing. A Pyrrhonist affirms no ontology and so is more skeptical than a phenomenalist, who assumes an ontology of sense data or ideas. The Bishop would gloat if she ended up in Pyrrhonism, and he'd declare victory if we ended up tying the believer's *de re*-ness to ontology. But the unified general theory of *de re* belief, stated in section O, does not force us into either of these scenarios. People's acceding to actuality a dominance over the referential aspects of their attitudes, which occurs primordially in their core indexical attitudes, is found again in a primitive way in the pre-ontological stage of perception: Lo, tree. At this stage the relational and notional aspects of attitudes have not yet bifurcated, and so the dominance applies globally in the form of extensive causal rapport prompting their assents.

We've left the Bishop speechless with the brilliance of our defense. We quickly depart before he recovers. Nevertheless, we raised an issue that needs to be addressed: Obviously Rep's neither an ontological innocent nor a Pyrrhonist. So if he's reporting a Pyrrhonist's or an innocent's beliefs, why can't he just introduce an about-position, since the reporter controls the about-position? I'd reply that he does not control whether or not there is an about-position, just what goes into it. This stricture is regimentation in the interest of saving the phenomenon of ontologized *de re* attitudes from going out of focus due to our sloppy ways of speaking. However we can accommodate Rep in his predicament of having to report an innocent's or a Pyrrhonist's beliefs without having to acquiesce in their pre- and post-ontological conditions. Suppose he's an evolutionary biologist working with a solipsistic species and must explain how its members' behavior is adapted to their environment. In section N we considered introducing a **concerning-position**, which occurs in reports just as an about-position does. In particular, it's under the control of extensive causal rapport. The difference is that the belief reported is entirely holophrastic and the believer may have no ontological theory. The causal rapport does not create a mental name.[13] The reporter is free to adopt any ontology he pleases to fill in the concerning-position; no conditions of concurrence need be observed. In section N I rejected it as the way to deal with beliefs in the first person. But there do seem to be beliefs about other things for which it makes sense.

# Notes

1. Quine, "In Praise of Observation Sentences," *Journal of Philosophy* 90 (1993) 107-116.

2. Quine, *Pursuit of Truth*, 41-43.

3. The quotation is from Quine's *Pursuit of Truth*, 43. Quine called attention to some of the counterfactuality of his definition of "observational for a group" in his "Response to Bergström," in *Inquiry*, 37 (1994) 496-8, where he exploits the fact that the witnesses need not assent, but would assent if queried. I think we need to push the counterfactuality to the witnessing itself: They would assent if they had been present and queried.

4. W. V. Quine, "In Praise of Observation Sentences," *Journal Of Philosophy* 90 (1993) 107-116. See p. 109.

5. Quine, *Pursuit of Truth*, 112.

6. Most of these examples come from W. V. Quine, *Word and Object* (1960) 51f. The cosmic complement example comes later in his *Pursuit of Truth*, 33f.

7. Quine allows that much of our truth functional conjunction is discoverable by experience from an analysis of speakers' "verdict behavior." See §20 of his *The Roots of Reference* (1974).

8. Gareth Evans, "Identity and Predication," *Journal of Philosophy* 72 (1975) 343-362. Evans may only have been making a point about developing translations, not a point about the determinacy of reference. Jerry Fodor revives the argument as an argument for the determinacy of reference in his *The Elm and the Expert* (1994), ch. 3.

9. Quine introduced the proxy function argument in his *Ontological Relativity and Other Essays* (1969) 55ff. Another statement of it is in his "Things and Their Place in Theories," published in his *Theories and Things* (1981) 19ff.

10. W. V. Quine, *The Pursuit of Truth*, 48.

11. W. V. Quine, *Word and Object* (1960) 43. Quine later admitted that this notion is useless.

12. This overlap of the categories and the need to get underneath ontology vitiate an argument for the primacy of *de re* attitudes to account for language learning and for justifying empirical knowledge, which Tyler Burge floated in part II of his "Belief *De Re*," *Journal of Philosophy* 74 (1977) 338-362, although his argument can be made independent of the false assumptions. I offer a Quinean account of these matters in section U.

13. This idea comes from John Perry, "Thought Without Representation"

(1986) and "I and Myself" (1998), both reprinted in his *The Problem of the Essential Indexical*, expanded edition (2000).

# U. Empathy, not Ostension of things, is the Primal Root of Discourse

Quine argued against non-notional perceptual belief, convinced that it begged the question of ontology. He gave us instead a notional perceptual belief that was nevertheless relational too. In its analyzed form, however, the perceptual belief which is both notional and relational gives way to the non-notional perception, one that Rep reports with an about-position which presupposes an ontology. Quine does not see much chance of this idiom being useful to science. What can we say in its defense? One might hope to create an argument for the scientific utility of non-notional, *de re* belief in its perceptual form at least, since the passing of the language on from one generation to the next depends on **ostension** (pointing to a thing is "ostending" it), which depends on relational perception. Children learn what to call things by having their attention drawn to them by ostension, and while they're attending they hear the things' names. Again Quine has a surprise for us: People have the power of **empathy**, a power to intuit the mental state of another, both its mood and its content. Empathy is more basic than ostension, for the reason that truth is more basic than reference. Empathy does not depend on ostension; ostension depends on empathy. For how does the ostender know that what he sees, the child sees, and how does the child know that what she sees, the ostender's words name? So any defense of the scientific utility of *de re* perception from its use in propagating language must also be a defense of the scientific respectability of empathy. Let me explain these ideas.

### §1. Our identification of the contents of each other's attitudes by empathizing.

Quine thinks that a sentence is observational for a community, not because all members of the community assign to it the same stimulus-prompts for assent and dissent—that would be the discredited "constancy of stimulus meaning from speaker to speaker"—but rather, it's observational for the community because the sentence is observational for each member, and

> . . .each would agree in assenting or dissenting on witnessing the occasion
> of utterance. We judge what counts as witnessing the occasion . . . by
> projecting ourselves into the [utterer's] position.[1]

In other words, Quine generates communal observation sentences from the
community's members' empathic (or empathetic[2]) abilities to "read" each
other's propositional-attitudinal states. One reads both the attitude and the
content of the attitude. In the case of belief and perception, one projects
oneself into the other's situation, intuiting what one would oneself assent
to there and imputing the same assent to the other.

Absent from this account of observation sentences is any shared
stimulus meaning between perceivers that's detectable objectively and
independently of their empathic agreement. The would-be objective test
of shared stimulus meaning has been revealed to be spurious, since Quine
defines stimulus meaning in terms of the stimulation of receptor neurons;
not only is it unlikely that human beings are exactly similar in their
receptual make-up, it's certainly not the case across species lines. So
there's no shared stimulus meaning.

In the flow of events in the mind as it processes the neural input, Quine
contrasts the receptual stage, which is the first level of stimulation, to the
perceptual stage, which results from the processing of the stimulation.[3] In
the flow of events, the receptual is upstream and the perceptual downstream. Might not the different streams in different individuals become
exactly similar in their downstreams? But any cross-person perceptual
isomorphism is undetectable by readily performed tests, since perceptual
isomorphisms would occur deep in the brain. So Quine and folk psychology turn to empathy as the basis for communal observationality.

In view of the primacy of holo-acquaintance (see the previous section),
we must give up the traditional thesis that observation sentences have a
foundational analyzed meaning-content that goes hand in hand with the *de
re* format of reports of perceptions. If empathy is to take the place of *de re*
perception as the basis for ostension, what makes empathy trustworthy?
What is the check we have on it that shows us our empathy is right? Quine
says of reports of perceptions,

> their distinctive factuality is blurred now by the disavowal of shared
> stimulus meaning. What is utterly factual is just the fluency of conversa-
> tion and the effectiveness of negotiation[4]

for instance, negotiation between Rep and Belia, facilitated by Rep's
empathic practices for "reading" Belia. The firmness of their agreement

on observation sentences—describe them holophrastically so that their truth-value^ is their only semantic relation—marks no more than their personal interactions' fluency and effectiveness. The only check on one's empathy with another is its prediction of the other's assent to a *dictum* or dissent from it. The results of one's empathy are testable. Empathy does not do any worse on these tests than observation sentences themselves.

## §2. Empathy as a way into ontology.

We've yet to account for the perceptually obvious ontology that all human beings and perhaps other primates share, namely an ontology of persons and enduring bodies. The part of folk psychology that theorizes about perception tells us these are the things human beings perceive. How did folk psychology get to that conclusion? (For that's what it is, a conclusion.) Even when Rep says in *de re* style, "Belia is perceiving the bowl," he, the empathizer, understands Belia to have just assented to an observation sentence, "Lo, bowl!" Furthermore, like the expression of perception itself, the expression of one's empathic understanding of another perceiver is initially holophrastically *de dicto*: For example, suppose Belia's observing the rain outside. Using a common holophrastic *dictum*, "it's raining," Rep, the empathizer, assents to, "Lo, Belia perceiving it's raining!" Think of those five words as a holophrastic utterance. Since stimulation causes assent only to holophrases, *a fortiori* so does perceptual empathy. Empathy also initiates the first step in analyzing that holophrase. For it causes two assents: One assent expresses Rep's act of empathy with Belia's attitude—she perceives. The other assent is to that which he detects Belia assenting to—it's raining. So how does folk psychology conclude from that the ontology of persons and enduring objects?

However mysterious, the point of the empathy is for the empathizer to get to the other's analyzed meaning and so to the other's ontology. How else understand ostension but as one's pointing to a thing one believes the other sees? But the *theory* of language propagation can be noncommittal on the ontology of the empathizer's particular analyses, even if the language teacher cannot be. Thus the emphasis in section T on the reporting of holophrastic content.

It's problematic how empathy can be appealed to in support of the scientific respectability of *de re* reports of perception. Quine argued that the *de re* format is indexical, that the rules for its proper use are context-dependent, as we saw in section J. The truth conditions of reports of belief and other standing propositional attitudes are so gerrymandered according to context that the locution is unsuitable for serious science. Might not the *de re* format at least for reporting perception, or equivalently, the observation sentence analyzed into subject and predicate, be salvageable for explaining perceptual empathy, just because the observation sentence is commonly true just around the time it's expressed, whereas sentences with more lasting truth-values are more common as the contents of the other attitudes? My reason for thinking there's hope is this: Uttering a sentence with a more ephemeral truth-value allows more stringent shaping^ of it to the communally accepted conditions for its being prompted.[5] This is fortunate for the science that explains how our language is propagated, since it must endorse the practice of perceptual empathy, an empathy about the assenting to utterances on the basis of the assenter's causal rapport with what the utterance is true to. The more control the rapport has, the less the context of reporting has.

But how make the jump to the *de re* format for perception? There's a hurdle to jump: One of the major conclusions of philosophy in the latter half of the twentieth century was that people's perceptions are imbued with theory. Sellars, Feyerabend, Hanson, and Quine made this case. Quine's distinction between holophrastic and analyzed utterances should be seen in the light of this conclusion. Holophrastic observation sentences are as pre-theoretical as they are pre-analyzed. Observation sentences, *qua* analyzed, however, are **theory-laden**, that is, they presuppose the truth of some system of conceptualization. People see people and bodies, and it's *theory* that the world is populated with persons and bodies. Distinguish between a test that something's so and an explanation why it's so: By empathy and successful negotiation a person *detects* a community's observation sentences and *tells* he's right in assenting to them, but we *explain* his success by the theory implicit in the decomposition of the holophrastic sentences into their terms. His observation sentences *are* ontologically committed theory just when the theory they're laden with describes them as analyzed into subjects and predicates.

A theory's explanatory power derives from the logical interconnectivity of the theory's sentences. By virtue of the analysis of observation sentences into terms, the sentences have relations of implication and probabilistic relevance to the rest of the theory's sentences, including other observation sentences. To see the dependence of a sentence's logical interrelations on how it's analyzed, consider three utterances taken first holophrastically. Logic sees no structure in them and simply lists them as

*p*

*q*

*r*

The third shows no more relationship to the first two than they do to each other. Now suppose these three sentences are analyzed to reveal their interior structure:

>Every F is G
>Socrates is F
>Socrates is G

You now see that the third is a consequence of the first two, but you see no connection to

>Socrates is the only F

However, suppose we dig deeper and find that the predicate G itself has internal structure, and that G stands for the predicate " = *a*." Now it also follows from our two premises that Socrates is the only F. By the relations revealed by grammatical analysis, the theory can predict observations and explain them by appeal to other sentences logically connected to them.[6]

It's not that there's no interconnectivity without logical structure, but that without logical structure all interconnectivity must be induced *ad hoc* by shaping.^ Indeed we do have much interconnectivity of that sort; our holophrastic observation sentences are not atoms assertable independently of each other. Refer back to the chart in section S of interconnected concepts developed by linguists decades ago. But now don't think of the terms as concepts; think of them as holophrastic observation sentences: Arm! Wrist! Joint! and so on. The holophrastic observation sentences are connected by either broken or unbroken lines. The unbroken line stands for the relation "__has a__," as in "arm has a wrist." The broken line stands for the relation "__is a__," as in "wrist is a joint." But don't think of the relations as that of set inclusion or part to whole, which are not ontologically neutral. Think of them on the model of Quine's observation categoricals: compounds of holophrastic sentences of the form "whenever this stimulation, that stimulation." In other words the relations make good sense simply as ways the stimulus conditions of the paired holophrases are related. Quine seems to have thought of his observation categoricals as expressing discoveries. But the ones we're considering seem to be such primitive discoveries that we must discover them in the very learning of the holophrases. These connections then are the results of conditioning, connecting our holophrastic observation sentences into holistic structures prior to any analyses into subsentential parts. Subsequent analyses generally respect these connections, unless the pressure of theory forces a change, as happened in the case of "whale is a fish." Since the analyses of holophrases are generally constrained by their preanalytic stimulus relationships, the picture still supports Paul Thagard's thesis that the core of any noun concept is a network of "is a" and "has a" relationships, as I mentioned in section S. Logic works on these analyzed components to yield a connectivity that transcends what *ad hoc* conditioning could achieve.

In one of Quine's last publications, he came to admit that observation sentences have a way of being theory-laden even in their holophrastic form. Although they're observational to the extent that people's assent to them is immediate, they're also theoretic to the extent that they're susceptible to recantation.[7] Recantation should be distinguished from the kind of changing of one's mind that occurs in vague or borderline situations. Unlike that sort of on-the-spot vacillation, recantation occurs when one has affirmed an observation sentence in stimulation conditions that are clear. Later, one comes to recant. Actually, I think Quine slipped here. One does not recant the observation sentence, since one no longer believes the sentence. After all, it, or rather its utterance, was only true on the occasion of its utterance. What one recants is the sentence in the past tense that at the time of the recanting expresses what was experienced.

Immediate affirmability and recantability can vary independently, so that one might affirm "Rabbit" but recant its past-tensed replacement among our standing episodic memories upon learning it was not a rabbit. But in the same context of experience, one might affirm "Rabbit-look-alike," where that's intended to cover genuine rabbits as well, and be unwilling to recant upon learning it was not a rabbit, for it was still a rabbit look-alike. Quine associates recantability with theoreticity because one's theoretic commitments can determine the interconnections of the standing records of utterances of observation sentences. To recant one observation sentence is to replace the memory record of it with another standing sentence endorsed by the underlying theory. The analyses that make the connections operate in the background, as do the observation categoricals that organize holophrases into a pre-analyzed network.

How can observationality and theoreticity be so entangled that we have to resort to such devices as holophrastic versus analyzed formats of a sentence, and distinguish between its immediate affirmability after stimulation and its recantability upon further stimulation? My own view is that to account for this residual theoreticity we must invoke the further distinction between public language and LOT, the language of thought. A child learns a public language more slowly than its language of thought matures, so that its public language is holophrastic when its LOT is already analyzed and so theory-laden.

Even the baby first learning its public language may have some theoreticity infecting the observation sentences it learns, if some of the theory is innate, built into LOT. That's how the analyses that make the inferential connections could operate in the background. We don't have to suppose that, by the time the child is learning holophrastic utterances in the public language, she's still confined to holophrastic mental utterances in the language of thought. If we imagine those first holophrastic utterances in the language of thought, at a stage before the innate theoretic commitments become operative, then we'll have imagined a pre-theoretic observationality. Perhaps this stage is nothing but a fiction. Quine seemed to think so.

### §3. Objectivity and the empathic detection of content.

By allowing Quine to define the stimulus meaning of holophrastic utterances in terms of the stimulation of our sensory neurons, we're departing from folk psychology or modernizing it. The innovation is trivial, however, because folk psychology can reformulate the prompting of holophrastic utterances in terms of eyes and ears. Nevertheless, this part of the definition of observationality is individualistic and subjective. What then is the origin of objectivity? It's the empathic detection of content. The empathy condition in Quine's definition of observationality implies that intersubjectively similar **distal stimuli** do underlie observation sentences; observations do focus a community on features of a world. Folk psychology introduces distal stimuli (the things people see or hear despite there being some distance separating them) as the referents of terms.

The folk psychological theory of perception is also consistent with evolutionary biology, the science that offers the ultimate explanation why our observation sentences are usually true when uttered, or true enough, to the world. So folk psychology can borrow some support from evolutionary biology for the empathy condition. If *de re* perceptions can play a role in its theoretical explanations, then there'll be a reason why the theory covers observation sentences and also *de re* reports of perception, whereas *de re* reports of beliefs may be too indexical, too contextually dependent to be covered. The reason will be the greater susceptibility of perception-empathy to being shaped^ by a sequence of *selection events* on our lineage. For example, because of a similar selection history of their lineages, Rep sees what Belia sees. In that situation, selection may have worked on Rep's ancestral line to make Rep realize *that* he sees what Belia sees, regardless of their perspectival differences. Given that ability in his ancestral line, selection may have worked on it so that he even has the ability to tell *what* Belia sees, whether or not he sees it too.

Empathy can start to be shaped only when isomorphisms of perceptual similarity happen to be occurring between the partners in empathy. An isomorphism exists between the perceptual states of two people when there's a one-to-one correlation between their states such that, when one of them believes a truth as a result of the state she's in, the other believes an equivalent truth also because of the state he's in. The goal of empathy is objective information. That may sound odd, since we tend to think of empathy as capturing the subjective state of another: She's upset; she's angry, she's sad, and so on. While that's so, we want to understand the propositional content of that state, and that's where the objectivity comes in. Empathy detects not just the mood of another person, but the proposition that mood is directed toward. It detects not the other's own sentence, but a content that the empathizer can assess. If Rep sees Belia take umbrage at being called a fool, he knows the propositional content of her attitude in such a way that it becomes a component content in his own empathic attitude. He must extract the content from the way Belia formats it, so that he can format it for himself. That process of extraction is called a transformation.

*Objective content is content that remains invariant through all appropriate transformations.*[8] Let's fill out this concept of objectivity of information by considering a case where the information is quantitative. What part of our information about temperatures is objective? Consider the following transformation equation. It relates the Fahrenheit scale of measuring temperature to the Celsius scale for measuring temperature. The letters F and C show where to insert the temperature measurement you're familiar with: $F^{\circ} = (9/5)C^{\circ}+32$. You then solve for the other temperature.

Calculate from the equation these six temperatures, which we'll refer to in the three examples that follow:

| Temperature in F° | Its Translation in C° |
|---|---|
| It's 70° | It's 21 1/9° |
| It's 65° | It's 18 3/9° |
| It's 35° | It's 1 6/9° |
| It's 30° | It's -1 1/9° |
| It's 0° | It's -17 7/9° |
| It's -40° | It's -40° |

If we think of the equation as telling us merely these equivalences, we're missing its deeper purpose as a test that reveals *objectivity*. Here are three examples to help us see that the equation distinguishes genuinely objective information from mere artifacts of people's choice of scaling:

> *I. An example of something a person can say that's only an artifact of the scale he uses, because it doesn't stay true if we translate what he says into another scale:*
>> F° talk: 70° is twice 35°. (true)
>> C° talk: 21 1/9° is twice 1 6/9°. (false)

What was true in F° talk becomes false when transformed into C° talk. (See 1$^{st}$ and 3$^{rd}$ rows above).

> *II. An example of something a person can say that's objective information, because it stays true even when we translate it into the other scale:*
>> F° talk: The difference between 70° and 0° is twice the difference between 35° and 0°.
>> C° talk: The difference between 21 1/9° and -17 7/9° is twice the difference between 1 6/9° and -17 7/9°.

Both are true. What was true in F° talk remains true when transformed into C° talk. (See first, middle, and fifth rows of the calculations from the transformation equation.)

> *III. Another example of something a person can say that's objective information:*
>> F° talk: The difference between 70° and 65° is the same as the difference between 35° and 30°.
>> C° talk: The difference between 21 1/9° and 18 3/9° is the same as the difference between 1 6/9° and -1 1/9°.

Both are true. What was true in F° talk remains true when transformed into C° talk. (Compare the first two rows with the second two rows of the list of temperature equivalences.)

Now for the moral which these examples teach us: Let's operationally define absolute *objective information* as the information that's not changed from true to false by transforming it from one frame of measurement to another. In other words, objective information remains invariant under transformation. What varies is subjective. The transformation equation corrects for two features, which immediately show themselves to be subjective: The first term in the transformation equation is a multiplicative factor which simply stretches or shrinks a scale. The second term is an additive factor which simply moves a scale up or down on the number line. These are artifacts. But the multiplicative factor must be positive, for a negative factor would flip the scale.

We should note one more feature of the definition: Since -40°F =

-40°C, and since -40° is an artifact of both scales, invariance may seem only indispensable for objectivity, not sufficient.[9] To get sufficiency, **objectivity** must be invariance in *all* equivalent scales. In measuring velocity according to the theory of relativity, something analogous to -40° does come out invariant on all the scales for measuring velocity, and that is $c$, the speed of light. So the speed of light is objective. The various sciences decide what to count as equivalent scales in other domains. In the case of the formal sciences, such as geometry, the relevant equivalencies are determined by *a priori* reflection on meanings, and the resultant invariances reveal the meanings of geometric terms. For example, the essence of a right triangle is the feature of shape that remains invariant through transformations of place, size, orientation, and being flipped over. In the case of the empirical sciences, however, the discovery of the equivalencies is part of the theorizing process, and the resultant invariances reveal, not the *a priori* meanings, but rather the objective information.

In the case of the two temperature scales, the only objective information they give people is comparisons of differences (or of intervals). This limitation is the result of the arbitrariness of their zero points and the arbit% rariness of what they count as a unit.[10] They're called "interval scales." But what emerge as objective by Einstein's transformation equations are the laws of nature, including the invariant speed of light, and a single extensive manifold we call spacetime. The individual spaces and indepen% dent times of the various frames of reference are artifacts of the scaling; they are secondary^ qualities. Galileo's transformation equations relate different observer's measurements of the locations of things in relative motion. What's invariant between observers is the laws of mechanics.

When people agree on information, we take that as a sign that it's objective information. Agreement is a form of invariance from one frame to another, since in a sense people themselves are frames of reference. Our example has been quantitative information, since it's easier to see the correspondence of the objective to the invariance through transformations. The point is not confined to quantitative information, however. *Empathy, insofar as it reads the content of another's attitudes, is the primordial ability to perform transformations.*

The evolution of people's empathic abilities we explain by a natural selection for an alternative to the impossible direct detection of perceptual isomorphism between speakers. Posit perceptual isomorphism between a perceiver and an onlooker whenever the onlooker feels empathy with the other's perception; it explains the success of the empathic alternative. Empathy does not detect the cross-person perceptual isomorphism by some indirect causal rapport with it; it simply substitutes for such detection well enough. For the empathic substitute to have evolved, ensuring empathy's reliability among us, we human beings must have been selected for greater inner similarity than would've been needed by members of a species that did not rely on empathy.[11] It's not just that our ancestors were selected for their ability to empathize in appropriate circumstances; our ancestors were selected also for their being easier targets for others to empathize with successfully. For the more empathic pairs of people should out-compete the less empathic pairs in situations where the members of a pair must cooperate. Hominids became more similar so that empathy would work better. Nevertheless empathy is more reliable in detecting others' perceptions than in detecting their other propositional attitudes.

Perception itself is the discovery of invariances through the transformations that occur because of perceivers' interactions with their environments. These invariances show up as the ontology of perception. As the physicist David Bohm expresses it after reviewing the evidence of developmental psychologists and brain scientists,

> . . .the infant begins with a limited set of inborn reflexes. When these are developed into the "circular reflex" he has the most basic feature of perception, i.e., the ability to be sensitive to a relationship between outgoing and incoming nervous impulses, a relationship that is characteristic of what is to be perceived. [We study the circular reflex in section Y.] From here on he is able to "attune" himself step by step with his environment, by abstracting from such relationships what is invariant in its general structure. In doing this he builds up his notions of space, time, causality, the division of the world into permanent objects (one of which is himself), the notion of permanent substance, permanent numbers of objects, etc., etc.[12]

Bohm draws a significant conclusion about the relationship of science and perception:

> . . . scientific investigation is basically a way of extending our *perception* of the world, and not mainly a mode of obtaining *knowledge* about it. That is to say, while science does involve a search for knowledge, the essential role of this knowledge is that it is an adjunct to an extended perceptual process. And if science is basically such a mode of perception, then, . . . it is quite reasonable that certain essential features of scientific research shall be rather similar to corresponding features of immediate perception.[13]

## §4. An argument against Quine in favor of *de re* perception.

Quine's account of perception shoots down two big epistemological motives for *de re* perception: The analysis of otherwise holophrastic reports of perceptions into subject and predicate is not what identifies them as foundational for knowledge, nor does the theory embodied in the analysis warrant recasting Belia's perceptions so that they're analyzed *de re*, which would seem to express a perceptually given ontology although in fact such perceptions are theoretical, that is, they are theory-laden; they presuppose the theory. Belia's perceptions are foundational evidence for theory only on the holophrastic reading of her reports of them. In their theoretical reading they're part of what the evidence is evidence for. We must realize the nongiven, nonfoundational status of analyzed *de re* perceptions. To put the point paradoxically, that one *assents* to an observation sentence provides evidence of its own truth noncircularly. We resolve the paradox thus: One's assent is foundational evidence only when the sentence is described as a holophrase; what it's evidence for is the theory implied in the analysis of it into subject and predicate.

I've so far given Quine's side of the story. At the beginning of this section I said I saw an argument here for my saving of analyzed relational perception. Here it is: Natural selection has honed people's observation sentences for truth from two directions, as prompted by stimulation and as empathically detectable by other observers. Observation sentences must be true when uttered or close to true much of the time, for language learning depends on the teacher's ostension of an object in contexts where he empathized that the learner has had a relational perception. The teacher's empathy depends on the teacher's analyzed meaning of the student's observation sentences. If no observation sentences in the analyzed stage are true when uttered, or true enough, in a way that contexts cannot rig, no language such as English could exist. For the teacher and the learner must agree and continue to agree, and truth or verisimilitude^ is the explanation of widespread and long lasting observational agreement. No science of language learning can so refuse to acknowledge its own basis without leading to skepticism. So science should accept not just the practice of perceptual empathy, but also some sort of analyzed perceptual reports that express it.[14]

I submit that these analyses make credible my original claim that relational beliefs are not only real, but they are suitable subjects for science to theorize about. My argument has been threefold, namely, the *de re* nature of empathic understanding in language learning (in this section) and of juries' verdicts (in section J), both supporting an idea of serious contexts, coupled with what so far is only a science fiction about names in the mind (in section L before the discussion of Burdick). I concede that my argument is inadequate to persuade others, not to mention Quine. So can you add to my account or correct it, to get something better?

Let's conclude with a perplexity: The more we say that people were selected to find minds in each other and in similar species, the less credible is the naturalization project, at least in its less radical form. For we're saying that people are constrained to find evolutionary steps up to their minds. There may only be material things, but some of them happen to be inveterate information categorizers who must read into the rest of what they see the story of their evolution into such beings, as if it all represented the lineage of their intentionality, rather than what it is, a projection of a presupposed theory.

Suppose it's so. Yet it would be a mistake to say that this constraint on people's thought constitutes an illusion. Rather it constitutes a secondary quality, that is, it does contain some truth about people's difference from non-mental reality.

# Notes

1. Quine, *Pursuit of Truth*, 43.
2. Quine dislikes the form "empathic." He says, "Not 'empathic', please. That, like 'phonemic' for 'phonematic', smacks of 'little Latin and less Greek'." ("Response to George" in Alex Orenstein and Petr Kotatko, eds, *Knowledge, Language and Logic: Questions for Quine* (2000) 410.) Quine follows what he takes to be learned rules of forming English words from Greek sources. He derives his "empathetic" from the participle form of a Greek verb. His derivation is supported by analogy with, for example, the adjective of "sympathy," which is "sympathetic." Despite Quine's plea to his expositors, I prefer "empathic" and will continue to use it in explicating Quine. The *Webster's Third New International Dictionary* gives priority to "empathic" by having the entry for "empathetic" refer to the entry for "empathic." The English "sympathetic" supports Quine, but the French (sympathique, apathique), Spanish, and Italian (simpatico) do not. I prefer the analogy of empathy to the English word "telepathy" anyway, whose adjectival form is "telepathic." I think Quine missed a pedagogical opportunity with this word: Since his empathy is directed more at the content of another's attitude than at its mood, whereas most people think they're detecting another's mood by empathy, Quine could've distinguished the empathic, which, like the telepathic, is directed toward content, from the empathetic, which, like the sympathetic, is directed toward mood. As for the word's formation from a Greek root, I see no reason to defer to schoolmarmish rules about forming English words from Greek

or Latin words, "rules" that only the superfastidious (control-freaks? show-offs?) have ever observed.

3. W. V. Quine, *The Roots of Reference* (1974), ch. 1. In §5 of the chapter Quine defines the perceptual stage as the detection of the similarities between stimuli that determine the perceiver's behavioral dispositions.

4. *Pursuit of Truth*, 43.

5. *Pursuit of Truth*, 67.

6. In the terms of probability theory, "one sentence; two descriptions of it" means that it makes no difference to the sentence's relations to other sentences if we distinguish the holophrastic $h_{holo}$ from the fully analyzed $h_{ana}$ such that,

where T stands for the theory that $h_{ana}$ is ladened with, $p(h_{ana}|T) > p(h_{ana})$.

In particular, we should not deny $p(h_{holo}|T) > p(h_{holo})$ simply because $h_{holo}$ is not theory-laden. Such a denial would be to accept a two-sentences thesis rather than a two-descriptions-of-one-sentence thesis. But it wrongly seems that neither should the positive relevance be asserted, because my subscripting notation promotes the illusion of two sentences. A more perspicuous expression of my point (and Quine's if he cashed out his appeal to "sense"?) would be at the metalevel of descriptions of statements. Only a holophrastic description of "*h*" is used in the analysis of truth as it occurs in the phrase: a perceptually prompted degree of belief in "*h*" counts toward the truth of "*h*." That is, truth is not analyzed here to the level of the satisfaction of predicates by sequences.^ Alternatively, instead of two syntactic descriptions of one sentence, we have only one and a description of it which is independent of the syntactic one. In other words, carry forward the gestalt shift that frees semantics from syntax—see sections H, note 5, Q, note 16, and V §1—to cover the emancipation of pragmatics also, pragmatics being the theory of the use of signs. "Holophrase" then refers to a pragmatic category of sentence.

7. W. V. Quine, "I, You, and It: An Epistemological Triangle" in Alex Orenstein and Petr Kotatko, eds, *Knowledge, Language and Logic: Questions for Quine* (2000) 1-6.

8. The concept of objectivity as invariance was stated over a half century ago in Hermann Weyl, *Symmetry* (1952), 132. The general idea traces back to the 1880's, particularly to the geometer, Felix Klein. See his *Geometry* (1959 [3rd ed., 1925 originally]), e.g., 24-25. For contemporary philosophical statements of the invariance criterion of objectivity, see Robert Nozick, "Invariance and Objectivity," *Proceedings and Addresses of The American Philosophical Association*, volume 72, no. 2 (1998) 21-48, and ch. 2 of his *Invariances: The Structure of the Objective World* (2001), also Patrick Suppes, *Representation and Invariance of Scientific Structures* (2002).

9. On the problem of sufficiency, see J. A. Winnie, "Invariance and Objectivity: A Theory with Applications to Relativity and Geometry" in Robert Colodny, editor, *From Quarks to Quasars* (1986). With hindsight, we see that Hendrik Lorentz, working before Einstein on the same problem, had the definition of objectivity reversed by interpreting the variable elements of the transformation equations as objective.

10. Modern theory of scaling has become more sophisticated than the classical "extensive" and "intensive" scales. See the pioneer article by S. S. Stevens, "On the Theory of Scales of Measurement," *Science*, 103 (1946), reprinted in B. Brody and N. Capaldi, *Science: Men, Methods, and Goals* (1968).

11. Roy A. Sorensen, "Self-strengthening Empathy" *Philosophy and Phenomenological Research*, 58 (1998) 75-98. (It would be ironic if the coincidence of different speakers' stimulus meanings, which was foundational for Quine in 1960 but later abandoned, were to return as a theoretical posit to explain the success of the empathy Quine now prefers. But it does not; what empathy requires is a perceptual similarity that's downstream from receptor stimulation.)

12. David Bohm, "Physics and Perception," *The Special Theory of Relativity* (1996 [1965]), Appendix. See p. 211 for the quotation.

13. Page 219.

14. This is the repair of Tyler Burge's argument, which I alluded to in section T ("Belief *De Re*" *Journal of Philosophy* 74 (1977), part II). He also notes that, insofar as science depends on a notion of justified true empirical belief, it must accept the primacy of *de re* attitudes.

# Second Subpart of Part III from V to X.
# Mind is Directed Toward Something other than Representations.

The remainder of Part III denies to representations the role of being the objects toward which attitudes are directed, for they're at best tools merely for pointing the mind toward the things which the representations represent. In order to notice the thing pointed at, one must notice the finger pointing, but one does not suppose the finger to be all there is. So this subpart is concerned with what the finger points at, whereas the first subpart concerned itself with the finger.

Just how Platonistic is this view of the content-terms of the directed-toward relation? All the views we'll consider are Platonistic in that they're committed to the existence of abstract entities. But they divide into those that accept only extensional abstract entities, for example, sets, and those that accept nonextensional entities, which are entities whose identity conditions are not extensional, for example, attributes and intensions.

In this subpart we consider three varieties of Platonism. Russell is the progenitor of extensional Platonism. Frege and Carnap created distinct varieties of nonextensional Platonism. Quine is a Russellian. Church and Montague are Fregean. Cresswell and David Lewis are Carnapian.

What am I? I think the objects of the directed-toward relation are not representations in people's minds, but rather the kind of abstract entities called eternal sentences and eternal predicates. My position is a form of nonrepresentationalism, because nobody utters eternal sentences or predicates. The author of the view is Quine. So I'm Quinean.

# V. When Believing the Same Thing Means Agreeing.

All the theories we've considered of the entity which an attitude is directed toward postulate representations as those entities. We located representations in the conceptual space between representings and representeds. Let's review that distinction:

We supposed **representations** to be distinct from a person's representings, which are components in her believings, desirings and other attitudes. Despite the distinction, we did allow Harman's identifying the concretization of an attitude in a person with the instantiation of a representation in that person. See section P, where I separated out Harman's thesis from the central thesis of representationalism as a possible common ground with nonrepresentationalism. See also section B, whose thesis fits nicely with Harman's identification. But if we think of a representation as a type, thinking of a sentence as a syntactic type, it's distinct from the attitudes that are at least the concrete representings, for types are distinct from their instances.

We also supposed that representations are distinct from the representeds, which we assumed were their referents or extensions. The representations are the ideas, images, and the syntactic, presyntactic, or connection ist structures we considered, the sentence-radicals mentioned in section D and other entities whose instances stand proxy in the mind for the representeds. Representations mediate the representing of the represented. In this subpart, we'll consider other representeds than extensions and intensions, entities whose whole reason for being is to solve two problems; one is the familiar problem of opacity and hyperintensionality, the other is the problem of accounting for agreement between attitudes in their content. (We might have called these entities meanings, were it not for the ing/ed ambiguity, for a meaning, despite ending in "-ing," would here belong on the "-ed" side of the distinction. Better to avoid the word.)

All the theories of reports that we've considered analyze the reports' that-clauses as referring to the representations in the mind of the one reported on. This followed from the theories' acceptance of the syntactic criterion for thought-objects (see section P). Meanings entered into these theories only as attached to representations (see section S). All the theories we've so far considered are therefore **representationalisms**. Representationalisms are all of one mind that the objects of the directed-toward relation, the contents of the attitudes, are representations, which meet syntactic criteria of identity, or at least formal criteria of identity, of which syntactic criteria are one kind. The theories also are unanimous that attitudes are individuated and concretized by the representations they instantiate. So far we've only been watching intramural disputes unfold within representationalism about the centrality of syntax for representations. Sententialism, one kind of representationalism, maintains that it's central; the other representationalisms deny that. The dispute over the width of content of a representation is another intramural one, although the advocates of wide content for representations may very well be reaching for nonrepresentationalism.

### §1. A nonrepresentational theory of the object of the directed-toward relation.

Looking beyond all these family quarrels, a case can be made for nonrepresentationalism. **Nonrepresentationalism** says the entity which is the object of the directed-toward relation is not a representation. The typical nonrepresentationalist denies the object that's the content of an attitude is anything meeting syntactic or formal criteria of identity. Such syntactic or formal things may individuate the represent*ings*, as Harman suggested, but they have no place as objects of the directed-toward relation, which is a semantic relation. As befits represent*eds* the objects of the directed-toward relation should meet a semantic criterion of identity only. Such a semantic object is not any mind-dependent entity which stands proxy for the represented. Rather it's a public thing. The that-clauses of reports refer to that public thing.

A representationalist may wonder what the fuss is about, since he too believes in referents and extensions of terms, which meet semantic criteria of identity, are public, and are the representeds. This representationalist has missed the point. The nonrepresentationalist wishes to solve the problems of opacity and hyperintensionality with his semantic objects, and we know that the two positions' common ground of referents and extensions is inadequate for that purpose. That's why the representationalist resorted to words and their conceptual roles. The nonrepresentationalist will resort instead to hyperintensions and various elaborations of the ideas of attribute and proposition.

Semantic identity conditions for the contents of attitudes include the extensional and intensional conditions we studied in section G, and they contrast with the syntactic criterion of their identity, which we discussed in section P. But it may seem that the criteria cannot be so different, for the traditional way to do semantics is to make it interpret the syntax. So conceived, semantics, in slavish subservience to syntax, formulates the relation of the syntactic elements to their extensions and referents. This relation supervenes on the roles the syntactic elements play, as suggested in section S. The two identity conditions therefore coincide. But the nonrepresentationalist can bypass syntax and still do semantics. Logicians have shown us how to do **semantics** independently of syntax and the other modes of structuring representations, referring simply to the things meant by the representations, bypassing the representations.[1] Having developed the semantics, one then may attach it to a language as the language's interpretation, if one wishes. It's clarifying to think of the nonrepresentationalist as doing semantics this second way, where the connection to representations is an optional add-on. For then the identity conditions for the objects of the directed-toward relation may not coincide with the identity conditions for representations.

Just as there was a representationalism that proposed a replacement strategy, making no room for propositions, so also there's a go-it-alone strategy for nonrepresentationalism, making no room for the representationalist's conceptual roles. This nonrepresentationalist strategy may invoke representations as Harman invoked them, to instantiate an attitude, but they're not object-terms of the semantical relation of directed-towardness.

Just as there were the two strategies of representationalism, replacement and supplement, so also there are two for nonrepresentationalism, go-it-alone and conciliatory. The conciliatory nonrepresentationalist strategy not only invokes representations as Harman invoked them, to instantiate an attitude, but they serve a subordinate role in individuating the object-termini of the central semantical relation of directed-towardness. The more extreme positions on the two sides are the representationalist replacement strategists and the go-it-alone nonrepresentationalists. Go-it-alone nonrepresentationalism presents arguments against representationalism, which we'll now consider. Let's take syntactic constructions as typical representations in the following criticism of representationalisms, although the argument is supposed to apply to all representations. There's this problem with sententialism and more generally with representationalism: Syntactic and other representational types seem to be the wrong types for denoting *shared* beliefs. By shared beliefs I mean the believers would say they agreed with each other.

Let's see that agreement is not a shared belief in sentences of the same syntactic type: I like logic and so I believe the sentence, "I like logic." You don't like logic, let's say. So you do not believe the sentence, "I like logic." Consider now another sentence; you believe of me, "You like logic." I don't believe that sentence of you. Despite your accepting and my not accepting this sentence and my accepting and your not accepting the previous sentence, we *believe the same two things, one about me and the other about you.* Consider what we both believe about me. That thing's the same belief-type, but not the same sentence-type. For you believe the sentence of me, "You like logic." I believe a different sentence of me, "I like logic." Despite the difference in the sentences we accept, we agree. Therefore belief is not directed toward sentences.

Furthermore, Belia believes it's noon. Rep says Belia believes it's noon. An hour later, Rep reports that Belia believed it was noon an hour ago. Note the change in his sentence to, "it was noon." Belia hasn't changed her mind about the occurrence of noon, yet she too uses a different sentence to express what she believes. Belia believes it was noon an hour ago. Same belief-type; different sentences. The sentences people utter simply don't correspond to the way they individuate belief-types.

The sentences as uttered don't serve the purposes of the reporter either, who must report correctly when two people disagree, despite their using the same sentence type, and even when a person changes her mind, despite using the same sentence type. ("He's opening the door—No, now he's opening the door.") The belief-types that people most commonly use in their judgments of agreement among themselves are based on semantic identity conditions.

The nonrepresentationalists refocus our attention on the conditions that make community possible across persons and across times. In doing that, however, they cannot ignore problems of opacity and hyperintensionality, which tie up with causal explanations of people's actions. Is not the causation of behavior an individualistic matter? If so, we're forced to choose between causality and community as that which is explained by the object of the directed-towardness.

## §2. The clash over content: Does it explain community or causality?

Private mental states may be causative of behavior, the nonrepresenta-tionalist concedes. The private mental states of different persons, which are the same based on the syntactic similarity of the sentences they instantiate or the similarity of their conceptual roles, may be useful for predicting that they'll behave similarly. Suppose Belia believes she's *messed her best dress*, and she desires *to keep it clean*. Anyone knowing that would predict she'll clean it at the first opportunity. Similarly, if a lady in Japan believes she's *messed her best dress*, and she desires *to keep it clean*, then they'd predict that she too will clean it at the first opportunity. These considerations are supported by semantic ascent to the reports: Although the representations in the reports of each person's attitudes are type-identical syntactically, the attitudes occur at different times and refer to different dresses and different soiling agents. So we wouldn't say they agree in their beliefs and desires. Yet they engage in similar behavior as a result of an isomorphism between their representations, which is reflected in the syntactic identity of the content clauses in the reports.

The representationalist reasons this way:

> The object, which an attitude is directed toward, contributes to the attitude's being a cause. So it must be part of what creates the attitude's concreteness in the mind, the attitude's shape so to speak, because causes are concrete events. So Belia's attitudes are instances of representations, instances of her own making. They are her private possessions, tucked away inside her.

Thus the representationalist identifies the object of the directed-toward relation with the sentence that individuates and concretizes the mental state, which is the attitude.

How might the nonrepresentationalists reply? Many accept the appeal to syntactic entities to explain the causal powers of people's attitudes over their bodily movements. One nonrepresentationalist gambit might be to accept the utter superfluity of the object of the directed-toward relation for this particular explanatory purpose. Communal agreement and individual behavior: here are two birds one cannot kill with one stone. Nevertheless the nonrepresentationalist playing this gambit stands up for the autonomy of semantics from psychology, saying that the propositions which Belia may believe in common with other people are public entities, foci for the different persons' attitudes to be directed toward. They're not made by Belia, nor are they in her mind—in mind, yes, but not inside her mind.

Perhaps I made this nonrepresentationalist gambit concede too much to the representationalist view of causal explanation, if we were to take John Perry's views in the early 1980's as paradigmatic of this position.[2] An early 80's Perry-style nonrepresentationalist did not admit that beliefs and desires are themselves sentence-instances that cause behavior; for he said sentences have nothing to do with concretizing the beliefs and desires.

Only explicitly *linguistic* attitudes *are* directed toward representations, such as the attitude of accepting a sentence, and *these* attitudes are causes of a person's behavior. But he did not agree that beliefs or desires are among these causative attitudes. The beliefs and desires belong to the group of attitudes defined in ways that identify the attitudes that people share. Obviously folks need to know when people are agreeing with each other, despite the different wordings of what they say.

However, other nonrepresentationalists, who accept Harman's thesis that mental sentence-instances are what concretize the attitudes in people, can avoid this dichotomizing of attitudes into the causative ones and the communally shared ones. There's no basis in folk psychology for such a division of types of attitudes. Indeed, the 1980's Perry-style nonrepresentationalist's concession, that an explicit linguistic attitude of accepting a sentence is what has a causal role in behavior, was based on an artificial separation of the belief of propositions from the acceptance of the sentences which express them, as if the two attitudes could vary independently. Of course they cannot, and perhaps we acknowledge their internal^ relationship to each other by accepting the Harman identification and not singling out the explicitly linguistic attitudes. So I won't say any more about the early 1980's Perry version.

Instead of the representationalists' behavioral criterion of identifying the object of the directed-toward relation, which we stated in section S §1, nonrepresentationalism offers a communicative agreement criterion. Nonrepresentationalism says of the attitudes,

> the object of the **directed-toward** relation is that which determines agreement and disagreement among *de dicto* attitudes. We picture the agreement this way: A *public entity* is the common object that the agreeing attitudes are directed towards. Two believings are directed toward numerically^ the same nonlinguistic thing, if and only if they're in semantical agreement. For *de re* attitudes to agree, they must be not only directed toward the same entity, but also about numerically the same things.

This agreement criterion for the directed-toward relation matches the semantic criterion of identity for the object of the relation, just as the representationalist's behavioral criterion for the relation matches the syntactical or formal criterion of identity for its object. So the agreement criterion excludes the ordinary sentences of our language, but **propositions** fit the criterion. (Their intensional identity criteria, mentioned in section G, may still disqualify them, however. We'll see in subsequent sections how nonrepresentationalists use propositions to build entities that account for opacity and hyperintensionality.)

The numerical identity of the object of numerically distinct attitudes is just a corollary of its being a public object. It's not a public object of the relation if each person's attitude is directed toward a private replica of it. In other words, the nonrepresentationalist rejects any analogy between propositions and rainbows. (Two people may tell each other over the phone to look out the window to see a rainbow. They each see *it*; but in one sense, there's no one thing they each see, only a correlation between two differently located physical events. Is the "it" that their propositional attitudes agree on the same sort of "it"? No, says the nonrepresentationalist.) Another corollary of its public nature is that it's an abstract object, since no public concrete object fills the bill. Abstract objects are simpler than concrete ones, certainly simpler than things like rainbows. This corollary therefore supports the first one. Another corollary of its public nature is that it's language-independent, since people speaking different languages can agree in what they believe.

A fourth corollary of the public nature of a proposition is its truth-invariance. Think of a proposition as the common target of the various sentences, which, though uttered by different people in different times and places, mean the same by expressing it. We'd expect that all the sentences targeting the same proposition for expression will agree in truth-value.^ They're all false or else they're all true. For it's absurd to say that one person's false belief agrees with another's true one. We can, if we wish, say that a proposition is itself true, if it confers truth on all the sentences targeting it, and is false otherwise. Another test for the object of the directed-toward relation is therefore invariance in truth-value. A reason for communicating is to share beliefs. When we communicate we're concerned with the truth or falsity of what we're told, or at least with the reliability of the testimony. Sentences that use the indexicals of person, place, and tense are not invariant in truth-value from person to person, from place to place, or from time to time. So it's not the truth-value of the sentences uttered that we're not concerned with, but rather the truth-value of the propositions. Propositions do have the requisite invariance in truth-value and meet the communicative agreement criterion.

In summary, four features of propositions follow from their being public:

- Two attitudes in agreement are directed toward numerically the same proposition.
- The proposition is an abstract entity.
- The proposition is not a linguistic object.

•The proposition confers the same truth-value on all the sentences targeting it; alternatively, it is itself invariant in its truth-value.

We mentioned the go-it-alone nonrepresentationalists. They're content with this characterization of the directed-toward relation. There are other nonrepresentationalists who are more conciliatory. Despite the displacement of representations as termini of the directed-toward relation, representations are indispensable to that relation, according to the conciliatory nonrepresentationalists, who add to the criterion that the directed-toward relation is never unmediated. Just as you cannot be the grandchild of someone directly, but require the intermediation of a parent who is a child of that person, so you cannot have an attitude toward a proposition without the intermediation of a representation of it. For a person's attitude to be directed toward a proposition, the relation must be mediated by her entertaining a representation expressing it for her. We'll discuss this addendum further in section W §3. Recall the discussion in section P of the two strategies of the representationalists, the replacement strategy and the supplement strategy. I noted that the supplement strategy of the representationalist coincides with the conciliatory strategy of the nonrepresentationalist, merging in effect the two positions.

Since the nonrepresentationalist concedes that the inner sentences expressive of a person's beliefs and desires may control the person's bodily movements, it may seem the nonrepresentationalist is not interested in having the objects of the directed-toward relation explain behavior. That's not quite so. The public objects are invoked in explaining strategic behavior or collective coordinated behavior. When many people share a common goal, such as converging on a place at a time, say for a picnic, how otherwise explain their common goal if one of them says to herself, "I should go north," a second says to himself, "I should go south," a third says to herself, "I should go east," and a fourth says to himself, "I should go west starting tomorrow," a fifth says to himself in a tizzy, "Dear me, I should go west starting today"? There need not be one sentence, instances of which are in the minds of each of them. Yet they share a goal, which is the truth of some complete proposition.

Not only do the nonrepresentationalists invoke the public objects, but so do the participants in group behavior. They each can project what the others are thinking. That does not mean they can tell which sentences occupy the others' minds. If they can tell, they discover the sentences by first knowing the semantic content of those sentences. If this is the correct account of how we think of each other, the nonrepresentationalist who gives this account is making a claim about the ontology of folk psychology. When people predict and explain how others are coordinating their activities with their own, they postulate that the others' attitudes are directed to the representeds, not the representations of those representeds. The representeds are propositions or at least public objects like propositions.

How reconcile this account of coordinated action with the earlier account of getting the soiled dress cleaned? In that example the causes were sentences, but the emphasis was not on coordinating with others, only on an individual's making the motions needed to achieve the desired outcome. The nonrepresentationalist might put the individual and group processes together this way: Coordination is a sophisticated form of action which supervenes on the individual bodily movements of many individuals. So coordination is built upon individual causal processes.

The nonrepresentationalist can also save the principle announced at the beginning of section N, upon which we based our no-name theory of indexical attitudes. In section S we derived this principle as a corollary of the representationalist account of the directed-toward relation. But now, it must be saved independently. I'll address this in subsection §4 in the context of the particular form of nonrepresentationalism I favor. Suffice it to say now that, even according to the nonrepresentationalist account of the directed-toward relation, enunciated earlier, the individual causal processes may have intentional components that are directed toward incomplete propositions, which are directly attributed.

Need we choose between representationalism and nonrepresentationalism? Might we not allow for two equally valid ways for believings to be instances of the same belief-type, namely, a syntactic or representational way and a semantic way? By allowing Harman's identification of mental sentence-instances with concretizations of attitudes, many nonrepresentationalisms already do allow this. But representationalism would have to have more than that, if it's to be combined with nonrepresentationalism, something that would amount to postulating that each attitude has two directed-toward relations. One of the two has its terminus in a representation and the other in the proposition represented. The representationalist smells a rather pungent redundancy. Unless there's a way to recover some parsimony, the representationalist avoids this option. There may be a way for a syncretist^ like me to recover some parsimony, after all. Back to Quine, who I take to be a sort of nonrepresentationalist, one who manages to keep his allegiance to the extensionalist ideal of intelligibility:

### §3. Nonrepresentationalism with eternal sentences.

Let's evaluate the nonrepresentationalist argument that sentences are unsuitable as the objects that beliefs are directed toward. Quine, once again, has a theory which may undermine the argument. He brings the type-instance distinction, as it applies to syntactically identical sentence-instances, into line with the way it has to apply to semantically identical belief-instances. If Quine can find a segment of syntax sufficient for creating sentence-instances of the same syntactic type that match up one-to-one with belief-instances of the same semantic type, he's undermined the argument presented in subsection §1. The instances of syntactic types, when syntax is not restricted to the segment Quine needs, are the sentences in LOT, but the restricted syntax, with which Quine creates match-ups to instances of semantic types, yields another batch of sentences which correspond to the intuitively correct units that attitudes are directed towards. Also he must not require the latter sentences to be uttered, since then there'd only be a finite number of them. If he succeeds, nonrepresentationalism may impute to folk psychology an ontology that's less different from that imputed by representationalism than it seemed to at first sight. In particular he'll have provided nonrepresentationalism with an ontology freed from nonextensional identity conditions.

As we proceed, be on guard against lapsing into a sententialist way of thinking. We're about to deal with sentences again. So the confusion is easy to fall into, but the concepts we're about to develop are not part of sententialism. They are not about mentalese sentences. They develop a nonrepresentationalist position, offering strange new sentences as public objects that do everything that propositions do as candidates for objects of the directed-toward relation, but do it better. Quine was a behaviorist, not inclined to put much weight on the speculations of sententialists, however rooted in material brains or the descriptive metaphysics of folk psychology they might've been.

The general procedure for finding a part of syntax that will mirror semantics, one that Quine has championed for purposes of logic, is to decontextualize sentences, that is, make them such that, if they're ever true, they're true at all times in all places as uttered by anyone. Following Quine's instructions,[3] we eliminate the tenses and the words "I," "you," "this," and "now" from the vocabulary. Decontextualizing requires that all the words that depend for their meaning on the context in which they're uttered, like these pronouns and demonstrative expressions, be replaced by proper names or definite descriptions used attributively. Even tenses are to be replaced by reference to dates. For example, if you said on New Year's Day, 2000,

> Arthur likes logic today,

what you said is regimented thus:

> Arthur like[s] logic sometime, perhaps all the time, between January 1, 2000, and January 2, 2000.

The bracketed suffix, "[s]," is supposed to represent a cancellation of the present tense on the verb. The tense is redundant since all the time indication is done by the dates in this regimentation. Suppose, instead of the present-tensed sentence, you said,

> Arthur will like logic.

The future tense is replaced by a quantification^ over times after now, and "now" is replaced by a date:

> Sometime after January 1, 2000, is such that Arthur like[s] logic then.

Quine even finds ordinary proper names like "Arthur" suspect because of a possible context-dependence of their meaning. (Standard names like "January 1, 2000 AD," which we defined in section F, are not suspect in this way, for although they depend on a system of naming—for instance, dates may be in the Julian or the Gregorian calendar system; the Gregorian Jan. 1, 2000 is the Julian Jan. 1, 1999—we can be explicit about the system being used rather than rely on context.) Quine extends Russell's analysis of definite descriptions to proper names to get rid of them. He can apply the analysis, because anything with a proper name has a property which belongs to it uniquely. It may be just the property of having that proper name, or it may be a modally rigid property. The latter is preferable, since we're not following Quine in rejecting modal logic. We replace the predicate "is Arthur" with something that means a modally rigid property of Arthur and sounds more like a predicate: "arthurizes." Replace the sentence containing a proper name with a three-clause Russellian paraphrase:

> Something arthurizes; nothing else arthurizes, and it like[s] logic sometime after January 1, 2000, Gregorian calendar.

The sentences that result once the process of decontextualizing is completed, Quine calls **eternal sentences**. Truth or falsehood attaches to each such sentence eternally in the sense that we can specify *any* time and place for evaluating the sentence and it will be true at *all* such times and places if it's true at *any* of them. Likewise for falsehood. The payoff of this maneuver is that every difference of meaning is now mirrored in a syntactic difference or difference in shape. The distinction between a type and its instance is less important for eternal sentences, since any two instances of the eternal sentence-type must agree in truth value. For any noneternal sentence-type that can be instantiated in different contexts to mean different things, corresponding to each of those distinct meanings is a distinct eternal sentence.

An argument, due to Felix Mühlhölzer, suggests that, if a sentence is truly eternalized, it's invariant under appropriate transformations and so is objective information in the sense we argued for in section U. We're to suppose a set of appropriate transformations do change a sentence from true to false. Since the theory that endorses the transformations as appropriate says the transformations should leave unchanged what is represented about the world, the change in truth-value reveals an inexplicit constituent in the sentence, and so the sentence is not yet eternalized. This argument allows us to state another definition of **objectivity** equivalent to the one in terms of invariance, namely, objective information is what eternal sentences state. This is Mühlhölzer's definition.[4] By analogy to theorems about soundness (correctness) and completeness in formal logic, we may think of this definition as sound, if all information that's objective by it is objective by the one in section U, and it's complete, if all information that's objective by the one in section U is objective by it. The little argument above pertains to the definition's soundness.

### §4. Reconciling eternal sentences with the essential indexical.

Eternalizing sentences involves replacing indexical terms in them with expressions whose meaning is fixed independently of context and filling in all ellipses that the context of utterance filled in for us. Even observation sentences, or rather the uttered instances of them, have an eternalized format. Consequently, no holophrastic sentence is an eternal sentence.

We must consider the ramifications of eternalizing for the thesis of the essential indexical, mentioned in section M. Our recourse to eternal sentences can be consistent with holding to the thesis of the essential indexical. For this thesis is really the thesis that direct attribution (defined in section N §4) is essential and acts of attributing fall squarely on the side of concrete events, distinct from that which is attributed. The procedure of eternalizing can eternalize the predicates (i.e., the incomplete sentences) which an agent, say Belia, directly attributes to herself and which this form of *de re* attitude would have to be directed toward, according to this nonrepresentationalist theory. The same can be said of the incomplete sentences which her acts of believing or desiring predicate *de re*.

One may wonder what point there is to eternalizing the predicates of direct attributions. Can a pair of them ever agree, or one of them ever agree with any other attitude? Review the example we started with: I directly attribute the incomplete eternal sentence, "like logic"; you attribute to me, *de re*, the same incomplete eternal sentence, "like logic." To fully characterize agreement of *de re* attitudes, however, the criterion requires that the subject of the attributions be the same also. For, if each of us were *directly* attributing one sentence, "like logic," that would not count as our agreeing. Although the attribute and the now, i.e., the temporal subject of our attributings, are the same, the personal subjects would be you for you and me for me. I do see  point, however, to eternalizing the attribute which a direct attribution is directed toward: Between two direct attributions, it reveals agreement at least on the property of a time, between a direct attribution and another attitude, it also reveals agreement on the property of a person, and even when agreement is not the immediate issue, it reveals the objective information in the attribution, as we noted at the end of the last subsection.

But Quine must face a dilemma that infects his combined views that all beliefs are *de dicto* and their *dicta* are complete sentences: Either he must reject the thesis of the essential indexical in making the sentences eternal so that they match our intuitive communicative semantic identity conditions for beliefs, or he must allow indexical sentences to be the complete sentences that indexical attitudes are directed toward, in which case he must reject our intuitions about the identity of beliefs, which we discussed in sections M and N. Quine does not address this issue. We on his behalf avoid both alternatives, particularly avoiding the rejection of the nonidentity of beliefs about oneself and beliefs *de dicto*. We avoid that and we avoid the undermining of the decontextualizing by allowing incomplete eternal sentences to be the objects of the directed-toward relation of *de re* attitudes. We acknowledge that a nonrepresentationalist who accepts the essential indexical must avoid elevating the agreement criterion to the level of a criterion for the numerical identity of attitudes. This is not even tempting except in the intrapersonal case. Reverting back to the examples in section M, David changed his mind, Mach changed his mind, Harriet changed her mind. So they had successive distinct beliefs, changing to *de se* from *de re* that was based on causal rapport. These successive beliefs agreed, in accord with the agreement criterion, but the criterion does not say that therefore the seemingly successive beliefs are therefore really numerically one belief. They are as they seem: two.

If attitudes are directed only toward eternal sentences, incomplete as well as complete ones, would the possible *content-types* of people's beliefs, desires, and other attitudes map one-to-one on to the eternal sentence-types? Yes, despite the semantical nature of the attitude-types and the syntactic nature of the sentence-types. Eternal sentences have an advantage over propositions in this respect, in that there's not a one-to-one matching by synonymy between the set of eternal sentences and the set of propositions. If there were, eternal sentences would be just as intensional as propositions, and so just as insufficiently differentiated to be objects of the directed-toward relation as propositions are. In fact here are two distinct eternal sentences:

> All equiangular triangles are equilateral.
> All equilateral triangles are equiangular.

They each express the same proposition, since they are provably equivalent, but they are distinct sentences nevertheless. This divergence from propositions is a mark in their favor, since someone could believe one of them and not the other.

### §5. An eternal sentence nonrepresentationalist theory of reports.

So much for the beliefs themselves. Let's now consider reports—how Rep might report beliefs directed toward eternal sentences. Direct attributions are reported in *de re* reports, either by Belia self-reporting or by Rep reporting on her. First, they could still use indexicals in the reports' about-positions, and, secondly, Belia's directly attributing an eternal predicate of herself and her present moment locates the two referents indexically. So eternalized incomplete sentences would be consistent with the thesis of the essential indexical. Indexicals are not essential inside the sentence. The same can be said of reports of other *de re* attitudes.

Rep's that-clause is correct if the sentence in his that-clause expresses numerically the same eternal sentence as Belia's sentence in LOT expresses. Rep need not have mastered the art of eternalizing sentences to make his reports. They figure only in our theory of the correctness of his reports. Belia's the only one who knows the sentence in LOT, and that's why she's in charge of the that-clause. She also need not know how to eternalize either her sentence in LOT or Rep's sentence. As an alternative to eternalizing, there's the procedure of applying "transformation equations," so to speak, directly to one of the sentences to produce the other. We discussed that in the previous section. The device of an eternal sentence is equivalent to a procedure that uses transformations.

It should be possible, however, for Rep to use eternal sentences in his that-clauses. And Quine should have the right to propose a regimentation of reports which reveals their true nature, according to his own theory. (This would not be regimentation as preparation of data, but as theoretic interpretation.) We have two models which the regimentation of attitudes as directed toward eternal sentences might emulate, namely, the two ways Rep might report what Belia *says*: direct **quotation** and indirect quotation. Let's consider each in turn. Direct quotation is committed to using the exact words of the person quoted, and the words are enclosed in quotation marks. This alternative has desirable consequences for ontology. Quotation marks are semantically powerful. The reference of an expression that begins and ends with quotation marks is constructed from its component expressions, but not in the usual way, which is to construct it from the references of the component expressions. Instead we construct it from the enclosed words themselves. What's the difference between quoting Belia in these two ways?

"There goes the woodchuck."
"There" "goes" "the" "woodchuck."

No difference that makes any difference, it seems. Indeed what's the difference between quoting a word and quoting its spelling?

"There"
"T" "h" "e" "r" "e"

The reference of a phrase that begins and ends with quotation marks is just the letters in a particular order inside the quotation marks. So Belia can say about the skunk the letters here quoted: "it is a woodchuck." Belia is in as much of a relation with other genuine entities, the skunk and some letters, when the abstract relation '$x$ says words "$y$" to be true of $z$' is applied to her, she being $x$, as she is with the lawn she's standing on.

So far we've only discussed quotation in the context of reporting the act of saying something. The notional sense of belief can also be put in terms of believes-true, where that which is believed-true is a complete sentence in quotation marks. Let's explore this analogy, if only to see why we must reject it in the end. If the regimentation of attitude reports were to use direct quotation, then, since logic does not snoop for pronominal anaphora (cross-references) inside quotations (since inside a quotation only the letters themselves are being referred to), all the logically embarrassing stuff, the failure of intersubstitution and generalization, would be out of sight for logic. Quine's glad of that. To emphasize that his analysis presupposes nothing but real things, Quine even replaces the words and the quotation marks around them with the *names* of the letters used to spell the words. Letters are well-defined entities, and naming them raises no problems for extensionality![5] So the ultimate motivation for Quine's device of eternal sentences is not to undermine nonrepresent-ationalism, but to legitimize and reinforce it by putting the entities it requires on a less controversial ontological footing. The entities are sup-posed to be public, and eternal sentences are taken to be constructed from public entities, and the sentences have extensional identity conditions.

The device of direct quotation of an eternal sentence does have the consequence, perhaps too stringent, of not even allowing substitution, preserving truth, of synonyms for synonyms in the quoted *dictum* of the propositional attitude. For synonyms consist of different letters. It would not even allow translation of the *dictum* into another language, when we translate the report into that language. Yet all these are equally valid ways of reporting Belia's beliefs, and we end up with a drastic overcount of Belia's beliefs. They all report the same belief. This may seem like the perfect solution to the hyperintensionality and opacity of that-clauses. It goes too far, however, for surely Belia may approve many synonym substitutions, perhaps an infinity of them, like affirmations, double nega-tions, quadruple negations, etc., as all equally expressive of her *one* belief. It's not the case (and not not not the case) that she has an infinity of beliefs, just because she admits an infinity of sentences as equally expressive of her belief.

We may try to amend the Quinean paraphrase, which refers to letters or words, to keep the distinction between indirect and direct quotation. Regimentations of Rep's reports of Belia's beliefs are indirect quotations. Rep says:

> Belia believes some phrase in her LOT, which is expressive of all the same eternalized phrases as my (Rep's) phrase "having gone into the bushes" is expressive of, to be true about the skunk.

And Rep might've used one of the eternalized phrases, which are all expressive of each other. What makes one eternal sentence expressive of another? That they are equivalent? That cannot be our criterion because we'd lose our solution to the problem of hyperintensionality, namely language's providing a greater multiplicity than intensions provide. We should go back to saying attitudes are directed toward single eternal sentences. Eternal sentences give us all the distinctions we need to meet the problems of opacity and hyperintensionality in reports. In fact, although they give us way too many distinctions for any one person, potentially all the distinctions are needed to account for all possible attitudes. To solve the problem of overcount of beliefs for some particular person, Belia for instance, we're being driven back into Belia's mind for the language, indeed the idiolect,^ to create eternal sentences in. Many a nonrepresentationalist pleads, let's not go back there!

Militating in favor of the idiolect strategy, however, there's the distinction I alluded to in section C between the child or student who believes a sentence true without understanding its import, that is, simply on faith. This is a case where the state of quoting a sentence and believing it true is distinct from the state of believing what the sentence says. Even if we accept that attitudes are directed toward eternal sentences, the distinction's been lost between believing in the truth of a sentence on faith and, understanding what the sentence says, believing what it says. To recapture the distinction, we eternal sentence nonrepresentationalists must now replace "believes-true" with "believes-true, with understanding of it" or alternatively, "without understanding of it." We can elaborate the difference between the phrases in accord with the inferential role semantics of section S, also decontextualized. Someone who understands a sentence exploits its analytic and probabilistic relations, and models the understood domain at a semantic metalevel, in addition to being able to see the purely deductive implications of the sentence. The result may be idiolectal for the person, in that the inferential role a sentence has for her may differ from a standard role for that sentence, by being poorer than the standard, richer than it, or just plain crazy in comparison.

It would be confusion on a critic's part to object that eternal sentences and their inferential roles cannot really do the work of being that which is in a believer's mind, for Quine never intended us to suppose that. So they're not the stuff of mentalese. Despite the recourse to sentences, Quine is not giving us a species of sententialism, as I described that position. It's rather just an ontological refinement of nonrepresentationalism. The regimentation it implies is for a clearer ontology and a clearer theory of meaning. (When I launched regimentation in section C, I mentioned that it also had uses in theory. Eternal sentences are theoretically motivated constructs.)

## §6. Problems with eternal sentence nonrepresentationalism.

Despite the easy improvements over Quine's version, such as incomplete as well as complete eternal sentences with a decontextualized semantics, the device of eternal sentences as a replacement for propositions has not met with much favor among nonrepresentationalists. It's a bit of a stretch to claim that folk psychology posits eternal sentences. The theory need not claim that, however. As a theory of directed-towardness, it may be going beyond folk psychology in a limited way in precisely the areas that folk psychology is either silent or confused about. In section W we'll discuss a puzzle that suggests just that. There we'll deal with the issue of specifying the language.

I declare myself satisfied with a nonrepresentationalism that posits incomplete as well as complete eternal sentences as the objects of directed-towardness. All the causal desiderata which motivate the representationalist are adequately captured by accepting Harman's identification of the psychological state with the uttered representation *in situ*. That representation occupies the causal role and is not the object of the directed-towardness, but from it Belia can project its decontextualized eternal sentential version, unuttered, abstract, and idealized, as the object of her state's directed-towardness. Rep can project in the converse direction by empathy. My syncretism is fulfilled in that the position does justice to the explaining of both community and causality. It's parsimonious ontologically, coheres with the extensionalist ideal of intelligibility, accommodates the indeterminacies of reference and translation, and solves the problems of hyperintensionality and opacity without abridging the believers control of the that-clause of reports. That said, I admit to a few unsolved problems:

Two features of eternal sentences are problematic. First, are there enough sentences to even match all the propositions? There would have to be a transfinite^ number of them. Quine believes we can simply stipulate a language sufficiently strong to generate that many sentences. We can allow infinitely long sentences, such as the conjunction of the infinitely many finite declarative sentences, which of course will be an inconsistent sentence. Some awfully strange consequences flow from this admission.[6] Second, a problem which has bothered even Quine is that eternal sentences, unlike propositions, are meaningful relatively to a language and to other devices for making meaning determinate, such as measurement systems. The problem is whether we can ever complete the process of decontextualizing, absolutizing, and eternalizing. For example, if we put a date in the sentence, must we say the date is in the Gregorian calendar? If we add 7 to 5 and get 12, must we specify our addition is in base 10 notation? Surely some of these, like the fixing of which language the sentence is in, must be left to context. For, if I say the language is "English," must I specify that *that* word is to be understood as an English word? A vicious regress lurks here.

One way to stop an infinite regress of absolutizing is to state the truth conditions for eternal sentences in a semantic interpretation of the language. If a person can distinguish between conditions in which a sentence is true and conditions in which it's false, perhaps that's a sufficient^ condition for her knowing the meaning of the sentence. (This is a fundamental thesis about meaning, like the context principle mentioned in section B. We'll not pursue it here.) Further, given a language's interpretation in a semantics, all eternal sentences need not be in just one language, for their logical interconnections can be represented semantically even if they're in different languages. We resort to a multiplicity of languages in section W.

Still another problem: How rich is the vocabulary of this language? Does it contain an expression for every possible concept? No, but its vocabulary is extendable, so that we can add words for newly invented concepts to the language and then extend its semantic interpretation. We can add concepts that Quine would avoid, such as modal idioms and ways of referring to intensional entities. In the next section we'll find reason to add vocabulary of no great interest just so Rep can accommodate the idiosyncratic conceptualizations that believers come up with. So it should never be the case that someone could point to a thought which no eternal sentence could express. Not that some haven't tried![7]

A more serious problem, if it were a problem, would be that directed-towardness must have meanings for its object, and sentences are not their meanings. This is not a problem though, for eternal sentence nonrepresentationalism can steal a page from the representationalist account of internal meaning. We appeal again to the conceptual role semantics of section S: Meanings are just the conceptual roles of the sentences and the words in the sentences. That semantics was applied to the actual representations in people's minds, but easy adjustments make possible its application to eternal sentences. Since the eternal sentences and many of the words in those sentences are not actually instantiated in the minds of the people whose attitudes are directed toward them, the roles cannot be causal roles nor can the meanings be psychological states. They are instead logical roles in implications and probabilistic relevance^ relations among eternal sentences and predicates. These roles are abstract, but then so are the eternal sentences. To call the roles "internal meanings" is therefore a misnomer, since nothing internal is intended by this nonrepresentationalist version of **conceptual role semantics**. Rather than being internal, role-meanings are just ontologically cost-free. That is to say, if you got the sentences, you got their roles at no added cost. So it's ok to amend eternal sentence nonrepresentationalism to say the object of directed-towardness is a meaning in the sense of the logical role of an eternal sentence or eternal predicate.

I find that eternal sentence nonrepresentationalism is at least as problem-free as any form of nonrepresentationalism, and probably more so. It also works well with the Davidsonian regimentation. We've been working with the common regimentation of reports, which require that-clauses, but recall the Davidsonian regimentation which I introduced in sections C and E. It analyzed a report into two sentences with distinct forces. The difference in their forces, pretense and nonpretense, prevented their being treated as a logical unit for the purposes of generalization, thereby blocking the illogical results we explored in section E. When the reporter utters the sentence which he says Belia believes, he neither quotes Belia nor states an eternal sentence. Instead he utters a sentence with tenses and pronouns appropriate for an utterance coming from himself at the time and place he's actually in. What is required for the truth of the report is that this sentence say "the same thing" as what Belia believes. They say the same thing if they express the same eternal sentence. So Quine could accept the Davidsonian regimentation, and in fact his remarks about it are favorable.

# Notes

1.  Refer to section H, note 5, and section Q, note 16, for the semantic conception of theories, which I am presupposing here. The moral I wish to draw is that what a person's attitudes are directed toward can be characterized semantically without reference to any sentences they may embody.

2.  Perry makes the contrast between accepting sentences and believing propositions in his "Belief and Acceptance" (1980), reprinted in his *The Problem of the Essential Indexical and Other Essays* (1993, expanded edition 2000). But acceptance becomes a mode of individuation of beliefs in "The Prince and the Phone Booth: Reporting Puzzling Beliefs," co-authored with Mark Crimmins (1989), reprinted in *The Problem of the Essential Indexical and Other Essays*. The later view is hardly distinguishable from Harman's identification, which was presented in section P.

3.  W. V. Quine, *Word and Object* (MIT Press, 1960), §§40 and 43.

4.  Felix Mühlhölzer, "On Objectivity" *Erkenntnis* 28 (1988) 185-230. See page 218 for the argument that suggested the one in the text. See page 192 for the definition of objectivity in terms of eternal sentences.

5.  *Pursuit of Truth*, 69-70.

6.  With this allowance, we can now prove that the number of sentences transcends even all the transfinite numbers: Omitting all sentences of the form, "*a* is humbug," "*a* is truly humbug," "*a* is truly, truly humbug," and so on, where *a* names your favorite bit of humbug, take the set of all other sentences which are finite in length. This set is the same size as the set of natural numbers. Now

consider the set whose members are the null set^, one-membered sets whose sole members are each of the sentences, two-membered sets whose members are each pair of them, three-membered sets whose members are each triple of them, and so on, up to the set of all of them. This is the set of all the subsets of the set of sentences. We can construct another set from this set, replacing each two-membered set with the conjunction of the two of them, each three-membered set with the conjunction of the three of them, and so on up to the one we just allowed in the text, the conjunction of all of them. We match the null set with the sentence "*a* is humbug." This set of sentences is the same size as the set of all the subsets of the set of natural numbers, which Cantor proved is larger than the set of natural numbers. (Yes, larger than infinite.) We can generate even larger sets of sentences similarly, starting with the set we just constructed, forming the set of all its subsets, and constructing a set of conjunctive sentences to match each subset, plus one of our humbug sentences to match the null set. Those familiar with set theory can read a defense of this idea in D. Terence Langendoen and Paul M. Postal, *The Vastness of Natural Languages* (1984).

7. One who has is George Bealer, "Universals," *Journal of Philosophy* 90 (1993) 5-32. He tries to show that an ontology of abstract entities that meet extensional identity conditions, such as an ontology of sentence-types, is insufficient for specifying all the possible objects of the directed-toward relation. He concludes that "'that'-clauses do not denote linguistic entities (either types or tokens)" (p. 25). He purports to derive an obviously false conclusion (that every-thing is a necessary being) from the supposition that an extensional ontology is sufficient, thereby disproving the supposition. He employs other controversial premises, and the argument is carried out in second-order quantified modal logic. We cannot evaluate it here because of its reliance on advanced logic.

# W. Singular Sentences and Singular Propositions

In section A, I stated alternative pairs of definitions of relational and notional belief. I favored the pair that distinguished the two in terms of the completeness or incompleteness of the propositions they were directed toward. The alternative definitions distinguished the two in terms of the singularity or generality of the propositions they were directed toward. These alternatives nagged us in Part II, in connection with the issue of the indispensability of causal rapport. Now again we must face the question which pair of definitions is correct. First we'll face the alternatives expressed in terms of singular eternal sentences, then in terms of singular propositions.

## §1. A puzzle about belief involving eternal sentences, and its solution.

Eternal sentence nonrepresentationalism manages to join the communicative agreement criterion of the directed-toward relation with the syntactic criterion of identity for the objects of that relation. It seems, however, we can generate paradox in the view that makes the words and sentences of our public languages the objects that our beliefs are directed toward, whether they be the uttered sentences (which in any case individuate and concretize our attitudes) or the unuttered abstract entities like eternal sentences, if the view also seeks to satisfy simultaneously the communicative agreement criterion for the directed-toward relation rather than the behavioral one. In short, we seem to generate paradox for eternal sentences. Beliefs may be concretized and individuated by mentally uttering sentences, but if Rep's that-clauses are not referring to them, and if they're not the objects of the directed-toward relation, we can ignore them. The paradox affects public sentences.

We set up the paradox: Belia has a belief in English that Florence is a beautiful city. She's had that belief since she was a child and looked at travel books. When Rep reported her belief to curious Italians, he told them truthfully in Italian that Belia believed *Firenze è bella*. However, although Belia has become fluent in Italian, she has never made the connection that Firenze is the Italian name for Florence. Nevertheless she cannot object to Rep's that-clause, for surely it's correct. When as an adult she went to San Marino (in section H), she was told in Italian that "Firenze non è bella." Perhaps the San Marinoans were envious of Florence, but, whatever the reason for their saying so, Belia heard it enough times so that she too came to believe in Italian, *Firenze non è bella*.

The case has immediate consequences for the view that eternal sentences are the objects of the directed-toward relation. We've been thinking of them all as being in the same language. How, then, if Belia has the two beliefs, are those beliefs directed toward distinct eternal sentences, unless eternal sentences may differ in language too? Surely they may. So, we now have eternal sentences in two languages. And why stop with two? We can even allow idiosyncratic versions of a single language, which happen to correspond to the idiolects^ of believers. That sort of distinguishing is more easily accomplished for eternal sentences than for propositions, which are not in languages. So major problems for propositions, but none for eternal sentences—yet.

Suppose we accept a principle of translation between public languages:

> If a sentence of one language expresses a truth in that language, then any translation of it into any other language also expresses a truth (in that other language).[1]

The **translation principle** applies to the sentences mentally uttered by Belia in English and Italian, and also to the unuttered eternal sentences which her two attitudes are directed toward, according to the eternal sentence version of nonrepresentationalism which we're considering. We'll only apply the translation principle to the eternal sentences. Inconsistency in the believer and contradiction in the reporter follow. Consider the several reports of her beliefs that Rep may make. Begin with the *de dicto* ones:

Belia believes that Florence is beautiful,

and translating from the Italian:

Belia believes that Florence is not beautiful.

That report is true too by the translation principle. Poor Belia. Is she in such an inconsistent state of mind though? She just doesn't know that Firenze is Florence.

And now for poor Rep. In Italian Belia has no inclination to assent to "Firenze è bella"; in fact everything suggests she does not believe it. So Rep, translating from the Italian, reports:

Belia does not believe that Florence is beautiful.

Rep has just contradicted himself, for this third report contradicts the first of his reports.

It makes no difference if we move to the *de re* format:

> Belia believes about Florence, that it is and that it's not beautiful.
> Belia believes and does not believe about Florence that it's beautiful.

The first makes Belia inconsistent, the second makes Rep contradict himself.

The curious Italians, who learnt from Rep when Belia was a child that she believed *Firenze è bella*, wonder why Belia has now changed her mind. She tells them in Italian she never changed her mind, and she's right. Poor Rep cannot explain why his Italian report of long ago was true, his current report is also true, and Belia never changed her mind in the meantime.

The nonrepresentationalist who defends the view that beliefs are directed toward eternal sentences can reply: The paradox is solvable for the *de dicto* cases by the simple expedient of distinguishing the translation *principle* from the particular translation manuals governing translations between particular languages. The paradox arises simply from Rep using the wrong manual. As long as we think of sentences about purely physical matters, such as whether eating gold is good for one's arthritis, the translation manuals are simply the ones compiled in our bilingual dictionaries and grammars. But as the principle is stated, it covers statements of psychological attitudes too, and there we must also observe the principle that *Belia's in charge of the report's that-clause.* In particular Rep may not use in his translations any identity of meaning which Belia positively denies. We saw that she denies the identity of Firenze with Florence. So he may not translate her "Firenze" as "Florence" in reporting her that-clauses. Particular translational equivalencies that work ordinarily may not work for the idiolect^ of the person being reported on. We should require of such equivalencies that they preserve idiolectal synonymy and not just extensional equivalence.

That feature of translation may be obscured by the fact that in our example we seem to be translating a proper name. The meaning of a logically proper name is the thing meant. We cannot simply declare that the name in her idiolect of English and the name in her idiolect of Italian are not two names of the same thing. For, since there aren't two things for them to name, at least one of them would not be a name at all in that case. She does not believe gibberish, nor can it be that she believes two true things, namely the beauty of Florence and the lack of beauty of Firenze. I see two solutions to this difficulty of applying the idea of synonymy to proper names. One is to bite the bullet, keeping proper names and spurning their having external meanings, thereby denying any force to arguments based on appeals to such meanings. The derivations of contradiction would assume synonymy where there was none. The other is to eliminate proper names from eternal sentences, so that the objects of directed-towardness are either complete general eternal sentences or incomplete eternal sentences. The first alternative would allow complete singular eternal sentences to be objects of directed-towardness; the second would not.

We might rationalize the spurning of external meanings by noting that we've already spurned such external meanings as propositions by positing eternal sentences as the objects of the directed-toward relation. Eternal sentences are *substitutes* for external meanings, of which propositions are one example, so let's not talk of the meanings they have! On this alternative we just go on blithely using the two words "Florence" and "Firenze" in positions reserved for singular terms, regardless of any criticisms that appeal to external meanings to establish their synonymy. There'd still be the meanings of eternal sentences, in the sense developed in sections S and V, namely, that predicates and sentences would have roles in implications and probabilistic relevance^ relations, abstract roles, not causal roles, since eternal sentences do not occur concretely in the people whose attitudes are directed toward them. The attitudes themselves have the causal roles.

The other solution takes the problem of proper names in the object of the directed-toward relation to be deeper than our puzzle intimates. For whatever the logical role of a proper name may be, it's at least to be a modally rigid designator of a thing in all its concreteness. We'll develop a thought experiment at the end of this section whose conclusion is that designators of contingent things, that purport to capture their designees in all their concreteness, are not properly part of any sentence which is an object of a directed-toward relation. In anticipation of this result, following Quine's lead, the second solution eliminates proper names from eternal sentences. It regiments logically proper names out of eternal sentences, putting modally rigid definite descriptions in their place. Descriptions abstract from the full concreteness of their designees. Demonstratives that accompany acts of pointing would also be eliminated, using in their place some descriptions salient to the pointing. (Belia's pronouns "I" and "now" would not be eliminated that way, but instead would indicate that eternal predicates, incomplete eternal sentences, were the objects of the directed-toward relation as suggested by the no-name theory in section N.) Following this alternative, we'd say her idiolects of English and Italian do not treat the two modally rigid definite descriptions "is Florence" and "è Firenze" as synonymous and intertranslatable, even though they have the same extension. Let's provisionally opt for this second alternative.

Have we been too facile in cooking up a "solution"? Certainly the philosopher who gave us this puzzle, Kripke, would say so, for he quite peremptorily dismissed any purported solution that appealed to translation between idiolects. He'd say that by invoking idiolects and eliminating proper names we simply rendered unanswerable the question he asked, which was, what does Belia believe as expressed in ordinary public languages? Does she or doesn't she believe Florence is beautiful?

To the latter question, I'd reply that Kripke has discovered a hole in folk psychology, in that it leads to incoherence when faced with the beliefs of bilinguals. There's no coherent answer in naive folk psychology to his question. The puzzle has no solution. Since the disease has no cure, it must be prevented from occurring. Therefore a theory that makes minimal amendments to folk psychology is justified, if it expands folk psychology enough to deal coherently with the case. The elimination of proper names does that. So does the appeal to idiolects.

The appeal to idiolects must be constrained, however. In section S, in the course of several thought experiments of the twin-earth genre, we considered a person whose use of the word "arthritis" was infected with misinformation, but which was properly translated as "arthritis" anyway, because she intended to use it in the standard way and would correct her use of it if she were aware of her mistakes. Does not the same apply to Belia's use of "Firenze"? If so, then it's correctly translated as "Florence" even for her Italian idiolect, and all the paradoxes remain unresolved.

We're making a lot hang on flimsy intuitions that can be pushed either way. If we let Belia choose the translation manual for Rep to use, we can imagine her choice governed by the title of the manual or by the particular rules contained in the manual. If she just goes by the title, she'll choose "Standard Italian Into Standard English." She'll be surprised by the results and will learn something. Alternatively, if she goes by her examination of the particular rules and ignores the title, she'll pick another manual that contains the rule, "leave the Italian 'Firenze' as is in the translation." She'll be pleased with the results. She won't learn anything, unless she looks at the manual's title, "Belia's Idiolectal Italian Into Standard English." When intuitions are unclear, we can regiment in the interest of clarity of theory. Clarity of theory requires her to choose in the latter way. For, if we're to suppose she hands Rep a manual, whose use causes Rep to contradict himself, contradiction enters the theory itself. The theory we're talking about is the eternal sentence version of nonrepresentationalism.

The situation and solution would be the same if Belia used an English name nonstandardly. For instance, she may use one person's name as if it were the name of two people. Kripke also considered this case. Suppose that Belia knows that Ignace Paderewski was premier and president of Poland and that Ignace Paderewski was a composer of classical music. She erroneously believes the nonidentity of Paderewski the president and Paderewski the composer. Kripke thinks there's only one language involved in this version of the paradox. Although we must admit Belia is now thinking only in English, and so the eternal sentences her thoughts would be directed toward would both be English and contain modally rigid definite descriptions created from the proper name in the way Quine recommends, nevertheless does not her language of thought differ from our English? Belia's idiolect is again distinct from the standard English we speak, because it contains the two proper names or the two predicates that happen to sound alike, unlike our language, which contains only the one.

It's not that *any* difference of opinion as to matters of fact leads to a difference of idiolect, but only that differences on matters of necessary truth do, and identities and differences are necessary truths, as noted in section F. Such differences pave the way to contradictory translations, for Belia may believe of Paderewski the composer that he was a good musician and of Paderewski the statesman that he was not a good musician. In the case of Florence, the languages for expressing eternal sentences became idiolectal when she came to believe the necessarily false nonidentity of Florence and Firenze. That's how Rep could translate her earlier belief correctly as he did, but could not maintain that translation after she acquired the necessarily false belief. So, *pace* Kripke, we may invoke idiolects and the translation principle to make folk psychology immune to the paradox.

For a nonrepresentationalist to appeal to idiolects is to endanger one of the key insights of the position, namely, that the objects of the directed-toward relation are common or public objects. To keep from undermining that insight, we must insist that idiolects are largely intertranslatable. How translate Belia's Paderewski beliefs from her idiolectal English into our standard English? If we translate both her names for the composer-statesman into the one name available in standard English, because she *intends* to be speaking standard English, we pin her and ourselves into contradictions. Therefore, we should not. Our rule of translation should say "translate her predicate 'is Paderewski' into English with one or other of two subscripts attached, depending on whether the discourse concerns politics or culture." More generally, we must face up to the fact that beliefs directed toward distinct objects may not be translatable into the standard language in ways that show their difference. Moreover standard language may need to be enlarged to enable it to express the object of someone's belief.

I'm not attacking the translation principle itself. The translation principle is as correct for idiolects as for public languages; rather I claim the rule for a certain word, which is for translating the word in the common language, may not be for translating its homonym in the idiolect.

That suffices to block the paradox for the *de dicto* cases. Does not this vaccination amount to rejecting the communicative semantic criterion for the objects of the directed-toward relation? It may seem to, for why grant Belia the veto over that-clauses for any reason other than that the that-clauses refer to the things in her mind? But there's an alternative reason to grant her the veto: She can hypothesize about the eternal sentences her own attitudes are directed toward, just as she can about the eternal sentences which others' attitudes are directed toward. She vetoes the that-clauses that express the wrong eternal sentences.

Nonetheless our resort to idiolects seems to go against the motivation to find public entities for attitudes to be directed toward. For an idiolect is one person's language even if its sentences are eternalized and not in the person's mind. Does it seem right that Belia should be in charge not only of the that-clause but of a whole language, since she has veto power over translation manuals? The community should be in charge of that. In reply we can agree that, insofar as Belia's idiolect does not conform to the public language, that's because of her ignorance and error, and there should be pressure on her to bring it into conformity. But let's not impose the ideal of conformity on the very analysis of her beliefs. As for her idiolect being private, that's not necessary. Her idiolect is in principle a public language, which happens to have only one speaker. If we eternalize the sentences of her idiolect, they'll be decontextualized and their truth-values will be independent of the circumstances in which they might be uttered.

The paradox seems to survive in the *de re* cases, for Belia's not in charge of the about-position; Rep is. He's entitled to use his own translation manual there. So about Florence, Firenze, the center of the Renaissance, or whatever else it is, it's so and it's not so that Belia believes it [to be beautiful during temporal interval *i*]. The bracketed portion of the report is an eternal incomplete sentence. Rep contradicted himself and also accuses Belia of inconsistency. He attributes to Belia an application of a contradictory predicate to the city, [to be and not to be beautiful during temporal interval *i*]. In response to this situation there'll be nonrepresentationalists who say, "One more nail in the coffin of *de re* propositional attitudes." They'll be happy to see the idiom of relational belief consigned to the heap of idioms not suitable for scientific thinking about the mind. Quine comes to mind.

But I say, "One more nail in the coffin of their version of nonrepresentationalism, which sets aside all the causal aspects of what's in the believer's mind in its monomaniacally pure pursuit of the directed-toward relation." The ellipsis theory broached in Part II makes the contradictions evaporate, for it requires that any report will expand to expose an elliptical reference to the believer's representations of the entities referred to in the report's about-position. (See section L.) Rep may use whatever name he wishes for Florence in his about-position, but when he reports her believing the predicate of being beautiful to be false of it, *he must say that Belia names it with the name, "Firenze."* Suppose Rep gives his *de re* report in Italian. Then he translates it into English. What happens to the reference to Belia's use of "Firenze" which appears in Rep's report in quotation marks? Rep must not apply the translation rule to his Italian *de re* report of Belia's beliefs *until after* he has made the elliptical element explicit. Doing that exposes Belia's reference to Florence by its Italian name, which stays Italian in the translation of the report into English since "Firenze" is in quotation marks in the report. Translation does not translate inside direct quotations, but leaves that material in the original.

In the previous section I stated a nonrepresentationalist definition of the directed-toward relation, and there I mentioned that some nonrepresentationalists concede that this relation is mediated by representations. Perhaps the conciliatory nonrepresentationalist must relax his account of reports to admit into their truth conditions a reference to the believers' representations. More on this concession in the next section. If he does that, this mediation becomes a solution available to the nonrepresentationalist, for the distinction between the noneternal, mentally uttered sentences concretizing and individuating attitudes (which he can accept) and their being the objects of the directed-toward relation (which he must reject), is unimportant for solving this puzzle.

How does the Firenze/Florence paradox raise any issues that were not raised by the paradox we considered in section K, (which was Belia's mistaking a skunk for a woodchuck and then not mistaking it for one)? The present paradox differs in invoking a translation rule between languages, which reporters must observe in making their reports, whereas the case in K invoked the substitution rule between coreferential terms in the same language. There the issue was opacity and hyperintensionality; but the current paradox is not about those features, for translation is the finding of synonymous expressions and so should work even in opaque and hyperintensional contexts. The paradox attacks specifically the view that sentences are the termini of the directed-toward relation. The paradox also attacks the Davidsonian regimentation of reports, which we presented in Part I. (We noted there that the Davidsonian regimentation is immune to paradox based on substitution.) The solutions, which we just presented to defend eternal sentence nonrepresentationalism, in terms of idiolectal names and sentences, will also save the Davidsonian regimentation from paradox.

## §2. Structured propositions and singular propositions.

In the subsection just completed I favored the eternal sentence version of nonrepresentationalism, allowing incomplete eternal sentences to accommodate *de re* beliefs. I also favored analyzing names out of the language for expressing what a person's beliefs were directed toward, so that ostensibly singular eternal sentences are really general eternal sentences. The puzzle about bilingualism might have left your faith in eternal sentence nonrepresentationalism shaken. It was meant to do that, although it was not meant to restore confidence in propositions, for singular propositions fare even worse than singular eternal sentences. This subsection and the remaining ones present the case for that negative assessment of singular propositions. Many intensionalist nonrepresentationalists are left for us to consider, some of whom prefer a language-independent concept of proposition. They feel they can capture the idea of *de re* beliefs in the thesis that all beliefs are directed toward complete singular propositions, and in fact, there are no other beliefs than these, for there are no other propositions than complete singular propositions, simple and compound. There are other philosophers, however, who deny there are any singular propositions at all! So let's wade back into this quagmire for a while. The upshot for nonrepresentationalism will be (in my opinion) that only the eternal sentence version of it is viable.

Propositions, as we've been using the word, are not sentences, not representations, but rather the entities that are represented by sentences, or more exactly by sentence-radicals. They're abstract, and they're public in the sense that many people can believe numerically^ the same proposition, however far apart they are in time and space, and however distinct their languages. Complete propositions are members of a broader family, which is the family of attributes, i.e., the family of propositions, complete and incomplete. I mentioned in section D that complete propositions, which are attributes of zero adicity, can be thought of as constructed from attributes of higher adicity by filling in some or all of the positions in those attributes and treating the composite as an attribute of lower adicity determined by how many positions remain to be filled. Thought of in this way, attributes have the formal properties of functions^ as mathematicians understand them. An attribute of adicity $n$, $n$ being greater than zero, when applied to a term, yields an attribute of adicity $n$ - $1$. For example, the dyadic "(1) loves (2)" becomes the monadic "(1) loves everyone" when the dyadic function is applied to the term "everyone." Complete propositions result when this process goes as far as it can.

An ambiguity occurs in our way of understanding any attribute that results from an attribute of higher adicity.[2] We can see the monadic attribute, "(1) loves everyone," as a new unity, or we can see in it the complexity of its derivation from the dyadic attribute "(1) loves (2)." How we understand attributes in the latter way, namely as functions, is similar to how in arithmetic we understand the addition of numbers as a function. If I add 2 to 3, in the language of functions I'm applying the function of addition to the two numbers, and the result is another number, the number 5. The inputs to the addition function are 2 and 3; its output is 5. I can think of 5 as a new unity, or I can see in it the complexity of its derivation, by referring to it as 2+3. The ambiguity of 2+3 is clear, but less clear in the case of propositions, since we're accustomed to thinking of 5 as having an existence side by side with 2 and 3, which are not literally its parts, but we're not accustomed to thinking of propositions as having their own existence separate from the attributes "in" them.

Nevertheless, try to feel this ambiguity in propositions. Just as the numbers 2 and 3 are inputs to the addition function and 5 is its output, so also the $n$ terms are inputs to the $n$-adic attributes, and propositions are their outputs. In the case of the number 5, it's easy not to think that 2 and 3 are its parts, because there's also 4+1 and 5+0 and 6+(-1) and so on, which provide alternative candidates for being parts of 5, if 5 had parts. The situation is similar with propositions. Because of their identity conditions (recall section G), different inputs can yield the same output proposition. For example, on intensional criteria of identity, the proposition

that the set of natural numbers is noninductive
and the proposition

that the set of positive and negative integers is reflexive

are the same proposition. (This proposition was discussed in section G.) If this proposition has parts, which set is a part of it, the set of natural numbers or the set of signed integers? The language of parts and wholes is simply inappropriate. It's less mind-boggling to just say the sets are alternative inputs to the function, and the one proposition is its output from both inputs.

In Part II we rehearsed some arguments against complete propositions being the sole objects of the directed-toward relation. Still another argument against that turns on the intensional identity condition for propositions. In most logics, the following schema represents the same proposition, no matter which proper name is inserted into the three blanks:

If $x$ exists, then $x$ is identical to $x$.

On my view of relational attitudes, their regimentation ensures that this attribute is separated from the thing it's applied to, so that Belia has distinct beliefs when she applies it to Rep and when she applies it to Arthur. On the alternative view of some nonrepresentationalists, these are beliefs directed toward the same complete proposition, which is counter-intuitive. In making this criticism I must avoid a confusion. Just because Arthur figures in one and Rep figures in the other, that does not make them different propositions. The intensional criterion of identity for propositions settles the matter. Recall the earlier example of there being only one proposition whether it's specified as the noninductiveness of the set of natural numbers or the reflexivity of the set of signed integers. In the case of Arthur and Rep, as in the case of those two sets, only one complete proposition is involved. This granted, nevertheless my view is clearly more in conformity with intuition. These beliefs of Belia's are distinct. So the unified proposition is the wrong object of the directed-toward relation.

We'll call a complete proposition, viewed as a unity, a proposition *simpliciter*. In contrast, some philosophers want a kind of proposition that shows its inputs: A **structured proposition** is a sequence^ consisting of an attribute of any adicity, say $n$, followed by all the $n$ things which are the proposition's logical^ subjects. A structured proposition is analogous to what we might call a structured number, as if we pictured 5 as the structure:

<+, 2, 3 >

Of course we're not picturing 5's parts, but the proponents of structured propositions do speak of their parts. In the case of a singular proposition, corresponding to the singular sentence,

"Jack loves Belia,"

there's a sequence, in this case an ordered triple,

< the relation of (1) loving (2), Jack himself, Belia herself >.

That's a structured proposition. Strictly, I should make a time one of the terms in the sequence, as a counterpart of the present tense of the sentence. Let's ignore how time figures in structured propositions. Literally both Jack and Belia are members of the structured proposition, *not* their names. Thus in contrast to propositions *simpliciter*, the language of parts and wholes is appropriate for structured propositions.

The structured proposition, with things in it, exists whether it's true or false of those things. For every *n*-adic property and every sequence^ of *n* things, the structured singular proposition exists which is the sequence of that property followed by that sequence of things. Since the things include all the things that ever were or will be throughout past and future time, microscopic things, and some philosophers would even include nonactual but possible things, clearly more structured singular propositions exist than I could possibly think. But these are language-independent and mind-independent entities. Whether anyone can think them is irrelevant to their existence.

Russell believed in structured singular propositions for a few years, and in 1904 declared in a letter to the puzzled Frege that, yes indeed, Mont Blanc itself was in the structured proposition that Mont Blanc was tall.[3] There are other strange consequences:

> Russell accepted such odd consequences as objectively existing false-hoods. If one acquiesces in falsehoods being citizens of the realm of being along with truths, just as red roses exist along with white roses, then one must justify discriminating against the falsehoods as objects of one's belief or else admit to unaccountable prejudice.[4] Russell concluded that the erroneousness of a belief in a false proposition consisted in the ethical badness of such belief.[5]

His acceptance of the objective existence of structured singular propositions did not survive beyond 1907, however. Despite his recantation and his philosophizing in another vein for the next sixty or so years, today many philosophers who believe in structured singular propositions show their knowledge of history by calling them "Russellian." I do not follow this practice, not because Russell does not deserve the credit, but because he deserves more credit for rejecting them.

I'll now argue that *singular propositions do not exist*. Since we've already dispensed with singular eternal sentences, it will follow that there cannot be **singular *de dicto* beliefs**.

What reason is there to believe some sequences are propositions? Putting the question another way, there are two ways to think of the contents of the attitudes. They're either disparate elements disassembled, some going into about-positions and others going into that-clauses, or they have the unity of a proposition. Why think that sequences are identical to the latter and not just the former? It would be better to avoid an uncritical use of the language of identity here; let's ask instead whether sequences *model* propositions and their logical properties. We can say, yes, on these grounds:

> ●There are formal relations between sequences that mimic the logical relations of implication and contradiction, which exist between propositions.
>
> ●We can identify by the intrinsic properties of sequences which ones mimic tautologies and which mimic inconsistencies.
>
> ●Since contingent truth and falsity are extrinsic properties of propositions, it does not matter that no intrinsic property of the sequence models truth or falsity.
>
> ●But just as propositions must be one or the other, so the sequences modeling propositions must be such that its first member is true of, or false of, the sequence which follows the first member.

So these sequences behave logically as if they were propositions. There's another payoff. Instead of the intensional identity conditions of propositions *simpliciter*, structured propositions have the identity conditions of sequences: Two sequences are identical if their first members are identical, their second members are identical, and so on. So if structured propositions are the objects of the directed-toward relation, that promises relief from the problems of opacity and hyperintensionality. For example, the pair of sentences from set theory, stated above, express the same proposition *simpliciter* because they meet the conditions of intensional identity, although they correspond to the following pair of structured propositions, which are distinct sequences. Even if the predicates provably express the same attribute, the sets they are applied to are provably distinct:

> < the attribute of (1) being noninductive, the set of natural numbers >
>
> < the attribute of (1) being reflexive, the set of positive and negative integers >.

Similarly, the attribute, "if *x* exists, then *x* is identical to *x*," yields distinct structured propositions when it's applied to Arthur and when it's applied to Rep. The nonrepresentationalist theory is providing us with the public objects for our private attitudes to be directed toward, objects which have identity conditions that fit our intuitions of which attitudes are directed toward the same objects and which are not. Thus it's important for this theory to solve the problems of opacity and hyperintensionality, which seem to arise from our intuitions of the distinctness of the objects.

Nevertheless, structured propositions cannot solve all the problems of opacity and hyperintensionality. One example would be, in the example from set theory, the identity of the attribute of being noninductive with the attribute of being reflexive, since identity for attributes is intensional. Their interchange in hyperintensional contexts within a truth could result in a falsehood. A remedy would be to reconstitute the structure of structured propositions so that predicates replaced attributes. The result would be a nonrepresentationalism that was just as extensional and just as language-relative as eternal sentence nonrepresentationalism. But it would not be as good. For it would still be susceptible to the problem of opacity: An example would be the problems associated with proper names of the same person. Let's focus on the difficulty. Recall the problem I posed at the end of section A. A new relative of mine learns from my nephews on my wife's side of the family about an uncle of theirs, Arthur. She comes to believe many nice things about him. She learns from my nephews on my side of the family, however, about an uncle of 'theirs, Sonny, and she comes to believe only terrible things about him. Unbeknownst to her, Arthur = Sonny. Are there two logically independent structured propositions such that she believes the first and disbelieves the second? Here's what you might suppose the two to be:

< the property of (1) being nice, Arthur himself >
< the property of (1) being nice, Sonny himself >

But no. There's only one structured proposition here, the distinct names notwithstanding. The names are not in the proposition; *I* am, since I'm the one they name. Surely my new relative has not committed an error of logic! So structured propositions do not solve the problem. The representationalist theory in section L, postulating an ellipsis referring to her vivid names for me, will solve it. In addition this ellipsis theory meets the non-representationalists' concern about common objects for our attitudes to be directed toward; it supposes them directed toward attributes or incomplete propositions, which we can replace with eternalized predicates.

Besides not solving the problems of opacity and hyperintensionality, the concept of structured propositions can promote confusion between the disparate inputs to a function and the function's output, which is a unity that does not have those inputs as its parts, although confusion is not an inevitable feature of the concept, I must admit.

## §3. The showdown between the incomplete proposition and the complete singular proposition theories of *de re*.

Returning to the matter of singular propositions, many nonrepresentationalists think of them as structured propositions and draw consequences for propositional attitudes. Reports of *de re* beliefs would not need the paraphernalia of about-positions if they were directed toward complete singular propositions. According to their view of belief, all our fuss over about-positions and incomplete propositions is just the tedious consequence of our failure to see that structured singular propositions are what these beliefs are directed toward. The incomplete proposition is just the first member of the sequence, and the things named in the about-position are just the other members of the sequence. The transparency of the about-position manifests the fact that things themselves, not their names or descriptions, are in the structured singular propositions. So they say.

They continue: Furthermore, the understanding of belief as involving a reference to a name makes about-positions superfluous for the purpose of providing an antecedent for the anaphoric pronouns in the that-clauses. To see this, observe that these two sentences really are equivalent in what they tell us about the content of Belia's belief:

> Belia believes about the skunk with name "VN" that it is a woodchuck.
> Belia believes that VN is a woodchuck.

Since VN is her own vivid name for that one thing, she cannot object to the second report's that-clause. But this report is *de dicto*.

(If for some reason logically proper names are to be excluded, then we combine "VN" with the identity symbol to create a term for a property, namely, the property of being identical to VN. We use it to create this version of the report:

> Belia believes that everything identical to VN is a woodchuck.

The universally quantified^ subject phrase in the sentence does all the work that the pronoun and reference to a name did in the first. For example, I am writing now if and only if everything identical to me is writing now. My self report and Rep's report use the same device. Again the reports are *de dicto*, though not directed toward a singular proposition.)

So, these nonrepresentationalists conclude, our ellipsis theory of *de re* reports, far from saving the analysis of *de re* belief as directed toward incomplete propositions, delivered its death-blow by finding the names that go in the sentences that express complete singular propositions!

Oof! I pick myself up and try to get my wind back. I resist this identification of my view of *de re* belief with their view of belief as belief in complete structured singular propositions. In subsection §5 I'll argue they don't exist. Although our access to *de re* content, which these philosophers take to be singular propositions, often depends on our causal rapport with the things in the proposition, and the rapport is indispensable on my view of *de re* beliefs about perceptible things other than ourselves, it's not indispensable for the expression of singular propositions. We already noticed such devices as

> • the reference fixing of a name by an attributively used definite description, which gives expression to a singular proposition (in section A),
> • also the demonstrative use of a description (in section H) and
> • the referential use of a description (in section A).

They all can give expression to singular propositions, i.e., their use creates singular sentences. Of these three devices, only the referential use of a description seems to depend on some causal rapport with the subject of the proposition. The more usual ways we have of expressing singular propositions, by means of

> • the common demonstratives and proper names,

also seem to depend on causal rapport, at least in the central cases. Nevertheless, the proponents of singular propositions accept the mind's noncausal access to singular propositions by way of singular terms that "denote strictly," that is, "individuate the [denoted] object in a context-independent manner," to quote Tyler Burge.[6] Their dubious mode of access from the nowhere makes me keep my position distinct from theirs. I'd do so even if singular propositions did exist.

My view seems to the nonrepresentationalists as though it fails to assemble the complete proposition from the elements, held apart so to speak by some of them being in the about-position and others being in the that-clause. Where, they ask of me, is the unity which is the output proposition? They do not think my representationalist solution to the paradoxes, which posits names in Belia's mind, answers this question. The unity must be the unity of the represented proposition, not the unity of the representing sentence or of the inner representation. My reply is that Rep's job is not to report any such unity as the propositional unity, but to report its inputs disassembled.

The distinction between my position and theirs is perhaps best argued for in the context of beliefs about oneself. I hope you noticed how bad an example was used a few paragraphs above:

> I am writing if and only if everything identical to me is writing.

It's true of course that I believe one if and only if I believe the other. That hardly shows the ellipsis theory makes about-positions unneeded. For according to that theory the "I" and "me" in that sentence correspond to no names at all in my mentalese! So neither side of that equivalence stands for a *de dicto* belief of mine.

Let's go over the defense of the no-name theory again. The thought experiment concerning Belia and Trixy (section N), was based on this staple of the literature: Heimson is a madman: He believes he's David Hume. So,

Heimson believes that he wrote *A Treatise of Human Nature*.

Heimson's belief is a false belief, since the *Treatise* was written by Hume. There are just two singular propositions which might be what his belief is directed toward:

<(1) wrote the *Treatise*, Hume>
<(1) wrote the *Treatise*, Heimson>

Of course he does believe the first, but the belief we're considering is not directed toward that proposition. Why not? Because this proposition is true, and the belief of his which we're considering is something false. Is it then that the belief is directed toward the second proposition? Heimson denies it vigorously. Nevertheless, proponents of the complete singular proposition view of *de re* belief say that, when he believes he himself wrote the *Treatise*, this second one is the proposition his belief is directed toward. I, however, recommend we accept Heimson's denial of that, in accord with our policy of letting the believer be in charge of the that-clause. What, then, is left for Heimson to believe? The solution is to expand the variety of believables: Add incomplete propositions and a way of using them that does not require names.

We saw in section M that, when people believe something in the first person, they may behave differently from the way they'd behave if they believed a proposition they'd express using a proper name of themselves or even a demonstrative pointing to themselves. For they may not know that the proper name is their own or that they are the ones they're pointing at. On the basis of that behavioral difference, I reject the identification of Heimson's belief about himself with a belief directed toward a complete singular proposition with Heimson as its logical subject. My rejection depends on the principle enunciated at the beginning of section N:

Suppose a person's believing, in a particular context, about $x$ that X and her believing to the same degree in that same context about $y$ that Y would have different effects on the believer's behavior, when all else that's independent is held constant. Then they are different believings, and since their difference is not a difference of location, mood, or any other difference besides one of content that would account for the difference in ensuing behavior, it must lie in their contents. So it's not the case that both $x = y$ and $X = Y$.

The nonrepresentationalist opposing us rejects this principle, interpreting the reference to content as a reference to just what the belief is directed toward (rather than to both what it's about and what it's directed toward). They believe a different principle:

When both $x = y$ and $X = Y$, and the beliefs about $x$ that X and about $y$ that Y issue in different behaviors, that's because of the difference in the mental states of believing which the believer reveals he's in by uttering the different sentences, "x is X" and "y is Y," which happen to express the same proposition.

Animals and people without the ability to speak could be in those different mental states too, for they have representations in mind despite their lack of speech. On that we both agree. Furthermore, all nonrepresentationalisms assert the public nature of the terms of the directed-toward relation. According to all, I and Aristotle can believe numerically^ the same thing. You and I can disagree over numerically the same thing. We can both follow numerically the same steps in a logical derivation. There's a domain of public entities, which people's private attitudes focus on. These are the things whose truth or falsity matters to them.

The issue then is whether a theory of the directed-toward relation should account for the role of attitudes in explaining the behavior of people. The believers in structured singular propositions are conceding its insufficiency, according to their view of the relation and its object. Don't look to this domain for the role of causes of people's behavior. So say the proponents of this view. But is not this dichotomizing between community and causality an oversimplification? We saw in the last section that coordinated action requires the actors to refer to the contents of each other's attitudes. Similarly it's right for us to infer difference in semantic content from difference in behavior, provided we go on to infer from the semantic difference a syntactic or formal difference embodied in the mental states that cause the difference in behavior.

### §4. Reduction of all propositions to singular propositions, and its consequences for causal rapport.

It's not right to criticize this view on the ground of parsimony about the things beliefs are directed toward. The view is parsimonious, indeed parsimony is its great virtue: Beliefs are all directed toward complete singular structured propositions. One might wonder how to understand general propositions as compound singular propositions. The general proposition expressed by the sentence,

"Something is tall"

is just the disjunctive compound of all the true and false propositions thus:

< tall, Mont Blanc> or < tall, Tiny Tim > or, etc.

The universal general proposition expressed by the sentence,

"Everything is tall"

is a conjunctive compound. Mixed general propositions, such as is expressed by the sentence,

"Everyone loves someone"

are conjunctions of disjunctions:

Jack loves himself, or Belia, or ...; and Belia loves herself, or Jack, or ...; and etc.

In the notation of sequences, this proposition is,

<(1) loves (2), Jack, Jack> or <(1) loves (2), Jack, Belia> or . . .; and <(1) loves (2), Belia, Belia> or <(1) loves (2), Belia, Jack> or . . .; and etc.

On the other hand, the reverse order of quantifiers as in,

"Someone loves everyone"

would interchange the "and"s and "or"s.

This analysis of general propositions as compounds of singular ones is disputable; Russell himself disputed it. And it's indisputable that it cannot work for general *sentences*. We cannot analyze a general sentence as a compound of singular sentences, for the constituents of sentences are predicates and names, not properties and things. It's certain that we don't have names for everything we talk about. Even when we do have names for all the things our general sentence is about, the analysis of the sentence into a compound of singular sentences would have to say so, and that introduces an element of generality back into the analysis, defeating the goal of reducing general sentences to compounds of singular ones. This objection about sentences does not hold against the analysis of general propositions into compounds of singular propositions.

A consequence these philosophers would draw from their reduction of general propositions is that all belief is *de re*, assuming their reduction of belief *de re* to belief in complete structured singular propositions. Bye, bye, *de dicto*, they say. (From my point of view, they analyze all belief as *de dicto*, since all belief becomes belief in complete propositions.)

Furthermore, if general propositions are just compounds of singular propositions, then all the more reason for proponents of this view to put causal rapport aside, for we could hardly be in causal rapport with the constituents of such compound propositions as these. Not that causal rapport has no relevance; obviously for some attitudes like perceiving and recalling, it does. As a criterion for dividing attitudes into two types, however, it's of no value in a theory of attitudes; worse, it's downright obfuscatory. So they say.

## §5. An argument against structured singular propositions.

If the nonrepresentationalism that rejects incomplete propositions is parsimonious in rendering uniform the terms of the directed-toward relation, it's not parsimonious in its separation of the role of cause of behavior and the role of common object that our private attitudes share. Although there's no *a priori* reason why the same thing cannot play both roles, in view of the argument in section V §1 it's unlikely that the same thing does serve both. Thus the principle I accepted in section N and restated earlier in subsection §3 may be simplistic in being more parsimonious than their alternative, also stated earlier, by allowing the terms of the directed-toward relation to serve both as common objects of our individual attitudes and as the individuators of states of believing along lines that account for their causal roles. There are ways to narrow the gap without simplistically denying it. The way I favor is to recognize the relation of **expression**. The semantical entity is expressed by the syntactic or formal entity, which would not have the causal powers it has were it not for the fact that it expresses that semantical entity. The syntactic entity is the instantiated sentence in LOT, which is expressive of the eternal sentence, the semantical entity. The expression relation is definable as a correspondence of the causal and logical roles of the syntactic entity, which we discussed in section S under the heading of conceptual role semantics, with the logical roles of the eternal sentences, which we discussed in section V. The causal roles of the former imitate in some way the logical roles of the latter. Some causal roles are innate and instinctual; in human beings some are habitual and some are chosen. Obviously from the nature of expression, either is incomplete if and only if the other is. Thus, if considerations of causality suggest that incomplete things are the causes, incomplete things are the things whose roles the causal entities imitate.

One argument favoring our kind of nonrepresentationalism would be that attitudes cannot be directed toward such things as complete structured singular propositions. I hinted at this line of thought in section H, when I suggested we might be able to state propositions we cannot think. Chisholm argued for the more radical thesis that singular propositions do not exist.[7] If he's not denying the existence of the sequences, which proponents of the view we're considering identify with singular propositions, then he's denying that identification. I mentioned in subsection §2 Russell's deserving credit for rejecting structured singular propositions. Chisholm's main argument against them is simply Russell's own, which he stated in 1918:

> When I say "Obviously propositions are nothing" it is not perhaps quite obvious. Time was when I thought there were propositions, but it does not seem to me very plausible to say in addition to facts there are also these curious shadowy things going about such as "That today is Wednesday" when in fact it is Tuesday. I cannot believe they go about the real world. It is more than one can manage to believe, and I do think no person with a vivid sense of reality can imagine it. One of the difficulties of the study of logic is that it is an exceedingly abstract study dealing with the most abstract things imaginable, and yet you cannot pursue it properly unless you have a vivid instinct as to what is real.[8]

Russell's choice of an example of a proposition is quite infelicitous, however. What does the word "today" express that is in a proposition? He might've made his point with the proposition that Tuesday is Wednesday, for that is a proposition. Is Tuesday's being Wednesday among the things that exist? Come on.

The identification of propositions with set-theoretical entities like sequences does not quiet the vivid sense of reality. One can very well accept the ontology of set^ theory without accepting the literal identity of structured singular propositions and sequences. Without literal identity, we're free to accept the sequences but reject the structured singular propositions. The relationship between singular propositions and sequences is merely that of the sequences modeling some of the logical properties the singular propositions would have to have, if they existed.

Chisholm says that Russell's instinct for what's real would have to be rejected, if the structured singular propositions did what they're supposed to do, and there were no plausible alternative. One argument that they don't do what they're supposed to do, the crucial step of which Chisholm attributes to Castañeda, is that the structured propositions, which our attitudes are supposed to be directed toward, should have the logical relationships among themselves that mimic the logical relations which we intuit between the attitudes. But *they don't*.

For example, if Heimson's belief that he himself wrote the *Treatise* is directed toward the singular proposition,

<(1) wrote the *Treatise*, Heimson>,

then this believing is logically equivalent to his believing that Heimson wrote the *Treatise*, because that attitude would be directed toward the same proposition. So when Heimson denies the equivalence, he'd have to be committing a mistake of logic. But intuitively, the content of what Heimson believes, when he believes that he himself wrote the *Treatise*, is *not entailed* by the content, that Heimson wrote the *Treatise*.[9] We might see no further irrationality if he came to deny that he himself wrote it and started to assert that Heimson did! So, contrary to the theory of structured singular propositions as contents, Heimson is not committing an error of logic by believing one without believing the other. We noted a similar failure to entail beliefs in the first person in section M in the argument concerning the two gods, who believe everything their beliefs in complete propositions entail.

You might think to preserve structured singular propositions by simply adding incomplete propositions and conceding that Heimson's belief that he himself wrote the *Treatise* is directed toward one of those. That would be a full concession to my point of view and a repudiation of the appeal to Ockham's razor^ in the theory of directed-towardness. Chisholm holds out for more: His argument tells against structured singular propositions themselves and not just against the thesis that they are the sole objects of directed-towardness. For, to capture the intuitions just elicited and conceded, you'd have to expand the set theoretic model so that it modeled the structured propositions' nonentailments of the supposed incomplete structured propositions, by adding to set theory notation to represent an incomplete sequence. It can be done, but why bother? Chisholm undermines the motivation of parsimony for the whole project of structured singular propositions.

I find this argument against complete singular propositions persuasive. One may hesitate, however, and wonder what logically proper names would be for, if not to create sentences expressive of complete singular propositions. There are two lines we might take: Deny the existence of logically proper names or find another job for them. The first alternative amounts to treating ordinary proper names as covert descriptions, not modally rigid. Then Russell's technique for eliminating descriptions would reveal the sentences they occur in to be general. The second alternative accepts logically proper names occurring in sentences, but they would not express singular propositions any more than the occurrence of the pronouns "I" and "now" do, as we noted in section N. Their primary job might be to be descriptively neutral labels on mental folders, dossiers, so to speak. A mental folder contains all the beliefs that are about the one named on its label. The proper names' occurrence in singular sentences would then be to tell the listener something about the organization of the speaker's mind.

Is there an alternative to complete singular propositions that does the job the nonrepresentationalists expected them to do? Sure: For the extensionalist nonrepresentationalist, there are the complete and incomplete eternal sentences. For the intensionalist nonrepresentationalist, there's the one we've been working with all along, namely, about-positions and attributes, with zero-adic attributes being unstructured propositions. All's not lost for the nonrepresentationalists. If they can use attributes instead of structured singular propositions to solve opacity and hyperintensionality problems, their theory's viable. We explore their efforts in section X.

### §6. An argument that no terminus of directed-towardness is singular.

When you're nailing a coffin lid on a menace that refuses to stay dead, an extra nail is worth having. So here's another argument, constructed by David Lewis. It attacks the idea that a singular proposition is ever a part of the content of any attitude directed at capturing a concrete state of affairs. Return to Belia's two mental states about Florence which contradict each other without her being aware of it. Lewis takes it as a datum that there's an important sense in which she's not contradicting herself, despite the fact that her two beliefs are directed toward contradictories. We developed the puzzle with eternal sentences in the role of the contradictories, but Lewis has us think of two singular propositions in that role instead. They share the same individual subject term, the city Florence, and each attributes to it one of a pair of opposite properties. In that important sense in which Belia's not contradicting herself, the supposition that these singular propositions are the objects of the directed-towardness is false.

How spell out that important sense? It's within the realm of possibility for all Belia's mental states to be the same as they've been throughout her life, and yet the languages and the concrete world have been different enough so that both her beliefs were true, which should not be possible if her beliefs are contradictory. It is possible, for it might very well have been that the English rigid designator "Florence" was the translation of the Italian rigid designator "Fiorenze," the name of a town that could've been in the hills twenty miles to the north of what's actually Florence, while in the counterfactual scenario we're imagining, the actual Florence existed but did not develop because of floods on the Arno river and other pestilential factors. Its Italian name was Firenze, but it was neither important nor beautiful. Instead, all the artistic, scientific, and commercial geniuses congregated in the hill town and developed a beautiful city there remarkably similar to the actual Florence.[10] If this were the way the world was, everything in Belia's mind would've stayed the same as it was in actuality. Nevertheless her two beliefs would be both true, not contradictory, and be about two cities, not one. So in some important sense her beliefs in the actual world are not contradictory. Therefore in that sense they're not directed toward singular propositions.

What's the proper way to understand the word, "Florence," as it occurs in her beliefs in the actual world? It is a modally rigid designator, even if "Florence" could've been the English translation of the hill town's name, "Fiorenze." It could've rigidly designated something else. According to Lewis, the word makes her belief be about whatever plays the Florence-role, whether or not it's the actual Florence. The Florence-role includes playing the role of referent of her mental name "Florence."

If we were to ask Belia, I suspect she'd heartily agree to this assessment, since she'd not want to be accused of a logical contradiction, and this solution protects her, not from actual inconsistency, but from something every rational person should be able to avoid by simple attention to logic, namely, logical contradiction. The point is deeper than just protecting Belia's rationality, however. The point is that singularity is not to be attributed to the object of the directed-toward relation.

David Lewis's version of this thought experiment targets singular propositions about the concrete world, but it applies just as well against singular eternal sentences about the concrete world. It gives us an additional reason for our earlier elimination of them from any sentences that play the role of objects of directed-towardness. Unlike Chisholm's argument, Lewis's argument does not deny the existence of singular propositions, but only denies them roles in thought. Nor does it deny the existence of logically proper names that are modally rigid; it just assigns them a certain job in thought. Since I'm inclined to accept the argument, I must return to the job of singular terms in mental states, which I made much of preserving in section F, and in section L as things that reports refer to elliptically, and in section Q as things that actualize attitudes in the mind (Harman's thesis). Looking back, I see nothing in our previous commitments at odds with these results. In fact, Lewis's idea that a mental name introduces a role its referent plays explicates more of what it could mean to believe something "with a name," the phrase I used in section L. Looking ahead to section Y, I'll develop further the suggestion made earlier in the previous subsection that names function as labels on mental dossiers.

# Notes

1. Saul A. Kripke, "A Puzzle about Belief," in A. Margalit, ed., *Meaning and Use* (1979) 254-256. The scenario I develop is similar to the one Kripke develops for his Pierre.

2. Introducing the concept of a structured proposition by way of the ambiguity of input and output of a function is due to Maxwell Cresswell, *Structured Meanings: The Semantics of Propositional Attitudes* (1985).

3. Gottfried Gabriel *et al.*, eds., *Gottlob Frege: Philosophical and Mathematical Correspondence* (1980) 169.

4. Bertrand Russell, "Meinong's Theory of Complexes and Assumptions (III)," *Mind,* 13 (1904) 523f. Reprinted in *The Collected Papers of Bertrand Russell: Foundations of Logic, 1903-05*, vol. 4 (1994) 474.

5. Arthur Falk, "The Judger in Russell's Theories of Judgment," *Russell: the Journal of the Bertrand Russell Archives*, new series 17 (1997-98) 105.

6. Tyler Burge, "Belief *De Re,*" *Journal of Philosophy* 74 (1977). See his part III.

7. Roderick Chisholm, "Why Singular Propositions?" in Joseph Almog, John Perry, and Howard Wettstein, eds., *Themes from Kaplan* (1989) 145-150.

8. Bertrand Russell, "The Philosophy of Logical Atomism," (1918), reprinted in Robert C. Marsh, ed., *Logic and Knowledge* (1956) 223.

9. Hector-Neri Castañeda, "He: A Study in the Logic of Self-Consciousness," *Ratio* 8 (1966) 130-157.

10. David Lewis, "What Puzzling Pierre Does Not Believe" (1981), reprinted in his *Papers on Metaphysics and Epistemology* (1999) 408-417. Alternatively and still consistent with all Belia's mental states remaining the same, we could've supposed the Italians called the beautiful hilltop town Firenze and the unbeautiful town on the Arno, Fiorenza. Then Belia's beliefs would both be false: "Firenze non è bella" would be false and "Florence is beautiful" false too, given the alternative translation of Florence, but there'd be no logical contradiction since two cities would be involved.

# X. Two Approaches to Hyperintensions.

Let's begin with a long look back over our train of thoughts.

## §1. A survey of results so far, to see where we are.

One of the more important things these notes have given you, I like to think, is an architecture for housing the many issues in your mind. The architecture consists of a progression of dichotomies: First, there was the contrast of the data and the theories of the data, which distinguished Part I from the remaining three parts. Second, there was the division of theory into descriptive and prescriptive. We've been concerned so far only with theory descriptive of folk psychology. Part IV will take us into theory that revises folk psychology. Thirdly, theories of attitudes have two components, the theory of the aboutness of relational attitudes and the theory of the directed-towardness, which all attitudes have. This division distinguished Part II from Part III. Fourthly, taking us to the two subparts of Part III, there are the two ways of thinking of the terms of the directed-towardness. The object-terms of that relation are either things dependent on the mind for their existence, or they are things in existence independently of the mind. Or both(!) Fifthly, the things in existence independently of the mind might be extensional or not. The extensionalists are the Quineans who accept eternal sentences and predicates. We studied their position in section V. The nonextensionalists subdivide fluidly as they think of the objects of directed-towardness as being Carnapian or Fregean in nature. We'll study them in this section.

The title of this section may mislead you, since many of these nonextensionalists (though not all) would object that the entities they investigate are simply intensions, not a new class of nonextensional entities to be referred to as hyperintensions. They work with subclasses of intensions to solve the problem of hyperintensionality. I'll continue to use the term "hyperintension," not to refer to a new nonextensional entity, but to the intensions of those supposed to solve the problem of hyperintensionality.

The house representing all these distinctions has a basement, two stories and an attic. The basement stores the data, above ground is for the theories. Basements are not tidy, and we had to work hard to prepare the data, and deal with that poltergeist, Bishop Berkeley. The ground floor is for the theories of aboutness. The loudest voices on that floor were the advocates of incomplete propositions and the dominance plus ellipsis theory of the about-position. They were opposed by the advocates of complete singular propositions and the skeptics of the about-position. The poltergeist interrupted us there too, forcing us to invent *faux de re*. We're now on the upper floor where the theories of directed-towardness are. And wouldn't you know, the poltergeist showed up again, requiring a dose of holophrastics.

The chief quarrel on this floor is between the representationalists and nonrepresentationalists. Part of the dispute from the lower floor continues up here, for representationalists divide into the complete singular sentence mob and the predicate clique, and the nonrepresentationalists divide into the complete proposition mob and the attribute clique. The two mobs, when they were downstairs, opposed the two cliques, who were united in their advocacy of the dominance plus ellipsis defense of the about-position. The mobs were their opponents. Naturally, whether you are a representationalist or nonrepresentationalist on the upper floor, I hope you join me as a member of one of the cliques, and have nothing to do with either mob.

In its purest form, the dispute between representationalists and nonrepresentationalists on the upper floor is between the representationalists who adopt the replacement strategy, avoiding all reference to propositions and attributes or such substitutes for them as eternal sentences and eternal predicates, and the go-it-alone nonrepresentationalists, who explicate directed-towardness without any reference to the sentences and predicates of LOT or other actual utterances. As befits the extremism of the two, they're at opposite sides of the floor, hurling gobs of disdain at each other. Each side also has its moderates, representationalists who adopt the supplement strategy and nonrepresentationalists who adopt a conciliatory stance toward the sentences of mentalese or spoken languages. It's hard to tell these two groups apart, since they mingle in the middle of the room arguing over minutiae. Over near the wall, where all the go-it-alone nonrepresentationalists gather, there's the additional dispute among them over the kind of entities to posit as the objects of the directed-towardness, extensionalist ones like eternal sentences or nonextensionalist ones of the Carnapian or Fregean kind. In this section, we're going to listen in on some of the strategizing by the Carnapians and Fregeans for solving problems of hyperintensionality.

And what's that din coming from the attic? That's where all the naturalizers and their critics are proposing their various revisionist theories. Not too many folk psychologists up there. We'll go up after this section.

I'd like to suggest that, in the dichotomy between things existing independently of mind or dependently on mind, the truth lies in accepting that one thing can be both, despite the glaring contradiction in my way of putting it. In the case of aboutness, we ended up with both sorts, the inner names and the things they name; might not the case of directed-towardness be similar? Eternal sentences would be likely candidates. Something else the mind makes might just be a tool with which it snares the eternal sentences out there to be found. The extreme representationalists and nonrepresentationalists adopt divergent criteria for something to be the object of the directed-towardness, the former saying it's the tool, the latter the thing snared with the tool. Although we've sided with the latter, and only the snared object is the object-terminus of directed-towardness, we can accept both objects, paired together in a relation of expression. Harman's thesis, that the concrete reality of an attitude is the instancing of the tool in the mind, shows how the tool figures into the picture other than as the object-terminus of directed-towardness.

We could even accept two directed-toward relations. However, we'd then have to face the justified disdain of those who mind parsimony. Because it's so obviously true, we must concede that the mind contains representations and that the instantiations of them (mental utterances) both concretize our attitudes and have some connection to the objects our attitudes are directed toward. So it's tempting to go one step further and concede that one kind of directed-towardness is directed toward things the mind makes. I resist that step. Some parsimonies are more parsimonious than the world is, however, for example the theories of the philosophers who want only a single kind of object. Cresswell is one; he opposes the subjective mind-made terms.[1] Fodor is another; he opposes the objective mind-found terms. Each shrugs at the vanity of the other's pursuits. I suggest we return both their shrugs.

We're digressing. Returning to the exploration of our house of controversies, how should we articulate the connection between the two views of the object-term of the directed-towardness, i.e, as a thing made and as a thing found, the latter to be understood in either of the two nonextensional ways which this section will be devoted to presenting?

Today few nonrepresentationalists are willing to make a go of go-it-alone nonrepresentationalism. Of the few, three are Collins, Cresswell, and Stoutland. Among the many others who opt for a conciliatory approach, some even go so far as to propose a hybrid theory, by which I mean a conception of directed-towardness that partakes of the nature of both the communicative agreement criterion and the behavioral criterion. Does this hybrid display "hybrid vigor," or is it a mule? The philosophers are, for instance, Crimmins, the Perry of the 1990s, Richard, Salmon, Schiffer, and Soames.[2] They steal a page from the representationalist's book. Their analyses of the content of attitudes postulate representations after all. First they postulate that the directed-toward relation is not an immediate or direct relation of a person to a proposition. The person requires a mode of access to the proposition, a way of its being presented to her, which we may think of as a sentence expressing it. The sentence mediates the person's being directed toward the proposition it expresses. Since different sentences can mediate a person's being directed toward the same proposition, this hybrid of representationalism and nonrepresentationalism has the conceptual resources to solve the problems of opacity and hyperintensionality without giving up its claim to have found the common objects of our private attitudes. The hybrid theory also steals a page from the ellipsis theories presented in section L, for it postulates that reports of persons' beliefs are elliptical in that their that-clauses make an implicit reference to the believer's representations of propositions. In one version of the hybrid theory, the sentence in a report's that-clause refers the hearers of the report not only to the proposition believed but to the sentence which presents that proposition to the believer. Failures of substitutivity *salva veritate* in that-clauses occur because the substitutions disrupt this second reference. Other versions of the theory don't admit there are failures of substitutivity of proper names of the same person.

We should note two differences between these hybrids and the theories presented in section L, for example, the theory of vivid names. First there's the difference between implicit reference to names in reports' aboutpositions and the purported implicit reference to sentences or sentence-like representations in reports' that-clauses. Secondly, there's the difference between the indispensability of causal rapport with the things named, when the names name perceivable particulars, and the dispensability of causal rapport with the propositions supposed to be expressed by singular sentences. There's also a difference with the no-name theory presented in section N, since a hybrid theory requires some propositions to be presented only by way of sentences in the first person. Otherwise it would be without a response to Chisholm's proof, which we presented in the previous section, that there are no singular propositions.

One could mount critiques of the hybrid theories on all three fronts. As section Q suggested, a solution to the problem of the unity of the subjective proposition forces us to see verbs as a surface phenomenon of language. So not all propositions can be presented by sentence-like representations. As the early sections of Part II suggested, if there's no causal rapport with a particular, then there's no access to it for the purposes of *de re* thoughts about it. So we're not given access to all propositions even if we can formulate sentences which express them. As section N suggested, the semantic specialness of the first person pronoun is best accounted for by a theory of the believer's directly attributing attributes to herself without benefit of a name for herself. So it's not even a complete proposition that we have access to in first-person beliefs.

## §2. The varieties of go-it-alone nonrepresentationalism.

Despite the temptations of the hybridizing form of conciliationism, there are several reasons to suppose the directed-toward relation is just one thing, and its only content-object is out there, and the mind finds it just by being directed toward it. That's the thesis of the nonrepresentationalist. I gave one reason for it in section V, namely, that two people agree, yet the things which are in each of their minds, which their minds made, are not even mental utterances of the same sentence. Since they agree, what is that thing which is the one thing they agree on? This is something that neither of their minds made, since the things that are in their minds are not numerically^ the same thing. Q.E.D. There are other arguments to the same effect. One person can have several attitudes all directed toward the same content or toward contents that are interconnected. For example, I might be angry about the fact that *p*, which I believe to be true. Thus my anger and my belief have the same content. Even if content is not the same, there may be overlap. I might desire that the one I believe to be rich be my benefactor, so that the same subject term is in the content of my desire and the content of my belief. Assume the desire and belief are *de dicto*, since we're not concerned here with the way about-positions provide for overlap. This argument, confined to considering one person, may not persuade you that the mind finds the contents of its attitudes rather than creates them. But the same situations of content-identity and content-overlap occur between people. More than one person's attitudes may be interconnected by shared content, so that the one you saw in your dreams may be the same one who appeared to me in my dreams. If that's too far-fetched, surely many people in ancient Greece all prayed to the same goddess. I assume that about-positions, which are extensional, are of no use in explaining these overlaps.

How account for all this anaphora, not only crossing between different attitudes of the same person, but between the attitudes of different persons? The image of a common arena of contents, around which we're all arrayed and to which we all latch on, is compelling. It's led some philosophers of the past century to simply acknowledge the existence of, in Popper's terms, a "third world" in addition to the world of material objects and the world of subjective states of mind.[3] If the supposition of such a third world of contents of propositional attitudes helps us to understand propositional attitudes, then so be it. That's the assumption of nonrepresentationalism that's been underlying this second subpart of Part III.

Popper thought this third world, though autonomous, was something the mind made and then explored. Recall my analogy in section P of Popper's idea to our exploring the properties of the numeral in the decimal notation that we created, which names the ratio of the circumference of a circle to its diameter. (By the way, in answer to the question I asked there, there is a sequence of six 9's in its first thousand digits.) The world of eternal sentences is just such a third world. But many other philosophers are content to make the Platonistic assumption, that this world exists as independently of us as does the physical world. We'll now consider two such. (There's a further Platonistic assumption, which we'll not, not!, not!!, get into, namely, that this third world exists independently of the physical world too. If you think our discussion of folk psychology has been arcane, wait 'til you get into that discussion, which started as a disagreement between Plato and Aristotle and has been going on ever since.)

### §3. The varieties of nonrepresentationalist intensionalism.

Within the Platonistic assumption that the third world exists independently of minds thinking it, one must show that the that-clauses, by referring to things in that world, are well-behaved logically. All theories must explain why substitution of predicates seems to fail in these that-clauses, and how it is that, when the true hyperintensional nature of what the predicates express is uncovered, substitution really does work. They must also deal with singular terms to dispel the appearance of opacity. And after they do all that, they must show their immunity to the translation difficulties of theories that posit language-dependent entities, which we presented in section V.

Some philosophers would like to keep the Platonistic ontological commitment within the confines of extensionality. I'd say Russell is the father of this approach, with Quine as its most acute proponent. Quine would like to capture all that this common arena of content helps us explain about the that-clauses of propositional attitudes with his concept of eternal sentences and the elimination of all singular terms except anaphoric pronouns. We might call this extensional Platonism, since the eternal sentences and their languages are Platonic objects, just as sets are. I covered extensional Platonism in section V.

Also there are nonextensional ways to be Platonistic, which are not so shy about ontological commitments beyond extensions. These are the approaches that explore the concept of hyperintension. I'll consider two: First, there's the Carnapian approach. It exploits the fact of sentential structure. The main trick is to replace mere intensions, including propositions, which are only good for modal logic, with structured intensions, intensions that preserve information about how they were constructed from component intensions. Carnap's approach is followed by Cresswell and David Lewis. Linguists also use this approach in lexical semantics to decompose the meanings of individual words. For many words' meanings are themselves structured, as their definitions show. The second of the nonextensional approaches is Frege's, which goes the way of hierarchies of intensions. This idea exploits the fact that a term like "the intension of 'being round'" has not only an extension, namely the unit set consisting of the attribute of being round, but also its own intension, the attribute of being the attribute of being round. Why stop there? There's also the term:

the intension of "the intension of 'being round'."

Its extension is the intension of the phrase in double quotation marks. And so we're launched into a hierarchy of terms. Richard Montague and Alonzo Church were the main expositors of this approach.

The two nonextensional approaches are not mutually exclusive. There's no reason not to mix both techniques. Nevertheless, the greater reliance on one rather than the other technique is characteristic of the two approaches. I shall refer to structured intensions and hierarchic intensions indifferently as hyperintensions.

Both nonextensional approaches require some sophistication in formal semantics. First, the Carnapian approach requires that you understand the difference between the intension of a compound phrase and its **structured intension**. They're different. Consider the phrase, "presidents of petroleum companies." There are no petroleum companies in the extension of that phrase, only people. Something similar is true of its intension. Its intension is simply the attribute that those people have which makes them and only them members of the extension. Granted that this attribute is a relational property of each of them, nevertheless the use of the phrase "petroleum companies" could be replaced by reference to Exxon, BP Amoco, Royal Dutch Shell, etc., and the same attribute would be picked out. We want to get at something unique to the phrase, "presidents of petroleum companies" such that Belia might believe something of presidents of petroleum companies, but not believe the same of presidents of Exxon, BP Amoco, Shell, etc. Thus, besides the intension of the predicate, "presidents of petroleum companies," there's its structured intension, which makes ineliminable reference to the intension of the predicate's component, "petroleum companies." See Carnap's discussion of intensional isomorphism.[4]

The Fregean approach requires a sophistication of another sort; one must understand type-theory or hierarchy theory. In set theory, we require the sets covered by our theory to be constructed in a particular way so that they have a determinate type. The lowest level of sets in the hierarchy of sets consists of the sets that do not have sets as members. There is at least one set at that level, namely, the null-set.^ But sets of people would be at that level too. Let the level or type of these sets be 1 and the type of their members 0. Then any other set that has as its highest type member a set of type $n$ will be of type $n+1$. So the set of all subsets of the set of people is of type 2. Set^ theory only theorizes about sets of determinate type in this hierarchy of types. What of the class of all things whatsoever? Sorry. It's easy to see that it must contain itself and so it cannot be of determinate type. In fact, set theory does not theorize about any class containing itself, nor about the class of all and only those sets which are not members of themselves. Russell generated a paradox from this last: If such a class exists, then a contradiction is true, namely that it both is and is not a member of itself. Set theory avoids proofs of its own self-inconsistency by ensuring that it only deals with sets of determinate type level, by a specification of this **cumulative type structure**. The word "cumulative" is used to distinguish this structure from the type structure Russell invented. He was the first to propose type structures as a way to avoid inconsistency in set theory. His structure is much more cumbersome than the cumulative type structure that mathematicians use today.

Analogous to the mathematic hierarchy of sets is a hierarchy of formal languages. The greater the language's expressive power the higher its order. Recall from section G the distinction between the referential and attributive (predicative) positions in sentences. When students learn logic today, usually they only see referential positions subjected to quantification.^ Variables appear only in referential positions; the symbols in predicative positions are treated as having extensions. The founders of modern logic did not restrict the device of variables and quantification to referential positions. The restriction came about because, when it's imposed, many powerful theorems can be proved about the resulting system that would not otherwise be provable. These languages, with quantification restricted to referential positions, are first order languages or languages of "order 1." (A language without quantification, as propositional logic is usually presented, is order 0.) An order 2 language allows variables in the predicative position and quantifies over them. Thus what an order 1 language predicates, an order 2 language generalizes about. An example of a sentence of order 2 is "for any two people $x$ and $y$, there's some relation $R$ such that $Rxy$." Advancing to order 3, one can ask what might be said of the relations themselves, what are their properties, so that the relations now constitute a domain for referential positions, and we quantify over their predicates. A language which can generalize about anything of up to order $n$ is a language of order $n+1$.

If you sense the opportunity for paradox, you sense acutely. Can a property describe itself? Is "English" English? Yes. What then of the property of properties of not being self-descriptive? Is it self-descriptive? Yes and no. A second hierarchy of languages comes about if we follow Tarski's solution to the semantical paradoxes. Unlike English, the sentence, "The sentence you're now reading is false," does not exist in any formal language in a Tarski hierarchy. This is good, since any language which lets this sentence exist in it is a language that's self-inconsistent, since such a sentence is simultaneously true and false. (If it's true, then it's false. If it's false, then it's true. But any sentence must be one or the other. So it's both.) Tarski required that consistent languages not contain their own truth or "true-of" predicates. Then, to say of a sentence that it's true, or of a predicate that it's true of something, requires a more expressively powerful language than the language in which the sentence or predicate occurs. Languages, ordered in terms of their power to say of sentences that they are true or false, are called **metalanguages**, and the languages, whose sentences they say are true or false, are their object languages.

As defined, a second order language may not be a metalanguage, and a metalanguage may only be a first order language. For the purposes of the nonextensional Platonist, the first way of thinking of a hierarchy of languages, in terms of quantificational power, is the more relevant, and so is the cumulative type structure of set theory.

Now apply the concept of order level to intensions. A phrase like "president" has an intension. What of the phrase, "the intension of 'president'"? Presumably its extension is the attribute which is the intension of "president." So its intension must be the attribute of possessing the attribute of presiding over something. Richard Montague, resorting to such intensions, proposed that a fairly elementary fragment of English is best modeled in a language of order 3.[5]

So there are these two nonextensional approaches: There's the approach that's not contented with simple intensions but decomposes meanings into structured intensions with parts corresponding to the parts of a phrase, and there's the approach that builds intensions upon intensions, creating a hierarchy of intensions. Structured intensions do not *prima facie* differ in type level from simple intensions. (Since structured intensions are usually represented by ordered sets, and ordered sets themselves are usually defined in ways that invoke the higher levels of types, in fact both approaches get into types. Type theory is not the device that the Carnapian approach exploits to solve problems of hyperintensionality, as it is in the Fregean approach.) Both nonextensional theories promise that they can analyze the contents of the directed-towardness relation so that we can get to the elements that won't block the application of the rule of substitution within the that-clauses of propositional attitudes.

### §4. An example of structured intensions in analyses of attitudes.

Although we've not had much recourse to the idea, we did note that a single instance of the directed-towardness relation can have more than one object. For example, any act of preference must involve more than one object. The Carnapian approach capitalizes on this possibility, so that even belief in one intension might take note of the elementary intensions which compose the one whole intension, all of which being collectively objects of the single belief.

Belia's given a logic problem. She's given a premise, from which she must draw a conclusion. She *takes it as given*

> that there is a burglar in the house who is either stealing the spoons and forks or stealing the spoons but not stealing the forks.

She is asked whether the burglar is stealing the spoons. She sees the logical equivalence:

> $x$ steals spoons = either $x$ steals spoons & $x$ steals forks, or $x$ steals spoons & $x$ does not steal forks.

Belia knows that these two clauses are intersubstitutable in the sentence, "a burglar $x$ in the house is such that . . . ." So she *concludes* that there's a burglar in the house who's stealing the spoons.

If unitary intensions were all that mattered, the equivalence between what she took to be given and what she concluded would entitle us to say she took to be given what she concluded. But that's obviously false, even though she did know the equivalence. Just ask her. One cannot interchange the that-clauses after "takes it as given" and "concludes"; she'll object vociferously. To avoid warranting the interchange, we suppose her attitude of taking-to-be-given reaches into the object-intension to the elemental intensions of its structure. The elemental intensions are themselves termini of the attitude's directed-towardness, as must be their composition into a unity also. In the example the elemental intensions included two monadic attributes and two functions in propositional logic that figured in her calculation of the equivalence. Much of the work of the Carnapian is to show how the elemental intensions can be objects of the attitude and also be constructed into a unitary object of the same attitude. A wise Carnapian posits structured intensions that have only intensions as parts, and so they differ from the structured singular propositions, now discredited, which supposedly had you, me, and Mont Blanc as parts.

There comes a point, however, when the Carnapian must swallow Mates's paradox, presented in section G, because it's unsolvable by these techniques. After much accommodating of intuitions generated by Belia's control of the that-clause, this intensionalist must tell Belia to stop insisting, because she's wrong about her own attitudes. The eternal sentence nonrepresentationalist never reaches that level of desperation. Mates's paradox is framed in terms of sentences and is solved by sentences.

### §5. An example of cumulative type structures in analyses of attitudes.

Let's suppose that Belia owes a dollar to Jack. The position filled by the noun phrase, "a dollar" is opaque. We cannot export from it and say there's a dollar, meaning some actual dollar, such that Belia owes that one to Jack. That could be true, if Belia owed Jack something to add to his coin collection, but by itself the sentence has no such implication. The situation is similar to wanting a dollar. Rarely is there a particular dollar that's wanted.

How might the Fregean nonrepresentationalist describe the logic of owing something without implying there's a particular something which is owed? Montague suggested that owing a dollar is being obliged to give a dollar, and being obliged to give a dollar is really two attributes. Giving a dollar is a triadic attribute, the attribute of something $x$ being a dollar which a person $y$ gives to a person $z$. It's a first order attribute because all three positions are filled by individuals of the lowest order. And it's a conjunctive attribute combining dollar and giving. But being obliged is a dyadic attribute, connecting a person to an attribute such as the attribute of giving a dollar, and it's second order, since it has a term that's first order. That's the consequence of the cumulative type structure.

The term "a dollar" is really part of the attribute, giving a dollar. Back in section D, where we introduced attribute abstraction from sentences, we did not note this way of dealing with positions reserved for singular terms. Generally in our examples of abstractions of attributes the singular terms were left behind. Thus from the sentence, "Belia owes a dollar to Jack," converted to "Belia is obliged to give a dollar to Jack," we would've abstracted the attribute of (1)'s giving (3) to (2), which is a legitimate abstraction, but not the only one. We might also have legitimately abstracted the attribute of (3)'s being a dollar which (1) gives to (2). Or we might have abstracted only a dyadic attribute, containing a quantifier: the attribute of *something's* being a dollar which (1) gives to (2). This last is what our Fregean nonrepresentationalist abstracts.

If quantifiers may be expressed inside attributes, logic must rule on the permissible ways of manipulating them. We'd like logic to deliver our intuition that it's invalid to infer from Belia's owing a dollar to Jack, that there's a particular dollar which Belia owes to Jack. Higher order intensional logic delivers. Its rules make the boundary of an attribute fairly impervious. Given a quantifier that's within the scope of the words, "the attribute of . . ." its exportation from the attribute has the effect of changing the attribute. In the example of Belia's owing a dollar to Jack, the first order attribute of something's being a dollar, which (1) gives to (2), is itself the second term of the second order attribute of (1)'s being obliged to (2). If the quantifier "a dollar" is exported from the first order attribute, the second term of the second order attribute is no longer the attribute of something being a dollar which (1) gives to (2). It's rather the attribute of (1) giving (3) to (2). Then why suppose Belia's obligation concerns that attribute? The whole sentence's truth value may have changed from true to false. If the quantifier "something" is exported, the attribute has changed to this one: (3)'s being a dollar which (1) gives to (2), and we can still doubt that Belia's obligation concerns that attribute. Consequently it's invalid to export the terms "a dollar" or "something" from the attribute.

At least that's what the nonrepresentationalist would like to say. Logic may not be so accommodating, however. If the operations of abstraction and concretion are implicative, that is, if we may infer from the truth of a sentence to the existence of the attribute formed from the sentence, and vice versa for concretion, the jig is up, because one could move back and forth among the attributes just distinguished. The nonrepresentationalist can prevent this extensionalization by allowing abstraction from false sentences and concretion to false sentences.

## §6. Problems with hyperintensions.

These nonextensional, nonrepresentational approaches to that-clauses revive the analogy that we dismissed in section F, between modal logic and theories of propositional attitudes. We saw there that the sentences of modal logic could be regimented with about-positions and that-clauses, suggestive of an analogy to the theory of propositional attitudes. We also saw that problems of opacity and intensionality in modal logic could be solved by resort to Russell's analysis of definite descriptions and Carnap's criterion for intensional identity of attributes. The approaches to propositional attitudes that we're now considering claim that all we need to solve similar problems afflicting the propositional attitudes is more of the same kind of medicine, just higher dosages; thus hyperintensions.

Belia is quite paranoid about these two approaches, and rightly so, for they both seek to deny her control over the that-clauses in Rep's reports of her attitudes. They seek to absolutize the contents of that-clauses so that we can analyze them in a way that implies the properties of opacity and hyperintensionality of their contexts, with the result that Belia's power of veto over equivalencies of that-clauses is abolished. They say Belia's consent has just been *ersatz* for the proper entities to have that-clauses refer to. When we get them right, Belia can keep her peace. Worse than that, Belia can go take a hike, for they might just decide that Belia is wrong about what she believes her attitudes are directed toward. Go-it-alone nonrepresentationalists do have to reject certain intuitions about truth and falsity of reports, about what is actually being believed. Such rejections are likely to occur in the translation paradox, discussed in section V, and in paradoxes involving substitutions of logically proper names of the same thing and hyperintensional problems which involve pairs of terms denoting the same structureless attribute.

Should we stand up for Belia? In rejecting "*salva veritate*" intuitions, her opponents are not following Plato's advice that theory should "save the appearances." For our intuitions of truth and falsity *are* the appearances in this case, and they're chucking the appearances to save the theory. Surely they put a good face on what they're doing; but how? They use the concept of conversational implicature.[6] Belia's control over the that-clause of reports of her attitudes is a matter of conversational implicature and may be canceled. Our regimentation of the data has obscured this fact, they'd say. Therefore they are saving the appearances after all. See section C's presentation of disquotation principles, which the nonrepresentationalists consider to be principles of implicature merely.

Let's concede their complaint that our regimentation has obscured the role of conversational implicature in reports. Of course, one may wonder about their canceling an implicature for metaphysical reasons, such as their treating two verbally different reports as reporting a belief in the same thing for metaphysical reasons, so that if the first report is true the second must be true too, no matter what Belia may say. Overriding Belia's protestations on the grounds that she's drunk is one thing; overriding them because metaphysical theory demands that Belia be treated as ignorant is another.

How decide between these alternative nonextensional views of the content-object of directed-towardness, as a thing the mind finds, if they and the extensionalist alternative all accomplish the main goal of making propositional attitudes conform to the law of substitution? Quine would argue that intensions assume the concept of analytic^ truth in the very statement of intensional identity conditions, and this assumption by itself is sufficient for doubt about nonextensionality.

### §7. Better and worse ways of being syncretist.

We conclude our discussion of the descriptive metaphysics of folk psychology with a look at syncretism. Ever since the Introduction I've presented myself as a syncretist, but warned that there's a taint to such a position. Here's the bad way to be a syncretist: Sections S and V presented alternative ways of thinking of the object of the directed-toward relation. In S the criterion was behavioral; in V it was communicative agreement. Which one is right? The disreputable syncretist says they're both right. On alternate days of the week? No; one must not say one accepts both representationalism and nonrepresentationalism, one's reason being one cannot make up one's mind about how to define directed-towardness.

A better way to be syncretist is to note that the representationalist criterion for the object of directed-towardness is superfluous, since the thesis we began section N with, does all the real work. We need not deduce it as a corollary from the behavioral criterion of directed-towardness. Harman's method of individuating attitudes can give it to us.

Therefore we need not accept the criterion proposed in section S and can go with the one in section V. Representations are important to our final theory since they're needed to individuate and concretize attitudes, thereby placing them in the flow of causes and effects. But they're not the objects of directed-towardness.

The nonrepresentationalist tends to be extravagant in ontology, however, when positing objects of directed-towardness, giving up on the ideal of extensionality. Our investigations in this section have not offered us much basis for optimism that such extravagance will pay off. The eternal sentence version of nonrepresentationalism is less extravagant and does pay off in solving the problems of opacity and hyperintensionality without giving up on the ideal of extensionality. Furthermore we can accommodate all varieties of *de re* attitudes by allowing incomplete eternal sentences to be the objects of that sort of directed-towardness. Concerning the *de dicto* attitudes, all the complete eternal sentences they are directed toward are general. The sentences can be in more than one language, and the languages they are in may be idiolects. The eternal sentence version of nonrepresentationalism not only has an ontology somewhat like the representationalists, but it steals a page from their theory of meaning as role, so that we might say that the real objects of the directed-towardness are the logical roles of eternal sentences. The representing that concretizes an attitude is a translation of, or expression of, the eternal sentence that the attitude is directed toward in this sense: It has a causal role that mimics the eternal sentence's logical role. The mimicking is either the product of natural selection, or training within a culture, or choice. The most spectacular examples of the last are acts of genius.

So there you have my syncretism, which is intellectually respectable, I hope. Helping me bring it to you was my supporting cast, whom I'd like to bring back for a final bow: Rep, who took much abuse from us, and Belia. For her magnificent performance, we present a gift to Belia, fresh from the taxidermist. Yes, the woodchuck that died in section O has been preserved and mounted. . . . Just a minute, now, is that a skunk?

# Notes

1. Maxwell J. Cresswell, *Structured Meanings* (1985).

2. Differences among these hybrid theorists are explored by Scott Soames, "Beyond Singular Propositions?" *Canadian Journal of Philosophy*, 25 (1995) 515-550. One difference is whether the supposed second reference of a report's

that-clause to the sentence which presents the believed proposition to the believer should count in assessing the truth or falsity of the report. Stephano Predelli, "Who's Afraid of Substitutivity?" *Nous*, 34 (2000) 455-467, finds the real differences between the hybrid theories to be less significant than is generally supposed.

3. Karl Popper, *Objective Knowledge: An Evolutionary Approach* (1972), chs. 3 and 4.

4. Rudolf Carnap, *Meaning and Necessity*, 2$^{nd}$ edition (1956) §§14 -15 and Appendix C.

5. See Richard Montague, *Formal Philosophy* (1974) 168 and 261 (rule T1(b)). Montague is very difficult for the nonlogician. For an introduction to what linguists call Montague Grammar, see David R. Dowty, R. E. Wall, and P. S. Peters, *Introduction to Montague Semantics* (1981).

6. Thomas McKay, "On Proper Names in Belief Ascriptions," *Philosophical Studies*, 39 (1981) 287-303.

# Part IV: The Naturalization Project, from Y to Z

The fourth part of these notes, consisting of two sections, assesses the prospects for naturalizing the science of the mind, in the light of what we learned about folk psychology. It also makes explicit the evolutionary element that has broken into our practice of analytic method.

As you may recall, earlier introductions to the parts contained warnings about proceeding. Evidently, you've not been heeding them. So once again it seems appropriate to append a warning label, this time from the New Testament. Many believe you're about to read God's own warning:

> See to it that no one deceives you by philosophy and vain deceit, according to human traditions, according to the elements of the world . . . (Colossians 2:8)

What's this? You continue? Ok, this time you're in big trouble.

# Y. The Prospects for Naturalizing the Science of the Mind.

You've worked hard. Time for recreation. Youthful metaphysicians, rejoice! For we're about to investigate a few key concepts in revisionary metaphysics, specifically in the naturalization project. Naturalization, you'll recall from the Introduction, is the project of showing that the properties of the mind, such as intentionality and consciousness, are fully explainable in terms of the physical properties of physical things. It's time for folk psychology to be judged to be either a partner in this project or an obstacle to it. My own view is that it needs to be supplemented and revised in accord with contemporary science. I say supplemented and revised rather than reduced or replaced, which naturalizers more radical than I am would say, because the ontology of folk psychology is sound. There really are the representational states which folk psychology is all about. In the ideally coherent modern worldview, which we metaphysicians seek, folk psychology survives largely intact.

Some naturalists may say that we've already departed irreconcilably from naturalism, for they define naturalism more severely than we did back in the Introduction. They say that naturalism rejects any claim to knowledge that's not a part of science. We only said that naturalism considers scientific knowledge to be the gold standard of knowledge, not that it constituted all the knowledge there is. So our acknowledging a peculiar form of knowledge in indexical beliefs (sections M and N), and later considering empathy to be an indispensable form of knowledge (sections T and U), not to mention our dalliance with knowledge of values and god (section O)—all that might seem to put us beyond the pale.

To be quite fair to ourselves, we only acknowledged forms of beliefs, not of knowledge. But I do go further and admit that there is indexical knowledge and empathic knowledge, and they're extra-scientific, a claim I'll defend in section Z. I don't think that admission puts me beyond the pale of naturalism, however, for my adherence to science's being the gold standard of knowledge means that I believe scientific knowledge is the only sort of knowledge that yields ontology, and that's naturalism enough. The indexical knowledge we've admitted imports no new ontology. As we saw in section N, indexical knowledge is a form of knowledge that can be fully understood without requiring an ontology additional to that recognized by science. The empathic knowledge does import the ontology of folk psychology, but science will grow to accept it, or so I claim.

### §1. Two kinds of naturalization project, stemming from two kinds of explanation.

First, let's introduce a distinction that evolutionary biologists find useful, namely, the distinction between proximate and ultimate causes, mechanisms, and explanations. The distinction was introduced in 1938 by J. R. Baker and popularized by Ernst Mayr.[1] Mayr suggested that if you're asking *how* something occurs, you want a proximate cause of it. If you're asking why it occurs, or *how come* it occurs, you want an ultimate cause. Proximate causes of biological features are the physical and chemical mechanisms that underlie them. Their ultimate causes are historical, why they came to be in the first place. The proximate causes are studied in functional biology; the ultimate causes in evolutionary biology. This same distinction divides two ways of conducting the project of naturalizing the mind.

The distinction between two kinds of explanation carries over into the naturalization project, yielding two naturalization projects: **Proximate naturalization** shows the mind is a physical and chemical system, and intentionality is a physical and chemical manifestation. **Ultimate naturalization** shows, by reference to evolution, that the mind is as continuous with the rest of nature as is life itself.

The word "why" suggests reasons as well as causes, but the intent here is only to give causes. People often describe a trait's "reason for being" in terms of its supposed purposes for existing, for instance, its contributions to the reproductive fitness^ of an organism possessing the trait. Purpose is something minds give to their creations, however, and so belongs among the things the naturalizers must explain, and not among the things assumed by their explanations. Ultimate naturalizers must avoid the pitfall of explanation by purpose. Explanations in terms of natural selection causing a lineage of organisms to become more adapted to its environment are not explanations in terms of purpose. For example, we sweat, and there's a proximate story of how we do and another story of why ultimately we do. According to the latter story, it happens that sweating is adaptive enough to make the organisms that sweated able to leave more descendants, and so natural selection operating on their lineage led to the prevalence of the gene for sweat glands in contemporary members of the lineage. Please satisfy yourself that no reference to purpose occurs in that story of adaptation. Not all stories of origins are stories of adaptation however. The ultimate cause of sickle cell anemia, which is a genetic disease, is a tale of the utter mindlessness of the evolutionary process. Natural selection worked in both cases, so it's hardly a teleological factor in evolution.

Naturalizers sometimes develop a predilection for one of the projects and a distaste for the other. They are either proximate naturalizers, disdaining the ultimate naturalizers, or vice versa. I, syncretist that I am, do not share this prejudice. Nevertheless, we must note something like a civil war going on among the naturalizers.

Some naturalizers are simply interested in the physical and computer-like underpinnings of intentionality. They're interested in proximate causes. It may be that proximate naturalization is the more revisionary of the projects, the less consistent with folk psychology. Thus it has the attractiveness of scandal. Nevertheless, it's just as interesting to show how an incremental evolution of intentionality can be true in a nonplatitudinous way, and how a belief in its evolution is consistent with folk psychology. Some of the proximate naturalizers are exclusively interested in the proximate causes, because they don't see anything but vapid truisms and untestable conjectures coming from the search for the ultimate causes of intentionality. They believe in the evolution of the mind, or at least of the brain, but, ho hum, that's all you can say. So, as one of these proximate naturalizers (Fodor) says, "So, please, spare me; no Darwin."[2] If it comes down to vapid truisms and untestable conjectures, however, both types of naturalizers exhibit plenty of that.

There's another motive for suspicion of the evolutionary naturalizer. The belief is very common today that with the coming of mankind one must recognize a jump to intentionality, which is next in magnitude only to the jump from nonlife to life. That is, both jumps are so great that, as the earlier jump went from the realm of chemistry into the realm of biology, the later jump went from biology into a third realm. Mind escapes biology and belongs to psychology, sociology, and anthropology. The proximate naturalizers take this to be, oh, so obvious that they dismiss anyone who looks for small incremental steps of intentionality connecting humanity to the rest of the animal kingdom. The fact that the brain is obviously a biological organ does not allay their impatience. For even if there are only small differences between our brains and, say, the chimpanzee's, and we can trace both species back by small decrements to an extinct common ancestor, nevertheless those small differences in brains lead to huge differences in mentality. It's a fallacy to argue from a small difference in brain or genes to a small difference in mind. So Fodor says.

We must grant the fallacious nature of the inference, but not grant that evolutionary naturalizers commit it. My own interest in the naturalization project stems mostly from a conviction that human intentionality is not so big a leap within the animal world as these proximate naturalizers think. I believe this can be proved directly from an examination of mentality, without resorting to inferences from brain studies. Mentality itself is something that evolved in small increments throughout evolution. Not all of the increments evolved as adaptations. I'm convinced that all of it, including our own intentionality, is very much a part of biology. Nevertheless, given the hostile intransigence the evolutionary naturalizers meet, they cannot even count on the support of the proximate naturalizers. It's not reciprocated; ultimate naturalizers don't have the same animus toward the proximate naturalizers as many of the latter have toward the evolutionary naturalizers, although I, for one, do yawn when the proximate naturalizers tell me what consciousness is.

Ultimate naturalizers often deserve the scorn directed toward them for their uncritical appeals to adaptation. As the example of sickle cell anemia shows, not everything that evolved is adaptive. Define **evolution** so that this can make sense, as the change in the frequency of genes in a population of organisms from one generation to the next. The causes of evolution are whatever causes changes in gene frequencies. Thus mutation is a cause, as is sexual reproduction, any act of which discards half the genes of the parents. So there's nothing in the definition of evolution that necessitates the changes being adaptive. Natural selection is the greater or less contribution by individuals of their genes to the pool of genes in the population's next generation, as a result of the environment facilitating some of the individuals and hindering others. Natural selection frequently prevents evolution when the environment is stable, but when a population is not adapted to its environment, only natural selection can lead to organisms with traits that help them survive and reproduce in their environment (i.e., adapt). The lazy idea of the job of the ultimate naturalizer of the mind is that it's simply to assert the adaptiveness of every mental trait, and presume natural selection formed it. Would that the project were that easy!

Let's put aside the internecine disputes: There are two naturalization projects, which should fit together the way functional and evolutionary biology fit together. There's proximate naturalization, and there's ultimate naturalization. Those two revisionary metaphysics can be pursued together, along with the descriptive metaphysics of folk psychology, without those interested in one of them being snooty about the pursuits of the others. Some of us pursue all three.

## §2. The fundamental mechanism of proximate naturalization: negative feedback.

There are two great successes of the proximate naturalizers, both stemming from discoveries made in the nineteenth century, but which the pressures of world war II forced into our technology. They're the negative feedback mechanism and computers. If you understand the former, you know how to naturalize purposiveness. If you understand the latter, you know how to naturalize rationality.

First, let's focus on the fundamental mechanism that captures within a naturalistic framework all purposefulness and meaningfulness. It's the **negative feedback mechanism**. As a mechanism it does something, but it's mechanical in a special way: It collects information about its own activities—that's feedback. It compares the feedback with a representation of the goal of its activities. The comparison is just the finding of a difference between the two by a process of subtraction—that's the negative. If the system is not yet successful, i.e., the result of the subtraction is not zero, it corrects its activities in directions which promote achieving the goal, i.e., getting a comparison result equal to zero. The control loop of the negative feedback mechanism is the fundamental principle of robotics.

That description employs mentalistic terminology to describe the machine: "collect information," "goal," "success," and so on. The underlying process is transparently purely physical, and we can eliminate all these terms from our descriptions, as I'll now show with a mini-course for philosophers about engineering. Demonstrating their eliminability also shows how they may be reintroduced by definition, if it were useful to do so, and indeed it is useful. We're giving a naturalistic analysis of the basic mentalistic notion, what it is to make a representation, what it is to be a made representation, not just a found one. The representations figure in contentful states such as intentions. Given a system sufficiently complex to warrant a mentalistic description of it, we can state a necessary^ condition for its state to be an **intention-to-act**, as distinct from an intention-to-refrain. If a state is an intention-to-act, then it establishes and activates a negative feedback mechanism within the system. The content of the system's intention, what it intends to do, is the foresign in it, about which more later. I only say this is a necessary condition for being an intention-to-act, not a full analysis, because obviously I've left out things like consciousness, which many think are also necessary.[3] Nonetheless, the machine's information states are the physical symptoms of the direct attributions and the holophrastic utterances discussed in sections N and U.

Not just any stabilizing mechanism will do as the generator of all purposefulness and meaningfulness, even if it's come to be called a negative feedback system. We must distinguish systems that merely tend toward an equilibrium from those systems that are true negative feedback systems. There are many kinds of systems that can return to equilibrium from an arbitrarily large range of different initial conditions. And many systems reach equilibrium by having some links of the system compensate for other links that have been disturbed from their equilibrium values. The compensations work to restore all states of the system to their equilibrium values. That's not enough to make a system one that operates by feedback, however. For example, the geyser in Yellowstone National Park, Old Faithful, is a regular mechanism reestablishing its equilibrium every fifty minutes or so by sending a stream of water and steam a hundred meters into the air. It does not operate by comparing feedback to a sign of a goal state. Another example: Processes that affect the reflectivity of clouds may stabilize atmospheric temperatures. When ocean surface temperatures rise and micro-organisms emit more aerosol particles into the atmosphere, clouds become whiter and reduce sunlight's warming of the atmosphere. The surface temperatures of the ocean will tend to stability. This so-called CLAW cycle does not respond to information, despite its having a counter-active link in the cycle. The albedo of clouds is not signaling the oceanic microorganisms to modulate their activities for the sake of the global ecosystem. No sky-high cirrus transducer is preserving an isomorphism between the input and output energies, analogous to sensing. Many systems in nature are just energy merry-go-rounds, with some steps that dampen the amplification of effects. For example, populations of predators and prey may constitute a cycle of predation and evasion that produces a stable population. The interlocking of many such cycles forms what we call the balance of nature. I'm not talking about any of that, when I talk about negative feedback systems.[4] On the other hand, I must distinguish the two kinds of systems in nonmentalistic terms if there's to be any hope of a naturalistic capture of a contentful state.

Three naturalistic and non-question-begging things distinguish true negative feedback systems from systems that merely tend to equilibrium. First, they compensate for disturbances of their states by having a causal path that's spatially distinct from the main path. Old Faithful has no such independent loop. Besides the main path where the input of energy is high and most of the work is done, there must also be distinct low energy paths. The low energy channels often begin at transducers and terminate in unusual arrangements of matter that trigger but don't power the high energy channels. Such a peculiar dimorphism cries out for explanation, which comes in the form of a semeiotic description of the same configuration. So, secondly, information collects at the sensors and flows along these low energy paths to comparators where it's exploited for the control of purposive behavior. A path that transports information is not like a path for transporting a material such as gas or hot air. Systems that exploit information through channels dedicated to relaying it are more robust in the face of disturbances and respond with more speed and discrimination. Thirdly, negative feedback systems need not have as goals their states of equilibrium as a physicist understands equilibrium, namely, thermodynamic equilibrium. The physicist will tell you that the equilibrium point of the human body is attained after death. The goal of a human being is not that. So the goal of a negative feedback system is some stable condition distinct from its physical equilibrium point. One cannot infer that, because a system stabilizes at a condition distinct from physical equilibrium, it also fulfills the first two conditions. Many systems fulfill the third condition without fulfilling the first two, for instance, the sun with its ample supply of fuel for fusion. The other two conditions are independent diagnosticators of genuine feedback systems, more sensitive than the third condition is.

**Information** must be distinguished from the energy that carries it. "The news" has at least three features that distinguish it from energy. As the ancient Greeks said, light that's reflected from the surface of an object carries away the *form* of that object, that is, its shape, size, texture, and color. More exactly, the light carries with it the mathematically describable structure of the surface. The forms in energy like light are information or, if you prefer, potential information. The information in the energy is therefore a relative property, the form *of* some object, but the energy carrying the form is not a relative thing; it has its existence in its own right. Secondly, energy is a conserved quantity, but information is not. It can be destroyed. And whereas energy is degraded in work and becomes useless, information does not have to disappear when it is used; that is, it need not be used up. It can be duplicated without destroying or depleting the information. (I assume that the entropy^ added by the use of information can be dumped, so that the information is kept after being used even if the totality of information in the universe is depleted by its use.) Thirdly, information is a macro-pattern distributed over energy. The whole pattern is not derived by adding up its parts, any more than the information in a paragraph is merely the sum of the information in each of its sentences or words or letters in the words. Suppose that the information in "all men are mortal" is the set of all the sentences it implies. Now create the union of that set with the set of all the sentences implied by "Socrates is a man." The union does not contain the sentence, "Socrates is mortal." There's more information in the two sentences together than in the sum of the information in each separately.

A negative feedback system exploits the information that comes its way as signs or representations. Its "setting" is its *foresign*, its sign of a possible state of the system, which because of the way the sign functions in the system we may identify as its goal state. A foresign's mood is imperative. The *feedback* is a sign too, a sign of conditions as they allegedly were when measured. It's declarative in mood. Feedback signs are good examples of the representations we discussed in section P. We noted there that some signs are simply found in nature, which organisms exploit. In appealing to found signs, therefore, we've not lapsed carelessly into using the mentalistic concepts we wish to explain.

The feedback, traveling along paths in the system, comes into proximity to the foresign, and the two get "compared": signs of conditions as they allegedly just were with signs of conditions as they allegedly should be. If we're not to beg any questions about the analysis of mentalistic notions, that description should be replaced by a physical description of the comparison process. Later I will show how a bimetal does it in a thermostat. In simple systems the signs are quantitative measures, and the comparison is like subtracting the feedback from the foresign. Any result other than zero triggers a correction, bringing results of later comparison closer to zero. Zero marks the end attained. These systems are self-governing, which is why the science of them is called cybernetics. If "governetic" were a word, we would see in it the Greek "cybernetic" (where "c" transliterates a Greek sound like the "c" in "actor"). Let's apply these ideas to figure Y-1. Four types of components occur in the control diagram:

> ● the dot = measurer: measures, e.g., temperature, and relays (i.e., feeds back) the measurement to comparators.
>
> ○ the circle = comparator: subtracts any feedback from a setting (foresign) or from another measurement, or it makes a more complex comparison than subtraction, and produces an error signal.

■ the square = operator: responds to non-zero difference signals in a way that makes later error signals tend toward zero.

– – the broken line = system's boundaries. Measurement can occur inside or on the exterior surface of a boundary.

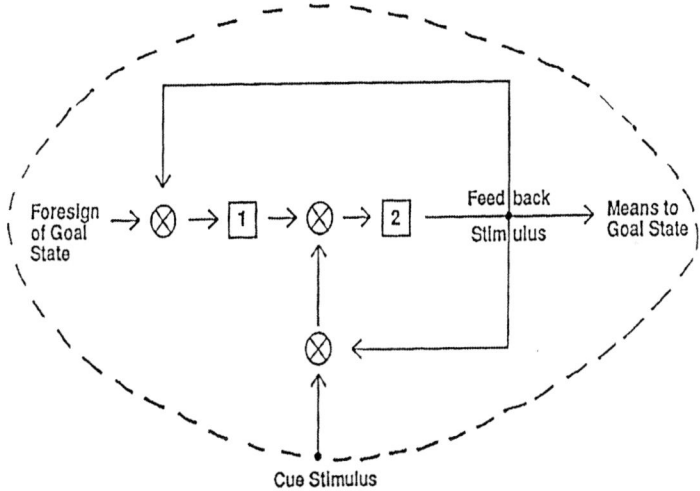

Figure Y-1. Control diagram for a negative feedback mechanism. The system responds to negative feedback, simulating purposeful action.[5]

Assume the control diagram is of a proportional regulator of temperature in a house. I'll describe its operation in terms of its signifying goals and existing conditions and its interpreting its signs. (Reminder: We do not interpret "signifying" and "interpreting" as mental or communicative.) The rightmost measurer measures the temperature of the air being pushed into the house from the furnace/cooler blowers. This measurement is relayed along feedback loops to the leftmost comparator and is subtracted there from the foresign of the desired temperature. The resulting error signal, if not zero, ultimately changes the action of the second operator, which is the furnace/cooler. If the difference turns positive, the furnace's activity is increased; if negative, the cooler's. Before the instruction is carried out it is further modulated:

> ●The first operator responds to the error signal by resetting the middle comparator to a sub-foresign. This signifies the amount of change in temperature that the system should make.

> ●The bottom measurer measures the temperature outside the house (more strictly, its own temperature at its surface) and

relays it to the bottommost comparator, which compares it to the interior temperature. (No foresign or output to an operator here.)
●The middle comparator compares the difference, just described, to the sub-foresign by more than mere subtraction. In effect it substitutes a new error signal for the original one to account for the rate of gain or loss of heat through the walls of the house.
The final operator is the furnace/cooler. Its level of activity adjusts so that the temperature fore-signified at the original comparator will be reached.

For example: Suppose the system's temperature is 15°C. The measurement goes to the comparator. It computes the difference between this measurement and the setting. Suppose it's set for 20°C. The difference is the number 5, called the error, *e*. The operator then receives the error signal and responds by directing a flow of gas to the furnace at a rate that will reduce the number *e* to zero. When $e = 0$, that's the end realized. The system then ceases changing the means; the rate of flow of the gas to the furnace stays constant.

Although the foresign of the goal is on the control diagram and the means to reaching it are there also, the end is not shown on it, for the end is not a cause of its own coming to be. The end is the temperature of the house at which the error signal equals zero. To show the end attained we need a time-flow diagram. We'll ignore the complicating effect of the cue stimulus and the first operator in figure Y-1, to emphasize the key concepts:

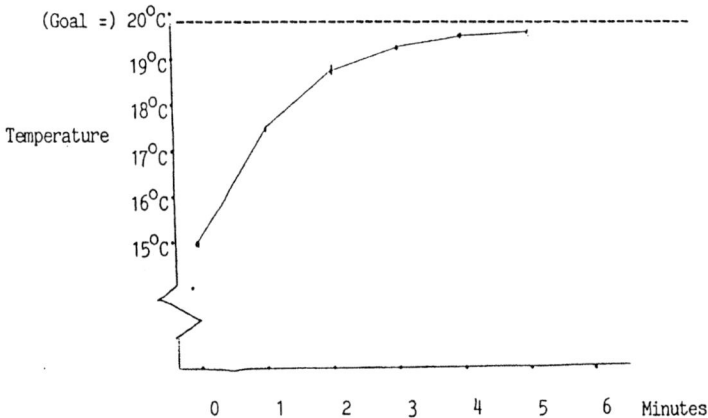

Figure Y-2. The response over time of a negative feedback system (simpler than the one in figure 1) to error signals. As time passes, the negative feedback system tends to reach the condition identified by the zero error signal and, once the system attains it, thereafter acts to maintain it.

We can write equations that describe the action of a negative feedback system. Equations can be written in various forms. For example, a linear equation may be written in slope-intercept form, or in point-slope form, or in other forms. Here's a form of linear equation that is especially important for the point we're making. Call it the goal-minus-feedback form:

$$r = (1/t)(g - f)$$

$r$ = the adjusted rate of action; $t$ = the time needed to achieve the goal at the initial rate of action; $g$ = the goal; $f$ = the feedback.

The formula approximates the operation of feedback in our continuously adjusting thermostat-furnace system.[6] The thermostat is set at 20°C. So 20°C is the goal, but it's winter, and the door's been opened and the house temperature has dropped to 15°C. So the feedback is 15°C. This difference of 5°C is the error, $e$, as I said. The "action" of this system is the burning of gas to heat the air in the house. The initial rate at which the gas was being burned was sufficient to raise the house temperature to 20°C in two minutes; let's say. The reciprocal of this number, 1/(2 min.), is constant in all our calculations. We can now put numbers for the variables.

$$r = (1/2\text{min})(20° - 15°) = 2.5° \text{ per minute}$$

Gas will now be burned at a rate that would increase the temperature to the desired level in two minutes. (Notice in figure Y-2 that each straight line segment, if doubled in length, would intersect the 20°C line.) We don't do that, since it would lead to overshoots and compensatory corrections that would cause a perpetual oscillation of the temperature. In fact, the burning of the gas increases the temperature to 17.5°C in one minute. Let's imagine that the operator adjusts the burning once every minute instead of continuously, so that we can avoid calculus. After one minute the rate of action adjusts again:

$$r = (1/2\text{min})(20° - 17.5°) = 1.25° \text{ per minute}$$

After the second minute the temperature has risen to 18.75°C and the rate of burning gas adjusts downward again:

$$r = (1/2\text{min})(20° - 18.75°) = 0.625° \text{ per minute}$$

So after the third minute, the temperature has risen to 19.375°. As the feedback temperature approaches the goal of 20°, the rate of action slows so that the feedback temperature approaches the goal only asymptotically. When the thermostat can *detect* no difference between goal and feedback, $e = 0$ and the goal is reached for all practical purposes.

Recall from section B the reciprocity of a desire's intensity for a goal and a belief's degree of certainty that it's been achieved. The former decreases as the latter increases, according to decision theory. Figure Y-2 shows an analogous reciprocity between the amount of the feedback's negativity and the action's intensity.

I mentioned earlier that I'd cash out the mentalistic connotations of the idea of comparison and subtraction, which we used to describe the feedback system's operations. To understand how the subtraction is done physically, we need the concept of a **bimetal**. A bimetal is a strip of one pure metal, say brass, bonded to another strip of metal, say iron. Since the different metals contract and expand differently in response to differences in temperature, a bimetal will curve in response to changes in temperature as one side of it expands more than the other side. Comparison of feedback to goal is the orientation of a bimetal within a circuit which the bimetal can open or close—that's the goal—and the degree of its bending in response to the attained temperature of the ambient air—that's the feedback. The bimetal's initial orientation determines how far it must bend to close the circuit—that's the comparison.

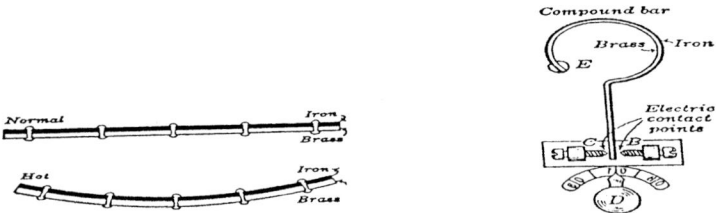

Figure Y-3. A bimetal. Left: Two states of a bimetal. The lower state is the effect of heating Right: A typical way a temperature is compared to a goal for the temperature is to insert a bimetal into a circuit in such a way that it closes the circuit if the temperature is too low, which the bimetal detects because bimetals bend and unbend in response to temperature. The dial at D controls the orientation of the bimetal at E.[7]

The goal-minus-feedback formula describes the behavior of the bimetal in the circuit and the operator's response to its opening and closing the circuit. I'd like, however, to say that here we have the toehold for a mentalistic description, as if it were the manual for translating this system's signs. You may doubt that the goal-minus-feedback form of the equation should be interpreted as a manual for the translation of nature's own signs into our own language. For even systems that are *not* negative feedback systems can be described by equations in so-called goal-minus-feedback form, systems like pendulums and populations of animals. Surely, a pendulum does not have a foresign of the position at which it comes to rest, as though that were its goal. How then do we know that the equation is a schema for translation for negative feedback systems, but not for pendulums? My reply is that, when the other distinguishing features of engineered negative feedback systems are in place, the three we mentioned earlier, the mentalistic reading of the formula begins to make sense. All that we need add is complexity.

Of course, the artifact of a furnace/cooler system controlled by a thermostat, which we used to introduce the concepts appropriate for negative feedback systems, is too simple to be like a living thing, but the needed complexities are easy to imagine. First, in place of each measuring device we put millions of them, whose measurements can be thought of as a long vector input to a parallel distributed network of the connectionist sort.[8] A human eye, for instance, is an organ with millions of sensors all feeding data to the brain. The connectionist network that's in the brain's optical cortex is sophisticated enough to analyze and classify its input. Its output is the signal we've called the feedback or a cue stimulus. Secondly, the output of the operator need not be the single discharge of energy, which the single arrow titled "means to goal state" seems to portray. Instead it may feed into another connectionist network that operationalizes the command and activates millions of muscle fibers coordinately. Finally, many negative feedback systems can be organized hierarchically so that there are goals, sub-goals, sub-sub-goals, and so on. They interlock for mutual protection and for increased range of adaptive response.

This complexity sinks any defining of sign-types by their functions; functions won't individuate them. In the last subsection we'll set in place the conceptual means to treat signs as definitionally prior to functions.

A sharp critic will challenge us, "Ok, supposing the negative feedback system does intend to heat up the place, why does it intend to? What are its reasons?" We might concede that we've so far captured only part of the folk psychological theory of purposefulness as it applies to us. But the theory applies to simpler beings also, for we may opt out of answering such questions about a spider's spinning a web, for instance, when we reply, "No reason; it's instinct for survival and reproduction." We cannot say even that much about our negative feedback system, however, since it does not have many goals subordinated to an overarching goal of fitness, as do all living things. Nevertheless, it does contain the primordial contentful states. Recall the boiler room analogy from sections N and P. There we looked into the room from above; here we've been inside inspecting the machinery. As we huff and puff our way back up, we note the long flight of stairs ahead of us, representing the continuities and growing complexities for the science of the distinctiveness of the human mind to explore. Let's resist the incessant calls of the antinaturalists to find just one major dichotomy splitting us off from all else. By the time we reach the last step up, much of the human mind will be already in place.

### §3. Intentionality comes from the mind's being interconnected computers.

At the other extreme of the continuum of life, we do want to understand naturalistically what it is for one to embed one's intention in a framework of reasons. We resort again to complexity for the account we seek. The mind computes, and the more rational we are the more resources of computation we make use of. This idea is old hat today. I'll not belabor the analogy of mind to computer. The proximate naturalizer's project is to show that the mind achieves all its intentionality by operating as a computer. Or rather the brain is like a beehive or ant nest, where each neuron is one bee or one ant. The individual bee and ant are computers, and each individual neuron is also. Bees communicate with each other, and so do ants, but their communications are not expressions of an inner meaningfulness. It's as if a bee's thought of where the nectar can be found is there for the first time in its dance in the hive, from which other bees learn where to collect more of it. The conceptual roles of the components of the dance are their social roles only. The thought is not first in its cephalic ganglion (proto-brain) in beementalese. The same emptiness or pure exteriority characterizes ant communications. Behaviorist theories of meaning say all there is to say that's true of these systems. Now suppose that ten billion ants get locked into fixed positions inside a robot and must make do with directing the robot to do all their work for them. The chat among the ants continues, but what had been a communication system without expressing anything inner finds itself on the inside. That which has no inner is now the inner. When its robot—we can call her Aunt Hillary[9] —meets a robot belonging to another ten billion ants in a similar fix, it's expedient for the two of them to develop another communication system expressive of the inner in each robot, so that they may cooperate. This communication system looks the very opposite of emptiness and pure exteriority. To collect the payoff of this analogy, convert all that talk of ants into talk of neurons, and you have a conception of human **intentionality**. So much excellent material already exists on this subject that here I only wish to examine the most vivid attack on the analogy and show why it's inconclusive.

In section S I disengaged a form of conceptual role semantics from the naturalization project, just as I did with respect to sententialism in section P, so that they might find a home in folk psychology. I did mention that conceptual role semantics is often an ingredient in naturalization projects. The goal of the naturalizing philosophers is to show that the states of brains and computers might play meaning-giving roles without defining the roles in terms that assume purpose or logic. We were not so confined when we were doing folk psychology. It's hard to delimit meaning-giving roles without making use of rationality and purpose. Perhaps there are naturalistic substitutes. Perhaps biological fitness will serve as goal, and the finding and using of means to reach that goal is rationality. The greater the stretch and convolution of connection between stimulation and the responses it prompts, the greater the rationality of the responder. If so, then the proximate naturalizers' conceptual role semantics can simply be called *causal role* semantics, because they are reductionists: The reduction of semantics to causal roles is explicitly a part of the naturalization project as they develop it.

Let's consider an objection to this form of naturalization, which goes so well with sententialism and conceptual role semantics. A thought experiment, part of what is called the **Chinese room Argument**, tries to break the connection the naturalizers draw between our understanding of meanings and our calculating in LOT, leading to appropriate, purposive action. The issue is whether thinking in LOT, which involves understanding, just is the naturalistic causal process of symbols being manipulated by a program of the sort that runs computers.[10] That would be the proximate naturalizers' reduction of folk psychology's sententialism and conceptual role semantics. The experiment in my words:

> Imagine a computer that manipulates symbols in such a way as to simulate the results of understanding, namely, it gives intelligent responses. It outputs in Chinese appropriate answers to questions formulated in Chinese. Does it understand the Chinese inputs and outputs?

You may not intuit that it need not understand the questions or its answers by virtue of what it does. To see that it does not, we continue:

> Analogously, if you just imagine yourself duplicating the symbol manipulation processes by which it arrived at the answers, you intuit that you don't. All you do is follow the rules of the computer program. You accept Chinese inputs, follow the program's rules for manipulating them, and send out the Chinese outputs.

The people fluent in Chinese who gave you the questions and accept the answers may be amazed at how clever you seem to be. But you know you don't understand the questions or answers. And neither did the computer!

Applying the result to the naturalizers' thesis that the mind is a computer, if thinking in LOT were just the manipulating of sentences according to a program, it would not include understanding meanings.

I criticized this argument in a note to section R on connectionism, and I'll just add here a defense of the naturalizers. The thought experiment is weak in that it trades on our confusing the way a computer might *simulate* what a mind does and the way it might *duplicate* the complete causal processes whereby a mind understands, down to the last essential detail.[11] All that could be understood as following a program. In the thought experiment where you play the part of a computer, you haven't been following the program that would constitute thinking in LOT; you've only been following a program that simulates it by delivering equivalent results. Notice that, while the computer emulates the results of intelligent processing, you emulated the computer's processing, not the intelligent processing. What if the computer had to emulate not just your appropriate purposive action but the processing by which you come to act appropriately and purposively?

One may intuit that a computer could act *as if* it had understanding, but actually not have any. But unless you're assured that the computer operates causally equivalently to the way human beings do and still doesn't understand, you cannot conclude that the connection which the naturalizer claims between action and understanding is false. When the thought experiment is reworked so that the computer operates causally equivalently to the way human beings do, we fail to intuit a lack of understanding. Now the interesting work begins; backing off from the equivalence, how much of the causal detail is inessential to understanding, so that a computer might leave it out and still understand?

In defense of the argument, you'll be told that the naturalizer can appeal only to the size and complexity of the mind's program for thinking in LOT and changes in such physical traits are insufficient to invalidate the results of the thought experiment. If you did not understand the Chinese inputs or outputs by mimicking the computer, you won't understand them by following another program that gets the same result by a longer more circuitous route. Computing is syntactic; understanding is semantic. The one does not suffice for the other. Therefore the intentionality of the mind is not accounted for by its being a computer. So say the critics of this form of proximate naturalization. The naturalizer's reply is to note that the size and complexity of the mind's program just might make the difference. As the saying goes, "God is in the details." But if so, it's premature for us to try to settle this dispute.

It is premature. Here's a thought experiment that fits the naturalizer's specifications for a thought experiment that might refute the naturalistic reduction: Suppose scientists make a syntactic processor out of silicon chips, which duplicates almost down to the last neural detail your brain's causal pathways. Suppose they tap into your memories and load into the syntactic processor a complete stock of your memories. Suppose they also arrange for a way to load the processor's memories, should it acquire any, back into your brain for you to remember. The scientists hook the processor into your nervous system as a backup to your brain. They also installed a switch that allows them to take your brain out of the causal loop and substitute your syntactic processor. Now comes the real experiment: You read a book. The scientists don't tell you this, but you read all the odd numbered chapters with your brain and all the even numbered chapters with your syntactic processor. At the end of each chapter the scientists transfer the accumulated memories of the chapter from the organ you used to the organ you will use for reading the next chapter. When you finish the book, they question you twice about your understanding of the chapters, once with your brain in the loop and once with the silicon syntactic processor in the loop. The scientists themselves find no difference in your understanding of the chapters in either sequence of questionings. Well, that lack of difference to spectators was granted by the critics of the naturalizers. Now the scientists ask you if *you* feel there's any difference in your understanding of the chapters. What's the answer?

Here are two possibilities: If when your brain is in the loop, you say that there's a curious feeling about every even numbered chapter, that in retrospect it felt a bit like having read Jabberwocky, then the critics win. Alternatively, suppose you say that nothing seems different to your introspections, and you say this even with your brain in the loop. Waiting out in the hallway are all the proximate naturalizers. When they hear what you say, they pop the champagne and abandon themselves to wild celebration.

Now here's the real thought experiment: Do you here and now know which of the two possible outcomes would occur? I don't. The Chinese room argument focuses one of the issues well, but it settles nothing.

This concludes our brief survey of proximate naturalization. Negative feedback systems and computation are the key ideas we explored and defended. Together they give the naturalizer a way to reduce purpose and rationality to physical properties of physical things. What of consciousness? I beg off that one.

### §4. Ultimate naturalization: there's more than one way to go about it.

Let's turn now to the other form of naturalizing, ultimate explanation. I assume that everyone will assign Daniel Dennett's philosophizing about the intentionality of the mind in an evolutionary way, in his *Darwin's Dangerous Idea*,[12] the status of Plan A for ultimate naturalizing. By calling it Plan A I mean it's the strategy which is generally considered the most promising of success. I'm in favor of philosophizing about the mind in an evolutionary way, but I disagree with Plan A. In this subsection I want to break the hold of certain ideas that might prevent you from seeing alternative ways of carrying out an ultimate naturalization of the mind.

Dennett's Plan A can be interpreted as an inversion of the ontology accepted in Europe in the time just before Darwin, graphically presented by the pre-Darwinian cosmic pyramid (p. 64):

God
Mind
Design
Or d e r
C h a o s
N o th i ng

The pre-Darwinians interpreted reality as flowing from the top of the pyramid downwards. They put a level of design between the levels of mind and order. Minds create the things that display design, and order is the result of design. Dennett's darwinizing of the pyramid accepts the level of design; he just reverses the direction of explanation. In place of the pre-Darwinian top-to-bottom order of the higher explaining the lower, the post-Darwinian posits a bottom-up direction of explanation. Top-down construction Dennett calls skyhook strategy, by which he wants us to think it's a phony strategy since a hook cannot be suspended from the sky. Bottom-up construction uses conceptual cranes, and is not phony, since we build skyscrapers with cranes. When the level of order is understood to include natural selection from a variety of heritable traits, it has as its outcome the level of design, and when the level of design is understood to include use-functions,^ it has as its outcome the level of mind. The bottom-up strategy is feasible, since there are conceptual analogs of cranes. I use cranes too, but not Dennett's, which fall down.

I'll have nothing to say about the top or the two bottom levels, just the middle three. What status should post-Darwinians accord the level of design? Is it objectively real, or is it in the mind of the beholder merely? Pre-Darwinians opt for the former, and so does Dennett. Dennett thinks the intermediate level of design helps us understand natural selection, how the succession of its products traces a path through what he calls design space, a logical space of possible designs. The design level also represents the functionality, i.e., the usefulness or adaptation to their environments, of the things that natural selection produces. (I'll speak of "use-functions" to distinguish them from the mathematical functions we've spoken of already.) So according to the design level ontology the heart is not just a pump-like thing, it *is* a pump. The ontology backs up the epistemology, namely, the claim that the conceptual framework of design yields scientifically adequate explanations of the phenomena.

Understanding the heart as a pump and consequently its evolution by selection for pumping-ability is a good instance of adaptationist thinking in biology. *Adaptationism* is a strategy for thinking about evolved things as adaptations to their environments, that is, their having evolved by natural selection *for* traits that help, and *against* traits that hinder, survival and reproductive success. Biologists don't insist that the strategy pays off for all the traits of interest, just most of them. One might be an adaptationist and deny that certain common traits (for example, senescence) evolved for adaptive reasons. Other traits evolve as maladaptive side effects of adaptations, as in the case of sickle cell anemia. Still other traits survive long after their contribution to adaptation has disappeared. For example, all vertebrate nervous systems have two pathways, one for the right side of their bodies and one for the left. The paths cross over each other just below the brain, switching sides. It's extremely unlikely that the switch is an adaptation for any extant species to its environment.

Despite these warning-signs, Dennett grounds adaptationism in metaphysics; he accords the design level the status of objective reality and thereby justifies not merely the utility of the adaptationist research methodology for thinking up evolutionary scenarios. It's more than that; its explanations are realistic, for they reveal an objective feature of things: design. Dennett ontologizes the design level, if I understand his writings since 1991, which back away from his earlier instrumentalism.[^13] Perhaps Dennett would only think of the epistemological dimension, the giving of realistic explanations, as divided into levels, while the ontological dimension, the backing for those explanations, is more a continuum of types of being. That's still an objectionable ontology to me. Another proponent, less equivocal in his support of the reality of the design level, is Fred Dretske.

My chief objection to the design level is that it authorizes explanations of a thing's existence and structure by reference to its ends. It's contrary to the naturalistic point of view, however, to countenance such teleology except in the case where the reference to an end can be reduced to an antecedent efficient cause which has that end in view, i.e., a cause which is a contentful state. We've seen the maximum naturalistically allowable expansion of such causes in our analysis of negative feedback systems. Dennett's level of design is not so restricted. It's just old fashioned teleology, no matter whether it derives from levels above it or below. The alternative I wish to develop is that the design level and use-functions, insofar as they're supposed to exist prior to intentionality, are simply pretense and the adaptationist stance is also. What scientists see when they adopt this stance are fictions or else intention-driven systems. The case of fiction does not make the biologists who adopt it any the less productive, although they're mentally prepared better for its frequent misguidance, if they're aware of the fictionality. The value of this alternative of pretense, mere as-if-ness, for philosophy is in the ridding ourselves of use-functions, and *a fortiori* the ridding ourselves of bad explanations of mental representations in terms of them.

Let's rethink the value of adaptationism in terms of the pretense alternative. Concerning intentionality, will adaptationism explain it? It might lead us astray. Recall section R on how connectionist systems can create memories of nonexistent persons. Representing the nonexistent and the false is a distinctive mark of intentionality. I attributed this ability or rather susceptibility to a flaw in the design of the system. In other words, I think the adaptationist strategy might fail to account for some of the distinctive features of mentality. Other features that are probably byproducts of an adaptation, but not themselves adaptations, are the egocentricity of beliefs and now-based perceptions of time, which were the focus of sections M and N. I recommend adaptationism as strongly as Dennett and Dretske do for its ability to help biologists hypothesize ultimate explanations, although I think we must be prepared to attribute some features of mentality to design flaws. Perhaps I could convince Dennett of that, but we differ fundamentally about the metaphysics he imports into adaptationism. I don't accept the metaphysical accretion to it, this pre-intentional level of design, which is Dennett's particular contribution. Virtually everything which natural selection has shaped has design flaws, and that fact shows adaptation is *not real design*. For example, the vertebrate eye, the traditional example of design, is flawed by having a blind spot close to the center of vision. This is no adaptation, but an instance of "the cumulative historical burden" we carry as products of eons of natural selection, as one biologist put it.[14] It's an utterly mindless process and its products always betray the fact by some flaw or other.

From the design level, Dennett builds the intentional level, the mind. His chief crane is the fact of use-functions. He thinks they exist objectively at the design level. Dretske agrees. With use-functions they build representations, which are the core components of the mind level. For representations are supposed to bring with them the distinctive marks of mentality such as semantic meaningfulness. Representations are constituted by use-functions, they say. X represents Y for Z, if and only if Z uses X in a Y-representing way to achieve its goals (roughly, and the definitional circle is mine). That thesis goes beyond conceptual role semantics. Conceptual role semantics is consistent with some representations existing prior to having a role, by virtue of their carrying information into the mind. They take on the role they have in the mind because of their being what I call found representations. To say all representations are representations solely by virtue of their use-functions amounts to denying the existence of found representations. For before these representations are found they represent without being used.

Natural use-functions, if they're to be distinguished from mind-constituted use-functions, involve history in the very concept of them, in particular, a history of being selected for. (The use-functions of artifacts, in contrast, are not conceptually bound to histories.) So Dennett's Plan A posits this order of definition:

> selection history —> use-function —> representation and other essentials of mind.

Given the use-function of a sign, he can say what it's a sign of. And he can say what it's a sign of only if given its use-function. Since representations are at the level of mind and use-functions are at the lower level of design, Dennett's construction of the aboutness of a representation is an example of a crane, building the higher from the lower.

## §5. Criticism of the argument for design coming before mind.

I wish to convince you that Dennett's crane fails and we don't need it anyway. Let's examine one of Dennett's defenses of his position against criticism, and see the defense fail. Dennett sees Putnam's twin-earth experiment (see section S) as a challenge to his account of representations in terms of use-functions. So he reanalyzes it, but in the course of doing so he sets up a dilemma: Either buy into his position or accept a sky-hook explanation. We must follow his analysis to see how there's a third way out:

Twin-earth is enough like earth to fool the ordinary person. Suppose Hume or any earthling of his generation were transported to twin earth while asleep. He wakes up on twin-earth, quite ignorant of the switch in his habitat. On twin-earth there's a stuff with all the common appearances of water, but it is not $H_2O$, but rather another potable, life-sustaining substance, $XYZ$. Hume, upon waking up, calls it "water." He's wrong. All twin-earthers call it "water"; they are right. Hume and they use the same sounds to mean different things. So far Dennett sides with Putnam. Suppose Hume stays there for the rest of his life. Dennett extends the scenario across the long time that Hume stays there. The extended scenario leads to a divergence of intuitions. There are two viewpoints to separate. There's Hume's, who's always oblivious to the switch. Yet he survives. Then there's our omniscient viewpoint, as we observe Hume. According to Dennett, from our point of view, as Hume continues his life none the wiser, the use-function of his word "water" changes from what it was on earth, so that it eventually begins to *mean* $XYZ$ stuff, even though nothing at all relevant to the semantics of "water" changes in Hume himself. According to Dennett that intuition supports his use-function account of the meaning of "water."

Some of Dennett's critics believe in "original intentionality," that is, intentionality not built up from a level below mind. According to their intuitions, if nothing semantical happens in Hume while he accumulates experience on twin-earth—for example, he does not himself decide to change the meaning of the word—then nothing happens at all to change the meaning of his word. He goes to his death on twin-earth misapplying his word "water." For the "original intentionality" folks, his word means the stuff pointed out to him on earth when he learned the word and whatever else shares the same essence as that stuff, unknown though that essence be to Hume. That the word works for Hume on twin-earth is irrelevant to what it means for him. The switch in use-function, as seen from our omniscient point of view, is irrelevant. That crane doesn't work. Hume himself must change the meaning of the word, if it's to change. So say the original intentionality folks.

Believers in original intentionality not only reject the definition of a word's meaning and reference in terms of its use-function, they reject all ontologizing of a pre-intentional design level and its use-functions. The heart is not a pump, says Searle, and, whatever the functions of teddy bears be, real bears don't have functions says Fodor.[15] There's no intention-independent design or use-function. This doctrine of no design independent of mind, if true, deprives Dennett of his chief crane. I'm inclined to think the "no mind, no design" doctrine true.

I'm siding with the underived or "original intentionality" folks in my assessment of the debate over use-functions, but not with their assessment of the outcome of the twin-earth thought experiment. I accept an account of it that allows Dennett the change in meaning of Hume's word "water," but not his explanation of the change by a change in the word's use-function. To set up my alternative account of the change, I quote Gareth Evans's "The Causal Theory of Names"[16]:

> Suppose I get to know a man slightly. Suppose then a suitably primed identical twin takes over his position, and I get to know him fairly well, not noticing the switch. Immediately after the switch my [mental] dossier [on the guy] will still be dominantly of the original man, and I falsely believe, as I would acknowledge if it was pointed out [to me], that *he* is in the room. Then I would pass through a period in which neither was dominant; I had not misidentified one as the other, an asymmetric relation, but rather confused them. Finally the twin could take over the dominant position; I would not have false beliefs about who is in the room, but false beliefs about, e.g., when I first met the man in the room.

To understand this quotation, think of our beliefs as connected both physically and semantically to their subject matter, physically by the subject matter somehow causing the belief to come into existence and semantically by the belief being about the subject matter. On the semantic side, beliefs and other attitudes about people are organized into **mental dossiers** about each of them. All the beliefs in a dossier at a time are at that time about the same person. That person's name is the label on the dossier. On the physical side, occasional confusions cause misfilings, but the dossier is *dominantly* caused by one person, and so *all* the beliefs in the dossier are about whichever individual is the cause of *most* of the beliefs in it. Now consider the dossier as it exists over the course of time: The idea of a single dossier, collecting filings as time goes by, changing from containing beliefs dominantly caused by one guy to containing beliefs dominantly caused by another guy. Consequently, all the beliefs in the dossier change semantically, from being about the first guy to being about the second guy. Yet it remains *the same dossier*, so that the label on the dossier changes its meaning. Well, that's the intuition pump that makes me agree that Hume's meaning changes, as Dennett thinks.

Use-functions have nothing to do with this story, however. To the junk yard with Dennett's two-bitsers in Panama, and all the other paraphernalia he trots out to show that changes in use-functions are at the bottom of this change! Having mental dossiers on people, water, and horses makes sense to me, and they are all we need to accommodate the intuition of meaning change. I reject the intuitions of the original intentionality folks on this thought experiment, and I don't agree with Dennett that it's use-function that matters. It's simply a matter of belief-count, based on the beliefs' causes. When the count of beliefs caused by twin-water in Hume's water dossier exceeds the count of beliefs caused by water, the meaning of Hume's word "water" changes to mean twin-water.

### §6. Plan B for implementing the naturalistic project.

Dennett's offered us the philosophical Darwinian's "Plan A." I suggest we consider a "Plan B" for ultimate naturalization of the mind. The chief feature of **Plan B** is to naturalize the mind by appeal to evolution without ontologizing the design level and without accepting as true the appearances of natural functionality. Objectively, there are no mind-independent designs or use-functions. That admission entails that we cannot use functionality as a crane for introducing representations. It would be circular, deriving mind from the mental.

Who needs a crane for introducing representations? Nobody. Consider the bimetal in a thermostat of a system for regulating temperatures by way of negative feedback loops. Do changes in the shape of the bimetal represent changes in temperature only because of the bimetal's function in the system? Of course not. Changes in the one represent changes in the other regardless of the use-function. In fact the very functionality of negative feedback systems depends on the antecedent existence of representations. The temperature regulator wouldn't work, if a bimetal's states did not already represent temperatures. Now extrapolate to all the naturally occurring systems. According to Plan B, representations are already in the pre-life world waiting to be found and exploited by life to serve the fitnesses of organisms. If bimetals had existed in nature, natural selection would most likely have exploited them eventually for temperature control, as it has exploited magnetite to help some species of migratory birds to navigate the globe. Magnetite free to move around represents north-south directionality, whether or not anyone uses it for a compass. Plan A had the story reversed. The order of explanation is:

representations —> selection for exploiters of representations, in
tandem with the use-functions which they endow things with.

More fundamentally, if there weren't representations of states of the environment and of goals, nothing would be good for anything, and there'd be no use-functions.

Plan B for the ultimate naturalizing of the mind is to see how the mind level can be built up using cranes from the levels of mere life and indeed from the pre-life level, directly and without benefit of a mediating level of design and functionality. One ingredient of Plan B is the fact that life does not have to invent representations. It simply has to find them and exploit them. What life does invent is purposes, which are representations of organisms' goal states. Biological theory posits the value called fitness, in terms of which we appraise organisms' purposes. Biological value, namely fitness, and the purpose to actualize it are there on the ground floor of life, mere life, along with representations. They're what's available for the construction of minds.

Natural selection, according to Plan A, entered into the definition of everything mental, because it entered into the definition of use-function. According to Plan B, natural selection does not enter into the definition of use-function or indeed of anything mental at all, either directly or indirectly. Natural selection only makes minds; what minds *are* is a distinct matter. The adaptationist stance, with its method of reverse engineering, is a frame of mind that helps us understand how natural selection makes minds, but it doesn't reveal a level of reality consisting of pre-mental functions. Instead it reveals that all the ingredients of mentality are there from the start of life. Think of life itself not as pre-mental but proto-mental.

When it comes to explaining how Hume's word "water" changed its meaning gradually as he lived out his life on twin-earth, I incorporate Evans's dossiers into my Plan B. Proper names and names of natural kinds are good candidates to be labels on mental dossiers, since there should be a division of labor between the label and the information. Hume's dossier on water came to be predominantly filled with material based on his acquaintance with water's twin. So that's what the dossier's label came to mean.

You may feel some residual doubts about the viability of Plan B. Let me try to allay them. First, there's something odd in saying there are representations in nature. It amounts to allowing two ways of describing material things. A representation is first just something physical with measurable properties. Secondly, a representation can be described as containing propositional content, namely, the information about something else which it contains. For example, a particular coiling of a bimetal makes it represent *that the temperature of the ambient air is 20 degrees Celsius*. Nevertheless, I see nothing wrong in having this mode of description of material things available, even though science itself makes most headway using the language of measured physical properties.

Furthermore, in the course of evolution, the primate brain latched onto this representational way of describing its own states, and perceiving them by introspection. The primate brain got it right to that extent. Brains exploit representations in nature because organisms are structured to carry the propagation of the information into their interiors so that internal states are representations too. There they get tied into negative feedback mechanisms. Selection hones the interior extension of representational states for fitness, and so for verisimilitude^ and appropriateness.

One might object that the brain has trouble seeing its representational states as being states also describable in materialistic measurable terms. That's because, having found one way of dealing successfully with its own states, there was no evolutionary need to find still another way. The difficulty translates into an argument from ignorance: "I do not know a second way; so there is no second way to be known." That's something the primate brain got wrong.

One thing that gets in the way of thinking of the mind naturalistically is the suspicion that a naturalistic account of misrepresentation is very difficult, if not impossible. A proponent of Plan A might grant me my found representations, but insist there is a gulf between the found representations that carry information naturalistically and the made representations that have semantic meaning. The gulf is so wide that falsehood is impossible on the naturalistic side. Information must be true or else it is not information; who can deny that? Proponents of Plan B are then without the conceptual resources to account for falsity, for the only way to bring it into the picture is to establish a concept of semantic meaning for made representations, and that requires the prior notion of use-functions.

This objection, popularized by Dretske,[17] is widely considered to be fatal to Plan B, but is it not based on a false dichotomy? Consider the connectionist memories in a Hopfield net, as described in Section R. The net connects feature detectors. The exogenous activation of some of them leads to the activation of the whole net, often in such a way that the activated set represents the presence of people truly, but sometimes in a way that represents no actual person. It's a representation nevertheless, fo in either case the result can rise to consciousness as a memory-thought or utterance, just because we cannot exploit the true ones for a certain purpose without risking getting false ones. Granted there's a processing that leads to a continuum of enhanced meaning; nevertheless it seems simply stubbornness always to insist on a later stage of processing as the onset of meaningfulness, and that prior to that stage use-functions have already come into being. The state of the net has a perfectly good meaning in terms of the same feature detectors that are activated in both cases by the components' interactions, independently of the fact that the organism processes the state further and acts successfully in the former case and unsuccessfully in the latter. I hope your intuitions agree with mine that the falsity is there in the representation independently of there being any use of it. If Dretske were to shift his dichotomy so that all examples of this sort are on the side of the gulf without semantic meaning and are only mimicking or presaging genuine false representations and representations of the nonexistent, one would have to wonder if the debate had become merely verbal.

Another thing that gets in the way of thinking of the mind naturalistically is that we tend to see all representation on the model of communication. According to Plan B, however, receivers of information just have to find it in the world, and there do not have to be intentional senders of the information. Plan B has the order right. Getting it comes before dishing it.

Summarizing Plan B:

- There is no ontological level of design. Natural selection shapes only close imitations of design, but always with some screwball defect that reveals the burden of history.
- Intentionality itself shows many instances of these nonadaptive screwball defects. Indeed some of them are the chief identifying characteristics of intentionality, like the ability to name nonexistent objects.
- The chief crane for constructing the mind is the prebiological fact that representations exist in nature. Life simply exploits that fact to produce minds.
- The representations found in nature independently of minds exhibit all the marks of intentionality, so that the traits that distinguish mind from non-mind are less fundamental traits, and mostly matters of degree.
- Consequently mind is not a fundamental ontological category, far less fundamental than life is.
- Use-functions are features of organisms emergent from life's exploitation of the representations it finds in nature. The representations make use-functions possible, not the other way round.

There's one more feature of Plan B, which I'll elaborate on in our last section:

- The techniques of philosophical analysis can reveal the

evolution of intentionality.
If this is so, then, since analysis is inherently a conservative procedure, perhaps ultimate naturalizing fits folk psychology very well.

# Notes

1. J. R. Baker, "The Evolution of Breeding Systems" in *In Evolution: Essays Presented to E. S. Goodrich* (1938) 161-77. Ernst Mayr, "Cause and Effect in Biology," *Science*, 134 (1961) 1501-6.

2. Jerry Fodor, *The Elm and the Expert* (1994) 20. For more in the same vein, see part IV of his *In Critical Condition* (1998).

3. Gilbert Harman argues that intentions-to-act are self-referential in the sense that, for one to intend to act, one must see that one's intention will cause the act intended and one must intend that causation. If that's so, I've not given a complete analysis. See part 1 of his "Desired Desires" in R. G. Free and Christopher W. Morris, eds., *Value, Welfare, and Morality* (1993) 138-157.

4. For a more detailed criticism of this conflation of terminology, see my "Gaia = Maya" *History and Philosophy of the Life Sciences*, 17 (1995) 485- 502.

5. The figure is copied from my two essays, "Gaia = Maya" and "Essay on Nature's Semeiosis." It was adapted from my "Purpose, Feedback, and Evolution" *Philosophy of Science* 48 (1981) 200, where it was adapted from Herbert Simon, "Applications of Servomechanism Theory to Production Control" in his *Models of Man* (1957) 219-240.

6. The mathematical treatment is derived from Jay Forrester, *Principles of Systems* (1968), ch. 2.2 on first-order systems.

7. These pictures come from pp 315ff. of James S. Perlman, *Science Without Limits* (1995).

8. See Paul Churchland, *The Neurocomputational Perspective* (1990) ch. 9, for a description of such a network.

9. The pun on "ant hill" comes from Douglas R. Hofstadter, whose playful "Prelude . . . Ant Fugue" develops the analogy between an ant colony and the brain. Reprinted in Douglas R. Hofstadter and Daniel C. Dennett, eds., *The Mind's I: Fantasies and Reflections on Self and Soul* (1981).

10. See John Searle's article on himself in *Blackwell Companion to the Philosophy of Mind*.

11. Ned Block's criticism in his "Advertisement for a Semantics for Psychology" in French, Uehling, and Wettstein, eds., *Midwest Studies in Philosophy*, vol. 10 (1986) 666. The article is reprinted in Stephen P. Stich and Ted A. Warfield, eds., *Mental Representation: A Reader* (1994).

12. Daniel Dennett, *Darwin's Dangerous Idea: Evolution and the Meanings of Life* (1995).

13. I may be misinterpreting Dennett as being a scientific realist about natural design, and he may only be an instrumentalist.^ His articles in the 1970s were instrumentalist. It seems to me, however, that since the late 1980s he has tried to

find a middle position between realist and instrumentalist theories of theories. See his "Real Patterns," *Journal of Philosophy*, 87 (1991) 27-51. To evaluate the coherence of this attempt would take us into the philosophy of science.

14. George C. Williams, *Plan and Purpose in Nature* (1996) 10. See also chs. 6 and 7. In America the title of this book is *How the Pony Fish Got Its Light*.

15. Dennett quotes Searle in *Darwin's Dangerous Idea*, 399. For Fodor on bears, see p. 87 of his *A Theory of Content and Other Essays* (1990). I argued for the inversion of Plan A's order of explanation, by putting signs before functions, in part II of my "Essay on Semeiosis."

16. Gareth Evans, "The Causal Theory of Names," *Proceedings of the Aristotelian Society*, supplementary volume 47 (1973) 187-208. Reprinted in A. W. Moore, ed., *Meaning and Reference* (1993). The quotation is on p. 220 of this reprint.

17. Fred I. Dretske, *Naturalizing the Mind* (1995), ch. 1. Also see his "Misrepresentation" (1986), reprinted in Stephen P. Stich and Ted A. Warfield, eds., *Mental Representation: A Reader* (1994).

# Z. Philosophical Method and Evolution.

Let's reflect on the nature of philosophical method and on the nature of philosophy. I believe it will help us understand not only what we've been up to during the previous twenty five sections and what the naturalization project is for, but also more generally how philosophy might best proceed.

## §1. Three conceptions of analytic method in philosophy.

Philosophy does not differ from empirical science in what it targets for investigation. Both target the world and ourselves in the world. They also don't differ in the kind of truth they uncover about the common target, or in the logical status of the premises their arguments appeal to, or in the source of their knowledge. Like the formal and empirical sciences, it's philosophy's goal too to amplify what we know, not just to clarify it and add attitude. To that end, there's a disciplined use of analogy for advancing knowledge toward the literal truth. We see the discipline in the history of accepted scientific hypotheses, as they move from being metaphor to being the literal truth, e.g., the hypotheses that light is a wave and that nature selects variants among organisms for reproduction, just as pigeon fanciers select breeding stock. Another example would be model-theoretic investigations in science, models being a kind of analogy. Extrapolation from familiar cases is another. Philosophy uses analogy, extrapolation, and modeling in this way too, as tools for amplifying what we know.

So philosophy does not differ from science in what it targets for investigation, nor does it differ in method. Some think that a philosophical method should be a method whose use distinguishes philosophy from other disciplines. It should divide knowledge into what belongs to philosophy and what belongs to the others. Well, this prescription is not one of the Ten Commandments, and it's reasonable to ignore it because it's a recipe for intellectual sterility. Philosophy and the other sciences are rather locked into a fruitful mutualism every bit as close as that between fig trees and fig wasps.

The methods of each discipline are open to use by the others. In particular, philosophy is not precluded from using the sciences' methods. Formal scientists, such as mathematicians, practice the methods of rationalism. In a way so do philosophers: We analyze and analogize in hopes of bringing precision and order to our thinking about the questions that a worldview must answer, and in hopes of bringing us a step closer to an adequate worldview. Perhaps philosophy will clarify the thinking enough to make the questions tractable to rationalist or empirical methods. Then, lo and behold, a formal or empirical question is also a philosophical question. Failing that, philosophical clarifications should be consistent with the results of formal and empirical science, so that a coherent worldview emerges.

Although philosophers use the techniques of the formal and empirical sciences when it serves their purposes to do so, one technique that philosophers tend to use more than scientists is the *semantic ascent* from talking of things to analyzing the talk itself. For example, some philosophers prefer to talk of the indexical formatting of some beliefs rather than of ego and subjectivity. We analytic philosophers do this, not to carve out a uniquely philosophical discipline, but just because the ascent sometimes sheds the sort of light we want to shed on the things talked of. At least that's all it's reasonable to claim for semantic ascent. A philosopher should never hesitate to talk of things directly, nor should a scientist hesitate to talk of the talk about things, if either's purposes were served. Nor would they be trading professions if they did so.

I say all this by way of a corrective and preemptive strike against overinterpretation of what I am about to say, since I'll focus on linguistic analysis, semantic ascent by another name.

The next advance in the philosophical practice of semantic ascent is for it to incorporate techniques for reconstructing our ancestral patterns of thought and speech, techniques similar to those used by paleontology and evolutionary systematics in reconstructing the past of organisms. I could argue that the mutualist interdependence of philosophy and the sciences calls for this development. Instead I'll make the case by showing this advance to be in line with earlier significant advances in the techniques of semantic ascent. In other words the next advance is called for by the autonomous growth patterns of one method favored by philosophers.

When semantic ascent is appropriate, there are several quite different techniques of analysis for use by the so-called **analytic philosophers**. Two distinctions, a trichotomy and a dichotomy, which cross-cut each other, yield six kinds.[1] Russell made the first distinction in his essay "On Denoting": Some analysts leave the syntactic structures of the sentences they analyze as they find them and posit entities, either senses or mere *possibilia,*^ for those structures to denote. Let's call them the ontologizers. Frege was one, because his analyses posited concepts and thoughts that existed independently of anyone thinking them. Russell recommended an alternative to ontologizing, namely being skeptical of the apparent syntax and allowing adjustments to it to avoid the need to denote odd entities. Let's call these analysts the grammatical reorganizers. The reorganizers were not opposed to the project of ontology, but they were minimalist ontologizers. The later Wittgenstein saw that the first dichotomy, between the ontologizers and grammatical reorganizers, was not exhaustive of all the alternatives, that an analyst could be neither an ontologizer nor a grammatical reorganizer, by looking instead to a sentence's social contexts, its use, for clarification of the sentence to be analyzed. He proposed an exhibition-analysis, in contrast with all the kinds of replacement-analysis.[2] To analyze a locution is to place it in contexts that suffice to exhibit the rules of its proper use. We can call analysts of this sort the social contextualizers. By acknowledging the relevance of contexts of usage to meaning, they can split the issue dividing the ontologizers and grammatical reorganizers. Concerning syntax, they side with the ontologizers against the utility of regimentation of the ways of speaking into a canonical notation. Concerning semantics, they side with the reorganizers against drawing lessons in ontology from grammatical forms. They thus avoid extravagances of both the syntactic and semantic varieties. For the contextualizers a deeper understanding depends on relating the contexts of use of problematic sentences to primitive contexts by a series of intermediate cases.[3] Thus these analysts preserve the ideal of understanding complexity by means of simples, which is the point of analysis, although they differ from other analysts about which simples yield that deeper understanding, and how they yield it.

Quine derives another distinction from Bentham's and Russell's ideas about definition: First, there are analysts who take the meanings of words as primitive, and construct the meanings of sentences from them, parasitically on a syntactic principle of compositionality. Let's call these the meaning-atomists, words being their atoms of meaningfulness. Quine recommends the alternative assumption, that sentences, or indeed groups of sentences, whole theories, are the units of meaning. The sentences' meanings have recursive definitions, the clauses of which bring in the whole sentence's components.[4] Let's call these analysts the meaning-holists, because they adapt Tarski's definition of truth so that it becomes a definition of sentence meaning, making the meaning of sentences to be their truth-conditions. For example, I know the meaning of another's declarative sentences if I can state their truth conditions in my language. Crossing the threefold distinction with the Quinean distinction, we have six ways of being an analytic philosopher, ignoring for now the last row:

| Ways of being an analytic philosopher, with exemplars | Atomist on compositionality; word is unit of meaning | Holist on compositionality; sentence is unit of meaning |
|---|---|---|
| Ontologizer | | Frege[5] |
| Grammatical Reorganizer | Russell often, after 1920[6] | Quine; earlier Wittgenstein |
| Social Contextualizer | | later Wittgenstein |
| Evolutionary Contextualizer | | us? |

Table Z-1. Ways of being an analytic philosopher.

Meaning holism is characteristic of the best current analytic methodology. Since Frege enunciated the context principle, namely, the principle that only in the context of a sentence does any word have meaning, there's been some backsliding to the reverse dependency. Notably Russell backtracked about the meanings of object-words. He says, "Object-words have a meaning which does not depend on their occurring in sentences," and "if sentences contain object-words, what they assert depends upon the meaning of the object-words."[7] He goes on to say, "At the lowest level of speech, the distinction between sentences and single words does not exist." What he supposes do exist are acts of naming of objects, a thesis Wittgenstein criticized.[8] But the context principle does not admit that object-words are exceptions, and a Tarski-style definition of sentence-meaning assigns a clause to each object-word no differently from the way it treats other words. As Quine says, "knowing words is knowing how to work out the meanings of sentences containing them."[9]

The key to an unproblematic adherence to the context principle in explanations of language learning, making sense of its application even to object-words, is the concept of a holophrastic sentence, which is a sentence not differentiated into a subject part and a predicate part, but also is not elliptical either syntactically or semantically. Examples are Quine's "Gavagai!" and Wittgenstein's "Slab!" These are not mere acts of naming, but useful sentences. Infants begin with them, not with nouns and verbs. They are the original sentences phylogenetically too. Many philosophers side with Russell, who did contrast one-word sentences with one-word ellipses, but the sentences consisting of one word are "used explosively," suggesting an unstated mental complex.[10] Russell did not have the concept of a self-sufficient holophrastic unit of sentence meaning, nor do those philosophers who take his line.

The context principle builds on an asymmetry between words and sentences, such that the sentences are the indispensable contexts in which the words have meaning. We must respect the asymmetry between the way words function in sentences, and the way sentences function in more complex sentences.[11] Sentences (and predicates) are the terms in the implication relation that logic studies, and sentences are the units with which we perform speech acts. So any sentence must have a meaning independently of its contribution to the meaning of more complex sentences in a way to which there's no parallel for words.

How are we to understand Quine's more radical holism, namely, that sentences themselves have meaning only in the context of theories? The single recursive definition that yields a truth value for each and every sentence defines a unitary language. Each sentence is in a language along with other sentences just because the definition which defines its meaning also defines theirs. Enough of them, in enough syntactic variety, can constitute an implicational structure that yields testable predictions. Quine says they then have the "critical semantic mass" for each of the sentences in the structure to be meaningful. Despite the extended holism, there's still an asymmetry between words and sentences.

In view of the validity of meaning holism, we may ignore the column for meaning atomism on the table.

## §2. A fourth method of analytic philosophy: evolutionary analysis.

I hope by now, dear reader, that you're poised at the edge of your seat in anticipation of the world-historical inevitability of a fourth row on our table. I shall not disappoint you. Still another way of being a holist analyst generalizes Wittgenstein's way so that it covers contexts more inclusive than a speech context. According to this broader analytic method of semantic ascent, sequences of episodes selected from long stretches of time provide the key to a holism complete enough for the extraction of all the information that's contained in our ways of speaking. Call it evolutionary analysis.[12] The evolutionary analyst criticizes the contextual analyst for attending to microcontexts to the exclusion of the macrocontext. One kind of macrocontext for a phenomenon would be an antecedent sequence of episodes of adaptation that brought the phenomenon into existence. Philosophers already use the technique, although not self-consciously. Two instances stand out: I already hinted at one sequence of contexts that begins phylogenetically with holophrastic sentences.[13] I developed this in sections T and U. Another hint in current philosophical discussion is the claim by Lewis, Chisholm, and others that all our propositional attitudes are variants of what Quine called egocentric attitudes.[14] Is it not plausible that this feature of our mental structure is a survival of a more primitive structure? Indeed, is not the dominance component of *de re* attitudes just such a survival?

I take myself to have given an argument, not just a rhetorical conceit, for the autonomous dynamics of the advance into an evolutionary contextualizing. To make the argument, I must defend the idea that Wittgenstein made a real advance in analysis, and did not reject analysis, when he extended the notion of a simple element from being an atomic component of the analysandum to being one end point in the series of intermediate cases connecting to the analysandum as the other end point. If you accept this extension, then evolutionary analysis simply temporalizes and stretches this series. Simples are simple beginnings.

The price of not taking this step is ignorance and error. The ignorance comes from overlooking philosophical information that a larger view of our speech practices can reveal. It's like the ignorance of all those on the east and west coasts who live near highly polished rock outcroppings. They never wonder why the polish, and never realize it tells a story of glaciers having passed over the rock thousands of years ago. As for the error, by ignoring evolutionary analysis the social contextualist defaults to unwarranted and misleading perfectionist assumptions about mind and language, and to dichotomies, dualisms, and essentialisms to describe what are just superficial differences and gradations among evolved things. However, I don't recommend the opposite error of claiming evolutionary analysis is sufficient as an all-purpose tool. For the other ways of performing semantic ascent have proved useful and continue to have a place in the philosopher's toolbox. We should contract their current range of application, however, to make room for evolutionary contextualism.

Before saying what evolutionary analysis is, I should say what it's not, since the scientific theory of evolution is so misunderstood. The evolution-ary analyst does not mean that philosophy's subject matter concerns evolution especially, but rather that philosophy's analytic methods of semantic ascent must be strengthened in the light of the evolutionary perspective, so that it can extract the information usually overlooked about evolved things. Whereas many philosophers over the last hundred years recommended a substantive Darwinism, the analyst recommends some-thing novel, a methodological Darwinism.

The evolutionary analyst does not mean what James Baldwin and John Dewey meant when they too called for philosophy to adopt an evolution-ary analysis. Evolutionary theory consists of two parts, the history of life and the mechanisms for producing that history, especially the mechanism of natural selection. Baldwin's and Dewey's inspiration was the mecha-nism. Baldwin noted that natural selection could be generalized to be a method for creating and criticizing ideas.[15] For ideas have four of the traits needed for natural selection to work:

- They're replicatable in the environment provided by brains in communication with each other;
- they're susceptible to variation in content, ease of replication, and resistance to corruption in transmission;
- the brain environment provides a limited number of niches, creating competition between the variant ideas to occupy them; and
- ideas are robust enough and rich enough in variation to compete enough times to reach conditions of adaptation.

Nevertheless, although Baldwin's proposal has won adherents, for instance Popper and Rescher, I'm struck more by the disanalogy between Baldwin's method and the real evolutionary process. There's a fifth trait of natural selection:

- Natural selection does not guide the making of the variation it selects from, nor does adaptation guide the natural selection that culminates in the adaptation; instead the first four traits connect up with each other in an unteleological process.

But Baldwin's step of varying the ideas takes place inside a teleological system, namely, inside a human being. The variation that results is not independent of a human being's purposed outcome. We deduce this from the fact that people do think up useful variants at better than chance. The natural evolutionary process, by contrast, is without foresight, and so cannot tip toward creating variants whose selection is more probable. For instance, some deleterious mutations have known rates of recurring; the fact that they're selected against does not affect the rate. But if a person kept on generating an idea that did not suit his purpose, he'd be considered dim-witted.[16] Also our selection procedures are guided by a rational goal; a scientist's is information; an entertainer's is striking an emotional chord; an advertiser's is memorability. Nature's selections are not goal-guided. Organisms are the products of evolution, and the products of evolution are teleological systems, but the evolutionary process is not.[17] How the products operate is fundamentally different from how the process operates. Much faulty theorizing arises from a failure to appreciate this disanalogy, so much of it in fact that I distance myself even from Baldwin's sensible proposal. I propose an evolutionary method of philosophical analysis that fits all five of the traits of evolution by natural selection as it occurs in nature, not just the first four. The method extends the first of the two features of the theory of evolution mentioned earlier, not the five-faceted mechanism but the history. We should generalize the historical part of evolutionary theory, its systematics and paleontology in other words, to our practice of semantic ascent.

A paleontologist sees the past enfolded into the present and explaining the present. More needs to be said, however, because there are ways of looking at the enfoldment that get the relationships all wrong. Absolutely antithetical to my evolutionary analysis is Husserl's intellectual "archeology." The *archae*, i.e., the origins, that evolutionary analysis uncovers are not the most purified and trustworthy, the most revelatory of truth, or superlatively anything except the oldest. Thus the goals of an evolutionary method are not those of, say, the philologist who compares the different manuscripts of an ancient text in order to construct a tree diagram of the succession of copies, in the hopes of revealing the lost original's wording. No.

We're used to thinking that traces of the past are erased as time passes because a tendency to disorder rules our universe. Thus, when we do detect the past, we tend to think, "here's pristine order not yet erased by the processes of degradation." This conception supports the philological view of a historical method. In contrast, Darwinism sees the introduction of designedness to be the culprit in erasing traces of history. Natural selection's not a process of degradation; it's the opposite. It's constantly reworking organisms to fit their changing environments, and in the process it must erase the traces of past environments left in organismic designs. Although selection tends to erase the traces of history, it's too weak to do a complete erasure. The trait which it does not erase has no claim to pristine designedness, like the autograph copy of an ancient author; rather it's simply what's not gotten in the way of fitness yet, or what's in the way and can't be undone, but can be worked around. In short, the suboptimalities, which show that natural selection is not foresightful or omnipotent, are the unerased traces of history. To find the history of a design, look for the flaws in the design. For example, the history of mentality is revealed by the defects and idiosyncracies of mentality, beginning with its oldest elements, insofar as their defects were incorrectable by subsequent selection. A mindless process produced our minds; let's not kid ourselves about their having any nonnaturalistic insight into *archae* such as Husserl attributed to them. And, if an analyst is to extract from linguistic practices some information that will help him understand mentality, he must be prepared to notice suboptimality in our speech practices; he cannot find it antecedently "clear that every sentence in our language 'is in order as it is',"[18] if that's to gratuitously assume the omnipotence and timeliness of natural selection. Now let me add some to my earlier characterization of a macrocontext as a sequence of episodes of adaptation: The philosopher of mind and language will look at how some features of the past don't get wiped out by the adaptations, but are carried into the present as vestigial or marginalized, perhaps as unremedied primitivity or even flaw.

Evolutionary analysis is analysis. An evolutionary analyst analyzes complexes into their simpler parts, but with an evolutionary twist, since the simple is seen as related temporally to the complex in an idealized time. Although some simples terminate a process of simplification, other simples began a process of complexification. These latter simples are not just parts of complexes but hypothetical forerunners as well. It's reasonable to practice a form of analysis on complex phenomena that reveals their aboriginal features. One would proceed much like the way a biologist, when classifying an organism within its family, order, class, and phylum, comes to discern in it some features of its ancestral species. For these higher taxonomic categories that affiliate today's species are the remnants of bygone species that evolved into today's.[19] Darwin said, "All true classification is genealogy."[20] So the taxonomist's synchronic tree diagram of today's species falls from its upright position down along the time line and becomes diachronic. With the tree trunk to the past, it becomes a tale of evolution. As time advanced, the tree grew branches; a few continued to grow and branched again, down to the present. Omitted from the tree are the many branches that left no descendants today, yielding the well-pruned look of taxonomic trees. See Figure Z-1.

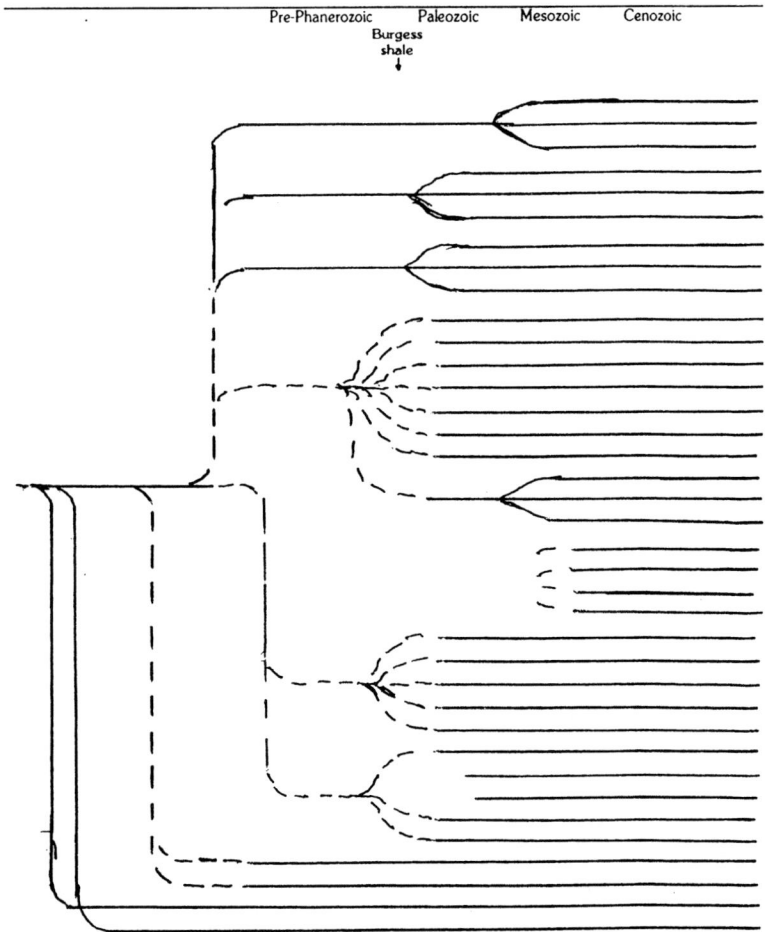

Figure Z-1. From Lynn Margulis and Karlene V. Schwartz, *Five Kingdoms*, 3rd ed. (W. H. Freeman, 1998), 204. The tree for Animals, reproduced lying on its side; so the future's to the right. The paleozoic, mesozoic, and cenozoic eras began 590, 248, and 66 million years ago respectively.

The study of ontogeny also reveals some aspects of the forms of ancestral species. Why else would we find gill slits and tails on human fetuses? Similarly for a philosopher, to analyze present complexities of our thought interestingly is to find the equivalent of gill slits and tails in our thought processes. When the analysis leads to something like a tree diagram, one finds oneself peering into the long past of mentality evolving. Recall that the tree diagrams of sentences, prescribed by grammars, do seem to describe how thought gets transcribed into speech; we should look to see if any phylogeny of acts of meaning is recapitulated in this brain-work. There are three continuities of relevance: the phylogeny of minds from non-minds, the ontogeny of a mind from its non-mental zygote, and the brain-work from the sensory inputs to a thought. They're revelatory of each other.

All the basic cleavages between the human mind and the rest of nature, all the temptations to dualisms of mind and matter, of prescription and description, of causal connection and implicative connection, can be set in an evolutionary macrocontext with antecedent case upon more antecedent case making today's dichotomies less and less contrastive. The connecting back to a more unified situation through a series of intermediate contrasts reveals the superficiality of the dualisms masking the underlying continuity. Although Wittgenstein's analysis showed us the way, in retrospect it was simplistic; his sequencing of cases was linear, connecting two end points. By contrast, evolutionary analysis is tree-like, connecting multiple branch-ends back to a single trunk-end.

An aboriginal feature of a phenomenon would be a basic one, capable of separation from the rest of the features and standing alone, while the rest depended on it. It's the root ancestral form out of which all the rest grew, the initial scenario of a macrocontext. The evolutionary analyst's practicing this paleontology-like analysis leads him to turn things around, arranging them oppositely from the way custom would have them, to find these stand-alone phenomena. Often finding a sequence that works requires shattering preconceptions. For example, when shells were found on mountain tops, the inference is clear that the tops were once submerged. How so? The easier answer is that water once covered them and has since subsided. This answer leaves us with a residual problem of the missing water. The true answer's the reverse: The mountains rose out of the waters. When we can't progress by thinking of things in a certain order, try the reverse order. The evolutionary analyst avoids the sterile version of this procedure, which is to reason from A to B whenever everyone else reasons from not-B to not-A. Rather than that, the evolutionary analyst reasons from A to B when others reason from B to A, and in order to succeed in that reordering the evolutionary analyst must be conceptually innovative. Often the analyst's reversals break the hold of analogies we find compelling. Perceiving's not so like imaging; thinking's not so like saying. Imaging and saying are rather more complex than perceiving and thinking. Dear reader, you probably found the topsy-turvy thinking took some getting used to! You may be familiar with famous instances of topsy-turvy thinking, say Kant's Copernican-style revolution in the theory of *a priori*^ knowledge or the Whorf-Sapir hypothesis that our public communication language's categories fix the limits of what we can think (which I grant is false). Other examples are Nietzsche's claim that happiness causes virtuousness, not the other way round, and Sartre's dictum that existence precedes essence. A better example for my point is Russell's argument that relations must be more fundamental than properties despite their seeming more complex, since properties can be contextually defined in terms of relations, but not the other way around. Definitional order suggests temporal order in that the ancestral type often supplies the genus which the descendent types are species of. Familiarity with enough such examples lets you know that one consequence of the evolutionary form of analysis is not so new after all. Even so, the approach still takes some getting used to, for it's counter-intuitive at every turn.

For example, phenomena that we tend to dismiss as too simple to manifest a mind are sometimes survivals that give us a rare glimpse at the elements of our mental structure. Thus the evolutionary analyst shines the spotlight on seemingly peripheral features such as one-word sentences and indexical terms.[21] Until you see their significance as ur-elemental survivals, it will be hard to work up any interest in them.

Again, belief in some truths must precede any beliefs in falsehoods. How can the original knowers have been so accurate? Furthermore selection is a pressure of variable strength. One does not explain its degrees of strength against falsehoods simply by describing its target in terms of the dichotomy between true and false. So one is led to suspect that falsehood's not the real target of selection against. Verisimilitude^ is the key to solving both of these paradoxes and showing evolution's relevance to the theory of knowledge. Think of organisms as collecting information in the form of propositions. A proposition's verisimilitude is its closeness to the whole truth.[22] If, for example, the truth is $p\&q$, then the two propositions, *p, but not-q*, and *neither p nor q*, are each entirely false, so equally false. Nevertheless, the former is closer to the truth than the latter. False propositions vary in verisimilitude. Verisimilitudes that are distant from the truth can only be selected against in environments where they compete with verisimilitudes closer to the truth. So there was pressure on organisms to get falsehoods that were closer to the truth. (We're not yet all the way there.) As for the truth, it can be as uninformative as a tautology. Among truths, the less informative will be selected against. Indeed verisimilar falsehood will be selected over uninformative truth.

A similar story can be told about the evolution of norms of rational thought and meaningful language. We start with the norm of each living thing, namely its fitness, as evolutionary theory posits. (I defend this claim of normativity later.) To this theory we add the comparative relations of one's thoughts being more rational than another's and one's words being more meaningful than another's. Then, as the competition for fitness plays itself out between the one and the other, the minimum rationality needed by an organism to be a contender rachets up and up and up. (And again, we are not yet all the way up.) Not only do minimum standards rachet up, but they ramify into structures of intermediate and ultimate norms which are the means and ends of one's way of life. The tentative and testable relations within our hierarchies of means and ends generate the ability to distinguish better from worse alternative norms and to edit the worse ones out of the hierarchies. Meaningfulness is also a matter of slow accretion of complexity from simple beginnings.[23] In developing these scenarios, one must recognize that the human form of life is the result of a coevolution of culture and mind over a million or more years. Evolutionary analysts will have to rely on human paleontologists, historical linguistics, ethology, and evolutionary psychology to flesh out the macrocontexts.

The mind's an evolved thing; so its existence and its nature must be explainable in evolutionary terms.[24] Needless to say, given what's been said, not all of the explanation need be in terms of adaptation. Some of the nonadaptive elements of the explanation can be discovered and supported by evolutionary analysis in semantic ascent. A picture emerges of what a mind must be, if it's to be the product of a process of natural selection. It understands by analogizing or modeling, and its models are more or less verisimilitudinous. Why is the mind this semanticizing sort of thing, rather than a program-driven symbol-manipulator? I speculate that a semanticizing thing, by virtue of its being just this sort of thing, breaks down bit by bit rather than catastrophically, and is tweakable, just the sort of thing that wins adaptive contests and can make the climb to optimal design. (But it's not there yet.)

Although the evolutionary paradigm for thinking is now more than a century old, philosophers still resist it. Why? For many, evolution belongs in biology, not in philosophy. It has little to do with philosophy's subject matter and even less to do with its methodology. The proposal of an evolutionary mode of analysis leaves them cold. All that a philosopher needs from analysis can be found without reference to evolutionary biology, or so they think. Moreover, importing evolution into analysis is likely to bring its own unwarranted assumptions, like reductionism and extensionalism and the naturalistic fallacy, distorting the uniquely human features of our form of life, or so they think. We reply first on the offensive: You cannot get the full explanation of the nature of evolved things except by this method.

### §3. Replies to some criticisms of evolutionary method.

On the defensive, note first that the objections are more to substantive Darwinism than to methodological Darwinism. I could then ignore them. Nevertheless I'll address the problem of the naturalistic fallacy, which is difficult for the substantive evolutionist in one respect, easy in another. It's easy because evolutionary theory splits into a theory of the evolutionary process and a theory of the products of the process, namely, the organisms. Although the theory of the process posits only an "as-if-it-were" a value, namely, directional selection optimizing fitness, the evolutionary theory *of organisms* posits value, namely, fitness. Here's another example of a scientific theory's literalization of what began as only an analogy. Organisms purpose their fitness, mostly unconsciously and with variable success. The theory does not say their ultimate values are chimaeric, but quite the opposite, since it does declare some subgoals of some species to be chimaeric (like the male Irish elk's goal of pursuing fitness by engaging in antler butting) relative to the ultimate value of fitness. Theory's not confined to prediction and explanation; it can appraise as well. The idea that scientific theory cannot posit value as one of its theoretical terms is simply false. Theory can do whatever we design it to do. Three hundred years ago the intellectual world was united in denying that energy could be a term in physical theory. How wrong they were! Today the intellectual world seems united in denying that value can be a term in an empirical theory of material things. How gratuitously dogmatic and self-shackling they are! Mackie expresses the naked prejudice when he remarks that value just is too queer to be in the world described by scientific theory or, if it were in the world, it would be too queer for us to become aware of it.[25] Berkeley thought something similar of energy, with an equally flagrant lack of cogency.

The issue over which the naturalistic fallacy poses difficulty is that *ethical* value seems unrelated, even in conflict with, the value posited for human beings by the evolutionary theory of organisms, namely, individual inclusive fitness. When ethics conflicts with other values it claims to trump them as value and unmask them, as mere semblance of values, by means of a question, for example, "Is individual fitness for a human being really good?" This is the format of an open question, open for challenging all claims of connectivity except the analytically^ necessary connections between concepts. Thus connections posited by theory will be susceptible to question in this way. I shall say no more except to deny that the method I advocate stacks the deck in favor of something called evolutionary ethics or worse, social Darwinism. I reject both; I repudiate individual inclusive fitness as an unconditioned value for human beings.[26] But I also reject the subsumption of all value, even all human value, under ethical value. I'm Nietzschean enough to dismiss any claim that a genuine value for human beings is not to be recognized by us by its power to motivate and sustain the roots of human motivation. Such a dissociation is total sham and deserving of our utmost scorn and ridicule.

The discussion of value has been a digression, since it does not pertain to methodological Darwinism. We must now address the criticisms, insofar as they are directed against methodological Darwinism. Does an evolutionary analysis entail reductionism and extensionalism in its analyses? Perfectionists and dualists will define reductionism as the denial of their prejudices. Ok, then evolutionary analysis is geared to prove reductionism. Even so, the reduction need not be located in the wrong place, too near the present in the macrocontext, so to speak, so as to dehumanize human phenomena. That would be objectionable in the sense of not being true to the data.

Other critics may argue that philosophy aims for theory, and a methodology centered on reconstructing history simply misses the goal of philosophy. We reply: Yes, philosophy aims for a comprehensive scheme of self-in-world that includes theory. Some theories are necessarily supported by evidence for a history. Philosophical theories of selfhood and information-exploitation are prime instances of that. But more, the contrast between theory and historical method is phony in this case of evolutionary semantic ascent, because the very method of extracting history from current evidence depends on the theory of natural selection. Without the theory of natural selection to correct us, we'd read the evidence of history as the philologist does and get it all backwards! The theory and the method are intertwined.

Still other critics will look at their agenda of unsolved philosophical problems and declare the method of evolutionary analysis to be irrelevant to solving them. Or they'll ask that solutions to their problems be produced as a precondition for their accepting the method. First in reply, we must concede that much on the philosophical agenda is better dealt with by more direct theorizing or by use of the other methods of semantic ascent. That conceded, consider just the agenda on evolved things. To what extent has the agenda been set by impasses engendered by the perfectionist and dichotomous thinking of the pre-Darwinian era? Part of the problem to be solved is the very agenda. Secondly, if a method did not have the effect of changing the agenda considerably by deletion and addition, it would not be much to shout about. Thirdly, what would you think of someone who heralded a new method and then added, "Oh by the way, I've milked the method dry; there's nothing left for you to do by means of it"? No, dear reader, this is unexplored territory and you're to be the explorer. If you want some results, I mentioned Quine's development of a pre-ontological stage of semeiosis with holophrastic observation sentences. I think there's another take on this stage as a form of solipsism-by-default, from which the Cartesian project of explaining the origin of our nonsolipsistic realism reappears in an evolutionary guise. With the emergence of realist ontology in the vertebrate line, we have intentionality. I've suggested that a design flaw is at the core of intentionality, giving rise to "the marks of the mental."[27] I mentioned earlier that Chisholm and Lewis argued that all our propositional attitudes are grafted into a fundamentally egocentric attitude, and I think it plausibly is a survival of our ancestral mental structure. We must also explain the origin of the fact that our mental life has both an inner psychological side and an outer social side, quite unlike, say, the bee whose "thinking" is contained entirely in its social behavior. Even more primitively, I proposed a precognitive, kinetic theory of reference to the self and the present time that can be attributed to all organisms.

Let's laugh off such caricatures of the method as the unsympathetic Frege's. He has us suppose an evolution of mathematical truth, for example, of $2+2=4$ from a previous truth, $2+2=5$, and prognosticate its evolution into the future truth, $2+2=3$.[28] Obviously, analysis of the macro-contexts of mathematical assertions is no substitute for proofs. On the rare occasions when mathematicians do resort to semantic ascent as in Cantor's diagonal argument and Gödel numbering, the ascent serves proofs, and it cannot serve proofs better by being given an evolutionary twist. The evolutionary method of analysis is applied mostly to the indexical features of information and anything else that promises to be aboriginal in an evolved thing; it does not apply to everything whatsoever of philosophical interest. It's not the abrogation of any eternal truth embodied in science's theories, or in its atlas and chronicle of the universe. Nevertheless, despite the character of these remarks as things "needless to say," it's incumbent on practitioners not to give credibility to the method's critics. We protect ourselves by respecting the method's limited range of application to just evolved things and by developing standards for evaluating the applications. Some may feel that reconstructions of the past are speculative to the extent of not being serious science. Yes, they can be that, but need not be that. Of this pudding, the only proof will be in the eating.

## §4. Evolutionary philosophy and one's worldview.

I've ignored the Kantian transcendental project for philosophy, perhaps the most important competitor of the naturalization project. The Kantian project is to determine *a priori* the indispensable conditions for the possibility of an experience of objects, of truth and more ambitiously, of meaningfulness. It's a project which contemporary analytic methods are well suited to be used to pursue, as R. C. Pradhan showed.[29] But it's not a project that's easily pursued conjointly with the naturalization project, because it lifts the mind, the object of our studies, out of the sphere of empirical knowledge, where the naturalization project would put it. I'm not inclined to follow Kant into the transcendental. His project presupposes several dichotomies which I think have no philosophical significance, such as the analytic-synthetic^ and the *a priori-a posteriori*^ distinctions and the transcendental distinction of form and content. It also presupposes there's a valid form of argumentation, called transcendental deduction, for establishing the indispensable conditions for the possibility of something. I accept the conclusion of the Kant scholar, Stephan Körner, that the argument form is really not valid.[30] Without the dichotomies and the argument for establishing its conclusions, the Kantian project is bankrupt. Needless to say, this assessment is controversial.

Let's now turn to the question, which any Kantian must want to ask, what philosophical purpose does an evolutionary extension of analytic method serve? Before answering, let's put aside one apparent presupposition of the question, namely, a sharp division between content and method. Contrary to what Kant supposed, one's methods of thought are not prior to worldviews and neutral between them. Ultimately, just as the substance of one's science flows into one's worldview, so one's methodology flows out of it. Evolution's at the heart of my worldview as it is of my method.

Having admitted the interpenetration of content and method, what's my purpose in adopting the method? I want a coherent worldview, and that's why I'm not content to stay within the classical analytic methods of folk psychology. To achieve a coherent worldview one must pursue the naturalization project from within folk psychology using a method that can succeed.

There's a division of labor between philosophers and empirical scientists. Philosophers keep alive the questions that remain intractable to empirical methods, but whose answers are fundamental to our worldview. When empirical methods do answer fundamental questions, philosophers are left the job of integrating the various scientific answers into a unified vision of the world. The integration of the sciences raises foundational issues, which are reputed to be "philosophical issues," but they're obviously as much a part of science as of philosophy. Philosophy can stake out an intellectual territory exclusively its own, however: Connecting up the results of the various sciences is a philosopher's job, insofar as connecting them helps philosophy extract their implications for our worldview, to criticize our current one and formulate a better one. In the twentieth century philosophers debated whether their field creates theories or engages in intellectual therapy. The debate was groundless; in elaborating a worldview to replace outmoded ones, philosophy does both and more.

Insofar as scientists and philosophers agree to a division of labor, the philosophers explore the egocentric frame of reference: We human beings are selves cast into a world; we're points of subjectivity with interests, but cast into an unconcerned objectivity. Philosophers must use indexical formulations of their claims about ourselves, that is, formulations in terms of "we" and "now." These words finger some feature of the circumstance in which they're uttered. Philosophers must use them, whereas physical scientists formulate indexically only their evidence and predictions, not their theories, atlases, and chronicles of the world. The scientists' theories state how some quantities are functions of other quantities; their atlases aim for the ideal that no place be labeled *terra incognita*; and their chronicles aim to state the events over all time, even the future. A **worldview**, on the other hand, is necessarily indexical, for it's our perspective on the world. It is:

- a sense of our scale and place here in the universe,
- a sense of our stage now in the history of things, and
- our sense of the worth of things.[31]

It adds, if you will, the richness of appearance to mere reality. It adds the slant of perspective to the boxy blueprint of the world.

For example, the time between one's birth and death is different from other times; it is one's own time, from which one views all the past and the future. Science's official chronicle of the universe takes no notice of this perspectival difference. Bertrand Russell was playing physicist to the exclusion of philosopher when he said, "The occurrence of tense in verbs is an exceedingly annoying vulgarity due to our preoccupation with practical affairs."[32] The vulgarity was the perspectival time that tense expresses, namely, the past, present, and future. Is the futurity of one's death just an exceedingly annoying vulgarity? Although it would be nice to think so, a philosopher does not so underplay the importance of indexicality as it applies to time. Our worldview must take it into account.

It may seem that the contrast of science to worldview that I draw is too stark, on the grounds that indexicality cannot be extruded from science's atlas, chronicle, and theory. For even if science avoided explicit use of indexical information in them, their very incompleteness betrays their origin in organisms living in a particular place and time. Our science's pattern of blank areas and filled-in areas shows where we are. Blanks may be irremediable, if what we call the universe is but a bubble in an infinite froth of universes, each with its own natural laws. We may only ever know our own. Furthermore, the uneven development of mathematics betrays its origin in organisms who began their mathematical studies with the natural numbers. I concede that the incompleteness and uneven development of our science does give away the position of its creators. Nevertheless, the ideal of science is the total de-indexicalization of its atlas, chronicle, and theory. Our worldview, then, is something distinct from science.

This indexicality of philosophical formulations does not justify the idea that philosophy precedes science or is a parallel science to natural science. It's only a way of formatting what we know, and natural science is what we know, if we know anything. Indexicality should be extricated from issues of epistemic justification. Philosophy's resort to indexicality is not to be confused with Descartes's resort to indexicality in his "*cogito ergo sum*." Philosophy comes after science and reformulates it so that the world and self are integrated into a coherent scientific worldview that corrects and expands our prescientific worldview.

There are other sciences besides the empirical ones we have so far alluded to. The formal sciences also contribute to our worldview by helping us to locate ourselves in respect to possibilities. Ours is not the best of all possible worlds. Alas for that, but thank goodness there are worlds better than this one. Philosophy is captivated by certain parts of the formal sciences, because theorems like those in the foundations of mathematics, for instance, the proof of the incompletability of arithmetic or the proof of an unending series of infinities, can have an effect on our conception of ourselves and our goals. So it's reasonable to define philosophy as the discipline that articulates and refines our worldview; that's a comprehensive enough definition to capture what has interested even logic-oriented philosophers.

Within philosophy there's also a division of labor. Few philosophers take up the whole aim of philosophy; they're not less philosophical because of the more modest goals they set for themselves. They'd be wrong, however, to delimit philosophy itself to just the part they engage in. And they'd be wrong to excommunicate other philosophers for not doing what they do. It may be that a worldview recommends political and educational activity in the service of reforms. Even so, not all philosophers need become reformers. Since science progresses so swiftly on so many fronts, and since worldviews lag in responsive development, philosophy can no longer consist of one-man shows. Nor can it be self-contained. If a coherent and informed worldview is ever to emerge from the joint efforts of the empirical scientist, the formal scientist, and the philosopher, then the philosopher must know the empirical and formal science that's relevant to the philosophizing.

Of the philosopher's two jobs, working shoulder to shoulder with scientists and constructing a worldview more responsive to science, it may seem the latter is far the less serious work. It will seem so, if one thinks science under-determines worldviews. If so, they must be vague emotings much more responsive to the idiosyncracies of personality and culture than to science. I concede that a person's worldview consists of three parts:

- parts that are normative for all mankind
- parts that are peculiar to the person's culture
- parts that are peculiar to the person's personality.

I must also concede that the second and third parts have swamped the first. The first should constitute more of our worldview. The spread of the historic world religions has limited the cultural and personal contributions. These religions seek to impose universality by not fully rational methods and fail. But scientific methods can work; cultural and personal factors will become less preponderant as science saturates the whole fabric of our life. A large part of all informed persons' worldviews, whatever their cultures and personalities, will be common to all, because the requirement of coherence with science will dictate it. Already our sense of the world has so expanded that we, chattering away in our hubbub of cultures, are called to attention to view this scene:

In the universal black and silent night of it all, a speck of light flickers briefly. If you approach it before it goes out, a tiny cacophony becomes barely audible there for a moment. That's the totality of us. Some of us have strayed from the cacophony into the silence, looked up, and shivered. We welcome the drawing of the curtain of daylight over the disturbing scene. We step back into our tiny noise, realizing that all excellence arises for us just there, but also realizing that excellence and worth will still arise if we give up our anthropocentrically circumscribed and cosmically teleological illusion. Then we look within ourselves as evolutionary psychology reveals us, and again we shudder at how limited a light on ourselves is shed by our natural self-knowledge. We live an illusion about ourselves. Yet, in overcoming the illusion, we cannot allow ourselves to disintegrate. Or perhaps we can. It will be a new kind of brave and noble death, death by enlightenment. The conditions will then be right for what Nietzsche called for, the revaluation of all values.

A scientific worldview trades in our cozy *umwelt* for the unimaginably alien real world, and we must come to terms with it. We're in danger of coming to be alien even to ourselves. To our old selves, farewell . . .

A worldview does not just add feeling to fact; it's an attitude that consists of ways of thinking that shape character and affect choices. Worth, the third ingredient of our worldview, goes beyond the physical sciences, which only deliver the factual ingredients of our worldview. It goes beyond the evolutionary science of organisms, which delivers the chief motivating value of fitness. It's a value which we can call into question, yet there's no indexicality without the value of fitness; indexicality generates this value, and all values are covertly indexical. Some philosophers of the past century thought that, since science cannot deliver our human ethical values, which therefore are not knowledge, value theory and ethics are not legitimate parts of philosophy; their claim to being part of philosophy is merely one of historical precedent, because so many of the master thinkers of the past mistakenly thought of values as legitimate objects of knowledge. So these philosophers said. But it's reasonable to agree with the precedent and include theory of value in philosophy, because philosophy's proper object is to elaborate a new science-based worldview, of which value theory is an indispensable ingredient, whatever its status as knowledge. We have reason to think that evolutionary theory should recognize biological value, i.e., fitness. This is not ethical value, and the two kinds of value overlap only accidentally. Nevertheless, if the one is knowledge, why not the other?

While it would be derelict of philosophers to leave our ethical values outside the scope of their rational scrutiny, some of us go further in our commitment to philosophize about values: Reflection on nature's ways forces an acknowledgment of the evil of the evolutionary process to which we owe our existence.[33] Because of that legacy, only by our living together to realize values reformed and transfigured by rational examination do we redeem in our own eyes our presence in this world and at last make this collective life of ours a life worth living.

# Notes

1. This paragraph and the next several appeared in "Whither Analytic Ontology?" in *Russell: the Journal of the Bertrand Russell Archives*, n.s., 18 (1998-99) 161-174.

2. Stephan Körner, *What is Philosophy? One Philosopher's Answer* (1969), ch. 2. A similar point is made by P. F. Strawson, *Analysis and Metaphysics* (1992), ch. 2. The seeming non-exhaustiveness of the first distinction is an artifact of my statement of it. In particular, I underplay the role of simple components of the complex to be analyzed. If I had made finding those simples central to the concept of analysis, I'd've been forced to treat the later Wittgenstein as rejecting analytic technique and favoring a comparative technique.

3. Ludwig Wittgenstein, *Philosophical Investigations*, §5. Cp. §§90-92.

4. W. V. Quine, "Russell's Ontological Development" *Journal of Philosophy* 63 (1966), reprinted in his *Theories and Things*. See pp. 75ff.

5. Frege's "senses" are a bit of ontology. Frege did enunciate a holistic "context principle" in 1884, but according to Michael Dummett, *The Interpretation of Frege's Philosophy*, (1981), ch. 19, Frege's later doctrines interfered with his continued explicit avowal of it, although he never denied it. Dummett has changed his mind, however, and now thinks that Frege continued to accept the principle. See Dummett, "The Context Principle: Centre of Frege's Philosophy," in Ingolf Max and Werner Stelzner, eds., *Logik und Mathematik: Frege Kolloquium Jena 1993* (1995) 3-19. See Johannes Brandl, "What is Wrong with the Building Block Theory of Language" in J. Brandl and W. Gombocz, *The Mind of Donald Davidson, Grazer Philosophische Studien*, 36 (1989). Carnap, who is known for his principle of ontological tolerance, would have denigrated this classification.

6. For the evidence, see my "Whither Analytic Ontology?"

7. *An Inquiry into Meaning and Truth* (1940) 26.

8. In view of *Philosophical Investigations*, §49. Even the earlier Wittgenstein did not allow names to be exceptions to the context principle. See *Tractatus* 3.3; 3.311; 3.314.

9. "Russell's Ontological Development," 76.

10. See Russell, *My Philosophical Development* (1959) 150f. In *Human Knowledge* (1948), ch. 5, his discussion of the ambiguity of one word sentences suggests the same mental completion by beliefs or desires which are not holophrastic.

11. Dummett, *The Interpretation of Frege's Philosophy,* 371, lines 1-4. I am emphasizing Dummett's "in succession . . . in a similar way." He repeats the contrast in the middle of p. 373. Also on p. 372 Dummett is appealing beyond Frege for his view of what Frege should have said. His later paper, cited earlier, does not retract this argument for the context principle.

12. My thanks to Pranab Kumar Sen who expressed skepticism about this feature of my thought, making me realize the need for defense.

13. Quine, then, should be seen as the first evolutionary contextualist, albeit hesitant. See his "Propositional Objects" in his *Ontological Relativity and Other Essays* (1969) 156.

14. D. Lewis, "Attitudes *De Dicto* and *De Se*" (1979), reprinted in his *Philosophical Papers,* vol. I (1983). R. Chisholm, *The First Person* (1981). Quine's discussion of egocentric attitudes is in his "Propositional Objects."

15. John Dewey, *The Influence of Darwin on Philosophy* (1910), ch. 1.

16. Appeal to this analogy with natural selection seems to entail a willingness to accept pure chance as the source of our creativity at least at a preconscious stage. One could then explain away my disanalogy this way: If by the time a creative insight becomes conscious its suitability to our purpose is already better than chance, then selection was already at work at the preconscious stage. Robert Kane incorporates something like this into his indeterminist theory of free will (*The Significance of Free Will* (1996) 161). Popper is another who combined indeterminist free will with this analogy to natural selection, and all who are inclined to press this analogy should consider whether they too must adopt an indeterminist theory of free will.

17. I argue this in "Gaia = Maya," *History and Philosophy of the Life Sciences,* 17 (1995), and earlier in "Purpose, Feedback, and Evolution" *Philosophy of Science,* 48 (1981).

18. *Philosophical Investigations,* §98.

19. G. Ledyard Stebbins, *Processes of Organic Evolution,* 3rd ed. (1977) 203ff.

20. Charles Darwin, *The Origin of Species,* ch. 13, thirteenth paragraph. It's at least evidence for a genealogy.

21. I argue the primitiveness of direct-attribution to the self in "Reference to Myself" *Behaviorism* (1987), and in "Consciousness and Self-Reference" *Erkenntnis* 43 (1995).

22. On the analysis of verisimilitude see I. Niiniluoto, *Truthlikeness* (1987); Graham Oddie, *Likeness to the Truth* (1986); Patrick Maher, *Betting on Theories* (1993) chs. 7 and 8; and I. Niiniluoto, "Verisimilitude: The Third Period," *British Journal for the Philosophy of Science,* 9 (1998) 1-29.

23. I argue this in "Gaia = Maya."

24. This is not an analytic^ implication, and distinguished evolutionists have

questioned the connection. I argue for the connection in "Williams's Domains and Reductionism," *Quarterly Review of Biology* 72 (June, 1997) 179-83.

25. J. L. Mackie, *Ethics: Inventing Right and Wrong* (1977), ch.1, section 9. His argument from relativity (section 8) does not apply, since the organismic value of fitness is universal.

26. The connection of ethics to biology I discuss in "Essay on Nature's Semeiosis," *Journal of Philosophical Research* 20 (1995) esp. 307-311.

27. I argue for this in "A Connectionist Solution to Problems Posed by Plato and Aristotle," *Behavior and Philosophy*, 23 (Winter, 1995/1996).

28. Gottlob Frege, *The Foundations of Arithmetic* (1960) xviiif.

29. Ramesh C. Pradhan, *Recent Developments in Analytic Philosophy* (2001) ch. 1.

30. Stephan Körner, "The Impossibility of Transcendental Deductions" *Monist*, 51 (1967) 317-331. See also Robert Stern, *Transcendental Arguments and Scepticism* (2000).

31. Georg Misch, *The Dawn of Philosophy*, 1926 (translation in 1951), one of the first philosophy books I ever read, and the definition of philosophy as a *Weltanschauung* stuck.

32. "The Philosophy of Logical Atomism," lecture VI, in Bertrand Russell, *Logic and Knowledge*, Robert C. Marsh, ed. (1956) 248.

33. Arthur Falk, "Reflections on Huxley's 'Evolution and Ethics'," *Humanist*, 55, number 6 (November/ December, 1995) 23-25. See also ch. 9 of my *Darwinism and Philosophical Analysis*.

# GLOSSARY

### *a posteriori* & *a priori*

Terms from the theory of knowledge distinguishing two ways of justifying your believing a statement. You're justified *a posteriori* in believing something, if any of your evidence is observational, more generally, if any of your evidence originates in the world's interacting with your mind. You're justified *a priori* in believing it if you have adequate evidence, none of which is of this sort. A noncontroversial example of *a priori* belief (knowledge in this case) would be if the totality of your evidence concerns the meaning of the terms in the statement expressing what you believe. Thus you are justified *a priori* in believing these: An uncle is a brother of a parent or a husband of a sister of a parent. Two sticks, each exactly the same length as a third stick, are exactly the same length as each other. You believe these are true when you realize their truth follows simply from what they mean. Some *a priori* justification must be teased out with much logic and calculation. In this way all the theorems of geometry are justified *a priori*.

It's controverted whether you can know anything about the world other than by observation, that is, without the world having any part in producing your evidence. If you do have such synthetic knowledge (for synthetic see the entry for analytic truth), perhaps the world told it to you by having selected the genes for your cognitive equipment with the effect that it spontaneously generates some beliefs with truth or verisimilitude.ˆ If so, it would seem more illuminating philosophically to recognize it as another mode of *a posteriori* knowledge or at least belief with verisimilitude. Then not all that we believe innately would be *a priori*, despite the prevalent opposite convention. In particular, the intuitions that thought experiments evoke would be a form of *a posteriori* knowledge or belief.

The Latin terms distinguish something epistemological, not to be confused with the distinction in logic or metaphysics between necessary truth and contingent truth. It may be that you can know some contingent truths *a priori*, and perhaps only know some necessary truths *a posteriori*. (Both theses are controversial, but you won't understand the controversies unless you keep the epistemological distinction separate from the metaphysical distinction.) Also avoid confusing genesis with justification. How you got the belief may not be relevant to how you justify it.

### absolute probability

In general, "absolute" contrasts with "relative," but in probability theory, absolute probability contrasts with conditional probability. The unconditional probability statement, $p(X)=n$, shows an absolute probability for the proposition X. A conditional probability statement for X, conditional on Y, is shown by $p(X|Y)=n$. The $p(X|Y)$ is defined, if $p(Y)>0$, as $p(X\&Y)/p(Y)$. (See the entry for relevance.)

In the personalist or subjective interpretation of probability, the symbol "$p(X)$" means any one of a family of functions assigning to proposition X, and to all other propositions, some degree of belief. One of the functions in that family will, under ideal conditions, describe someone's total belief state at one time, assigning a degree of belief to each proposition. The context of use of the symbol determines the person and time being referred to. As the person learns, the function is superceded by another one from the family of functions, one which describes the person's degrees of belief after having learned. It makes no difference to the meaning of the absolute probability, $p(X)$, whether the person has already learned many things or is starting out with a clean slate (ignorant of all but truths known innately). We can single out the former of these two states, if we wish, by subscripting the function letter, p, with a K, standing for all that has been learned, thus $p_K(X)$. Contrary to common opinion, the subscripted formula should not be taken to mean the same as the conditional probability formula, $p(X|K)$. For the K may have been learned without certitude or with certitude; if without certitude, the common opinion has unfortunate consequences; if with certitude, the supposed equation creates redundancy. (Proofs: According to the proposed equation of subscripting with conditional probability, this holds: $p_K(X|Y)=p(X|Y\&K)$. If K is not learned with certainty, then the person should be able to form degrees of belief conditional on not-K, but the formula $p(X|\text{not-}K\&K)$ is not well defined. If K is learned with certainty, $p(X|Y\&K)$ is defined as $p(X\&Y\&K)/p(Y\&K)$. But in view of K's certainty, this reduces to $p(X\&Y)/p(Y)$, and so the reference to K is redundant.)

### analytic truth

A term from the theory of meaning (semantics). An analytic truth is true either by virtue of its logical form alone or by virtue of that together with the meanings of its terms. For an example of the latter sort, an uncle is a brother of a parent or married to a sister of a parent. True because that's what "uncle" means. Another example: Two sticks, each exactly the same length as a third stick, are exactly the same length as each other. The truth of an analytic truth may not be so obvious as it is for these two. But what you do to reveal the unobvious truth is "analyze" its terms (an *a priori*^ method). A truth that's not analytically true is called a synthetic truth. You should not assume that philosophers who use the so-called analytic method confine themselves to discovering analytic truths; perhaps synthetic truths come to their attention by analysis. Quine challenged the comprehensiveness of such a sharp dichotomy between analytic and synthetic, and seriously undermined its philosophical significance.

**associationism**
Associationist psychology explained the flow of thoughts in the mind as occurring in accordance with laws of association of ideas either by their similarity or by their connection in space or time. Associationism was the dominant theory in the 18th and 19th centuries. Hume is a good representative of the theory. The stimulus-response theories of the 20th century were heirs to this tradition in psychology.

**cognitivism**
A term used for many things in many areas of philosophy and psychology. Generally, it refers to positions that emphasize the role of knowledge and belief. For example, in theories of the meaning of judgments of the goodness or badness of things or actions, cognitivism is the position that says the judgments are beliefs rather than noncognitive attitudes. A noncognitivist alternative is emotivism. The term is used in psychology for a position that contrasts with behaviorism in the way it explains behavior. In these pages the term stands for a position about how the subject of attribution is established for indexical attitudes, namely, through the attributor's knowledge about it, and contrasts with the kinetic theory of such reference.

**commutation**
Commutation is the logical operation of switching the order of terms in a formula. When two propositions are joined by an "and" or an "or" or an "if and only if," their commutation is valid: "$p$ or $q$" is equivalent to "$q$ or $p$." Commutation of $p$ and $q$ is not valid in "if $p$, then $q$." Commutation of the terms of an identity statement is also valid: $a=b$ if and only if $b=a$. When it seems to fail, we invoke conversational implicature, as in this

example, due to David Kaplan: "The man in dark glasses is John's brother" and "John's brother is the man in dark glasses." The latter but not the former implicates that John has just one brother.

### contrapositive
In propositional logic, the contrapositive of "if $p$, then $q$" is "if not-$q$, then not-$p$." If we take the probabilities of the indicative conditionals of ordinary language to be conditional probabilities (see the glossary entry for absolute probability, where conditional probability is defined), then contrapositives are not equivalent except in the special case in which the conditionals are known with certitude. Contraposition is used in this book only when this condition holds true. The reason contraposition is not valid in general is that in a valid argument the probability of the conclusion cannot be less than the probability of the premise. Assuming the probabilities of indicative conditionals are conditional probabilities, it's easy to find models where, if a conditional is less than certain, its contrapositive is still more uncertain. (See the article by D. Edgington and the book by E. Adams.)

In predicate logic, the contrapositive of "All $A$ are $B$" is "All non-$B$ are non-$A$." In predicate logic, contraposition of the universally quantified forms preserves equivalence. But probability affects the validity of contraposition of the indefinite forms. "$A$'s are $B$'s" is not necessarily equivalent to "Non-$B$'s are non-$A$'s." See Adams's *Primer*, appendices 7 and 9.

### converse
The converse of a proposition is another proposition created from the first by conversion, which is a commutation^ of terms. We'll consider four examples: First, the conditional sentence, "if $p$, then $q$." Conversion is just switching antecedent and consequent. The resultant converse proposition is: "If $q$, then $p$." Conversion does not preserve equivalence, nor is it valid here. The second example is conversion of a valid rule of inference. Instead of inferring the conclusion from the premise, we infer the premise from the conclusion. Often this works in algebra, since the rules are rules of equivalence. But it doesn't work for such valid rules as, "Infer $p$ from $p\&q$." The converse inference would be invalid: "inferring $p\&q$ from just $p$." The third example, the converse of "All $a$ are $b$" would result from switching subject and predicate terms: "All $b$ are $a$." These are not equivalent, nor does one follow from the other. However, conversion preserves equivalence in this pair: "No $a$ are $b$" and "No $b$ are $a$." Fourthly, the converse of a relation, $a$ R $b$ is the relation that $b$ bears to $a$

whenever *a* R *b*. "Being parent of" is the converse of "being child of."

## counterfactual

A counterfactual is a conditional sentence whose antecedent is so stated as to presuppose it's false. Here's a counterfactual conditional: *If Oswald had not shot Kennedy, Kennedy would not have been shot.* Here's another conditional which does not presuppose its antecedent false (although it happens to be): *If Oswald did not shoot Kennedy, Kennedy was shot by someone else.* Note that the content of their antecedents is the same, and the contents of their consequents are contraries. Yet they're both probably true. Therefore they're really different kinds of conditionals. Starting with breakthroughs around 1968, the logic of counterfactuals has been worked out. Sometimes counterfactuals are called "subjunctive conditionals." When the antecedent of the conditional is about past time, the name "counterfactual" is appropriate. But their antecedents may also be about future time, and the antecedents may come true in the actual future. These conditionals still have the same logic as those whose antecedents are contrary to past fact, and so the name "subjunctive" for the whole class of them is less misleading.

## counter-intuitive

A philosophical thesis may be asserted despite its seeming false according to one's intuitions. In view of these intuitions, the thesis is said to be counter-intuitive. That does not mean it's false; the intuitions may themselves be faulty. But a greater burden of proof falls on the one who asserts a counter-intuitive thesis.

## domain

In logic, we interpret quantifiers, like "some" and "all" as "quantifying over" a domain of objects. Thus the domain of "everyone" is the set of people. A domain is either empty or nonempty. Thus a domain consisting of unicorns is empty, the domain of people is nonempty. Another use of the word "domain" is to specify the set of entities a function applies to, that is, the things that $x$ stands for in the functional notation, $f(x)=y$. The set of things from which the values^ of $y$ may come is called the function's counter-domain. For more, see the glossary entry for function.

## entropy

Entropy is a measure of a machine's capacity for doing work, the higher the entropy the less it can do and the less efficiently it can do it. Low entropy requires differences, for example in a steam engine, the difference between the temperature of the steam and the temperature of the parts of the machine. For a hydroelectric generator, the difference is in the height of the water behind the dam and in front of it, determining how far the water can fall. Since the development of statistical thermodynamics, entropy is defined more generally as a measure of the degree of disorder of a system. The second law of thermodynamics says that a system's entropy does not decrease, it tends to increase.

Entropy is also a measure of degree of residual uncertainty left by information. The negative of entropy is a measure of the amount of information in a system. The lower the entropy the greater the amount of information. All three conceptions of entropy are intimately connected, as reflections on the thought experiment called "Maxwell's demon" show. See H. S. Leff and A. F. Rex, eds., *Maxwell's Demon: Entropy, Information, Computing*, (1990). Because of this connection, a consequence of the second law is that information tends to decrease. It's customary to warn that the order in a system that constitutes its low entropy cannot be the carrier of information in the sense we use the term in, unless it's causally connected to earlier ordered states of the system in such a way that the later states are *about* the earlier ones. The warning is misguided, since, according to the second law of thermodynamics, order only comes from order, usually greater order, and so only the universe's initial states of order are not information in the sense of being about something else. The limit on extracting from current order what it's about is entirely our own limitation. As for the universe's initial order, high temperature is an indicator of disorder, and so the initial state of the universe does seem to have been a state of very high entropy. Presumably its entropy was not so high as to exclude the existence of any information then or thereafter. We await the physicists' solution to this problem.

In probability theory, where the entropy of a description of a system is a measure of the residual uncertainty it leaves about the system, entropy is confusingly called a measure of the information that could be gained by performing experiments on the system. Of course, this is not the information of the original description, but the additional information that would overcome the uncertainty it left. Nor is this way of speaking, which entails decrease in entropy, to be taken as denying the second law. For the collecting of information increases entropy enough to more than offset the increase in information.

**fitness**
The reproductive, or Darwinian, fitness of an organism or gene is its reproductive success. Its absolute attained fitness can be measured numerically by counting its offspring. By extension, the fitness of an organism is its adaptedness to its environment, because adaptations are the traits and behaviors that contribute to the organism's reproductive success. Fitness is the central concept of the theory of evolution by natural selection. Biological evolution of a population of organisms is defined as the change in gene frequencies in the population. Many mechanisms can cause evolution, but only one mechanism, natural selection, causes frequencies to change in the direction of greater fitness. A generation of organisms in a lineage (i.e., a line of inheritance) with an advantage in fitness over competing lineages will leave more offspring, and so the genes of later generations of that lineage will be more frequent in the population. Not only has the population evolved, but it has evolved toward greater average fitness. For more, see the glossary entry for inclusive fitness.

**formalism**
In the philosophy of mathematics, formalism is the thesis that mathematics is just the putting forth of strings of symbols, the so-called mathematical truths, and the manipulation of strings of symbols, the so-called mathematical proofs, in accordance with explicit rules for constructing the strings of symbols and manipulating them. Reference to what the symbols mean is eliminated. The rules for manipulating the symbols should be both fecund and consistent. Their fecundity is their sufficiency for producing all the theorems of mathematics; their consistency is their not also producing the negation of any of the theorems.

**foundationalism**
In the theory of knowledge, foundationalism is the thesis that, for there to be knowledge of the world, there must be experiential certitudes that provide a foundation (whether deductive or probabilistic) for inferring the rest of what we know of the world. Descartes was a foundationalist.

**frequency interpretation**
The formulas of the calculus of probability can be interpreted to mean different things. We've been interpreting them to refer to a person's degrees of belief at a time. That's the subjectivist interpretation. The frequency interpretation takes formulas to refer to the frequency of events within a larger class of events. For example, we say the probability of a coin falling

heads is one-half. On the subjectivist interpretation that refers to a person's degree of belief that it will fall heads. But on the frequency interpretation it refers to the event of coming up heads having a frequency of one-half within the larger class of events consisting of tosses of that coin. There are other interpretations of probability besides these two, and all can be complementary and combinable into a single interpretation.

### function

A function in the mathematical sense is a kind of relation which one or more values of variables in the "domain" of the function have to another variable in the "counter-domain" of the function. In particular, it's either a many-to-one relation or a one-to-one relation. For example, the operation of squaring a signed integer is a many-to-one relation, in that the square of 2 is 4, and the square of negative 2 is 4 also. Thus, many signed integers in the domain of the function, such as 2 and negative 2, are related to the same signed integer in the counter-domain of the function, namely 4. What's not allowed in a function is that one element in the domain be related to more than one element in the counter-domain. Thus square-rooting a positive integer is not a function into the counter-domain of signed real numbers, since some numbers, 4 for instance, have two square roots. The "range" of a function is the set of entities in its counter-domain to which the function relates some member of the domain. A function can have a domain that's a set of sequences of elements. Thus addition is a function, relating a sequence of numbers to their sum. A function can be total or partial, depending on whether or not it assigns an element from its counter-domain to each item in its domain. An example of a partial function is division. If its domain consists of all pairs of numbers, interpreting the second as dividing the first, nothing in the counter-domain is assigned to those pairs in the domain that have zero in second position. That function is not defined for all the members of that domain.

"Function" in a non-mathematical sense of the word is just a use or job. See the glossary entry for "use-function."

### holism

Holism (from the Greek word, *holos*) describes any theory that says the parts of a thing are internally related to each other so that nothing works unless they all work together. Thus theories of organisms are usually holistic. Although "merism" would be better, the opposite of holism is generally referred to as atomism, which means here a belief that one can deduce the explanation of a whole from the independent contributions of its particulate elements. Thus holism is the claim that the whole is more than the sum of its parts. Fodor defines a holistic property as one which, if it applies to any one thing, it applies to lots and lots of them. However, the property of being a number turns out to be holistic on this definition.

### idealism

Idealism in metaphysics means the thesis that all that exists is either the things whose existence depends on their being the object of awareness, or the minds that are aware of them. Some idealists even analyze minds into bunches of awarenesses. Anti-idealists believe that some things are neither minds nor depend on minds being aware of them for them to exist. This philosophical meaning of the term "idealism" should not be confused with the common meaning of having ideals to live by.

### idiolect

An idiolect is a language or dialect unique to one speaker. "*Idios*" is a Greek word meaning unique, as in "idiosyncratic." Just as people all speak some dialect of their language, each one of them has idiosyncracies of language which make them speak idiolects of their language.

### inclusive fitness

The fitness of an organism is its survival to reproductive maturity and its reproducing fertile offspring. More exactly, that's its reproductive fitness. (See the glossary entry for fitness.) Inclusive fitness takes into account that one's genes are shared by one's siblings and cousins, and if you aid in their reproduction, even at some cost to your own reproduction, your genes may achieve a greater representation in the next generation, than if you had not aided them. Counting that aid along with your reproductive fitness yields your inclusive fitness.

### inconsistency

An inconsistent proposition is one that cannot possibly be true. In the elementary logic of propositions, it would be one whose truth table entries were false in all cases. But inconsistent propositions can be found in higher branches of logic and in mathematics where the truth table technique doesn't work. To say that $2+3=6$ is to say something inconsistent. Distinguish inconsistent propositions from contradictory sentences. A contradiction is a sentence that affirms and denies the same thing. The two are connected in this way: To demonstrate something is inconsistent involves deducing a contradiction from it by logic alone. Not all inconsistencies are demonstrably inconsistent. This was proved by Gödel for mathematics. Another instance of inconsistency without contradiction comes from identity theory, when one thing has more than one proper name, say *a* and *b*. Then to deny the identity *a=b* is to affirm an inconsistency. But it cannot be demonstrated by logic alone. I am recommending a usage that allows us to say there can be inconsistencies that are not contradictions in those areas where logic and mathematics are incompletable.

### instrumentalism

Instrumentalism is a thesis about the ontological commitments involved in accepting a scientific theory. It says that one does not have to believe in the existence of the entities which a theory posits in order to justify using the theory as an instrument to predict and control events. Instrumentalism contrasts with scientific realism. Copernicus's book on the structure of the solar system was published posthumously with the editor's preface, which was perhaps the first statement of instrumentalism.

### internal relation

Around 1900, the phrase "internal relation" was customarily used to mean a relation to something which a thing had to have to be the thing it is. In other words, an essential relation. This use of the word "internal" has nothing to do with the semantic internalism discussed in section S.

### intersection

In set theory the intersection of two sets is a set whose members are in each of the two sets. Thus the intersection of green things and triangular things is the set of green triangular things.

### logical subject

In ordinary grammar, the singular terms in a sentence are subjects, direct and indirect objects of the verb, and objects of prepositions. In logic, all these singular terms are called subjects, or logical subjects. It's common today to also call the things that the terms name the logical subjects.

### mathematical induction

In proofs by mathematical induction, one proves that all things in an infinite domain have a property by showing that each individually has the property. One first establishes a base clause, for example in the domain of natural numbers, that 0 has a certain property. Then one establishes the inductive clause, for example, that if a number has that property, then its successor does also. Once the two clauses are proved, they establish that 1 also has that property. Since the inductive clause is general, if 1 has it, so does 2, and if 2 has it, so does 3, and so on for all the natural numbers. Mathematical induction may proceed by identifying the things in any way, including by their structural properties. Thus suppose the inductive clause to be such as, for any proposition $p$, if it's true, so is $pvq$. By recursion, that is, by feeding the output of this clause back into it, as input to its antecedent, putting $pvq$ for $p$, we establish the truth of $pvqvq$, and so on forever.

### metaphysics
See the glossary entry for ontology. Metaphysics may be more inclusive in that it can cover the dynamics of systems of entities.

### metatheorem
A metatheorem is the conclusion of a proof that a system of logic has a particular property. In contrast, a theorem is just the conclusion of a proof done in the system, which is presupposed. An example of a metatheorem is that the logic of propositions has the property of decidability: If a sentence in the language of the system is a logical truth, that's provable, and if it's not a logical truth, that too is provable. Quantificational logic is complete: If a sentence in the language of the system is a logical truth, that's provable. But it's not decidable because if a sentence in the language of the system is not a logical truth, that may not be susceptible of proof. Arithmetic is not complete because no finite set of axioms suffices to ensure that all arithmetic truths are provable.

### *modus tollens*
In logic, the inference from two premises: If $p$, then $q$. Not $q$. Therefore, not $p$. This inference is valid. The Latin name means "the denying way [of inference from a conditional]," because one infers the denial of the conditional's antecedent from the denial of its consequent.

### necessary condition
X is a necessary condition for Y (if and only if) in any case in which Y occurs, X occurs. I also call X an indispensable condition, since Y cannot occur unless X occurs. Contrast indispensability with sufficiency—see the entry for sufficient condition. Necessary conditions, like sufficient conditions, can be either causally or conceptually indispensable.

A tendency to confuse necessary conditions and sufficient conditions is partially vindicated if we generalize the concepts within probability theory. Probabilistically, X is more or less strongly necessary for Y, if and only if $p(X|Y)>p(X)$, the amount of the difference governing the "more or less." Since it's a theorem that if $p(X|Y)>p(X)$, then $p(Y|X)>p(Y)$, if X is probabilistically necessary for Y, then Y is probabilistically necessary for X. Furthermore, we define sufficiency similarly: X is more or less strongly sufficient for Y, if and only if $p(Y|X)>p(Y)$, so that X is sufficient for Y if and only if Y is sufficient for X. (Our definitions are appropriate only for conceptually necessary or sufficient conditions.)

Thus we vindicate the tendency to blur the two ideas together, but only partly. To see where error does lie, we define the strongest form of condition by adding to the definition, just given, the clauses that $p(Y|X)=1$ for the limiting case of X's sufficiency for Y, and $p(X|Y)=1$ for the limiting case of X's necessity for Y. From X being sufficient for Y in this limit sense, it follows neither that X is necessary for Y in this limit sense, nor that Y is sufficient for X in this limit sense. Another form of error is to assume that, if the difference between $p(X|Y)$ and $p(X)$ is large, then the difference between $p(Y|X)$ and $p(Y)$ is also large. Probability theory contains no such theorem.

## null extension

General terms, like common nouns, have extensions, namely the sets of things they're true of. The noun "dog" is true of each thing in the set of dogs. So that set is the extension of the word "dog." What is the extension of the noun "unicorn"? The noun is true of nothing at all. So its extension is the null set (also defined in this glossary). When the null set is thought of as the extension of a word, it's called the null extension.

## null set

The null set is the set that has no members in it. Also called the empty set. We call it "the" null set, because there is only one set that's empty, even though it can be specified in myriad ways, for example, the set of five-sided circles and the set of dinosaurs living in the year 2000ad. Why are they the same set? They both have exactly the same members, namely, none.

## numerical identity

Numerical identity contrasts with qualitative identity. When we say that something is numerically the same as something, or numerically identical to something, we mean there's just one individual, particular thing there.

Norma Jean Baker is numerically identical with Marilyn Monroe. Qualitative identity occurs when there are more things than just one, but they are exactly similar, for example, identical twins and the three "i"'s in the term "identical twins."

## Ockham's razor

Also called the principle of parsimony, it's a methodological recommendation that, when two theories can account for all the same data, but one does it more simply, with more economy in postulating entities and causes, it should be the one accepted. William of Ockham (also Occam), a philosopher who died in 1349, often used it. But so did many before him. Priority belongs to Aristotle; see his *Physics*, Book 8; 259a8ff.

## ontology

Ontology is an account of the basic kinds of entities. Descriptive ontology is meant to contrast with "revisionary ontology," an allusion to Peter Strawson's book, *Individuals; an Essay in Descriptive Metaphysics* (1959). Descriptive ontology, like Strawson's descriptive metaphysics, is just an attempt to faithfully describe the ontology of an area of discourse, such as people's talk about their own mental states. Revisionary ontology (prescriptive ontology) would tell what things a person really ought to believe in, because they're the things that really exist.

## *possibilia*

The Latin word *possibilia* is plural and neuter, and means possible entities. The singular neuter form is *possibile*, pronounced "po-SEE-bill-aye." The possibility intended is logical, that is, mere self-consistency. Among the *possibilia* is Santa Claus, since a world is not self-contradictory by virtue of its containing a man who has reindeers fly him to the houses of every child all in a single night (I think).

## prenex form

In logic, compound sentences have connectives, like "and," "not," "if ... then ....," etc., and quantifiers, "all," "some," etc. The quantifiers and connectives have "scopes." A sentence in prenex form has the scopes of all its connectives within the scopes of all its quantifiers. It's a theorem of logic that for any sentence there's a sentence in prenex form equivalent to it. Quine's *Elementary Logic* shows how to create prenex equivalents to any sentence.

## psychologism

Psychologism is the thesis that logic is a part of psychology. If you believe that logic is just the laws of thought, you're a psychologizer of logic. Some who think psychologism is an error believe logic to be normative, necessary, and *a priori*, whereas psychology is descriptive, contingent, and *a posteriori*. Others who think psychologism an error believe that logic along with mathematics describes the most general structural features of the world.

## quantifier

"Quantifier" and "quantification" are terms from logic. They're best understood by starting from the idea of an incomplete proposition, which contains pronouns untied to any antecedent: "I gave it to him." What's "it"? It might be obvious to you from context. Suppose he's been bad. So you assume I mean "I gave him the devil," that is, I scolded him. Or it might be that it's just an incomplete sentence which cannot be understood. The first and most obvious way of completing the sentence would be to put names in place of the pronouns "it" and "him." Quantifiers are the second and less obvious way: Quantifiers are phrases which you prefix to the incomplete sentence to act as antecedents of the pronouns. One prefix is called the universal quantifier: Everything is such that I gave it to him. Another is called the existential quantifier: Something is such that I gave it to him. You could prefix another quantifier to act as antecedent of the "him": Somebody is such that everything is such that I gave it to him. More compactly stated, the pronouns might not show: I gave everything to a certain person. When more than one pronoun is tied to the same quantifier, none, some, or all of the pronouns might be concealed: Everything is such that, if it's solid it's matter. Or we might suppress the first of the two pronouns: If anything is solid it's matter. Or we might suppress both of them: Whatever is solid is matter.

## *reductio ad absurdum*

A form of valid argument, also called "indirect argument." If you want to prove A, assume for the sake of argument the opposite, not-A. Now show that not-A leads to absurdity. So A must be true. The purity of the argument depends on how many assumptions you must add in order to prove that not-A leads to absurdity. The more questionable they are, the more questionable is your conclusion that A's true. Also what's the absurdity you prove from not-A? If it's an out-and-out self contradiction, that's indeed absurd. But if you only prove something outrageous to common sense, well, maybe, common sense needs revising! So arguments by *reductio ad absurdum* range in validity from fully demonstrative, when the proof invokes no extra assumptions other than not-A and concludes a self-contradiction, to various degrees of persuasiveness. The conclusion that there's no barber who shaves all and only those who don't shave themselves is absolutely demonstrative and conclusive. Ask if he shaves himself.

**reflective equilibrium**
Reflective equilibrium of one's intuitions on a particular subject occurs when, after comprehensive and detailed deliberation, further deliberations don't tend to sway them any more. It's a sign that you've come to closure on the subject by as rational a process as the subject matter admits of. John Rawls introduced the term in 1951 as a test for the trustworthiness of intuitions about fairness and other moral matters. But the term's useful generally.

*relata*
*Relata* is a Latin word, plural, meaning the things that are related. The singular form is *relatum*. I use it because it's a convenient word for the terms in a relation. I also use *termini* as a synonym for *relata*.

**relevance**
Two propositions are relevant to each other if the probability of one, conditional on the other, is different from its absolute probability (defined in another glossary entry). If the probability of one of them is greater, the relevance of the two is positive; if less, negative. If one proposition is relevant to a second, the second is relevant to the first. For the connections to conditions necessary or sufficient, see the entry for necessary condition.

**scope**
Quantifiers, modal operators (e.g., "it's necessary that"), negation, and the other logical connectives all have scope, which is the extent of the sentence they govern, to indicate which parentheses are used. For example, quantifiers in sentences act as antecedents for pronouns that follow in the sentence. For example, "If anyone (=quantifier) hides his (pronoun) talents, then he (pronoun) will go to hell and the devil will taunt him (pronoun) for being a couch potato." The scope of the quantifier is the extent of its coverage, so that pronouns may refer back to it. Here it was the whole of the sentence.

**secondary and primary qualities**
Primary qualities of a thing are those qualities which our best science attributes to it. For example our best science of matter attibutes mass and charge to material things. So mass and charge are primary qualities of those things.

Secondary qualities of a thing form a system that's the joint product of the thing's primary qualities and our sensory systems, and they have features which should not be attributed to the thing. The colors, tastes, and other sensory qualities of things are secondary. Obviously, a color like brown does not correspond to a single wave length of light the way red does. Nor is the timbre of a sound a quality of the dominant note, but rather it's the quality of being accompanied by overtones.

Nevertheless, we attribute secondary qualities to things because they're not illusions but carry information about those things. Descartes, in his Sixth Meditation, was perhaps the first to say exactly how secondary qualities conveyed information:

> And to be sure, from the fact that I sense a wide variety of colors, sounds, odors, tastes, levels of heat, and grades of roughness, and the like, I rightly conclude that in the bodies from which these different perceptions of the senses proceed there are differences corresponding to the different perceptions—though perhaps the latter do not resemble the former.

The seventeenth century physicist Robert Boyle named the two classes of properties "primary" and "secondary."

**sequence**
In set theory, sets consist just of their members, and if you enumerate the members (usually by naming them inside curly brackets thus {a, b, c}) it doesn't matter which order you name them in. A sequence, however, is a set where the order of the members counts, and members are usually enumerated in corner brackets thus < a, b >, which is a different sequence than < b, a >. A sequence with only two members is called a pair, one with three members a triple, and so on. A sequence can have any number of members. But different orderings of them are different sequences. The relation "kill" is true of the pair < Brutus, Caesar >, but not of < Caesar, Brutus >.

**set theory**
A branch of mathematics, which studies sets (or collections, or classes), sometimes called Zermelo set theory. Zermelo was a mathematician who

stated a group of axioms from which could be derived the standard theorems of the field, especially Cantor's theorems dealing with sets with an infinity of members, while avoiding the paradoxes that had been discovered when set theoretic proofs were only presented in an intuitive and informal way.

**shaping**
Shaping is a procedure in behavioral psychology applying the laws of conditioning to an animal, so that it comes to manifest a learned, perhaps skillful form of behavior.

**sorites**
An ancient conundrum, also called the heap, which says that if you have a heap of sand, and take away just one grain, you still have a heap. That is a general statement, which, if true, entitles you to repeat the process of taking away one grain from a heap, and you'll still have a heap. But clearly it must be false, since eventually you'd have nothing at all. So where's the divide between a heap and something too small to be a heap? Does there have to be a nonstipulative answer to that? The conundrum can be worked in the other direction: Add one grain of sand to what's not a heap, and you still don't have a heap.

**subjunctive conditional**
See the glossary entry for counterfactual conditional.

**sufficient condition**
X is a sufficient condition for Y (if and only if) the presence of X suffices for the presence of Y, that is, Y occurs in any situation in which X occurs. Contrast sufficient condition with necessary condition, a separate entry. The sufficiency of X for Y may be causal or conceptual. Thus putting a lit match into prolonged contact with dry paper in an oxygen atmosphere is causally sufficient for the paper to catch fire. But being a poodle is conceptually sufficient for a thing's being a dog. For a generalization of the concept of sufficient condition within probability theory, see the entry for necessary condition.

**syncategorematic**
A kind of term that goes with (*syn* in Greek) a categorematic word. A categorematic word, such as ordinary nouns, carry meaning, which is at least to have an intension and extension. Syncategorematic words don't

carry meaning by themselves, but only in combination with the words that do carry meaning. Thus the word "the" has no meaning by itself, but only in combination with nouns like "stone" in the phrase "the stone." Other syncategorematic words are "a" and "of." Traditionally, verbs and adjectives are categorematic, but in section Q I boldly and perhaps wrongly call them syncategorematic.

### synchronic
For an investigation to be synchronic, it must consider only what happens at one time. An investigation which is diachronic considers what happens across times. Thus synchronic investigations look at correlations that exist at one time and are ahistoric.

### syncretist
Syncretism is the name for the claim that conflicting positions are really complementary. It ain't "either—or"; it's "both—and." Usually the syncretist is just showing superficial understanding of the positions he combines. I claim I'm syncretist (in the Introduction) concerning the content of belief. Let's see if I too am only showing how shallow my comprehension is. (Pronounced "SING cru DIST")

### tautology
There's a restrictive sense of the term in which it just means the proposition in the truth-functional logic of propositions that's true in all cases on a truth table. More generally, a tautology is the proposition that's true no matter what. There's arguably only one such, since there'd be nothing to distinguish it from another that's true no matter what. Although there's one tautologous proposition, many sentences express it. Sentences which express the tautologous proposition are truths of logic, instances of logically valid forms. For example, "if $p$, then $p$", "$x=x$", and "All $A$ are $A$."

### transfinite
A transfinite number numbers one of the infinities. Cantor proved in the late nineteenth century that the number of members of a set A, whose members are all the subsets of a set B, is greater than the number of all the members of set B, even if set B has an infinite number of members. It follows that there is a series of transfinite numbers, starting with the infinite set of all the natural numbers, 0, 1, 2, ... One of the sets larger than this set is the set of real numbers.

**unit set**
A unit set is a set with exactly one member. The set of natural satellites of the earth is usually taken to have just one thing in it, namely the moon. How does the moon differ from the unit set of the moon? In many ways! The set has many properties the moon does not have, like being a member of a set of sets. The moon is not a set and so is disqualified from being a member of that set.

**univocal/equivocal**
A statement is univocal if it bears only one interpretation. Otherwise it's equivocal, that is, ambiguous. Univocity is what we strive for; equivocity is a defect (except perhaps in poetry).

**use-function**
My neologism to distinguish functions, in the sense of the purposes or jobs of a thing, from mathematical functions.^

**value**
Three uses of the word, "value," have nothing to do with goodness, worth, or what ought to be. They are "semantic value," "truth value," and "value of a variable." The semantic value of a phrase is the thing the phrase refers to or means. A valuation rule is a function that assigns to each phrase its semantic value. The truth value of a proposition or sentence is just its truth or falsity. They're the two truth values. The value of a variable is the thing it's taken to stand in for.

**verisimilitude**
A proposition has similitude to the truth (*verum* in Latin), i.e., verisimilitude, if it's close to the truth. We're accustomed to judge propositions as either wholly true or wholly false. But surely among falsehoods, some are closer to the truth than others. Some philosophers develop precise versions of this idea. One version preserves the principle of bivalence and builds an analysis of verisimilitude that presupposes it. (The principle of bivalence says there's only one way for a proposition to be not true, and that's to be false.) So this assigns a degree of verisimilitude less than perfect to propositions that are false. (Examples of an objective approach of this sort can be found in Niiniluoto and Oddie; a somewhat more subjective approach can be found in Maher.) Another version denies the principle of bivalence and directly assigns to propositions either maximal verisimilitude or some distance from the maximal value. Some so-called

fuzzy logics and multi-valent logics approach verisimilitude in this way. The bivalent version often treats verisimilitude holistically,^ i.e., as closeness to the whole truth, whereas the non-bivalent approach treats verisimilitude particulately, not taking the totality of maximal verisimilitude into account in judging the distances of the less-than-maximally verisimilar propositions from the maximum.

# WORKS CITED

Abbott, E. A., *Flatland: A Romance of Many Dimensions* (2nd ed., 1884). **[P]**

Ackerman, D., "*De Re* Propositional Attitudes Toward Integers" in R. W. Shahan and C. Swoyer, eds., *Essays on the Philosophy of V. W. Quine* (U. of Oklahoma Press, 1979). **[O]**

Adams, E. W., "Probability and the Logic of Conditionals," in J. Hintikka and P. Suppes, eds., *Aspects of Inductive Logic* (North-Holland Publishing Co., 1966) 265-316. **[B]**

Adams, E. W., *A Primer of Probability Logic* (CSLI Publications, 1998). **[P]**

Anscombe, G.E.M., "The First Person" (1975) reprinted in her *Metaphysics and the Philosophy of Mind* (U. of Minnesota Press, 1981) ch. 2. **[M,N]**

Anselm, *Proslogion*, M. J. Charlesworth, translator (Oxford, 1965). **[D]**

Aristotle, *De Anima*. **[A]**

Aristotle, *Metaphysics*. **[A]**

Aristotle, *Nicomachean Ethics*. **[D]**

Aristotle, *Physics* **[Glossary]**

Aristotle, *Posterior Analytics*. **[H]**

Aristotle, *Topics*. **[E]**

Bach, K., *Thought and Reference* (Clarendon, 1987). **[I,J]**

Bach, K., "Do Belief Reports Report Beliefs?" *Pacific Philosophical Quarterly*, 78 (1997) 215-241. **[D]**

Baker, J. R., "The Evolution of Breeding Systems" in *In Evolution: Essays Presented to E. S. Goodrich* (Oxford, 1938) 161-77. **[Y]**

Baker, L. R., *Explaining Attitudes: A Practical Approach to the Mind* (Cambridge University Press, 1995). **[H]**

Bealer, G., "Universals," *Journal of Philosophy* 90 (1993) 5-32. **[V]**

Bechtel, W., "Connectionism and Intentionality," *Program of the Eleventh Annual Conference of the Cognitive Science Society* (Hillsdale, N. J.: Laurence Erlbaum Assoc. Pub., 1989) 553-560. **[R]**

Berkeley, G., *The Principles of Human Knowledge* (1710). **[M]**

Berkeley, G., *Three Dialogues Between Hylas and Philonous* (1713). **[B,J,T]**

Bever, T. G., and Rosenbaum, P. S., "Some Lexical Structures and Their Empirical Validity," in R. A. Jacobs and P. S. Rosenbaum, eds., *Readings in Transformational Grammar* (Ginn and Co., 1970). **[S]**

Block, N., "Advertisement for a Semantics for Psychology" in French, Uehling, and Wettstein, eds., *Midwest Studies in Philosophy*, vol. 10 (U. of Minnesota Press, 1986). **[Y]**

Boër, S. E., "Neo-Fregean Thoughts," in James Tomberlin, ed., *Philosophical Perspectives*, vol. 3 (Ridgeview Publishing, 1989). **[I]**

Boër, S. E., and Lycan, W. G., *Knowing Who* (MIT Press, 1986). **[C, Part II, J]**

Bohm, D., "Physics and Perception," *The Special Theory of Relativity* (Routledge, 1996 [1965]) Appendix. **[U]**

Bradley, F. H., *The Principles of Logic* (Oxford, 1883). **[Q]**

Brandl, J., "What is Wrong with the Building Block Theory of Language" in J. Brandl and W. Gombocz, *The Mind of Donald Davidson*, Grazer Philosophische Studien, 36 (1989). **[Z]**

Brandom, R., *Making It Explicit: Reasoning, Representing, and Discursive Commitment* (Harvard University Press, 1994). **[J]**

Brentano, F., *Psychology From an Empirical Standpoint* (1874); 2nd ed. O. Kraus, ed. (1924); English translation (Routledge, 19950. **[G]**

Burdick, H., "A Logical Form for the Propositional Attitudes," *Synthese* 52 (1982) 185-230. **[L]**

Burdick, H., "A Notorious Affair Called *Exportation*," *Synthese* 87 (1991) 363-377. **[L]**

Burge, T., "Belief *De Re*," *Journal of Philosophy* 74 (1977). **[T,U,W]**

Burge, T., "Other Bodies" (1982) reprinted in the Pessin and Goldberg, 142-160. **[S]**

Burks, A., "Icon, Index, and Symbol," *Philosophy and Phenomenological Research*, 10 (1949) 673-89. **[M]**

Carnap, R., *Meaning and Necessity*, 2nd ed. (U. of Chicago Press, 1956). **[F,G,X]**

Carnap, R., "Empiricism, Semantics, and Ontology" (1950) reprinted as supplement A to his *Meaning and Necessity*, 2nd edition, 205-221. **[A]**

Carroll, L., *Through the Looking-Glass* (1897). **[P]**

Castañeda, H., "He*: On the Logic of Self-consciousness," *Ratio* 8 (1966) 130-157. **[M,W]**

Caston, V., "Connecting Traditions: Augustine and the Greeks on Intentionality" in D. Perler, ed., *Ancient and Medieval Theories of*

*Intentionality* (Brill, 2001) 23-48. **[Intro]**

Chatterjee, S., *The Nyaya Theory of Knowledge*, 2nd edition (U. of Calcutta, 1950). **[A]**

Chierchia, G., and McConnell-Ginet, S., *Meaning and Grammar: An Introduction to Semantics* (MIT Press, 1990). **[P]**

Chisholm, R., "Intentionality" in Paul Edwards, ed., *Encyclopedia of Philosophy* (Macmillan, 1967). **[G]**

Chisholm, R., *Perceiving: A Philosophical Study* (Cornell, 1957). **[G,R]**

Chisholm, R., "The Indirect Reflexive" in C. Diamond and J. Teichman, eds., *Intention and Intentionality: Essays in Honour of G. E. M. Anscombe* (Cornell University Press, 1979). **[N]**

Chisholm, R., *The First Person* (U. of Minnesota Press, 1981). **[N,Z]**

Chisholm, R., "Why Singular Propositions?" in J. Almog, J. Perry, and H. Wettstein, eds., *Themes from Kaplan* (Oxford, 1989) 145-150. **[W]**

Chisholm, R., ed., *Realism and the Background of Phenomenology* (Free Press of Glencoe, Illinois, 1960). **[Intro]**

Chomsky, N., *New Horizons in the Study of Language and Mind* (Cambridge University Press, 2000). **[P]**

Church, A., "Review of Carnap's *Introduction to Semantics*," *Philosophical Review*, 52 (1943) 298-304. **[G]**

Church, A., "A Remark Concerning Quine's Paradox About Modality" (1982) reprinted in Salmon and Soames, 58-65. **[F]**

Churchland, P. M., *A Neurocomputational Perspective* (MIT Press, 1989). **[R, Y]**

Churchland, P. M., "Conceptual Similarity across Sensory and Neural Diversity: The Fodor- Lepore Challenge Answered" in Churchland, P. M., and Churchland, P. S., *On the Contrary: Critical Essays 1987-1997* (MIT Press, 1998). **[S]**

Churchland, P. M., "To Transform the Phenomena: Feyerabend, Proliferation, and Recurrent Neural Networks" in Churchland, P. M., and Churchland, P. S., *On the Contrary: Critical Essays 1987-1997* (MIT Press, 1998). **[S]**

Clark, A., "language of thought (2)" in Guttenplan, *A Companion to the Philosophy of Mind*, 408-412. **[P]**

Collins, A., *The Nature of Mental Things* (U. of Notre Dame Press, 1987). **[P]**

Corrado, M., "What *De Re* Belief is Not" *Analysis*, 35 (1975) 188-192. **[J]**

Crane, T., "The Efficacy of Content: A Functionalist Theory," in J. Bransen and S. E. Cuypers, eds., *Human Action, Deliberation and Causation* (Kluwer, 1998) 199- 223. **[C]**

576

Crawford, S., "In Defence of Object-Dependent Thoughts," *Proceedings of the Aristotelian Society*, vol. 98 (1998) 201-210. **[I]**

Cresswell, M. J., "Hyperintensional Logic," *Studia Logica*, vol. 34 (1975) 25-38. **[G]**

Cresswell, M. J., *Structured Meanings: The Semantics of Propositional Attitudes* (MIT Press, 1985). **[W,X]**

Crimmins, M., and Perry, J., "The Prince and the Phone Booth: Reporting Puzzling Beliefs" (1989) reprinted with postscript in Perry's, *The Essential Indexical and Other Essays*. **[L,V]**

Darwin, C., *The Origin of Species* (1st ed. 1859). **[Z]**

Davidson, B. L., "Belief *De Re* and *De Se*," *Australasian Journal of Philosophy*, 63 (December, 1985) 389-406. **[L]**

Davidson, D., "Moods and Performances," reprinted with additional notes as ch. 8 of his *Inquiries into Truth and Interpretation* (Oxford, 1984). **[D]**

Davidson, D., "On Saying That," in Davidson and Hintikka, reprinted with an added note as ch.7 in his *Inquiries into Truth and Interpretation* (Oxford, 1984). **[C]**

Davidson, D., and Hintikka, J., eds., *Words and Objections: Essays on the Work of W. V. Quine* (Reidel, 1969). **[A,C,E,H,K,L,R]**

Davies, M., and Stone, T., eds., *Folk Psychology: The Theory of Mind Debate* (Blackwell, 1995). **[H]**

Davies, M., and Stone, T., eds., *Mental Simulation: Evaluations and Applications* (Blackwell, 1995). **[H]**

Dennett, D., "Intentional Systems," *Journal of Philosophy* 68 (1971) 3-22. **[S]**

Dennett, D., "Three Kinds of Intentional Psychology" in Richard Healey, ed., *Reduction, Time and Reality* (Cambridge University Press, 1975) 37-60; reprinted in David Rosenthal, ed., *The Nature of Mind* (Oxford, 1991). **[Intro]**

Dennett, D., "Real Patterns," *Journal of Philosophy*, 87 (1991) 27-51. **[Y]**

Dennett, D., *Darwin's Dangerous Idea: Evolution and the Meanings of Life* (Touchstone, 1995). **[Y]**

Devitt, M., and Sterelny, K., *Language and Reality*, 2nd edition (MIT Press, 1999). **[P]**

Dewey, J., *The Influence of Darwin on Philosophy* (Henry Holt, 1910). **[Z]**

Donnellan, K., "Reference and Definite Descriptions," *Philosophical Review* 75 (1966) 281-304; reprinted in many anthologies. **[A]**

Donnellan, K., "The Contingent *a priori* and Rigid Designators" (1977) reprinted in French, Uehling, and Wettstein, eds., 45-60. **[F,H]**

Dowty, D. R., Wall, R. E., and Peters, R. S., *Introduction to Montague Semantics* (Reidel, 1981). **[X]**

Dretske, F. I., *Naturalizing the Mind* (MIT Press, 1995). **[R, Y]**

Dretske, F. I., "Misrepresentation" (1986) reprinted in Stephen P. Stich and Ted A. Warfield, eds., *Mental Representation: A Reader* (Blackwell, 1994). **[Y]**

Dummett, M., *The Interpretation of Frege's Philosophy* (Harvard, 1981). **[Z]**

Dummett, M., "The Context Principle: Centre of Frege's Philosophy," in I. Max and W. Stelzner, eds., *Logik und Mathematik: Frege-Kolloquium Jena 1993* (Berlin: Walter de Gruyter, 1995) 3-19. **[B,Z]**

Eames, E. R., *Bertrand Russell's Dialogue with his Contemporaries* (U. of Southern Illinois Press, 1989). **[Q]**

Edgington, D., "Conditionals," in Lou Goble, ed., *Blackwell Guide to Philosophical Logic* (Blackwell, 2001) 385-414. **[D]**

Elga, A., "Self-locating belief and the Sleeping Beauty problem," *Analysis* 60 (2000) 143-147. **[M]**

Evans, G., "The Causal Theory of Names" *Proceedings of the Aristotelian Society*, supplementary volume 47 (1973) 187-208. Reprinted in A. W. Moore, ed., *Meaning and Reference* (Oxford, 1993). **[S,Y]**

Evans, G., "Identity and Predication," *Journal of Philosophy* 72 (1975) 343-362. **[T]**

Falk, A., "Purpose, Feedback, and Evolution" *Philosophy of Science* 48 (1981). **[Y,Z]**

Falk, A., "Knowledge of Myself," *Prajna*, Journal of Utkal University, India, 6 (March, 1986) 1-26. **[N]**

Falk, A., "Reference to Myself," *Behaviorism* 15 (1987) 89-105. **[N,Z]**

Falk, A., "Consciousness and Self-reference," *Erkenntnis* 43 (1995) 151-180. **[M,N,Z]**

Falk, A., "Gaia = Maya," *History and Philosophy of the Life Sciences*, 17 (1995) 485-502. **[Y,Z]**

Falk, A., "Essay on Nature's Semeiosis," *Philosophy Research Archives*, 20 (1995) 297-348. **[R,Y,Z]**

Falk, A., "Reflections on Huxley's 'Evolution and Ethics'," *Humanist*, 55, number 6 (November/ December, 1995) 23-25. **[Z]**

Falk, A., "A Connectionist Solution to Problems Posed by Plato and Aristotle," *Behavior and Philosophy*, 23, no 3/24, no 1 (Winter 1995/1996) 1-12. **[R,Z]**

Falk, A., "The Judger in Russell's Theories of Judgment," *Russell: the*

*Journal of the Bertrand Russell Archives*, new series 17.2 (Winter 1997-98) 101-122. **[Q,W]**

Falk, A., "Williams's Domains and Reductionism," *Quarterly Review of Biology* 72 (June, 1997) 179-83. **[Z]**

Falk, A., "Whither Analytic Ontology?" in *Russell: the Journal of the Bertrand Russell Archives*, n.s., 18 (1998-99) 161-174. **[Z]**

Falk, A., "Singular Knowledge," D. P. Chattopadhyaya, Sandhya Basu, Madhabendra Nath Mitra, and Ranjan Mukhopadhyaya, eds., *Realism: Responses and Reactions; Essays in Honour of Pranab Kumar Sen* (New Delhi: Indian Council of Philosophical Research, 2000) 382-404. **[Q]**

Falk, A., "Time Plus the Whoosh and Whiz" in Q. Smith and A. Jokic, eds., *Time Tense and Reference* (MIT Press, 2002). **[M,N]**

Falk, A., *Darwinism and Philosophical Analysis*, Utkal Studies in Philosophy, vol. (?) (New Delhi: Decent Books, 2003). **[L,M,O]**

Falk, A., "A Decision-Theoretic Analysis of Faith" *Philo* 5 (2002) 174-195. **[O]**

Feldman, F., "Two Questions about Pleasure," in D. F. Austin, ed., *Philosophical Analysis* (Kluwer, 1988) 59-81. **[B, N]**

Feldman, J. A., "A Connectionist Model of Visual Memory," in G. E. Hinton and J. A. Anderson, eds., *Parallel Models of Associative Memory* (Erlbaum, 1981). **[R]**

Ferejohn, M., *The Origins of Aristotelian Science* (Yale, 1991). **[D]**

Field, H., "Logic, Meaning, and Conceptual Role," *Journal of Philosophy*, 74 (1977) 379-409. **[S]**

Fine, K., "Quine on Quantifying In" in C. Anderson and J. Owens, eds., *Propositional Attitudes* (Stanford Center for the Study of Language and Information, 1990) 1-25. **[E]**

Fodor, J. A., "Methodological solipsism considered as a research strategy in cognitive psychology" (1980) reprinted in his *Representations* (MIT Press, 1981). **[S]**

Fodor, J. A., *Psychosemantics* (MIT Press, 1987). **[P]**

Fodor, J. A., *A Theory of Content and Other Essays* (MIT Press, 1990). **[Y]**

Fodor, J. A., *The Elm and the Expert: Mentalese and Its Semantics* (MIT Press, 1994). **[S,T,Y]**

Fodor, J., *In Critical Condition: Polemical Essays on Cognitive Science and the Philosophy of Mind* (MIT Press, 1998). **[S,Y]**

Fodor, J., and Lepore, E., *Holism: A Shopper's Guide* (Blackwell, 1992). **[P,S]**

Forrester, J., *Principles of Systems* (Cambridge, Mass.: MIT Press, 1968). **[Y]**

Fraenkel, A., *Abstract Set Theory*, 2$^{nd}$ ed. (North-Holland Publishing Co., 1961). **[G]**

Frege, G., *The Foundations of Arithmetic* (1884) translated by J. L. Austin. **[B]**

Frege, G., "On Sense and Reference" (1892) in P. Geach and M. Black, *Translations from the Philosophical Writings of Gottlob Frege* (Blackwell, 1960). **[G,K]**

French, P., Uehling, T., and Wettstein, H., eds., *Contemporary Perspectives in the Philosophy of Language* (U. of Minnesota Press, 1979). **[A,F,H]**

Geach, P., "On Beliefs About Oneself" (1957-58). Reprinted in his *Logic Matters* (U. of California Press, 1972) section 4.1. **[M]**

Geach, P., *Mental Acts*, 2$^{nd}$ edition (Routledge, 1971). **[Q]**

Gelperin, A., Hopfield, J. J., and Tank, D. W., "The Logic of *Limax* Learning" in Allen Selverston, ed., *Model Neural Networks and Behavior* (Plenum, 1985). **[R]**

Gilbert, D., "How Mental Systems Believe," *American Psychologist*, (February, 1991) 107-130. **[D]**

Gödel, K., "Russell's Mathematical Logic" in Paul Arthur Schilpp, ed., *The Philosophy of Bertrand Russell* (Library of Living Philosophers, 1944). **[G]**

Golding, J. L., "Toward a Pragmatic Conception of Religious Faith," *Faith and Philosophy* 7 (1990) 486-503. **[O]**

Gopnik, A., "How we know our minds: The illusion of first-person knowledge of intentionality," *Behavioral and Brain Sciences* 16 (1993) 1-14. **[H]**

Graham, G., "The Origins of Folk Psychology," *Inquiry* 30 (1987) 357-79. **[H]**

Graham, P. J., "Conveying Information," *Synthese*, 123 (2000) 365-392. **[I]**

Grice, H. P., "Meaning" (1957) reprinted in P. F. Strawson, *Philosophical Logic* (Oxford, 1967). **[D]**

Grice, H. P., "Logic and Conversation," published in part in Davidson and Harman, eds., *The Logic of Grammar* (Dickenson, 1975) and the whole of it in Paul Grice, *Studies in the Way of Words* (Harvard University Press, 1989) 22-40. **[E]**

Griffiths, P. J., *On Being Mindless* (Open Court, 1986). **[B]**

Guttenplan, S., "An Essay On Mind" in Guttenplan, 3-107. **[L]**

580

Guttenplan, S., ed., *A Companion to the Philosophy of Mind* (Blackwell, 1994). **[Intro, A,E,L,K,P,R,S,V]**

Hahn, L., and Schilpp, P., *The Philosophy of W. V. Quine* (Open Court, 1986 [2nd, expanded edition 1998]). **[B,G]**

Hardin, C. L., *Color for Philosophers* (Hackett, 1986). **[S]**

Harman, G., *Thought* (Princeton University Press, 1973). **[P]**

Harman, G., "Desired Desires" in R. G. Free and Christopher W. Morris, eds., *Value, Welfare, and Morality* (Cambridge University Press, 1993) 138-157. **[Y]**

Harsanyi, J. C., "Acceptance of Empirical Statements: A Bayesian Theory Without Cognitive Utilities," *Theory and Decision* 18 (1985) 1-30. **[O]**

Hilpinen, R., "Deontic Logic," in Lou Goble, ed., *Blackwell Guide to Philosophical Logic* (Blackwell, 2001) 159-182. **[D]**

Hintikka, J., *Knowledge and Belief: An Introduction to the Logic of the Two Notions* (Cornell University Press,1962). **[J]**

Hintikka, J., "Semantics for Propositional Attitudes" (1969) reprinted in Hintikka's *Models for Modalities* (Reidel, 1969). **[H]**

Hinton, G. E., McClelland, J. L., and Rumelhart, D. E., "Distributed Representations" in D. Rumelhart, J. McClelland and the PDP Research Group, *Parallel Distributed Processing: Explorations in the Microstructure of Cognition* (MIT Press, 1986) vol I, ch. 3. **[R]**

Hofstadter, D. R., "Prelude . . . Ant Fugue" (1979) reprinted in D. R. Hofstadter and D. C. Dennett, eds., *The Mind's I: Fantasies and Reflections on Self and Soul* (Basic Books, 1981). **[Y]**

Holt, E. B., *et al*, *The New Realism* (Macmillan, 1912). **[D]**

Holton, R., "Attitude Ascriptions and Intermediate Scope," *Mind* 103 (1994) 123-130. **[D,J]**

Hughes, G. E., and Cresswell, M. J., *A New Introduction to Modal Logic*, 2nd or later printing (Routledge, 1996). **[F,H]**

Hull, D. L., "Are Species Really Individuals?" *Systematic Zoology*, 25 (1976) 174-91. **[O]**

Hull, D. L., "A Matter of Individuality," *Philosophy of Science*, 45 (1978) 335-360. **[O]**

Humphrey, N., *A Natural History of the Mind* (Simon and Schuster, 1992). **[N]**

Humphreys, P., and Fetzer, J., eds., *The New Theory of Reference: Kripke, Marcus, and Its Origins* (Kluwer, 1998). **[A]**

James, W., *The Principles of Psychology* (Dover Publications, 1890). **[A,M]**

James, W., "The Sentiment of Rationality" in his *The Will to Believe and Other Essays in Popular Philosophy* (1897). **[H]**

Jeffrey, R., *The Logic of Decision*, 2nd ed. (Chicago, 1983, corrected edition, 1990). **[B]**

Jeshion, R., "Acquaintanceless *De Re* Belief," in Campbell, J. K., O'Rourke, M., and Shier, D., eds., *Meaning and Truth: Investigations in Philosophical Semantics* (Seven Bridges Press, 2001). **[H]**

Jeshion, R., "Donnellan on Neptune," *Philosophy and Phenomenological Research* 63 (2001) 111-135. **[H]**

Jones, W. T., and Fogelin, R. J., *The Twentieth Century to Quine and Derrida*, 3rd edition (Harcourt Brace, 1997). **[E]**

Kane, R., *The Significance of Free Will* (Oxford, 1996). **[Z]**

Kant, I., *Prolegomena to Any Future Metaphysics* (1783). **[Intro]**

Kaplan, D., "Quantifying In," *Synthese* (1968) reprinted in Davidson and Hintikka, 206-242. **[H,K,R]**

Kaplan, D., "Dthat" (1978) reprinted (without the errors of the original printing) in French, Uehling, and Wettstein, eds., *Contemporary Perspectives in the Philosophy of Language* (U. of Minnesota Press, 1979) 383-400. **[H]**

Kaplan, D., "Opacity" in L. Hahn and P. Schilpp, *The Philosophy of W. V. Quine* (Open Court, 1986 [2nd, expanded edition 1998]). **[B,G]**

Kaplan, M., *Decision Theory as Philosophy* (Cambridge University Press, 1996). **[B]**

Keenan, E., "A Note on Marking Transparency and Opacity," *Linguistic Inquiry* 4 (1973) 421-24. **[A]**

Keller, H., *The Story of My Life* (1903). **[P]**

Klein, F., *Geometry* (Dover, 1959 [3rd ed., 1925 originally]). **[U]**

Körner, S., "The Impossibility of Transcendental Deductions" *Monist* 51 (1967) 317-331. **[Z]**

Körner, S., *What is Philosophy? One Philosopher's Answer* (Penguin, 1969). **[Z]**

Kraut, R., "Worlds Regained," *Philosophical Studies*, 35 (1979) 239-255. **[J]**

Kraut, R., "There are no *De Dicto* Attitudes" *Synthese* 54 (1983) 275-294. **[J]**

Kraut, R., "Love *De Re*," in French, Uehling, and Wettstein, eds., *Midwest Studies in Philosophy*, 10 (1986) 413-430. **[B]**

Kripke, S., "Naming and Necessity," in D. Davidson and G. Harman, eds., *Semantics of Natural Language*, 2nd ed. (D. Reidel, 1972) 253-355; "Addenda" 763-769. **[A,F,H]**

582

Kripke, S., "A Puzzle about Belief," in A. Margalit, ed., *Meaning and Use* (D. Reidel, 1979) 239-283, reprinted in Salmon and Soames. **[C,V]**

Kyburg, H. E., Jr., *Probability and Inductive Logic* (Macmillan, 1970). **[B]**

Langendoen, D. T., and Postal, P. M., *The Vastness of Natural Languages* (Blackwell, 1984). **[V]**

Leff, H. S., and Rex, A. F., eds., *Maxwell's Demon: Entropy, Information, Computing* (Princeton University Press, 1990). **[P, Glossary]**

Lewis, D. K., "Attitudes *De Dicto* and *De Se*" (1979) reprinted in his *Philosophical Papers*, vol. I (Oxford, 1983) ch. 10. **[B,H,M,N,O,Z]**

Lewis, D. K., "Counterfactual Dependence and Time's Arrow" (1979) republished with postscripts in his *Philosophical Papers*, vol. II (Oxford, 1986) ch. 17. **[O]**

Lewis, D. K., "Veridical Hallucinations and Prosthetic Vision" (1980) reprinted in his *Philosophical Papers*, vol. II (Oxford, 1986) ch. 24. **[H]**

Lewis, D. K., "What Puzzling Pierre Does Not Believe" (1981) reprinted in his *Papers on Metaphysics and Epistemology* (Cambridge University Press, 1999) 408-417. **[W]**

Lewis, D. K., "Lewis, David: Reduction of Mind" in Guttenplan, 412-430. **[P,S]**

Lewis, D. K., "Finkish Dispositions" (1997) reprinted in his *Papers in Metaphysics and Epistemology* (Cambridge University Press, 1999). **[B]**

Loar, B., "Social Content and Psychological Content," reprinted in Pessin and Goldberg, 180-191. **[S]**

Mach, E., *Analysis of Sensations* (Open Court, 1897). **[M]**

Mackenzie, I. E., *Introduction to Linguistic Philosophy* (Sage Publications, 1997). **[Intro]**

Mackie, J. L., *Ethics: Inventing Right and Wrong* (Penguin, 1977). **[Z]**

Maher, P., *Betting on Theories* (Cambridge University Press, 1993). **[Z]**

Makinson, D. C., "The Paradox of the Preface," *Analysis* 25 (1965) 205-207. **[B]**

Malle, B. F., Moses, L. J., and Baldwin, D. A., eds., *Intentions and Intentionality: Foundations of Social Cognition* (MIT Press, 2001). **[B]**

Maloney, J. C., "language of thought (1)" in Guttenplan, 401-407. **[P]**

Marcus, R. (Barcan) "Modalities and Intensional Languages," *Synthese*, 27 (1962) 303-322. **[G]**

Mates, B., "Synonymity" (1950) reprinted in Leonard Linsky, ed.,

*Semantics and the Philosophy of Language* (U. of Illinois Press at Urbana, 1952). **[G]**

Matthews, R. J., "The Measure of Mind," *Mind*, 103 (1994) 131-146. **[D]**

Mayr, E., "Cause and Effect in Biology," *Science*, 134 (1961) 1501-6. **[Y]**

McCawley, J. D., "On Identifying the Remains of Deceased Clauses" (1974); reprinted in his *Adverbs, Vowels, and Other Objects of Wonder* (U. of Chicago Press, 1979) ch. 10. **[B]**

McFetridge, I. G., "Propositions and Davidson's Account of Indirect Discourse," *Proceedings of the Aristotelian Society*, 76 (1975) 131-145. **[C]**

McKay, T., "On Proper Names in Belief Ascriptions," *Philosophical Studies*, 39 (1981) 287-303. **[E,X]**

McKay, T., "Actions and *De Re* Beliefs," *Canadian Journal of Philosophy* 14 (1984) 631-635. **[I,J]**

McKay, T., "Names, Causal Chains, and *De Re* Beliefs" in J. Tomberlin, ed., *Philosophical Perspectives*, vol. 8 Logic and Language (Ridgeview Publishing, 1994) 293-302. **[I]**

McKinsey, M., "The Semantics of Belief Ascriptions," *Nous* 33-4 (1999) 519- 557. **[D]**

Mellor, D. H., "I and Now" (1989) reprinted in his *Matters of Metaphysics*, Cambridge University Press, 1991). **[N]**

Mill, J. S., *A System of Logic* (1843). **[A,F]**

Miller, R., *Meaning and Purpose in the Intact Brain* (Clarendon Press, 1981). **[R]**

Misch, G., *The Dawn of Philosophy*, 1926 (translation in 1951, Harvard University Press). **[Z]**

Mitchell, P., *Introduction to Theory of Mind: Children, Autism, and Apes* (Arnold, 1997). **[H]**

Montague, R., "On the Nature of Philosophical Entities" (1969) reprinted in his *Formal Philosophy* (Yale University Press, 1974). **[B,X]**

Morgan, L., *Instinct and Experience* (1912). **[D]**

Morton, A., "Because He Thought He Had Insulted Him," *Journal of Philosophy*, 72 (1975) 5-15. **[N]**

Mühlhölzer, F., "On Objectivity" *Erkenntnis* 28 (1988) 185-230. **[V]**

Murphy, M. C., "The Simple Desire-Fulfillment Theory," *Nous* 33 (1999) 247-272. **[O]**

Newman, J. H., *A Grammar of Assent* (1892 [1$^{st}$ edition 1870]). **[D]**

Newman, J. R., *The World of Mathematics* (Tempus, 1956). **[O]**

Niiniluoto, I., *Truthlikeness* (Reidel, 1987). **[Z, Glossary]**

Niiniluoto, I., "Verisimilitude: The Third Period," *British Journal for the*

*Philosophy of Science*, 49 (1998) 1-29. **[Z]**

Noonan, H. W., "Object-dependent Thoughts and Psychological Redundancy," *Analysis*, 51 (1991) 1-9. **[I]**

Nozick, R., "Invariance and Objectivity," *Proceedings and Addresses of The American Philosophical Association* volume 72, no. 2 (American Philosophical Association, 1998) 21-48. **[U]**

Nozick, R., *Invariances: The Structure of the World* (Harvard, 2001). **[U]**

Oddie, G., *Likeness to the Truth* (Reidel, 1986). **[Z, Glossary]**

Olson, K., *An Essay on Facts* (CSLI Publications, 1987). **[G]**

Orenstein, A., and Kotatko, P., eds., *Knowledge, Language and Logic: Questions for Quine* (Kluwer Academic Publishers, 2000). **[U]**

Ørstrøm P., and Hasle, P., *Temporal Logic* (Kluwer Academic Publishers, 1995). **[M]**

Pagin, P., "Is Compositionality Compatible with Holism?" *Mind and Language*, 12 (1997) 11-33. **[S]**

Peirce, C. S., *Collected Papers* (Harvard, 1960). **[D]**

Penner, T., and Rowe, C. J., "The Desire for Good: Is the *Meno* Inconsistent with the *Gorgias*?" *Phronesis*, 39 (1994) 1-25. **[I,O]**

Perlman, J. S., *Science Without Limits* (Prometheus Press, 1995). **[Y]**

Perry, J., *The Problem of the Essential Indexical and Other Essays* (Oxford, 1993); expanded edition (CSLI Publications, 2000). **[L,M,N,T,V]**

Perry, J., "The Problem of the Essential Indexical" (1979) reprinted in his *The Problem of the Essential Indexical*. **[M]**

Perry, J., "Beliefs and Acceptance" (1980) reprinted in his *The Problem of the Essential Indexical*. **[N,V]**

Perry, J., "Thought Without Representation" (1986) reprinted in his *The Problem of the Essential Indexical*. **[T]**

Perry, J., "I and Myself" (1998) reprinted in the expanded edition of his *The Problem of the Essential Indexical*. **[N,T]**

Perry, J., *Knowledge, Possibility, and Consciousness* (MIT Press, 2001). **[N]**

Perry, J., *Reference and Reflexivity* (CSLI Publications, 2001). **[N]**

Pessin, A., and Goldberg, S., eds., *The Twin Earth Chronicles: Twenty Years of Reflection on Hilary Putnam's 'The Meaning of "Meaning"'* (M. E. Sharpe, 1996). **[O,S]**

Pinker, S., *The Language Instinct: How the Mind Creates Language* (William Morrow and Co., 1994). **[P]**

Pinker, S., *How the Mind Works* (Norton, 1997). **[R]**

Plato, *Euthyphro*. **[E]**

Plato, *Gorgias*. **[D]**

Plato, *Laches*. **[E]**

Plato, *Philebus*. **[N]**

Plato, *Republic*. **[I]**

Plato, *Symposium*. **[D]**

Plato, *Theaetetus*. **[R]**

Popper, K., *Objective Knowledge: An Evolutionary Approach* (Oxford, 1972). **[B]**

Pradhan, R. C., *Recent Developments in Analytic Philosophy* (Indian Council of Philosophical Research, 2001). **[Z]**

Predelli, S., "Who's Afraid of Substitutivity?" *Nous*, 34 (2000) 455-467. **[W]**

Prior, A., "Thank Goodness That's Over," *Philosophy* 34 (1959) 12-17, reprinted in his posthumous *Papers in Logic and Ethics* (Duckworth, 1976). **[M]**

Putnam, H., "Meaning and Reference," *Journal of Philosophy*, 70 (1973) 699-711. **[S]**

Putnam, H., "The Meaning of 'Meaning'"(1975) reprinted in Pessin and Goldberg, 3-52. **[S]**

Quine, W. V., "On What There Is," in *From a Logical Point of View* (Harvard University Press, 1953, 1961 revised 2$^{nd}$ edition). **[O]**

Quine, W. V., "Reference and Modality," in his *From a Logical Point of View*. **[G]**

Quine, W. V., "Quantifiers and Propositional Attitudes," *Journal of Philosophy* 53 (1956) reprinted in his *The Ways of Paradox and Other Essays*, revised and enlarged edition (Harvard University Press, 1976) ch. 17. **[A,B,D,E,H]**

Quine, W. V., *Elementary Logic*, revised edition (Harper and Row, 1965). **[Glossary]**

Quine, W. V., *Word and Object* (MIT Press, 1960). **[A,C,D,G,K,T,V]**

Quine, W. V., "Speaking of Objects" (1958) reprinted in his *Ontological Relativity and Other Essays* (Columbia University Press, 1969) ch. 1. **[A]**

Quine, W. V., "Propositional Objects" (1965) reprinted in his *Ontological Relativity and Other Essays*, ch. 6. **[B,K]**

Quine, W. V., "Russell's Ontological Development" *Journal of Philosophy* 63 (1966) reprinted in his *Theories and Things* (Harvard University Press, 1981). **[Q,Z]**

Quine, W. V., "Ontological Relativity," reprinted with corrections in his *Ontological Relativity and Other Essays* (Columbia University Press,

1969). **[C,K,T,Z]**

Quine, W. V., "Reply to Davidson," in Davidson and Hintikka, 333-335. **[C,E]**

Quine, W. V., "Reply to Kaplan" in Davidson and Hintikka, 341-345. **[A]**

Quine, W. V., *The Philosophy of Logic* (Prentice-Hall, 1970). **[Q]**

Quine, W. V., *The Roots of Reference* (Open Court, 1974). **[R,U]**

Quine, W. V., "Five Milestones of Empiricism" (1975) reprinted in his *Theories and Things* , ch. 7. **[A,B]**

Quine, W. V., "Intensions Revisited" (1977) reprinted in French, Uehling, and Wettstein, eds., and in his *Theories and Things*, ch. 13. **[A,B,D,K,Q]**

Quine, W. V., "Burdick's Attitudes," *Synthese* 52 (1982) 231-233. **[L]**

Quine, W. V., "Reply to Jaakko Hintikka" in Hahn and Schilpp, eds., *The Philosophy of W. V. Quine.* **[J]**

Quine, W. V., "Reply to David Kaplan" in Hahn and Schilpp. **[G]**

Quine, W. V., *Theories and Things* (Harvard University Press, 1981). **[A,B,D,T]**

Quine, W. V., *Pursuit of Truth*, revised edition (Harvard University Press, 1992). **[T,U,V]**

Quine, W. V., "In Praise of Observation Sentences," *Journal of Philosophy* 90 (1993) 107-116. **[T]**

Quine, W. V., "Promoting Extensionality," *Synthese* 98 (1994) 143-151. **[G]**

Quine, W. V., "Response to Bergström," in *Inquiry*, 37 (1994) 496-8. **[T]**

Quine, W. V., "Response to Gibson," *Inquiry* 37 (1994) 501-502. **[M]**

Quine, W. V., *From Stimulus to Science* (Harvard University Press, 1995). **[L]**

Quine, W. V., "Reactions" in P. Leonardi and M. Santambrogio, eds, *On Quine* (Cambridge University Press, 1995). **[A]**

Quine, W. V., "I, You, and It: An Epistemological Triangle" in Alex Orenstein and Petr Kotatko, eds, *Knowledge, Language and Logic: Questions for Quine* (Kluwer Academic Publishers, 2000) 1-6. **[U]**

Quine, W. V., "Response to George," in Orenstein and Kotatko, eds. *Knowledge, Language and Logic: Questions for Quine* (Kluwer Academic Publishers, 2000) 408-410. **[U]**

Reshotko, N., "A Reply to Penner and Rowe" *Phronesis* 40 (1995) 336-341. **[I]**

Reshotko, N., "Do Explanatory Desire Attributions Generate Opaque Contexts?" *Ratio (New Series)* 9 (1996) 153-170. **[O]**

Rose, S., *The Making of Memory* (Doubleday, 1992). **[R]**

Rumelhart, D., McClelland, J., and the PDP Research Group, *Parallel Distributed Processing: Explorations in the Microstructure of Cognition* (MIT Press, 1986). **[R]**

Rumelhart, D., and McClelland, J., *Handbook on Parallel Distributed Processing* (MIT Press, 1988). **[R]**

Rumfitt, I., "Content and Context: The Paratactic Theory Revisited and Revised," *Mind*, 102 (1993) 429-454. **[C]**

Russell, B., *The Principles of Mathematics* (1903). **[Q]**

Russell, B., Letter to Frege (1904) in Gabriel, G., *et al.*, eds., *Gottlob Frege: Philosophical and Mathematical Correspondence* (Blackwell, 1980) 169. **[W]**

Russell, B., "Meinong's Theory of Complexes and Assumptions (III)" *Mind,* 13 (1904) (*Collected Papers of Bertrand Russell* 4). **[W]**

Russell, B., "On Denoting," *Mind*, (1905) reprinted in his *Logic and Knowledge*, 39-56. **[A,B,M]**

Russell, B., *The Problems of Philosophy* (Henry Holt, 1912). **[Q]**

Russell, B., *The Collected Papers of Bertrand Russell* (George Allen and Unwin, 1984) vol 7. **[B]**

Russell, B., "The Philosophy of Logical Atomism" (1918) in his *Logic and Knowledge* 175-282. **[B,D,G,Q,W,Z]**

Russell, B., "On Propositions" (1919) reprinted in his *Logic and Knowledge* 283-320. **[B,Q]**

Russell, B., *Introduction to Mathematical Philosophy* (1919). **[A]**

Russell, B., *An Inquiry into Meaning and Truth* (George Allen and Unwin, 1940). **[L,Z]**

Russell, B., *Human Knowledge: Its Scope and Limits* (Simon and Schuster, 1948). **[F,Z]**

Russell, B., "Politically Important Desires," Nobel Prize speech, reprinted in his *Human Society in Ethics and Politics* (Simon and Schuster, 1955). **[D]**

Russell, B., *Logic and Knowledge*, R. C. Marsh, ed. (George Allen and Unwin, 1956). **[B,D]**

Russell, B., *My Philosophical Development* (George Allen and Unwin, 1959). **[A,G,Z]**

Russell, B., *Autobiography* (George Allen and Unwin, 1967-69). **[Q]**

Ryle, G., *Dilemmas* (Cambridge University Press, 1954). **[E]**

Salmon, N., and Soames, S., eds, *Propositions and Attitudes* (Oxford, 1988). **[F]**

Sayers, D., *Gaudy Night* (1936) **[M]**

Schiffer, S., "Naming and Knowing" (1977) reprinted in French, Uehling, and Wettstein, eds., 61-74. **[H]**

Schiffer, S., *Remnants of Meaning* (MIT Press, 1989). **[C, S]**

Searle, J., "Searle, John R.," in Guttenplan. **[R,Y]**

Searle, J., "Is the Brain's Mind a Computer Program?" *Scientific American*, Jan. 1990. **[R]**

Sellars, W., and Chisholm, R., "The Chisholm-Sellars Correspondence on Intentionality," *Minnesota Studies in the Philosophy of Science*, vol. 2 (U. of Minnesota Press, 1958). **[P]**

Sellars, W., "Naming and Saying" (1961) reprinted in his *Science, Perception and Reality*. **[Q]**

Sellars, W., *Science, Perception and Reality* (Humanities Press, 1963). **[Q,S]**

Sellars, W., *Science and Metaphysics: Variations on Kantian Themes* (Routledge and Kegan Paul, 1968). **[P,Q]**

Shoemaker, S., "Introspection and the Self," *Midwest Studies in Philosophy: Studies in the Philosophy of Mind*, 10 (1986) 101-120. **[N]**

Shope, R. K., *The Analysis of Knowing* (Princeton University Press, 1983). **[A]**

Simon, H., "Applications of Servomechanism Theory to Production Control" in his *Models of Man* (John Wiley and Sons, 1957) 219-240. **[Y]**

Sleigh, R. C., "On a Proposed System of Epistemic Logic," *Nous* 2 (1968) 391-398. **[H]**

Smith, M., *The Moral Problem* (Blackwell, 1994). **[D]**

Smith, Q., "The Multiple Uses of Indexicals," *Synthese*, 78 (1989) 167-191. **[M]**

Smith, Q., "Marcus and the New Theory of Reference: A Reply to Scott Soames," in Paul Humphreys and James Fetzer, eds., *The New Theory of Reference: Kripke, Marcus, and Its Origins* (Kluwer, 1998) 37-61. **[A]**

Smullyan) A. F., Review of Quine's "The Problem of Interpreting Modal Logic," *Journal of Symbolic Logic*, 12 (1947) 139-141. **[F]**

Smullyan, A. F., "Modality and Description," *Journal of Symbolic Logic* 13 (1948) 31-37. Reprinted in Linsky, ed., *Reference and Modality* (Oxford, 1971). **[F]**

Soames, S., "Beyond Singular Propositions?" *Canadian Journal of Philosophy*, 25 (1995) 515-550. **[W]**

Sorensen, R. A., "Self-strengthening Empathy," *Philosophy and Phenomenological Research*, 58 (1998) 75-98. **[U]**

Spinoza, B., *Ethics* (1677). **[D]**

Stalnaker, R., *Inquiry* (MIT Press, 1984). **[C,G,S]**

Stebbing, L. S., *A Modern Introduction to Logic* (Methuen, 1930). **[A]**

Stebbins, G. L., *Processes of Organic Evolution*, 3rd ed. (Prentice Hall, 1977). **[Z]**

Stenius, E., "Linguistic Structure and the Structure of Experience" *Theoria* 20 (1954) 153-172. **[Q]**

Stenius, E., *Wittgenstein's 'Tractatus'* (Cornell University Press, 1960). **[D,Q]**

Stern, R., *Transcendental Arguments and Scepticism* (Oxford, 2000). **[Z]**

Stevens, S. S., "On the Theory of Scales of Measurement," *Science*, 103 (1946). Reprinted in B. Brody and N. Capaldi, *Science: Men, Methods, and Goals* (W. A. Benjamin, 1968). **[U]**

Stich, S., *From Folk Psychology to Cognitive Science* (M.I.T. Press, 1984). **[K]**

Stoutland, F., "Real Reasons" in J. Bransen and S. E. Kuypers, eds., *Human Action, Deliberation and Causation* (Kluwer Academic Publishers, 1998) 43-66. **[P]**

Strawson, P. F., *Individuals: An Essay in Descriptive Metaphysics* (Methuen, 1959). **[Glossary]**

Strawson, P. F., *Analysis and Metaphysics* (Oxford, 1992). **[Z]**

Suppes, P., "Probabilistic Inference and the Concept of Total Evidence," in J. Hintikka and P. Suppes, eds., *Aspects of Inductive Logic* (North-Holland Publishing Co., 1966) 49-65. **[B]**

Suppes, P., *Representation and Invariance of Scientific Structures* (CSLI Publications, 2002). **[U]**

Tank, D. W., and Hopfield, J. J., "Collective Computation in Neuronlike Circuits" *Scientific American* 257 (Dec. 1987) 104-114. **[R]**

Thagard, P., *Conceptual Revolutions* (Princeton University Press, 1992). **[S]**

Thomas, O., *Transformational Grammar and the Teacher of English* (Holt, Rinehart, and Winston, 1965). **[P]**

Turing, A. M., "Computing Machinery and Intelligence," *Mind* 59 (1950) 433-460. **[R]**

Tye, M., "The Puzzle of Hesperus and Phosphorus," *Australasian Journal of Philosophy*, 56 (1978) 219-224. **[L]**

Tye, M., "Belief (1): Metaphysics of," in Guttenplan, 140-146. **[A]**

Wasserman, P. D., *Neural Computing: Theory and Practice* (Van Nostrand Reinhold, 1989). **[R]**

Weyl, H., *Symmetry* (Princeton University Press, 1952). **[U]**

Whitehead, A. N., *The Concept of Nature* (U. of Michigan Press, 1957

[1920]). **[A]**

Whitehead, A. N., and Russell, B., *Principia Mathematica* (Cambridge University Press, 1910 [2nd edition 1927]). **[G]**

Williams, G. C., *Plan and Purpose in Nature* (Weidenfeld and Nicolson, 1996). **[Y]**

Winnie, J. A., "Invariance and Objectivity: A Theory with Applications to Relativity and Geometry" in Robert Colodny, ed., *From Quarks to Quasars* (U. of Pittsburgh Press, 1986). **[U]**

Wittgenstein, L., *Notebooks, 1914-1916*, 2nd edition, revised (Blackwell, 1979). **[Q]**

Wittgenstein, L., *Tractatus Logico-Philosophicus* (Routledge and Kegan Paul, 1922). **[G,Q,Z]**

Wittgenstein, L., *Philosophical Investigations* (Macmillan, 1953). **[D,Z]**

Wordsworth, W., "The Tables Turned" **[Part I]**

# INDEX OF TERMS

The names of persons are omitted; see instead the key included in the list of Works Cited. The page citations for the terms are to the places in the text where the words occur in bold face type and are defined, or otherwise to definitions in the Glossary. Other occurrences are cited only if they add to the definitions. Almost all the terms are common in the philosophical literature. The few that I invented solely for this book are asterisked to warn you that only readers of this book are likely to recognize them. But the concepts underlying these terms are common.